Charlotte Brontë

Charlotte Brontë

REBECCA FRASER

METHUEN LONDON

First published in Great Britain 1988
by Methuen London
Michelin House, 81 Fulham Road, London SW3 6RB
Reprinted 1988 (twice), 1989

Typeset by Wyvern Typesetting Ltd, Bristol
Printed in Great Britain by
Butler & Tanner Ltd, Frome, Somerset

British Library Cataloguing in Publication Data

Fraser, Rebecca
Charlotte Bronte.
1. Fiction in English. Brontë Charlotte –
Biographies
I. Title
823′.8

ISBN 0–413–57010–X

Contents

Illustrations

The photographs in this book are reproduced by kind permission of the following: the Brontë Society: 1a, 1b, 1c, 2a, 2b, 3a, 3b, 4b, 4c, 5a, 5b, 6a, 6b, 6c, 7a, 7b, 8c, 10a, 10b, 11b, 11c, 12a (original copyright-holder not known; reproduced by courtesy of the Brontë Society), 12b, 13c, 14a, 14b, 14c, 14d, 15a, 15b, 15c, 16a, 16c; the National Portrait Gallery, London: 4a, 13a, 13b, 16b; M. René Pechère: 8a, 8b; Bibliothèque royale Albert Ier, Brussels (Cabinet des Estampes): 9a (collection: 'Georges Frédéric'), 9b (collection: 'Edifices Civiles Pensionnats'); the British Library: 11a. Illustration 13d is taken from *In the Steps of the Brontës* by Ernest Raymond (Rich and Cowan, 1948).

Introduction

'If the Public will only see Charlotte as she really was . . . I shall feel my work has been successful': thus Mrs Gaskell expressed her aim in 1857 for the first published life of Charlotte Brontë. Some 130 years later, a biographer may humbly echo the same plea.

There have of course been innumerable studies of Charlotte Brontë since that of Mrs Gaskell, in particular Winifred Gerin's authoritative and distinguished biography, which is generally considered to be the last word on the subject. In fact it is over twenty years since that was published, and in the intervening time much new material has emerged. The Seton-Gordon papers and Charlotte Brontë's marriage settlement, in particular, are vital new documents unavailable to previous biographers. They give, among other things, a far fuller picture of the nature of Charlotte's husband, Mr Nicholls, and their relationship; likewise that between Charlotte and her publisher, Mr George Smith. Along with the photograph now proved beyond doubt to be of Charlotte Brontë, these have been recent major discoveries. Meanwhile, assiduous Brontë scholars have been steadily filling in the mosaic of Charlotte Brontë's life with a multitude of new detail. Old evidence is continually being sifted and re-analysed, until nothing will have escaped the keen-eyed, unsentimental scrutiny of the late twentieth century.

A most important aspect of this is the feminist revolution, which has created a major shift of emphasis in nineteenth-century scholarship. To quote Elaine Showalter, in *A Literature of their Own: British Women Novelists from Brontë to Lessing*, 'As scholars have been persuaded that women's experience is important, they have begun to see it for the first time. With a new perceptual framework, material hitherto assumed to be non-existent has suddenly leaped into focus.' The 'lost continent' of the mores and taboos hedging women round in the mid-nineteenth century has surfaced, and the sort of constraints under which the woman writer worked, and the inimical way she was perceived, have only recently become as clear to us as they were to Charlotte Brontë's contemporaries.

In the case of Charlotte Brontë the different landscape now visible is particularly electrifying, for Charlotte Brontë offended gravely against the standards of her day. Her assertive, passionate, realistic heroines were a threat to the concept of the 'angel in the house', the unprecedented moral influence ascribed to women from around 1820 onwards. Her brave and honest depiction in *Jane Eyre* of what was termed with horror 'the natural heart', her bold attack on the clergy and religious hypocrisy, swiftly earned the novel, despite its runaway success, the reputation of being pornographic and irreligious. When it was discovered that it had been written by a woman, and an unmarried woman at that, it lent Charlotte a notoriety which overshadowed the rest of her life. Furthermore, in an age which seemed threatened by revolution, the questioning of the status quo by her individualistic heroines was seen as 'moral Jacobinism'; the author of *Jane Eyre*, in which the rights of a poor governess were insisted on as of equal importance to those well above her in rank, must be 'an alien from society and amenable to none of its laws'.

Reviewers thought her dangerous enough to be fulminated against, and her reputation for immorality was such that it was the main reason why Mrs Gaskell undertook to write her *Life*, for she wished to show how her friend had been misjudged. 'A noble true Christian woman was what she was', she wrote, 'even more than a gifted author and it is in the first character I wish her to be thought of.'

Without considering contemporary reaction to Charlotte Brontë's novels, a most important dimension of her character and life is lost – her bravery in responding to her critics and stalwartly refusing to be cowed by them, though it cost her dear. Despite her lifelong battle with convention, she was enough a product of her society to be appalled by the reaction to her novels. Nevertheless, she continued defiantly to write as the spirit took her, calling boldly for sexlessness in authorship, regardless of what was considered proper or becoming for her gender, with a missionary commitment to the truth, unpalatable as it might be, that was the product of an upbringing by an Evangelical father.

My intention in writing this biography has been to try to show Charlotte Brontë as she appeared to her era, to reveal what a phenomenon she was considered. At the same time I wanted to show how the life of this complex, passionate woman, so tragic in many ways, was also almost remarkable in its ordinariness, its daily preoccupations with domestic duties, family and friends.

This book would not have been possible without the work of many scholars, past and present, whose works are listed in the Bibliography. The following have, however, been of particular inspiration and worth: Inga-Stina Ewbank, *Their Proper Sphere, A study of the Brontë sisters as Early-Victorian Novelists*; Kathleen Tillotson, *Novels of the 1840s*; Miriam Allott (ed.), *The Brontës, The Critical Heritage*, which has been the main source for contemporary reviews of Charlotte Brontë's novels; Martha Vicinus (ed.), *Suffer and be Still: Women in the Victorian Age*; Margot Peters, *Unquiet Soul*; Enid L. Duthie's researches on Brussels and Constantin Heger in *The Foreign Vision of Charlotte Brontë*, which have been indispensable, as has Dr Christine Alexander's *The Early Writings of Charlotte Brontë* for the juvenilia. The many publications of Dr T. Winnifrith and Dr Edward Chitham are too numerous to mention here, but are gratefully acknowledged. And naturally every Brontë biographer must owe a debt to Winifred Gerin and John Lock for their tireless researches into the Brontë family.

I also had the benefit of the expert knowledge of Dr Juliet Barker, the Curator of the Brontë Parsonage Museum, and am deeply grateful to her for her seemingly inexhaustible patience in answering my queries, for her stimulating ideas for lines of research and for her kindness in reading this manuscript and making many helpful suggestions. I would also like to thank the Assistant Librarian at Haworth, Miss Sally Johnson, for her unstinting help over the past three and a half years, and the Council of the Brontë Society for permission to quote from Brontë source material.

I most gratefully acknowledge the assistance of the following: M. René Pechère, Professeur of the Haute Ecole Nationale Supérieure d'Architecture et des Arts Visuels, M. Heger's great-grandson, for his kindness in furnishing me with much information, including previously unpublished material; M. François Ferrers; Dr Lola L. Szladitz, the Curator of the H.W. and A.A. Berg Collection at the New York Public Library; Mr Chris Sheppard of the Brotherton Collection at Leeds University; Sheffield University; Mr Paul Woudhuysen of the Fitzwilliam Museum Library; Mlle C. Gheysen of the Cabinet des Estampes, at the Bibliothèque Royale Albert Ier, Brussels; Mrs Virginia Murray and John Murray Ltd for allowing me to read the Seton-Gordon papers in their possession; the Department of Manuscripts of the National Library of Scotland; the staff of the British Museum; the Curator of the Library of the State University of New York at Buffalo; Mrs Lesley Byrne of the Penzance Library; Mr P.A.S. Pool for his help with the Branwell family and for showing me notes of her family by Frances Branwell; Dr Peter Dally for his discussion of the causes of Charlotte Brontë's death; the British Medical Association.

Others who have been very kind with their time are M. Alain Camu, Lady Mary Clive, Mr Adrian Fortescue, Miss Gillian Greenwood, Dr Rana Kabbani, Mr Paul Keegan, Mr and Mrs Laurence Kelly, Miss Nigella Lawson, Miss Giulia Ajmone Marsan, Mr William Mostyn Owen, Miss Kathy O'Shaughnessy, the Hon. Mrs Michael Pakenham, Mr Harold Pinter, Mrs Joan Rees and Mr Peter Willes.

Especial mention should be made of Mr Christopher Falkus, former Chairman of Methuen London, whose enthusiasm for this project and encouragement have meant so much to me over the past three and a half years; likewise Ms Alexandra Bennion and Ms Ann Wilson of Methuen. I would like to thank Mr Ed Victor for his support and Miss Betty Prashker of Crown Books for her constant interest, and Ms Fiona Clarke for typing the manuscript.

I would like to thank Mr Stephen Pickles for kindly reading the proofs, and my grandmother Elizabeth Longford for reading this manuscript at a very early stage and criticising it in the minutest detail. The greatest thanks of all go to my mother Antonia Fraser for her ceaseless help, way beyond the call of maternal duty. Lastly, I dedicate this book to the memory of my father, the late Sir Hugh Fraser, M P.

Rebecca Fraser

CHAPTER I

Origins

The first record of the name of Charlotte Brontë is to be found in the diary of Miss Elizabeth Firth of Kipping House, near Bradford in the West Riding of Yorkshire. On Sunday, 21 April 1816 she noted the birth of a baby girl to her friends, the Irish incumbent of the neighbouring small town, Thornton, the Reverend Patrick Brontë and his Cornish wife Maria. They were on sufficiently close terms for her to have been asked to be godmother to Charlotte's older sister Elizabeth, and as she methodically entered the information 'C. Brontë was born' she may have paused to wonder what sort of life lay ahead for this third Brontë daughter born in the humble stone terraced house in narrow Market Street. Something perhaps similar to her own, as chronicled by her diary – a typically dutiful quiet feminine life, unprotesting, Godfearing, unadventurous and undisturbed; a series of meals followed by sermons followed by household tasks undertaken in a decorous modest fashion. In fact such stuff would make up the external fabric of Charlotte Brontë's life, to the surprise of the Victorian reading public. Born a clergyman's daughter, she would end her days a clergyman's wife, who had taught at Sunday School, sewed religiously and listened to a thousand sermons with the best of them.

Nevertheless, the tempestuous spirit Miss Firth ushers into the world so quietly would revolt against an existence which seemed to enmesh and suffocate her. The parson's little daughter with her pale calm face, framed on each side by the smoothly bandolined hair, could not be satisfied by an inner life restricted to prayer and meditation. Beneath the quiet dresses with their faintly printed patterns burnt a fire and a hunger that would demand more from her brief existence than the terrible inaction of the feminine life. The strong, impatient nature would crave a place to exercise her exceptional faculties as it chafed against convention. While never able to abandon wholly the

1

feminine self-abnegation the age demanded, she would heroically articulate her creed of feeling with a power and frankness that was completely new in the writing of her sex.

Charlotte was the first of her parents' offspring to be born in their new home. She was their third child; her elder sisters Maria and Elizabeth had been born in the two previous years during their father's curacy at Hartshead, a neighbouring parish. The Thornton house had no running water, and for the delivery water would have been brought specially from the trough in the centre of town by the two maids, Sarah and Nancy Garrs, and heated up in the kitchen at the back of the house. It was customary in these parts to turn the parlour into the delivery room, and for Charlotte's birth the bed which Mrs Brontë normally shared with her husband was brought downstairs from their bedroom, next door to the dressing room which served as a study. This unprepossessing ground floor room facing onto the street may still be seen today. In it, in the course of the next four years, were born Patrick Branwell, Emily Jane and Anne Brontë, to an exhausted, fragile, middle-aged woman who was thus delivered of six children in as many years.

From the window the landscape which greets the eye is one of great tracts of moorland which rear up opposite the town and run on to Haworth, four miles away due west. This bleak brown terrain which surrounds the town and stretches away in all directions is nowadays known as the South Pennines and it surrounds the Pennine Chain for thirty miles between the Yorkshire dales and the Peak district. The scenery is a curious mixture of valleys which were once the place of early manufactures, and empty moor, unified by the underlying rock of hard grey millstone grit, whose non-porous quality accounts for the area's myriad rushing rivers and streams. The prevailing tones in this landscape are dark and wintry. Blossom appears on the trees a month and a half later than in the south, in mid-June, and Charlotte Brontë herself would write that summer never really came to Haworth, that the countryside only took on a more burnished glow. Although there are parts of the land which are more domestic with small wooded copses and sheltered meadows, pale with buttercups, dusted with Old Man's Beard, more characteristically it consists of range after range of exposed scrubland, edged by sagging stone walls. In the thickly wooded valley bottoms can be seen the little dark villages and high factory chimneys built out of millstone grit which blackens when exposed. The villages were small and mean, the halls undistinguished, the natives dour and puritanical; so much so that it comes as a surprise to find charming echoes of Chippendale lurking in the pretty balustrade within a small girls' school, or statuary brought back from Italy by some busy merchant, or a Shakespeare First Folio.

2

The Methodists, in their golden age fifty years before Charlotte Brontë's birth, achieved a painless conquest amongst fearless Yorkshiremen whose ancestors had welcomed Nonconformism. The chapels, with their harsh, uncompromising architecture, were often the only human dwellings to break up the grim rugged vistas – stark granite outcroppings silhouetted against the sky.

The town of Thornton itself had been a haven for Nonconformists since the seventeenth century. Charlotte Brontë's own uncompromising life was spent amongst men and women whose consciousness had been formed by fierce Methodist preachers; her cast of mind was very close to theirs. Her vehement, charismatic, Evangelical father brought his children up to worship Truth, and Truth for her became the cause of feeling. Charlotte Brontë's later life, when she continued to write in solitude, often suggests the image of a prophet crying in the wilderness. The Methodist preachers who came to the moors before her, who also listened only to their consciences, would have found not a little to recognise in the parson's daughter who would not bow before public opprobrium and enmity.

The country's bleakness appealed strongly to the austere, powerful nature of her father, the Reverend Patrick Brontë. Despite his Cambridge education and literary pursuits, a certain primitive quality informed his personality. A man of almost ferocious vigour and willpower, his letters and sermons reveal an original and energetic mind full of ideas, and strong and obstinate prejudices about the world. Ignorance of convention, intelligence and discontent with a life of manual labour which might be the natural destiny of the son of a peasant ditchmender in Northern Ireland got him to Cambridge at the age of twenty-five, via schoolmastering. Over the years that followed, he established no little reputation in the West Riding for fearless action and independent views, so independent that they seemed a little eccentric. This does not really seem to have bothered him. One visitor records him alluding to his eccentricity and independence of other people's views 'with a certain pride'.[1] Nearing the end of his long life, he would describe himself thus: 'Being in early life thrown on my own resources – and consequently obliged under Providence, to depend on my own judgement and exertions, I may not be so ready as some are to be a follower of any man, or a worshipper of conventionalities and forms, which may possibly, to superficial observers, acquire me the character of a little eccentricity.'[2]

His daughter Charlotte's biographer, Mrs Gaskell, would describe his head as 'nobly shaped' – an oval face with 'straight Greek lines', but there is little such elegance to be found in the photographs of him taken in old age. The face crowned by white bristles which stares out at one boldly and fiercely resembles a North American Indian, or perhaps some cunning old sea salt. There is something a little sly about the bright eyes in the broad strong face with its great high cheek bones. The nose is broad and strong too; a very determined chin juts beneath the mouth that is so tightly controlled it looks graven. It turns down at the corners, tucked in against the many blows life has dealt him. But they have done nothing to wear away the strength and forcefulness of a face which even at eighty looks as if it would never brook much contradiction. Many people found him alarming, and one can see why. Although a foot and a half shorter than him, it would be Charlotte who would inherit his broad countenance, his strong jaw, and above all, his ambitious determination.

Patrick Brontë was born on St Patrick's Day, 17 March 1777, the eldest child of Hugh and Alice Brunty of the parish of Drumballyroney-cum-Drumgooland in County Down, Northern Ireland. The name Brontë was fixed on by Patrick himself when he was a student at Cambridge, but previously the family seem to have been known variously as Brunty, Bronty, Branty, Bronte, Prunty, O'Prunty or, in Gaelic, O'Pronntaigh. According to new research by the Brontë scholar Edward Chitham, it is possible that Patrick Brontë was the grandson, or at least a relative, of an eighteenth-century Gaelic poet, Padraig O'Pronntaigh, who lived in County Louth bordering on County Armagh, and was part of a school of Irish poets and scribes in Louth, Meath and south Ulster.[3] However, the Bruntys in general seem to have been peasants and tenant farmers, too poor even to memorialise themselves in stone at death. Hugh Brunty, though, had a reputation as an extraordinarily skilled story-teller, and it may well be that the heroic legends he used to relate were owed to such a father as Padraig O'Pronntaigh.

Delving around the bogs of Ireland for clues to the ancestry of the Brontës, it is difficult to sort out the truth from myth, although various sources concur that the Bruntys had a reputation for wild behaviour.

Patrick's father Hugh, an Ulsterman brought up by his tenant farmer uncle and aunt in the Boyne valley, met his future wife while working in a lime kiln in Ballymascanlan, through her brother who was a fellow labourer. She was Eilis McClory, member of a local family with some smallholdings. Their life together was led in cramped and squalid conditions. Patrick, the first of their ten children, was born at Emdale, Lougbrickland, in their two-roomed bothy with a mud floor and straw roof, which also contained the kiln in which Mr Brunty roasted corn for the neighbourhood – one of his several hand-to-

4

mouth jobs. The family diet consisted largely of oatmeal and potatoes, and was probably responsible for Patrick Brontë's habitual abstemiousness throughout the rest of his life. How many of the couple's children were born here is not clear, but when Patrick was about ten years old, his mother's family rented their kinsfolk some land, on which the Bruntys built a two-storey house with five rooms.

We have some idea of the original Brunty stock: they seem to have been strong, well-favoured, fair-complexioned people, tall with large bones and high colouring. Of the ten Brunty children, nine lived to be over eighty. Mr Brunty is described as having sandy hair, which the red-headed Mr Brontë would pass on to Charlotte and Branwell. But none of the Brontë children inherited the strong Brunty constitution, nor the height. Emily Brontë, at around five foot six inches, would be the tallest of Patrick Brontë's children, but all of them were delicate – a legacy from their mother's side of the family.

In his early thirties Patrick Brontë described the sort of home he was born in with considerable distaste in his didactic novelette *The Maid of Killarney*, pointing up the ignorance and stupidity of the peasantry and ridiculing their primitive customs. He must certainly have been most dissimilar from the rest of his family, who settled into their lot like their ancestors before them as innkeepers, shoemakers and roadmenders. During what seems to have been a rudimentary education, supplemented by Patrick's passion for poetry – he knew much of *Paradise Lost* by heart as a boy – he often also worked as a hand in his parents' few fields, as well as taking odd jobs in a linen draper's and at a blacksmith's; it was during his apprenticeship to the smith, according to his own account, that one of the formative experiences of his life took place.

The blacksmith and a gentleman having his horse shod were discussing what constituted a real gentleman. According to the mighty smith there were three kinds of gentlemen: 'the born gentleman, the gentleman by good fortune, and the gentleman by nature'. He then pointed at Patrick and said, 'Now, for instance, that boy standing there, though he is only between six and seven years of age [sic], is what I call a gentleman by nature'. According to our informant, the stationer at Haworth, Patrick Brontë nodded solemnly and said that those words had had an inestimable effect upon him for the rest of his life.[4]

Hugh Brunty seems to have had links with the Presbyterian Church, probably because of an active ministry in the area, although his children were baptised into the Church of Ireland. In 1793 his promising son's quality was recognised by the local Presbyterian minister, and Patrick Brontë became a teacher at the school attached to the Presbyterian meeting house at nearby Glascar. He taught there until about 1800, when he was taken up by a local wealthy landowner, the Reverend Thomas Tighe, who supposedly engaged Patrick as his sons' tutor, but who probably also coached him.[5]

This patronage was Patrick Brontë's much needed leg-up from fate. The Reverend Thomas Tighe was a friend and supporter of John Wesley's, and a distinguished former Fellow of St John's College, Cambridge. As a boy Patrick had probably heard John Wesley preach on his visits to Ireland every other year, when he travelled through Patrick's parish and stayed at Rosanna, the mansion belonging to Thomas Tighe's half-brother William. Wesley described his itinerant ministers being housed here in 'richly furnished apartments' attended by liveried servants and meeting 'with Senators, Ministers and ladies of rank and talent, while within a day or so they stopped in a mud cabin with a little straw for a bed'.[6]

Patrick's early notions of religion, unlike those of the greater part of his fellow Britons, thus contained a strong pietistical element, with an emphasis on the need for personal holiness, the sinfulness of man, and the glorious salvation available through Christ, which was the peculiar contribution of the Wesleys to the religious climate of the eighteenth century. In the company of the Reverend Thomas Tighe, Patrick Brontë learned the religion of Wesley at even closer hand, and it must have assumed its most attractive guise to the naïve but ambitious young schoolteacher with its close links to a way of life that seemed impressively elevated, both spiritually and materially. He was surrounded by distinguished former Fellows of St John's College in the shape of the Tighes, and visions of Cambridge University and eminence must have shimmered before him. They were shortly made reality. Through the Reverend Thomas Tighe's influence a young man of Irish peasant stock – commonly held to be the most miserable people in Europe – made the astonishing leap to Cambridge, one of England's most prestigious institutions which, if it had lost its reputation as a temple of learning, remained a nursery for politics and power.

The Reverend Patrick Brontë's journey from being a barelegged blacksmith's assistant at the age of twelve to a member of the Establishment – as one of the clergy he became a 'gentleman' and one of the first men of the area mentioned in the county guide books in the same paragraph as that describing the 'gentry of the locality' – was considered quite remarkable by his contemporaries at Cambridge. His friend, the Cornish Wesleyan missionary Henry Martyn, was amazed by his life story. Writing to his patron Wilberforce about the background of the bright young Evangelical recruit while Patrick was a student at Cambridge, Martyn said that

its singularity has hardly been equalled, I suppose, since the days of

Bishop Latimer. He left his native Ireland at the age of 22 [sic] with seven pounds, having been able to lay by no more after superintending a school some years. He reached Cambridge before that was expended and then received an unexpected supply of £5 from a distant friend. On this he subsisted some weeks before entering St John's, and has since had no other assistance than what the college afforded.[7]

St John's had been founded as a training school for the clergy – though not every graduate took orders. In the early part of the nineteenth century Simeon was only just beginning his reign there as one of the most important leaders of the Evangelical party in the Church of England, but by the mid century the college had become synonymous with fierce, poor, Evangelical sizars, the 'Sims' whom Samuel Butler describes so eloquently in *The Way of All Flesh*. It is not certain that Patrick Brontë had made up his mind to enter the Church before he left Ireland. The way in which his path was cleared by the Reverend Tighe suggests that there was some strong affinity between them which was most likely to have been based on religion, as do the subsequent helping hands Patrick Brontë received from the grand old luminaries of the Wesleyan movement, Mrs Fletcher and her friends.[8] What is certain is that two years after he arrived at Cambridge, Patrick Brontë had determined to take Holy Orders and was moving in the inner circle of the Evangelicals, the dedicated revolutionary sect committed to renewing the Church of England from within.

In the eighteenth century the Churches of England and Ireland had reached a spiritual nadir, despite such figures as Bishop Butler. While the leaders of the Church engaged in endless controversy, they failed to look after their flocks, or maintain church discipline. The political corruption of the age was mirrored in the clergy at all levels: absentee pluralist livings were the norm; considerable numbers of the population had no regular ministry; the clergy came into disrepute as being venal, and congregations fell away. It was a commonplace among some concerned contemporaries that sermons given even by as exalted a person in the church hierarchy as the prebendary of York, 'excepting a phrase or two . . . might be preached in a synagogue or mosque without offence'.[9]

Into this desert, of which the abuses in the distribution of ecclesiastical revenue were only finally investigated in 1836, had come the feverish contagion of Wesleyan Methodism, with its meetings, hymns and the joyful news of salvation for all, decried by High Church cleric Sydney Smith as 'one general conspiracy against common sense, and rational orthodox Christianity'.[10] He could not have been so bold thirty years later, for by then the Methodists in the

7

Church, as the Evangelicals were tagged, had transformed the face of nineteenth-century England, and charismatic religion was the order of the day, dictating the manners and mores of Victorian society.

The chief immediate difference between the Evangelical party and what would become the Methodist Church was a formal one: although the Evangelicals were actuated by the same enthusiasm, they remained within the Church of England. Common to both sides was a belief in 'conversion', that is, one had to receive some kind of spiritual experience or revelation before one could be certain of being one of the 'saved', or as Simeon put it, one of the very few 'certainly vital Christians'.[11]

Patrick Brontë put pen to paper at least twice to describe this phenomenon for the benefit of parishioners, and the frequent pepperings of later letters with other-worldly appeals rather call into doubt depictions of his being a somewhat lukewarm celebrant of his faith. There can be no doubt of the presence in the parsonage of a religion of black and white ferocity and conviction; against such a background his children would be brought up, their every action informed by consciousness of sin and the imminence of the world to come. He evidently moved with ease in the company of men like Henry Martyn, Senior Wrangler and Fellow of St John's and one of the leading lights of the Evangelical movement, whose diary reminds him of 'the infinite necessity of an ardent pursuit of holiness',[12] and who could sometimes hardly bear to see his students because they meant that he was unable to concentrate on God's presence. His zeal in the cause of true religion was sufficient to secure him Martyn's friendship, and the latter obtained a grant for him via Wilberforce from the Evangelical Church Missionary Society. In his letter of recommendation Martyn said that 'there is reason to hope that he will be an instrument of good to the Church as a desire of usefulness in the ministry seems to have influenced him in no small degree'.

This was high praise indeed. 'Useful' was an Evangelical code word signifying commitment to the Evangelical cause and the struggle against the High Church party. Patrick was evidently quite vocal in his support of the Evangelical movement, for the historian of the Evangelicals has named him as one of the 'several actors contributed to the Orthodox–Evangelical drama by St John's College'.[13]

Although by 1820 the lay leadership of the philanthropist member of Parliament Wilberforce had taken Evangelicalism in thirty years from an unpopular sect of perhaps fifty clergymen to a body 70,000 strong with royal patronage, the party was still very small — perhaps two to three hundred influential people. They were very unpopular with the High Church party, from whom they never managed to wrest control, and with their fellow Anglicans. Consequently it was often difficult to get Evangelical clergymen ordained and to find livings for them. In fact before 1815, when Ryder became Bishop of Gloucester, there was a great deal of trouble finding bishops willing to ordain Evangelical candidates. It was not until 1855, when the Evangelical Lord Shaftesbury was given control of ecclesiastical patronage, that there were many Evangelicals above the rank of an incumbent, since it was almost impossible for any clergyman known as an Evangelical to obtain preferment. The great Simeon himself, of whom Macaulay wrote 'if you knew what his authority and influence were, and how they extended from Cambridge to the most remote corners of England, you would allow that his real sway in the Church was far greater than any primate'[14] never rose above the level of vicar.

To combat such attitudes, only a dedicated freemasonry and the unashamed use of power and influence would succeed. Evangelicalism was also a worldly and energetic religion, and it may well be that the ambitious Patrick, who as a young minister is recorded as boasting of his grand connections, was attracted by the great and the good who had begun to flock to its ranks. A certain natural grandeur caused him to identify almost obsessively with the heroes of the age, and on arrival at Cambridge he had repudiated with magnificent dash the plebeian name of Brunty in favour of Brontë as a tribute to Nelson, who had just been created Duke of Brontë by the King of Sicily. The man who had what amounted to a proprietorial feeling for Wellington and a passion for politics, who tried to invent a new musket and who joined the corps of volunteers drilling against the threat of Napoleonic invasion with alacrity, might not have been drawn to the priesthood in the heady theological days of the seventeenth century; he was always something of a warrior priest. The Evangelicals' battle, to bring true religion to the atheistical, potentially revolutionary masses of post-1789 Britain, was peculiarly well suited to Patrick Brontë's notably soldierly character. His ministry would always be rather warlike, whether he was bombarding the working classes with improving Christian poetry of his own invention or defending the Church against the insidious forces of Roman Catholicism and Dissent. Nevertheless, however much contemporaries opined that he could have had a distinguished military career if he had not entered the Church, his life demonstrates an unswerving faith and pursuit of his mission, to be a light in the darkness. To him must be given the credit for the Brontës' belief in themselves.

The early Evangelicals' belief in the awful operation of Providence in their favour – often tantamount to superstition – was also shared by Patrick Brontë in his youth. However, although he expresses himself along party lines on the corruption that could be engendered by the novel and poetry, when it came to his own bookshelf, 'forbidden'

9

works, the improper literature of Byron, Cervantes, and the irreligious Walter Scott, could be found there in abundance. The early school of Evangelicals to whom Patrick Brontë belonged, in effect the eighteenth-century ones, were a more cultured and less puritanical breed than those who followed. The Brontës were not brought up in the rigid and hushed atmosphere that Samuel Butler describes; pictures were not turned to the wall of the parsonage on Sundays, as in the Ruskin household, and the many toys and games, as well as Charlotte's own descriptions of childhood, suggest a happy and uninhibited atmosphere. The man who in later life would boast of his amorous conquests was no believer in the mortification of the flesh. Full-blooded, the tracts he embarked on as a minister for the benefit of the working classes are not dry theological discussions, but novelettes. 'The Cottage in the Wood', notable for its richness of colouring, allows Mr Brontë to go to town with a sort of religious *Pamela*, and indeed Patrick Brontë in a foreword would write that he derived 'indescribable pleasure' from writing 'from morning till noon, and from noon till night'.

On leaving Cambridge, after taking holy orders in 1806 under the patronage of Jowett, Regius Professor of Civil Law, Patrick Brontë was promoted by the Evangelical/Methodist network, first to Wethersfield and Wellington in Shropshire – one of Mrs Fletcher's 'precious young men'[15] – and then to an obscure yet spiritually important curacy in the wilder parts of the West Riding of Yorkshire, with the additional responsibility of being the Scriptural Examiner to Wesley's school in the area. His ministry began amongst the turmoil produced in West Yorkshire by the Napoleonic Wars and the continental trade embargo which hit Yorkshire's woollen trade at the time when the introduction of new technology into the mills was already causing rising numbers of unemployed. For two years Yorkshire seemed to hover on the brink of revolution. The country was constantly rife with rumours of armies of men on the march to destroy the new machinery.

Patrick Brontë, with typical fire, was out at every opportunity with the millowners defending the mills against night attacks, very much like Mr Helstone in *Shirley*. The original of that formidable man was one of the local vicars, the Reverend Hammond Roberson. He bore a marked resemblance to Patrick Brontë – and was a great friend of his. Robeson was known as the 'Duke Ecclesiastic', because he was a 'very Wellington in the Church'. Mr Brontë in later years would delight in recalling his exploits with this man: one of Charlotte's best friends related how 'many a breakfast hour he enlivened by his animated relations of his friend's unflinching courage and dauntless self-reliance – and how the ignorant and prejudiced population around misunderstood and misrepresented his worthiest deeds'.[16] Probably Mr

Brontë's happiest days were during that period of 1811 to 1812 when the threat of Luddite uprisings forced every man in Yorkshire to carry arms; until the day of his death, though the Luddites themselves were long in their graves, he wore a brace of pistols at his belt, like a pirate king.

Patrick Brontë soon fulfilled his promise of usefulness in the ministry. In his early days in Yorkshire he became a close friend of the vicar of Christ Church, Bradford, a leading Yorkshire Evangelical who was very active in the area. He had a reputation for being hot-headed, sometimes difficult, but he was quite popular and became known in the district for writing and reciting light occasional verse. He also wrote three volumes of didactic poetry to aid the cause of converting the working classes to true religion. His natural gregarious-ness and volatility, which his children would inherit, could at times be overlaid by sensitivity about his Irish origins. He was certainly over-conscious of affronts to his dignity, as two, perhaps apocryphal, stories about him demonstrate. Apparently he set about him with his cudgel when the Dewsbury bellringers practised for a competition without his permission on a Sunday, and on another occasion, when he felt that he had been insulted by his vicar's father-in-law, he vowed that he would never preach again from the Dewsbury pulpits. There was a slightly hysterical quality to his nature which showed itself in his tendency to self-pity and sulking, and to take offence where none was intended. Tales abound of his short temper, and whatever his servants' later loyal denial of such legends, it appears that he was an irascible, difficult, choleric sort of man, and that these traits would increase with age. But as he himself would remark, 'Had I been numbered amongst the calm, sedate, concentric men of the world, I should in all probability never have had such children as mine have been.'[17]

By 1812, when Patrick met Maria Branwell, he was thirty-five, a minister with a considerable reputation which had certainly reached and impressed Miss Branwell. She was the niece of John Fennell, the headmaster of Woodhouse Grove School where Patrick Brontë was Scriptural Examiner. After the death of both parents within a year of each other three years before, she had come to help her aunt with the teaching at the school, one of the key establishments for the sons of Wesleyan Methodist preachers, and perhaps to seek a husband. A tiny, neat woman, now aged thirty, she was well-read and intelligent, with a gentility and sweetness of character that, combined with her strong Methodist faith, immediately attracted Patrick Brontë.

Maria Branwell came from a very different background to Patrick Brontë. She was a member of an old and modestly prosperous commercial Cornish family based in and around Penzance, known variously as Bromwell, Bremble and Branwell. According to one family legend, the Branwells had originally been pirates. Her great-great-grandfather John Bromwell married a woman called Constance in about 1657 (surname unknown), and their son, Martyn Bremble, became a butcher in Penzance and seems to have been a man of property, in that he owned two houses with gardens. He married a Jane Tremearne, who was probably a descendant of John Tremearne, the vicar of Paul, near Penzance, at the end of the sixteenth century, and they had six children. Their third son, Richard, baptized in 1711, was Maria Branwell's grandfather. His occupation is unknown, but he married the daughter of a blacksmith, by whom he had six children, and with him the name changed to Branwell.

The generation that this marriage produced – Maria Branwell's father Thomas Branwell and her paternal aunts and uncles – were very caught up in the Methodist movement, being supporters of the revival of 'serious religion' in Penzance. Maria's mother's family, the Carnes, were also well-known local Methodists, and Maria Branwell and her brothers and sisters therefore had an unusually devout upbringing. Maria's aunt Elizabeth married a shopkeeper who was a pillar of the Methodist Society for thirty-six years; her aunt Jane married the class leader among the Wesleyans of Penzance, John Fennell; and Maria's own sister Jane married a Methodist minister (though he was later disgraced and expelled from the ministry for immorality in 1807). According to the reminiscences of the eminent Wesleyan Divine, Dr Rigg, of the time when he was stationed in Penzance:

Among the intelligent and superior mercantile families in Penzance in 1846 was the Branwell family which still flourishes with increasing prosperity and influence, though those that were the heads of the family have now passed away beyond. Miss Branwell appears to have been the first matron or housekeeper of Woodhouse Grove School. She must have been a cousin of the heads of the family at Penzance whom I remember more than half a century ago. One young and more than ordinarily attractive daughter of the family I remember, who became, in mature life, leader in works and companies of Christian philanthropy and fellowship. . . . There was also, in 1846, another branch of the same family, a widow and daughters, refined, superior women, who spoke vaguely of cousins in a northern parsonage who 'were clever and who wrote'.

Poetic licence after the event? (The account was written in 1903.)
Thomas Branwell married Anne Carne, the daughter of a pros-

12

perous Penzance silversmith and watchmaker, cousin of the town's first banker. The union produced seven surviving children – Anne, born in 1769, Jane in 1773, Benjamin in 1775, Elizabeth in 1776, Maria in 1783 (15 April), Margaret in 1789 and Charlotte in 1791, as well as four children who died in infancy. Thomas was sufficiently well-off to patronise an artist, and the resulting portraits show Anne Carne as a mild-looking woman, with neat, small features, and her husband to have rather sharp, refined looks. Maria inherited something of his cast of countenance, though her features were rather more pointed and she had a noticeably long nose. Charlotte Brontë is said to have been the 'spit' of her mother's youngest sister Charlotte, although unfortunately no portrait of the latter exists.

It was probably Thomas Branwell who was responsible for establishing the Branwells as leading townsfolk in Penzance. His relatives lauded him as having 'more than ordinary talents', and he was also said to be very musical, a gift that his grandson Patrick Branwell Brontë and Emily Brontë were also to have.

In 1790 he was admitted to the Penzance Corporation, an honour reserved for the town's leading tradesmen and professional people, and at the time of his death he had a considerable amount of property in and around the town – three or four houses (one of which was let to the Methodist preachers), The Golden Lion Inn, and some cellars. From the rents of the property would come the £50 annuities which he left to each of his four daughters alone, suggesting that his own income may have been in the region of £500 a year, a not inconsiderable sum. The family themselves lived in a comfortable red-brick house, one of a terrace of three in a prosperous street in a fashionable part of town.

His son Benjamin Branwell was also admitted to the Corporation in 1797 and was Mayor and Justice of the Peace before he died at the early age of forty-three. Maria Branwell would have moved in an increasingly prosperous mercantile society, among tradesmen, merchants and professional men. One of Mr Branwell's businesses may have been a draper's shop, as there is evidence that one of Maria's sisters helped another in a draper's shop before she married. Thomas's brother Richard was a builder and stonemason, who lived at Thomas's inn. His firm was responsible for part of the pier and the Assembly Rooms. This branch of the Branwells flourished commercially, and continued to be prominent in the town for the next century. The flour business begun by Richard's son, who was also a clockmender in Penzance market, became a very successful grain business, R.M. Branwell and Sons, which was run by four generations of the Brontës' cousins. By the 1860s the Branwells owned two of the more imposing houses in Penzance, one of which, Penlee House, is now the Penzance Museum.[18]

Amidst her energetic, commercially minded relatives little Maria Branwell seems to have had more intellectual pursuits. About the time of her marriage she wrote an essay on 'The Advantages of Poverty in Religious Concerns'. She seems to have been held in high regard by the rest of her family; her nieces and nephews were anxious to convey an impression of her 'great amiability of disposition' to Mrs Gaskell. She and her sisters were well-read and must have pursued the concerns becoming fashionable for the daughters of the burgeoning middle classes: charity work and reading. They were perhaps members of the Ladies' Book Club, a subscription library which proved very successful.[19] Books at this time were extremely expensive (about five shillings a volume) and Maria Branwell mentions her books as an important part of her effects once lost at sea. Founded in 1770, the Ladies' Book Club was symptomatic of a new, consciously elegant, more cultured and enlightened age. In the case of Penzance it heralded a move away from a coarser world of smuggling, cockfighting, drinking and gambling to one dominated by societies of all kinds and by the revival of religion.

By Maria's twenties, Penzance had become a social centre in Cornwall, second only to Truro. Genteel society had expanded so much as to require the erection of new Assembly Rooms. In 1818 there was a Royal Geological Society of Cornwall, the agreeable private subscription library in Morrab Gardens, the Royal Institute of Cornwall, and the Penzance Public Dispensary and Humane Society. By her own account Maria Branwell was happy enough in her quiet existence. Why was she still unmarried at thirty? History does not relate. Perhaps she had found no one who was sufficiently congenial to her pious and serious mind. She was well enough off not to need to marry for financial reasons, and she was clearly an independent character. She seems to have prided herself on this latter quality. When he was courting her she told Patrick that 'for some years I have been perfectly my own mistress, subject to no control whatever', that 'even my dear mother used to consult me in every case of importance and scarcely ever doubted the propriety of my opinions and actions'.

That whirlwind courtship began in August 1812, and by December they were married. At the beginning, Maria told Patrick Brontë with her usual evidently attractive candour: 'I will frankly confess that your behaviour and what I have seen and heard of your character has excited my warmest esteem and regard.' There were picnics, visits to the picturesque beauty spots around Kirkstall Abbey, and poetry written by the admiring curate. In the school's handsome Scriptural Examiner Maria found someone whose views were strikingly similar to her own. Patrick Brontë was a converted Christian too, someone with whom she could share the importance of her religion, someone who

14

would understand her view of life, which was very much in the shadow of eternity. As a member of a strongly Methodist family she would not have found the manifestations of religious awakening at the school that year – what her uncle termed the 'marks of God's most blessed work among the children' shown by many of them being 'deeply affected . . . sighs and tears were on all sides'[20] – unnatural, alarming or laughable. To a Methodist this would be something to rejoice over, and no doubt Maria's fervent religious character did.

She also shared Patrick's political views, insofar as hers were articulated, that religion was a very useful antidote to revolution. Like him, she was inspired by the Evangelical impulse to write (though she would not be published until a century after her death); like him she devoutly kept the Sabbath and believed in family prayer – still a novelty in Regency England.

The attraction was not purely religious, however. In Maria Branwell Patrick Brontë found a partner who could respond to his own feeling nature in equal measure. Their shared religion seems to have paved the way to an instant bond of frankness and familiarity. Maria's letters are full of a breathless exultation in which the language of Methodism lends her utterances a rare passion and freedom from inhibition, a passion and freedom that her daughter Charlotte would inherit. Thus she writes to Patrick, 'O my dear friend, let us pray much that we may live lives holy and useful to each other and all around us.' And 'I firmly believe the Almighty has set us apart for each other; may we by earnest frequent prayer, and every possible exertion, endeavour to fulfil His Will in all things! I do not, cannot, doubt your love, and here I freely declare I love you above all the world besides!' How could she resist his need for intimacy, his demand for her to 'write my thoughts' and therefore 'as they occur I freely let my pen run away with them'.

But he is also her 'saucy Pat', who was demanding and extravagant as a lover. Miss Branwell wrote in reply to one of his evidently rather over-dramatic letters: 'I really know not what to make of the beginning of your last; the winds, waves, and rocks almost stunned me. I thought that you were giving me the account of some terrible dream, or that you had had a presentiment of the fate of my poor box, having no idea that your lively imagination could make so much of the slight reproof conveyed in my last. What will you say when you receive a *real, downright, scolding*?'[21]

She was probably particularly attracted to Patrick's sense of mission as a clergyman. In one of her letters to him, she writes, 'In all my addresses to the throne of grace I never ask a blessing for myself but I beg the same for you, and considering the important station which you are called to fill, my prayers are proportionately fervent that you may

15

be favoured with all the gifts and graces requisite for such a calling.'

Many years later Charlotte read her love letters and said that there was a 'rectitude, a refinement, a constancy, a modesty, a sense of gentleness about them indescribable' which she was pleased to think her own mind had sprung from. The reader today might be more struck by Maria Branwell's ardour, her intelligence, her frankness and her feeling – qualities which she passed on in plenty to her daughters.

Unfortunately, none of Mr Brontë's letters to his wife has survived, but the following attempt to renew affection in the heart of a former sweetheart when he was in search of a second wife after Mrs Brontë's death suggests something of his simple urgency and attractive desire for intimacy:

> I *have not* the *least doubt* that if you had *been mine* you would have been happier than you *now* are or *can* be as one in *single* life. You would have had other and kindlier views and feelings. You would have had a *second self* – one nearer to you than Father or Mother, sisters or brothers; one who would have been continually kind, and whose great aim would have been to have promoted your happiness in *both* the worlds. Our rank in life would have been in every way genteel, and we should together have had *quite enough* of the things of this life.

Love overcame Maria Branwell's reluctance to leave her comfortable home in Cornwall, the friends and relatives by which her affectionate nature put such store, for the life of a minister's wife in the wilds of Yorkshire. Within six months, she had agreed to exchange an atmosphere 'so bland as to foster myrtles and other tender plants' for the freezing northern winter. They were married in December 1812 in a double wedding; at the same time her cousin Jane Fennell married Mr Brontë's friend Mr Morgan in Guisely Church. Coincidentally, on the same date, Maria Branwell's sister Charlotte married their cousin Joseph Branwell in Penzance.

Patrick Brontë's marriage to Maria helped tame a spirit that could flash out into unwise behaviour. She was content to be the helpmeet to her 'dear companion on his pilgrimage' as she put it, but she was also coolly capable of reprimanding her husband for his suspiciousness and tendency to unexpected rages, and of tempering with her sweetness his over-austere qualities. Ministerial duties and the children that followed so quickly on each other did not mean that their life in Yorkshire was without social enjoyment. The town of Thornton where Charlotte was born was near enough to Bradford for them not to miss out on concerts and oratorios, and they moved in a social round amidst the cultured middle-class families of the district. Patrick Brontë's reputation for writing and declaiming light verse helped bring invitations from such families as the Firths, who lived in seventeenth-century Kipping House, with its porticoed entrance of Corinthian columns, high-ceilinged panelled rooms and gardens sloping pleasantly down to the river. Patrick Brontë's artistic instincts led him also to redecorate the interior of Thornton's rather grim Nonconformist Bell Chapel, and his sense of history and pride is shown in the notice he put up there recording his work.

Of the first four years of Charlotte Brontë's life little is known. She and in turn Branwell, Emily and Anne were baptised in the Bell Chapel, and the family attended services there every Sunday. They would probably have all slept together in what seems to have been the night nursery next door to the maids' room at the top of one of the house's two staircases, while Mr and Mrs Brontë slept at the front of the house, approached by the main staircase. The children played in the high-walled cobbled yard behind the house, running up and down the three stone steps which led to it from the kitchen.[22] They were taken round the district on visits to all the Brontë acquaintances, and were looked after by their mother and the two servants. The latter would recall the very affectionate relations between husband and wife. It was a pleasant and rewarding life, which continued without major incident until January 1820 when Anne's birth coincided with the death of the curate of Haworth – an event that was to have far-reaching consequences for the Brontë family.

CHAPTER II

Early Youth: Haworth and Cowan Bridge

The small village of Haworth lay out on the moors north of Thornton, ten miles from the borders of Lancashire, a remote place whose people were notorious locally for their roughness and individuality. Nevertheless, the Haworth curacy was a more attractive proposition than Thornton – better paid, with a larger house and greater responsibilities. By the end of February 1820 Patrick Brontë, with his usual vigour, had convinced the trustees of Haworth that they should appoint him Perpetual Curate, as the position was termed. The care of 5,000 souls was now his, as was an income of £200 a year. It was not a large sum but it was an improvement on his previous £140, and the curacy had the advantage of what he satisfiedly described as 'a good house which is mine for life also, and is rent free'. It seems that he had recognised he would go no further, whatever his earlier dreams of advancement.

It was a wrench to leave their pleasant life in Thornton, particularly so soon after the birth of Anne. This had been a difficult confinement, which seriously affected Mrs Brontë's health and it seems likely that there was some complication in her sixth pregnancy which led to sepsis of the blood. Nevertheless, by 20 April, the day before Charlotte's fourth birthday, mother and baby and the other five young children were making the day-long journey across the crests of the moors from Thornton to Haworth, travelling in one of the seven crude bumpy carts containing all the Brontës' furniture and possessions, and protected from the keen winds only by thin canvas. It is difficult not to question the sensitivity of Mr Brontë in letting her make the journey a short while after her difficult confinement.

Even in a landscape remarkable for dramatic effects – Daniel Defoe had crossly described it ninety years before as 'frightful country . . . no sooner we were down one hill but we mounted another'[1] – the situation of Haworth is unique. Although only four miles from the

18

then flourishing manufacturing town of Keighley, the moors have such dominance here, so mighty is their breadth and swell, that the village seems to sit uneasily among them. Its single street, a long stretch of small grey houses, perches on the side of the vertiginous moor, out of place amid the hills and valleys. Nevertheless, this is very much an industrial landscape, where mills sent up smoke from the leafy floor of the Worth valley, which coaches had to cross to get up to the parsonage. Charlotte later wrote dispassionately of her environment, contradicting the usual impression: 'The scenery of these hills is not grand – it is not romantic; it is scarcely striking. Long, low moors – with heath, start in little valleys, where a stream waters, here and there, a fringe of stunted copse. Mills and scattered cottages chase romance from these valleys.'[2]

One of Charlotte's Yorkshire friends would describe her first journey to the parsonage thus:

> The scenery for some miles before we reached Haworth was wild and uncultivated, with hardly any population; at last we came to what seemed a tremendous hill, such a steep declivity no one thought of riding down it; the horse had to be carefully led. We no sooner reached the foot of this hill than we had to begin to mount again, over a narrow, rough stone-paved road; the horses' feet seemed to catch at boulders, as if climbing. When we reached the top of the village there was apparently no outlet, but we were directed to drive into an entry and then saw the Church close at hand, and we entered on the short lane which led to the parsonage gate-way.[3]

Something of her surprise may have been shared by the Brontës as they arrived at Haworth, where most of the populace had turned out to see the new parson and his wife. Whatever the associations which hung about the house in later years – 'cold', 'dead-coloured', a 'bleak oblong', observers shuddered romantically – to the Brontë children it must simply have appeared a great deal bigger than their home in Thornton. It was surrounded on two sides by the church graveyard, but there was the novelty of a proper garden to play in, even if the grass and vegetation were rather sparse. The house itself, built in 1799 out of the local grey millstone grit, has a pleasing rough neo-classical simplicity, with an elegant pediment above the door. Set above the village and separated from it by the graveyard and Church of St Michael and All Angels, the parsonage gave a fine view over the valley of the Worth to the moors beyond, while behind it rose further steep moorland. The situation must have seemed promising, and the disadvantage of the house's exposed position less apparent. No trees then

19

sheltered the building, and the wind came sweeping across the open country making a wild piping sound.

The parsonage itself was very scantily decorated by the Brontës, a reflection of Patrick Brontë's abstemious way of life and dislike of luxury in any form – legacy of his impoverished youth? – although there was probably also not sufficient money to provide for comfortable furnishings, even if they had been to his taste. The two front rooms, the sitting room and Mr Brontë's study, were about fifteen feet square, with windows facing on to the graveyard, and were separated from one another by a narrow passage leading back into the rest of the house. Behind Mr Brontë's study was the main kitchen – the hub of the house, where the servant Tabby would later reign supreme, and beyond it the back kitchen. A small store room lay behind the dining room. A narrow stone staircase led up past the great-grandfather clock which Mr Brontë wound up every night to the four bedrooms – three looked down over the churchyard – and the little slip of a room five feet by nine which became the 'children's study'. Outside at the back was the water pump from which the water for the house was drawn – although it is possible that there was a pump in the back kitchen. The privy was an earth closet in the back yard. Peat was probably what the family burnt for heat. This was kept in one of the outhouses at the back, and eventually Emily and Anne would keep geese there.[4]

There were no curtains, evidently because of Patrick Brontë's fear of fire; he had witnessed casualties of fires that resulted from the local cottage wool industry, and it was only when Charlotte was thirty-six, with the income from *Shirley*, that curtains were added to the sitting room. A schoolfriend of Charlotte's from a typically comfortable and crowded Victorian upper-middle-class home recalled in later years her first impression of the parsonage. She was clearly taken aback by the austerity of the house, though she politely tried to conceal it:

Mr Brontë's horror of fire forbade curtains to the windows: they never had these accessories to comfort and appearance till long after Charlotte was the only inmate of the family sitting room. There was not much carpet anywhere except in the sitting room, and on the study floor. The hall floor and stairs were done with sandstone, always beautifully clean, as everything was about the house; the walls were not papered, but stained in a pretty, dove-coloured tint: hair seated chairs and mahogany tables, book shelves in the study but not many of these elsewhere.

She adds that though many people would have thought it scanty and bare, 'it was not a scantness that made itself felt'.[5] One wonders. Mr Brontë's sweeping decision about curtains was typical of his approach.

Despite the sparseness of the upholstery, the parsonage was rich in books; engravings by the apocalyptic painter John Martin hung on the walls; and there was a constant flow of newspapers and periodicals. In fact the home provided a wealth of material that would stimulate young minds. As in all things, Patrick Brontë held strong views on the importance of education, which he considered to be 'the last and most intense and abiding fortune'[6] parents could give their children, and all of his children were taught to read and write with exceptional rapidity. He also believed strongly in the importance of exercise. Dressed in the flannel that he considered conducive to good health, the children were thrust out on to the hills at the back of the house almost as soon as they could walk. He himself would stride for miles over the moors to bring the message of Christ to his far-flung parishioners.

Methodism was the chief religious influence on the wild, proud people amongst whom Patrick Brontë had now taken up his ministry. Until the construction of the Worth Valley railway, the area was almost completely cut off, and isolation had fostered a spirit of remarkable independence. A strong streak of folklore still flourished in these northern hills, and tales of fairies and the wee folk – tales which the servant Tabby probably related to the delight of the Brontë children – went alongside Methodist teaching, with its emphasis on the marvellous.

Years later, Charlotte recounted to Mrs Gaskell stories of the 'ungovernable families' living 'here and there in the gloom of distant hollows'. They made even *Wuthering Heights* seem comparatively tame to Mrs Gaskell:

Such dare-devil people – men especially – and women so stony and cruel in some of their feelings and so passionately fond in others, They are a queer people up there. Small landed proprietors, dwelling on one spot since Q. Eliz – and lately adding marvellously to their incomes by using the water power of the peaks in the woollen manufacture which had sprung up during the last fifty years – uneducated – unrestrained by public opinion – for their equals in position are as bad as themselves. . . . These people build grand houses, and live in the kitchens, own thousands of pounds and yet bring up their sons with only just enough learning to qualify them for onlookers during their father's lifetime and greedy grasping money hunters after their father's death.[7]

Mr and Mrs Brontë soon established that they did not care to visit with them, although Mr Brontë, and later his daughter Emily, would delight in their doings, and it would become his frequent habit to relate stories about them to his enthralled family. However, while Mrs

Brontë lived she seems to have acted as a brake to the more unrefined side of his nature. He was deeply suspicious of the uneducated working man, whom he would fearlessly maintain on the hustings should not be given the vote, and inevitably he was not interested in mixing with inhabitants of Haworth, who were mainly employed as factory hands in the textile industry. With the exception of the Heatons who lived in Ponden Hall, the big house out on the moor, and the Taylors of Stanbury who were Church trustees, the Brontës were extremely isolated socially. More than most families they would have to rely on each other for companionship and amusement.

The sense of foreignness – Mr Brontë's relatives were all in Ireland, Mrs Brontë's in Cornwall – would become a theme in the Brontës' lives. They were encouraged in this by Mr Brontë in his gloomier moods, who made a point of telling them that they were strangers in a strange land. He missed tremendously the friends he had made at Thornton. The children picked up on this actual geographical isolation and would find that it suited their poetic concept of life, which was strongly coloured by the alienation to be found in the works of their heroes, the Romantic poets, particularly Shelley and Byron. It is probable that, had Mrs Brontë lived, she would have provided a kinder, more homely atmosphere in the parsonage and dispelled this.

There are many legends about Mr Brontë's character, and all kinds of rumours abound about him. They first reached the public with Mrs Gaskell's biography of Charlotte Brontë, and were based on information spread by a former maternity nurse of Mrs Brontë's, who had been sacked by him. From her, no unimpeachable source, came rumours of Mr Brontë being 'strange' and 'half-mad', which were delightedly exaggerated by gossipy Lady Kay Shuttleworth. On one occasion he was said to have sawn up all the chairs in his wife's bedroom when one of her confinements went wrong, and another time he was supposedly so angry that he put the hearthrug on the fire in the grate, 'and sat before it with a leg on each hob, heaping on more colds [sic] till it was burnt, no one else being able to endure the room because of the stifling smoke'. Other stories were that he burnt the children's coloured boots because he thought that they would encourage vanity, and that he cut up his wife's favourite dress because it displeased him. Mrs Brontë was said on her deathbed to have repeated over and over again 'Oh my poor children' at the thought of leaving them to such untender mercies.

Charlotte herself evidently believed the story of the dress being cut up and there seems to be some basis of truth in the story, as the maids confirm it.[8] She would later represent her father to Mrs Gaskell and others as being solitary and misanthropical in his habits, though far from mad.[9] However, the record of his years at Haworth as Vicar must also convince one otherwise.[10] He was extremely active in the parish, faithful to Evangelical and Wesleyan tenets of pastoral care. Letters show him taking an intimate interest in his parishioners' affairs: advising them not to go to law and so on. He sought jobs for them: in 1858, aged 82, he was writing asking for employment for Greenwood Wood, a tailor: 'He is labouring under the effects of indigestion and is very reduced and feeble – his employment as a Tailor being ill-suited to his condition.' Letters to his parishioners show a thorough knowledge of their circumstances, and where positive steps are needed to ensure their well-being, mental or moral, he took steps to do so. Thus when one of his churchwardens, Mr Enoch Thomas, was suffering from melancholia he requested a fellow church trustee 'to have a tea party, soon, and to invite him among [sic] the number of the guests; his mind, which is, in a very disordered state should be diverted, as much as possible, from his present way of thinking.'

Despite his reclusive tendencies, he never neglected the parish: in 1832 it was his initiative to build Haworth's first Sunday School, and providing suitable preachers for the two Sunday sermons at 2.30 p.m. and 6.00 p.m., was a subject which constantly preoccupied him. As someone who despite his very limited means would hire both music master and drawing teacher for his children it is unsurprising to find that he was responsible for raising the money for Haworth's first organ, and the first bell for St Michael and All Angels. The sense of justice which had compelled him, during his first curacy at Dewsbury, and despite being a newcomer, to spearhead a campaign to release a man wrongfully accused of desertion, also prompted him to attack the Criminal Code as too 'bloody'. Public meetings, whether to address the problems of law and order, or to combat disease in cottages by whitewashing them, became the order of Haworth under Mr Brontë's active ministry. His tall black figure was often to be seen – when not striding amongst his parishioners or out on the moor – in the White Lion Hotel in the centre of Haworth, where the Conservative Club held its meetings. It would be he who for years would try and rally the village into getting a Public Health Inspector in to investigate the water supply and drainage system, as his logical mind had concluded that pollution there might account for the extraordinary disease rate. The public meeting he organised in 1837 to raise a petition to Parliament to repeal the New Poor Law Act was a typical action, as was his practice of contributing articles to the local papers throughout his lifetime on issues that interested him such as Catholic Emancipation. 1835 saw him fulminating against the democratic tendencies of the day in a twenty-four-page political pamphlet, 'The Signs of the Times'. As in his earlier Evangelical publications, he advocated religion and education as the antidote to revolution, and the following year he produced a treatise on baptism in answer to the local Baptists. Nevertheless, his attitude to the Nonconformists was in general broad-minded and sensible. He would urge moderation over the sensitive issue of church rates, against his fellow Anglican colleagues. Indeed, towards the end of his life he used to attend services at the Wesleyan chapel behind the parsonage, evidently deriving pleasure from the absolute conviction of the preachers whose intensity of feeling was in many ways so akin to his own.

Little or nothing of Mr Brontë's formidable work at Haworth appeared in Mrs Gaskell's book. The campaigner and committee man, thought highly of in Evangelical circles, whose speech on the Poor Law had been published in the *Times*, was obscured by the domestic tyrant, who gave his children nothing but potatoes to eat, who 'did not speak when he was annoyed or displeased, but worked off his volcanic wrath by firing pistols out of the back door in rapid succession'.

Mrs Gaskell met Mr Brontë under peculiar circumstances. The atmosphere in the parsonage was fraught with tension due to Mr Nicholls the curate's pursuit of Charlotte. Mr Brontë was in a particularly difficult mood, and Mrs Gaskell was already predisposed to dislike him for what she considered to be his selfish attitude towards his daughter; her opinion of him had already been prejudiced by his former nurse's gossip. Furthermore, judging by *The Life of Charlotte Brontë*, her novelist's mind was perhaps already searching for an explanation for the soil which had produced her vehement new friend, whose frankness about sexual feeling in women had so outraged Victorian England. For all her own outraging of propriety by examining taboo topics (such as 'fallen women' in *Ruth* – which caused some of her husband's congregation to cut her), like many of her contemporaries Mrs Gaskell disliked much of the 'coarseness' of *Jane Eyre* while she admired its power. It was only her meeting with Charlotte Brontë that convinced her of her 'purity', and thenceforth she became her champion.

It was in such guise that she took up her pen to write Charlotte's biography. She was determined to make her brilliant unconventional friend acceptable to her contemporaries, as her many letters and the biography itself shows. The charges of coarseness, at worst pornography, were to be assuaged by producing a portrait of a woman who was, in Mrs Gaskell's words, 'forced to touch pitch'.[11] Part of the touching pitch, aside from the debauched, corrupting presence of Branwell in the parsonage, was revealed to be Mr Brontë himself and the village of Haworth.

Mrs Gaskell was at pains to stress the wild, uncivilised nature of the inhabitants of the West Riding of Yorkshire, in order to explain the extraordinary roughness and crudeness in the Brontë writing which so alarmed contemporaries – one reviewer thought that they must be a wild brotherhood of Lancashire weavers. The population of Haworth itself was even singular within 'this wild, rough population' for its unmannerliness: 'the people so independent, wilful, and full of grim humour, there would be found much even at the present that would shock those accustomed only to the local manners of the south'. Mr Brontë's curate Mr Nicholls, later Charlotte's husband, would later comment that Haworth might be a queer place, but it was nowhere quite as queer as Mrs Gaskell had made out.[12]

Mr Brontë himself she described as having opinions 'often both wild and erroneous, his principles of action eccentric and strange, his views of life partial and almost misanthropical . . . he had strong vehement prejudices and was obstinate in maintaining them' (though she had to admit admiringly that 'not one opinion that he held could be stirred or modified by any worldly motive'). She goes on, building up the defence's case for what she terms Charlotte Brontë's 'strong mind and vivid imagination' – too strong for Victorian England – 'I have named these instances of eccentricity in the father because I hold the knowledge of them to be necessary for a right understanding of the life of his daughter.'[13] In addition, Mrs Gaskell believed, as further reasons for lack of propriety in Mr Brontë's daughters' books, the death of Mrs Brontë so soon after her husband had moved into the district, and the distances and the bleak country which had to be travelled, meant that the wives of Mr Brontë's clerical friends 'did not accompany their husbands, and the daughters grew up out of childhood into girlhood bereft, in a singular manner, of all such society as would have been natural to their age, sex, and station.'[14]

In point of fact such an upbringing probably did play an important role in the unfeminine and unusual quality of the Brontë books, which would so astonish their contemporaries. Likewise, the experience of being brought up in the care of a man who held impassioned opinions on most topics was almost certainly responsible for his daughter's strong views, and for Charlotte Brontë's defiant reaction to critics' attacks.

The uncouth customs of the village, the remoteness of the Brontës from any opinion other than their own and their father's contributed to an absence of polite manners and an informal, intellectual way of life, an informality and roughness encouraged by the surprisingly (to Mrs Gaskell) intimate and friendly relations between kitchen and parlour.

Charlotte herself, after the outcry that *Wuthering Heights* caused, would suggest that their environment forced an acceptance of the

25

crude and the brutal: to strangers 'unacquainted with the locality' *Wuthering Heights* 'must appear a rude and strange production':

> Men and women who, perhaps, naturally very calm, and with feelings moderate in degree, and little marked in kind, have been trained from their cradle to observe the utmost evenness of manner and guardedness of language, will hardly know what to make of the rough strong utterances, the harshly manifested passions, the unbridled aversions, and headlong partialities of unlettered moorland hinds and rugged moorland squires, who have grown up untaught and unchecked, except by mentors as harsh as themselves.[15]

For Patrick Brontë's children, there was not much chance of being naturally very calm, or being trained to observe evenness of manner and guardedness of language. Not only did his excitable children feel a temperamental affinity with their environment, but everything they read or heard disposed them to exult in strong feeling, to despise the polite. An insistence on the real and the true would be quite marked in Charlotte and Branwell by the age of thirteen and fourteen. In Charlotte's case, the combination of Evangelicalism and Romanticism colouring her upbringing would result in an ineradicable feeling of responsibility for her 'gift' of writing, a necessity to write the truth even if it offended. Patrick Brontë's Evangelical fervour and sense of mission were turned towards art.

Reading between the lines, it seems that the genteel upper-middle-class matron Mrs Gaskell found the unaffected and forthright Mr Brontë, in his language and behaviour, quite unlike anyone she knew. His lack of polish and unconventionality made him seem half mad to her. It was indeed his custom, as she would describe, and would be for forty years after his wife died, to dine alone in his study. Mr Brontë's habit of wearing his loaded pistol at all times of the day – 'There was this little deadly pistol sitting down to breakfast with us, kneeling down to prayers at night to say nothing of a loaded gun hanging up on high, ready to pop off on the slightest emergency' – and the force of his personality made her believe that the nurse's stories were true. Charlotte Brontë herself would never remember her father dressing himself in the morning without putting a loaded pistol in his pocket just as regularly as he put on his watch.[16]

Certainly, all authorities agree that this powerful man insisted on nursing his wife himself when in January 1821, some nine months after the move to Haworth, the ailment that Mrs Brontë had incurred after the birth of Anne flared up into an excruciating illness. This has been attributed to cancer of the stomach but latest medical opinion points to infection of the blood following a complex delivery. Perhaps there was a family weakness, passed on to all her children, for two of her sisters died before the age of thirty and her brother died at forty-three.

Mrs Brontë spent the next seven months dying in the hushed atmosphere of the little house, so ill that Mr Brontë expected her death almost every day. It was a terrifying long-drawn-out experience for the children, whose father was too impatient and distraught to be of comfort. They were, according to the nurse who attended their mother, grave children anyway, so quiet that 'you would not have known there was a child in the house, they were such still noiseless, good little creatures'. The older ones clung together in the children's study, where the eldest, the precocious Maria, would shut herself up with a newspaper and be able to 'tell me everything when she came out; debates in Parliament and I don't know what all'. The nurse went on in wonder: 'There never were such good little children. I used to think them spiritless, they were so different to any children I had ever seen.'[17]

Mr Brontë was overwhelmed with grief and anxiety, made worse by his dearth of companions. He poured out his loneliness and despair to his former vicar at Dewsbury in his usual vivid and poetic prose:

Had I been at D. [Dewsbury] I should not have wanted kind friends; had I been at H. [Hartshead] I should have seen them and others occasionally; or had I been at T. [Thornton] a family there who were ever truly kind would have soothed my sorrows: but I was at H. [Haworth] a stranger in a strange land. It was under these circumstances, after every earthly prop had been removed, that I was called on to bear the weight of the greatest load of sorrows that ever pressed on me. One day, I remember it well; it was a gloomy day, a day of clouds and darkness, three of my little children were taken ill of a scarlet fever; and, the day after, the remaining three were in the same condition. Just at that time death seemed to have laid his hand on my dear wife in a manner which threatened her speedy dissolution. She was cold and silent and seemed hardly to notice what was passing around her.

In desperation Mr Brontë applied to his wife's elder sister, Miss Elizabeth Branwell, to come and help nurse his wife and aid Mr Brontë with the six children, all under eight years old. In her dutiful way the forty-year-old spinster made the long journey from Cornwall to comfort her sister's last months in this harsh land, and remained there for the rest of her life.

Perhaps it is merely a picturesque legend, but during Mrs Brontë's

27

illness it is said that she used to like to sit up in bed to watch the servants clean the grate because that was how they did it in Cornwall. She was probably delirious at the last, and fearful of death. Mr Brontë wrote of her end: 'During many years she had walked with God, but the great enemy, envying her life of holiness, often disturbed her mind in the last conflict.' She died in early September 1821 'if not triumphantly, at least calmly and with a holy yet humble confidence that Christ was her Saviour and heaven her eternal home.' She was buried in the crypt of the church, thirty yards from the house across the churchyard.

Mr Brontë did not suffer his loss stoically, and seems to have found his children's presence a painful reminder of his wife rather than a comfort:

> Oppressive grief sometimes lay heavy on me . . . there were seasons when an affectionate agonising *something* sickened my whole frame, and which is I think of such a nature as cannot be described, and must be felt in order to be understood. And when my dear wife was dead and buried and gone, and when I missed her at every corner, and when her memory was hourly revived by the innocent yet distressing prattle of my children, I do assure you, my dear sir, from what I felt, I was happy at the recollection that to sorrow, not as those without hope, was no sin.

He would also have had the added burden of debt after his wife's illness, if friends had not helped him out. He had at least one specialist's bill for £50 to pay – a quarter of his income. But people seem to have realised the plight he was in, and he recorded that 'good and wealthy' friends in Bradford sent him £150; a further £50 was sent by an Evangelical Society in London. As usual the Evangelicals looked after their own.

With Mrs Brontë's death, a cheerful and alleviating influence in the parsonage was removed, and the children were left in the charge of a man who, though brilliant, was little interested in the material comforts of life. The gay, gregarious side of his nature slowly became submerged; he withdrew into himself, beginning the habit of dining alone, theoretically on account of his poor digestion.

Charlotte would later confide to Mrs Gaskell that 'he did not like children' and that when they had six in six years 'the consequent pinching and family disorder . . . and noise made him shut himself up and want no companionship – nay, be positively annoyed by it'.[18] In later life Charlotte, although five at the time of her mother's death, said that she could remember almost nothing about her, apart from a dim recollection of her playing in the parlour in the evening light with

Branwell. Perhaps she consciously tried to blot out this period of her life because it was too painful to live with. Most of the characters in her juvenilia would be orphans, and of the heroines of her adult fiction, only Caroline Helstone was not one.

Meanwhile, the sweet-natured seven-year-old Maria took over the mother's role that her reserved aunt found difficulty in assuming. Although Miss Branwell and Mr Brontë suited one another – she was a courageous intelligent woman with firm opinions which she enjoyed expressing in debate with her brother-in-law – and though he himself considered that she had 'behaved as an affectionate mother to my children', she was not the kind of woman to compensate adequately for the loss of her sister. She made a point of doing her duty by the children, but she does not seem to have been a very sympathetic presence. None of the Brontë children's letters except Branwell's includes an affectionate mention of her. Nevertheless, to see her as the prototype of Mrs Reed in *Jane Eyre* seems to read too much into the coincidences of the relationship. Certainly she does not appear to have frightened her nieces, judging by Anne's diary entries where the girls enjoyed themselves teasing her. She was strict with the servants, who resented how little beer allowance she gave them and who considered her 'a bit of a tyke'.[19] But the report of one of them that she was not very affectionate to the little girls, and that their 'wild eyes' frightened her, may be taken with a very large pinch of salt. What is certain is that she was a very independent-minded woman, who insisted that she pay her brother-in-law for her keep for the twenty years she lived with him, and who was so frugal in her habits that she was able to leave what would amount to about £1,300, all saved from her £40 annuity.

In appearance she stuck resolutely with the fashions of her youth, wearing the large respectable lace caps of her girlhood in the 1790s long after they had been replaced by the smaller ones worn from the 1820s on, so that one visitor to the house described her amusedly as 'a very small antiquated little lady'.[20] Like many women she wore what was known as a 'false front' of auburn curls over her forehead. Judging by the portrait of her as a young girl, she had the long nose of the Branwells which both Anne and Emily inherited.[21] She always dressed in dark silk, which met with Mr Brontë's approval. He considered silk and flannel to be safe from fire hazard, and was swift to show his disapproval of visitors to the parsonage foolish enough to wear cotton or wool.

Miss Branwell distrusted the climate so far north and feared the stone floors of the parsonage. To guard against damp, she somewhat eccentrically wore wooden pattens inside the house, and when the children reached their late teens, she retreated more and more to her

29

bedroom,[22] which she turned into a bed-sitting room, leaving the run of the house to the children. They were left to form a little society of their own, as one of the servants remembered, mothered by the sweet and religious Maria. However, Miss Branwell, like her sister, was a devout Methodist, a member of the Methodist Society in Penzance, and it may be that Wesley's religion of love provided some comfort against the children's grievous loss.

With time, Patrick Brontë came to the conclusion that he was happier within the cocoon of marriage. He was too purposeful a man to allow his wife's death to destroy the fabric of his family's life, and within two years he began in his determined way to cast about for a suitable candidate. In the process he met with a savage rebuff from a still unmarried (and apparently sensitive about it) girlfriend of his Essex days fifteen years before. He also seems to have made overtures to Miss Firth and to the Rector of Keighley's sister, Isabelle Dury. The latter's reaction to the rumours of this sheds light on how Mr Brontë was viewed in the neighbourhood:

> I heard before I left Keighley that my brother and I had quarrelled about poor Mr Brontë, I beg if you ever hear such a report that you will contradict it as I can assure you it is perfectly unfounded. I think I never should be so very silly as to have the most distant idea of marrying anybody who had not some future, and six children into the bargain. It is too ridiculous to imagine any truth in it.

With this last refusal Mr Brontë abandoned all ideas of marriage, and became increasingly odd and anti-social. Around the same time he came to the conclusion that he was no longer equal to the task of educating his children and performing his extensive parish duties, and in 1823, probably on the advice of Miss Firth, he sent the two elder girls to the famous girls' school run by Miss Mangnall in Wakefield. However, the expense made it impossible for this to be a lasting arrangement, and by the end of 1823 they were once again back home.

Such affectionate feeling as Patrick Brontë possessed he poured out on his children, for whom he would depend in the future for most of his companionship. He fed them a thrilling intellectual diet, which took little account of the modern concept of childhood as a discrete entity, with its own systems of thought requiring different books and approaches, although they certainly had toys (some of which were found under the floorboards of the parsonage many years after the Brontës were dead). Mr Brontë's own childhood had, after all, been largely undifferentiated from adolescence and adulthood. Under his tutelage they took a close interest in 'public characters' and the local, domestic and foreign politics discussed in the newspapers. He later said that he could converse with Maria long before she was eleven years old on any of the leading topics of the day with as much freedom and pleasure as with any grown-up person, and he wistfully remembered this marvellous child's 'powerfully intellectual mind'.[23] A printer from Thornton also remembered this precocious child helping to correct the proofs of one of Mr Brontë's long poems. At this time Charlotte was very much the third sister, in awe and in the shadow of the eldest.

The precocity of the Brontë children must in some measure be attributed to Mrs Brontë's death. Had she lived it is doubtful that the children would have been thrust into adult habits as soon as they were, or that Maria Brontë would have been correcting proofs. With his wife's death Patrick Brontë's idiosyncratic way of going about things would no longer be restrained and he could try out his odd quasi-scientific ideas on his children, as the following account he gave of their childhood reveals:

When my children were very young, when, as far as I can remember, the oldest was about ten years of age, and the youngest about four, thinking that they knew more than I had yet discovered, in order to make them speak with less timidity, I deemed that if they were put under a sort of cover I might gain my end; and happening to have a mask in the house, I told them all to stand and speak boldly from under the cover of the mask.

I began with the youngest [Anne, afterwards Acton Bell], and asked what a child like her most wanted; she answered, 'Age and experience.' I asked the next [Emily, afterwards Ellis Bell] what I had best do with her brother Branwell, who was sometimes a naughty boy; she answered, 'Reason with him, and when he won't listen to reason, whip him.' I asked Branwell what was the best way of knowing the differences between the intellects of man and woman; he answered, 'By considering the difference between them as to their bodies.' I then asked Charlotte what was the best book in the world; she answered, 'The Bible'. And what was the next best; she answered, 'The Book of Nature'. I then asked the next [Elizabeth] what was the best mode of education for a woman; she answered, 'That which would make her rule her house well.' Lastly, I asked the oldest what was the best mode of spending time; she answered, 'By laying it out in preparation for a happy eternity.' I may not have given precisely their words, but I have nearly done so, as they made a deep and lasting impression on my memory. The substance, however, was exactly what I have stated.[24]

*

31

The complaint of both schools that Charlotte would attend was that she knew nothing systematically, though she surpassed even her teachers in her knowledge of poetry. This assessment sheds some light on Mr Brontë's teaching methods. The lack of methodical knowledge of French grammar, for example, probably reflects the harried parson's lack of hours in the day to sit down and go over grammatical principles with his children. His great gift to his children was his encouragement and enthusiasm, and pride in their progress; he wrote to Mrs Gaskell that 'I frequently thought that I discovered signs of rising talent, which I had seldom or never before seen in any of their age.'[25]

The preface of a poem written for his Sunday School pupils in 1824 when Charlotte was eight shows the intelligence of his methods and his encouragement of the spirit of enquiry and endeavour in children: 'You are now, as I suppose, in the first class of your Sunday School and consequently are able to read considerably well. This is one reason why I have not been careful to select for you the easiest words and phrases, judging it proper that you should have a dictionary, and be able to find out in it the meaning of such phrases and words as you do not clearly understand.'[26] He had not spent many years teaching children in Ireland for nothing.

Maria was the stellar presence in the parsonage, greatly looked up to by Charlotte and Branwell; Emily and Anne, being that much younger, were less involved. According to Charlotte's own account, she was a serious and rather silent child, although this is belied in a letter Charlotte wrote years later to a friend recounting the visit of a small child to the parsonage: 'She amused Papa very much – chattering away to him very funnily. . . . Papa says she speaks as I did when a child – says the same odd unexpected things.'[27] In yet another letter her father says she always was a 'chatter box'. Nevertheless, her father seems to have found the tiny Charlotte quite difficult to get to know. Asked by Mrs Gaskell to 'state something respecting the development of her intellectual powers', he writes: 'A difficulty meets me in the very commencement, since she was from a child prone to say very little about herself and averse from making any display of what she knew.' He went on to say: 'However, in her childish days she often gave proofs of intelligence and quickness, so that the servants often said that they never saw such a clever little child, and that they were often obliged to be on their guard in regard to what they said and did before her. Yet she and the servants always lived on good terms with each other.'[28]

Despite Charlotte's portrayal of herself as very much in her older sister's shadow, she was clearly an imaginative child with a strong personality of her own. There is a story that at about the age of six, she was retrieved from running away to Bradford, the nearest big town, because she thought it must be the Celestial City from *Pilgrim's Progress*; and from the same time comes a memory of seeing an angel hovering over Anne's cot. According to Mr Brontë, during the plays the children used to act, 'the Duke of Wellington, my daughter Charlotte's hero, was sure to come off the conquering hero – when a dispute would not infrequently arise amongst them regarding the comparative merits of him, Bonaparte, Hannibal and Caesar.'[29] It was a characteristic that would increase as time went by. This little girl – the most puny of her father's entire brood as she would say in later life, who by default took on the responsibilities of the eldest child, would dominate the family.

Mr Brontë's dramatic temperament was swift to use natural phenomena to demonstrate the omnipotence of the Creator to his children. In 1824 the three youngest, who were out on a walk over the hills, were in danger of being killed when a bog erupted high up on the moors, bringing trees and earth down in a great landslide of earth and water. Mr Brontë responded to the occurrence with all the fervour of like meeting like. A poem celebrating the awefulness of God and the minatory nature of the avalanche immediately swelled within him. And lest the lesson be lost to any of his congregation, he not only constructed the sermon for that Sunday out of it, but the poem became the standard text for the first class of the Sunday School to learn.

But he also imparted to his children a dislike of cant, instilling in them the value of the sacred truth above anything materialistic. They were taught to believe in the validity of their own opinions from a very early age. In their father they had an example of a man willing to perish for his beliefs, a man unafraid of unpopularity. Patrick Brontë's own career was constantly before his children as an example: the books of poetry he had written; his ascent to respectability entirely through his own efforts: his reverence for 'genius' and great men – the passion for culture of the auto-didact. Mrs Gaskell would be very struck by his intense curiosity which amounted to almost a craving for knowledge.

In 1824 a solution to Patrick Brontë's problems of educating his growing children on little income, with all the responsibilities of his ministry, seemed to arise when a new school was established for the daughters of poor Evangelical clergy at Cowan Bridge in Lancashire. It was a preventive measure to curtail the spread of High Church teaching. Only about fifty miles from Haworth, it must have seemed like a god-send. It was under the patronage of his own patron, Wilberforce, and a host of other important figures among the Evangelicals were subscribers to it, including Mr Brontë's former mentor, Simeon, and the influential and famous female Evangelical educator, Hannah More, as well as several Members of Parliament. Parents of the girls were to pay £14 a year, and the rest of the fee would be subsidised by subscription among Evangelical supporters. From the school would go forth a new generation to spread the word. As the prospectus put it: 'In all cases, the great object in view is [the girls'] intellectual and religious improvement; and to give that plain and useful education, which may best fit them to return with respectability and advantage to their own homes, or to maintain themselves in the different stations of life to which Providence may call them.'

The director of the school had impeccable qualifications: Carus Wilson was an independently wealthy clergyman, a landowner with a large house named Casterton Hall near the school, who was very highly thought of in Evangelical circles. In his obituary the Bishop of Rochester would describe him as having 'the singular felicity of improving, if not anticipating, in his various plans of benevolence, the leading ideas of his age, and his name has long been a household word in every Christian family'. He was not unqualifiedly admired by some of his fellow clergy, and was at first refused ordination for being too Calvinistic in his beliefs, though one must allow for anti-Evangelical feeling among the ministry.

Unfortunately for the well-meaning Mr Brontë, the worst side of Evangelicalism was personified in Carus Wilson. In the hands of this plump chosen vessel the peculiar later Evangelical attitude towards the claims of the flesh, in combination with the delicacy of the Brontë children and an unpleasant staff, transformed a school whose sanitation and food were probably no worse than any other, into a death chamber. Something of his attitude towards illness is indicated by the following letter to his daughter, who had become a bedridden invalid, in constant pain due to a spinal disorder: 'You are early learning, my child, to carry the cross. I would have spared you the cross if I could; but in so doing how I should have marred your real welfare.'[30] The literature which poured out of him, his penny periodicals for children, *The Friendly Visitor* and *The Children's Friend*, begun in 1824 probably to coincide with the opening of the school and printed locally, while typically Evangelical in their emphasis on the edifying deathbed, are unusually emphatic about the natural sinfulness of little children. And their prevalent theme, that a holy death of a child is better than an unholy life, does not suggest a man who would concern himself with the physical well-being of his charges.

The school's prospectus, however, gave no hint of any cause for concern, and to Mr Brontë the education outlined would have appeared excellent and most suitable for women. 'The system of education comprehends History, Geography, the Use of Globes, Grammar, Writing and Arithmetic; all kinds of Needlework, and the nicer kinds of household-work, such as getting up fine linen etc. If Accomplishments are required, an additional charge is made, for French, Music, or Drawing, of £3 a year each.' Mr Brontë promptly paid the extra for music lessons for the infant prodigy Maria. Since the educators were very much aware of training some of the girls to earn their own livings, and of practical ends for education, it was particularly requested 'that the wishes of the friends may be stated regarding the line of education for each pupil, as will best suit their future prospects, as well as their respective dispositions and abilities'. Maria, Charlotte and Emily all paid higher fees to get the higher standard of education, suitable for training governesses. Elizabeth must have been designated the family housekeeper, as she had the lower scale.

Pupils were requested to bring £3 with them to pay for the frocks, pelisse, bonnet, tippet and frills which the school would provide. In summer the girls were to wear white frocks on Sundays and nankeen on other days. In winter they were to wear purple stuff dresses and purple cloth pelisses. There was to be five weeks' holiday at midsummer, but any of the pupils might remain at the school during the holidays, for which a fee of £1.1s was to be paid. The parents were requested to state what diseases their children had had. It all seemed very decent and carefully thought out. Even the rule, 'All letters and parcels will be inspected by the Governess' had no sinister overtones; it was a standard practice in schools of the time.[31]

The arrangements were duly made, and on 1 July 1824 Maria and Elizabeth Brontë, aged ten and nine years old, arrived at Cowan Bridge. They were still rather weak from attacks of measles and whooping cough which had been epidemic in Haworth that summer, and there was at first doubt as to whether they were well enough to be admitted. The little girls were apparently happy enough, for on 10 August Mr Brontë sent eight-year-old Charlotte to join them. The Brontës' kind friend Miss Firth, now Mrs Franks, who cared for the children's welfare and who was the frequent donor of money and clothes, stopped by there with her new husband on her honeymoon to give them a present. She evidently found nothing amiss, and six-year-old Emily was sent to join her sisters in late November. Presumably the girls had sent no letters of complaint, but they were young and probably would not have considered doing so.

The school would have appeared quite attractive, though not particularly imposing. Cowan Bridge was a small hamlet on the coach road between Leeds and Kendal which had grown up round the bridge crossing the pretty little River Leck. The countryside was gentler than that round Haworth, but it was still upland and could

35

become very cold in winter. The school was about seventy yards from the river, the distance between being the school garden, which a contemporary woodcut shows to be just as Charlotte later described it in *Jane Eyre*: 'a covered verandah ran down one side, and broad walks bordered a middle space divided into scores of little beds'. The school buildings themselves comprised a long, low series of cottages converted into one building; the dormitories were on the top floor, over the various school rooms.

Mrs Gaskell afterwards visited it during the summer and found 'the air all around was so sweet and thyme-scented' that it was hard to believe the position was not ideal. As Charlotte would write in later years, it was 'assuredly pleasant enough, but whether healthy or not is another question'; in fact it was 'a situation as unhealthy as it was picturesque', for the school was an ill-thought-out project conceived by a novice who had never run a school before. It was too near the river and consequently too damp. Too many girls were crowded into too few rooms; sanitation, as in almost all early nineteenth-century housing, was hardly planned for – there was one stone privy between about sixty girls and staff. Under such conditions, particularly among sickly children, disease could flourish, and then run rife.

The educational standards of the Brontë girls were assessed by the school authorities and found lacking, whatever their father's pride in them. The register reads:

Maria Brontë, aged 10 . . . reads tolerably. Writes pretty well. Ciphers a little. Works badly. Very little of geography or history. Has made some progress in reading French, but knows nothing of the language grammatically. Elizabeth Brontë, aged 9 (Vaccinated. Scarlet fever, whooping cough.) Reads little. Writes pretty well. Ciphers none [sic]. Works very badly. Knows nothing of grammar, geography, history or accomplishments. . . . Charlotte Brontë . . . Writes indifferently. Ciphers a little, and works neatly. Knows nothing of grammar, geography, history or accomplishments. Altogether clever of her age, but knows nothing systematically. . . . Emily Brontë . . . aged $6\frac{1}{4}$. Reads very prettily, and works a little.[32]

But what was the reality of life at the school? Can Lowood in *Jane Eyre* have really been identical in all particulars to the Clergy Daughters School at Cowan Bridge? Who can forget those extraordinary scenes – the disgusting food and near starvation; the cold; the cruelty of Miss Scatcherd to the mild and gentle Helen Burns? The modern reader shudders at the saintly resignation of Helen Burns, and applauds Jane Eyre's savage spirit of resistance to Miss Scatcherd when she says, 'if she struck me with that rod, I should get it from her hand; I should break it under her nose'. Was the sadistic Mr Brocklehurst, who thought it better that children should imitate Christian martyrs than have their bodily wants taken care of, who would reply to Miss Temple's pleas 'Oh, Madam, when you put bread and cheese, instead of burnt porridge, into these children's mouths, you may indeed feed their vile bodies, but you little think how you starve their immortal souls', a portrait, as opposed to a caricature, of Charlotte's headmaster Carus Wilson? Hard as it is to believe, Charlotte Brontë's later claims that Lowood *was true* and pretty well 'photographed' from life are borne out by most of the evidence. In particular, Ford K. Brown notes that Mr Brocklehurst's reply could be 'taken as gross caricature by someone who has not read Evangelical literature, but by no one who has'.[33]

The school records show that the food was hardly adequate for growing girls. It seems as if the authorities had tried to cut the costs (probably because the subscribers had not all contributed in quite the way it had been anticipated). Breakfast was scanty – milk and a slice of dry bread (with a thin scraping of butter on Sundays only) or milk and porridge. Dinner, at one, was a pudding as first course (mostly baked rice) – possibly Yorkshire pudding – presumably to take the edge off the girls' appetites – which indeed suggests that the meat course of 'Hot Roast', 'Pie of Odds and Ends', 'HotchPotch' or 'Boiled Beef' was fairly small; the vegetables were served separately from the meat. Tea was at five, the last meal of the day, and consisted of milk and dry bread. In the subsequent dispute about the school on the publication of Mrs Gaskell's *Life of Charlotte Brontë* in 1857, there was some consensus that the food was indeed poorly cooked. The husband of Anne Evans, the original of *Jane Eyre*'s kind Miss Temple who braved the wrath of Mr Brocklehurst to feed the starving girls a cheese lunch, said that his wife talked only admiringly of Mr Carus Wilson's personal sacrifices and 'the parental affection he manifested towards the pupils', and that 'of the food and treatment of the children she always spoke in terms of general approval'. But he did say that 'I have heard her allude to some unfortunate cook, who used at times to spoil the food, but she said she was soon dismissed'.[34]

Again, the school registers are a testament to the poor health record at Cowan Bridge. A typhoid epidemic that swept the school in the spring of 1825 was later claimed to be 'not an alarming one', but out of a total of fifty-one children entered into the new school, eight – which is almost a sixth – had left between February and June 1825.[35] It must be assumed that most of these had gone because of concern for their health. The pathetic entries include, for example, 'left school in ill health, 13th February, died April 28, 1825'; 'left on account of ill health which incapacitated her for further study'; 'left

37

school in good health April 2nd 1825, died of typhus fever April 23rd'.[36] These entries do not inspire confidence in the regime.

Some twenty years after she had left, Charlotte was asked if she could recommend the school and replied that she understood that the regime was much altered and the school moved to a healthier situation, but that as she had known it, the school was not a fit place for children: 'The establishment was at that time in its infancy, and a sad, ricketty infancy it was. Typhus fever decimated the school periodically, and consumption and scrofula in every variety of form, [which] bad air and water, and bad, insufficient diet, can generate, preyed on the ill-fated pupils.'[37]

The regime broke down the already weak constitutions of Charlotte's older sisters. By the winter of 1824 her adored, wise, brave Maria was seriously ill with consumption, and Elizabeth's health was deteriorating. In a letter written to her publisher when she was grown up Charlotte spoke of herself as probably having been 'very grave' at school, 'for I suffered to see my sisters perishing'. Her feelings of rage and helplessness must have been made worse by the school reading matter, Carus Wilson's parables of children welcoming death. Most of the phrases which Brocklehurst uses come almost verbatim from Carus Wilson's writings, taken in indelibly by a silent, appalled child: the need for God to take away the wicked heart of stone and give you a heart of flesh; the horrors of the fiery pit. The book which Mr Brocklehurst presses into Jane Eyre's hand, *The Children's Guide*, containing 'an account of the awfully sudden death of Martha G. – a naughty child addicted to falsehood and deceit' is identical in form to many of the stories of sudden death and eternal damnation in *The Children's Friend*. While she must have encountered these ideas at home,[38] the affection of her father and aunt must have removed some of their horror. In any case they did not wallow in morbid imaginings. The atmosphere at the school must have been worsened by Carus Wilson's cruel streak as exhibited in a work of his entitled 'Thoughts Suggested to the Superintendent and Ladies'. Written in 1824, he describes his way of thinking in tones which uncannily echo Mr Brocklehurst when he orders all the girls' top knots to be cut off, and announces that his mission is to mortify in these girls the lusts of the flesh, to 'teach them to clothe themselves with shamefacedness and sobriety, not with braided hair and costly apparel'. Wilson writes: 'The pupils are necessarily put into a very simple and uniform attire. Many of them no doubt feel it. They have been unfortunately accustomed, perhaps even to excess in this very prevailing and increasing love of dress, for alas, clergymen's families are not exempt from the mania – not even the poorest. With me it was always an object to nip in the bud any growing symptom of vanity.' He everywhere insists that the pupils be 'made useful and kept humble'; and he again echoes Mr Brocklehurst's description of Lowood being a 'nursery of chosen plants' when he writes that the school is 'a nursery for Christ's Spiritual Church on earth, and a nursery for Heaven'.[39] A real nursery to prepare children for everyday life never seems to have bulked large in his plans.

Mrs Gaskell wrote that Charlotte had been 'suffering her whole life long, both in heart and body, from the consequences of what happened' at Cowan Bridge, though she admitted that Charlotte 'had not considered it necessary, in a work of fiction, to state every particular with the impartiality that might be required in a court of justice'.[40]

Nevertheless, according to Mrs Gaskell, 'Helen Burns is as exact a transcript of Maria Brontë as Charlotte's wonderful power of reproducing character could give. Her heart, to the latest day on which we met, still beat with unavailing indignation at the worrying and cruelty to which her gentle patient dying sister had been subjected by this woman [Miss Scatcherd]. Not a word of that part of *Jane Eyre* but is a literal repetition of scenes between the pupil and the teacher. Those who had been pupils at the same time knew who must have written the book from the force with which Helen Burns' sufferings are described.' And she went on to write that one of the Brontës' fellow pupils had given her the following description of the behaviour of the original of Miss Scatcherd to Maria:

The dormitory in which Maria slept was a long room, holding a row of narrow little beds on each side, occupied by the pupils and at the end of this dormitory there was a small bed-chamber opening out of it, appropriated to the use of Miss Scatcherd. Maria's bed stood nearest to the door of this room. One morning, after she had become so seriously unwell as to have had a blister applied to her side [a common remedy for consumption] (the sore from which was not perfectly healed), when the getting-up bell was heard, poor Maria moaned out that she was ill, so very ill, she wished she might stop in bed, and some of the girls urged her to do so, and said they would explain it all to Miss Temple, the superintendent. But Miss Scatcherd was close at hand, and her anger would have to be faced before Miss Temple's kind thoughtfulness could interfere; so the sick child began to dress, shivering with cold, as, without leaving her bed, she slowly put on her black worsted stockings over her thin white legs (my informant spoke as if she saw it yet, and her whole face flashed out undying indignation). Just then Miss Scatcherd issued from her room, and, without asking for a word of explanation from the sick and frightened girl, she took her by the arm, on the side to which the blister had been applied, and by one vigorous movement whirled her out into the middle of the floor, abusing her all the time for dirty and untidy habits. There she left her. My informant says Maria hardly spoke except to beg some of the more indignant girls to be calm; but in slow, trembling movements, with many a pause, she went down stairs at last – and was punished for being late.

It is impossible to believe that the naturally kind-hearted Patrick Brontë could have known how ill his elder daughters were or that cruelty of this kind was being perpetrated at the school and not have taken action, however sympathetic he was to Evangelical principles of education for children. The exceptional delicacy of the Brontë children which made them particularly susceptible to the harsh regime, the poor diet, the damp, the freezing walks in rain without adequate clothing, was probably not recognised. Mr Brontë's colleague, the Rector of Keighley, the Reverend Theodore Dury, had also sent his child Isabelle to the school and there is no record to indicate that she did not continue at Cowan Bridge quite happily for some years. There must have been lighter moments. Charlotte herself, aged thirteen, remembered days of paddling in streams, and she evidently thought highly of the Principal Miss Evans, who in turn spoke in laudatory terms of Charlotte's 'intelligence, quickness and good conduct'.

By February 1825, however, the school authorities admitted that Maria Brontë was too ill to remain and in that month Mr Brontë withdrew her from the school. By then, whatever chances of sparing her life had gone; the tuberculosis from which she was suffering was already far advanced. She lingered on at Haworth for a further three months and finally died there on 6 May. Elizabeth was left at the school, getting paler and thinner through the spring, and it was only on 31 May that she was brought home. An immediate alarm must have been raised because on the next day, 1 June, Charlotte and Emily were also removed from the school. It was too late to save Elizabeth, who died on 15 June two weeks after coming home.

Thirty-two years later, after Charlotte's own death, the publication of Mrs Gaskell's biography aroused instant controversy because of its claim that Cowan Bridge was identical to Lowood. In the ensuing battle waged in the columns of the *Halifax Guardian* of 1857 by Charlotte's husband Mr Nicholls against the defenders of Carus Wilson, each side produced equally impressive evidence of the regime having been both perfectly pleasant, and perfectly unpleasant. Carus Wilson's son claimed to have 300 testimonials of satisfied former pupils in his father's favour, while Mr Nicholls produced women who had been removed from the school because they had become so ill from starvation and consumption. It was pointed out by Mr Wilson's faction that Charlotte Brontë had been a mere child at the time, incapable of evaluating the true significance of events, seeing them through the magnifying glass of childhood. And it is true that to a child whose sisters the administrators of the school had not been able to preserve from death, her view of it must inevitably have been clouded by emotion.

But the strongest piece of evidence vindicating the regime was considered to be a letter produced by Carus Wilson supporters from a certain 'A.H.', who was said to have been the superintendent during Charlotte's residence at Cowan Bridge. She thus must have been the 'good' Miss Temple. A.H. discredited Charlotte's claims that there was not enough to eat, saying that the daily dinner consisted of 'meat, vegetables, and pudding in abundance' (although the principal criticism in *Jane Eyre* is actually the poor quality of the food and the way it was cooked). A.H. dismissed claims that when a physician had been called in to deal with what she described as an 'unalarming' low fever, he had spat out the food in disgust, denouncing it as not fit for pigs: 'I recollect that he spoke rather scornfully of a baked rice pudding, but as the ingredients of this dish were chiefly rice, sugar and milk, its effects could hardly have been so serious as have been affirmed.' She also said that Charlotte had been a 'general favourite, a bright, clever, happy little girl, never in disgrace; punishment she certainly did not experience while she was at Cowan Bridge'.

This calm voice of reason went on to say that the real question to be addressed was how far young and delicate children were able to contend with the necessary evils of a public school. She pointed out that 'thoughtless servants will occasionally spoil food, even in private families, and in a public school they are likely to be far less particular, unless they are well looked after. But in this respect the institution in question compares very favourably with other and more expensive schools, as from personal experience I have reason to know.'

In fact it emerged in 1975 that the real Miss Temple, Anne Evans, had died in 1856 (which was known at the time but not computed) and that the *soi-disant* superintendent on whom so much evidence depends, and who wrote the exoneration of the school, was the original of Miss Scatcherd,[41] one of the chief villainesses of *Jane Eyre*. Her evidence thus becomes very tainted indeed. After all, the cruel Miss Scatcherd is one of the book's chief targets. It is she who persecutes Helen Burns unmercifully for untidiness, flogs her cruelly and humiliates her, binding 'slattern' round Helen's 'large, mild, intelligent and benign-looking forehead'. She would have very good reason to deny everything.

It is probable that the defence of the school by former pupils was dictated by Carus Wilson's sacrosanct status as a clergyman. As 'A.H.'

41

wrote, and she was speaking for many, 'There were not wanting, however, those even then, who more than doubted the tendency of the much admired volume, and a leading Review did not hesitate to pronounce *Jane Eyre*, an "eminently irreligious book".'[42] Many of his defenders felt (correctly) that Evangelical religion was being attacked through the attack on him and that *Jane Eyre* had brought disgrace upon religion.

Although Carus Wilson's son complained that the portrait of Mr Brocklehurst was a monstrous caricature, and others that the character of the founder had been cruelly and falsely assailed, the man who emerges from Carus Wilson's writings is remarkably similar to Mr Brocklehurst. It seems very unlikely that Charlotte, who described herself as 'plodding and industrious' at the time and her career as 'a very quiet one', was ever punished by Mr Wilson. It seems equally unlikely that she showed outward signs of rebellion and was treated like Jane Eyre was by the black marble clergyman, but it is probable that scenes similar to those she described in *Jane Eyre* took place before her eyes. Her experience at Cowan Bridge was almost certainly responsible for her taking what she would describe as 'a clouded and repulsive view of religious matters' until the age of twenty. There is no record of how the six-year-old Emily was affected, but for the rest of her life she had a strong aversion for schools of all kinds.

That the portrayal of Cowan Bridge was somewhere close to the truth is borne out by an incident related by Charlotte to her publisher's reader shortly after the publication of *Jane Eyre* in 1847 – a decade before Mrs Gaskell's biography stirred up such controversy. Charlotte said that she had seen an elderly clergyman reading the book and 'had the satisfaction of hearing him exclaim, "Why – they have got — school, and Mr — here, I declare! and Miss —" (naming the original of Lowood, Mr Brocklehurst and Miss Temple). He had known them all: I wondered whether he would recognise the portrait, and was gratified to find that he did and that moreover he pronounced them faithful and just – he said too that Mr — (Brocklehurst) "deserved the chastisement he had got"'.[43]

CHAPTER III

That Visionary Region of Imagination

It was to a sombre house that Charlotte and Emily returned, following the journey of their all too evidently dying sister. In two weeks, Elizabeth's pitiful remains joined those of her mother and sister in the family vault below the church floor. The service was taken once again by William Morgan, Mr Brontë's old friend, who had married him, and buried his wife and eldest child. Living across from the dark old church, the surviving children would be reminded of their sisters every day. The serried ranks of tombstones which filled the view from every window must now have taken on a new, more dreadful meaning.

Branwell was particularly deeply affected by Maria's death. He had witnessed her dying months at the parsonage, alone of the children except for five-year-old Anne, who was too young to have shared his feelings towards the beloved eldest sister who had taught him to say his prayers and taken on so much of the mother's role for him. During his troubled adolescence, Branwell, conscious of his inadequacies *vis-à-vis* the proper conduct of a clergyman's son amidst the impossibly high standards of holiness that the Evangelicals expected their offspring to maintain, would refer in poem after poem to Maria's death, to the end of her holy inspiration:

> What was the star which seemed to rise
> To light me on and guide me through?
> What was that form so heavenly fair,
> Untouched by time, unmarked with care,
> To whose fond heart I clung to save
> My sinking spirit from its grave.[1]

His poem 'Caroline' describes a funeral which is almost certainly a description of Maria's. It follows the procession under the churchyard arch to the sound of the organ, and the details of the burial; his horror at the obsequies gives the poem great poignancy, as does the little girl narrator's inability to accept leaving her sister in the earth:

> How bitter seemed that moment when,
>   Earth's ceremonies o'er,
> We from the filled grave turned again
>   To leave her evermore;[2]

Elizabeth's death appears to have had a similarly strong effect on Charlotte. She may have had an extreme immediate reaction to it, since she was apparently sent at this time to stay with some friends of Mr Brontë whom he had made during the Thornton years, the Kay family of Allerton Hall. A niece remembered seeing the rather comic sight of the very small figure of Charlotte in a nightcap sitting up in an enormous four-poster bed.[3] Certainly, both Branwell and Charlotte were exceptionally morbid children and adults, and in Branwell's case death became an obsession.

The passing of Maria and Elizabeth meant the end of an era for the Brontë children. They exchanged the tutelary influence of the gentle, religious and loving Maria for that of Miss Branwell, while Maria came to represent to the bereft parent and children a perfect state of virtue, an unattainable state of purity that was an example to which they should aspire. Charlotte's almost painful sense of duty and responsibility were traits that were always remarked on by her contemporaries. They can partly be ascribed to her overwhelming sense of inadequacy when she compared herself to her wonderful sisters, any faults they had forgotten, their virtues imperishably enshrined. At the age of nine she became the eldest of the family and she no doubt felt that upon her now fell the burden of mothering her brother and sisters.

The regime which was instituted after June 1825 by the adults of the household set the pattern for the next six years. An important new influence was introduced by the servant, Tabitha Aykroyd. The maids Nancy and Sarah Garrs had left in the winter of 1824, to be replaced by Tabby, as she rapidly became known, a local woman then aged fifty-six, who was a Methodist class leader, and a fund of wonderful stories. She formed a motherly presence in the parsonage, and the kitchen from which she reigned supreme became the centre of life for the young Brontës. They sat there basking in the warmth of her loving, if sharp-tongued character. The children particularly delighted in her rough Yorkshire dialect, sometimes mimicking it in their writings.

Miss Branwell meanwhile was responsible for inculcating in her nieces the necessary feminine domestic virtues of sewing and light cleaning, while Mr Brontë once again gave the girls their lessons. Charlotte, although she found it tedious and would rather have been reading, learned to sew, though surprisingly not proving as dextrous as she was at drawing with her tiny delicate hands. More than one observer would remark upon them, 'tiny taper fingers with perfect circular nails'.[4] One of her dresses, a turquoise frock printed with small flowers, to which a collar and false hem has been added, shows that she was nevertheless a competent seamstress. Aunt Branwell made sure that all three nieces, like young middle-class girls all over nineteenth-century England, sewed samplers for the good of their souls. Emily, though she early had the reputation of being a tomboy, was a neater seamstress than Charlotte, whose sampler is noticeably more untidy. Her sampler, with Charlotte's and Anne's, still hangs at the parsonage. Anne too was unconfident of her sewing, and as a young woman would wonder whether she was capable of turning a 'grey figured silk'. Sewing for the household or for the 'Jews' Basket' – articles for the needy in the neighbourhood – occupied much of the girls' time, although later Emily became more taken up with bread-making. She excelled at this and enjoyed doing it partly because it allowed her to get on with her reading.

What the girls learned in the lessons with their father was probably similar to that taught to most girls of their class and time. They would read and learn by rote sections of the Bible, and the greater part of their knowledge would come from 'Mangnall's Questions', a hodgepodge of information about ancient history and geography (rather like the answer sections of a quiz book) which was the standard – and only – text for most young women in schoolrooms. Although Branwell, as the boy, was the only child to be given a thorough education, it seems that Mr Brontë taught Anne at least some Latin and Greek as there is a reference to her teaching them as a governess. The father took pride in the precocious brilliance of his only son and carefully tutored him in the classics. By the age of ten, when Patrick Brontë gave him a New Testament in Latin, Branwell had read Homer and Virgil, and had a thorough grounding in ancient and modern history.

Whatever the scantiness of the daughters' formal education and the Brontës' physical isolation from the outside world, there was no lack of stimulus to the imagination and intellect in the parsonage. Mr Brontë made every effort to obtain a very wide range of reading matter for his children, joining the Keighley Mechanics Institute shortly after it was founded in 1825 in order to borrow books. His enthusiasm for poetry meant that the children had access to all the works of Byron and Wordsworth, and much of his small stipend was used to supply his home with newspapers, books and magazines. That these were expensive items for him is shown by the fact that from 1825 onwards he used to borrow *Blackwood's Magazine* from the local doctor and he later had an arrangement with a woman friend to receive her day-old copy of *The Times* after she had finished with it.[5] In the afternoons there would be discussions of the week's political events, new poetry, articles in literary magazines, all of which gave the Brontës a sophistication and knowledge of art, poetry and cultural and political affairs quite beyond any of their neighbours.

Religious teaching was of course central to the children's upbringing, though what kind of religious attitudes were imparted to them by Miss Branwell and Mr Brontë is a vexed question. In adolescence, Charlotte, Branwell and Anne all underwent serious religious crises, which have been linked to the effects of harsh and frightening doctrines instilled in earlier childhood. Miss Branwell has been seen as the villain of the piece, blamed for upholding Calvinistic ideas. But she and Mr Brontë can both be absolved of specifically terrifying their charges with such beliefs. Elizabeth Branwell had an impeccable pedigree as a supporter of Wesleyan Methodism, which followed what was known as Arminian theology, and firmly repudiated the Calvinism adopted by George Whitefield's Methodists. And Mr Brontë is on record for opposing Calvinist teachings, saying that he could not 'feel comfortable with a coadjutor who would deem it his duty to preach the appalling doctrines of personal Election and Reprobation'.[6]

However, as committed Evangelicals and Methodists, Miss Branwell and Mr Brontë undoubtedly impressed on the children the ever-present danger of hell-fire and eternal damnation and the constant need to be conscious of sin, which would leave such an ineradicable mark on their psyches. Recent scholarship has pointed out that Patrick Brontë's religious beliefs, while not Calvinist, were heavily laced with threats of damnation. In Professor T.J. Winnifrith's view, Mr Brontë preferred to dwell on damnation rather than salvation. Much of his didactic verse contains descriptions of hell and threats of hell-fire, and his writings are full of references to 'the stock themes of the terrors of the last judgement, unquenchable fire, never-ending woe, ever-living worm, opening hell, and deathbed thoughts of demons'.[7] Nor was this creed only part of the domestic furniture. Every Sunday the little Brontës would listen to their father declaiming it to the world from his pulpit.

Patrick Brontë, indeed, also felt sufficiently strongly about the theme of personal conversion, what Wesley himself described as a 'warming of the heart', to write about it both in his novelette *The Maid of Killarney* and in a five-part article for the Vicar of Bradford's Evangelical magazine. For a sinner to be saved, he had to have 'undergone that change without which no man shall see the Kingdom of

46

Heaven . . . not only must the outward conduct be holy, but all the inward views changed and the feelings sanctified, before you can have any just ground for hope'.[8]

The earliest Methodists were meant to 'testify' in public to their state of mind and to the weekly progress of religion in their hearts. Although Miss Branwell would be very unlikely to encourage the more raucous manifestations of Methodist behaviour, of what became known as the Primitive sort, there would have been present in the parsonage some display of the zeal which made supporters of Methodism 'witness' to their belief in their cause. Apart from their aunt and father, the children had the influence of Tabby, herself a Methodist class leader.

The *Methodist Magazine* was taken at the parsonage and, along with the Bible, the Book of Common Prayer and the *Imitation of Christ*, probably formed some of the Brontës' earliest literature. John Fennell was a regular contributor to it and Miss Branwell no doubt approved of her brother-in-law's description of the behaviour of a young Methodist woman who died at the age of nineteen. 'She saw that God must be feared and loved at all times. When among her young companions she generally employed the time in telling them what God had done for her soul.'[9] Furthermore, despite its Arminianism, by the 1820s and 1830s the *Methodist Magazine* was particularly preoccupied with the question of hell and damnation, salvation from the burning lake, and included descriptions of deathbeds as numerous as in the writings of Carus Wilson, although deathbeds of course played a heavy role in all Evangelical literature. It was alarming reading matter for the young particularly, and may explain the hostile references in both *Shirley* and *Villette* to childhoods spent reading 'mad Methodist tracts' with their 'excitation to fanaticism'.

One of the more telling indications of the intractable religious teaching the Brontë children seem to have received comes from a Moravian Bishop, James de la Trobe, who was called in by Anne in the midst of the religious crisis she underwent at sixteen, when she was also very ill from gastric poisoning. He recounted:

Her voice was only a whisper; her life hung on a slender thread. She soon got over the shyness natural on seeing a perfect stranger. The words of love, from Jesus, opened her ear to my words, and she was very grateful for my visits. I found her well acquainted with the main truths of the Bible respecting our salvation, but seeing them more through the law than the gospel, more as a requirement from God than His Gift in His Son, but her heart opened to the sweet views of salvation, pardon and peace in the blood of Christ, and she accepted His welcome to the weary and heavy laden sinner, conscious more of her not loving the Lord her God than of acts of enmity to Him.[10]

Charlotte voiced this idea of universal salvation through Helen Burns, her portrait of her sister Maria in *Jane Eyre*: 'I hold another creed, which no one ever taught me, and which I seldom mention, but in which I delight, and to which I cling, for it extends hope to all; it makes eternity a rest – a mighty home – not a terror and an abyss', which suggests that there may have been a common reaction amongst the children against the harshness and fervour of their religious upbringing. Nevertheless, they could never quite escape the hold of Evangelicalism, its exaggerated sense of sin, leading to terrifying consequences. Finally Branwell's lack of feelings of holiness and consciousness of grace, which his aunt had drilled into him were evidence that he was one of the saved, would convince him of his irredeemable damnation for what on the whole were really very minor peccadilloes.

The Brontës' view of the world, then, had an essentially otherworldly frame. It was a world in the grip of a mysterious supernatural force, which achieved its most impressive plastic expression in the imagery of the artist John Martin, whose engravings were scattered around the parsonage. Martin's work was illumined by an apocalyptic vision: the plains of heaven were as real as the plains of earth. But if Martin served to reinforce the inexorable power of God to the Brontë children, he also had a remarkable effect on their imaginations. The completeness of his vision, his capacity to evoke the reality of other fantastic worlds, utterly captivated them. What the dazzled Charles Lamb described admiringly as 'his towered structures . . . the highest order of the material sublime. Whether they were dreams, or transcripts of some elder workmanship, Assyrian ruins old',[11] Martin's vast moonlit palaces were brooded over by the children and became an inspiration for the imaginary world in which they increasingly took refuge.

Years later Charlotte told Mrs Gaskell of her desire 'amounting almost to illness' to express herself as the result of such visual stimulation. At first she wanted to learn to express her ideas by drawing, but 'after she had tried to draw stories and not succeeded, she took the better mode of writing'.[12] The written world that she and Branwell, joined by Emily and Anne, created for themselves was called Glass Town, a world complete with its own landscapes and magnificent buildings all in the manner of John Martin's fantastical constructions.

It began after a visit to Leeds in June 1826 by Mr Brontë, who brought back a gift of twelve wooden soldiers for nine-year-old Branwell – or Brannii as he was known to the family – whose other sets

48

of soldiers had been broken. His sisters and he, already used to making up secret plays, were unexpectedly captivated by the brightly painted soldiers and began to weave stories about them, in the process inventing the name the 'Young Men' for them. The twelve soldiers were transformed into a band of young adventurers, headed by Charlotte's hero, the Duke of Wellington. Under the domination of the two elder Brontës, their imaginations probably stirred by reading in *Blackwood's* of the recent exploits of the Arctic explorers Parry and Ross, the children sent the soldiers off to explore the continent of Africa and found a colony. Within three years the colony, called Glass Town by its founders, and which was situated at the mouth of the Niger on the site of the real-life town of Fernando Po, had become a complete world peopled by the now teeming descendants of the twelve soldiers.

In her 'History of the Year' written on 12 March 1829, Charlotte describes the origin of their first play, 'Young Men', in June 1826.

Papa bought Branwell some wooden soldiers at Leeds; when papa came home it was night, and we were in bed, so next morning Branwell came to our door with a box of soldiers. Emily and I jumped out of bed, and I snatched up one and exclaimed, 'This is the Duke of Wellington! This shall be the Duke!' When I had said this Emily likewise took up one and said it should be hers; when Anne came down she said one should be hers. Mine was the prettiest of the whole, and the tallest, and the most perfect in every part. Emily's was a grave-looking fellow, and we called him 'Gravey'. Anne's was a queer little thing, much like herself, and we called him 'Waiting-Boy'. Branwell chose his and called him 'Buonaparte'.

Over the next four years, the play evolved around these characters, though the curious names of Gravey and Waiting-Boy were rapidly exchanged for Parry and Ross. The children themselves featured in the story as the four Genii – inspired by their reading of the *Arabian Nights* – with Branwell as Chief Genius Brannii, the nastiest of the four, Charlotte as the terrible Chief Genius Tallii, and Emily and Anne as the considerably less fierce Emmii and Annii. Charlotte and Branwell wrote stories about the goings-on in this world almost daily in a tiny, almost indecipherable hand, which was intended to imitate print. The two younger children do not appear to have written anything, although they were clearly involved. It was Branwell who invented the language for the imaginary country, the Young Men's Tongue, and he shows a natural bent for historiography as he attempts to bring order to the fragments of manuscript written in this strange tongue and reconstructs the colony's origins. Maps still exist at the parsonage showing the geographical divisions of the imaginary country.

The Glass Town World – and the other plays invented by the children in these years – were fed by the rich diet of the Brontës' reading matter. They found inspiration in the *Arabian Nights*, the works of Sir Walter Scott – Charlotte would later declare that 'all novels after Scott's are worthless' – Shakespeare, Ossian and of course the Bible, which, whatever Charlotte's dislike of religious fanaticism, she found an enthralling narrative. But above all the world that Charlotte and Branwell were creating together was under the romantic spell of Byron. Whether out of intention or neglect, Mr Brontë's eldest daughter and son had read most of Byron's complete works by the time they were twelve and thirteen. Certainly, they knew *Lara*, *The Corsair*, *The Bride of Abydos*, *Manfred* and *Cain*. The only act of censorship that Mr Brontë seems to have performed was to have burnt copies of Miss Branwell's *Ladies Magazine* 'because they contained foolish love stories'. He might perhaps have done better to have kept them from Byron.

The Byronic hero took a hold on their imaginations which both children would find it almost impossible to break. The rebel, the outcast, the swashbuckling anarchist, the foe of hypocrisy, had a fascination that would eventually dictate Branwell's every movement. By the age of seventeen both his chief protagonist in the imaginary world, Northangerland, and Charlotte's Zamorna were immediately recognisable imitations of Byron's ubiquitous fallen angel, the stranger with the mysterious darkling eye. Branwell took Byron's rebellious attitudes for his own and Emily too, following behind and rarely reading consistently, became increasingly taken with the figure of the outlaw.

That volcanic quality to Charlotte's writing that caused one reviewer to remark that *Jane Eyre* was written in fire is partly explained by the intensely Romantic influences that surrounded her in childhood. Brought up on a diet of the heroic and gigantic, she naturally gravitated towards excitement. How could it be otherwise? Tranquillity was never an outstanding feature of the parsonage. As David Cecil summed it up, she dealt with the 'least romantic classes of humanity, governesses, schoolmasters, clergymen ... yet the impression they make is more like the Brothers Karamazov. ... Lit by its [her imagination's] lurid glare, these prosaic schools and parsonages stand out huge, secret, momentous. .... Their loves, hates and ambitions are alike fiery and insatiable. Their smallest misdeed is dark with the shadow of hell, their briefest moment of elevation haloed by a heavenly glory.'[13]

The unhappiness and uncertainty of their early childhood predisposed Charlotte and her precocious bookish siblings to escape more than most children into the world of the imagination, where people and events were controllable, unlike real life. There was little to interrupt the children from the reveries induced by their reading, which provided the consolation in unhappiness that they were so much in need of. The charming 'Lines on Bewick', which Charlotte wrote at seventeen a few years after the death of Thomas Bewick, suggest what hours of pleasure contemplation of his illustrations had given to her and her brothers and sisters:

> again we turn
> With fresh delight to the enchanted page
> Where pictured thoughts that breathe and speak and burn
> Still please alike our youth and riper age
> We turn the page: before the expectant eye
> A traveller stands lone on some desert heath;
>
> I cannot speak the rapture that I feel
> When on the work of such a mind I gaze

The earliest of the children's astonishing number of drawings include many copies of Bewick's woodcuts. The Brontës seemed to revel particularly in the 'tail pieces' which Bewick interspersed with the natural history engravings in his best-selling books *A General History of Quadrupeds* and *A History of British Birds*. Often macabre, always fascinating, these black and white tales in miniature were sedulously redrawn by the children. Wordsworth himself wrote of Bewick's work that 'the narrative or anecdotal content, compressed within so small a space conveys an intensity of feeling in a way entirely fresh'.[14] Charlotte in turn conveyed this intensity of feeling when describing Bewick's power to remove the unhappy child Jane Eyre from her hateful surroundings:

> I returned to my book – Bewick's *History of British Birds*: the letter press thereof I cared little for, generally speaking; and yet there were certain introductory pages that, child as I was, I could not pass quite as a blank. They were those which treat of the haunts of sea-fowl; of 'the solitary rocks and promonteries' by them only inhabited . . . Of these death-white realms I formed an idea of my own: shadowy, like all the half-comprehended notions that float dim through children's brains, but strangely impressive. The words in those introductory pages connected themselves with the succeeding vignettes, and gave significance to the rock standing up alone in a sea of billow and spray; to the broken boat stranded on a desolate

51

coast; to the cold and ghastly moon glancing through bars of cloud at a wreck just sinking. . . .

Each picture told a story: mysterious often to my undeveloped understanding and imperfect feelings, yet ever profoundly interesting: . . . With Bewick on my knee, I was then happy: happy at least in my way.

Branwell later summed up the Brontës' wild excitement for matters literary in his description of his almost contagious love for *Blackwood's Magazine*: 'I cannot express the heavenliness of associations connected with such articles as Professor Wilson *read and re-read while a little child*, with all their poetry of language and divine flight into that visionary region of the imagination which one very young would believe reality, and which one entering into manhood would look back upon as a glorious dream.' With characteristic extravagant self-regard, Branwell continued: 'I speak so, Sir, because while a child "Blackwood's" formed my chief delight, and I feel certain that no child before ever enjoyed reading as I did, because none ever had such works as "The Noctes", "Christmas Dreams", "Christopher and his Sporting Jacket" to read.'[15]

The children were also probably sometimes able to use the library of Ponden House, three miles away across the moors on the way to Colne in Lancashire, judging by the wideness of their reading. It belonged to the ancient family of the Heatons, who were hereditary trustees of the church at Haworth. The great panelled room on the second floor held an astonishing collection of books and manuscripts, including a Shakespeare First Folio, and was particularly rich in sixteenth- and seventeenth-century English and French literature, which was quickly imitated by the fluent pens of Charlotte and Branwell. By the age of fourteen Charlotte was mocking the poetical effusions and attitudes of her brilliant younger brother, who was already self-consciously posturing as a Romantic poet, in an ambitious imitation of Jacobean drama, 'The Poetaster', a play in six acts.

Ponden Hall had further significance for Emily, who is sometimes considered to have used it as a model for Thrushcross Grange in *Wuthering Heights*. In fact the house is far from being the gracious mansion set in parkland that Thrushcross Grange is and, although not set up on the moors, it has more of the feel of Wuthering Heights itself. Built in 1513 by a Heaton ancestor, the long low house with its thick greenish-grey slabs of stone is far more of a farmhouse. It certainly has a mysterious feel to it, partly due to its concealed position.

Although Emily and Charlotte shared a bedroom, and in December 1827 and March 1828 established what Charlotte called their 'bed plays [which] are secret plays; they are very nice ones',[16] Emily was much more closely associated with Anne, probably as a result of Charlotte going away to school. The two younger children spent much of their time roaming about the moors around the house. The wild landscape was already beginning to take possession of Emily's mind and became part of the imaginary land of Gondal that she and Anne later established together. From Charlotte's juvenilia, it appears that the reserved, unsociable Emily and the quiet, passive Anne found the extravagance of their elders' imaginings and predilection for aristocratic Byronic life not to their taste. The imaginary kingdom which they were inventing for themselves was, in contrast to Charlotte and Branwell's, rooted much more in the everyday life around them, its inhabitants more like the gruff local Yorkshire people than the lordly careless gallants about whom Charlotte wove her own fantasies.

Nevertheless, the four children all participated in common imaginary worlds, even if these were at the instigation of Charlotte and Branwell. In July 1827 they had invented the play 'Our Fellows', inspired by *Aesop's Fables*,[17] and in December 1828 the play 'Islanders'. Charlotte's description of how the 'Islanders' began gives a rare glimpse into childhood life at the parsonage:

One night about the time when the cold sleet and dreary fogs of November are succeeded by the snow storms and high piercing night winds of confirmed winter, we were all sitting round the warm blazing kitchen fire having just concluded a quarrel with Tabby concerning the propriety of lighting a candle from which she came off victorious, no candle having been produced a long pause succeeded which was at last broken by B saying, in a lazy manner, 'I don't know what to do'. This was re-echoed by E and A.
T: Wha ya may go t'bed.
B: I'd rather do anything [than] that.
C: You're so glum tonight T. [?Well] suppose we had each an Island.
B: If we had I would choose the Island of Man.
C: And I would choose Isle of Wight.
E: The Isle of Arran for me.
A: And mine should be Guernsey.
C: The Duke of Wellington should be my chief man.
B: [?Heries] should be mine.
E: Walter Scott should be mine.
A: I should have Bentinck.
Here our conversation was interrupted by [the], to us, dismal sound of the clock striking 7 and we were summoned off to bed. The next day we added several others to our list of names till we had got almost all the chief men in the kingdom.[18]

Those chief men show an impressive range of acquaintance on the part of the Brontë children. At an age when most children's knowledge is of a fairly limited kind, they are naming the leading figures of the day. Thus seven-year-old Anne chose the social reformer Michael Sadler, the royal physician Henry Halford and Tory politician Lord Bentinck; Branwell chose, besides John Bull, the king's surgeon Astley Cooper and Leigh Hunt, Byron's poet friend; Emily wanted Walter Scott's son-in-law and grandson, Mr Lockhart and Johnny Lockhart, to accompany Scott. Charlotte's 'History of the Year' of March 1829 shows how important newspapers were in the parsonage, and how closely interwoven were domestic reality and the world of make-believe.

> Once papa lent my sister Maria a book. It was an old geography book; she wrote on its blank leaf, 'Papa lent me this book'. This book is a hundred and twenty years old; it is at this moment lying before me. While I write this I am in the kitchen of the Parsonage, Haworth; Tabby, the servant, is washing up the breakfast things, and Anne, my younger sister (Maria was my eldest), is kneeling on a chair, looking at some cakes which Tabby had been baking for us. Emily is in the parlour, brushing the carpet. Papa and Branwell are gone to Keighley. Aunt is upstairs in her room, and I am sitting by the table writing this in the kitchen. Keighley is a small town four miles from here. Papa and Branwell are gone for the newspaper, the *Leeds Intelligencer*, a most excellent Tory newspaper, edited by Mr Wood, and the proprietor, Mr Henneman. We take two and see three newspapers a week. We take the *Leeds Intelligencer*, Tory, and the *Leeds Mercury*, Whig, edited by Mr Baines, and his brother, son-in-law, and his two sons, Edward and Talbot. We see the *John Bull*; it is a high Tory, very violent. Dr Driver lends us it, as likewise *Blackwood's Magazine*, the most able periodical there is. The editor is Mr Christopher North, an old man seventy-four years of age; the 1st of April is his birthday; his company are Timothy Tickler, Morgan O'Doherty, Macrabin Mordecai, Mullion, Warnell, and James Hogg, a man of most extraordinary genius, a Scottish shepherd.[19]

In the same year, the thirteen-year-old Charlotte wrote an impassioned account of the passing of the Catholic Emancipation Bill which in 1830 brought down the government of the Duke of Wellington and Robert Peel.

> I remember the day when the Intelligence Extraordinary came with Mr Peel's speech in it containing the terms on which the Catholics

were to be let in! With what eagerness papa tore off the cover and how we all gathered round him, and with what breathless anxiety we listened as one by one they were disclosed, and explained, and argued upon so ably and so well; and then, when it was all out, how aunt said she thought it was excellent and that the Catholics could do no harm with such good security. I remember also the doubts as to whether it would pass the House of Lords and the prophecies that it would not; and when the paper came which was to decide the question, the anxiety was almost dreadful with which we listened to the whole affair: the opening of the doors, the hush; the royal dukes in their robes and the great duke in green sash and waistcoat; the rising of all the peeresses when he rose; the reading of his speech – papa saying that his words were like precious gold; and lastly, the majority of one to four in favour of the Bill.[20]

It is not surprising that political issues played a key part in the continuing Glass Town saga, the growing verisimilitude of which is attested to by the fact that the children in January 1829 started to write magazines for Glass Town full of jokes and puns. The magazines thrived alongside the romantic novelettes in imitation of Scott that Charlotte was continuing to write. Increasingly, Arthur Wellesley, the Iron Duke's son, was coming to the fore in the Glass Town world as a romantic hero whose life and loves were beginning to obsess Charlotte. Branwell's particular forte was to describe with remarkable thoroughness Glass Town's system of government, the details of its constitution, the geography and language.

The first issue of the children's magazine was, like all Glass Town literature, written on tiny bits of paper fashioned into booklets about $2\frac{1}{4}$ by $1\frac{1}{4}$ inches, in minute, almost indecipherable writing. The size of the magazine was intended to correspond to the actual size of the wooden soldiers, but the tiny writing seems also to have been used to prevent prying adult eyes from reading the children's secrets. There is in existence an exercise book with a warning in Mr Brontë's hand thus: 'All that is written in this book must be in a clear and legible hand.'

The cover of the first issue of the magazine was made from a printed pamphlet which advertised books by and about John Wesley. As paper was expensive, the make-shift nature of their books, sometimes made from old laundry books and sugar paper, were a constant in the Brontë children's productions. The leading article in the four-leaved magazine described a fabulous fish, with a horn about twenty-foot long which, when cut off by sailors, grew back in half an hour, and it was accompanied by illustrations. There was also a poetry section, containing an adaptation of the English National Anthem to fit it for

Glass Town dwellers, and an editorial in the Young Men's Tongue.[21]

The June 1829 issue, the next magazine to survive, was considerably more sophisticated, and its title page announced that it was 'Printed and sold by Sergeant Tree' – a witty reference to the ultimate origins of the paper from which the magazines were made. As with the children's enjoyment of the Genius/Genii joke, there is a vein of humour and gaiety running through the little magazines. Mrs Gaskell, meeting Charlotte after the death of her siblings, could not believe her to have ever been anything but sad and repressed. But the Charlotte to be met in the magazines and juvenilia bubbles over with excitement and jokes, and one can imagine her and Branwell's constant badinage.

The 'Noctes Ambrosianae', a celebrated feature of *Blackwood's* – which was in some ways similar to the *New Yorker's* 'Talk of the Town' and presented apparently informal discussions of the world's affairs in a convivial but philosophical way round a fireside – were enthusiastically mimicked. Wellington would discuss 'military science, politics, literature and art' in the famous local tavern, the Grand Inn. The tyranny of the Genii was another favourite topic at most of the Glass Town gatherings, as reported in the magazine. There are reviews of a major new painting, by the (real) English painter De Lisle of 'The Chief Genii in Council', and also a description of 'Characters of the Celebrated Men of the Present Time' by Captain Tree.

These character studies display an early gift for trenchant characterisation by Charlotte, as well as demonstrating how real the characters of Glass Town had become to its two creators. The Duke of Wellington has 'a certain expression of sarcasm about his mouth which showed that he considered many of those with whom he associates much beneath him' – and here it is evident that Charlotte was enjoying the very idea of the great Iron Duke participating in this imaginary kingdom.

She described two of Branwell's alter egos, Captain Bud the historian of Glass Town and Young Soult the poet, and playfully mocked Branwell's tendency to being prolix and over-scholarly as Captain Bud, and his taste for absurd melodramatic effusions. She had to admit, however, that Branwell was 'the ablest political writer of the present time and his works exhibit a depth of thought and knowledge seldom equalled and never surpassed. They are, however, sometimes too long and dry, which they would be often if it was not for their great ability.'[22]

The portrait of Young Soult, the French poet (Branwell had a passion for all things French, and Young Soult's writing has notes on the title page to the effect that it was edited by Chateaubriand), is a curiously accurate foreshadowing of the character that Branwell would become in later years. But Charlotte's object in writing about Soult seems affectionate – to amuse rather than to warn Branwell about the dangers of lack of discipline and extravagant self-delusion:

His apparel is generally torn and he wears it hanging about him in a very careless and untidy manner. His shoes are often slipshod and his stockings full of holes. The expression of his countenance is wild and haggard, and he is eternally twisting his mouth to one side or another. In his disposition he is devilish but humane and good natured. He appears constantly labouring under a state of strong excitement occasioned by excessive drinking and gambling to which he is unfortunately much addicted. His poems exhibit a fine imagination but his versification is not good. The ideas and language are beautiful but they are not arranged so as to run along smoothly, and for this reason I think he should succeed best in blank verse. Indeed I understand that he is about to publish a Poem in that metre which is expected to be his best. He is possessed of a true genius which he has cultivated by great effort. His beginnings were small, but I believe his end will be great and that his name will be found on the pages of history with those of the greatest men of his native country.[23]

Branwell was indeed considered destined for great things by his family, and not merely by his own estimation. From the age of eleven, he thought that he would be a great poet; there was no one other than a slightly mocking but loving Charlotte to gainsay him as he flung himself about the house. His father sympathised with such ambitions – he had once had them himself – and his fond aunt would soften when Branwell quoted snatches of poetry at her in such an enchanting way. The literary world was there, virgin territory, clearly awaiting his embrace.

It was evidently very hard to resist Branwell's charm and brilliance. He was extremely precocious, as fluent and articulate in expressing himself as his sister Charlotte. He was boisterous, exuberant and affectionate; above all, he made life fun. Branwell's effervescent temperament was marked by a nervousness that was perhaps congenital and exacerbated by the early deaths of his mother and sisters. His first biographer, Francis Leyland, who knew Branwell well, told of an incident in Branwell's boyhood at the annual Keighley feast, which was related to him by a village friend of Branwell's:

Branwell's excitement, hilarity and extravagance knew no bounds: he would see everything and try everything. Into a rocking boat he and his friend gaily stepped. The rise of the boat, when it reached its full height, gave Branwell a pleasant view of the fair beneath;

but, when it descended, he screamed out at the top of his voice, 'Oh! my nerves! Oh! my nerves!' On each descent, every nerve thrilled, tingled and vibrated with overwhelming effect through the overwrought and delicate frame of the boy.[24]

Branwell, like Charlotte, was very small – he would grow up to be five foot three inches tall, a great contrast to his father who stood over six feet – and again like Charlotte he was very short-sighted. His delicate frame did not, however, denote any lack of energy. When he was about ten or eleven, Mr Brontë's friends seem to have urged him to send the irrepressible Branwell to school. Mr Brontë decided against it, either for financial reasons or because he felt that all Branwell's teaching requirements could just as easily, or better, be satisfied by himself. There is, however, a rumour that Branwell had to be removed from Haworth Grammar School because of a nervous breakdown, and furthermore that this may have occurred because Branwell had been bitten by a mad dog and never had the wound cauterised.

In later life Charlotte and her sisters would be convinced that it was over-indulgence of Branwell in youth which lay at the root of his problems. Mrs Gaskell, probably reflecting Charlotte's opinion, regarded Mr Brontë's decision not to send his son to school as the beginning of Branwell's troubles. Because the father was taken up with parish duties, Branwell 'was thrown into chance companionship with the lads of the village – for youth will to youth, and boys will to boys'.[25] This supposedly had a corrupting and roughening effect on Branwell. More importantly, their father's decision that Branwell should remain at home meant that Charlotte did not lose her collaborator, who led on the world of the dream to new heights, inspired it to further twists and turns, and together they were able to inhabit this visionary region without a break for five years.

The children were still subject to the constraints of childhood whatever their omnipotence in the world of the imagination, where the Duke of Wellington did their bidding and Charlotte and Branwell entered into energetic, clubmanlike correspondence over the control of the various newspapers read in Glass Town. In September 1829 the four children, in company with Aunt Branwell, went to stay with her uncle and their great-uncle John Fennell at his parsonage at Cross-Stone near Todmorden, about twelve miles from Haworth. His wife had died in May and it may be that he and Aunt Branwell had some family business to discuss, as he was one of her executors. His daughter Jane had died two years ago at the age of thirty-six, cursed by the same shortlivedness as her first cousin, Mrs Brontë. Mr Fennell lived in the new parsonage, a plain rustic Georgian dwelling built three years before, just along from the church. The country was even more precipitous than that by Haworth with very dramatic views across the Pennines. The party of children and Miss Branwell travelled across the Cockhill Moors on a frosty autumn day, and then wound up and up the exceptionally steep hill to the parsonage. This lay across the road from the church itself, a great black barn of a building more suited to a big town than the few scattered houses round the hamlet of Cross-Stone. Like the parsonage, it was in a very elevated position looking down over a drop so sharp and steep that it is almost a cliff.

The schoolmaster's house stood next to the church on the cliff top, and the adventurous Brontë children must have observed a stone tablet at the far end of the building. Piquantly, prophetically, two tiny children are stretching their little arms towards the quote inscribed on it, 'Train up a child in the way he should go and when he is old he will not depart from it.' Did the sensitive little Charlotte cease from play and, having read the lines with her usual grave care, ponder their future application to her family all brought up in the shadow of Methodism?

Charlotte's restrained and dignified first letter to her father[26] showing what an industrious holiday they were having makes an amusing contrast to the world where she reigned as Chief Genius Tallii, able to destroy a thousand men and cities in a second, to reduce 'the world to a desert, the purest waters to streams of living poison'.[27]

Parsonage House
Cross-Stone

September 23 1829
My dear Papa,
At Aunt's request I write these lines to inform you that 'if all be well' we shall be at home on Friday by dinner-time, when we hope to find you in good health. On account of the bad weather we have not been out much, but notwithstanding we have spent our time very pleasantly, between reading, working, and learning our lessons, which Uncle Fenell [sic] has been so kind as to teach us every day. Branwell has taken two sketches from nature, and Emily, Anne, and myself have likewise each of us drawn a piece from some views of the lakes which Mr Fenell brought with him from Westmoreland, the whole of these he intends keeping. Mr Fenell is sorry he cannot accompany us to Haworth on Friday, for want of room, but hopes to have the pleasure of seeing you soon. All unite in sending their kind love with your affectionate daughter,

Charlotte Brontë

They returned, to continue the ceaseless elaboration of their imaginary world, writing in the dining room, the children's room upstairs or their bedrooms. By this time the constant practice, the imitation of *Blackwood's*, of poetry, of novels, had given Charlotte an extraordinary proficiency in the written word, and a commonsensical, professional attitude to the art of writing which for a girl of thirteen is remarkably mature:

> How much people in general are deceived in their ideas of great authors. Every sentence is by them thought the outpourings of a mind overflowing with the sublime and beautiful. Alas, did they but know the trouble it often costs me to bring some exquisite passage neatly to a close, to avoid the too frequent repetition of the same word, to polish and round the period and to do many other things. They would soon lower the high standard at which our reputation is fixed. But still the true poet and proser have many moments of unalloyed delight while preparing their lucubrations for the press and public.[28]

Perhaps it is not surprising, given the extreme precocity of Branwell and Charlotte, that they should meditate on the world they were creating, but the sophistication of their concept of fictions aged thirteen and fourteen is fairly extraordinary. The speaker is Lord Charles Wellesley:

> While I was listlessly turning over the huge leaves of that most ponderous volume, I fell into the strangest train of thought that ever visited even my mind, eccentric and unstable as it is said by some insolent puppies to be.
> It seemed as if I was a non-existent shadow – that I neither spoke, eat, imagined, or lived of myself, but I was the mere idea of some other creature's brain. The Glass Town seemed so likewise. My father, Arthur, and everyone with whom I am acquainted, passed into a state of annihilation; but suddenly I thought again that I and my relatives did exist and yet not us but our minds, and our bodies without ourselves. Then this supposition – the oddest of any – followed the former quickly, namely, that WE without US were shadows; also, but at the end of a long vista, as it were, appeared dimly and indistinctly, beings that really lived in a tangible shape, that were called by our names and were US from whom WE had been copied by something – I could not tell what.[29]

By 3 August 1830, still aged only fourteen, Charlotte was able proudly to draw up a list of her life's work so far. It was an impressive twenty-two volumes, the majority written around the subject of Glass Town. By fourteen, she had an astonishing knowledge of literary form and, if she was very heavily influenced by Scott's and Byron's romanticism – the atmosphere of most of the Glass Town writing towards the end of 1830 is full of romantic intrigue between aristocratic personages who are as passionate and swaggering as they are high-born – in most of her stories she managed to retain an ironic edge.

By the end of the year the name Glass Town has been transmuted to the more patrician Verdopolis, a compound of (imaginary) Greek and French. Charlotte's final manuscript for 1830 was 'Albion and Marina'. It was the tale of a pair of tragic lovers, one of whom dies and is seen in a vision, and contains a motif Charlotte would use in *Jane Eyre* – that lovers can communicate through a sort of telepathy.

But this life of the imagination was interrupted towards the end of 1830. In the wet summer Mr Brontë fell ill with inflammation of the lungs and for several weeks he lay in danger of his life. Once again the spectre of death raised its head – but this time, if Mr Brontë were to die, the very roof over the children's heads would be removed from them. The inflammation gradually cleared but he was left feeling weak and, on his own admission, often in low spirits; at one point he was again too ill to be able to do his church duties. His illness seems to have jerked him out of his somewhat laissez-faire attitude to the children's future and in January 1831, on the advice of friends, the Chief Genius Charlotte was sent off to be formally taught at a girls' school at Roe Head which would enable her to earn her living as a governess.

CHAPTER IV

The Misses Wooler's School at Roe Head

Roe Head school was at Mirfield Moor near Dewsbury, twenty miles from Haworth. It was lower, more sheltered country, protected by copses and woods, with gently winding lanes. A large, double-fronted building with extensive grounds looking down the plain towards Dewsbury, it was more like a country house than a school, although to the south the smoke from the factories of Huddersfield could be seen. Altogether, it was a very different proposition to Cowan Bridge. Roe Head was run by Miss Margaret Wooler and her three spinster sisters, kindly, high-minded women connected through family marriage with the wealthy of the district of the Spen Valley. There were only ten girls at the school and, far from being charity pupils, they came – except for Charlotte – from the newly wealthy manufacturing families of the area, at whose hands new baronial halls were springing up all over Yorkshire. As Charlotte would write in Chapter 2 of *The Professor*, there were 'tall cylindrical chimneys, almost like slender round towers' indicating the factories which the trees half concealed, and 'here and there mansions, similar to Crimsworth Hall, occupied agreeable sites on the hillside; the country wore, on the whole, a cheerful, active, fertile look. Steam, trade, machinery had long banished from it all romance and seclusion. At a distance of five miles, a valley opening between the low hills held in its cups the great town of X——. A dull, permanent vapour brooded over this locality.' It was only Charlotte's status which remained similar to that at Cowan Bridge; her fees were being paid by her godparents, the Atkinsons, and her arrival in a covered cart, generally used to ferry produce to market in Keighley, can have done nothing to alleviate the sense she would always have of being a charity child.

Charlotte's arrival was noticed by another new pupil, Mary Taylor, a member of a local family of Radicals and Nonconformists, who was to become one of Charlotte's most intimate friends. She remembered vividly Charlotte getting out of the cart, seen at its worst before the bow windows of the school, in old-fashioned clothes and looking very cold and miserable. When Charlotte reappeared in the schoolroom, her dress had been changed, but for another which was just as curious-looking.

'She looked a little, old woman,' wrote Mary later, 'so short-sighted that she always appeared to be seeking something, and moving her head from side to side to catch a sight of it. . . . When a book was given her she dropped her head over it till her nose nearly touched it, and when she was told to hold her head up, up went the book after it, still close to her nose, so that it was not possible to keep from laughing.'

It was as a tiny prostrate figure, abandoned to her unhappiness, that Charlotte was first encountered by her other great support in the years to come, the daughter of another of the better families of the district, Ellen Nussey:

Arriving at school about a week after the general assembling of the pupils, I was not expected to accompany them when the time came for their daily exercise, but while they were out, I was led into the schoolroom, and quietly left to make my observations. I had come to the conclusion it was very nice and comfortable for a school-room, though I had little knowledge of school-rooms in general, when, turning to the window to observe the look-out I became aware for the first time that I was not alone; there was a silent, weeping, dark little figure in the large bay-window; she must, I thought, have risen from the floor. As soon as I had recovered from my surprise, I went from the far end of the room, where the book-shelves were, the contents of which I must have contemplated with a little awe in anticipation of coming studies. A crimson cloth covered the long table down the centre of the room, which helped no doubt to hide the shrinking little figure from my view. I was touched and troubled at once to see her so sad and tearful.[1]

Anxiety about her father's health – Mr Brontë had written to his old Thornton friend Mrs Franks expressing doubts that he would ever recover – and fear for her family's future must have contributed to Charlotte's desperate unhappiness. Cut off from her home and from the world of Glass Town, she wrote on the inside cover of a French text book on 17 January 1831 when she had just arrived at the school: 'Like a vision came those sunny hours to me. Where are they now? They have long since joined the past eternity.'

Both Mary Taylor and Ellen Nussey commented on how tired and old Charlotte looked at this time. Mary remembered telling her, with the impetuous frankness typical of Mary, that she was very ugly, and even the ever-loyal Ellen, who claimed that Charlotte never seemed to her 'the unattractive little person others designated her', did admit that 'certainly she was at this time anything but pretty . . . even her good points were lost. Her naturally beautiful hair of soft silky brown being then dry and frizzy looking, screwed up in tight little curls, showing features that were all the plainer from her exceeding thinness and want of complexion, she looked "dried in". A dark, rusty green stuff dress of old-fashioned make distracted still more from her appearance'.

Consciousness of her oddity, her utter dissimilarity to the girls around her, must have greatly increased Charlotte's painful shyness and nervousness in the company of strangers. She even sounded different: to the Roe Head girls her voice had a strong Irish accent. But worst of all, she was considered exceedingly ignorant and was relegated to the lowest class. Mary Taylor discovered that she had never learned grammar at all and very little geography. To Charlotte, conscious of her own precocity and intelligence, the entire experience was an overwhelming humiliation. After all, only a few months before, she had written a poem (a little tongue in cheek perhaps) on the pains of being especially gifted with divine fire and feeling, an attitude she and Branwell had slavishly adopted from their favourite Romantic poets. Whether conditioned to be so or not, she had been brought up with an attitude to knowledge and culture wholly different from that of these stolid manufacturers' daughters.

Ellen Nussey was sure that Charlotte's shyness did not stem from vanity or self-consciousness but from feeling an outsider among her fellow-pupils: 'They did not *understand* her, and she keenly felt the distance.' Despite Charlotte's lack of elementary education, Ellen noted that 'she far surpassed her most advanced school-fellows in knowledge of what was passing in the world at large and in the literature of her country. She knew a thousand things in these matters unknown to them.' Her knowledge of poetry appeared quite phenomenal. 'She was acquainted with most of the short pieces of poetry that we had to learn by heart: would tell us the authors, the poems they were taken from and sometimes repeat a page or two, and tell us the plot.' During her time at the school she could be observed committing long pieces of poetry to memory, which she did with the ease of long practice. Mary Taylor observed with wonder that her new friend picked up 'every scrap of information concerning painting, sculpture, poetry, etc. as if it were gold'.

Her fellow pupils used to complain that Charlotte was always talking about 'clever people – Johnson, Sheridan, etc.' and to this she replied, 'Now you don't know the meaning of *clever*. Sheridan might be clever; yes, Sheridan was clever – scamps often are – but Johnson hadn't a spark of cleverality in him.' According to Mary Taylor, no one appreciated the opinion: 'They made some trivial remark about "cleverality", and she said no more.'

Too short-sighted to play games – Charlotte could not see the ball – she was considered by her energetic school fellows as a dreamy, strange creature: 'She took all our proceedings with pliable indifference, and always seemed to need a previous resolution to say "No" to anything.'[2] Rather than playing games, she would stand under the trees in the playground, saying that it was pleasanter. Looking back, Mary Taylor realised how little they had understood what sort of aesthete had been nurtured at the parsonage and how she languished amongst them. The girl who at the age of thirteen had made a list of the great painters she wished to see – 'Guido Reni, Julio Romani, Titian, Raphael, Michael Angelo, Anibal Carracci, Leonardo da Vinci, Fra Bartolomeo, Carlo Cignani, Vandyke, Rubens, Bartolomeo Ramerghi' – tried to explain why it was more enjoyable to stand under the trees in the playground, 'pointing out the shadows, the peeps of sky, etc. We understood but little of it.' She told them of how she used to like to stand in the burn, on a stone, to watch the water flow by.'[3]

The girls were very impressed by her drawing ability. 'She used to draw much better and more quickly, than anything we had seen before, and knew much more about celebrated pictures and painters. Whenever an opportunity offered of examining a picture or cut of any kind, she went over it piecemeal, with her eyes close to the paper, looking so long that we used to ask her "what she saw in it". She could always see plenty, and explained it very well.'[4] To Mary Taylor, who had hitherto not been able to see the point of drawing and poetry, Charlotte's explanations were a revelation.

But though a friendship began to develop between Mary, Ellen and Charlotte, life was still difficult for Charlotte. Her friends probably seemed rather tame to her once she had got over her shyness and Charlotte said years later that Ellen had appeared to her as 'no more than a conscientious, observant, calm, well-bred Yorkshire girl. She is without romance.' If Ellen attempted to read poetry or poetic prose aloud, 'I am irritated and deprive her of the book – if she talks aloud of it, I stop my ears.' But with time affection would grow.

The memory of her sisters, six years after their deaths, continued to dominate her, and she seems to have spoken of them often to Ellen and Mary, who both mention this in their recollections of her. Mary Taylor remembered Charlotte telling her of a dream: 'She had been told that she was wanted in the drawing-room, and it was Maria and Elizabeth. I was eager for her to go on, and when she said there was no more, I said, "But go on! *Make it out*! I know you can." She said she would not: she wished she had not dreamed, for it did not go on nicely; they were changed; they had forgotten what they used to care for. They were very fashionably dressed, and began criticising the room, etc.'

Ellen Nussey noticed how intense Charlotte's love for her dead sisters continued to be, despite the years which had passed: 'a kind of adoration dwelt in her feelings which, as she conversed, almost imparted itself to her listener.' Charlotte would still weep and suffer when thinking of them, in particular Maria. 'When surprise was expressed that she should know so much about her sisters when they were so young, and she herself still younger, she said she began to analyse character when she was five years old.'

Charlotte seems to have given some idea of her life at home to Mary, telling her about a magazine in which no one wrote or read but her brother and two sisters. She promised to show Mary some of the issues and told her a story out of one, but afterwards retracted her promise. To the vigorous, outspoken Mary, as lively a supporter of the Radical party as Charlotte was of the Duke of Wellington, there seemed something a little unhealthy about living so exclusively in the realms of the imagination: 'This habit of "making out" interests for themselves, that most children get who have none in actual life, was very strong in her. The whole family used to "make out" histories, and invent characters and events. I told her sometimes they were like growing potatoes in a cellar. She said, sadly "Yes! I know we are!".'

Although Charlotte slowly blossomed in the kindly atmosphere at Roe Head, her time there was characterised by an almost frantic industriousness. From being the lowest in the class she rapidly rose to the head of it, and vied for prizes with Ellen and Mary; after her first term she took home the silver medal for good conduct. She felt that a great responsibility rested on her; that she was an object of expense to those at home and she must use every moment to obtain the purpose for which she was sent to the school – to fit her for making her way in the world. She pushed herself to the limit with study and, according to Ellen Nussey, had almost too much opportunity for her conscientious diligence. The girls were so little restricted in their doings that the industrious might accomplish the appointed tasks of the day and enjoy a little leisure, 'but she chose in many things to do *double* lessons when not prevented by class arrangement or a companion. . . . All her fellow pupils by the end of her stay regarded her as a model of application and high rectitude.' 'She did not play or amuse herself when others did. When her companions were merry round the fire, or otherwise enjoying themselves during the twilight, which was always a precious time of relaxation, she would be kneeling close to the window busy with her studies, and this would last so long that she was accused of seeing in the dark.'

There seems to have been some deep-seated nervous anxiety in Charlotte Brontë's make-up, which was increased by being outside the family circle and which would later manifest itself in psychosomatic migraines and illness. Since Mr Brontë had always encouraged his children to walk on the moors, it may have been a reflection of Charlotte's nervousness that she now seemed so sickly and ill-at-ease out of doors. The games played enthusiastically by the other girls seemed to jar on her and Ellen thought that she was physically not up to the exercise of muscle which strong healthy girls both older and younger than herself enjoyed. The anxiety also seems to have expressed itself in her taste in food.

One of the charges made by Mrs Gaskell, on the evidence of the gossipy maternity nurse who had attended Mrs Brontë at her confinements, was that the children were not allowed to eat meat by Mr Brontë, which made them particularly spiritless and quiet. 'It was from no wish for saving, for there was plenty and even waste in the house . . . but he thought children should be brought up simply and hardily: so they had nothing but potatoes for their dinner.' Mr Brontë afterwards wrote a letter to Mrs Gaskell categorically denying this: 'The principal mistake in the Memoir which I wish to mention is that which states that I laid my daughters under restriction with regard to their diet, obliging them to live chiefly on vegetable food. This I never did.'[5] And indeed Emily and Anne's secret diary papers of 1834 mention that boiled beef was for luncheon one day, without any indication of this being an extraordinary occurrence.

Nevertheless, in their independent accounts of Charlotte Brontë at school, one written in New Zealand, the other in Yorkshire, both Mary Taylor and Ellen Nussey said that she ate no animal food. Ellen went into great detail on this point: 'Her appetite was of the smallest; for years she had not tasted animal food; she had the greatest dislike to it; she always had something specially provided for her at our midday repast. Towards the close of the first half-year she was induced to take, by little and little, meat gravy with vegetable, and in the second half-year she commenced taking a very small portion of animal food daily. She then grew a little plumper, looked younger and more animated, though she was never what is called lively at this period.'

This is too detailed an account to be dismissed. Interestingly, Charlotte herself – who would wear children's chemises all her life and described herself as 'undeveloped' when she first met Mrs Gaskell – ascribed her diminutive appearance to the scanty supply of food she had had as a growing girl when at Cowan Bridge school. Is it possible that Charlotte at Roe Head was deliberately trying to make herself the focus of attention?

The difference in social status between Charlotte and her new friends also contributed to her nervousness. Roe Head emphasised anew her sense of being an object of charity, first experienced so young at Cowan Bridge and which would later find expression in bitter resentment in her work (particularly in *Jane Eyre*). Her benefactors, the Atkinsons, who lived only a mile away at Green House, and her father's former circle of friends all kept an eye on her and she was often bidden to spend the weekend with the Atkinsons. The servant sent to fetch her remembered in old age how unhappy Charlotte had been on these visits,[6] amongst the many relatives who were part of country house life then. On one occasion Mrs Franks and Miss Outhwaite, Anne Brontë's godmother, were so struck by her shabby clothes that they sent her a new frock and muslin, and a shawl, which, though welcome, were embarrassingly lavish presents, as a stiff little letter of thanks shows.[7]

Through such connections, and through invitations to the homes of her school friends, Charlotte was introduced into the life conducted in the large, affluent houses of the district, which are such a feature of her novels. Some were transformed by her imagination into places of terror. Thus in *Jane Eyre* the red-room at Gateshead Hall is apparently just a large empty room (though with hints of trouble to come) which rapidly assumes the dimensions of nightmare:

> The red-room was a spare chamber, very seldom slept in: I might say never indeed, unless when a chance influx of visitors rendered it necessary to turn to account all the accommodation it contained; yet it was one of the largest and stateliest chambers in the mansion . . .
>
> My seat, to which Bessie and the bitter Miss Abbot had left me riveted, was a low ottoman near the marble chimney-piece; the bed rose before me; to my right hand there was the high dark wardrobe, with subdued, broken reflections varying in the gloss of its panels; to my left were the muffled windows; a great looking-glass between them repeated the vacant majesty of the bed and room. I was not quite sure whether they had locked the door; and, when I dared move, I got up and went to see. Alas, yes! no jail was ever more secure. Returning, I had to cross before the looking-glass; my fascinated gaze involuntarily explored the depths it revealed. All looked colder and darker in that visionary hollow than in reality: and the strange little figure there gazing at me with a white face and arms specking the gloom, and glittering eyes of fear moving where all else was still had the effect of a real spirit.

However, Mary Taylor's home, the Red House (nowadays just behind the road from Gomersal to Bradford, and a mile up the road from

Birstall, where Ellen lived) enchanted Charlotte – as it must do anyone who visits it – and she later immortalised it as Briarmains in *Shirley*. A low, gabled red-brick house, built in 1660, it had been italianised by eighteenth-century ancestors of the Taylors, who had added a gallery to the grand staircase surmounting the matted hall – striking to Charlotte coming from a home without any carpeting – with its lovely mouldings, where statues brought back from Italy by Mary's father filled the niches. The elegant drawing room had a coloured neo-classical frieze running round it, interspersed with alcoves also containing white marble statuary. What particularly took Charlotte's fancy was a curious nineteenth-century ornament, a stained glass window in the parlour, which she describes in *Shirley* and which is now at the parsonage at Haworth: 'Those windows would be seen by daylight to be of brilliantly stained glass – purple and amber the predominant hues, glittering round a gravely tinted medallion in the centre of each, representing the suave head of William Shakespeare, and the serene one of John Milton.'

Mary Taylor's family, like Mary herself, were a welcome antidote to Charlotte's morbidity and introspection. In their house, she was treated without condescension and found there kindred spirits to her own family. The Taylors were as intellectual and argumentative as the Brontës themselves, far more interested in culture and politics than in social connections, as the Nussey family were. The children had a 'rage for practicality and laughed all poetry to scorn' according to Mary Taylor. Neither Charlotte nor she 'had any idea but that our opinions were the opinions of all *sensible* people in the world, and we used to astonish each other at every sentence . . . We used to be furious politicians, as one could hardly help being in 1832 . . . [Charlotte] would launch out into praises of the Duke of Wellington, referring to his actions; which I could not contradict, as I knew nothing about him. She said she had taken interest in politics ever since she was five years old. She did not get her opinions from her father – that is, not directly – but from the papers, etc., he preferred.'

Mr Taylor was an attractive personality with a somewhat volatile temperament and strong political views. He came from a family with a long history of Nonconformism, and had his own bank (carried on in a small stone building at the back of the house) as well as holding the monopoly on army cloth manufacture in the district. The business was now, however, in financial trouble and it was typical of him that when he later went bankrupt, he vowed to pay back all his creditors, and did so before he died. He took a fancy to Charlotte, and, as is clear from her portrayal of him in the figure of Mr Hunsden in *The Professor* (and Hiram Yorke in *Shirley*), she thought of him as a sort of unfathomable bluff magician. Like Mr Hunsden, he was much involved in business on the Continent; he spoke French and Italian as well as he did English and was a connoisseur of French and Italian literature. Observing Charlotte's thirst for knowledge and love of art, when she was grown up he sent her French and German books, once forty volumes at a time, and it was through him that she was introduced to the work of George Sand and Eugène Sue, among others. Charlotte would later say that the company of what she called the 'peculiar, racy, vigorous Taylors' was one of the most rousing pleasures she had ever known. So striking were the Taylors as a family – the father, his sons Joshua Taylor junior, John and Joe (a chemist with a very flirtatious disposition) – that Charlotte could not forbear from portraying them all pretty well to the life as her friends observed in *Shirley*, as the typically unorthodox and independent breed which were the peculiar glory of Yorkshire:

Take Mr Yorke's family in the aggregate, there is as much mental power in those six young heads, as much originality, as much activity and vigour of brain, as – divided amongst half-a-dozen commonplace broods – would give to each rather more than an average amount of sense and capacity. Mr Yorke knows this, and is proud of his race. Yorkshire has such families here and there amongst her hills and wolds – peculiar, racy, vigorous; of good blood and strong brain; turbulent somewhat in the pride of their strength, and intractable in the force of their native powers; wanting polish, wanting consideration, wanting docility, but sound, spirited, and true-bred as the eagle on the cliff or the steed in the steppe.

Mary Taylor inherited her father's strength of character and carried on the family tradition of independent thinking. Charlotte's description of Rose Yorke in *Shirley* was a portrait of the radical feminist as a young woman: 'Rose is a still, sometimes a stubborn girl now: her mother wants to make of her such a woman as she is herself – a woman of dark and dreary duties – and Rose has a mind full-set, thick sown with the germs of ideas her mother never knew. It is agony to her often to have these ideas trampled on and repressed. She has never rebelled yet; but if hard driven, she will rebel one day and then it will be once for all.' And later the resolution of Rose, when she demands a life that 'shall be a life . . . [not] a long slow death like yours in Briarfield Rectory. . . . Better to try all things and find all empty, than to try nothing and leave your life a blank' is the fiery talk of the admirer of Harriet Martineau who would sail half a world away in pursuit of 'action!'. At fifteen the rather formidable face to be seen in the only known portrait of her, an engraving taken from a photograph when she was in her fifties, had yet to develop. According to Ellen Nussey she was then very pretty, so much so that in later years Miss Wooler said that Mary seemed too pretty to live. We may imagine the three girls strolling about the school's extensive grounds, Charlotte feeling a natural affinity to Mary temperamentally and intellectually, helped perhaps because Mary's clothing too was not quite as good as the rest of the pupils. On account of Mr Taylor's financial difficulties, Mary's household was permanently on an economy drive. She and her younger sister Martha, who was also at the school, had to stitch over their new gloves before wearing them, under instructions from their mother, to make them last longer. Ellen admired both Taylor girls for their philosophical acceptance of their lot, which to fashion-conscious Ellen seemed particularly dismal – the dark blue cloth coats worn 'too short' and black beaver bonnets 'quite plainly trimmed'. Ellen's own taste mirrored the current fashion for adornment. Her own wide-set eyes, blonde curls and mild broad countenance, as seen in Charlotte's drawing of her, were conventionally appealing feminine looks.

Though a forceful personality, Mary was not talkative at school. She was hardworking and very persevering, and had a tendency to be touchy. It was difficult to know how an estrangement came about with Mary, but it always lasted a long time. One of Ellen's anecdotes about her two friends is revealing of their characters at this period:

The time came that both Charlotte and Mary were so proficient in schoolroom attainments there was no more for them to learn, and Miss Wooler set them Blair's *Belles Lettres* to commit to memory. We all laughed at their studies. Charlotte persevered, but Mary took her own line, flatly refused, and accepted the penalty of dis-obedience, going supperless to bed for about a month before she left school. When it was moonlight, we always found her engaged in drawing on the chest of drawers, which stood in the bay window, quite happy and cheerful. Her rebellion was never outspoken. She was always quiet in demeanour.

Mary Taylor would in the end incite Charlotte to rebellious behaviour, but of this aspect of Charlotte's character there was little or no outward sign at the age of fifteen. The outspoken rebel at the school was Martha Taylor, who was known as little Miss Boisterous and who was a favourite with Charlotte, as with everyone else, despite her cheek. Martha on one occasion annoyed Miss Wooler to the point where she threatened to box her ears, whereupon Martha talked of the danger of boxing ears and quoted in support of her argument Miss Wooler's clergyman brother. Ellen's description of her many years later indicates her infectious charm: 'She was not in the least pretty,

71

but something much better, full of change and variety, rudely outspoken, lively, and original, producing laughter with her own good humour and affection. She was her father's pet child. He delighted in hearing her sing, telling her to go to the piano, with his affectionate "pretty lass".'

Ellen Nussey's family was similar in origins to that of the Taylors – their fortune had been made in manufacturing in the middle of the eighteenth century, and the family had been in the district for several centuries. Unlike the Taylors, they put great stock in their gentility. At the time when Charlotte and Ellen met, Ellen's widowed mother was living in a large country house called Rydings set in its own parkland off the Birstall to Halifax road and only about three and a half miles away from the Taylors. A stately, rather gloomy building in dark stone, it lowers over its lawn; with its castellated roof, rookery and thorn trees, it would provide part of the inspiration for Mr Rochester's house, Thornfield, in *Jane Eyre*:

> It was three stories high [Rydings was in fact two], of proportions not vast, though considerable; a gentleman's manor house, not a nobleman's seat: battlements round the top gave it a picturesque look. Its gray front stood out well from the background of a rookery, whose cawing tenants were now on the wing. They flew over the lawn and grounds to alight in a great meadow from which these were separated by a sunk fence, and where an array of mighty old thorn trees, strong, knotty and broad as rakes, at once explained the etymology of the mansion's destination.

Rydings had belonged to the Nussey family since the early eighteenth century, when it had been acquired by Ellen's great-uncle, Reuben Walker, Justice of the Peace for Leeds, Bradford, Huddersfield and Halifax. His courts had been held there; the county candidate, Earl Fitzwilliam, had been a house guest during the 1809 parliamentary elections, and Reuben Walker himself was no stranger to the fashionable world, having been a Court apothecary. Four other members of Ellen's family held this post, including her brother John. The Nusseys were very well-connected in the district. Most of the local mansions were owned by their relatives, including the imposing Elizabethan Oakwell Hall, with its sinister twisting Jacobean furniture and dark panelling, which would be the inspiration for Fieldhead in *Shirley*. Financial vicissitudes would ultimately result in Ellen's family having to leave Rydings, but she remained very much a product of her background. Though snobbish, extremely conventional and blindly pious, she was nevertheless a great comfort to Charlotte. She irritated her at times, but her soothing common sense, like Miss Wooler's, had a salutary effect on Charlotte's easily overwrought personality.

Miss Wooler's emphasis in the curriculum on orderliness and method, on a certain code of behaviour, which to a twentieth-century view might seem restrictive, was probably a source of stability for Charlotte. She certainly came to respect, and be respected by, the high-minded Miss Wooler, who was genuinely kind-hearted, if a little awe-inspiring in her stateliness. To her pupils she resembled a lady abbess in the white embroidered dresses which were her habitual attire. Her long hair, worn plaited in an elaborate style to form a coronet with long ringlets falling to her shoulders, increased her digni- fied appearance. Her nun-like quality seems to have been generally recognised since, according to one of her relations, she was looked up to with the greatest respect by her family and was called 'Sister' by her brothers and sisters all her life.

But she also had an intimate, convivial side, and made a point of joining the girls at the fireside during their evening hour of relaxation and conversation. She apparently had a rare talent for conversing with her pupils, for they used to hang about her as she walked up and down the room, delighting to listen to her and to be nearest to her in the walk. It was a habit which Charlotte would bring home with her to the parsonage; night after night she and her brother and sisters would pace up and down the room, composing and talking about their writing.

Charlotte's resolute emphasis on self-denial and duty, which would be both a prop and a terrible restriction in later years, was more than probably modelled on the example of Miss Wooler and also to some extent Ellen. Miss Wooler approximated far more closely to a living rule than Miss Branwell, who does not seem to have earned Charlotte's intellectual respect even if she was lively enough at argument. To the girls Miss Wooler was an imposing presence, 'nobly scrupulous and conscientious, a woman of the greatest self-denial'. Although her income was small, she gave half of it to charity; she read the Bible through each year and read a chapter out of her Italian Testament every day because, she said, she 'never liked to lose anything she had learnt'.[8] To her, over the years, Charlotte would air her views in formal letters which imitated the elevated tone of Miss Wooler's favourite *belles lettres*.

Under Miss Wooler's regime of studies – based on Mrs Chapone's *Letters on the Improvement of the Mind* – French grammar, Rollin for ancient history, 'Mangnall's Questions' for history and biography, Hume, Milton and Shakespeare for poetry, Charlotte had little time to think of Glass Town. All her pursuits had changed so much. When to her joy Branwell, whom she wrote to weekly, came to visit her unex- pectedly, she confessed that lately she had begun to think 'I had lost

73

all the interest which I used formerly to take in politics'. But the 'extreme pleasure I felt at the news of the Reform Bill's being thrown out by the House of Lords, and of the expulsion or resignation of Earl Grey, etc., etc., convinced me that I have not as yet lost *all* my penchant for politics.'[9]

Although in the summer holidays she had written a short fragment of a Glass Town tale, in December 1831 Charlotte evidently decided that the secret world must be abandoned and destroyed. She expressed this in a stirring poem, 'The Trumpet has Sounded', heavily influenced by Byron's 'The Destruction of Sennacherib', which ends:

> The morning rose over the far distant hill,
> And yet the great city lay silent and still.
> No chariot rode thunderous adown the wide street,
> No horse of Arabia, impetuous and fleet.
> The river flowed on to the foam-crested sea,
> But, unburdened by vessel, its waves murmured free.
> The silence is dreadful. O city, arise!
> The sound is ascending the arch of the skies.
> Mute, mute are the mighty, and chilled is their breath,
> For at midnight passed o'er them the Angel of Death!
> The king and the peasant, the lord and the slave,
> Lie entombed in the depth of one wide solemn grave.[10]

Despite her resolutions she was evidently still contemplating Glass Town two weeks later, as on Christmas Day she wrote another poem brooding on its destruction:

> The bright sun in vain to this far land is given,
> And the planets look forth from the windows of heaven;
> And the birds sing unheeded in words fresh and green,
> And the flowers grow unscented, ungathered, unseen.[11]

Branwell's enthusiasm, however, continued unabated, although most of his writings on Glass Town were written when Charlotte was on the point of returning home after the school term or during the holidays together. They were still close – she wrote her weekly letters from school to Branwell because, she said, it was he to whom she had most to say. But school was distancing them more than physically. Charlotte's energies had been diverted into Roe Head and by the end of her stay there in May 1832, after three terms at the school, she had lost much of her initial shyness and had become quite a figure in her own way.

Her schoolfriends had had a hint of her extraordinarily vivid imagination when she had frightened the entire dormitory with a ghost story, and it was Charlotte who had taken over writing the playlets and ceremonials of the school. She would be remembered afterwards for her kindness and cleverness. Martha Taylor wrote to Ellen Nussey in the early summer of 1832 that she wondered 'how we shall go on next half year without you and Miss Brontë. I think that the schoolroom will look strange without Miss Brontë at the head of the class.'

On her very last day Charlotte was seized by a sudden desire to drop her dignified ways. She said to Ellen, 'I should for once like to feel *out and out* a schoolgirl; I wish something would happen! Let us run round the fruit garden [running was what she never did]; perhaps we shall meet someone, or we may have a fine for trespass.' But, as Ellen remarked, she left school as calmly and quietly as she had lived there.

CHAPTER V

Minds Out of the Same Mould

Charlotte returned to Haworth in the early summer of 1832 a little plumper, having lost what Ellen Nussey had described as her 'dried-in' look. A new world had been opened up to her by Roe Head, peopled by beings very different to the family circle which was almost all she had previously known. She had been made aware of another pattern of life; she now had the regulated path of duty to follow. Jane Eyre's description of the influence on her of Miss Temple was probably an echo of Miss Wooler's on Charlotte: 'I had imbibed something of her nature and much of her habits; more harmonious thoughts; what seemed better regulated feelings had become the inmates of my mind. I had given in allegiance to duty and order; I was quiet . . . to the eyes of others, usually even to my own, I appeared a disciplined and subdued character.'

Above all, she had made two friendships which would stand her in good stead for the rest of her life, although at first she was wary of trusting her new friends. When Ellen took the initiative in sending her a letter, it came as an agreeable surprise. Charlotte wrote back in her restrained, adult way that Ellen must excuse her if she had put little faith in her friend's promises to write, for she had thought that schoolgirl friendships were of necessity of short duration. Both Ellen and Mary were to prove her wrong. Charlotte's diffidence and strange lack of self-confidence were manifesting themselves here. She found it hard to estimate what sort of an impression she made on people.

In response to Ellen's request for a description of how her friend now spent her time, Charlotte gives a telling if strictly factual reply:

. . . this is soon done, as an account of one day is an account of all. In the morning from nine o'clock till half past twelve, I instruct my Sisters and draw, then we walk till dinner, after dinner I sew till tea time and after tea I either read, write, or do a little fancy work or draw, as I please. Thus in one delightful, though somewhat monotonous course my life is passed. I have only been out to tea twice since I came home. We are expecting company this afternoon and on Tuesday next we shall have all the Female teachers of the Sunday-school to tea. . . .

There is no hint in Charlotte's correspondence with Ellen of her secret writing, and little of her attitude to wider issues. Probably her letters to Mary Taylor were much closer to the real nature of the woman, but this correspondence was burnt by Mary expressly to protect Charlotte from the prying eyes of posterity. Charlotte laughingly admitted that her letters to Mary were 'rhodomontade' and contained long disquisitions on books and politics. To the timid, conventional Ellen, whom Charlotte characterised as having a 'naturally confiding and affectionate disposition', Charlotte's correspondence is self-consciously decorous but also very emotional. She is very much the dominant personality and in these early letters often adopts a lofty tone towards her friend. When Ellen had ventured into discussing Scott's *Kenilworth*, Charlotte responded in the Olympian manner of a distinguished contributor to the *Edinburgh Review*:

I am glad you like 'Kenilworth', it is certainly a splendid production, more resembling a Romance than a Novel, and in my opinion one of the most interesting works that ever emanated from the great Sir Walter's pen. I was exceedingly amused at the characteristic and naive manner in which you expressed your detestation of Varney's character, so much so, indeed, that I could not forbear laughing aloud when I perused that part of your letter; he is certainly the personification of consummate villainy, and in the delineation of his dark and profoundly artful mind, Scott exhibits a wonderful knowledge of human nature, as well as surprising skill in embodying his perceptions so as to enable others to become participators in that knowledge.[1]

Alongside such statements went ardent expressions of affection for 'my *dear dear dear* Ellen' and also a stout cheeriness that co-existed with the morbidity and fearfulness in Charlotte's nature and had already manifested itself in her keen although benevolent dissection of Branwell's flightier poetic aspirations. In response to Ellen's fears, at eighteen, of a tendency to 'pulmonary affection', she briskly enjoins her friend: 'If you remember I used frequently to tell you at school that you were constitutionally *nervous* – guard against the gloomy impressions which such a state of mind naturally produces, cheer up, take constant and regular exercise and all I doubt not will yet be well.'

77

Ellen would much later write a rebuttal of Mrs Gaskell's depiction of Charlotte as 'a victim to secret terrors and superstitious fancies': 'The fellowship of the school society knew the secrets of her heart far better than did any who became acquainted with her in after life. To such the real Charlotte Brontë, who knew no timidity in their presence, was a bold, clever outspoken girl; ready to laugh with the merriest, and not even indisposed to join in practical jokes with the rest of the schoolfellows.'[2]

Nevertheless, Charlotte's life of the imagination, so long shared with Branwell, remained secret from Ellen. Although for about a year following her return from Roe Head, she showed a lack of real interest in Glass Town, Branwell's influence was soon paramount again. During her absence his wilful streak had been allowed to grow unchallenged. Rebellious adolescent feelings were acted out by the inhabitants of Glass Town, and he had moved into increasingly sophisticated descriptions of Glass Town life. Between September 1830 and August 1832 he wrote six small manuscript booklets, 'Letters from an Englishman', which were supposedly written by a London banker visiting Glass Town. They detail the revolt against the rule of the Twelves and the Duke of Wellington by a new Byronic alter ego of Branwell's, Alexander Rogue. His delirious invention of detail after detail is formidable in its prolificness and scope, but also rather unbalanced and obsessional. The booklets display a mind which at the age of fourteen had lost its grip on reality a little, while it shows an extraordinary imagination and considerable wit in such inventions as the African Olympic games and an Academy of modern Athenians.

Charlotte's only manuscript for 1832, written in July, soon after her return from Roe Head, was 'The Bridal', a drama of romantic love. It is surprisingly little, given that the years 1829 and 1830 saw the creation of a manuscript almost every month. In this drama, The Marquis of Douro, perhaps influenced by the figure of the cultured Mr Taylor, is revealed at home in his palace to be the owner of 'one of the most splendid, select, and extensive libraries now in the possession of any individual. His picture and statue galleries likewise contain many of the finest works, both of the ancient and modern masters.' It seems that Charlotte had recently seen a representation of the popular statue, the Apollo Belvedere, because Lady Zenobia, who is wildly in love with the Marquis of Douro, gives him a little figurine of it as a token of her love. With the romantic themes of 'The Bridal', fed by Scott and Byron, Charlotte was moving away on her own, leaving the Glass Town world as conceived by Branwell.

The relationship between sister and brother, however, was still exceptionally close. In September 1832 he escorted Charlotte to Rydings after Ellen had persuaded her friend to come and stay with her. Ellen was very struck by how much Branwell, now fifteen, was the apple of Charlotte's eye: 'Happy, indeed, she then was, *in himself*, for she, with her own enthusiasms, looked forward to what her brother's great promise and talent might effect.' Ellen described Branwell's characteristically feverish, intense reactions at the time:

> . . . he was *then* a very dear brother, as dear to Charlotte as her soul: they were in perfect accord of taste and feeling, and it was mutual delight to be together. . . . Branwell probably had never been far from home before. He was in wild ecstacy with everything. He walked about in unrestrained boyish enjoyment, taking views in every direction of the old turret-roofed house, the fine chestnut trees on the lawn (one tree especially interested him because it was 'iron-girthed', having been split by storms, but still flourishing in great majesty), and a large rookery, which gave to the house a good background – all these he noted and commented upon with perfect enthusiasm. He told his sister he 'was leaving her in Paradise, and if she was not intensely happy she never would be!'

The influence on Charlotte of Rydings, which had a legend of a mad woman attached to it, would show later in *Jane Eyre*. The split chestnut tree that entranced Branwell also took hold of Charlotte's very visual imagination, and it became a memorable symbol of Mr Rochester's love and doom: 'Descending the laurel walk, I faced the wreck of the chestnut-tree; it stood up, black and riven: the trunk, split down the centre, gaped ghastly.'

On the visit Ellen Nussey relates that Charlotte spent much of her time in the garden away from the rest of the household. She enjoyed walking up and down through the plantations, or being sequestered from the rest of the world in the fruit-garden. She was safe from the Nussey visitors there. According to Ellen, 'Notwithstanding her excessive shyness, which was often painful to others as well as herself, she won the respect and affection of all who had opportunity enough to become acquainted with her'.

Ellen remembered Charlotte trembling and almost bursting into tears when a fellow guest had to escort her into dinner. Years later in a confidential letter to an early Brontë biographer, T. Wemyss Reid,[3] she expressed her opinion that the Brontës' extremely unconventional way of life, their 'unrestrained talk', meant that they reacted very badly when among strangers. They had 'no power of asserting themselves' because of their exceptional sensibilities, and 'they suffered intensely from what to another would at once have been cast aside and forgotten. Few, very few people unless they were the closest observers could be aware of the pain they inflicted, and would have been infinitely sorry for had they known.'

Ellen went on to say, coming unconsciously close to a definition of romanticism, that 'Charlotte had a painful conviction that living in other people's houses was to all of them an *estrangement* from their real characters, it compelled them to adopt an exterior which was a *bona fide* suppression and alienation from themselves, and they suffered accordingly.'[4]

During the visit to Rydings, Charlotte and Ellen's friendship had thrived and the ardent letters that followed were full of resolutions for self-improvement, no doubt influenced by Ellen's pious aspirations. Charlotte's letter of thanks was written in French: 'If you do not like me to write French letters tell me so, and I will desist, but I beg and implore your reply may be in the universal language, never mind a few mistakes at first, the attempt will contribute greatly to your improvement. Farewell. Write soon, very soon: I shall be all impatience till I hear from you.' In her next letter, shortly after New Year 1833, Charlotte told Ellen that the first day of January 'always presents to my mind a train of very solemn and important reflections, and a question more easily asked than answered, frequently occurs, viz. "How have I improved the past year, and with what good intentions do I view the dawn of its successor".'

Charlotte probably found the pull between the conventionally moral attitudes to life, exemplified by Ellen, and the imaginative world of her writings increasingly hard to cope with, on top of the confusions of adolescence. In March 1833 Branwell addressed 'A Few Words to the Chief Genii' in another Glass Town miniature newspaper, *The Monthly Intelligencer*, complaining that Glass Town was being abandoned:

When a parent leaves his children, young and inexperienced, and without a cause absconds, never more troubling himself about them, those children, according to received notions among men, if they by good fortune should happen to survive this neglect and become of repute in society, are by no means bound to believe that he has done his duty to them as a parent merely because they have risen, nor are they indeed required to own or treat him as a parent. This is all very plain and we believe that four of our readers will understand our aim in thus speaking.

However, by the end of May Charlotte was at work on a novelette set in Glass Town, entitled 'The Foundling'. It shows considerable collaboration with Branwell[5] and is full of crude verses, low-life scenes and Byronic swearing and swaggering – a far cry from the priestess-like code of behaviour Charlotte had been endeavouring to maintain. Midway through it she wrote anxiously to Ellen that her feelings were so much less holy than Ellen's:

> Your last letter Ellen revealed a state of mind which seemed to promise much. As I read I could not help wishing, that my own feelings more nearly resembled yours: but unhappily all the good thoughts that enter *my* mind evaporate almost before I have had time to ascertain their existence, every right resolution which I form is so transient, so fragile, and so easily broken that I sometimes fear I shall never be what I ought. Earnestly hoping that this may not be the case, that you may continue steadfast to the end I remain Dearest Ellen, Your *ever* faithful friend, Charlotte Brontë.

In 'The Foundling' and another manuscript from about this time, 'Something About Arthur',[6] the Marquis of Douro has moved to centre stage and is evolving into a fully fledged Byronic hero. Life passes in an exotic eastern fashion among velvet couches and ottomans where aristocratic guests recline, whiling away the time sipping sherbert and coffee. In 'Something About Arthur' it is clear that Charlotte had lingered with pleasure over the love scenes between Byron's Don Juan and Haidée, 'passion's child' – although she would later appear to Ellen to disapprove of such literature. Over the next two years Charlotte immersed herself deeper and deeper in Douro's largely illicit amorous adventures, and the atmosphere in which she and Branwell wrote their spirited romances became increasingly like a hothouse.

They were temporarily interrupted when in the late summer of 1833 Ellen paid her first visit to the parsonage. Charlotte had been anxious to keep up her friendship and return Ellen's hospitality but Aunt Branwell had prudently advised, as Charlotte reported, that the visit should wait until the summer as 'the winter, and even the spring seasons are remarkably cold and bleak among our mountains'.

Ellen later described in some detail her reactions to the family, and despite her somewhat sentimental approach, her narrative gives us a sense of family life at Haworth which was so unlike her own. Mr Brontë, at this time fifty-six years old, looked very venerable to her, with his snow-white hair and powdered coat collar. He sported an extraordinary cravat – like an enormous white neck bandage – which would become even larger in later years:

> He was in the habit of covering this cravat himself. We never saw the operation, but we always had to wind for him the white sewing-silk which he used. Charlotte said it was her father's one extravagance – he cut up yards and yards of white lutestring [silk] in

covering his cravat: and like Dr Joseph Wolff (the renowned and learned traveller) who, when on a visit and in a long fit of absence 'went into a clean shirt every day for a week, without taking one off', so Mr Brontë's cravat went into new silk and new size without taking any off, till at length half his head was enveloped in cravat. His liability to bronchial attacks, no doubt, attached him to this increasing growth of cravat.

Mr Brontë, Ellen related, frequently made efforts to stir up his parishioners to improve the sanitary conditions of the village but:

the needful outlay was not to be thought of, Haworth like many other places refused to acknowledge the real remedy for prevalent sickness and epidemic. The Passing-bell was *often* a dreary accompaniment to the day's engagements, and must have been trying to the nervous temperaments of those who were always within sound of it as the Parsonage inmates were, but *every thing* around, and in *immediate vicinity* was a reminder of man's last bourn: as you issued from the Parsonage gate you looked upon the stone-cutter's chipping shed piled with slabs ready for use, and to the ear [also remarked upon by Mrs Gaskell] there was the incessant sound of the chip, chip of the recording chisel as it ground in the dates of births and deaths.

The graveyard was so full of gravestones that hardly a strip of grass could be seen, but a comic feature in all this apparatus of death was provided by the ongoing battle between the housewives of Haworth and Mr Brontë about the right to use the graveyard as a place to hang out the village washing. Mr Brontë finally won, and having expelled them, commemorated the episode in some of his humorous verse:

The females all routed have fled with their clothes
To stockyard and backyards: where no one knows
And loudly have sworn by the suds which they swim in
They'll ring off his head, for his *warring with women*,
Whilst their husbands combine and [?vow] in their fury
They'll *lynch* him at once, without trial by jury,
But saddest of all, the fair maidens declare,
Of marriage and love, he must ever despair.[7]

It appears that Ellen found Mr Brontë quite alarming – indeed perhaps, reading between the lines, rather sadistic. She shuddered at the stories he told of some of the curiouser inhabitants of the moors. 'I can still see his eyes now as they gleamed at my (I am sure) blanched look, for I was frightened in my innocence and ignorance of such beings as he described. These stories were always given in early days as we sat around the breakfast and tea table where Miss Branwell presided. I understood, though I tried to hear as little as I could, that he was relating what others had told him.'

Mr Brontë's health made him retire early. At eight o'clock the family was gathered together for family worship. 'At nine he locked and barred the front door, always giving as he passed the sitting room a kindly admonition to the "children" not to be late; half way up the stairs he stayed his steps to wind up the clock.' Ellen's apprehensiveness of him cannot have been helped by the sound of his pistol being fired from his bedroom every morning as he discharged the loading made every night. She observed that his 'tastes led him to delight in the perusal of battle scenes, and in following the artifice of war. The self-denials and privations of camp-life would,' she thought, 'have agreed entirely with his nature, for he was remarkably independent of the luxuries and comforts of life.'

She noted that Mr Brontë was appreciated by his parishioners, because, as one of them said, 'he lets other folks' business alone'. But this lack of involvement, so prized by the village, redounded poorly on his children in Ellen's later view. 'If Mr Brontë had lived more in his family circle and turned his knowledge of human nature upon his own children, he would surely have influenced them to have chosen any vocation other than that of governess life – there never could have been temperaments *less adapted* to such a position.'[8]

Nevertheless, despite the many restrictions of their circumstances, Ellen considered this period of the Brontës' lives a very happy one: 'They were beginning to feel conscious of their powers – they were rich in each other's companionship, their health was good, their spirits were good, there was often joyousness and mirth; the perfection of unrestrained talk and intelligence brightened the close of the days which were passing all too swiftly.'

Emily and Anne did everything together. Ellen thought that they were like twins, so closely attuned were they to one another then. Like Charlotte, Emily wore what Ellen considered naturally beautiful hair in an unbecoming way – in a tight curl and frizz. Like Charlotte, she too had little complexion. 'She had very beautiful eyes – kind, kindling, liquid eyes; but she did not often look at you: she was too reserved. The colour might be said to be dark grey, at other times dark blue, they varied so.' She talked very little.

Emily lived in a self-sufficient world of the parsonage, the imagination and domestic tasks. One of her few reported utterances was given by Ellen when describing what was an annual visit of some of the female Sunday school teachers for tea at the parsonage. They were 'huge, cheerful, healthy light complexioned young creatures, with an astonishing amount of brusquerie in their manner, they were nearly all earners of their daily bread at the factories, but they manifested none of that deferential respect towards their employers which was the general tone of the well-employed in most other localities. They talked very freely of their masters but always by their Christian names as "Jack" or "Joe". When it was suggested they should be taught better manners, the Brontës were greatly amused, Emily especially so, who said, in her way which was always peculiarly quaint, "Vain attempt!".'[9]

Emily's manner could appear abrupt to the point of rudeness to anyone outside the family, and Ellen relates that 'it used to be a matter of surprise to Charlotte that she made an exception in my favour – she used to wish for my visits and was always kind and polite in her behaviour which was not often the case to other guests. Charlotte said she liked me because I never *seemed* to mark her peculiarities and I never pained her by treating her as a peculiar person. I remember after her death Charlotte spoke of Emily having valued me next to her sisters. This was the nearest approach she ever made I believe to anything like friendship apart.'[10]

Anne, 'dear gentle Anne', struck Ellen as being quite different in appearance from the others. 'Her hair was a very pretty, light brown, and fell on her neck in graceful curls. She had lovely violet-blue eyes, fine pencilled eyebrows, and clear almost transparent complexion.' Her voice, Ellen thought, was weak but very soft in tone. Anne was at this time only thirteen, and still largely being instructed by her aunt.

In the evenings the girls processed round and round the room in the way done at Roe Head:

The evening march in the sitting room kept time with their thoughts and feelings, it was free and rapid, they marched in pairs, Emily and Anne, Charlotte and her friend [i.e. Ellen] with arms twined round each other in child-like fashion, except when Charlotte in an exuberance of spirit would for a moment start away and make a graceful pirouette (though she had never learned to dance) and return to her march – sometimes she would dramatise on the impulse of the moment whatever came into her head making us all so merry – Emily or Anne would give out a cautious Hush! and say, Papa will wonder what we are about if he hears us laughing so much![11]

Ellen was enchanted by the unconventional way in which the Brontës amused themselves – rambling on the moors up behind the house in all weathers, for miles and miles and hours and hours. It felt as if they were on the roof of the world. It was a far cry from the sedate and measured stroll in the safety of the shrubbery at home.

The rugged bank and rippling brook were treasures of delight. Emily, Anne and Branwell used to ford the streams, and sometimes placed stepping stones for the other two; there was always a lingering delight in these spots – every moss, every flower, every tint and form, were noted and enjoyed. Emily especially had a gleesome delight in these nooks of beauty – her reserve for the time vanished. One long ramble made in these early days was far away over the moors to a spot familiar to Emily and Anne, which they called 'The Meeting of the Waters'. It was a small oasis of emerald green turf, broken here and there by small clear springs; a few large stones served as resting places; seated here we were hidden from the world, nothing appearing in view but miles and miles of heather, a glorious blue sky, and brightening sun. A fresh breeze wafted on us its exhilarating influence; we laughed and made mirth of each other, and settled we would call ourselves the quartette. Emily half reclining on a slab of stone, played like a young child with the tadpoles in the water, making them swim about, and then fell to moralising on the strong and the weak, the brave and the cowardly, as she chased them with her hand.

In later years Ellen emphasised that 'what the Brontës cared for and *lived* in most were the surroundings of nature'. And who, reading *Wuthering Heights*, can doubt that, like her creation Catherine Earnshaw, Emily Brontë found a heaven on earth in the moors she lived on?

Despite their reclusive situation, the Brontës appeared to Ellen completely happy with one another's companionship, because it was 'solitude and seclusion shared and enjoyed with intelligent companionship, and intense family affection'. That intense affection manifested itself also in a love of animals. They owned several cats and dogs, though in 1833 there was only one dog, which during Miss Branwell's regime was admitted to the parlour only at certain times. Emily and Anne always fed him part of their breakfast, which obviously startled the genteel Ellen; by their own choice it was the old north country dish of oatmeal porridge. Apparently the Brontës' love of dumb creatures made them very sensitive to treatment bestowed on them: 'For any one to offend in this respect was with them an infallible bad sign and a blot on the disposition'.

Tabby's influence remained important. She still kept to her duty of walking out with the 'childer' if they went any distance from home, unless Branwell was sent by his father as protector. She was very proprietorial towards her charges and thought she alone was capable of looking after them. When the villagers expressed curiosity about the parson's family, who kept themselves so much to themselves, Tabby refused to talk. Asked once if the Brontës were not 'fearfully larn'd', she left in a 'huff', but told the 'childer' about it.

Branwell was at this time still studying with his father. Ellen observed that amidst his sisters he sparkled, talking with extraordinary speed and brilliance. Although she thought his face handsome, she found his appearance generally rather grotesque. His red hair hung down in ragged locks behind his ears, in the romantic fashion appropriate to his being a poetic 'genius', and like all the Brontë children, he was in Ellen's eyes curiously dressed. 'He was neither full grown man nor yet a boy, and he had not yet acquired the art of attending to his appearance, none of the Brontës understood dress with its right and simple advantages till Charlotte and Emily had been in Brussels, they then began to perceive the elegance of a well-fitting garment made with simplicity and neatness and they adopted the better taste for themselves.'[12]

At the end of Ellen's visit the Brontës clubbed together their small pocket money in order to make an excursion to the famous nearby beauty spot of the ruins of Bolton Abbey. Branwell obtained a small, rather shabby double gig at a cheap rate to carry the party, which included a driver. They started between five and six in the morning from Haworth, and Branwell, showing off his extraordinary encyclopaedic memory, regaled them with the names of all the hills, views and places en route, and their exact height above sea level.[13]

They had arranged to meet up with a party of friends and relatives of Ellen's, who were to carry her on back to her home in Birstall, and the Brontë party arrived in high excitement at the hotel which was the meeting place. The disdain with which the hotel attendants greeted the old gig cast rather a blight over their spirits, although the ostlers changed their tune when they found that the Brontë party was recognised by the handsome carriage and pair arrivals. Both parties breakfasted together and afterwards strolled through the grounds. Emily and Anne would speak only to each other, but Branwell remained unabashed by the grandeur of the other party, who paid for the breakfast. He obviously had considerable charm of manner and the ability to fascinate, although from Ellen's later recollection his manic energy did give at least one of her party cause to fear for his stability:

Branwell, who probably never knew the feeling of shyness, amused everyone. He was in a phrenzy of pleasure, his eyes flashed with excitement and he talked fast and brilliantly, a friend who was of the party and herself a great admirer of scenery, said, she had never passed such a day of enjoyment in her life, she thought Branwell very eccentric but recognised his rare talent and genius, she presaged the *danger* though of those flashing impulses which came so sorely and surely in after time. He had any amount of poetry ready for quotation and this day he was well off in an appreciative audience whenever he chose to recite, and it was one of the things he did well.[14]

Ellen returned home to prepare for a season in London, a mark of her social superiority that could not have been lost on the Brontës as they returned to the isolated parsonage to immerse themselves with even more vehemence than before in the luxury of Verdopolis. When Ellen wrote to her from London, Charlotte replied in only semi-playful amazement that Ellen should find time to write to such an insignificant person as herself, 'while surrounded by the splendours and novelties of that great city, which has been called the mercantile metropolis of Europe'. Her imagination was set alight by the idea that Ellen might have seen 'the Great Personages which the sitting of Parliament now detains in town' and she says that if she were Ellen, she would not be too anxious to spend her time reading, as Ellen was doing. She should make use of her own eyes for the purposes of observation now, and 'for a time at least lay aside the spectacles with which authors would furnish us in their works'. Leave that to those with no chance of seeing the world, she might have added, who were forced to create new ones through their imaginations. At the end of the letter she asks if Ellen could find out the number of performers in the King's Military Band as Branwell wanted to know, presumably for authenticity in one of his stories.

Ellen's first season in London inspired Charlotte to begin a new manuscript, 'High Life in Verdopolis'. It featured the Duke of Zamorna, the title – taken from a Portuguese river – awarded the Marquis of Douro after a victory against the Ashantees. In the voice of Zamorna lounging at his ease in Verdopolis, Charlotte wrote a *cri de coeur* for her own existence:

I like high life, I like its manners, its splendours, its luxuries, the beings which move in its enchanted sphere. I like to consider the habits of those beings, their way of thinking, speaking, acting. Let fools talk about the artificial, voluptuous, idle existences spun out by Dukes, Lords, Ladies, Knights and Squires of high degree. Such cant is not for me, I despise it. What is there of artificial [in] the lives of our Verdopolitan Aristocracy? What is there of idle? Voluptuous they are to a proverb, splendidly magnificently

87

voluptuous but not inactive, not unnatural.[15]

She was amused by Ellen's nonchalant tone 'while treating of London and its wonders, which did seem to have excited anything rather than surprise in your mind'. Ellen's calm stance was quite bizarre to one of Charlotte's temperament: 'Did you not feel awed while gazing at St Paul's and Westminster Abbey? Had you no feeling of intense and ardent interest, when in St James's you saw the Palace? where so many of England's Kings had held their courts, and beheld the representations of their persons on the walls.' Ellen should not feel embarrassed to appear country-bred, Charlotte lectured. It was perfectly acceptable to be amazed: 'The magnificence of London has drawn exclamations of astonishment from travelled men, experienced in the World, its wonders, and beauties.'

Charlotte was hungering to see 'all the vista of proud salons glowing with brilliant fires and dazzling chandeliers' over which she waxed lyrical in novelettes of Zamorna's adventures at this time. The year 1834 marked his emergence as the consummate Byronic hero and it saw the expansion of Glass Town with the foundation of the Kingdom of Angria, given to Zamorna in recognition of his labours in the Ashantee wars. Characteristically, it was Branwell who provided the plot and moved the action forward, while Charlotte elaborated on the characters and relations between them. She had Zamorna's first wife die of a broken heart in response to Branwell's introduction of a new heroine and wife for Zamorna, Mary Percy, daughter of Branwell's hero, the Earl of Northangerland. The rivalry and love–hate relationship between Northangerland and Zamorna gave plenty of room for plots of revenge and cruelty, which were seized on energetically by Charlotte and Branwell. Glass Town finally moved towards civil war under Branwell's impetuous sway, as Northangerland became increasingly dissatisfied and rebellious, echoing Branwell's own state of mind.

Charlotte, meanwhile, elaborated on Zamorna's love affairs. Mistresses and illegitimate children, captured in highly coloured portraits written in voluptuous admiration by Charlotte, litter the manuscripts. Passion throbs from every line; gone is the ironic self-awareness, submerged in a long idyll of yearning. Zamorna's name is on the lips of all the swooning female inhabitants of Verdopolis: 'Zamorna, the god-like Zamorna, our idol, the idol of all my sex.' By 1835 his regiment of followers all dress in black satin! In a typical statement his wife cries '. . . were Zamorna to leave me and marry another, I should die, not of consumption, but of a sudden paroxysm of life-quenching agony that would cut me down like a scythe. Good God, at times I have had glimpses of the anguish she [Zamorna's first wife] endured so patiently. I have had sudden pangs of jealousy and moments of unutterable darkness, and while they lasted my spirit boiled in lava. I had feelings of suffocation and terrible degrading sensations that almost drove me mad.'[16]

These writings over the year amounted to some 140,000 words, about 350 pages, and were concealed from all but her brother and sisters. The Byronic fantasies that were engrossing her and Branwell, which conflicted so strongly with the pattern of piety for women laid down by Miss Wooler, would have appalled and amazed the unimaginative Ellen. Byron was considered unsuitable reading matter for women, as was Shakespeare, and a letter of July 1834 to Ellen, who had timidly asked for advice, shows how unorthodox Charlotte's attitudes to literature were as a young woman of eighteen. She was beginning to rebel against the narrow ideas of the age, even if in her lecture to Ellen she maintains the impression of frowning conventionally on Byron's 'Don Juan'. She evidently thought that Ellen's views needed to be broadened:

You ask me to recommend some books for your perusal; I will do so in as few words as I can. If you like poetry let it be first rate, Milton, Shakespeare, Thomson, Goldsmith, Pope (if you will though I don't admire him), Scott, Byron, Campbell, Wordsworth and Southey. Now Ellen don't be startled at the names of Shakespeare and Byron. Both these were great men and their works are like themselves. You will know how to choose the good and avoid the evil, the finest passages are always the purest, the bad are invariably revolting you will never wish to read them over twice. Omit the Comedies of Shakespeare and the Don Juan, perhaps the Cain of Byron though the latter is a magnificent Poem and read the rest fearlessly. That must indeed be a depraved mind which can gather evil from Henry the 8th from Richard 3rd from Macbeth and Hamlet and Julius Cesar [sic], Scott's sweet, wild, romantic Poetry can do you no harm nor can Wordsworth nor Campbell's nor Southey's, the greater part at least of his, some is certainly exceptionable. For History read Hume, Rollin, and the Universal History if you can – I never did. For fiction read Scott alone; all novels after his are worthless. For biography, read Johnson's Lives of the Poets, Boswell's Life of Johnson, Southey's Life of Nelson, Lockhart's Life of Burns, Moore's Life of Sheridan, Moore's Life of Byron, Wolfe's Remains, For Natural History read Bewick, and Audubon, and Goldsmith and White – of Selborne. For divinity, but your brother Henry will advise you there. I only say adhere to standard authors and don't run after novelty.

*

Although Charlotte hid the secret of her writing from Ellen, she revealed something of her and Branwell's devotion to art, which reached its height at this period. According to Ellen, Charlotte would pass the greater part of the day drawing, sometimes for nine hours with hardly an interval if she were greatly interested in the subject. She and Branwell would endlessly copy the engravings of Woollett, Brown, Fittler and others with great exactitude, almost line for line, and their meticulously copied engravings of fashionable beauties were transformed into Verdopolitan ladies as an accompaniment to their stories. Branwell later told his biographer Francis Leyland that he and Charlotte had at one time had a theory that 'the art-faculty consisted of little more than manual dexterity, and could be obtained by long study and practice in manipulation'.

During these years the talents of the brilliant Branwell were thought increasingly to lie in an artistic direction. He appears to have finally decided to be a painter after a visit the family made to the 1834 Summer Exhibition of the Northern Society of Arts in Leeds, which featured the work of two outstanding Yorkshire artists, the portrait painter William Robinson and the sculptor J. B. Leyland, brother of Francis. The sculptor was particularly famous for a colossal bust of Satan, about six foot high; an awed reviewer wrote that it was 'truly that of Milton's Archangel ruined'. Branwell would have seen it exhibited in 1834, and it would undoubtedly have particularly appealed to his love of the fiendish and grandiose which he was celebrating in his manuscripts at this time. Leyland had studied anatomy under the great sculptor Haydon and was coming to the peak of his fame; he had been eulogised several times in the London and local press, which may help explain why Branwell was seized anew by enthusiasm for such a career. After all, Leyland was a local man, who came from the town of Halifax only seven miles from Haworth.

William Robinson was a no less distinguished 'favourite son'. In 1820 he had been a pupil of Sir Thomas Lawrence; he had met Fuseli, and studied at the Royal Academy. He had a growing reputation as a portrait painter, whose commissions included portraits of the Earl de Grey's family, the Duke of Wellington for the United Services Club and Princess Sophia. It was therefore a move of some splendour when Patrick Brontë hired Robinson to teach his son. His children, his marvellous son, were to have nothing but the best.

From this, it appears that Mr Brontë was now determined that Branwell should have some kind of profession. The decision that Branwell should train as an artist probably indicates that the ever-practical Mr Brontë had judged his son, despite his wit and intellect, to be temperamentally unsuited to university and a career in the Church. Quite possibly, too, Branwell himself had been firmly against the idea of going into the Church. He was certainly very anti religion at this time (although his behaviour and the wicked fantasies of his writings would soon give rise to guilt), and he showed no tolerance as a teacher at Sunday School. He was remembered by one pupil for his 'violent temper and impatience'; he had difficulty in containing himself and often laid about him. According to this witness: 'They were not impressed by his tantrums, and on one occasion that he screamed at a pupil to "Get on! Get on! or I'll turn you out of the class!" the pupil sat there and slowly articulated "Tha' will'nt, tha old Irish —" and slowly picking himself out of his desk, took his own departure from the school.'

This man also remembered that after Sunday School the boys would stream out of the school a little way from the parsonage, down the green lane beside the graveyard to the church, where they occupied one of the big box pews under the north gallery. Branwell sat with them but retired to a corner of the pew close to the window 'where he read with avidity during the service some book which was not the Prayer-Book. If any of us disturbed him, he was very cross. He would come to the interrupter, and, turning a lock of the lad's hair round his finger, he would lift the offender from the floor and finish by giving him a sharp rap with his knuckles . . .'[17]

Branwell's character was beginning to assume the unhappy shape that it would take on for the rest of his life. His insistence upon intense feeling above all else appears to have led to his being incapable of tolerating the commonplace; life had to be lived at a high emotional pitch. The way of achieving this ecstasy might be through music, art or literature and, beginning at this time, drink. He also started to take a keen interest in boxing, and over the coming years would pass increasing amounts of time boxing or carousing at his local haunt, the Black Bull.

Sharp little Charlotte observed her companion's antics with her customary amusement, and then set her pen to work. In her manuscript of October 1834, 'My Angria and the Angrians', she gives a satirical portrait of seventeen-year-old Branwell in the person of Patrick Benjamin Wiggins: 'There advanced a low slightly built man attired in a black coat and raven grey trousers, his hat placed neatly at the back of his head, revealing a bush of carroty hair so arranged that at the sides it projected across a prominent Roman nose, black neckerchief adjusted with no great attention to precision. . . .'

Wiggins is both absurdly boastful – he claims to have walked sixty-five miles in twelve hours – and absurdly sycophantic. He tells Lord Charles Wellesley that his tomb will have the following inscription on it as a memorial to him: 'As a Musician he was greater than Bach, as a Poet he surpassed Byron, as a Painter, Claude Loraine [sic] yielded to him, as a Rebel he snatched the Palm from Alexander Rogue. . . .'[18]

Branwell, who played the organ, was enthusiastically fond of sacred music and Francis Leyland gave a telling description of his reaction to music at this time:

> although he could not perform their elaborate compositions well, he was always so excited when they were played for him by his friends that he would walk about the room with measured footsteps, his eyes raised to the ceiling, accompanying the music with his voice in an impassioned manner, and beating time with his hand on the chairs as he passed to and fro.[19]

Charlotte turned this extreme attitude of her brother's into high comedy through the character of Wiggins, who listens to a performance of 'I Know That My Redeemer Liveth':

> 'Then' said I, 'this is a God and not a Man.' As long as the music sounded in my ears, I dared neither speak, breathe nor even look up. When it ceased I glanced furtively at the performer. . . . Instantly I assumed that inverted position which with me is always a mark of the highest astonishment, delight and admiration. In other words I clapt my pate to the ground and let my heels fly up with a spring . . .

When Branwell seemed set on a new career as an artist, Charlotte did not pass up another opportunity to make fun of her brother. Perhaps she was partly motivated by envy for a profession open only to men. She seems to have seriously considered becoming a miniature painter – which would have been appropriate to her minute, detailed style – but probably soon realised the impossibility of achieving such an ambition as a woman, even though she continued to draw for hours and hours, head bent almost to the page, frequently very critical of the results. In her manuscripts of this time she created a new character for Branwell, William Etty R.A. (There was a real Sir William Etty living contemporaneously, who was a Yorkshire painter and fellow of the Royal Academy.) Lord Charles Wellesley wades in to mock the sensitive artist; as usual Charlotte could be quite biting.

> 'Well, Etty,' said I, as I entered the artist's studio at Adrianopolis, one fine afternoon last week, 'What's the last news with you? anything fresh on the canvass?' I knew that this mode of address was likely to be the most unpleasing possible to so sensitive a person as William Etty Esqr. R.A. and therefore I was not at all surprised when instead of answering me he turned his back on me and con-

tinued the assiduous prosecution of some works he was then engaged on. Undaunted by so cold a reception I calmly walked in and began to amuse myself by examining the pictures framed and unframed that hung around. Portraits, landscapes, half-finished historical scenes . . . single figures, comical sketches formed the splendidly variegated canvass panelling of this apartment.[20]

One of the first fruits of Branwell's new-found career was to embark on a family portrait, of himself and his three sisters, in oils. Dated to around 1834, for all its historical fascination, the painting is a crude object. Mrs Gaskell referred to it disparagingly and accurately as being not much better than sign-painting. It shows the girls seated around a small table; slightly behind them the figure of a man who must have been Branwell has been painted out, leaving what appears to be a pillar. As his biographer Leyland remarked, Branwell never mastered the medium of oil painting, and despite evidence of his quite superior skill as a draughtsman in the many sketches to be found at the parsonage and in the cross-hatching which infra-red rays have discovered beneath the wooden painting of his sisters, the portrait is very leaden.[21]

In the portrait Charlotte looks rather bovine; her hair, as befitted a young lady of eighteen, is put up in a topknot with curls hanging down beside it and she is wearing what Mrs Gaskell described as 'the womanly dress of the day of jigot sleeves and large collars'. She also, contradicting the descriptions of her as being sickly and thin, appears quite plump. But if Charlotte's face has none of the intensity of expression to be found in the later Richmond portrait, its proportions – 'the overhanging forehead' noticed by Mrs Gaskell, the broad though rounded and rather childlike planes of the face and the mild expression – bear a considerable resemblance to the photograph of Charlotte taken when she was thirty-eight. As authority for the likeness we have Mrs Gaskell's own reaction; when later shown the portrait by Charlotte, she thought the resemblance 'striking . . . though it must have been ten years and more since the portraits were taken'. Later Mary Taylor would write of her 'veritable square face and large disproportionate nose'.[22] We must also imagine a noticeably wide mouth (for her day), which appeared 'firm' and 'determined' to one observer, and a reddish complexion, which may have been natural high colouring or the results of being weather-beaten. The mouth would gradually become misshapen, as her teeth rapidly fell out. Her eyebrows were thin, but her eyes large and noticeably lambent.

Both Emily and Anne at the ages of sixteen and fourteen still had their hair shorn quite short. If we may assume that Branwell achieved fidelity to likeness, Anne was a rather wistful child. She bore considerable resemblance to her mother, with her long nose, rather pouting, full lips – which she shared with Emily – and small, rounded chin. Emily's hair blows in an invisible romantic wind which affects her alone and she stares mysteriously into the distance, calm, composed and grave, as she is in Branwell's other painting of her.

There is a brief glimpse into the characters of the shy and silent duo, into their occupations and preoccupations, in the first surviving entry of their jointly kept secret diaries, dated 24 November 1834. They were inspired by Byron's dashing diaries in which he noted his action at a precise minute of the day, but Emily's entry at the age of sixteen – poorly spelt, abominably punctuated and covered with blobs – gives no sign that thirteen years later she would produce *Wuthering Heights* or her visionary poems:

I fed Rainbow, Diamond, Snowflake, Jasper phaesant [alias] this morning Branwell went down to Mr Driver's and brought news that Sir Robert Peel was going to be invited to stand for Leeds. Anne and I have been peeling apples for Charlotte to make us an apple pudding and for Aunt nuts and apples Charlotte said she made puddings perfectly and she . . . was of a quick but limited intellect. Taby said just now Come Anne pilloputate [i.e. peel a potáto] Aunt has come into the kitchin just now and said where are your feet Anne. Anne answered On the floor Aunt. Papa opened the parlour door and gave Branwell a letter saying Here Branwell read this and show it to your Aunt and Charlotte. The Gondals are discovering the interior of Gaaldine. Sally Mosley is washing in the back kitchin.

It is past Twelve o'clock Anne and I have not tid[i]ed ourselves, done our bedwork, or done our lessons and we want to go out to play. We are going to have for Dinner Boiled Beef, Turnips, potatoes and applepudding. The Kitchin is in a very untidy state Anne and I have not done our music exercise which consists of *b major* Taby said on my putting a pen in her face Ya pittering pottering there instead of pilling a potato I answered O Dear, O Dear, O Dear I will derectly With that I get up, take a knife and begin pilling. Finished pilling the potatoes. Papa going to walk Mr Sunderland expected.

Anne and I say I wonder what we shall be like and what we shall be and where we shall be if all goes on well in the year 1874 – in which year I shall be in my 57th year Anne will be in her 55th year Branwell will be going in his 58th year and Charlotte in her 59th year hoping we shall all be well at that time we close our paper.

Beneath a drawing of a lock of hair on this manuscript is written: 'A

94

bit of Lady Jul[i]et's hair done by Anne.'

Whatever its literary merits or lack of them, the diary reveals a cheerful, carefree atmosphere in the parsonage. Sharp-tongued Charlotte appears in charge of running the house, while Branwell is clearly given priority by the father in being given a letter to read first and pass on. Emily and Anne, bantering with Tabby and in Anne's case not fearing to cheek her aunt, are quite different from their bookish brother and sister, their untidiness, laziness and almost dreamy contentment in marked contrast to Charlotte's studious purposefulness and to the intensity and sophistication of her and Branwell's writing. But the reference to 'the Gondals' shows that Emily and Anne had by now established their own imaginary kingdom, as important in the scheme of their lives as what was on the kitchen table.

'Gaaldine' was 'a large Island newly discovered in the South Pacific', according to Anne's definition written into Goldsmith's *Grammar of General Geography* which is still in the Brontë Parsonage Museum. This very early reference to the kingdom of the Gondals is one of the few prose fragments about Gondal to survive, probably because Charlotte destroyed much of her sisters' early writings after their deaths. The land of Gondal has to be pieced together largely from the poetry Emily and Anne wrote about it.[23] Although just as vivid to its creators as Glass Town and Angria to Charlotte and Branwell, it was a more rough and ready affair, with little of the elaborate geographical constructs and detail of Charlotte and Branwell's world. Its climate seems to have been very similar either to Scotland, on account of the influence of Scott on Emily, or to the Yorkshire moors near Haworth. What is particularly interesting about the Gondal world is that the chief actors are passionate women. Gondal was ruled by the ruthless, immoral Augusta Geraldine Almeda, a *femme fatale* who ruins men's lives and who is finally murdered by the lover of one of her former loves.

Although Emily and Anne were allowed to participate in Charlotte and Branwell's imaginary world until at least 1837, they remained essentially bystanders to the extraordinary creative output of their brother and sister. In the year following the summer of 1834, Branwell and Charlotte were absorbed in mimicking in Angria the rise and fall of government ministries in London and the canvassing for the parliamentary elections of 1835, held under the new, wider franchise of the recent Reform Act passed by the Whigs. Manuscript after manuscript, written alternately by Charlotte and Branwell in response to one another, describes the opening of the new Parliament in Angria, speeches from Zamorna, inspiring speeches in return from Northangerland, who is constantly trying to inspire revolt against the rule of Zamorna. Zamorna's rallying call to the Angrians gives rise to provincial meetings throughout the country, ministers resign and Northangerland becomes premier again. Meanwhile Northangerland is striking up another alliance to reform the Verdopolitan constitution; Zamorna now demands that Northangerland relinquish his seals of office.[24]

By early 1835 the parsonage was gripped by real election fever. The arch-Conservative Mr Brontë, pessimistic about the wisdom of extending the franchise, made impassioned speeches on the Tory hustings, undaunted by the hecklings from the crowd in this mainly Whig area. According to an eyewitness account by the son of Mr Brontë's tailor, when Mr Brontë spoke on the 'Blue' hustings outside the Black Bull he was heckled so repeatedly that Branwell leapt up, quite out of control with rage, and shouted: 'If you won't let my father speak, *you* shan't speak!'[25] Patrick Brontë was later burned in effigy for his pains, holding a potato in one hand and a herring in the other, the potato being a symbol of his Irish origins.

Charlotte wrote in excitement to Ellen at Birstall, trying to conjure up the electric atmosphere within the parsonage as her father and brother stamped in and out and held meetings at the White Lion in the centre of the village, just down from the church:

> The Election! The Election! that cry has rung even amongst our lonely hills like the blast of a trumpet, how has it roused the populous neighbourhood of Birstall? Ellen, under what banner have your brothers ranged themselves? The Blue or the Yellow? Use your influence with them, entreat them if it be necessary on your knees to stand by their Country and Religion in this day of danger.

The Tory government of Robert Peel had fallen in April 1835, paving the way to elections in May. It was the month of Charlotte's nineteenth birthday, and it also marked the end of her childhood years in the close family life of the parsonage. She had received an offer from Miss Wooler to teach at Roe Head, with a free place for one of her sisters. It came at the time when her father had decided that Branwell should apply to the Royal Academy of Arts in London the coming autumn. Assuming that he was successful, the expense would severely deplete Patrick Brontë's income. Charlotte had previously received a couple of proposals to be a private governess but Miss Wooler's generous offer, on top of Charlotte's wish to help her father's finances, finally decided her that she ought to embark on the governess role she had been trained for. '*Duty – necessity* – these are stern mistresses who will not be disobeyed,' she wrote with her usual drive.

Emily would accompany her, which was a source of consolation, as was the thought of having Ellen and her dear 'Mad Pag' – Mary Taylor – nearby. Despite her sadness at leaving home she wrote optimistically to Ellen, ' "My lines have fallen in pleasant places" . . . I both love and respect Miss Wooler. . . .'

CHAPTER VI

My Dreams, the Gods of My Religion

Charlotte and Emily left Haworth for Roe Head on 29 July 1835. Their father had written to the kindly Mrs Franks, their old friend Miss Firth from Thornton, to ask her to keep an eye on them:

> They both have good abilities, and as far as I can judge their principles are good also, but they are very young, and unacquainted with the ways of this delusive and ensnaring world; and though they will be placed under the superintendence of Miss Wooler who will I doubt not do what she can for their good, yet I am well aware that neither they nor any other can ever, in this land of probation, lie beyond the reach of temptation.

His fears of worldly temptations were more appropriate to Branwell, but his pessimistic tone was justified. Although Charlotte entered on this new phase of her life quite confidently, the next three years were marked by intense unhappiness. She had underestimated the power that the imaginary world, the 'darling dream' as she called it, held over her. She found the school routine and the teaching monotonous and restricting; there was rarely any time for herself and happiness was only to be found when she could be alone, free to summon up Zamorna and the glorious life of Byronic adventure enjoyed by her and Branwell. The surviving fragments of her 'Roe Head Journal' reveal the torment of her existence, her longing to escape and her dependence on the dream world. By February 1836 she was writing:

> It is seven o'clock at night; the young ladies are all at their lessons; the schoolroom is quiet, the fire is low; a stormy day is at this moment passing off in a murmuring and bleak night. I now assume my own thoughts; my mind relaxes from the stretch on which it has

been for the last twelve hours, and falls back onto the rest which nobody in this house knows of but myself. I now, after a day of weary wandering, return to the ark which for me floats alone on the billows of this world's desolate and boundless deluge. It is strange I cannot get used to the ongoings that surround me. I fulfil my duties strictly and well. I, so to speak – if the illustration be not profane – as God was not in the fire, nor the wind, nor the earthquake, so neither is my heart in the task, the theme, or the exercise, and it is the still small voice alone that comes to me at eventide, that floats like a breeze with a voice in it over the deeply blue hills and out of the now leafless forests and from the cities on distant river banks of a bright and far continent; it is that which takes up my spirit and engrosses all my living feelings, all my energies which are not merely mechanical . . . Haworth and home wake sensations which lie dormant elsewhere.[1]

The diary contains many references to her 'power', urgent invocations that it 'may never grow less', and the poetry she wrote reveals how she remembers the happiness of the children's shared world of the imagination at the parsonage:[2]

We wove a web in childhood
    A web of sunny air;
We dug a spring in infancy
    Of water pure and fair;

We sowed in youth a mustard seed,
    We cut an almond rod;
We are now grown up to riper age –
    Are they withered in the sod?

She goes on to wonder whether those past joys have now in her 'darkly shaded' life faded away. But no:

Faded! the web is full of air,
    But how its folds are spread,
And from its tints of crimson clear
    How deep a glow is shed.
The light of an Italian sky
Where clouds of sunset lingering lie
    Is not more ruby red.

For Emily, being away from her home and beloved moorlands proved unendurable. Charlotte later wrote with sympathetic understanding:

99

Liberty was the breath of Emily's nostrils; without it, she perished. . . . Every morning when she woke, the vision of home and the moors rushed on her, and darkened and saddened the day that lay before her. Nobody knew what ailed her but me – I knew only too well. In this struggle her health was quickly broken; her white face, attenuated form, and failing strength threatened rapid decline.[3]

Always conscious of her elder sisters' fate and convinced that Emily would die if she stayed on at Roe Head, Charlotte arranged for her to return home after less than three months at the school. Anne, now fifteen, was sent in her stead. Her more passive nature enabled her to fit better into the school life, although she too was home-sick and unhappy. Partly because she was the youngest child, she was much less close than Emily to Charlotte. The latter continued to suffer on at the school without any release, driven only by her strong sense of duty. She struggled daily to overcome the acute sense of separation from the land of thought in a way that Emily had found impossible. The call of Gondal, the hours of writing poetry and ballads about its heroic denizens with their uncontrolled passions, had been too strong for Emily. Her obdurate nature could not brook interference and the restrictions of the school room.

Charlotte later wrote that Emily's failure at Roe Head was a source of mortification to Emily.[4] It certainly may have increased the latter's fascination with the theme of a Byronic outcast that begins to make its presence felt in her poetry and was quite probably influenced by Branwell. When she had arrived home in mid-October, Branwell's mood was gloomy and cynically despondent, and increasingly beset by religious doubts and fears. His recent visit to London with the intention of applying to the Royal Academy of Arts had been a humiliating failure. What exactly happened is difficult to ascertain, but with his unbalanced nature and absurdly heroic view of himself, Branwell seems to have exaggerated the setback into proof of his unworthiness and predestined tendency as a sinner to failure. Mary Taylor thought that it was around this time that he took Cowper's poem of Calvinistic fear, 'The Castaway', for his own, as did all the Brontës at periods during their lives. Emily, mortified by her own failure at Roe Head, watching her brother frustrated and angry, chafed by his surroundings, may have absorbed something of his Calvinistic fears. Her mind had already been made receptive by Byron's own rebellious heroes and she began to write about a dark, doomed man, the prototype of Heathcliff.

Branwell's strong feelings of personal disappointment over the London episode, of having behaved badly, may have been the result of over-indulgence in the inviting inns of the capital. It is possible that he lost his nerve when he arrived at the Royal Academy and saw the work of other students; it is also possible that he was told that his work was not of a high enough standard to meet the requirements of the Academy, although given William Robinson's interest in Branwell this seems unlikely. The only factual information about the episode comes from a man named Woolven, who became an engineer on the Leeds and Manchester railway, and who was so taken by what he saw of Branwell one evening in a long session in the Castle tavern in Holborn as to recognise him four years later.

The Castle was kept by a great boxer of the time, Tom Spring, and Branwell would have read about it in the sporting papers that he took as a member of the Haworth boxing club. Branwell's particular gift for entertainment, for conviviality, would quickly have made him welcome as a stranger. Mr Woolven was greatly impressed by the young man's 'unusual flow of language and strength of memory'; appreciating his ever ready erudition and sparkling wit, 'the spectators made him umpire . . . about the dates of certain celebrated battles'.[5]

Some light on what happened to Branwell in London is shed by his manuscript 'Adventures of Charles Wentworth', written in May 1836. Wentworth, armed with many letters of introduction and recollecting the sort of advice doled out in the parsonage that 'you can never have real happiness without working for it', wanders restlessly about the streets of London 'with a wildish dejected look of poverty-stricken abstraction. His mind was too restless to stop and fully examine anything. . . . He felt the want, that restless uneasy feeling with which rest is torment, and ease begets stupor. The flashes of feeling which were constantly scintillating thrilled his soul, and he cared and thought of nothing more.' One biographer has suggested that this may have heralded an epileptic fit.[6] It certainly reads like a truthful self-portrait.

Wentworth's fourth day in London:

found him still unknown and unvisited, without participating in the splendours of wealth, no more than if he had not had a pound in his pocket. Nor was he bent studiously on ransacking the great libraries or studying in the picture galleries. He was restlessly, aimlessly, and with the same anxious face feeding his feeling with 'little squibs of rum', as he called them to himself, since he was perfectly aware that they would only the more depress him afterwards.[7]

Whatever the truth, Branwell returned to the parsonage after about two weeks. The rumour in Haworth years later was that 'before he had really reached the City he had fallen a prey to "sharpers" and had been robbed of most of his money';[8] Branwell himself may have put this story about. There is no mention of the episode in any of the Brontë records. Ellen Nussey later told Mrs Gaskell that she did not know 'whether it was conduct or want of finances that prevented Branwell from going to the Royal Academy'.

The news from home can only have increased Charlotte's unhappiness. Her self-sacrifice in taking the teaching post had been made particularly on behalf of Branwell, who had now failed to take his opportunity in London. Frustrated, bored, drinking more, he ricocheted from the idea of being a great artist back to being a great writer. In late November, when James Hogg, one of Branwell and Charlotte's childhood heroes on *Blackwood's Magazine*, died, Branwell was convinced in a typical wild fit of enthusiasm that this was his moment. He dashed off three letters to the magazine's editor, beginning imperiously in huge letters 'Sir – Read what I write', offering to take over Hogg's services, and sat back to await a call to the Edinburgh offices of the paper. None came. The letters were kept by the staff of the journal as curiosities, the correspondence of a madman, and were found years later by Mrs Oliphant.

Branwell's poetry from this time is increasingly preoccupied with death, his own sinfulness and fear of divine retribution, as well as the hypocrisy of practising Christians. The swashbuckling existence he lived in his dream writing could not be reconciled with the reality of his obscure life at the parsonage. He seems to have begun to doubt the existence of God, perhaps in rebellion against patriarchal authority; then, aghast, his early intensive religious training rose up against this, and he felt that such thoughts must show that he was one of the damned. In 'The Doubter's Hymn'[9] he writes that life is now 'a passing sleep/Its deeds a troubled dream', death is 'the dread awakening/to daylight's dawning beam'. He asks, 'Where will that waking be?' –

> How will that Future seem?
>   What is Eternity?
> Is Death the sleep? – Is Heaven the Dream?
>   Life the reality?

By March 1836 he had completed the second half of a long poem entitled 'Misery', which is informed by Calvinism and haunted by the image of Maria, who in this crisis appeared as the perfection he felt he could never attain. If a Heaven exists, Branwell will not be part of it for 'Hell's dread night must close my day!'.

For Charlotte, previously so intimately entwined with Branwell in their glorious imaginative kingdom, the anguished figure of her brother probably contributed to the intense religious crisis which she herself now began to experience. Back home for the Christmas holidays, she wrote a long piece of doggerel in which Angrian visions are mixed with appalling anxiety about her newfound desire for piety and dreadful fears of her own unworthiness. Meditating on the martyrdom of St Stephen, she longs for 'that lofty faith which made him bless his foes'. As Christine Alexander has movingly written,[10] Charlotte 'agonises over whether her supplication to Christ is motivated by a contrite heart or merely by her inward agony. She yearns for her childhood dreams of Heaven when she was blindly pious, unconscious of evil; now sinful terrors plague her mind, spectral visions foretell her death and the church tower bears down on her spirit like an awful giant. She is afraid to pray. She speaks of the "ghastly power" and "grinding tyranny" of her thoughts, fed in infancy by books "of ghostly and spectral dread".'

She ponders on the dream world of which she is so much a part, the 'divine creations' that are 'my soul's unmingled themes'.

> Succeeding fast and faster still
>   Scenes that no words can give,
> And gathering strength from every thrill
>   They stir, the[y] breathe, they live.
>
> They live! they gather round in bands,
>   They speak, I hear the ⟨tone⟩;
> The earnest look, the beckoning hands,
>   And am I *now* alone?
>
> Alone! there passed a noble line!
>   Alone there thronged a race!
> I saw a kindred likeness shine
>   In every haughty face.
>
> I know their deeds, I know their fame,
>   The legends wild that grace
> Each ancient house, and round each name
>   Their mystic signals trace.

On the day she is about to return to Roe Head, she goes on to reveal how important Zamorna has been to her in the past years and the solace her 'mental King' has provided in her lonely, unhappy existence as a governess where she is unable to love those around her:

> I owe him something, he has held

A lofty, burning lamp to me,
Whose rays surrounding darkness quelled
    And showed me wonders, shadow free.

And he has been a mental King
    That ruled my thoughts right regally,
And he has given a steady spring
    To what I had of poetry . . .

He's moved the principle of life
    Through all I've written or sung or said
The war-song rousing to the strife
    The life-wind wakening up the dead

He's not the temple but the god
    The idol in his marble shrine
Our grand dream is his wide abode
    And there for me he dwells divine[11]

Charlotte's guilt at the obsessive nature of the imaginary world, her hatred of the one she lived in and the painful awakening of a hitherto suppressed but powerful religious conscience in the enclosed female world of Roe Head assorted so ill with the free life of the imagination she and Branwell had created at Haworth that over the next two and a half years she teetered on the brink of a breakdown. The verse and prose of her journal repeatedly show the conflict and the irresistible pull of her imagination. Life in Angria remained her secret joy and only escape from misery. At the end of 1835, when Branwell had brought about another crisis in this imaginary world by expelling Angria, with Zamorna and his supporters, from the Verdopolitan union, Charlotte was greatly affected:

My dreams, the Gods of my religion, linger
    In foreign lands, each sundered from his own.
And there has passed a cold destroying finger
    O'er every image, and each sacred tone
Sounds low and at a distance, sometimes dying
Like an uncertain sob, or smothered sighing.[12]

Her journal continues:

Last night I did indeed lean upon the thunder-waking wings of such a stormy blast as I have seldom heard blow, and it whirled me away like heath in the wilderness for five seconds of ecstasy; and as I sat

104

by myself in the dining room while all the rest were at tea, the trance seemed to descend on a sudden, and verily this foot trod the war-shaken shores of the Calabar, and these eyes saw the defiled and violated Adrianopolis shedding its lights on the river from lattices whence the invader looked out.

Such vehemence, which only her brother could understand, was quite alien to the orderly life of the school, with its reined and gentle pleasures. Possessed by the dream world, Charlotte seemed almost to revel in the role of rebel, making little attempt to control her intense reactions. Her journal entry of 11 August 1836 seems written by someone delirious:

All this day I have been in a dream half-miserable and half-ecstatic miserable because it showed in the vivid light of reality the ongoings of the infernal world. I had been toiling for nearly an hour with Miss Lister, Miss Marriott and Ellen Cook striving to teach them the distinction between an article and a substantive. The parsing lesson was completed, a dead silence had succeeded it in the school-room and I sat sinking from irritation and weariness into a kind of lethargy. The thought came over me am I to spend all the best part of my life in this wretched bondage, forcibly suppressing my rage at the idleness the apathy and the hyperbolical and most asinine stupidity of those fat-headed oafs and on compulsion assuming an air of kindness, patience and assiduity? Must I from day to day sit chained to this chair prisoned within these four bare walls, while these glorious summer suns are burning in heaven and the year is revolving in its richest glow and declaring at the close of every summer's day the time I am losing will never come again? Stung to the heart with these reflections I started up and mechanically walked to the window . . . I shut the window and went back to my seat. Then came on me rushing impetuously, all the mighty phantasms that we had conjured from nothing to a system strong as some religious creed. I felt as if I could have written gloriously – I longed to write. The spirit of all Verdopolis – the mountainous North, all the woodland west of the river-watered East came crowding into my mind. If I had time to indulge it I felt that the vague sensations of that moment would have settled down into some narrative better at least than anything I ever produced before. But just then a Dolt came up with a lesson. I thought I should have vomited.

Years later Mary Taylor gave an account to Mrs Gaskell of Charlotte's life at this time. Mary sometimes saw her old schoolfriend at services in Gomersal Church and paid her a visit at the school:

[I] asked how she could give so much for so little. She owned that, after clothing herself and Anne, there was nothing left, though she had hoped to be able to save something. She confessed it was not brilliant, but what could she do? I had nothing to answer. She seemed to have no interest or pleasure beyond the feeling of duty, and, when she could get the opportunity, used to sit alone and 'make out'. She told me afterwards that one evening she had sat in the dressing room until it was quite dark, and then observing it all at once had taken sudden fright.

Mary also recounted that Charlotte told her that one night while sitting alone she heard a voice repeat the following lines:

Come, thou high and holy feeling,
Shine o'er mountain, flit o'er wave,
Gleam like light o'er dome and sheiling.

There were eight or ten more lines which I forget. She insisted that she had not made them, that she had heard a voice repeat them.

Charlotte's surviving letters to Ellen Nussey from the middle of 1836 give some idea of her increasing desperation and feelings of sinfulness. Her friend's excessive piety, which Charlotte had once found amusing, was now something she envied. 'It is from religion you derive your chief charm, and may its influence always preserve you as pure, as unassuming, and as benevolent in thought and deed as you are now. What am I compared to you?' Convinced of how different her thoughts were from her contemporaries she wrote in pathetic agony:

I feel my own utter worthlessness when I make the comparison. I am a very coarse, commonplace wretch, Ellen, I have some qualities which make me very miserable, some feelings that you can have no participation in, that few, very few people in the world can at all understand. I don't pride myself on these peculiarities, I strive to conceal and suppress them as much as I can, but they burst out sometimes, and then those who see the explosion despise me, and I hate myself for days afterwards.

The warm-hearted, bewildered Ellen responded with sympathy and well-meaning religious exhortations that tended only to deepen her friend's despair. Discussions of Calvinist dogma which Ellen had probably imbibed from her clergyman brother Henry added to the burden.[13] Charlotte wrote passionately that she had 'stings of conscience – visitings of remorse – glimpses of Holy, inexpressible things, which formerly I used to be a stranger to'. She hated her 'former flippancy and forwardness' but had 'a horror at the idea of becoming one of a certain set – a dread lest if I made the slightest profession I should sink at once into Phariseeism, merge wholly into the ranks of the self-righteous. In writing at this moment I feel an irksome disgust at the idea of using a single phrase that sounds like religious cant – I abhor myself – I despise myself.'

Branwell's influence, the years of mockery, could not easily be shaken off. In her novelette 'Passing Events' of April 1836, she had breathed defiance against convention, satirising religion in an exuberant skit on Methodist ranting, which is very similar in feel to Emily's later description of Lockwood's dream of Jabez Branderham's sermon on the seven times seventy-seven sins in *Wuthering Heights*. Unable to reconcile the conflict between her imaginings and what her awakened conscience told her were unholy thoughts, Charlotte clung more and more to Ellen and her calm, conventionally religious attitudes. If only, she wrote, Ellen knew her thoughts, 'the dreams that absorb me; and the fiery imagination that at times eats me up and makes me feel Society as it is, wretchedly insipid, you would pity and I dare say despise me.'

But it was only Branwell who could really know her thoughts, not Ellen, for whom passion was a closed book. Ellen could not 'imagine how hard rebellious and intractable all my feelings are – when I begin to study on the subject I almost grow blasphemous, atheistical in my sentiments, don't desert me' she adds piteously, 'don't be horrified at me, you know what I am – I wish I could see you my darling, I have lavished the warmest affections of a very hot, tenacious heart upon you – if you grow cold – it's over –'

It has been suggested by some biographers that these ardent letters are indicative of a lesbian tendency in Charlotte. The notion of a physical relationship must be dismissed, but perhaps Charlotte was a little in love with Ellen. Certainly, she used her friendship with Ellen as an outlet for her increasingly violent emotions, which had no other respite, except in her writings – and these frequently reveal how she lived a vicarious life of heterosexual love through the Duke of Zamorna's adventures. In the many sensual scenes involving Zamorna's mistress, Mina Laury, it is as if Charlotte herself is the passionate Mina of the 'sweet West': 'She hardly felt that his Majesty's arm had encircled her waist, and yet she did feel it too and would have thought herself presumptuous to shrink from his endearment. She took it as a slave ought to take the caress of a Sultan, and obeying the gentle effort of his hand slowly sank on to the sofa by her master's side.'[14]

Charlotte continued to live half in and half out of the dream, which she now began to perceive as dangerous but without which she could not exist. Letters from Branwell describing changes he had made to Angria brought her temporary calmness. 'It is astonishing what a soothing and delightful tone that letter seemed to speak – I lived on its contents for days. In every pause of employment – it came climbing in like some sweet bar of music'.[15] She longed for the moments when she could be alone, away from the girls:

> Delicious was the sensation I experienced as I laid down on the spare bed and resigned myself to the luxury of twilight and solitude. The stream of Thought, checked all day came flowing free and calm along the channel, my ideas were too shattered to form any defined picture as they would have done at home, but . . . thoughts soothingly flitted round me and unconnected scenes accumulated and then vanished producing an effect certainly strange but to me very pleasing. . . . What I imagined grew morbidly vivid. I remember I seemed to see with my bodily eyes a lady standing in the wall of a gentleman's house as if waiting for someone. . . . No more I have not time to work out the vision. A thousand things were connected with it, a whole country, statesmen and Kings, a Revolution, thrones and princedoms subverted and reinstated – meantime the tall man washing his bloody hands in a basin and the dark beauty standing by with a light remained pictured in my mind's eye with irksome and alarming distinctness. I grew frightened at the vivid glow of the candle at the reality of the lady's erect and symmetrical figure. . . . I felt confounded and annoyed I scarcely knew by what. At last I became aware of a feeling like weight laid across me. I knew I was wide awake and that it was dark and that moreover the ladies were now come into the room to get their curl-papers. They perceived me lying on the bed and I heard them talking about me. . . . I have had enough of morbidly vivid realisations – every advantage has its corresponding disadvantages.[16]

On 6 December 1836 she wrote to Ellen that she wished she could visit her before Christmas so that she could benefit from Ellen's piety, and repeated her idea of their living together. If she could read the Bible daily with Ellen, 'if your lips and mine could at the same time drink the same draught from the same pure fountain of mercy, I hope, I trust, I might one day become better, far better, than my evil wandering thoughts, my corrupt heart, cold to the spirit, and warm to the flesh will now permit me to be.'

She goes on to castigate herself for 'constantly seeking my own pleasure, pursuing the gratification of my own desires, I forget God and will not God forget me? . . . I adore the purity of the Christian faith, my theory is right, my practice horribly wrong.' However hard she tried, Charlotte was unable to be a party to her age's religious practice of outward forms of piety without believing every word she said. All the Evangelical preaching of her childhood which she had previously scornfully dismissed now flooded back to haunt her. Her eyes filled with tears when she suddenly realised that 'ghastly Calvinistic doctrines are true', and that she must be spiritually dead: 'If Christian perfections be necessary to Salvation I shall never be saved, my heart is a real hot bed for sinful thoughts and as to practice, when I decide on an action, I scarcely remember to look to my Redeemer for direction'.

Out of a new determination to come to terms with her life, almost twenty-one when she arrived home for Christmas, Charlotte took the step of seeking an outside opinion on her writing. With the same marvellous boldness which had impelled Branwell's letters to *Blackwood's*, and that winter to Wordsworth, Charlotte sent off some of her poetry about Glass Town to the Poet Laureate, Robert Southey, asking for his opinion. The dream might be 'drug-like' as Margaret Lane describes it; nevertheless it had originally been inspired by grand ambitions, and despite the maelstrom of emotion Charlotte was living in, she never quite lost sight of them.

The more urgent mood of Charlotte and Branwell is revealed in Branwell's letter to Wordsworth. Was there any point in continuing to pour out their souls onto tiny pieces of paper? Did they have any talent? Branwell's wild explanation of his need for self-expression makes interesting reading: 'from the day of my birth to this the nineteenth year of my life I have lived among secluded hills, where I could neither know what I was or what I could do. I read for the same reason that I ate or drank, because it was a real craving of nature . . .'

Perhaps the Brontës should have been forewarned by their idol Byron's contemptuous dislike for both Wordsworth and Southey. Wordsworth never replied; he thought Branwell's letter sycophantic. Southey did at least respond, but Charlotte had made an unfortunate choice in him. He was an arch-reactionary, pessimistic, declining in health and years. In his dispiriting letter of March 1837, he admitted that 'you evidently possess, and in no inconsiderable degree, what Wordsworth calls "the faculty of verse" '. This was not an unflattering or inaccurate judgement, particularly given that poetry was Charlotte's weak point, but, Southey continued, she should not be encouraged to high hopes as there were nowadays so many poets writing. 'Whoever, therefore, is ambitious of distinction in this way ought to be prepared for disappointment.'

Nevertheless, he thundered, 'Literature cannot be the business of a woman's life, and it ought not to be.' Expressing the general nineteenth-century view of women, which was only very slowly being

109

undermined among a few enlightened critics by the time of Charlotte
Brontë's death – despite the rapidly increasing numbers of women
writers – he went on: 'The more she is engaged in her proper duties,
the less leisure will she have for it, even as an accomplishment and a
recreation. To those duties you have not yet been called, and when
you are you will be less eager for celebrity.' There was a danger that
'the daydreams in which you habitually indulge are likely to induce a
distempered state of mind; and in proportion as all the ordinary uses
of the world seem to you flat and unprofitable, you will be unfitted for
them without becoming fitted for anything else.'

This was the view on women writers put forth in innumerable
etiquette books for women. Although views had progressed a little
from the attitude marked by Dr John Gregory's *A Father's Legacy to
his Daughters* at the end of the eighteenth century – 'if you happen to
have any learning keep it a profound secret' – he was nevertheless still
read, and the standard etiquette books of the 1820s continued to
counsel that women's only professional knowledge should be in the
domestic sphere. Mrs Barbauld's successful *A Legacy for Young
Ladies consisting of Miscellaneous Pieces, in Prose and Verse* (1826)[17]
reflected popular ideas when it advised almost boldly:

> Every woman should consider herself as sustaining the general
> character of a rational being, as well as the more confined one
> belonging to the female sex; and therefore the motives for acquiring
> general knowledge and cultivating the taste are nearly the same for
> both sexes. The line of separation between the duties of a young
> man or a young woman appears to me chiefly fixed by this – that a
> woman is excused from all professional knowledge. . . . Men have
> various departments in active life; women have but one, and all
> women have the same, differently modified indeed by their rank in
> life and other incidental circumstances. It is, to be a wife, a mother,
> a mistress of a family. The knowledge belonging to these duties is
> your professional knowledge, the want of which nothing will
> excuse.

Female Improvement by Mrs Sandford (1836) stated that although
women might nowadays improve themselves by study, they should do
so in private; they should not acquire knowledge to use in 'practical
pursuits in the public sphere' to satisfy personal ambition or 'for
financial advancement in the masculine manner'.[18]

It was a barely modified acceptance of this code of behaviour that
Mrs Gaskell later expressed in her defence and discussion of Charlotte
exercising her talents as an author:

When a man becomes an author, it is probably merely a change of employment to him. . . . But no other can take up the quiet regular duties of the daughter, the wife or the mother, as well as she whom God has appointed to fill that particular place. A woman's principal work in life is hardly left to her own choice; nor can she . . . drop the domestic charges devolving on her as an individual for the exercise of the most splendid talents that were ever bestowed.'[19]

But this divinely imposed duty did not mean one should shrink from the extra responsibility implied by possessing such talents, she ended spiritedly.

Southey did not want Charlotte to think that he disparaged the gifts that she possessed; he only suggested that they should be used for her good. She should write poetry for her own private use, 'and not with a view to celebrity . . . so written, it is wholesome both for the heart and soul; it may be made the surest means, next to religion, of soothing the mind, and elevating it. You may embody in it your best thoughts and your wisest feelings, and in so doing discipline and strengthen them.'

It was advice which in some ways could not have cut more against the bone, given Charlotte's own fears about her daydreams. Years later she told Mrs Gaskell that it had been a salutary lesson, despite the bleak future it held out for her. The letter's envelope has written on it: 'Southey's advice to be kept for ever. My twenty-first birthday. Roe Head, April 21, 1837.'

Charlotte wrote back to Southey immediately, anxious to disabuse him of certain of his ideas about her: 'I know the first letter I wrote to you was all senseless trash from beginning to end; but I am not altogether the idle, dreaming being it would seem to denote.' She told him that her father was a clergyman of limited though competent income who had expended quite enough on her education as could be afforded in justice to the rest. 'I thought it therefore my duty, when I left school, to become a governess. In that capacity I find enough to occupy my thoughts all day long, and my head and hands too, without having a moment's time for one dream of the imagination. In the evenings,' she went on apologetically, 'I confess I do think, but I never trouble anyone else with my thoughts. I carefully avoid any appearance of preoccupation and eccentricity which might lead those I live amongst to suspect the nature of my pursuits.'

It also appears from the letter that Mr Brontë's enthusiasm for developing his daughter's intellect was limited by the common view of women's duties:

Following my father's advice – who from my childhood has counsel-led me, just in the wise and friendly tone of your letter – I have

111

endeavoured not only attentively to observe all the duties a woman ought to fulfil, but to feel deeply interested in them. I don't always succeed, for sometimes when I'm teaching or sewing I would rather be reading or writing; but I try to deny myself; and my father's approbation amply rewarded me for the privation. Once more allow me to thank you with sincere gratitude.[20]

And indeed Southey believed that he had done Charlotte a service. He told a friend:

I sent a dose of cooling admonition to the poor girl whose flighty letter reached me at Buckland. It seems she is the eldest daughter of a clergyman, has been expensively educated, and is laudably employed as governess in some private family. About the same time that she wrote to me her brother wrote to Wordsworth, who was disgusted with the letter, for it contained gross flattery and plenty of abuse of other poets, including me. I think well of the sister from her second letter, and probably she will think kindly of me as long as she lives.[21]

Southey's words did not stop the dream continuing, nor Charlotte writing to Ellen of the peace that she was endeavouring to find from reading the Bible. During the summer holidays she wrote another two stories of 15,000 words each, one containing another heavily satirical skit on Methodism, while concurrently she continued her struggle to make herself more of a pattern of Christian virtue. Branwell was now drinking more, and the characters in his writing were becoming increasingly debauched. Nevertheless the old collaboration and closeness between the pair continued, even if Branwell's circle of drinking friends in Haworth and Charlotte's own preoccupations were making for their increasing estrangement.

The pattern of teaching at Roe Head went on, with Charlotte often near breaking point. One of her journal entries reads: 'a teacher nearly killed me between the violence of the irritation her horrid wilfulness excited and the labour it took to subdue it to a moderate appearance of calmness. My fingers trembled as if I had 24 hours' tooth-ache. . . .' Miss Wooler was kind to her but 'I could not have roused if she had offered me worlds . . . if those girls knew how I loathe their company they would not seek mine so much as they do.'[22]

Around Easter of 1837 the school had moved from the gracious environs of Roe Head high up on Mirfield Moor to a new situation on Dewsbury Moor, in order for Miss Wooler to be nearer to her elderly parents. It was a far less pleasant location, low-lying and damp. Miss Wooler was on the point of retiring and the greater part of the burden of teaching was falling on Charlotte's shoulders. Physical exhaustion was now added to mental anxiety, and as the year progressed both Charlotte and Anne became enveloped in an impenetrable religious gloom that was finally accompanied in Anne's case by serious physical illness.

She was suffering from gastritis and at one point, fearing that she was about to die and in the grip of religious torments, called in a minister from the Moravian Church at Mirfield, James de la Trobe, whose Moravian doctrine of love, so different from the harsh religion of her father, brought her some kind of relief. She continued very ill throughout the winter and Charlotte, unbalanced and always mindful of Maria and Elizabeth's deaths, turned on Miss Wooler, accusing her of being insensitive to Anne's illness and not taking it seriously enough. Shocked and hurt, Miss Wooler wrote to Mr Brontë, and Anne was removed from the school. Charlotte in a passionate rage was on the point of going too, until Miss Wooler, showing admirable tolerance, 'gave me to understand that in spite of her cold repulsive manners she had a considerable regard for me and would be very sorry to part with me'. An uneasy peace was restored.

Charlotte again turned to Ellen for comfort, writing in the same highly coloured hysterical prose of the past miserable two years: 'We have entered on a New Year – will it be stained as darkly as the last – with all our sins, follies, secret vanities, and uncontrolled passions and propensities? I trust not – but I feel in nothing better – neither humbler nor purer. . . . Come to see me my *dear* Ellen as soon as you can – however bitterly I sometimes feel towards other people, the recollection of your mild steady friendship consoles and softens me. I am glad you are not such a passionate fool as myself –'[23]

From the beginning of February 1838, Charlotte was isolated at Dewsbury, beset by severe mental depression that more and more affected her physical health. Her condition was made worse when her Easter holidays at Haworth were shortened by being called back to the school on account of the death of Miss Wooler's father. The melancholia that possessed her became so serious that, as she told Ellen:

at length I neither could nor dared stay any longer. My health and spirits had utterly failed me, and the medical man whom I consulted enjoined me, if I valued my life, to go home. . . . A calm and even mind like yours, Ellen, cannot conceive the feelings of the shattered wretch who is now writing to you, when after weeks of mental and bodily anguish not to be described, something like tranquility and ease began to dawn again. I will not enlarge on the subject; to me every recollection of the past half-year is painful – to you it cannot be pleasant.[24]

113

By June Charlotte was back home. She was aware that the state she had been in amounted to a kind of illness, which she described as 'hypochondria'. Some years later she wrote to Miss Wooler:

I can never forget the concentrated anguish of certain insufferable moments, and the heavy gloom of many long hours, besides the preternatural horrors which seemed to clothe existence and nature and which made life a continual waking nightmare. . . . When I was at Dewsbury I could have been no better company for you than a stalking ghost, and I remember I felt my incapacity to *impart* pleasure fully as much as my powerlessness to receive it.

CHAPTER VII

The Slave of Feeling

Within a few weeks of returning home, Charlotte made a remarkable recovery in her health and spirits. In early June Mary and Martha Taylor came for a visit, which was enjoyed by all, although Charlotte's extreme concern for Mary's health shows that she was still over-wrought. She wrote to Ellen on 9 June that she had watched Mary 'narrowly':

> Her lively spirits and bright colour might delude you into a belief that all was well, but she breathes short, has a pain in her chest, and frequent flushings of fever. I cannot tell you what agony these symptoms give me. They remind me strongly of my two sisters whom no power of medicine could save. I trust she may recover; her lungs certainly are not ulcerated yet, she has no cough, no pain in the side, and perhaps this hectic fever may be only the temporary effects of a severe winter and a late spring on a delicate constitution.

But Charlotte also gives Ellen a much more cheerful picture of the Taylors' visit: 'They are making such a noise about me I cannot write any more. Mary is playing on the piano; Martha is chattering as fast as her little tongue can run; and Branwell is standing before her, laughing at her vivacity.' Branwell's company had not lost its charm and Charlotte at this point may have had renewed hopes for his future.

Since May Branwell had been living in the burgeoning manufacturing town of Bradford, where he was endeavouring to earn his living as a portrait painter and from which he was able to return at weekends to Haworth, only six miles away. The previous winter his aunt had generously paid for further lessons under William Robinson in Leeds, and it was hoped that these could be put to good effect portraying the prosperous, confident citizens of Bradford. Branwell had been found lodgings very near the Town Hall, in Fountain Street, by his father's kindly friend, the tract-loving clergyman William Morgan, who had also commissioned Branwell to paint him. Amidst the artistic circles to which he was introduced by his artist friend John Hunter Thompson, and which centred on the George Hotel bar, Branwell must have felt that at last he was leading the sort of existence for which his spirit had so long pined. Here was bold, daring, masculine society, so different from a household dominated by his elderly, religious aunt and domineering father.

To his landlady's niece he appeared 'a very steady young gentleman, his conduct was exemplary, and we liked him very much'. She also recollected that Charlotte came to visit him, – and she remembered 'her sisterly ways'. There were other friends of the Brontë family living in Bradford, among them Miss Fanny Outhwaite, Anne's god-mother, and the children's former nurse, Nancy Garrs; Charlotte may well have visited them at the same time. But although initially Branwell's fortunes seemed to have changed, the outward favourable appearances were gradually belied. Charlotte's manuscripts from that summer show that she found her brother's behaviour curious and worrying.

Branwell was finding that he was not the only portrait painter seeking his fortune in Bradford and it soon became obvious that his own opinion of his artistic genius was not shared by the good citizens of Bradford. As ill luck would have it, his period as an artist coincided with the rise of the daguerrotype, or early photograph, and this, in combination with the competition of artists already established in the city, many of whom had made reputations in London, meant that there simply was not a large enough market for portraiture for him to be able to survive financially. The commissions did not flood in as had been hoped, and over the coming year Branwell was gradually reduced to varnishing other painters' canvasses – work his arrogant nature rebelled at.

In these depressing circumstances Branwell had been introduced to opium, probably through his friend Thompson. The continued popularity of Thomas De Quincey's book, *The Confessions of an Opium Eater*, first published in 1821, had helped make opium fashionable; the drug was available over the counter from chemists, and was a far cheaper intoxicant than alcohol. It was also thought – a view particularly propagated by De Quincey – to help in the prevention of consumption. Fear of succumbing to their sisters' disease haunted both Charlotte and Branwell, and De Quincey's moving descriptions of his own young sister's death of consumption when he was a similar age to Branwell probably gave opium an added appeal for him, who found the release its intoxication created difficult to resist.

The dangers of opium addiction were not then recognised, but the effects on Branwell were not lost on Charlotte. In her manuscript, 'Stancliffe's Hotel', which she began in the summer of 1838, she gives a detailed description of the behaviour of an opium addict in Lord Macara Lofty:

> There was vacancy in his aspect and dreamy stupor. Meantime the ecstatic smiles which had every now and then kindled Macara's eye and passed like sunshine over his countenance began to recur with fainter effect and at longer intervals – the almost sensual look of intense gratification and absorption gave place to an air of fatigue . . . 'My head throbs' said he 'I must not try this experiment often'. As he spoke his hand shook so convulsively that he could hardly replace the glass on the table.

Macara's justification for taking opium was no doubt Branwell's: 'I injured no fellow creature by this – I did not even brutalise myself. probably [sic] my life may be shortened by indulgence of this kind – but what of that, the Eternal sleep will come sometime and as well sooner as later.'[1] Recalling her own experience of depression, Charlotte was probably sympathetic to 'the gloom, the despair [which] became unendurable' and from which opium provided relief, although she was alarmed at the self-destructive tendencies of the antidote. Her affection for Branwell is mixed with awareness of the feckless nature of his charm: 'However infamous may be the position in which he is surprised, he turns round without a blush, instead of defending himself and denying that matters are as appearance would warrant you to suppose, coolly admits all the disgrace of his situation and begins with metaphysical profundity to detail all the motives and secret springs of action – which brought matters to the state in which you found them.'[2]

Branwell's presence encouraged Charlotte in her new, relaxed mood to write another funny set-piece on a Methodist service in 'Stanclyffe's Hotel'. Her writings over this and the following year take on a more realistic key. With playful irony, she wrote that her 'Duke of Zamorna' novelette, begun in the summer of 1838, was intended to be something 'high and pathetic' but she found that 'One cannot continually keep one's feelings wound up to the pitch of romance and reverie'. Her masculine narrator, Charles Townshend, says he is growing 'weary of heroics and longed for some chat with men of common clay.'[3]

In this mood, Charlotte's attention turned to considering the contrast between the reality of the individual and the suppression of it which her experience of society, outside the freedom of her home, seemed to her to demand. How difficult Charlotte found the

117

conventionally foolish behaviour demanded of young women of the time, as if they were no more complex than dolls – a theme to be repeated in her novels – is shown by this scene in Angria concerning the courtship of Jane Moore by Lord Hertford:

> His Lordship was leaning against the arm of a sofa where Lady Thornton was sitting, talking to her and watching the play of that discreet young woman's dark ringlets and darker eyes, as she shook about her head, and laughed and jested with him as naively and of course as innocently as possible.
> 'Good evening to your Lordship' says Miss Moore – quite frank and open. O that openness – it's a convenient thing isn't it, Townshend? So interesting you know – such a mark of a pure mind which is not afraid of its thoughts being known to the whole world.
> 'Your Lordship will dance with me to-night?' says the beauty . . .
> 'I will waltz with you Miss Jane – come.'
> 'Oh! waltz!' she screams with a pretty and certainly most affected scream etc. . . .
> I could not during the whole night satisfactorily unravel the puzzle of our heroine's character. . . .[4]

In the autumn and winter of 1838 Charlotte went to stay with Ellen and also visited Lascelles Hall, home of the oppressively grand Walker family, relations of Ellen's whose daughter Amelia was a former Roe Head schoolfellow of Charlotte and Ellen's. Again, the theme of the necessity to conceal the real self from society appears in Charlotte's writing: the character in one of her 'Duke of Zamorna' stories, the unobtrusive governess Miss West who savagely represses her true nature, is an embryonic precursor of her later passionate heroines Jane Eyre and Lucy Snowe. One of the heroes declares that strength of character and feeling are more important qualities in a wife than beauty: 'Beauty is given to dolls – majesty to haughty vixens – but mind, feeling, passion, and the crowning grace of fortitude are the attributes of an angel.'[5] Here for the first time in Charlotte's manuscripts is a heroine whose chief charm lies in such qualities, though she must feel guilty about possessing them and strive to hide them:

> The Adventuress is by herself, now in her own humble bedroom – wearing her own costume, countenance and character – How does she look thus freed from disguise and restraint? . . . What kind of thoughts are those contracting her marked forehead and (?) burning in her quick eyes? You see little of beauty to admire on those features – but surely they are aglow with meaning and a strange meaning too – What is it that all at once colours her face as she sits

118

alone and when as it fades away leaves it of a warmer hue than before?

Skilfully as the disguise was adjusted a penetrating eye could still see through it and Miss West was aware of this – There were one or two cool observers – people of strong mind, fixed principles and acute sagacity whom she shunned as if by instinct – She felt that her quiet modest manners – her seeming discretion and reserve did not altogether pass current with them. She was aware that those moments of awakened feeling, those sudden flashing fits of excitement which she could not always control – had betrayed her real disposition to one individual at least who was as capable of estimating character as herself – and she knew that there must appear in his eyes something sinister in the constant mask which hid and soothed her natural features.[6]

The teacher Miss West, reflecting what one imagines were Charlotte's own feelings, does not betray her inward scorn for the outpourings on the subject of love confided to her by her schoolgirl charges. To her, there is 'something weak and low and vapid' in their confessions; intellect, passion, 'intense energy of enthusiasm', are absent.

The contrast between the reality of matters matrimonial and Charlotte's wildly romantic attitude to love, expressed so ardently in countless novelettes, came home sharply, even comically, in the spring of 1839. On 4 March she received a proposal of marriage from Henry Nussey, Ellen's twenty-seven-year-old curate brother. He could not have been further from the lover of Charlotte's imaginings. Like Charlotte's father, he had sat at the feet of Simeon at Cambridge, but unlike Patrick Brontë he was a thorough-going Calvinist, and utterly devoid of that streak of passion and romance that at times could take over Patrick Brontë's rigid nature. Indeed he was pragmatic in the extreme.

His motive for marriage was that he now needed a wife, having recently become curate of Donnington in Sussex. It may have been Ellen who first mooted the idea of Charlotte to him, as her urgent invitations for her friend to come and stay during the winter of 1838–9 suggest that she had such an alliance in mind. Henry had first proposed to the daughter of his former vicar, but he met the refusal of what he admiringly termed 'a steady, intelligent, sensible and, I trust, good girl, named Mary' with such equanimity that the very same day he received it, he sent off a proposal of marriage to Charlotte. His diary entry for that day gives something of the flavour of his approach: 'On Tuesday last received a decisive reply from M.A.L.'s papa; a loss but I trust a providential one. Believe not her will, but her father's. All right, but God knows best what is good for us, for His church, and for

119

His own glory. Write to a Yorkshire friend, C.B.'[7]

Charlotte may not have known whether to laugh or to cry when she received his missive. Clearly there had never been anything in his regard on the occasions they had met before to make her think that Ellen's moon-faced though courteous brother thought of her in a romantic fashion, or indeed that he thought of her at all. And yet he now proposed that they should be yoked together, utter strangers, in intimacy for life. Charlotte's account of the proposal to Ellen[8] makes one think that she was keeping her tongue firmly in her cheek while describing it:

You ask me, my dear Ellen, whether I have a letter from Henry. I have, about a week since. The contents, I confess, did a little surprise me, but I kept them to myself, and unless you had questioned me on the subject, I would never had adverted to it. Henry says he is comfortably settled at Donnington, that his health is much improved, and that it is his intention to take pupils after Easter. He then intimates that in due time he should want a wife to take care of his pupils, and frankly asks me to be that wife.

A wife to look after pupils! Would, *could*, any of Charlotte's characters have behaved in such a fashion? Repressing a tremor of merriment she went on: 'Altogether the letter is written without cant or flattery, and in a common-sense style, which does credit to his judgement.'

Perhaps she was attracted a little by the idea he threw into the package that she should open a school near Donnington. She told Ellen that the thought that Henry's sister could live with her if she married him made the proposition more tempting. But, she declared ringingly, in tones worthy of Jane Eyre and of all the feeling heroines of her novelettes, she could not marry him because 'I had not, and could not have, that intense attachment which would make me willing to die for him; and, if I ever marry, it must be in that light of adoration that I will regard my husband.'

She faced the fact that she might never have such a chance again. But it was also a decision founded on common sense and knowledge of her own character. What Henry wanted in a wife, as she told him in her typically candid letter of refusal, was that her 'character should not be too marked, ardent and original, her temper should be mild, her piety undoubted, her spirits even and cheerful, and her *personal attractions* sufficient to please your eyes.' She was not right for him – she was not the serious, cool-headed person he thought she was. Moreover, she said, 'I scorn deceit, and I will never, for the sake of attaining the distinction of matrimony and escaping the stigma of an old maid, take a worthy man whom I am conscious I cannot render happy.'

To Ellen, she said she thought that Henry knew so little of her that he could hardly be conscious to whom he was writing.

> Why, it would startle him to see me in my natural home character; he would think I was a wild, romantic enthusiast indeed. I could not sit all day long making a grave face before my husband. I would laugh and satirise, and say whatever came into my head first. And if he were a clever man, and loved me, the whole world weighed in the balance against his smallest wish should be light as air. Could I, knowing my mind to be such as that, conscientiously say that I would take a grave, quiet, young man like Henry?

And the grave young man, who to his credit remained rather fascinated by Charlotte, would certainly have been amazed if he could have read any of the prose that wild, romantic enthusiast was writing in 1839. He recorded, 'Received an unfavourable reply from C.B. The will of the Lord be done.'

The manuscript she was at work on that spring, 'Henry Hastings', contained proposals of a very different nature. Basically a novelette about Elizabeth Hastings, a prototype of Jane Eyre – plain, intellectually superior, but passionate – it describes her attempts to shield her renegade brother Henry from justice. In the course of it she attracts the attention of Sir William Percy, the hero who has announced his intention to find a woman in whom mind, feeling and passion are predominant qualities. Despite such admirable intentions, his actual behaviour leaves a good deal to be desired and on a walk through the countryside he asks Elizabeth to become his mistress. Elizabeth, who is a being 'made up of intense emotions . . . always smothered under the diffidence of prudence and a skilful address', and strongly physically attracted to him, unlike the usual decorous Victorian heroine, is tempted to yield to Sir William's proposal. She goes through the 'hard conflict of passionate love – with feelings that shrank horror-struck from the remotest shadow of infamy'. But like Jane Eyre, and unlike Charlotte's earlier passionate heroines such as Mina Laury and Marian Hume, Elizabeth makes conscience and self-respect triumph over her emotions. Her self-respect is more important to her than what the world thinks of her. The Brontë heroine was progressing a stage further.

Henry Hastings was Branwell's most recent alter ego, and in the manuscript he is on the run after shooting his superior officer. Hastings is revealed to be a coward and a turncoat, and one suspects that Charlotte was sadly coming to the same sort of conclusions regarding Branwell. His drinking and general behaviour were becoming increas-

121

ingly undisciplined, and he had probably begun to run into debt with his friend Thompson; he had already been borrowing from his aunt and father.

Branwell's own manuscripts now revel in rather self-conscious and fantastic debauchery – page after page describes drunken carousings. By May 1839, his career and financial position almost hopeless, Branwell had all but left Bradford and was spending his time at Haworth. Henry Hastings is described as being now under a new influence, George Frederick Ellen of Hallows Hall, whose goal was 'to root out morality from the natures of all his acquaintance'. Surely it cannot have been coincidence that he used the name of Charlotte's strongly religious friend Ellen for this renegade character's surname.

Judging from her own manuscript, Charlotte had great compassion for her wild brother's state of mind. Elizabeth Hastings understands that Henry's passions are 'naturally strong, and his Imagination . . . warm to fever'. When Henry escapes and is sheltered by Elizabeth, she 'instead of softening the renegade's excited ferocity, and reasoning against his malignant vindictiveness . . . caught his spirit and answered in a quick excited voice'. Their sympathy remained of the closest:

> It was very odd that his sister did not think a pin the worse of him for all his dishonour: it is private moments not public infamy that degrade a man in the opinion of his relations. Miss Hastings had heard him cursed by every mouth, saw him denounced in every newspaper, still he was the same brother to her he had always been – still she beheld his actions through a medium peculiar to herself, saw him go away with a triumphant Hope – that his future actions would nobly blot out the calumny of his enemies. Yet after all she knew he was an unredeemed villain – human nature is full of inconsistencies – natural affection is a thing never rooted out where it has once existed.[9]

Despite the depths of Charlotte's natural affection for Branwell, he was now becoming a rather embarrassing problem to the family. In June his desperate father settled on a scheme for them to read through the classics together, with the intention of preparing Branwell for a teaching post, although this plan does not seem to have got very far. At the beginning of the year, Emily had returned home with intense relief after a spell as a governess, but the family's circumstances brought a continual sense of obligation on the daughters to earn their way, although no spoken pressure was ever put on them by their father.

To the surprise of all within the parsonage it was frail, quiet Anne who found herself employment at this time. In April she went as a governess to some connections of Miss Wooler's, the Ingham family of Blake Hall near Mirfield. None of the Brontës felt particularly confident of Anne's chances of retaining her position for long. Charlotte, who thought of herself *in loco parentis* to Anne, worried that her sister's slight stammer when nervous might put her employer off. In fact, Anne was to remain a governess for far the longest of the Brontës, in total about five and a half years. It seems that her more evenly balanced character was better able to tolerate the restrictions of such work than her elder sister.

Charlotte, still seeing nineteen-year-old Anne as the delicate baby of the family, was relieved and startled by the 'sensible, clever letter' that Anne wrote after her arrival at Blake Hall. The Inghams, Anne informed home, were kind, although she had a very low opinion of her pupils. Both were 'desperate little dunces' – neither of them could read; it was sometimes doubtful whether they had actually mastered the alphabet; and worst of all she had no power to subdue them by punishment – a typical situation for a governess.

Charlotte herself was enjoying the freedom of simply being at home at Haworth. She told Ellen that since Tabby had been ill she had discovered a most unladylike talent for cleaning: 'sweeping up hearths, dusting rooms – making beds etc. so if everything else fails – I can turn my hand to that – if anybody will give me good wages, for little labour. I won't be a cook – I hate cooking – I won't be a nursery-maid – nor a lady's maid, far less a lady's companion – or a mantua maker – or a straw-bonnet maker or a taker-in of plain-work – I will be nothing but a house-maid.' But despite these words, the offer of a temporary governess post in the summer of 1839 was too tempting to turn down, and June found Charlotte ensconced with the Sidgwick family at a house called Stonegappe, near Skipton and about twenty miles north of Haworth. The attractive house, which still stands, is a large, roomy mansion built at the end of the eighteenth century by the father of Charlotte's employer, Mr John Sidgwick, with some of the fortune he had made from cotton spinning in his mills at Skipton. Beautifully sited on a hillside overlooking the valley of the Lother, it had extensive grounds with terraces and lawns backed by shrubberies.

Charlotte probably obtained the post via the Reverend Edward Carter, brother-in-law of the Misses Wooler who had earlier recommended Anne to the Inghams. As curate of Mirfield, he had prepared Charlotte for her confirmation in 1832 and was now living on the Stonegappe estate after his appointment as curate to the nearby church at Lothersdale, which was under the patronage of John Sidgwick. Charlotte reports on the kindness of Reverend Carter and his family – Mrs Carter gave birth to their fourth child in the July of

123

Charlotte's employment – and from him she had news that Anne was 'looking uncommonly well'. It was evidently news that Charlotte refused to take on board, for in the next sentence of the same letter she writes, 'Poor girl, she must indeed wish to be at home'. She imagined that Anne's experience must be as unendurable as hers.

Charlotte had been hired as the nursery governess to the Sidgwicks' two youngest children, Mathilda, aged six and a half, and John Benson, aged four. Mrs Sidgwick, who was expecting her fifth child at this time, was by all accounts, including Charlotte's own, an agreeable woman. She was the daughter of a Keighley manufacturer whose family the Brontës had probably been on visiting terms with, and this may partly account for Charlotte's unhappiness at Stonegappe. The position of the private governess was one full of anomalies: too well-bred to be treated as the other servants but nevertheless an employee without the social standing to be included as an equal in the family. Meals could not be taken in the servants' hall nor, except on particular occasions, in the family dining room, so Charlotte would be brought her meals, by a resentful servant, to eat alone. As the old saying went, the governess was 'neither flesh, nor fowl, nor good red herring'.

Perhaps because of her previous acquaintance with Mrs Sidgwick, Charlotte had not anticipated the social distance that almost inevitably followed from her professional relationship with the family. She did not appreciate her employer's position and complained in a letter to Emily of 8 June that Mrs Sidgwick did not know her, that 'I now begin to find that she does not intend to know me, that she cared nothing in the world about me except to contrive how the greatest possible quantity of labour may be squeezed out of me, and to that end she overwhelms me with reams of needlework, yards of cambric to hem, muslin night caps to make, and above all things, dolls to dress.'

To Ellen she complained of Mrs Sidgwick's boisterous animal spirits: 'But, oh! Ellen, does this compensate for the absence of every fine feeling, of every gentle and delicate sentiment.' She was made particularly miserable brooding over the unwelcome fact that she would probably have to spend the rest of her life as a governess: 'The chief requisite for that situation seems to me to be the power of taking things easily as they come, and of making oneself comfortable and at home wherever we may chance to be – qualities in which all our family are singularly deficient', she admitted ruefully. She used to think that she would enjoy 'the stir of grand folks' society but I have had enough of it – it is dreary work to look on and listen.'

She was expected to be entirely devoted to her charges, over whom Charlotte had no control and with whom she had little patience – 'more riotous, perverse, unmanageable cubs never grew'. Their constant presence took away the charm of the beautiful surroundings;

Charlotte thought the country, the house and its grounds 'divine', with its pleasant woods, and winding white paths. To Emily, she sighed for freedom, writing that she would prefer working in a mill to this hateful drudgery. 'I could like to feel mental liberty. I could like this weight of restraint to be taken off. But the holidays will come. *Corragio* [sic].'

It was Mrs Sidgwick against whom Charlotte directed her complaints. To Mr Sidgwick, as to her later male employers, she had a rather different attitude; perhaps she even found him attractive. 'Mr Sidgwick is in my opinion a hundred times better – less profession, less bustling condescension, but a far kinder heart'. It was very seldom that he spoke to her, sometimes in the hall, sometimes in the dining room, but she observed that when he did, she always felt happier and more settled for some minutes after. He never asked her to do degrading things like wipe the children's noses or tie their shoes or fetch their pinafores or set them a chair. And indeed Charlotte must have felt how much were all her attainments and education worth, if this was the end to which they were to be used. 'One of the pleasantest afternoons I have spent here – indeed the only one at all pleasant – was when Mr Sidgwick walked out with his children, and I had orders to follow a little behind. As he strolled on through his fields with his magnificent Newfoundland dog at his side, he looked very like what a frank, wealthy Conservative gentleman ought to be.'

At the end of June the family moved to a summer residence, a house at Swarcliffe, near Harrogate, on the coast. It belonged to Mrs Sidgwick's father, Mr John Greenwood, and was full of relations, an experience which Charlotte found agonising and which intensified her consciousness of being close to a servant in the eyes of these people. She wrote to Ellen, in pencil because she could not face going into the drawing room for ink: 'Imagine the miseries of a reserved wretch like me, thrown at once into the midst of a large family – proud as peacocks and wealthy as Jews – at a time when they were particularly gay, when the house was full of company – all strangers, people whose faces I had never seen before – in this state of things having the charge given me of a set of pampered, spoilt, and turbulent children, whom I was expected constantly to amuse as well as instruct.'

Though surrounded by beautiful, rich agricultural land to which her visual nature responded, she found the whole experience a terrible drain on her:

At times I felt and I suppose seemed depressed. To my astonishment I was taken to task on the subject by Mrs Sidgwick with a stress of manner and a harshness of language scarcely credible. Like a fool, I cried most bitterly; I could not help it – my spirits quite failed me at first. I thought I had done my best – strained every nerve to please her – and to be treated in that way merely because I was shy and sometimes melancholy was too bad. At first I was for giving all up and going home, but after a little reflection I determined to summon what energy I had and to weather the storm.

Her employers, not surprisingly, had not found in Charlotte quite the governess they would have wished for. In later years, after reading *Jane Eyre*, Elizabeth Barrett Browning would exclaim at the idea of having such a savage free-thinking person as governess. The author A.C. Benson, son of and biographer of Archbishop Benson, who was a cousin of the Sidgwicks and who frequently went to Stonegappe, gave an account of Charlotte's governess-ship and although it is offered in extenuation of the family, and he never personally met Charlotte at Stonegappe, it gives an enlightening view from the other side:

> She was, according to her own account, very unkindly treated, but it is clear that she had no gift for the management of children, and was also in a very morbid condition the whole time. My cousin Benson Sidgwick, now vicar of Ashby Parva, certainly on one occasion threw a Bible at Miss Brontë! and all that another cousin can recollect of her is that if she was invited to church with them, she thought she was being ordered about like a slave, if she was not invited, she imagined she was excluded from the family circle. Both Mr and Mrs John Sidgwick were extraordinarily benevolent people, much beloved, and would not wittingly have given pain to any one connected with them.[10]

However miserable the period was for Charlotte, it provided her with novelist's material. It is more than likely that Benson Sidgwick formed the prototype for the odious little John Reed in *Jane Eyre* who throws a Bible at Jane and cuts her forehead. Charlotte may have been reticent about such an incident actually taking place at Stonegappe but, according to Mrs Gaskell, who was presumably told by Charlotte herself, John Benson did indeed throw stones at her.

It is also very likely, although there is no documentary proof, that Charlotte visited a house at Norton Conyers when staying at Swarcliffe. This house, originally Elizabethan, had the legend of a mad woman attached to it. It contained 'a low room in the third storey' where she had supposedly been confined, and Norton Conyers, as well as Ellen Nussey's Rydings home, has been claimed as the original of Mr Rochester's Thornfield in *Jane Eyre*. To Sir Reginald Graham Bart, a later owner of Norton Conyers, it seemed that Charlotte

126

Brontë must have had access to the house 'as in *Jane Eyre* the interior of the Norton Conyers mansion from beginning to end is very precisely described even to the most minute details'.[11] The house did indeed have a rookery, a church at its gates and a ha-ha, just as at Thornfield. Ellen Nussey felt particularly proprietorial about the Thornfield/Rydings connection, and there is little reason to doubt her claims. Nevertheless, England is not lacking in large country houses with legends of mad women associated with them, and Thornfield's wood-panelled interior, antique furniture, fine oak staircase and long gallery were all features of the halls lived in by Charlotte's friends and acquaintances, and which she had visited since the age of fifteen.

An end to Charlotte's hated drudgery came in mid-July, probably to the relief of both sides. She afterwards jokingly referred to the period as 'the long history of a Private Governess's trials and crosses in her first situation'; behaviour, manners, were absorbed, and, flavoured with resentment, would surface years later in *Jane Eyre*. On her return home a greater naturalism pervaded her Angrian characters,[12] and the Angrian countryside itself came closer to Yorkshire in a new novelette, 'Caroline Vernon', which she wrote from July to December 1839. Even the somewhat surprising subject matter for a shy Victorian lady of twenty-three – the seduction of the daughter of one of Northangerland's former mistresses by Zamorna – is treated with a certain distance by the narrator. Caroline's succumbing to Zamorna's advances is produced as a natural corollary to what is recognised to be her undisciplined and over-romantic temperament. Zamorna himself bears a greater resemblance to Mr Sidgwick than the Corsair and is described as hovering round his prey like 'a great Tom cat'. It is his very degeneracy that attracts Caroline, her folly unchecked by conscience, as she realises that Zamorna is 'a man, vicious like other men – perhaps I should say, more than other men – with passions that sometimes controlled him, with propensities that were often stronger than his reason, with feelings that could be reached by beauty, with a corruption that could be roused by opposition'.[13]

As Charlotte embarked on this manuscript, she received, totally unexpectedly, a second proposal of marriage. Her surprise suitor this time was a young Irish clergyman fresh from Dublin University, Mr Bryce, who had been appointed curate to Mr Brontë's former curate, Mr Hodgson, now a vicar of Colne in Lancashire, just across the moors. At the beginning of August Mr Hodgson took the path over the crest of the hills, bringing Mr Bryce with him on a visit to the Brontës, a meeting that was so without significance for Charlotte that she did not even quite hear his name – she thought he was called Price. It was the first time any of the assembled company had met him but,

127

as Charlotte wrote to Ellen, 'after the manner of his Countrymen he soon made himself at home'. She thought him witty and lively, though lacking the dignity and discretion of an Englishman, and she laughed and joked with him, for 'At home, you know, Ellen, I talk with ease and am never shy – never weighed down by that miserable "mauvaise honte" which torments and constrains me elsewhere.' Mr Bryce was obviously dazzled by her vitality. Charlotte's letter to Ellen continues:

> Though I saw faults in his character, [I] excused them because of the amusement his originality afforded – I cooled a little indeed and drew in towards the latter part of the evening – because he began to season his conversation with something of Hibernian flattery which I did not quite relish. However they went away and no more was thought about them. A few days after I got a letter the direction of which puzzled me it being in a hand I was not accustomed to see – evidently it was neither from you or Mary Taylor, my only Correspondents – having opened and read it it proved to be a declaration of attachment – and proposal of Matrimony – expressed in the ardent language of the sapient young Irishman! well thought I – I've heard of love at first sight but this beats all!

With such a hero as Zamorna in her mind, it is not surprising that Charlotte found this proposal comical, if cheering to her spirits. As she said to Ellen, 'I leave you to guess what my answer would be, convinced that you will not do me the injustice of guessing wrong.' Mr Bryce, unlike Henry Nussey, at least had some romance in him, but he could not begin to match the heroic qualities of Zamorna, nor the faults in character, so similar to Branwell's, that Charlotte was equally drawn to. In turning the proposal down, she laughingly said to Ellen that she was certainly doomed to be an old maid, and had been ever since she was twelve years old. But with two marriage proposals within six months, this must have seemed more of a pleasingly unlikely prospect.

Shortly before this incident, Ellen – concerned by Charlotte's unhappiness at Stonegappe – had proposed what was evidently considered a most daring plan: she and Charlotte should go alone and unchaperoned to the seaside for a holiday. Mary Taylor had suggested Burlington, now called Bridlington, on the north coast of Yorkshire. Charlotte wrote back to Ellen delightedly: 'I never had such a chance of enjoyment before . . . the idea of seeing the SEA – of being near it – watching its changes by sunrise, Sunset – moonlight – and noonday – in calm – perhaps in storm – fills and satisfies my mind'. The idea was made even happier knowing she should be with someone whom she knew and liked, and 'who knows me', that vital prerequisite.

After at first being in favour of the trip, Charlotte's father and aunt began to fuss about it raising all kinds of objection from expense to unsuitability. They had an alternative plan, which never came off, to take Charlotte and Emily with them on a trip to Liverpool. This was probably intended as a check on Branwell who was spending his time in that city secretly running up debts. There were anguished letters from Charlotte to Ellen as Aunt Branwell irritatingly chatted about Liverpool and Charlotte's plans to accompany Ellen got nowhere. She had packed her bags but could not make the necessary arrangements to travel from out-of-the-way Haworth to Ellen's home at Birstall. On 14 August she wrote to Ellen, that she was unable to secure a conveyance either that week or the next. The only gig for hire at Haworth was away at Harrogate and her father 'decidedly objects to my going by coach' or to her walking the four miles to Birstall. She was evidently plunged into despondency when Ellen, with uncharacteristic forcefulness, arrived at the parsonage in her brother's carriage and carried Charlotte off to the railway station at Leeds. Branwell, observing the scene laconically declared that it was 'a brave defeat, that the doubters were fairly taken aback'.

The idea of two young women travelling alone by the novel method of the railway – a first for both – and then on by coach and open fly to the seaside town of Burlington had created quite a stir back at home – so much of a stir that Henry Nussey had arranged for his friends the Hudsons to seize the bold travellers on arrival and take them to the Hudsons' farmhouse at Easton, about two miles west of Burlington. To their chagrin, Charlotte and Ellen, instead of being allowed to stay on their own in the seaside rooms they had rented, found themselves detained for the next few weeks with John and Sophia Hudson. Their hosts, however, were extremely kind and generous; Sophia plied them with farm food and they were free to enjoy the pleasant country around the pretty red-tiled house as well as play with the Hudsons' little niece, whom they christened Hanchion. Six years later when Ellen returned to Burlington, Charlotte asked to be remembered to Mrs Hudson: 'Tell her that our stay at Easton is one of the pleasant recollections of my life – one of the green spots that I look back on with real pleasure.'

According to Ellen's recollection, the two friends were not to be kept from the sea and the day but one after they arrived Charlotte insisted on walking to the coast. On her first sight of the waves, Charlotte was quite overcome and, in Ellen's words reported by Mrs Gaskell:

She could not speak till she had shed some tears – she signed to her friend to leave her and walk on . . . her friend turned to her as soon as she thought she might without inflicting pain; her eyes were red and swollen, she was still trembling, but submitted to be led onwards where the view was less impressive; for the remainder of the day she was very quiet, subdued and exhausted.

Writing afterwards to Henry Nussey, who was wishing to get up a 'literary' correspondence with Charlotte, she said that she would not tell him what she thought of the sea 'because I should fall into my besetting sin of enthusiasm. I may, however, say that its glories, changes, its ebbs and flow, the sound of its restless waves, formed a subject for contemplation that never wearied either the eye, the ear, or the mind.'

And she would later write ecstatically to Ellen: 'Have you forgot the sea by this time Ellen? is it grown dim in your mind? or can you still see it dark blue and green and foaming white and hear it – roaring roughly when the wind [is] high or rushing softly when it is calm?' The almost overwhelming physical effect of the sea on her, which went along with Charlotte's extraordinary sensual response to colour and other forms of natural beauty, never lessened and on her honeymoon many years later she would ask her husband to leave her so that she could watch the ocean's swell alone.

In the last week of their month's stay, Charlotte and Ellen were finally allowed to go into lodgings on their own, in a house opposite the quay with views over the sea. Mr and Mrs Hudson insisted on visiting them every day, bringing fresh eggs, milk and other farm produce – for which the young women were most grateful when they discovered what the cost would have been of catering entirely for themselves. They particularly enjoyed the merry evenings on their own, with Charlotte finding much amusement watching the solemn ritual of the crowds parading round the pier. One night, in high-spirited mood, she was keen to go to the Ranters' meeting-house across the way from their lodgings because of the howls and moans coming out of it, though the awfulness of the noise finally deterred her. And there was always the sea; as Ellen recalled, whenever the sound of it reached Charlotte's ears, 'she longed to rush away to be close to it'.

To twentieth-century eyes, such a holiday may seem very quiet and unexciting, but to Charlotte it was something quite outside her normal experience, a taste of independence away from anyone's government – father, aunt, employer; as she told Henry Nussey, she enjoyed the stay 'with the greater zest because such pleasures have not often chanced to fall in my way'.

She returned to Haworth, healthy and relaxed, although she was annoyed by having lost her wire-rimmed glasses. Writing to Henry Nussey, she said that she now felt so well that she was impatient of 'a prolonged period of inaction. I feel I ought to be doing something for myself.' Though the idea of being a governess remained as hateful as ever, she was determined to get another position. For the time being, however, she was able to put the prospect aside because towards the end of the year Tabby developed an ulcer on her lame leg and had to stop work. Charlotte and Emily took on all the household tasks, work which Charlotte shouldered with gusto. 'Human feelings are queer things,' she wrote. 'I am much happier – blackleading the stoves – making the beds and sweeping the floors at home, than I should be living like a fine lady anywhere else.'

With *Caroline Vernon* Charlotte had mocked many of her old romantic enthusiasms. Now, finally, in late 1839, a Charlotte newly awakened to the world by her experience of it steeled herself to turn away from the infernal magnates and concentrate on reality. Although she never wholly kept to the resolution of the document known as 'The Farewell to Angria' the unrelieved realism of *The Professor* and *Shirley* are here prepared for. In lyrical prose she bravely describes the need 'to quit for awhile that burning clime where we have sojourned too long – its skies flame – the glow of sunset is always upon it – the mind would cease from excitement and turn now to a cooler region where the dawn breaks grey and sober, and the coming day for a time at least is subdued by clouds'.

She went on:

I have now written a great many books and for a long time I have dwelt upon the same characters and scenes and subjects. I have shown my landscapes in every variety of shade and light which morning, noon and evening – the rising, the meridian and the setting sun can bestow upon them . . . So it is with persons. My readers have been habituated to one set of features, which they have seen now in profile, now in full face, now in outline, and again in finished painting – varied but by the change of feeling or temper or age; lit with love, flushed with passion, shaded with grief, kindled with ecstacy; in meditation and mirth; in sorrow and scorn and rapture, with the round outline of childhood, the beauty and fullness of youth, the strength of manhood, the furrows of thoughtful decline; but we must change, for the eye is tired of the picture so oft recurring and now so familiar.

She confesses that it is not easy for her to dismiss from her imagination the images which filled it for so long; 'they were my friends and my intimate acquaintances'.[14] But despite the manifesto she would solve the problem of abandoning her characters by continuing to scribble away at a manuscript in which the Angrians are transported wholesale to Yorkshire and feature one Alexander Percy of the West Riding of Yorkshire.

As the year closed even Branwell seemed temporarily settled. He had found himself a position as a tutor to the family of Mr Postlethwaite of Broughton-in-Furness, and the household was busy preparing for his departure with shirt-making and collar stitching. A more experienced Charlotte viewed these preparations with a distinctly weather eye: while recognising that the parsonage would be a duller place without Branwell, she wondered to Ellen whether he would be able to stay the course. 'I, who know his variable nature, and his strong turn for active life, dare not be too sanguine.'

CHAPTER VIII

Governessing

The year 1840 opened inauspiciously, with two deaths in January within the space of two weeks. Mr Bryce, Charlotte's unsuccessful clergyman suitor, despite his strong, athletic appearance when Charlotte met him, had been in delicate health for some time and on 17 January he died of a ruptured blood vessel. Although she knew little of him, Charlotte registered her shock and sadness. News of the death of Anne Carter, the young daughter of Reverend Carter, brought further mournfulness; when Charlotte had last seen her at Stonegappe, she had been a beautiful, happy girl. With unconscious prescience of her own future, Charlotte wrote elegiacially to Ellen: 'A bereavement of this kind gives one a glimpse of the feeling those must have who have seen all drop round them, friend after friend, and are left to end their pilgrimage alone.'

Prospects of employment also seemed dim, and as distasteful as ever. Anne's arrival home at Christmas after being dismissed by her employers at Blake Hall must have reinforced the message; Anne would later write of the miseries and injustice of that time in *Agnes Grey*. Charlotte had answered an advertisement from a Mrs Edward H. and planned to leave home at New Year. However, according to Ellen's grapevine amidst her relations and connections, this prospective employer had an 'undesirable character' – strong criticism to issue forth from the genteel conclaves held over bone china tea services – and Charlotte's plans were rapidly cancelled.

For once, however, a diversion was brought to the quiet parsonage, generally so empty of any eligible male presence, by the arrival of the new curate, William Weightman. In 1839 Mr Brontë, by then aged sixty-two, had applied to the Evangelical Pastoral Aid Society for a grant to finance a clerical assistant. He specified in his letter that the candidate should be zealous and active; he was also most anxious that he should not be a Calvinist, as so many clergymen were nowadays.

He told Miss Firth's husband, the Reverend Franks, that he would not feel comfortable with an assistant who would feel it his duty to preach what Mr Brontë termed 'the appalling doctrines of personal Election and Reprobation'. They were ideas he considered 'decidedly derogatory to the Attributes of God', and he was also fearful of their effect on his parishioners.[1]

Nothing less of a harsh Calvinist could be imagined than the charming Willie Weightman, and something rather less than what a clergyman should be, according to the sharp-tongued and sometimes over-puritanical Charlotte. Willie Weightman was handsome, lively and clever. A native of Westmoreland, he had just come down from Durham University where he had read classics, and, aged only twenty-five when he came to Haworth in August 1839, he was very interested in the opposite sex – and they in him. He certainly knew how to exercise his powers of attraction, but he seems to have been equally at the mercy of Cupid's dart.

Cupid indeed must have spent most of his arrows in 1840 on the young curate. Willie Weightman bounced inexhaustibly from passionate infatuation to passionate infatuation, scarcely drawing breath, with his ready captive field in the unmarried and unoccupied young women living round about Haworth. All this Charlotte came to look upon with a very sardonic eye, but at first she was disposed to like him and seems to have found him attractive. There must indeed have been something very appealing about him. He thoroughly enjoyed life and introduced some much needed youthful gaiety into a quiet and rather sedate household, teasing the irritable Miss Branwell in a way that even her naughty nephew would not have dared to do. When Ellen came to stay in February, there were lively evening gatherings, in which he introduced them to the latest popular songs. When he heard that none of the girls had received that exciting new fashion, the Valentine card, he copied out verses to each lady, such as 'Away Fond Love', 'Soul Divine', and, addressed with apparently special meaning to Ellen, 'Fair Ellen – Fair Ellen'. He walked ten miles to post them so that Mr Brontë and Miss Branwell should not find him out.

Charlotte painted his portrait, and to Ellen, who was taken by looks which were almost feminine in their fineness, his blue eyes and pink-and-white complexion set off by a mop of curly auburn hair, she rather cruelly nicknamed him Miss Celia Amelia. Long walks were taken on the moors, with Mr Weightman making himself so agreeable to Ellen that Emily began to feel the need to chaperone her, earning for herself the sobriquet 'The Major'. He even contrived that the young women should come one evening to his lecture on the classics at the Keighley Mechanics Institute. Understanding the weight of convention surrounding young ladies, he arranged that an invitation to the event should come from the Reverend Dury and, after much humming and hawing, Mr Brontë gave his consent.

The little expedition, the ladies stoutly clad against the cold March winds, set off with great excitement for this treat. The walk, eight miles there and back over vertiginously steep hills, would today in streamlined modern clothing be something of an effort even for a dedicated health enthusiast, but it was a walk the Brontës performed without a thought in unwieldy long skirts as often as once a week. To the consternation of Miss Branwell the party did not return until after midnight, in high spirits and with the unwelcome presence of two other clergymen, which necessitated Miss Branwell making fresh coffee. Charlotte was upset but Mr Weightman refused to be cowed by Miss Branwell's scolding and twinkled away at the situation.

Ellen's three weeks were soon up and, after she left, Charlotte admitted to her friend that they were now very dull without her. Ellen wrote teasingly about the attractive young man, but if there had been anything in Charlotte's feeling for Mr Weightman, she was now abandoning it. He had discovered a new light o' love and Charlotte amused herself by painting portraits of the latest inamorata. She told Ellen, 'You would laugh to see how his eyes sparkle with delight when he looks at it, like a pretty child pleased with a new plaything.' But, she added gruffly, 'let me have no more of your humbug about Cupid etc. You know as well as I do it is all groundless trash.'

Unexpected excitement was provided in April by a fracas over Church rates, which dissenters objected to paying when they did not attend the Church of England. There was a stormy meeting in the new brick schoolhouse just down the lane from the parsonage which was a chance for all concerned to display their not inconsiderable eloquence – and passions were running high. For once Charlotte's blood was stirred. It was yet another proof, in Mr Brontë's colourful phrase, that 'without our Citadel we have numerous vigilant, inveterate, and active enemies', while the citadel was threatened from within by the Oxford Movement. Mr Brontë was in the chair, with the two local curates, Mr Collins and Mr Weightman, as his supporters flanking him on either side. Notwithstanding his usually rather explosive temperament, Mr Brontë seems to have acted as a peacemaker when the violent opposition from the dissenters set Mr Collins' Irish blood in a ferment, so that he was only restrained with difficulty.

The next Sunday Weightman and Collins mounted a two-pronged attack on the dissenters, one in the afternoon sermon and one in the evening. All the dissenters were invited, and they actually shut up their chapels and came *en masse*. Willie Weightman delivered a 'noble, eloquent high-Church, Apostolical succession discourse – in which he banged the dissenters most fearlessly and unflinchingly', wrote Charlotte admiringly, watching from the front pew. She thought the dissenters really had had enough for the present, 'but it was nothing to the dose that was thrust down their throats in the evening'. Expressing herself with that compound of violence and excitement so strange coming from her small fragile form she told Ellen that if she was a dissenter she would have taken the first opportunity of kicking or horsewhipping people who made such bitter attacks on her religion or its teachers. Mr Collins' harangue impressed her greatly because he did not rant or speak high-flown cant, 'he just got up and spoke with the boldness of a man who is impressed with the truth of what he is saying, who has no fears of his enemies and no dread of consequences'. Though the sermon lasted an hour, something that usually bored her, she told Ellen she was sorry when he had finished. Although she could not agree with either Mr Collins or Mr Weightman in most of their opinions – she considered them 'bigoted, intolerant and wholly unjustifiable on the grounds of common sense' – always one to like boldness, she for once was rather carried away by 'the noble integrity which could dictate so fearless an opposition against so strong an antagonist'.

Something of the high order of thought existing in such a far away place reached the Yorkshire newspapers and Charlotte commented to Ellen with sarcastic amusement that it was mentioned as 'a matter of wonder that such displays of intellect should emanate from the village of Haworth "situated amongst the bogs and mountains and until very lately supposed to be in a state of semi-barbarism" such are the words of the newspaper.'

As the year proceeded, Charlotte continued to toy with the opening chapters of a novel about the old Angrian characters transplanted to a Yorkshire setting, but she later destroyed her writings from this time, no doubt dissatisfied with her early attempts to write without romance. Branwell meanwhile, still in his position as tutor to the Postlethwaites, refused to let the fires of literary ambition die down. En route to his employers, he had fallen in with some roisterers at an inn in Kendal and evidently had a good deal to drink. This episode, probably unexciting enough, was described with his usual imaginative vigour to his admiring friend, Haworth's sexton John Brown, and transformed into a great adventure. He had, he wrote, with many an absurd flourish, taken a 'half year's farewell of old friend whisky'. But he was now being a model tutor: he was thought 'a most calm, sedate . . . virtuous gentlemanly philosopher – the picture of good works and the treasure house of righteous thoughts.' Little did the old ladies with whom he sat and drank tea know 'the sort of devil sitting so near them'. Indeed the old ladies might have been very surprised if they could have been party to the fantastic thoughts of the shabby little tutor.

He successfully kept up the appearance of diligence and sobriety over the next few months, while dreams of glory continued to obsess him, helped by the proximity of the country that the Lake Poets had made famous. His circle at Bradford had included the poet and professional man of letters Hartley Coleridge, the strange but gifted son of Samuel Taylor Coleridge, and he had written to him to solicit an opinion of his writings. Coleridge, through his father, wrote drama and literary criticism irregularly for *Blackwood's* and the *London Magazine*, while teaching in boys' schools, after drink had lost him his Fellowship at Oriel. Like Branwell he had created an imaginary world, Ejuxria, in which he had dwelt quite happily in childhood. Coleridge invited him to spend May Day at his cottage at Ambleside, close to Lake Windermere, where he had retired to in 1837. The day was an experience that quite overwhelmed Branwell. The two men were extraordinarily alike in their extreme sensibility, their alcoholism and their passionate devotion to poetry. The following is a description of Coleridge written four years later by the Irish poet Aubrey de Vere:

> He could scarcely be said to have walked, for he seemed with difficulty to keep his feet on the ground, as he wavered about near us with arms extended like wings. Everything that he said was strange and quaint . . . always representing a mind whose thoughts dwell in regions as remote as the antipodes. After 50 years of ill fortune the man before us was still the child described by Wordsworth. . . . There was some element wanting in his being. He could do everything but keep his footing, and, doubtless, in his inner world of thought, it was easier for him to fly than to walk, and to walk than to stand. There seemed to be no gravitating principle in him.[2]

The last two sentences could have been Branwell's epitaph. Charlotte's fire and feeling were constantly tempered by her strong feeling of duty and reason; Branwell's, alas, never. Encouraged by his reception and enchanted by his 'first conversation with a man of real intellect in my first visit to the classic lakes of Westmoreland', he threw himself into translating the first two books of Horace's *Odes*, which he subsequently sent to Coleridge. The response, from an eminent literary figure whose opinion was not to be reckoned with lightly, must have given Branwell great cause for hope and self-congratulation on his persistence. In the existing, unfinished draft of his reply, Coleridge wrote that:

> you are, with one exception, the only young Poet in whom I could

find merit enough to comment without flattery or stuff enough to be worth finding fault with. I think I told you how much I was struck with the power and energy of the lines you sent before I had the pleasure of seeing you. Your translation of Horace is a work of much greater promise. . . . Your versification is often masterly – and you have shown skill in great variety of measure. . . .

Somewhat surprisingly, he then went on to praise the 'racy English' of the translation.[3]

Filled with elation, Branwell became careless of his role as the modest tutor. Rambles in the countryside, with stops for alcoholic refreshment in the company of local roisterers, made increasing depradations on his time with the Postlethwaites, who finally dismissed him, wrathfully claiming that their two sons seemed to have spent their time doing nothing but sketches and making up stories to accompany their tutor's fine drawings.

By early June the unrepentant Branwell had returned to Haworth. Some gauge of his influence on Charlotte is that in the late summer she sent off a few chapters of her Yorkshire version of Angria to Hartley Coleridge, soliciting his opinion in her turn. When he finally returned her manuscript, it seems that he had not been impressed by it and did not hold out any 'brilliant hopes' for her imagination, unlike that of Branwell.[4]

Writing back to thank him for reading it, Charlotte said that she would now commit her characters to oblivion, despite what it cost her, but she said, fairly cheerfully, that she hoped she would get over it. Once again, she hinted that she was conscious that this way of carrying on was not fitting her for 'normal life':

It is very edifying and profitable to create a world out of one's own brain and people it with inhabitants who are like so many Melchisidecs – 'Without father, without mother, without descent, having neither beginning of days, nor end of life'. By conversing daily with such beings and accustoming your eye to their glaring attire and fantastic features – you acquire a tone of mind admirably calculated to enable you to cut a respectable figure in practical life – If you have ever been accustomed to such society Sir you will be aware how distinctly and vividly their forms and features fix themselves on the retina of that 'inward eye' which is said to be 'the bliss of solitude'.[5]

It appears from her letter that Hartley Coleridge had thought her writing more suited to ladies' magazines. She told him that the idea of applying to a regular novel-publisher and seeing all her characters in print was very tempting, but after his comments she thought on the whole she would lock up her precious manuscript, and not approach any publishers for a while. She was pleased that he could not decide whether she was female or male, although she had not intended to mystify him on such an issue, but she would now deliberately withhold her identity from him. She wrote quite sharply: 'The ladylike tricks you mention in my style and imagery – you must not draw any conclusions from those – Several young gentlemen curl their hair and wear corsets – Richardson and Rousseau often write exactly like old women – and Bulwer and Dickens and Warren are like boarding school misses'.

Despite her decision to put away her manuscripts, between December 1840 and March of the following year Charlotte could not resist the temptation to write about her Angrians in Yorkshire. The manuscript relates the early life of Branwell's monstrous alter ego Alexander Rogue, but now named Alexander Ashworth. In it Charlotte found herself slipping back into the Angrian past, which she pulls herself back from, as an *'ignis fatuus'*. The characters of Ashworth's sons, Edward and William – Edward and William Percy in earlier novelettes – are meditated on and the disparity between them contrasted. They would eventually emerge, almost unadulterated, as the Crimsworths in *The Professor*. As usual Charlotte inserted much autobiographical material into the narrative: Mary Ashworth, Ashworth's daughter, the Mary Percy in a previous incarnation married to Zamorna – is depicted at her boarding school, with her schoolfellows Amelia De Capell, an odious Yorkshire heiress, and Ellen Hall, a poor pupil who like Charlotte herself, has some of the functions of a servant at the school. Charlotte was then very preoccupied by the affectation and grandeur of her godparents' niece Amelia Walker.[6]

But whatever Charlotte's slightly defiant attitude, Coleridge's words weighed upon her. When Henry Nussey insisted on sending her some of his poetry, hoping to receive her effusions in return – at long last the 'literary correspondence' he so earnestly desired – she told him she was no longer poetical: 'Once indeed I was very poetical, when I was sixteen, seventeen, eighteen and nineteen years old – but I am now twenty-four approaching twenty-five – and the intermediate years are those which begin to rob life of some of its superfluous colouring. At this age it is time that the imagination should be pruned and trimmed – that the judgement should be cultivated – and a *few* at least, of the countless illusions of early youth should be cleared away.'

They were vanishing fairly rapidly. Her observations of the behaviour of Willie Weightman and of Branwell over the summer of 1840, and perhaps fear of her own distempered daydreams, had inclined Charlotte to repudiate all her youthful views on love and passion. In June Mary Taylor had come to stay, an enjoyable visit during which Mary played several games of chess with the now famed Willie Weightman. But it was Branwell whom she found more attractive. They had sparkled in each other's company on her previous visit and this time Mary clearly showed her attraction, which Branwell at first reciprocated but then took fright at and coldly turned his back upon.

His treatment of Mary now warned Charlotte, ever preoccupied in her manuscripts with analysing affairs of the heart, as she wrote to Ellen, of 'the contempt, the remorse – the misconstruction which follow the development of feelings in themselves noble, warm – generous – devoted and profound – but which being too freely revealed – too frankly bestowed – are not estimated at their real value'. She saw now how much better it was to have a quiet, tranquil character like Ellen's. Though she never thought she would see a more truly noble character than Mary's – 'she would *die* willingly for one she loved' – she thought it was quite likely that Mary would never marry. And herself too, she might have added, for similar reasons.

Nor had her opinion of Mr Weightman improved. It had emerged that during the period when he was so pointedly paying attention to Ellen he had been carrying on a regular correspondence with a lady in Swansea, whom he had now cut off (sending back her letters in a gentlemanly fashion) in favour of one of the Rector of Keighley's daughters, Miss Caroline Dury. He had made his attentions plain in his usual courtly and poetic fashion, sending his *beau idéal* a copy of passionate verse. By July Charlotte was convinced that he was 'a thorough male-flirt', and worried that Ellen had fallen prey to his charms, like the rest of the area. She had, she told her friend, liked him when he was rather melancholy and she could cheer him up, but now he had such a large smitten acquaintance she no longer cared for him.

Charlotte's correspondence with Ellen at this period offers a touching picture of the innocence of pre-Freudian life. In Charlotte's case, the past six years of chronicling Zamorna's love affairs inexhaustibly lends her utterances the air of some disillusioned mondaine, a Colette even. Her complete lack of any kind of experience might lend a faintly comic air to her earnest theories, were it not for the dangers posed by such tremendous expectations of relationships.

Ellen was now more preoccupied with the rather mysterious pursuit of her by a Mr Vincent who, although he discussed her endlessly with her many relations and seemed always on the point of declaring himself, was never quite able to bring himself to do so. Matters were complicated by the fact that Ellen, as she told Charlotte, felt a curious sort of disgust for him. Charlotte, with her new-found philosophy that

140

'mediocrity in all things is wisdom – mediocrity in the sensations is superlative wisdom – the secret to a pain-free existence', advised Ellen not to wait for the folly of *une grande passion*', and thought, somewhat over-optimistically, that once Ellen got to know him, the disgust would disappear.

She dispensed her advice freely, telling Ellen that she now realised the truth of all those hitherto despised worldly maxims 'whose seeming coldness shocks and repels us in youth – are founded in wisdom'.

Did you not once say to me in all childlike simplicity 'I thought Charlotte – no young ladies should fall in love, till the offer was actually made . . . I now reply after due consideration . . . no young lady should fall in love till the offer has been made, accepted – the marriage ceremony performed and the first half year of wedded life has passed away – a woman may then begin to love, but with great precaution – very coolly – very moderately – very rationally – if she ever loves so much that a harsh word or a cold look from her husband cuts her to the heart – she is a fool. . . .

It was more important to marry a man whom one could respect, she lectured Ellen. 'Moderate love at least will come after; as to intense *passion*, I am convinced that that is no desirable feeling.' She was now pessimistically convinced that passion 'never meets with a requital'. If it did, 'the feeling would be only temporary: it would last the honeymoon, and then, perhaps, give place to disgust, or indifference, worse perhaps than disgust. Certainly this would be the case on the man's part: and on the woman's – God help her, if she is left to love passionately and alone.' She was now sure that she would never marry at all, she told Ellen dramatically. 'Reason tells me so, and I am not so utterly the slave of feeling but that I can *occasionally hear* her voice.' Ellen meekly absorbed Charlotte's directions. It was all a little above her head, but the letters sent to Haworth for advice, and the didactic replies from the mistress of love, continued with unabated energy.

To add to Charlotte's disillusioned mood, her mother's first cousin, John Branwell Williams, and his wife and daughter arrived in August on a visit to Uncle Fennell at Cross-Stone. Charlotte thought that they gave themselves airs; reckoned themselves to be 'very grand folks indeed – and talk largely – I thought assumingly.' She did not admire them much. There seemed to be an attempt to play 'the great Mogul' down in Yorkshire. She preferred Mr Williams himself to the 'womenites', as she called his womenfolk. 'He seemed a frank, sagacious kind of man – very tall and vigorous with a keen active look – the moment he saw me he explained that I was the very image of my Aunt

Charlotte [Mrs Brontë's youngest sister].' She had little in common with the daughter, who had thoroughly embraced the Branwells' tradition as a Methodist family, and talked mainly of the clergy and her own conversion, to the boredom of her sophisticated cousin.

August came and went. Charlotte continued to look for a position as a governess, without success. Kindly Mr Taylor, having some idea of her situation, sent her another bale of books – over forty volumes. The best thing about them, she told Ellen, was that they gave her a real idea of France and Paris, and she thought that they were the best substitute for French conversation which she could imagine.

Then once again sickness struck at Haworth: one of Charlotte's best Sunday School pupils, Susan Bland, the daughter of the Superintendent John Bland, was terminally ill. Much to her surprise Charlotte found that there was another side to the curate. On asking whether the Blands would like a little port wine, she was told that after Mr Weightman's last visit he had expressly sent them a bottle of wine and a jar of preserves. The woman added that he had always been particularly kind to the poor. Charlotte felt rather ashamed of herself, and though she and Mr Weightman continued to be estranged – perhaps she still felt piqued at his wandering attentions – she was honest enough to acknowledge to Ellen his good as well as bad points. What she failed to notice was that it was her sister Anne whose feelings were most deeply caught up by the curate.

While Charlotte and Anne repeatedly answered advertisements for situations through the autumn and winter, Branwell, despite his renewed sense of calling after Hartley Coleridge's encouragement, had found himself another job, as a booking clerk on the recently opened Leeds–Manchester railway, and left home at the beginning of October. It was very far from the sort of grandeur he and Charlotte had imagined for him. She wrote rather sarcastically to Ellen: 'A distant relation of mine, one Patrick Boanerges, has set off to seek his fortune in the wild wandering, adventurous, romantic, knight-errant-like capacity of clerk on the Leeds and Manchester Railroad.'

The year ended as dourly as it had begun. To Charlotte's great sorrow, her benefactor Mr Taylor finally died after a long and painful illness, leaving his business affairs still in disarray and the future of the apparently portionless Taylor girls in question. It seemed probable that the family would go their separate ways. Charlotte wrote warmly of all the Taylors' 'restless active spirits'; Mary alone had 'more energy and power in her nature than any ten men you can pick out in the united parishes of Birstall and Gomersal'. As she told Ellen admiringly, 'It is vain to limit a character like hers within ordinary boundaries, she will overstep them. I am morally certain Mary will establish her own landmarks, so will the rest of them.'

But Charlotte attributed no such high destiny for herself. She now constantly had to face the fact that the life of a governess was all that was open to her, however alien such employment was to her. If it were only teaching she felt she would be able to perform it easily, but it was 'the living in other people's houses – the estrangement from one's real character – the adoption of a cold frigid apathetic exterior that is painful'. It was with this aspect of her personality in mind, conscious of how much her nature needed sympathy and affection, that she accepted a position as governess to two children of a Bradford merchant named White. She thought that the Whites were genial people and that she would enjoy, as she told Ellen in her dramatic way, 'the society of cheerful faces, and minds and hearts not dug out of a lead mine, or cut from a marble quarry'. In exchange for this comfort she took a considerable drop in salary; most governesses would have earned about £40 per annum, and she was paid £20 – little more than a quarter of what Branwell was making as a clerk on the railway.

She left home in early March 1841 for Upperwood House, the Whites' home in the village of Rawdon, about six miles from Bradford, which consisted mainly of the houses of well-off Bradford professional men and tradesmen. Anne too had finally found a governess position and went later in March to Thorp Green Hall, near York. A first letter to Ellen from Upperwood House shows how the novelist continued to ferment in Charlotte: 'As to my employers, you will not expect me to say much respecting their characters when I tell you that I only arrived here yesterday. I have not the faculty of telling an individual's disposition at first sight. Before I venture to pronounce on a character I must see it first under various lights and from various points of view.'

Mr White she came to like; Mrs White was a more difficult matter. The house was on a much smaller scale than any of the homes of Charlotte's previous employers or of her friends and acquaintances around Gomersal and Birstall, and although she indeed found life there much preferable to Stonegappe, in moments of frustration she allowed herself several snobbish remarks on Mrs White's origins. 'Well can I believe that Mrs White has been an excise-man's daughter,' she wrote to Ellen after she had seen her mistress's 'very coarse unladylike temper'. Nevertheless, though cast into agonies over what she recognised to be absurdities – her intense shyness made it almost impossible for her to repel the rude familiarity of the children, to say what she wanted to the mistress or the servants, to ask for days off, or for visitors – and though she found it dreary and solitary work, she managed to survive it until the end of the year. Furthermore, living day to day with people was simply a tremendous strain to one as sensitive as her. She sighed over 'the heavy duty of endeavouring to seem always easy and cheerful and conversible with those whose ideas and feelings are nearly as incomprehensible to me as probably mine (if I shewed them unreservedly) would be to *them*.'

The misery of the endless sewing which was part of her duties, as well as teaching what seemed 'wild and unbroken' children – a girl of eight and a boy of six – was, however, considerably alleviated in July. Back at Haworth for the holidays – 'Paradise' – it turned out that her father and aunt had been giving thought to the future of their charges, and they proposed the idea of the three girls opening a school. Charlotte had often wished for this but had never had sufficient capital to consider it further. Now, it seemed that Aunt Branwell was in a peculiarly benevolent mood, and though the amount of money that she was likely to lend them would inevitably not to be very large – about £150 – it would be enough to establish a small school perhaps somewhere in the East Riding of Yorkshire, which was less well served by schools than the West.

All three Brontë girls were enthusiastic about the plan and Miss Wooler, to whom Charlotte appealed for advice, offered that they should take over the Wooler school at Dewsbury Moor. This was a tempting proposal, though Charlotte secretly rebelled at the idea of returning to Dewsbury, which had such unhappy memories for her. However, the whole scheme lost something of its glamour, and took on a new dimension, with a letter in August from Mary Taylor in Brussels.

The break-up of the Taylor family which Charlotte had predicted on Mr Taylor's death had taken place: Martha Taylor had been sent off to a finishing school in Brussels the previous year and Mary Taylor had joined her for a while. In fact Mary and her youngest brother Waring Taylor had conceived a plan that scandalised their relations and connections: it was to emigrate to New Zealand and open a business there. Mary had finally come to the conclusion that the restrictions of life in England made it impossible for her to stay. The choices of employment open to women were hopeless: she would not be a governess, or a mantua maker or a milliner; as she declared energetically. Meanwhile, with her usual fiery enthusiasm, she raved to Charlotte about the glories of Brussels that she was now enjoying. Charlotte, always full of artistic urges, was totally seduced, as she told Ellen:

Mary's letter spoke of some of the pictures and cathedrals she had seen – pictures the most exquisite – and cathedrals the most venerable – I hardly know what swelled to my throat as I read her letter – such a vehement impatience of restraint and steady work. Such a strong wish for wings – wings such as wealth can furnish – such an urgent wish to see – to know – to learn – something internal seemed

144

to expand boldly for a minute – I was tantalised with the consciousness of faculties unexercised – then all collapsed and I despaired.

The despair was much more than the frustration of financial restrictions. It is hard to imagine today the stifling effect of nineteenth-
century codes of behaviour for middle-class women, the 'cult of
domesticity' that had been growing from the turn of the century
onwards. The solitary, leisured, middle-class woman was part of a
new picture in which a combination of the agrarian and industrial
revolutions had turned the centre of production away from the household, from the private to the public sphere. The change in the nature
and scale of commercial farming made it impossible for women to
carry on their former occupations such as dairy-farming, running
small businesses, inns – which had been an exclusively female
preserve.[7] Similarly, the revolution in textile manufacture had rid
most women of the need to spin linen and wool for the family clothes.
For the rapidly burgeoning, newly wealthy middle classes, the home
was becoming an oasis in the new business world that was the result of
unparalleled economic growth and rationalisation, with its hard commercial ethic and cash nexus, which women had no part of. With that
development, manners and roles for women underwent a complex but
subtle transformation. The role that remained for women was to be a
lady, that elusive and mysterious ideal. She had been transformed into
a mystical goddess of the hearth – the 'Angel in the House', in
Coventry Patmore's later phrase – who as chaste wife and mother was
to safeguard the moral welfare of the nation through her 'influence',
as well as, by her gracious unemployed presence, testifying to the
wealth and power of husbands and fathers.[8] Let Elizabeth Barrett
Browning sum up the wearisome, pretty near universal dictates under
which she and the Brontës and the Misses Taylor and Nussey lived,
with Aurora Leigh's deeply sarcastic description of 'Woman's
Mission':

> I read a score of books on womanhood
> To prove, if women do not think at all,
> They may teach thinking (to a maiden aunt
> Or else the author) – books that boldly assert
> Their right of comprehending husband's talk
> When not too deep, and even of answering
> With pretty 'may it please you', or 'so it is' –
> Their rapid insight and fine aptitude,
> Particular worth and general missionariness,
> As long as they keep quiet by the fire
> And never say 'no' when the world says 'ay',

145

For that is fatal – their angelic reach
Of virtue, chiefly used to sit and darn,
And fatten household sinners – their, in brief,
Potential faculty in everything
Of abdicating power in it:

(*Aurora Leigh*, First Book, ll.427–441)

By the 1860s, it was quite conceded that in the sphere of moral influence women had won: they were morally superior to men. Nevertheless, as John Stuart Mill would point out,[9] it was a hollow victory:'(women) are declared to be better than men; an empty compliment which must provoke a bitter smile from every woman of spirit, since there is no other situation in life in which it is the established order, and considered quite natural and suitable, that the better should obey the worse.' For of course in 1841 a wife was at the mercy of her husband: she could not divorce him, although he could divorce her; if a wife left her husband, he could force her to return. There was no question of her taking children with her; the wife did not even control her own property: she scarcely had access to it in her own right. Yet her husband might confiscate the income from it if he liked, by force if he chose. With Jane Eyre, Charlotte Brontë – no 'true wife' – smashed a brick through the window. Jane Eyre demanded, was not pure; she was certainly no angel in the house. But all this lay in the future; in the meantime her creator was just as much a prey to these ideas as any other woman.

Single women, above all single women without money like Charlotte Brontë and Ellen Nussey, did not fit easily into this picture. As one historian has recently put it, 'Increased wealth and the consolidation of bourgeois social values in the early nineteenth century condemned spinsters to unremitting idleness and to marginal positions in the home, church, and workplace.'[10] Florence Nightingale summed it up in 1836: 'Why have women passion, intellect, moral activity – these three – and a place in society where no one of the three can be exercised?'[11]

However, Charlotte's restlessness reflected an equally strong and opposing current in the spirit of the age amongst middle-class women, particularly and mainly single women. The moderate feminist, Frances Power Cobbe, expressed the new thinking about women when she wrote:

But it is an absurdity, peculiar to the treatment of women, to go on assuming that all of them have home duties, and tacitly treating those who have none as if they were wrongly placed on God's earth, and had nothing whatever to do in it. There must needs be a purpose for the lives of single women in the social order of Providence . . . she has *not* fewer duties than others, but more extended or perhaps laborious ones. Not selfishness – gross to a proverb – but self sacrifice more 'entire' than belongs to the double life of marriage, is the true law of celibacy.[12]

The 'problem' of the single woman was highlighted because of the large number of unmarried women in nineteenth-century England who, in the words of Mrs Gaskell's liberal friend, the critic W.R. Greg, 'have to earn their own living, instead of spending and husbanding the earnings of men; who, not having the natural duties and labours of wives and mothers, have to carve out artificial and painfully sought occupations for themselves; who, in place of completing, sweetening, and embellishing the existence of others, are compelled to lead an independent and incomplete existence of their own.'[13] A solution, he proposed, was to send the bulk of what was thought to be 750,000 single women over thirty to Canada, Australia and the United States, where men were in the majority by 440,000:1. It was rather similar in some ways to pre-Civil War American proposals to solve the black problem by founding a new colony in Liberia.

By the 1840s even Mrs Sarah Ellis, who represented the traditional-role-for-women camp at its strongest in her 'Women of England' series of manuals,[14] had had to adapt her views to tally with the fact that some middle-class women who were unmarried had to work from sheer economic necessity. In effect she was forced to provide two branches of female education: in *Education of the Heart* she wrote that for a married woman 'the turn or tone of character should be different': she should fill her position 'with discretion and tact, and yet with grace and loveliness'. The unmarried woman should do her work 'with strength, determination and thorough efficiency'. As she wrote: 'How to meet these two requirements is a great perplexity in the present day, and it is one which presses closely upon all engaged in female education.'[15]

By the 1840s, the debate about women was in full swing, part of the spirit of protest which swept through English life under the presiding genius of Thomas Carlyle. The reformers, originally very much part of the Evangelical movement, were demanding political justice in recognition of women's rational nature. Higher education, teachers' training colleges, were being advocated. The popular writer Harriet Martineau, Charlotte and Mary Taylor's heroine, summed up the general view for the reformers:

As for women not wanting learning, or superior intellectual training, that is more than anyone should undertake to say in our

147

day. . . . Formerly every woman was destined to be married; and it was only a matter of course that she would be: so that the only occupation thought of for a woman was keeping her husband's house, and being a wife and mother. It is not so now. From a variety of causes, there is less and less marriage among the middle-classes of our country; and much of the marriage that there is does not take place till middle life. A multitude of women have to maintain themselves who would never have dreamed of such a thing a hundred years ago.[16]

In this situation, according to Miss Martineau:

What we have to think of [now] is the necessity – in all justice, in all honour, in all humanity, in all prudence – that every girl's faculties should be made the most of, as carefully as boys. While so many women are no longer sheltered, and protected, and supported, in safety from the world (as people used to say) every woman ought to be fitted to take care of herself. Every woman ought to have that justice done to her faculties that she may possess herself in all the strength and clearness of an exercised and enlightened mind, and may have at command, for her subsistence, as much intellectual power and as many resources as education can furnish her with.[17]

Charlotte would later say that it was Harriet Martineau whom she admired above all other women. When the two women finally met, as a result of Charlotte seeking her out, the former told her that her novel, *Deerbrook*, published in 1839, had had a tremendous influence on her. She may well have read it at the behest of Mary Taylor, whose own strong views would have been totally in sympathy with it. Harriet Martineau writes:

But, for an educated woman, a woman with the powers which God gave her religiously improved, with a reason which lays life open before her, an understanding which surveys science as its appropriate task, and a conscience which would make every species of responsibility safe – for such a woman there is in all England no chance of subsistence but by teaching – that almost ineffectual teaching, which can never countervail the education of circumstances, for which not one in a thousand is fit – or by being . . . the feminine gender of the tailor and hatter.[18]

In her letters of this period to Charlotte, Mary would have communicated some of her ceaseless meditation on the condition of women. They were fully articulated finally in her novel *Miss Miles, or a Tale of*

148

Yorkshire Life 60 Years Ago. It was actually published in 1890, but it mainly addresses itself to the problems of the female condition in the 1830s, the time of Mary and Charlotte's youth. Didactic in the extreme, it follows the fortunes of a group of women – mainly middle-class, with one working-class woman to illuminate the moral – and has a simple point: women can only be happy if they are well-educated and economically independent, which working-class women are shown to be. Without this they are subject to the vagaries of chance.

The position of the Turner girls in the novel, whose father's mill goes bankrupt, is no doubt a reflection of the Taylors' own predicament, and Mary's savage attack on the concept of the 'lady' suggests that her upbringing had many of the worst features of the most restricting female codes: 'A life of hard work and self-denial is, or may be, one of the noblest lives on earth. But self-denial without effort is mere mockery, good for no human soul. The more zealously it is followed the more it destroys the human faculty and feeling.'[19] When Amelia Turner expresses her wish to work, she is considered to have insulted her father: 'As if other people's insults were not enough, you must show him up to strangers because he can't provide you with everything you please to want.'[20]

Certainly Mary's elder brothers had a typically middle-class mid-nineteenth-century view about women of the family working – that it was a derogation of caste. It was a view almost unknown to Charlotte Brontë with her more unorthodox upbringing, less constrained by the expectation of keeping up the appearances required of such a long-established family as the Taylors. When Charlotte had turned down a governess job in Ireland, she had offered it to Mary only to find that, as she told Ellen, 'She is so circumstanced that she cannot accept it – her brothers – like George [Ellen's brother] – have a feeling of pride that revolts at the thought of their sister "going out". I hardly knew it was such a degradation till lately'.

For Charlotte, the struggle was more with what John Stuart Mill would describe in 1861 as the 'exaggerated self-abnegation which is the present artificial ideal of feminine character. All women are brought up from the very earliest years in the belief that their ideal of character is the very opposite of that of men: not self-will, and government by self-control, but submission and yielding to the control of others.'[21] She did not have Mary's radical political spirit. The 'urgent wish to see – to know – to learn', the 'vehement impatience of restraint and steady work', which Charlotte had felt on receipt of Mary's letter from Brussels – and which would be the natural feelings of any bright young woman of the present day wanting to expand her experience – had the effect of making Charlotte feel guilty. She told Ellen that she would hardly make that confession to anyone but her, and would

149

rather say so in a letter than in person: 'These rebellious and absurd emotions were only momentary. I quelled them in five minutes. I hope they will not revive – for they were acutely painful.' And of course such thoughts were not appropriate for a young Victorian woman to have, according to prevailing notions.

But the thought of Brussels lingered, encouraged by Mary. By late September Charlotte was inspired by a new idea that had emerged from all the thoughts of going abroad. If she and her sisters were to succeed with their own school against the competition of the many schools in the area, it must have some special quality, some drawing power. What she now proposed to her Aunt Branwell was that she and Emily spend six months on the continent to master their French, improve their Italian and learn some German. With such language qualifications, they could truly offer something special. She had broached the idea with her employers and the Whites had endorsed it.

The long letter that she wrote to her aunt on 29 September, outlining the scheme, was written by Charlotte at her most determined and persuasive, having finally made up her mind. She pointed out all the advantages of Brussels: it was much cheaper than other parts of the continent, living there being little more than half as expensive as England, and the facilities for education were equal or superior to anywhere else in Europe. She was sure that the Taylors, with the assistance of the wife of the British Embassy Chaplain, whose brother came from the West Riding, could find her a 'cheap and decent residence and respectable protection'. That Charlotte included Emily in the scheme but not Anne was a recognition that Aunt Branwell's money could not stretch so far; Anne, Charlotte suggested, could perhaps also go abroad for further education at a later date, when the girls had successfully established themselves. She ended with an emotional plea *ad hominem*, betraying an ambition and vigour which were hardly conventionally feminine:

Of course, I know no other friend in the world to whom I could apply on this subject except yourself. I feel an absolute conviction that, if this advantage were allowed us, it would be the making of us for life. Papa will perhaps think it a wild and ambitious scheme; but who ever rose in the world without ambition? When he left Ireland to go to Cambridge University, he was as ambitious as I am now. I want us *all* to go on. I know we have talents, and I want them to be turned to account.

Charlotte here ignored the separate sphere – that man was 'the doer, the creator, the discoverer; that 'woman's power' was 'for rule, not for battle'. But who could resist such eloquence? Both Aunt Branwell and Mr Brontë were persuaded. All that remained was to make the arrangements, which was a daunting task for, apart from the details of clothing and travel, talking over Emily's doubts at leaving Anne, and considering the running of the parsonage, there was the question of finding a suitable school. Martha Taylor's school was too expensive to be contemplated, but Mary busily looked into other possibilities and provided Charlotte with information about other establishments in Brussels.

As Charlotte pondered her future while looking after the children – putting them to bed and performing the myriad petty functions of the nursery governess – Ellen, meanwhile, had been left in the dark. The mysterious Mr Vincent had now disappeared from her life and she was presently staying with her brother Henry in Sussex. At the beginning of November, Charlotte wrote to Ellen, who was clearly offended at not hearing of Charlotte's scheme directly, apologising for her neglect. We have a glimpse of that burning ambition in her letter to Ellen. She had been 'deliberating on plans important to my future prospects . . . the plain fact is, I was not, I am not now, certain of my destiny. On the contrary, I have been most uncertain, perplexed with the contradictory schemes and proposals.' Miss Wooler had proposed that she should revive the Dewsbury Moor school but, she wrote yearningly, expressing her longing to 'become something better than I am' with something close to anguish: 'a fire was kindled in my very heart, which I could not quench. I so longed to increase my attainments, to become something better than I am; a glimpse of what I felt, I showed to you in one of my former letters – only a glimpse; Mary cast oil upon the flames – encouraged me, and in her own strong, energetic language heartened me on . . .'

It was not until January 1842 that a school in Brussels was finally fixed on. In the long and often dispiriting search, the Brontës had had the help of Mrs Jenkins, the wife of the British Chaplain in Brussels, the Reverend Evan Jenkins. The Chaplain was the brother of the Reverend David Jenkins, who had many years before succeeded Patrick Brontë as curate of Dewsbury and who was an acquaintance of Ellen's as well as Mr Brontë's. In response to Mr Brontë's request for advice, the Reverend David Jenkins had put the Brontës in contact with his brother and sister-in-law. Their connections included an English woman who had been a governess in the French royal family and who had accompanied Louis-Philippe's daughter, Princess Marie Louise, to Brussels when she married King Leopold of Belgium. It was because of this English woman's delighted account of the education her granddaughter was receiving at the Pensionnat Heger in Brussels that Mrs Jenkins reported back to Yorkshire in January recommending the Heger school.

151

Accordingly, Charlotte wrote off to the Pensionnat de Demoiselles, run by Madame Heger. Her husband was a professor at Brussels' prestigious boys' school, the Athénée Royale, and also gave lessons to pupils at the Pensionnat. As a young man he had been very poor, and he and his wife – now in their thirties – were serious-minded people, devoted to their profession, and to each other. He later told Mrs Gaskell that he and Mme Heger had been so impressed by the simple and earnest tone of Charlotte's letter of application, with its very particular enquiries about the cost of 'extras' from two young women who had the admirable desire to impart learning to others, that they had decided to name a specific sum within which all expenses would be included. How great was the sum involved is not clear, but it was satisfactory enough for Charlotte to accept the terms and arrange passage to Brussels in February.

Whatever hopes Charlotte had of seeing Branwell before she left, on what she intended to be a year's stay abroad, went unrealised, for Branwell was deliberately keeping out of his family's sight. They may have thought that his promotion in the spring to the clerk in charge of a new minor station on the Leeds–Manchester railway augured well, but in reality he was now living in greater confusion and disarray than ever before. Nor was it possible for Charlotte and Ellen to meet up to say goodbye. Charlotte wrote to her towards the end of January, reporting that Willie Weightman was 'looking delicate and pale. . . . He sits opposite to Anne at Church sighing softly and looking out of the corners of his eyes to win her attention – and Anne is so quiet, her look so downcast – they are a picture – He would be the better for a comfortable wife like you to settle him. . . .' She did not seem to have considered the possibility of that wife being Anne, who had now been persuaded by her employers to return to her position at Thorp Green rather than, as Charlotte had originally planned, stay at home in place of Emily. Aunt Branwell and Mr Brontë were to manage on their own, with extra domestic help. The parsonage was nowadays full of animals: two geese, Victoria and Adelaide (for the queen and her aunt) who lived in the peat house. They had had a wild goose, but it had flown away. There was also a hawk in a cage named Hero, and Keeper, Emily's huge mastiff.

Since it would not be fitting for Charlotte and Emily to travel to Brussels alone, it was arranged that their father should chaperone them, although in the event the seasoned travellers Mary Taylor and her brother Joe, who were at this time back in England, also accompanied them. Their first stop was London, for which the party set off from Yorkshire on the wet, dank day of 8 February 1842.

CHAPTER IX

The Pensionnat Heger

Now that the organising was finished and the journey begun, a joyousness irradiated Charlotte's spirits. After weeks of tedious manufacturing of clothing – a trousseau of chemises and nightgowns judged necessary for the cosmopolitan city – she was at last free to thrill to the new sights whirling past her eyes as the train made its eleven-hour journey from Leeds to Euston Square. The party finally arrived in London at about eight in the evening, and made their way to the Pater Noster Coffee House, where they were to spend the next few nights.

This curious inn in the shadow of St Paul's had once been a voguish literary meeting place; at the end of the eighteenth century both Dr Johnson and Goldsmith had been habituées. But those high days were long past. It had become a place which catered to university men and clergy passing through London. Mr Brontë had stayed there thirty years before when he was a young curate on his way north, and he saw no reason to question why a place used by clergymen was not respectable enough to put up his daughters as well as himself. According to the conventional notions of the day, his was an unrefined approach. Later, the mother of Charlotte's publisher, Mrs Smith – an inhabitant of respectably middle-class Bayswater – would declare it a most unsuitable place for young ladies to stay, for it had only one female servant and was in the middle of the city.

For Charlotte, probably as unaware as her father of such strictures and, as the consummate Romantic, foe of refinement where it restricted sensation or activity, the whole experience was something in which she exulted. Her feelings about the city would later be revealed through Lucy Snowe in a passage in *Villette*:

> I got into the heart of city life. I saw and felt London at last: I got into the Strand; I went up Cornhill; I mixed with life passing along; I dared the perils of crossings. To do this and do it utterly

alone gave me, perhaps an irrational, but a real pleasure. Since those days, I have seen the West-end, the parks, the fine squares; but I love the city far better. The city seems so much more in earnest: its business, its rush, its roar, are such serious things, sights and sounds. The city is getting its living – the West-end but enjoying its pleasures. At the West-end you may be amused, but in the city you are deeply excited.

The hum of St Paul's bells in their colossal dome – 'a solemn, orbed mass, dark-blue and dim – THE DOME' – which she and Emily could see from their bedroom window, felt like a summons to awaken to freedom the next morning. As she wrote so poignantly and perhaps ironically in *Villette* as Lucy Snowe sets off on her journey, the details of which were in many ways identical to Charlotte's own two journeys to Brussels: 'While I looked my inner self moved; my spirit shook its always-fettering wings half-loose; I had a sudden feeling as if I, who had never yet truly lived, were at last about to taste life.'

Indeed, she was about to experience the definitive emotional experience of her life. But, like Frances Henri in *The Professor*, so far she felt that she had 'done but little, learnt but little, and seen but little . . . I walked the same road every day; I could not get out of it; had I rested – remained there even till my death, I should never have enlarged it.'

Meanwhile, in the three days they had to spend in London before the packet left for Ostend, Charlotte threw herself into sight-seeing, alert to everything around her including what she afterwards called in *Villette* the strange, chopped-up speech of the southerners. Mary Taylor later told Mrs Gaskell that Charlotte seemed to think it their duty to see all the pictures and statues they could: 'She knew all the artists and where other productions of theirs were to be found.' Emily shared Charlotte's enthusiasm for the plastic arts, but it was Charlotte who initiated the expeditions, although according to an amused Mary, the extraordinary, uncouth Emily then always had her own opinions and never accepted Charlotte's.

Early on Saturday morning, the 12th of February, the party embarked on the boat to Ostend. Mr Brontë, in his characteristically determined fashion, had written out his own selection of French phrases in a thirty-six-page-long French phrasebook stitched into a grained calf cover. He added a forceful command to himself: 'The following conversational terms, suited to a Traveller in France, or any part of the Continent of Europe – are taken from Turenne's New French Manual for 1840 – and must be fully mastered, and ready – *semper* – All these must be kept – *semper*.'[1] He was delighted to find on his return how much cheaper travel was on the continent than in

England – it was a fifth less – and at his cunning in obtaining his passport at the Belgian Consul's office in London as opposed to the French where it would have cost him twice as much, i.e. ten shillings.

To Charlotte on board the packet, as to Lucy Snowe, the golden gleaming coast seemed like the whole continent of Europe spread out before her, 'like a wide dreamland, far away' – the dreamland it had truly been until so recently. William Crimsworth's ecstatic reaction was hers, too: 'Liberty I clasped in my arms for the first time, and the influence of her smile and embrace revived my life like the sun and the west wind.'

The crossing in theory took fourteen hours, but could take much longer in adverse weather, and it was past midnight before they docked in Belgium. In his note-book Mr Brontë observed that since on landing at ports 'numbers of porters bellow out, in recommending their respective houses, it is best directly to name your Inn – when they will cease, and the porter will take you to it without delay.' Saturday and Sunday were spent in a hotel at Ostend, where the travellers were very struck by the fashion for painted floors, the airy rooms and general air of sparkling cleanness, and the black stoves, the chamber-maids in wooden shoes, short red petticoats and printed cotton bedgown. They gave the whole country the novel atmosphere of a fairy-tale.

On Monday morning they set out for Brussels itself in the old-fashioned 'diligence', the French equivalent of a stage-coach. The small scale of the Belgian landscape clearly surprised Charlotte, used as she was to the grandeur of the wild fell country and endless moors she had grown up in; nevertheless, though 'not a beautiful, scarcely a picturesque object met my eye along the whole route', to her in her excitement 'all was beautiful, all was more than picturesque' Belgium today, though dissected by great autoroutes, is essentially the same landscape, presided over by the same grey low-lying skies that Charlotte described in *The Professor*, though those painted Flemish farm-houses are hard to find:

I gazed often, and always with delight, from the window of the Diligence . . . Well! and what did I see? I will tell you faithfully. Green, reedy swamps; fields fertile, but flat, cultivated in patches that made them look like magnified kitchen-gardens; belts of cut trees, formal as pollard willows, skirting the horizon; narrow canals, gliding slow by the roadside; painted Flemish farm-houses; some very dirty hovels; a grey, dead sky; wet road, wet fields, wet house-tops. . . .

They arrived at Brussels in darkness, entering through the gate which

155

was the main entrance to the city, the Porte de Flandre, and put up at the fairly modest Hôtel d'Hollande, in a street close to the diligence terminus on the Rue de la Madeleine. Presumably they had been attracted by its advertisement that it was 'distinguished by the persons of rank who sojourned there'. The next morning Mary and Joe Taylor departed for Mary's more expensive finishing school, the Château Koekelberg, a large white typically continental building which lay without the city walls on the Chaussée de Sette,[2] while the Brontës set off for the Rue d'Isabelle and the Pensionnat Heger. They were accompanied by the kindly Mr and Mrs Jenkins, who had looked after their interests so well and who now came in from their home outside the centre to greet the Brontës.

The quaintness of the town, with its curious churches on every corner and diverse styles of architecture bearing mute witness to the many vicissitudes and occupations the country had undergone – Burgundian, Spanish, Austrian Hapsburg, Napoleonic – was not lost on such visually aware young women as Charlotte and Emily Brontë. Brussels had built up around a hill, with the king living at the top in a small palace in the Park Royale, surrounded by smart, white, neo-classical squares. Below these spacious, neat and clean streets were clustered the tall, narrow, characteristically Flemish gabled houses that lined the precipitous little medieval streets of the lower part of the town. No two houses were the same; painted and whitewashed, with peaked and carved gables whose grotesque shapes would fire Charlotte's imagination, they looked over the many canals that ran through the city. Thackeray, who visited Brussels at the same time as Charlotte was there, thought rather unkindly that the city had 'an absurd kind of Lilliput look with it'.[3] And Charlotte may well have been influenced later by his disrespectful impressions, since she gave the capital city the diminutive title of Villette, from which her novel took its name.

The destination of the Brontë party on that February morning was 32 Rue d'Isabelle, below the Park Royale, which could be gained from the Pensionnat in five minutes by means of a steep flight of stone steps that came out at the statue of General Belliard on the stately Rue Royale, opposite the park entrance. The tiered construction of the city meant that the Rue d'Isabelle had a curiously sunken effect; it was towered over on all sides by high buildings, and the old city walls ran alongside much of it. Above lay the spacious, aristocratic quarters; below, the busy commercial town, with overcrowded slum area; and sandwiched between them, forming the middle level, was the area around the poorly lit Rue d'Isabelle.

The street had been built in the early seventeenth century during the Spanish occupation and named in appreciation of the Infanta

156

Isabella, under whose governorship the powerful guild of crossbow-men, 'les Arbeletriers du grand serment', had been forced to allow a road to be made through their exercise grounds to give a much-needed public short-cut to the Cathedral of St Michel and St Gudule. To compensate the guild, the Infanta Isabella had a 'great mansion' built for them in front of their exercise ground, which Mrs Gaskell mistakenly imagined to be the Pensionnat. In fact the school, with its long, low, straggling façade and shuttered windows looking on to the cobbled street, had been built, like the other houses on the Rue d'Isabelle, around 1800. Only the heavy, elaborate gate that gave a separate entrance into the Pensionnat garden, and bore a Latin inscription to the grounds created in the time of the Arbeletriers, remained of the Infanta's building.[4]

Today, the Pensionnat and the Rue d'Isabelle, along with much of old Brussels, has been knocked down and built over, but visitors up to the early part of this century could make their way to the Pensionnat following Charlotte's exact description of Lucy Snowe's journey in *Villette* or such passages as the following from *The Professor*, probably written about eighteen months after Charlotte's return to England, in which she makes no attempt to disguise place names:

> I saw what a fine street was the Rue Royale, and, walking leisurely along its broad pavement, I continued to survey its stately hotels, till the palisades, the gates, the trees of the park appearing in sight, offered to my eye a new attraction. I remember, before entering the park, I stood a while to contemplate the statue of General Belliard, and then I advanced to the top of the great staircase just beyond, and I looked down into a narrow back street, which I afterwards learnt was called the Rue d'Isabelle. I well recollect that my eye rested on the green door of a rather large house opposite, where, on a brass plate, was inscribed, 'Pensionnat de Demoiselles'.

The stately hotels of white stucco are still there, as is the park, with its gates, palisades and thin black trees, all too often dripping with wet from Brussels' moisture-laden atmosphere; and the great marble statue of portly General Belliard still marks the entrance to steep steps leading down to a narrow back street. You can stand on the level of the Rue Royale and look down to where the chimneys of the houses of the Rue d'Isabelle would have appeared at Charlotte and Emily's feet, and imagine the house where the Hegers once kept their flourishing seminary. As Mrs Gaskell noted, 'Anyone might drop a stone into it from the back windows of the grand modern hotels in the Rue Royale, built and furnished in the newest Parisian fashion.'[5]

Earlier biographers with a copy of *Villette* and *The Professor* in hand were able with ease to find their way around the Pensionnat. The house, a white building in unpretentious French style, struck Charlotte as rather large. The great door was opened by a portress who sat in a cabinet beside it, and immediately in view was a passage, exactly as described in *The Professor*: 'paved alternately with black and white marble; the walls were painted in imitation of marble also; and at the far end opened a glass door, through which I saw shrubs and a grass plot. . . . This, then, was my first glimpse of *the* garden.'

The ivy-covered walled garden, which would play such a large part in *Villette*, was unusually large for a city, and had a very long history. In the Middle Ages it had been attached to the hospice of a religious order, before forming part of the grounds of the Arbeletriers in the sixteenth and seventeenth centuries. The magnificent, ancient pear trees at the bottom of the garden were famed throughout Belgium for their massive snowy blossom and magnificent fruit, and were visited by fruiticulturists because of their marvellous qualities. Quantities of their pears lay bottled in cellars beneath the Pensionnat, providing the base for the compote eaten all year round. At the foot of one tree was a moss-covered slab, just as there was one in *Villette* beneath which Lucy Snowe buries Dr Bretton's letters, and which the pupils of the Pensionnat believed was the entrance to an underground passage.

The French window at the end of the hall passage led through to a vine-clad covered walk, with an acacia tree towering over it. This tree which 'shadowed the Grand Berceau and rested some of its branches on the roof of the first classe' would enable Ginevra Fanshawe's lover to climb up to visit her in the attic from over the wall of the adjoining Athénée Royale buildings. The whole garden, with its luxuriant flowering shrubs and deciduous trees, hidden walks and arbours, produced a feeling of deep seclusion that strongly appealed to Charlotte. She described its setting in *Villette*: 'The windowless backs of houses built in this garden, and in particular the whole of one side was skirted by the rear of a long line of premises – being the boarding-houses of the neighbouring college.' These were the buildings belonging to the boys' grammar school where M. Heger taught – the Athénée Royale in the Rue Terarcken to the south. It can still be seen today down a flight of steps from the Rue Ravenstein. Nowadays the Palais des Beaux-Arts covers some of the land where the school was, to the immediate left on descending the stone steps below General Belliard. On the skyline were the great towers of the Cathedral, the deep, frequent toll of its bells echoed by the smaller, sweeter note of St Jacques sur Coudenberg, high above in the Rue Royale, reminding Charlotte that the passage of time here was under the sway of Roman Catholicism.

Madame Heger was there to greet the Brontës on their arrival at the

Pensionnat on 15 February. Aged thirty-eight, only twelve years older than Charlotte, she presented a formidable figure of womanhood quite different to Charlotte's previous experience of schoolteachers. Dignified and imposing, she was the continental woman at her most polished and efficient, while managing to be serenely attractive at the same time. Her severe points had been softened by marriage, Charlotte thought later. She had a great admiration for the clergy and the English, even if they were Protestant – her own children's nurse was English – and she gave a hearty welcome to the two shy young women who had been introduced to her by the Chaplain of the English community and who were in the company of an English clergyman. All seemed to bode well. She probably led the weary travellers into the salon to the left of the hallway. As described in *The Professor* and confirmed by Francis Wheelwright,[6] it had a beautifully painted highly varnished floor, and was rather imposing. The chairs and sofas were draped with white fabric, unlike the black horsehair sofa at home, and the room contained a green stove, that characteristic feature of the northern European home. The walls were covered with pictures in gilt frames and mirrors above console tables. The mantelpiece was full of ornaments, and the windows were framed by soft muslin curtains. In the middle of the room was what one visitor described as a 'handsome centre table'. Though glittering the effect was somewhat chilling, and Charlotte was better pleased by a second room which was more snugly furnished. Two folding doors led into this carpeted room, which had a piano, a couch, a chiffonière, and an enormous window with dark red drapery looking onto the rainwashed garden.

Monsieur Heger was not in evidence, so Mr Brontë never met the man who would so radically affect his daughter's life. Before he departed for home a few days later, he was shown some of the sights of Brussels by the Jenkinses and also made a trip round the battlefield of Waterloo – an attraction which may have been part of the inducement for him to accompany his daughters. Meanwhile the Jenkinses extracted a promise from Charlotte and Emily that they would come to visit them on every holiday in their home outside the city walls on the Chaussée d'Ixelles.

The school that the Brontës had arrived at almost by accident was run by no ordinary couple. All contemporary accounts tally in describing M. Heger as an incomparable, almost charismatic teacher; at the age of twenty-five he had been singled out for the honour of making the annual speechday address at the Athénée Royale, which was one of the major events of the Brussels year. He was now thirty-three, just seven years older than Charlotte, and at the height of his teaching powers. Mrs Gaskell would tactfully present M. Heger as a 'kindly, wise, good and religious man'. This description scarcely does justice to the virile man painted by the distinguished Belgian painter Joseph Gerard. At the age of fifty-eight, twenty-five years after he met Charlotte Brontë, he still radiates magnetism and authority. Over the following decades he would become a considerable figure in the Belgian community so that on his death in May 1896 he would be described as possessing 'une sorte de magnétisme intellectuel'.[7] Charles Tardieu would recall 'combien son influence pédagogique fut considérable; sa position de partisan résolu de l'intervention de l'Etat; qu'il était croyant et profondément chrétien, mais sans étroitesse ni intolérance, ayant le respect des convictions sincères et des recherches de bonne foi.' *L'Indépendence Belge*, one of the leading Belgian newspapers, wrote a lengthy appreciation of the work of the Hegers on their fiftieth wedding anniversary in 1886. It deemed the occasion to be worthy of public notice since the Heger establishment had had the monopoly of the education of the daughters of the bourgeoisie for such a long time that the couple had in effect brought up an entire society, and consequently the country owed them much: 'Le père Heger s'était acquis une véritable renominée dans cet art qui consiste à dégourdir les intelligences et à rechauffer les coeurs.'[8]

Constantin Romain Heger was born in July 1809 into a family of well-to-do jewellers whose Viennese ancestors had moved to Belgium two hundred years before. Their German ancestry continued to be suggested by the fact that Heger does not take an acute accent on the first 'e', though pronounced as if it does. Constantin had been brought up to expect to train as a barrister, as he would tell Charlotte Brontë, but his father's rash if generous loan of a large sum of money to a friend which the latter was unable to repay had ruined the family overnight. Constantin was sent to Paris to find a living, and perhaps to escape the ignominy of his personal circumstances – the ruin of the respectable bourgeois. He had a kind of legal training as a solicitor's secretary for four years, and it was while he was in Paris that he was able to indulge that taste for the dramatic which so many pupils remembered pervading his teaching, for to earn extra funds he spent time at the Comédie Française as a *claqueur*.[9]

The death of his father in 1829 brought him back to Belgium, where he married one Marie-Josephine Noyer, and resumed his close family ties with his brothers Vital, a carpet manufacturer, and Jules, a stationer and printer. By returning he was at hand to fight in the September Days – the 1830 Belgian War of Independence against the Dutch, to whom the Belgian provinces had been united at the Congress of Vienna in 1815. This event, commemorated in marble form by innumerable patriotic statues dotted around Brussels in Charlotte's time, was slugged out all over the city, including on the roof of the

Pensionnat, where M. Heger fought. His wife's brother was killed while fighting on the barricades alongside him.

In October 1830, in the reorganisation following the war, he was appointed a schoolteacher at the Athénée Royale by the Provisional Government. A period of calm followed, during which his wife had a baby. But tragedy then struck. In September 1833 Marie-Josephine and the baby died on the same day in a cholera epidemic that swept through Brussels that year. (She would later be the inspiration for M. Paul Emanuel's dead fiancée Justine-Marie in *Villette*, whose father's profession, a jeweller, was that of M. Heger's own.)

It was not until he married his second wife, whom he met at the home of a schoolteacher friend, that he achieved real happiness. Mademoiselle Claire Zoë Parent, then thirty-two, was five years older that Constantin Heger and, like him, was a committed teacher, who had her own school at which he began to give literature lessons. She was a pretty woman with auburn hair and blue eyes; photographs of her in old age show delicate, neat features, and contemporary accounts remark her habitual calm, in contrast to her volcanic partner.

The Parent family were not Belgian but French – refugees from the French Revolution, when her father had fled to Brussels. There he had married a charming young woman named Charlotte Legrand and had been joined by his sister Anne-Marie, a nun whose convent had been disestablished in the Revolution. She began her new life outside the Church by opening a small school in her brother's house on the Rue de Bois Sauvage, which was attended by her four nieces – Claire Zoë, born in 1804, was the third eldest – and their friends.

This strong-minded aunt had a far-reaching effect on the family: two of the nieces became nuns, while Zoë, who was noted for her piety, took over the school on her aunt's death, setting up at No. 32 Rue d'Isabelle, which had become vacant after the 1830 Revolution. Such a background partly explains Mme Heger's rather formal demeanour and air of serene control. There was a little something of the Jesuit about her attitude to life – a cool recognition of the follies and problems of the world and a concomitant suave executive prudence. A Bruxelloise described her to Mrs Gaskell, having seen her once as having something cold and stiff in her demeanour – 'quelque chose de froid et de compassé dans son maintien' – though she knew, however, that she was loved and appreciated by her pupils.[10] They were qualities which would stand her in good stead in the running of something as volatile as a girls' school.

She married Constantin Heger in September 1836 and he moved into his wife's Pensionnat, where her widowed mother also lived. Based on mutual physical attraction, devotion to teaching and profound Roman Catholic beliefs, their extremely happy marriage would last over fifty years. It was soon blessed with three daughters and shortly after the Brontës arrived at the Pensionnat in 1842, a son was born – who would be followed by another two children, a girl born in November 1843 at the end of Charlotte's second year at the school, and a boy in 1846. M. Heger's main work continued to be in the Athénée Royale, while the Pensionnat was run entirely under his wife's direction, but living on the premises as he did, his role as *père de famille* became closely intertwined with a quasi-fatherly role in the school. The arrangement encouraged the sort of intimate paternal relationship which he liked to establish with pupils outside the classroom. According to one perceptive pupil, he almost demanded it, and grew angry if it was denied him.[11] It was his habit to share the brioches or bons bons he always seemed to have about his person with the pupils, particularly the young ones; he was always there to chat at the odd moment, to encourage the cleverer girls' interest in literature, to draw out the shyer, for despite the rages to which he was prone, he was very tender-hearted.

Despite his relative youth, he was a philosophical and mature thinker. Teaching was a complete way of life for him, a vocation requiring 'un devou absolue' as he stressed to a young teacher, with corresponding passionate convictions about the importance of education in the new industrial age. He was one of the most zealous members of the Society of St Vincent de Paul, giving much of his spare time to evening classes for the poor and factory workers. A devout Catholic, he would resign from his post at the Athénée Royale as a protest when religious instruction was made non-compulsory.[12] His habit of wearing clerical black – the *paletôt* and *bonnet grêe* M. Paul Emanuel would dress in – added to the impression that he had some priestly affiliation.

Despite authoritarian political views, which might be guessed at from the imperious behaviour which made him a 'terror' to his pupils, he was a highly emotional and impulsive man. His great knowledge of and unusual enthusiasm for the contemporary writing of the French Romantics undoubtedly stemmed from a temperamental affinity to them. He adored every nuance of the emotional: personal relations between pupil and teacher were profoundly important to him, and much cultivated. Something of his electric, febrile quality is suggested by the author of the article in *L'Indépendence* who seems to have been taught by him: 'Sans compromettre la gravité nécéssaire à l'homme de l'école, sans rien perdre de son autorité, il égayait la grammaire, il faisait vivre la syntaxe. Il avait le mouvement, le mot et le trait avec un grain de fantaisie. Ses exemples, qui parfois faisaient la bizarrerie, ne s'en gravaient que mieux dan la mémoire.'

In appearance he was rather short, with a shock of black hair and an 'important' nose, a determined chin and dark eyes below strongly marked black eyebrows. These Italianate looks matched a personality that while being too easily moved, egotistical and probably vain, was always fascinating. He ruled the Pensionnat like a little kingdom, its impatient, fiery, kindly and slightly absurd god. As Leslie Stephen would sum up, rather cruelly, he was 'an Aeolus of the duckpond'.

Such emotional involvement, such intimacy, such intellectual passion: they were qualities that would act like a match to dynamite on his fervent, brilliant, emotionally starved pupil, Charlotte Brontë. At first, however, he was only a stocky dark figure, to be glimpsed sometimes in corridors and the courtyard or at meals, as Charlotte and Emily strove to come to terms with their strange new life, the regulated timetable and hours of lessons and *devoirs*, which at the ages of twenty-five and twenty-three they were sharing with fifteen-year-olds. Apart from the boarders, there were about forty day girls at the school at this time, who ranged in age from seven years onwards. The two young women shared a dormitory for twenty pupils, although in acknowledgement of the Brontës' age, Mme Heger had given them their own space, partitioned off by a curtain. Charlotte's fantastic Angrian imaginings about the glamour of continental life bore no resemblance to her present, curious position.

But any lowering of spirits that she and Emily felt were resolutely pushed aside: they were in Brussels to a greater end, to learn, so that they might return and set up their own school. Emily's stoical approach was more surprising, although she had carried her private world of Gondal across the Channel. She certainly wrote the poem headed 'H.A. and A.S.' while in Brussels, and on 20 August 1842 drafted 'Aspin Castle', one of the pivotal poems of the Gondal cycle, which she revised and completed at Haworth the following February. It seems from Charlotte's 'Biographical Notice' of 1850 that the sisters had not been showing one another their poetry for some years, and Emily's poems must have been written in stolen moments in the school's large dormitory.

Separated as they were from most of the girls by age, language, culture and religion, the first month was undoubtedly very hard, even though they as usual found one another's company all-sufficing. Used to plain-speaking Protestant Yorkshire where truthfulness was a *raison d'être*, Belgian politeness and interest in keeping everything running smoothly struck Charlotte, as it did Mary Taylor, as odiously sly and false. Brought up by a vehemently anti-Papist father, she found it easy to attribute it to the Belgians' despotic religion which stifled independent thought. Although the school's prospectus had described the course of instruction as being 'basé sur la Religion', Charlotte had not foreseen how much of a barrier religious differences

163

would be, or how much of school time would revolve round religion. In any event it soon became a scapegoat for cultural divides. There was an oratory on the second floor of the Pensionnat where a mass would be held in the mornings, from which the Brontës were obviously excluded, and in the evening M. Heger would give the *lecture pieuse* – just as M. Paul Emanuel did in *Villette* – in the long, narrow refectory; the Brontës disliked it and would usually not attend.

They could find little in common with the Belgian girls, whom Charlotte thought stiff and over-refined. She told Ellen with some amusement: 'To lace the stays without a handkerchief on the neck is considered a disgusting piece of indelicacy.' And she had harsh words for the Belgian nature in general – 'It is a character singularly cold, selfish, animal and inferior.' Typically, one of the few people in the school whom Charlotte and Emily liked was a mistress named Mademoiselle Marie, because she was 'talented and original', despite her 'repulsive and arbitrary manners', which had made the whole school her enemy.

For their part, the Brontës, with their old-fashioned clothing and sincere Protestant outlook, did not find favour with the Belgian schoolgirls. According to Mrs Gaskell, who must have been repeating what M. Heger told her, they were too full of earnest thought to be ready for careless conversation or merry games – for which they were in any case too old. The Belgian girls thought the new English pupils 'wild and scared-looking, with strange odd insular ideas about dress; for Emily had taken a fancy to the fashion, ugly and preposterous even during its reign, of gigot sleeves, and persisted in wearing them long after they were "gone out". Her petticoats too had not a curve or wave in them, but hung down straight and long, clinging to her lank figure.'[13]

A little of the isolation the sisters felt was hinted at in Charlotte's first letter to Ellen towards the end of March: 'You will have heard that we have settled at Brussels instead of Lille. I think we have done well – we have got into a very good school – and are considerably comfortable. Just now we are at Koekelberg spending the day with Mary and Martha – to us such a happy day – for one's blood requires a little warming, it gets cold living among strangers,' she ended picturesquely. This trip to the Taylors' school was the first time they had been able to see Mary and Martha since their arrival in Brussels, and they must have admired its gardens with its plantations approached by a long avenue. The house was large, with high-ceilinged rooms and a broken pediment – this was the ruin of the tower of the old Château de Koekelberg, pulled down in 1820. The finishing school was conducted by Mme Goussaert, born Catherine Philips, whose husband was a 'rentier' and railway employee. Joan Stevens argues convincingly that the site of Château Koekelberg in modern Brussels is where the Boulevard Leopold II crosses the railway line going north from the Gare de L'Ouest.[14]

The standing invitation to visit the Jenkinses on Sundays and their Thursday half-day holiday proved more of a social embarrassment, with Emily in particular silent and awkward in the face of polite company.[15] Their time outside school hours was mainly spent with each other, and former pupils remembered their complete absorption in one another; one supplied a vignette of the pair walking quite tirelessly round the garden, Emily so much taller than Charlotte that she would rest on the latter's shoulder.

After Mme Heger had recovered from the birth of Prosper Edouard Augustin, born on 28 March, the Brontës began to see more of her, and of M. Heger himself, hitherto seen at a distance when he performed one of his dramatic evening readings after the *lecture pieuse*, which formed entertainment for the whole school.[16] With the advent of spring, the Hegers, as was their custom, arranged many little excursions into the pretty countryside round Brussels, and by now, too, M. Heger had begun to appreciate the calibre of these English pupils and to give them private lessons.

In his idiosyncratic fashion he had observed the English girls for several weeks, as he told Mrs Gaskell when she visited him years later, and saw that with their unusual characters and extraordinary talents a different method had to be adopted from the one in which he usually taught French to English girls. After discussion with his wife, M. Heger decided to dispense with the usual training in grammar and vocabulary, and use one he had occasionally used with the elder of his French and Belgian pupils. The proposal he made to the Brontës, he told Mrs Gaskell, was that he should read to them some of the masterpieces of 'the most celebrated French authors (such as Casimir de la Vigne's poem on the Death of Joan of Arc, parts of Bossuet, the admirable translation of the letter of St Ignatius to the Roman Christians in the Bibliothèque Choisie des Pères de l'Eglise etc.), and after having thus impressed the complete effect of the whole, to analyse the parts with them, pointing out in what such-and-such an author excelled, and where were the blemishes. He believed that he had to do with pupils, capable from their ready sympathy with the intellectual, the refined, the polished or the noble, of catching the echo of a style, and so reproducing their own thoughts in a somewhat similar manner.'[17]

According to M. Heger, Emily, who spoke first in reply to this proposal, disapproved of the idea, as she thought that they would lose all originality of thought and expression. She would have entered into an argument on the subject, if Monsieur had been open to such a possibility. Charlotte then said that she also doubted that the plan had much chance of success, but she would follow M. Heger's advice, because she was bound to obey him while she was his pupil. In an enthusiastic letter to Ellen in May, Charlotte, now twenty-six, admitted that it had felt very strange at first to have to submit to authority, to obey orders instead of giving them, but she had come to the conclusion that it was very natural to her to submit, and unnatural to command.

On the whole she was indeed happy under the regime. M. Heger was the first teacher Charlotte had come across who really understood contemporary literature and was passionately interested in it. Through him the Brontës were exposed to a much higher level of French literature than the French novels which had hitherto found their way to the parsonage through the kindness of Mr Taylor. From Charlotte's point of view she was exceptionally lucky to find someone who taught the French Romantics at a period when they were still liable to be excluded from the syllabus – in most schools the corpus consisted of classical French literature – and to find a teacher who was liberal enough to read Victor Hugo. As she told Ellen, despite the differences of country and religion which made such a broad line of demarcation between the Brontës and the rest of the school, she was never unhappy because she was so busy learning: 'My present life is so delightful, so congenial to my own nature, compared with that of a governess. My time, constantly occupied, passes too quickly.' It was a great change from the boredom of the past four years. How Charlotte would have benefited had university been open to her.

Her first, light-hearted and disrespectful description to Ellen of the man who would finally inspire the creation of the great romantic character of Mr Rochester bears a much closer resemblance to the despotic, unreasonable little hero of *Villette*, M. Paul Emanuel:

There is one individual of whom I have not yet spoken – M. Heger, the husband of Madame. He is professor of rhetoric, a man of power as to mind, but very choleric and irritable as to temperament; a little black ugly being, with a face that varies in expression. Sometimes he borrows the lineaments of an insane tom-cat, sometimes those of a delirious hyena; occasionally, but very seldom, he discards these perilous attractions and assumes an air not above 100 degrees removed from mild and gentlemanlike. He is very angry with me just at present, because I have written a translation which he chose to stigmatise as *peu correcte*. He did not tell me so, but wrote the accusation on the margin of my book, and asked in brief, stern phrase, how it happened that my compositions were always better than my translations? adding that the thing seemed to him inexplicable. The fact is, some weeks ago, in a high-flown humour, he forbade me to use either dictionary or grammar in translating the most difficult English compositions into French. This makes the task rather arduous, and compels me now and then to introduce an English word, which nearly plucks the eyes out of his head when he sees it. Emily and he don't draw well together at all. When he is very ferocious with me I cry; that sets all things straight.

M. Heger, speaking to Mrs Gaskell of the Brontës fifteen years later, appears to have had an even higher estimate of Emily's genius than Charlotte's: 'Emily had a head for logic, and a capability of argument, unusual in a man, and rare indeed in a woman.' In his opinion, which Charlotte herself would echo, the force of this gift was impaired by her stubborn tenacity of will, which rendered her obtuse to all reasoning where her own wishes, or her own sense of right, was concerned. 'She should have been a man – a great navigator,' said M. Heger. 'Her powerful reason would have deduced new spheres of discovery from the knowledge of the old; and her strong imperious will would never have been daunted by opposition or difficulty; never have given way but with life.' *Wuthering Heights* was not translated into French until the end of the nineteenth century and M. Heger, whose English was not fluent, would not have read it. But in talking to Mrs Gaskell he recognised that Emily's 'faculty of imagination was such that, if she had written a history, her view of scenes and characters would have been so vivid, and so powerfully expressed, and supported by such a show of argument, that it would have dominated over the reader, whatever might have been his previous opinions, or his cooler perceptions of its truth.'[18]

Charlotte, in M. Heger's eyes, allowed the egotistical, exacting Emily 'to exercise a kind of unconscious tyranny over her' in her concern to see her younger sister contented.[19] To him, Charlotte always appeared unselfish in comparison and it was in this pupil above all that his devotion to teaching and literature would be more than repaid. An exercise book still exists at Haworth Parsonage of twenty-one transcriptions from French authors which reflect M. Heger's own taste. It shows marked religious and poetic quality: the extracts include passages from Chateaubriand's *La Génie du Christianisme*, *Les Martyrs*, *Atala*, Victor Hugo's *Etude sur Mirabeau*, Michaud's *Histoire des Croisades*, and work by Lamartine, Nodier, Millevoye and Soumet. Although Romantic authors have by far the largest share, the eighteenth century is represented by Buffon and the Abbé Barthélémy, and the seventeenth by Bossuet and Massillon.[20]

A Romantic by temperament, those tendencies in her strengthened by a childhood and adolescence spent devouring the work of the English Romantics, her commitment to individual feeling intensified by the Brontës' sense of alienation from their surrounding Yorkshire neighbours, Charlotte came to the French Romantics with a sense of recognition. Their handling of language, the inversion of syntax, the use of metaphor to express meaning in a wholly new way, was peculiarly suited to her genius. As one scholar has put it, 'In French Romanticism . . . she found abundant confirmation of her inborn sense that the novelist may also be a poet.'[21]

The tutelage of M. Heger produced a new awareness in her of the possibilities of prose style, of the many effects it is possible to make by varying rhythm and language. It was a direction in which her own naturally colourful and expressive style was naturally tending, but with M. Heger's guidance she began to appreciate what was redundant and over-ornamental in her writing. Such did Charlotte feel her debt to M. Heger that she would later tell him she would like to write a book and dedicate it to her 'Maître de littérature'; the only master of literature she had ever had, she said, in an access of gratitude and enthusiasm.

By the end of the year M. Heger would show his tacit acknowledgement that Charlotte's French prose style was the language of an artist, as Enid Duthie has pointed out, by 'the care he took to supply from time to time, slight modifications of word or phrase whose function is simply to throw into relief an original thought or vivid image [in her exercise books]. This sort of correction is almost a collaboration.' M. Heger gave more attention to choice of words than to slips of grammar, 'still more to style and expression and most of all to the total impression made on the reader'.[22]

The more time that Charlotte spent with him, the more keenly she came to admire him. Not only was he dedicated to a personal quest, he was also committed to the State regenerating society through education; he considered a moral education to be of primary importance in an increasingly scientific age. 'Il est bien coupable celui qui s'occupe de remplir la tête et laisse la coeur vide: C'est faire de la science auxiliaire de l'égoisme, c'est voiler cette difformité morale sous des dehors séduisants . . . enfin, c'est armer l'égoisme de toutes pièces et rendre irrésistible son action dissolvante sur la société.'[23]

His passionate beliefs must have struck many a chord with Charlotte and Emily. Furthermore, he made no attempt to hide his admiration for the English girls, whose essays he would regularly read out to the rest of the class because they were immeasurably superior to the rest. It was exciting to have the admiration of M. Heger, who was so easily irritated by stupidity and was so frequently stern. Accounts by other pupils of their experiences of M. Heger all attest that in most particulars of looks and behaviour M. Paul Emanuel in *Villette* was an outstanding portrait of him: imperious, alarming, domineering, arbitrary, explosive, 'the velvet blackness of his close shorn head, the sallow ivory of his brow', his tigerish look. There was many a classroom scene when M. Heger, like M. Paul was 'raging like a pestilence! Some pupil had not spoken audibly or distinctly enough to suit his ear and taste, and now she and others were weeping, and he was raving from his estrade almost livid.'

To Charlotte, emotional and excitable, there was something peculiarly satisfying in being in the presence of a personality who could feel as intensely as she. Ten years later when she could look at him more objectively, she would describe his power to stir up his pupils, which he exercised almost at will: 'Still there was certainly something in M. Paul's anger – a kind of passion of emotion – that specially tended to draw tears. I was not unhappy, nor much afraid, yet I wept.' And of course his quality of domination was very closely akin to her imaginary hero, the Duke of Zamorna.

A pupil less sympathetic to these methods, Frederika Macdonald, thought that they could err on the side of emotional bullying. Taught by him years later, she described his teaching methods with interesting detail: 'His sympathy for his pupils, *as his pupils*, led him to work upon their sympathies, as a way of inducing a frame of mind in them and an emotional state of feeling, rendering them susceptible to literary impressions, and putting them in key with himself, in this very fine enthusiasm of his, not only for enjoying literature himself but for throwing open to others, and to young votaries especially, the worship of beautiful literature.' More coldly, she stated: 'M. Heger liked to foster a certain amount of sensibility in his relationship with his pupils – it did not amount to more than a taste for dramatic situations where he had an interesting part to play that he gave his histrionic talents a good field of exercise.'[24] He became irritable if he could not achieve this.

By July the Brontës had made such progress that Mme Heger proposed that they should stay another half-year, continuing their studies in French and German in exchange for teaching services. The English teacher would be dismissed and Charlotte was to teach English, and Emily to give music lessons to some of the pupils. There were to be no salaries but their board was to be free. It was a reasonable enough bargain, perhaps a little more to the Hegers' advantage than to the Brontës', and soon agreed on. Charlotte, looking back on the past six months, felt that despite occasional home-sickness the time had been spent happily on the whole, fully occupied with learning. Emily was making rapid progress in French, German, Music and Drawing; furthermore, she told Ellen, M. and Mme Heger were beginning to recognise 'the valuable points of her character under her singularities'.

They were friendly with the Hegers but outside school hours had little contact with them and their private family life. When they could, they visited Mary and Martha Taylor out at Koekelberg. The school there was full of English and German girls, and was thus much less successful than the Pensionnat Heger for acquiring knowledge of French, as Mary complained. She occupied herself mainly with learning German and would later find herself a position teaching English in Germany via one of her new friends at the Château, for a time becoming independent and free of what she called her 'confounded "patrie"'. The company of piquant little Martha Taylor, with her comic way of expressing herself, was a source of cheer for the Brontës. As Charlotte put it in *Shirley* of Martha's inspiration, Jessie Yorke, 'she was made to be a pet'. Cheerful joint letters written to Ellen at this time suggest that their spirits were high, even girlish, and that they were filled with a sense of purpose.

Charlotte did, however, come to confide to Mary that she felt rather confined. 'She used very inconsistently to rail at money and money-getting, and then wish she was able to visit all the large towns in Europe, see all the sights, and know all the celebrities.'[25] The ideal of the society of these 'clever people' was constantly before her. By no stretch of the imagination could the few Brussels acquaintances of the Brontës be considered 'clever' in the sense that Charlotte meant it. Mary recalled Charlotte longing for literary fame so she could know artists and authors. They were in touch with the English community of the city through their attendance of Anglican services in the Chapel Royal, formerly the Temple du Musée, in the crescent wing of the great white rococo palace built by Charles of Lorraine, which was about eight hundred yards up the hill from the Pensionnat. The small, highly ornate chapel with its exuberant plaster swags of flowers, shells, fruit, cherubs and musical instruments, which had been given to the Protestant community by Napoleon, only further impressed the decadence of the Roman Catholic religion upon the two Brontë girls – and showed up the dowdiness of the predominantly English congregation.

Afterwards they would often be dutifully entertained by the Jenkinses. The two Jenkins sons who used to escort them on the long walk down to the centre of town and then out beyond the city walls could scarcely coax a word out of them, and Mrs Jenkins would recall that once at the Jenkinses' home Emily would rarely utter more than a monosyllable. If the Jenkinses had company, the Brontës' outlandish taciturnity often gave offence, and although Charlotte was sometimes sufficiently excited to become eloquent on certain subjects, according to Mrs Jenkins, she had the unfortunte habit of gradually wheeling round on her chair, so as almost to conceal her face from the person to whom she was speaking.[26]

The only other people whom the Brontës knew in Brussels were a family called Wheelwright, whose five daughters were day-boarders at the Pensionnat. Their father, Dr Thomas Wheelwright, had practised medicine in Edinburgh and London, until a cataract and failing eye-sight had necessitated the sale of his practice. He had moved to Brussels, where the cost of living was considerably lower than in England, and where his daughters could be educated at one of the excellent, cheap schools for which the city had a reputation. The five girls, Laetitia, Emily, Frances, Sarah-Anne and Julia, ranged in age from fourteen to seven, and when the Wheelwright parents went away on a trip up the Rhine, Charlotte was left in charge of them. She became particularly friendly with Laetitia, despite the twelve-year disparity in age. The friendship was initially based on a common sense of enmity: Charlotte told her that it was the sight of her standing up in the classroom and glancing round with a semi-contemptuous air at all the Belgian girls which had first attracted her. 'It was so very English,' she later remarked laughing.

Motherly Mrs Wheelwright made a point of inviting the Brontës to meals, though the invitations only became more frequent the next year, when Emily had left Brussels. Laetitia Wheelwright confessed later that she 'would have thought it too high a price for a visit from Charlotte to receive as a fellow guest the apparently unamiable Emily'.[27] The Wheelwright girls particularly disliked Emily because she insisted on teaching them the piano during play hours, so that her own study time should not be forfeited. But whatever their opinion and the myth that has arisen that Emily rarely spoke to anyone in Brussels, she did become friends with fellow-pupil Louise de Bas-sompierre, whose name partly inspired Paulina Home de Bassom-pierre's name in *Villette*, and gave her a drawing of a tree. Years later Mlle de Bassompierre said that 'Miss Emily était beaucoup moins brilliante que sa soeur mais bien plus sympathique'.[28] Exceedingly reserved, Emily would not respond to the Wheelwrights' joshing except to say 'I wish to be as God made me'. Like M. Heger, Laetitia Wheelwright found Emily's intractable nature irritating and, like him, she thought that Emily dominated and rather tyrannised Charlotte.

Doubtless the latter and the sharp-tongued Emily amused them-selves observing the inmates of the school very closely. Though it was always Charlotte's way to be friendly and polite, unlike the brusque Emily, she made mental notes of character traits and behaviour. Ginevra Fanshawe was partly inspired by a girl named Maria Miller who was as gay, foolish and selfish as Ginevra, but with something

171

taking about her. She was famous for refusing to cut off a lock of her own hair to put in a keepsake ring – instead she cut some fur off the hearth rug! In later years such enforced observation of female character would stand Charlotte in good stead; when she came to write her books she could not allow conventional portrayals of idealised female character current in the novel to pass. *Jane Eyre*, *Shirley*, *Villette* and *The Professor* would all offer a very different picture of female character; 'the dreamers about earthly angels and human flowers' would be shown real women with hopes and unacceptably strong passions, whose character was 'a palpable substance enough; very hard too sometimes, and often heavy; there was metal in it, both lead and iron'.[29]

Charlotte could not help sometimes seeing the school as a pageant of the seven ages of woman, and a pageant where the life of the unhappy, ageing spinster was over-represented, particularly when on her own after Emily left. In her account of Charlotte's life in Brussels, Mary Taylor told Mrs Gaskell that Charlotte was particularly alarmed by the behaviour of one of the mistresses, who was very anxious to marry because she was getting so old. This woman used to get her father or brother to take letters to different single men who she thought might be persuaded to do her the favour, 'saying that her only resource was to become a sister of charity if her present employment failed, and that she hated the idea. Charlotte naturally looked with curiosity to people of her own condition. This woman almost frightened her. 'She declares there is nothing she can turn to, and laughs at the idea of delicacy – and she is only ten years older than I am! I did not see the connection till she said, "Well, Polly [Mary's nickname], I should hate being a sister of Charity; I suppose that would shock people, but I should".'

Charlotte was particularly concerned that in the process of turning into a person so alien to her nature as a sister of charity, she should have to lose or apparently repress all her natural feelings. Mary Taylor's feminist principles were outraged by this: 'I promised her a better destiny than to go begging any one to marry her, or to lose her natural feelings as a sister of charity. She [Charlotte] said, "My youth is leaving me; I can never do better than I have done, and I have done nothing yet." At such times she seemed to think that most human beings were destined by the pressure of worldly interests to lose one faculty and feeling after another "till they went dead altogether".' In an access of Romantic sensibility, after this incoherent outburst, Charlotte said, 'I hope I shall be put in my grave as soon as I'm dead; I don't want to walk about so.' Here, according to Mary, she and Charlotte always differed. Mary thought that the degradation of nature she feared was a consequence of poverty and that she should

172

give her attention to earning money. 'Sometimes she admitted this, but could find no means of earning money. At others she seemed afraid of letting her thoughts dwell on the subject, saying that it brought on the worst palsy of all.' It was a classic example, in Mary's view, of all that was wrong with women's lives. Mary's words and philosophy would take a long time to bear fruit, but bear fruit they would.

From the evidence of *Villette*, the Brussels triennial Salon, which took place in 1842 and which Charlotte would have had plenty of opportunity to visit in the August vacation, appears to have reinforced her meditations on the course her life was taking, dictated by her sex. The visit to the picture gallery in *Villette* describes three or four paintings listed in the catalogue to the 1842 Salon exhibition,[30] and from the accuracy and detail it seems that they impressed themselves deeply on her. What she calls 'The Cleopatra' in *Villette* was a painting entitled 'Une Almée', that is, a dancing girl. Charlotte's puritan spirit revolted at this slave of sensuality: 'Out of abundance of material – seven and twenty yards, I should say of drapery – she managed to make inefficient raiment.' That the flesh should be worshipped in this way offended her, the worshipper of intellect, and one who was ever miserably conscious of her deficiency in physical charms. She also resented the fact that such sensuality was not deemed suitable for the unmarried woman to look at.

In contrast, but with no greater appeal, was the painting entitled 'La Vie d'Une Femme' in both the salon and *Villette*. The life of the average bourgeois was the beloved subject of many Belgian artists of this period, celebrated in cosy genre paintings of domestic bliss, and this particular painting depicted four scenes of the supposedly glorious destiny of woman.

They were painted rather in a remarkable style – flat, dead, pale and formal. The first represented a 'Jeune Fille' coming out of a church-door, a missal in her hand, her dress very prim, her eyes cast down, her mouth pursed up – the image of a most villainous little preco-cious she-hypocrite. The second, a 'Mariée' with a long white veil, kneeling at a prie-dieu in her chamber, holding her hands plastered together, finger to finger, and showing the whites of her eyes in a most exasperating manner. The third, a 'Jeune Mère', hanging disconsolate over a clayey and puffy baby with a face like an unwholesome full moon. The fourth, a 'Veuve', being a black woman, holding by the hand a black little girl, and the twain studiously surveying an elegant French monument, set up in a corner of some Pere la Chaise [sic]. All these four 'Anges' were grim and gray as burglars, and cold and vapid as ghosts. What women to live with! insincere, ill-humoured, bloodless, brainless nonentities! As bad in their way as the indolent gipsy-giantess, the Cleopatra, in hers.

For Charlotte the painting summarised the frustratingly limited life of what was considered to be appropriate for women – the steady submission to a destiny which could only be biological, attendant upon which was a code of behaviour which was unnatural and stupid, the hypocritical manners her free frank nature chafed at. Moreover, the contrast between the destinies of the married woman and the spinster would be demonstrated in increasingly painful fashion to Charlotte, as the figure of the happily married, physically attractive and fecund Mme Heger swelled. As yet, however, teaching and learning were enough to bring contentment.

The Asiatically hot summer in Brussels was a new experience for the Brontës, whose lives had been spent amidst the rain and cold of the Yorkshire moors. The garden began to take on that luxuriant quality which is such a feature of *Villette*, and the pupils almost lived out of doors. Most of their lessons were now taken among the rose bushes and fruit trees, in the green bower that the vast vine-covered berceau had become, and Charlotte's extraordinarily visual and sensuous nature could not but expand amidst it all. The generally rather alarmist Mary Taylor noticed that the Brontës, so often a prey to melancholia, were thriving; she told Ellen:

> Charlotte and Emily are well; not only in health but in mind and hope. They are content with their present position and even gay and I think they do quite right not to return to England though one of them at least could earn more at the beautiful town of Bradford than she is now doing . . . if you can't see or rather feel why they are right I could not make you understand them. It is a matter of taste and feeling, and I think you feel pent up enough when you are there to see why they are right in staying outside the cage – though it is somewhat cold.

Mary's trenchant analysis of the position of women in the 'cage' would be shown in her book *Miss Miles*, satirising contemporary attitudes about women. The book's constant refrain is that women are barred from knowing about business, yet such knowledge is time and again proved to be their salvation, enabling them to view clearly the economic basis of their lives, as opposed to 'the dim, undecided way in which most women see the powers that are weaving their destiny'. The character, Dora, at twenty-five writes: 'I sit by myself till I know myself on the verge of idiocy. I know too, what I have so long

dreaded, that this is an ordinary fate. Women die off so sometimes.
The first step is, of course, that they sink out of sight – no one knows
what becomes of them. Perhaps they take to drink, to make the
process of dying a little shorter, and, at least, less painful.'

The lover of Dora's friend Maria attacks his sweetheart for encouraging Dora in her outrageous idea of wanting to give lectures, in a
passage which reveals the power of the etiquette book, and brilliantly
analyses the cult of true womanhood it propagated in Mary Taylor and
Charlotte Brontë's society:

> You little know the contempt and ridicule such attempts excite.
> You have hitherto been guarded by the respect of the community
> you live amongst. To them you are a living example of patient,
> quiet, Christian womanhood. But once you throw away the charm
> of seclusion, you become a prey to all that slander can do to annoy
> and degrade you.
>
> My white flower in the shade! – till now untouched by stormy
> winds or too burning sunshine! – do you not know how sacred your
> solitude has been to those compelled to face the workaday world?
> With all my heart I beg you not to soil your purity by mixing with
> those who misunderstand a woman's position and duties. . . . My
> white dove! My helpless lady! Wait! Wait a little longer, and be
> sure help will come!

To which Maria replies with spirit: 'Your white dove and white flower
are merely decorations to hide fetters too heavy for me to bear.'[31]

Mary's determined attitudes had helped rescue Charlotte from
being buried alive at Haworth but the positive report to Ellen of how
well everything was going in Brussels for the Brontës proved
premature. In September came news of the completely unexpected
death of William Weightman from cholera, which was only the
prelude to a dreary winter of death and change. At twenty-eight he
was only two years older than Charlotte, and three older than
Branwell, to whom he had been a kind and understanding friend, and
a good influence. Branwell had been fired from his railway clerk's job
that spring in shameful circumstances; money was missing from the
accounts, for which Branwell was held responsible as the person in
charge, although it was the porter who was technically guilty. Since
then he had been living at home again, without employment, and
Willie Weightman's end now confirmed his increasingly dark view of
life; it was one of unending sorrow, in which he gave way to ceaseless
morbid thoughts, seeming to feel the brush of death's wings every
day, till even his adoring circle at Bradford began to remonstrate with
him for his unremitting gloom.

175

At the funeral Branwell broke down, listening to his father's simple, heartfelt sermon in which he praised the young man for his character and for having been a model priest: 'His character wore well, the surest proof of real worth. He had, it is true, some peculiar advantages. Agreeable in person and manners, and constitutionally cheerful, his first introduction was prepossessing. But what he gained at first he did not lose afterwards. . . . We were ever like father and son, giving and taking mutual advice.'[32] A more satisfactory son, Mr Brontë would be forgiven for thinking, than the wretched fellow sobbing uncontrollably before him.

And then in late September, the ever lively and charming Martha Taylor went down with what at first appeared to be dysentery, and which was diagnosed too late as cholera. Charlotte had no idea of the severity of her illness until the day before she died. She rushed off to the Château on 13 October, only to hear that Martha had died during the night. Charlotte, like the rest of Martha's family and friends, was stunned by the news. There had been nothing to suggest how short Martha's life would be. She was only twenty-three.

She was buried in the Protestant cemetery on the Chaussée de Louvain, far out beyond the city walls, and Mary was taken away to stay with her cousins the Dixons who lived in Brussels. Mary, Charlotte and Emily visited her grave two weeks later and spent the evening with the Dixon family. The sombre sky, the special nature of the trees common to graveyards – the cypress, the willow, the yew – the stone crosses with their garlands of evergreens and flowers, all impressed themselves on Charlotte's memory. Mary's demeanour moved her profoundly: 'She who had nursed Martha so tenderly, who was more than a mother, more than a sister, appears calm and serious now: no bursts of violent emotion, no exaggeration of distress.' But the thought of Martha's ashes lying in foreign soil, surrounded by aliens, separated by religion, haunted Charlotte, and years later she evoked the memory of that day in *Shirley*, in the description of the visit to the grave of Jessie Yorke, who was based on Martha Taylor.

This evening reminds me too forcibly of another evening some years ago: a howling, rainy autumn evening too – when certain who had that day performed a pilgrimage to a grave new made in a heretic cemetery, sat near a wood fire on the hearth of a foreign dwelling. They were merry and social, but they each knew that a gap, never to be filled, had been made in their circle. They knew they had lost something whose absence could never be quite atoned for, so long as they lived; and they knew that heavy falling rain was soaking into the wet earth which covered their lost darling; and that the sad, sighing gale was mourning above her buried head.

176

Two days after their visit to the grave, a letter arrived telling them that Miss Branwell was ill of an internal obstruction and not expected to live. Charlotte and Emily immediately made preparations to go home, but before they could set off a second letter arrived informing them of her death, on 29 October. Too late by now for her funeral, they nevertheless determined to return home to sort out domestic affairs. Someone would be needed to replace Miss Branwell in looking after their father's needs.

Emily was thankful to be shaking the inimical Belgian dust off her feet. Charlotte departed with considerable regret. The Hegers for their part would not accept a break in the studies of such a promising pupil, and Charlotte carried with her a letter from M. Heger to Mr Brontë appealing to him not to let this sad event interfere with the rest of his daughters' course of studies. Perhaps she might return.

CHAPTER X

The Black Swan

Aunt Branwell may have been fussy and set in her ways, with a tendency to restrict her nieces' behaviour, but she was a kindly woman who had been a part of their lives since early childhood, and with her death the last fleshly link with their shadowy mother vanished. Although Charlotte was not overwhelmed with grief, it would be mistaken to see Aunt Branwell as the inspiration for Mrs Reed. Her nieces felt her loss, symbolised by their aunt's empty room, full of those personal possessions that evoke the dead so powerfully – her workboxes, her eye-glass, her rings, her clothes. Three of Charlotte's intimate circle were gone in two months; 'how dreary and void everything seems', she wrote wearily to Ellen from the house made still more grey by the sad November weather.

Branwell made up for his sisters' restraint. As his aunt's favourite and the only Brontë child at home when she died, he had found the spectacle of her final illness an agonising experience, coming so soon after William Weightman's death. The melancholic state in which he had been living since his dismissal from his post on the railway in April increased, to the point where he wallowed almost voluptuously in his grief and leaned towards an enthusiasm for sentimental effect that even his friends found difficult to tolerate. He wrote to his friend Grundy that he must excuse his scrawl as he was attending at his aunt's deathbed and 'my eyes are too dim with sorrow to see well'. Grundy's sister had taken him to task for over-indulgence in 'gloomy visions of this world or another', and Grundy himself had suggested he check his tendency to complain about his lot.

According to Grundy, Branwell had been dismissed from his job for 'constant carelessness'. When he and the porter were hauled up before the Company after the auditors had found a discrepancy of £11 1s 7d in the accounts, Branwell was not suspected of theft but he could not account for the loss. Investigation of the ledgers, which were

Branwell's responsibility to keep as clerk to the railway, showed a sorry record of hours of daydreaming: instead of rows of neat figures, the margins, like so many of the books the Brontës owned, were covered with caricatures and drawings. Branwell's absences from the office drinking with friends had sometimes turned into bouts of days, during which time the porter had been left alone in the ticket office and had been able to purloin the not inconsiderable sum missing from the accounts.[1]

Branwell would castigate himself for his life at Luddenden Foot: 'I would rather give my hand than undergo again the grovelling careless-ness, the malignant yet cold debauchery, the determination to find how far mind could carry body without both being chucked into hell, which too often marked my conduct when there, lost as I was to all I really liked.' To those with a less exaggerated sense of sin, Branwell did not appear so horrifying. He was sufficiently liked and respected by the worthies of the area for them to get up a petition to the railway company to ask that he should be re-employed. But it was to no avail, and Branwell had since been loafing around Haworth, drinking too much, still partly living in the more satisfactory world of Angria. He was encouraged some way in his ideas of being a poet by his artist friend Leyland, and by his poem on the Afghan War being published in the *Leeds Intelligencer* on 7 May. This poem, as morbid as much of his poetry, considers the twenty thousand-odd troops and camp fol-lowers murdered at the Khyber Pass in January 1842. With its patri-otic call to arms it is fairly predictable, if vigorous. Thus a typical verse:

> Breasts and banners, crushed and gory,
>   That seemed once invincible;
> England's children – England's glory,
>   Moslem sabres smite and quell!

Branwell was also partially employed by the sexton, his friend and fellow mason John Brown, to do his correspondence for the commis-sioning of gravestones and their design. The post of clerk to the railways had been far from the glittering future his family had fondly envisaged for him ever since he was a precocious little boy; now it seemed that even the discipline of clerical work was beyond his capabilities.

In her will, Miss Branwell left no money to Branwell. Mrs Gaskell believed mistakenly that Branwell had been cut out of it because his reckless expenditure had distressed her. In fact the will had been drawn up over ten years before, in 1833, when Branwell's scutcheon was still brilliant and unblemished, so one must conclude that the reason she left him no money was because she had no fears that he would be able to earn his own living with so many talents at his disposal. Instead, brought up in an age when women did not work, and perhaps mindful of the pleasure of the measure of independence her own money had given her, she divided her small fortune between her four favourite nieces – the fourth being one of the daughters of her sister Jane Kingston. Through immensely frugal living, and despite her insistence on paying her brother-in-law for her keep these past twenty years, she had managed to accrue a sum in the region of £1,200 from the small annuity of £40 per annum left to her by her father.

In addition, she bequeathed Charlotte her Indian workbox, Emily her workbox with a china top and, rather curiously, in view of Emily's extreme reclusiveness, her ivory fan. Branwell received her japanned dressing box, and Anne the most valuable of her individual belongings – her watch with all its fobs. Her other personal effects, her eye-glass and its chain, her rings, her silver spoons, books and clothes, she left to be divided between the three girls, the division to be made by Mr Brontë, 'according as their father shall think proper'. She also made it plain that she wished to be buried as she had lived, 'in a moderate and decent manner', and requested that her remains should be deposited in the church as near as was convenient to her sister.

Her death left the pressing question of the domestic arrangements at the parsonage. Filial duty for the Victorians taking precedence over any independent feminine life, it obviously fell to Charlotte or Emily to take their aunt's place. Anne, reassuring her sisters about her delicate state of health, was to continue in her governess's post at Thorp Green. Even as a little girl Charlotte had shown her keen sense of responsibility as the eldest surviving daughter – driving herself exceptionally hard at Roe Head so that she could pass on to her sisters all the knowledge she possibly could, taking on the teaching post at Roe Head to contribute to her father's pocket when he would have been stretched financially by trying to pay for Branwell at the Royal Academy and Anne at Roe Head – and she now had to balance this strong sense of duty against her wish to return to Brussels.

On the surface the decision appeared easy. Emily, always happier at home than anywhere else, would not be averse to taking on the role of their father's prop. On the sisters' return she had willingly taken up her old domestic duties – baking the bread and doing some of the housework; it left her free to dream about Gondal, to continue to write poetry about her imaginary cruel race of heroes, which she could now do uninterrupted by lessons or small children. Charlotte, less contentedly, borrowed books from the Keighley Library and visited Ellen at Brookroyd. Her friend was beset as usual by family problems relating to her many brothers and sisters, in which as an unmarried

1a Patrick Brontë's birthplace at Emdale
in County Down, Northern Ireland.

1b A portrait of Maria Branwell,
aged sixteen, by J. Tonkin.

1c Patrick Brontë in the early 1800s,
in his late twenties. Artist unknown.

2a The moors beyond the parsonage. The farmhouse is known as Top Withens, and may have been the inspiration for *Wuthering Heights*.

2b Nineteenth-century engraving of Haworth. The parsonage is the building on the horizon to the left of the church tower.

3a The steep Main Street of Haworth at the turn of the century.

3b Haworth parsonage, probably photographed in the mid-1850s.

4a Group portrait of Charlotte, Emily and Anne by Branwell Brontë, c. 1834. Branwell originally included himself in the painting, but then painted himself out, hence the presence of what appears to be a pillar. The atrocious condition of the painting is a result of the fact that the canvas was taken back to Ireland by Charlotte's husband, Arthur Nicholls, and kept folded up for approximately forty years.

4b Recently discovered self-portrait of Branwell, aged about twenty-three.

4c Anne Brontë aged fourteen, drawn by Charlotte Brontë.

5a Engraving of Cowan Bridge School in 1824, the year Charlotte attended it, by O. Jowett. As in *Jane Eyre*, 'a covered veranda ran down one side, and broad walks bordered a middle space divided into scores of little beds'.

5b The Rev. William Carus Wilson, the inspiration for Mr Brocklehurst: 'his features were large, and they and all the lines of his frame were equally large and prim'. Drawing by J. Dickson.

6a Engraving hanging in the parsonage of
'Belshazzar's Feast' by John Martin. The
monumental palaces in his visionary paintings
helped inspire Charlotte and Branwell's imaginary
world of Glass Town.

6b The Duke of Zamorna,
Charlotte's Byronic hero, drawn by Branwell.

6c Four little books of early juvenilia.

7a Miss Wooler's school at Roe Head, drawn by Charlotte Brontë.

7b Drawing of Ellen Nussey
as a girl by Charlotte Brontë.

8a *left* Constantin Heger aged fifty-nine, painted by Joseph Gerard in 1868. **8b** *right* The Heger family painted by Ange François in 1848, four years after Charlotte left Brussels. Judging by later photographs, the Gerard portrait is the better likeness. L. to r. back row: M. Heger, Prosper, Louise; l. to r. front row: Victorine, Mme Heger, Paul, Marie, Claire.

8c The Rue d'Isabelle and the Pensionnat Heger in 1909, a last view of the school and garden in which the greater part of the action of *Villette* takes place, much as Charlotte Brontë would have seen them, before they vanished when the area was redeveloped. The pear trees were uprooted before this picture was taken.

daughter sitting at home all day she was endlessly embroiled. In early January Ellen was persuaded to venture out from the greater comfort of her own home and the security of her relatives to make a return visit to the brilliant, nervous Brontës at Haworth, where Branwell would tease her for her airs and graces and pronouncements on what was proper and improper. By then the relaxed atmosphere of home had wrought its usual magical effects on Charlotte and she was back to twitting Ellen about the Taylor brothers' pursuit of her mild, fair person, and her final dismissal of the vacillating Mr Vincent. These girlish matters could be enjoyed because they no longer seemed to be the horizon of her life. The Hegers' interest in her held out a promise of greater things.

M. Heger's strongly persuasive and eulogistic letter to Mr Brontë about his daughters urged the necessity of the girls returning to Brussels. It had been closely followed by a warm personal letter to Charlotte from Mme Heger, which repeated the message. In excited French, the voluble M. Heger felicitated Mr Brontë on being the father of two young women who had made such remarkable progress in all branches of teaching. The education and sentiments he had found in Mr Brontë's daughters could only give him and Mme Heger a very high opinion of his merit and character. The progress of his children was entirely due to their love of work and their perseverance, for which he could claim no credit; it must all be Mr Brontë's doing. As a teacher he frankly could not hide the fact of his own 'chagrin et de l'inquiétude' at losing his 'two dear pupils'.[2]

In his view Mr Brontë's daughters needed a year or more in order to be 'quite prepared for any eventuality of the future, each of them while receiving instruction was at the same time acquiring the science of teaching'. Miss Emily was learning the piano, 'receiving lessons from the best professor in Belgium, and she herself already had little pupils: she was losing whatever remained of ignorance, and also of what was worse, timidity. . . . Miss Charlotte was beginning to give lessons in French and to acquire that assurance, that aplomb, so necessary to a teacher.' Charlotte was emphasised more than Emily. For her, 'Only another year and the work would have been completed, and well-completed.' After that period the Hegers would be able, if it were convenient to Mr Brontë, to offer 'to your daughters, or at least to one of them, a position according with her taste, and that pleasant independence so difficult for a young person to find'.

The letter ended in M. Heger's characteristically warm personal fashion, perhaps a little high flown for Mr Brontë's taste: 'This is not, believe me, Sir – this is not a question of personal interest: it is a question of affection. You will pardon me if I speak of your children, if we interest ourselves in their welfare, as if they were part of our

181

family: their personal qualities, their good nature, their intense zeal, are the sole reasons which impel us to run the risk of your displeasure.'[3]

Such an accolade, such distinct professional encouragement of her ambitions, was enough to convince Charlotte – and her father – that she should go back to Brussels. She would return home in a year, as would Anne, and then all three would open what Emily happily imagined would be a 'flourishing seminary', the money from Aunt's legacy enabling them to make suitable alterations to the parsonage. The lingering problem of Branwell had even been taken care of, at least for the present, for Anne had managed to find him a position as tutor to Edmund Robinson, the eleven-year-old son of the family to which she was governess at Thorp Green, at a very decent salary.

Greatly as Charlotte desired to go back to Brussels, it can have been no easy step for her to take. It was against the notions of the age for a young woman to follow wholeheartedly her own wishes; she was abandoning her role as eldest daughter and allowing Emily, of a far less practical, organised nature than herself, to look after their father. A vein of self-sacrifice, accentuated by social conditioning, was always very close to the surface in Charlotte, and in going back to Brussels she was in a sense kicking over the traces. The motives that enabled her to act so seemingly out of character have been questioned, particularly in the light of her remark to Ellen Nussey three years later: 'I returned to Brussels after Aunt's death against my conscience – prompted by what then seemed an irresistible impulse – I was punished for my selfish folly by a total withdrawal for more than two years of happiness and peace of mind.'[4]

This has been taken as evidence that Charlotte in effect recognised that she was drawn back to Brussels by her adulterous love for M. Heger. But it is clear from her puzzled letters to Ellen from Brussels over the next year that she was scarcely capable of articulating what she felt for M. Heger during that time, and it seems extraordinarily unlikely that Charlotte would have returned to Brussels on account of any acknowledged irresistible love for M. Heger. She and Branwell had frequently expressed an unorthodox attitude to adultery in the Angrian novelettes, and it is possible that at some later point in her writings she did contemplate the idea of adultery with M. Heger, but that is fiction and fantasy, not the real life, where Charlotte was a clergyman's daughter and only too conscious of sin. Indeed, if she had really analysed her feeling for M. Heger and found it to be (adulterous) love, she would surely not have decided to return to Brussels.

For Charlotte, ambitious, wanting to make something of herself, stimulated intellectually as never before by her teacher, M. Heger's opinion that she needed another year's study must have been sufficient 'irresistible impulse', leaving aside any inadmissible personal attraction she felt for him. Her statement made in the light of her subsequent terrible unhappiness that she returned to Brussels 'against my conscience', a phrase which on its own could be taken as an admission of sin, must be seen in conjunction with the phrase that follows: '. . . I was punished for my selfish folly'. 'Selfish folly' only makes sense in relation to Mr Brontë or Emily, not in relation to the Hegers, as the context of the letter makes clear. Charlotte was relating to Ellen why she could not leave home to start a school with her:

> Had I no will or interest to consult but my own, were I an isolated being without ties or duties connected with others, I should probably with pleasure and promptitude have cast in my lot with yours. . . . More than one very favourable opportunity has now offered which I have been obliged to put aside – probably when I am free to leave home I shall neither be able to find place nor employment – perhaps too I shall be quite past the prime of life – my faculties will be rusted – and my few acquirements in a great measure forgotten – These ideas sting me keenly sometimes – but whenever I consult my Conscience it affirms that I am doing right in staying at home – and bitter are its upbraidings when I yield to an eager desire for release.[5]

Immediately after this sentence, Charlotte cites the parallel case of her return to Brussels against her conscience. The misery of her experience there had by this time convinced her of the rectitude of following the path of filial duty, and in another letter earlier that year she would urge Ellen to follow the path of greatest self-sacrifice, making the case for duty and religion in a way which was by 1846 increasingly becoming second nature to her. The woman who had loathed cant and hypocrisy and regarded religion as abhorrent now wrote as follows:

> You cannot decide whether duty or religion command you to go out into the cold and friendless world and then to earn your *bread* by governess drudgery, or whether they enjoin your continued stay with your aged mother, neglecting *for the present*, every prospect of independency for yourself, and putting up with daily inconvenience, sometimes even privations. . . . The right path is that which necessitates the greatest sacrifice of self-interest – which implies the greatest good to others; and this path, steadily followed, will lead, I believe, in time, to prosperity, to happiness.[6]

When she left Haworth on 27 January 1843 for her second year at the

Pensionnat, Charlotte seemingly had no premonition of her fate. She was in a nervous, rather excited mood, perhaps feeling a twinge of suppressed guilt at her enthusiasm for M. Heger, and though the journey went badly from start to finish, she refused to allow it to bow her spirits. She was travelling unaccompanied, an adventurous way for a young woman to behave. By ill luck the train that she caught from Leeds at 9.00 in the morning was two hours late in arriving, not reaching London till 10 o'clock at night, and thus put paid to Charlotte's plan to stay at the Chapter Coffee House. By Yorkshire habits to have arrived so late would be unseemly. She perhaps panicked a little as her next step was still more unseemly: she decided to go straight on board the Ostend packet, and commanded her cab to take her straight from the station to London Bridge Wharf, where she ordered startled watermen to row her out to the boat. The scene, which Mrs Gaskell tells us is 'pretty much as she has since described it in *Villette*', with the watermen ribbing her and frightening her with their rough oaths, must have been made more startling by the diminutive size of the watermen's doughty little passenger sitting firmly upright amidst the darkness and the waves. It was a strange quirk in her character that despite her isolation, 'with two rude rowers for companions, whose insane oaths still tortured my ear', she found that she was neither terrified nor made wretched. 'Often in my life have I been far more so under comparatively safe circumstances. "How is this" said I. "Methinks I am animated and alert, instead of being depressed and apprehensive?"'

But such behaviour always took it out of her physically. She arrived in Brussels by her own admission completely exhausted from the three days of travelling, and was received with great kindness by Mme Heger. With the sympathy that many of her former pupils attested to, Madame realised that Charlotte would miss Emily's companionship and at first she made an effort to include Charlotte in the Hegers' social life. Charlotte was told to consider their sitting-room her own, and to go there whenever she was not engaged in the schoolroom.

The first month passed pleasantly enough. Charlotte was now addressed as Mademoiselle Charlotte, and though it appears from the evidence of *Villette* that she found it hard at first to maintain order, her small size, youthful appearance, soft voice and nervousness not being immediate aids to authority, the teaching became easier. Meanwhile she had found a congenial household to visit in the Dixon family, those relatives of Mary Taylor resident in Brussels, and was in a positively gay mood.

Mary Dixon was thirty-two, only five years older than Charlotte, who admiringly considered her 'an elegant and accomplished person' and very ladylike. The two women spent many happy hours together, during which Mary sketched Charlotte. On one envelope containing a letter to Mary she has written with some brio: 'Lest you think this comes from some mustachioed young gent, I beg to inform you that it is from Miss Brontë, and may be forwarded with propriety. C.B.'[7] Mary was keeping house for her widowed father, Abraham Dixon, who had been married to Mary Taylor's aunt Laetitia. He was an inventor, living at 11 Rue de la Régime in Brussels, who made a living of sorts selling industrial patents to the Belgian government and Belgian woollen manufacturers. Mary Taylor had valued the Dixons' company highly in the immediate aftermath of Martha's death, describing them as 'the most united affectionate family I ever met with. They have taken me as one of themselves, and made me such a comfortable happy home that I should like to live here all my life'. And they evidently made Charlotte equally welcome. Mary Dixon called on her one afternoon a few days after she arrived back from London. It was a lively household full of young people: Mary's brother Tom was still involved in his studies – he took lessons in German from King Leopold's librarian in the royal palace itself – and the other two Dixon sons, Abraham and George, were frequently over from Yorkshire on commercial business.

As usual Charlotte was dismissive of these specimens of the flower of English manhood. George Dixon, as a member of a firm of Birmingham export merchants dealing with Belgium, travelled between the two countries and obligingly carried Charlotte's letters to England for her. (Postal costs were considerable and made frequent correspondence impossible for people for whom every penny counted like the Brontës.) But in some way George Dixon aroused her irritation: she told Ellen that he was 'a pretty-looking and pretty-behaved young man, apparently constructed without a backbone; by which I don't allude to his corporeal spine, which is all right enough, but to his character'. George Dixon would in fact become an educational reformer and Liberal M P. Charlotte's caustic tongue was perhaps a defensive measure against what she felt to be her glaring lack of physical attraction; Mrs Gaskell reports her being convinced that a gentleman had averted his eyes from her. With such painful self-doubts, the contrast must have been all the more marked in her dealings with M. Heger, to whom her looks appeared to be of no importance, and who was so admiring of her intelligence.

Although Charlotte could no longer visit Mary Taylor, who was now teaching in Germany, the Wheelwright family continued to be very kind and invited her to their hotel in the Rue Cluysenaar more frequently now that she was no longer accompanied by Emily. Their apartments would be the inspiration of the Hotel Crécy in *Villette*: 'It was a hotel in the foreign sense: a collection of dwelling-houses, not an inn – a vast lofty pile, with a huge arch in its street door, leading through a vaulted covered way, into a square, all built round.[8] However, the age difference between Charlotte and the daughters, and the ten-year gap between her and the parents necessarily made the friendship rather distant, and the very carefree atmosphere of the home had been affected by the death of seven-year-old Julia Wheelwright, the youngest child, in November of the previous year, shortly after the Brontës had left for England. She had died of cholera, for which, in the Wheelwrights' opinion, the school's poor sanitary arrangements were partly to blame.[9] Whatever the truth, it is interesting that both Charlotte and Emily, whose health was a constant source of anxiety, enjoyed on the whole exceptionally good health during the period they were in Brussels.

But despite the efforts of the Hegers and her English friends, Charlotte was very lonely without Emily's companionship. Teaching would always be a strain to her; nor could she completely support herself on the £16 per annum which Mme Heger was paying for her services. She had to make what she called an 'unconscionable demand for money' from her father so that she could have German lessons, which were ten francs a month: 'This, with the five francs per month to the Blanchisseuse, makes havoc in £16 per annum.'

Deprived of Emily's comforting presence, with Mary Taylor now far away in Germany, there was no one with whom Charlotte could exchange observations and ideas on the daily basis which was so necessary for her confiding nature. She felt she was a good deal by herself, which as she realised could so easily mean her falling into low spirits. Although as she angrily told Ellen in early March, M. and Mme Heger were the only people in the Pensionnat for whom she felt esteem or regard, she felt she could not and would not intrude on their family life in the evening as they had suggested.[10] Perhaps if she had availed herself of the Hegers' invitation to spend the evenings *en famille* in their sitting room, M. Heger would not have taken on such a god-like image, with his attentions appearing a life-saving oasis in the midst of her self-imposed desert; rather, he would have been reinforced in her eyes as the contented paterfamilias he so evidently appeared to the rest of the world. During the day, their sitting room was a busy public room where music masters and mistresses were constantly passing in and out.

The Hegers' youngest son Paul, who was born three years after Charlotte left Brussels, and who would become Professor of Physiology at the Université Libre de Bruxelles, wrote of his childhood:

Nous n'avons connu pendant notre jeunesse que des jours heureux: une grande intimité règnait entre le Père, la mère et les enfants; je

ne me souviens pas avoir entendu maman élèver la voix: elle était
douce et d'une grande fermeté: elle n'eut d'autre orientation dans
toute sa vie que de créer du bonheur autour d'elle. . . . Elle était
pieuse, très croyante, mais pas cléricèle du tout. Le Père était d'un
tempérament généreux et ardent, il aimait sa profession, il s'y
adorait de tout coeur. Il avait parfois des accès de colère, mais si vite
passés et suivis de ces effusions de bonté qui montaient toute la
générosité de son coeur.

A la table de famille on causait très librement; le Père avait un
esprit très vif, beaucoup d'humour, il adorait la plaisanterie: nous
avions beaucoup d'amis et la maison était hospitalière.[11]

Although this was written many years later, after Charlotte had
become famous and her relationship with M. Heger had come under
scrutiny, there is little doubt of the central importance of family life to
the Hegers. To Charlotte, so much by herself out of school hours,
each ordinary encounter with the Professor became imbued with a
significance it did not merit, and the English lessons which she had
begun to give him and his brother-in-law became the high spot of the
day. She told Ellen proudly on 6 March: 'They get on with wonderful
rapidity, especially the first [i.e. M. Heger]. He already begins to
speak English very decently. If you see and hear the efforts I make to
teach them to pronounce like Englishmen, and their unavailing
attempts to imitate, you would laugh to all eternity.'

At the recent Carnival preceding Lent, M. Heger had enthusiastically and perhaps unwisely taken Charlotte and another pupil into the
town to see the revelries and the masks. She had found the whole
experience, she told Ellen in the same letter, 'animating', with 'the
immense crowds and the general gaiety'; it would be brilliantly
transmogrified with the patriotic fête later on in the summer to the
surreal fête scene in *Villette*, when Lucy wanders out in the town by
night. Her third reference to M. Heger in the letter is still more
telling: she worried about Mary, who she thought did not sound
particularly happy in Germany, for 'she has nobody to be as good to
her as M. Heger is to me; to lend her books, to converse with her
sometimes, etc.'

Perhaps unsurprisingly in view of their obvious rapport and his
sympathetic interest in her, Charlotte was becoming increasingly emotionally reliant upon M. Heger, but from her letters to Ellen, which
are the main source of evidence of the progress of her feelings, it seems
that she deliberately blinded herself to the way they were tending, and
the necessary consequences. Those who knew M. Heger protested
that the portrait of M. Paul Emanuel was identical to him up until the
moment when he falls in love with Lucy Snowe. Yet certain aspects of

M. Paul's behaviour which betray his growing feeling for Lucy Snowe may well have been based on M. Heger's idiosyncratic behaviour, and to a lonely, excitable and naïve young woman, they could well lend themselves to misinterpretation. He certainly pressed books on Charlotte, as he did on all his pupils, and given his slightly childlike nature, his love of surprise and excitement, it is not unlikely that those books, like M. Paul's presents to Lucy, would appear overnight in her desk: 'I saw the brownie's work, in exercises left overnight full of faults, and found the next morning carefully corrected: I profited by his capricious goodwill in loans full welcome and refreshing. Between a sallow dictionary and worn-out grammar would magically grow a fresh interesting new work, or a classic, mellow and sweet in its ripe age.' The acrid smell of cigars, sign of M. Paul having been there, must have been suggested by M. Heger, who was permanently wreathed in cigar smoke.

The *devoirs* of Charlotte's that have survived showing M. Heger's comments reveal his enthusiasm for her brilliance. 'Très bon', and 'excellent' are scribbled in the margins.[12] Lessons were a delight for pupil and teacher. Three Angrian manuscripts which turned up on a second-hand book stall in Brussels at the turn of the century suggest that she was sufficiently encouraged by his enthusiasm to bring them back from Haworth on her second visit to Brussels to show them to him[13] – a mark of her high regard to him and of a certain intimacy, for no one else had ever been privileged to see them outside her brother and sisters. What he made of these curious, wildly romantic effusions, history does not relate.

She certainly told him of her literary ambitions, and in an essay on Millevoye's *La Chute des Feuilles* poured out a theory of writing which might almost be a personal manifesto:

If for instance the sentiment possessing for the moment the empire of our mind is sorrow, will not the genius sharpen the sorrow and the sorrow purify the genius? Together, will they not be like a cut diamond for which language is only the wax on which they stamp their imprint? I believe that genius, thus awakened, has no need to seek out details, that it scarcely pauses to reflect, that it never thinks of unity: I believe that the details come naturally without search by the poet, that inspiration takes the place of reflection and as for unity, I think there is no unity so perfect as that which results from a heart filled with a single idea. . . . The nature of genius is related to that of instinct; its operation is both simple and marvellous.[14]

M. Heger, in response, measuredly told her to study form: 'If you are a poet, you will be more powerful – your works will live – if the

188

contrary is the case, you will not create poetry, but you will enjoy with discrimination its merit and charm.'[15] As a vocational teacher himself, who was expending much time and effort on preparing Charlotte Brontë for a teaching career, it seems unlikely that he encouraged her in her literary ambitions. Furthermore, his general attitude towards the capabilities of the female sex, although progressive in mid-nineteenth-century terms, was not quite advanced enough to view women as anything other than appendages of their husbands and children, judging by the maxims he sent to an old pupil: 'Housewifery is essential for a woman, but it is not enough by itself and is even a drawback in society. The bee, admirable in its hive, is nothing more than an annoying fly'; and 'It is not desirable for a woman to be a blue stocking, but she must be educated. Without education she can neither supervise her children's studies nor share her husband's ideas. Education is a bond between husband and wife – ignorance is a barrier.'[16] In the sharp Frederika Macdonald's view, 'Personally he would have preferred and recommended *religious* methods of prayer, and docile submission to spiritual direction, to any philosophy, especially in the case of women.'[17]

M. Heger has generally been presented as blameless in his conduct towards Charlotte. But can one really acquit him of any untoward behaviour? A letter from Mme Heger to a woman called K, who had been at the Pensionnat in 1860, seventeen years later than Charlotte, and which was written twenty-four years after that, in 1884, shows that there was at least one occasion when M. Heger was overcome by a pretty pair of eyes. The letter is particularly interesting for the light it sheds on M. Heger and his relationship with Mme Heger, to whom he apparently told everything, or to whom all was known:

> You remember, dear K—, having been scolded by M. Heger for . . . a kiss! I take your word for it, but, for my part, I remember that K— gave M. Heger a sharp lesson! K— was ill, or rather convalescent, and her large languid eyes were somehow irresistible. Moved by them, M. Heger allowed himself to make a sort of discreet declaration. 'Who' he asked the little invalid, 'is my best girl?' 'Your wife,' said K— dryly, turning her face to the wall. If you have not forgotten anything, you see, dear K—, that we remember, too . . . We send, dear K—, our sincere expression of goodwill to you, to your husband, and to all your family, and, in spite of the scornful manner with which you received M. Heger's respectful avowal of more tender sentiments, he joins me in kissing you, with your husband as intermediary, on both cheeks, as a proof of affection which endures in spite of time, country or sea.[18]

Perhaps, too, Charlotte's lambent brown eyes gazing adoringly at her teacher produced behaviour in M. Heger that was a little more tender and more flirtatious than was suitable. An idea of the emotional rapport that he encouraged with his pupils, the affection that was all to him, is shown by a letter from M. Heger himself to another former pupil, although it was written forty years later, when he was eighty years old:

> . . . it is true that I have not written, I have nevertheless answered you frequently and at length, and this is how. Letters and the post are not, luckily, the only means of communication, or the best, between people who are really fond of one another: I am not referring to the telephone, which allows one to speak, to have conversations, from a distance. I have something better than that. I only have to think of you to see you. I often give myself the pleasure when my duties are over, when the light fades. I postpone lighting the gas lamp in my library, I sit down, smoking my cigar, and with a hearty will I evoke your image – and you come (without wishing to, I dare say) but I see you, I talk with you – you, with that little air, affectionate undoubtedly, but independent and resolute, firmly determined not to allow any opinion without being previously convinced, demanding to be convinced before allowing yourself to submit – in fact, just as I knew you, my dear M— and as I have esteemed and loved you.
>
> In thinking it over you will have no difficulty in admitting that you yourself have experienced a hundred times that which I tell you about communication between two distant hearts, instantaneous, without paper, without pen, or words, or messenger, etc. a hundred times without noticing it, without its having attracted your attention, without anything extraordinary.[19]

Did that famous telepathic call from Rochester to Jane which pulls her back to her master stem from some similar discussion? Telepathy featured in one of the earliest Glass Town saga stories, and Charlotte herself said that she had undergone a similar experience.

In 1843, despite that 'affection presque paternelle' which he felt for Charlotte and Emily, M. Heger was very far from being a father figure for them. He was still youthful, only a few years older than Charlotte, swarthily handsome, relishing his powers over his pupils. According to one, his literature lessons were

> veritable dramas. . . . He was a magnificent reader – you saw, you felt . . . you went through a riot of emotion, exactly in proportion as he wished. He was compelling. His face was the most mobile poss-

ible; he could express anything he liked in it . . . in talking perhaps he made his profoundest impression by a steadfast often half-mocking gaze at the person. . . . I believe he liked to watch the emotions he could produce with his ever-changing facial expressions and amazing turns of thought and temper.[20]

By April Charlotte's increasing emotional dependence on this compelling figure had produced a new mood. She was considerably less gay. Miss Dixon had left Brussels so she did not have her companionship, the weather had been bitterly cold, and she was very lonely. She sounded off at Ellen, whose most recent letter had hinted that Yorkshire gossip had it that the reason she remained on the continent for such a low salary was because her future husband was there: '. . . if these charitable people knew the total seclusion of the life I lead – that I never exchange a word with any other man than M. Heger and seldom indeed with him – they would perhaps cease to suppose that any such chimerical and groundless notion influenced my proceedings.' It was not that she considered it a crime to marry, or to wish to marry, but it was 'an imbecility which I reject with contempt' for women who neither had money nor looks 'to make marriage the principal object of their wishes and hopes and the aim of all their actions – not to be able to convince themselves that they are unattractive'; 'They had better be quiet and think of other things than wedlock,' she ended savagely.

She could refuse to acknowledge her feelings to herself, remain unconscious of resentment of Mme Heger's marital happiness, but one person in the Pensionnat was not deceived. By 1 May the English lessons had come to an end, at what seems to have been Mme Heger's doing; M. Heger's English would remain idiosyncratic to the end of his life, so lack of need because of the pupil's high standard was not a reason for terminating them. Madame was no longer as friendly, and the ending of the English lessons helped ensure that Charlotte rarely saw her husband. In a revealing letter to Branwell of this time, Charlotte referred to Monsieur as 'the black swan', a romantic term that she might easily have used about the Duke of Zamorna in the fantasies of their youth. The eternal romantic and enemy of convention, she returned to her criticism of the Belgian character, telling her brother: 'They are very false in their relations with each other, but they rarely quarrel, and friendship is a folly they are unacquainted with. The black swan, M. Heger, is the only sole veritable exception to this rule (for Madame, always cool and always reasoning, is not quite an exception). But I rarely speak to Monsieur now, for not being a pupil I have little or nothing to do with him. From time to time he shows his kind-heartedness by loading me with books, so that I am still indebted to him for all the pleasure or amusement I have.'

She begged Branwell to ask Anne to send her a letter in his reply, to liven her existence. 'It will be a real charity to do me this kindness. Tell me everything you can think of.' To Branwell alone she could confess that once again Angria was creeping up on her, to comfort her as it had when she was a teacher at Roe Head: 'It is a curious metaphysical fact that always in the evening when I am in the great dormitory alone, having no other company than a number of beds with white curtains, I always recur as fanatically as ever to the old ideas, the old faces, and the old scenes in the world below.' It was not a good sign.

Perhaps to distract herself, perhaps to regulate Angria, perhaps in defiance of the teaching career M. Heger was so anxious for her to follow, she scribbled the following scheme for a 'magazine tale' on the cover of her German exercise book:

Time – from 30 to 50 years ago
Country – England
Scene – rural
Rank – middle
Person – first
Subject – Certain remarkable occurrences
Sex of writer – at discretion
No. of characters – at discretion
Plot – domestic – the romantic not excluded
Opening – cheerful or gloomy
Occurrences – 1st, reverses of fortune
                2nd, new arrival
                3rd, loss of relatives
                4th, crosses in the affections
                5th, going abroad and returning
                6th [blank]
Characters – Hero – heroine – family of do. – Rival or rivaless – villains. N.B. Moderation to be observed here.
            Friends – avoid Richardsonian multiplication.
P.S. As much compression – as little explanation as may be.
Mem. To be set about with proper spirit.
            To be carried out with the same.
            To be concluded idem.
Observe – no grumbling allowed.[21]

Charlotte was also reworking many of her earlier poems, possibly, at the back of her mind, with the intention of publishing them. But despite her valiant resolution to set about her writing with proper spirit, 'no grumbling allowed', she was becoming increasingly despondent, almost hysterical, in her daily life. By the end of May she was convinced that one of the mistresses, Mademoiselle Blanche, was spying on her and reporting what she said to Mme Heger. She scarcely saw the Hegers from one day to the next. She told Emily she could not tell why Mme Heger did not like her, 'nor do I think she herself has any definite reason for the aversion'. She thought that Mme Heger could not understand why she would not become friends with the other mistresses, as indeed would perhaps have been natural. Apparently unaware of the implications, she went on to Emily:

M. Heger is wondrously influenced by Madame, and I should not wonder if he disapproves very much of my unamiable want of sociability. He has already given me a brief lecture on universal *bienveillance*, and, perceiving that I don't improve in consequence, I fancy he has taken to considering me as a person to be let alone – left to the error of her ways; and consequently he has in great measure withdrawn the light of his countenance, and I get on from day to day in a Robinson Crusoe-like condition – very lonely.

Depressed, her tendency to have what she called 'indefinite fears' about those at home – a legacy of her overcast youth – increased. A letter from her father in June relieved her mind: all was well, and despite losing the girl who had been assisting the seventy-year-old Tabby he had decided to keep Tabby on, a decision Charlotte applauded, both as a charitable act that would be rewarded by the faithful Tabby's services and because it would mean company for Emily.

Charlotte was by now making an effort to behave in a *convenant* and sociable way, and on the early June holiday went on a long walk into the Belgian countryside with Mlle Haussé, one of the despised mistresses, and three of the schoolgirls. Try as she might though, her mercurial, sensitive temperament could find nothing in common with her slow, passionless companions. She wrote angrily to Branwell:

They have not intellect or politeness or good-nature or good-feeling. They are nothing. I don't hate them – hatred would be too warm a feeling. They have no sensations themselves and they excite none. But one wearies from day to day of caring nothing, fearing nothing, liking nothing, hating nothing, being nothing, doing nothing – yes, I teach and sometimes get red in the face with impatience at their stupidity. But don't think I ever scold or fly into a passion. If I spoke warmly, as warmly as I sometimes used to do at

Roe Head, they would think me mad. Nobody ever gets into a passion here. Such a thing is not known. The phlegm that thickens their blood is too gluey to boil.

And chief among these women whose ideas on life presented such a contrast to her own was Mme Heger. Her good looks, her obvious serene fulfilment as a wife and mother, her enlarging figure, pregnant with her fifth child, symbol of the Hegers' happy marriage, her quiet presence directing the life of the Pensionnat, began to grate on Charlotte. Mme Heger's sensible custom of wearing soft slippers so that she might move quietly about the classrooms (the continental habit of *surveillance* that the forthright English Wheelwright girls said they too found rather disturbing) began to take on sinister overtones; it seemed to Charlotte that Mme Heger was preventing her from seeing Monsieur.

To Mme Heger, Charlotte's nervous excitability, so easily fired by poetry or literature, that tendency to enthusiasm which was never controlled or checked – at first so charming, was now a dangerous quality. Miss Brontë was more dependent on her husband than was suitable, however much their relationship was based on a common passion for poetry – and was that all it was? The incident in *The Professor* when Mlle Reuter tries to discourage Mr Crimsworth from singling out Frances Henri for her skill in composition may reflect an actual situation when Mme Heger behaved in a similar way. For Charlotte Brontë would put what are almost exactly the same words Southey used to her to discourage her from writing into Mlle Reuter/ Mme Heger's mouth:

> . . . it appears to me that ambition, *literary* ambition especially, is not a feeling to be cherished in the mind of a woman: would not Mdlle Henri be much safer and happier if taught to believe that in the quiet discharge of social duties consists her real vocation, than if stimulated to aspire after applause and publicity? She may never marry . . . but even in celibacy it would be better for her to retain the character and habits of a respectable decorous female.

To Mme Heger, who told a former pupil almost with tears in her eyes that she should not write poetry, 'that is not a girl's work, and will not add to her usefulness as a woman',[22] to whom being a mother was the greatest of human roles, Charlotte was an incomprehensible being.

The '*surveillance*', depicted to such claustrophobic effect in *Villette*, was stepped up. In her deft way, without informing either party, Mme Heger contrived to make sure that her husband and Miss Brontë rarely saw each other, and were never alone. She could not dismiss

Miss Brontë because it would create a scandal, perhaps wrecking the school's considerable reputation, but if Miss Brontë were made sufficiently uncomfortable, she might leave of her own accord. To one in a state of nervous tension, apparently incapable of facing what she really felt about M. Heger, only aware of her need for him but subsuming it under the mantle of that true friendship which he had been so anxious to encourage, Mme Heger's behaviour began to force it to Charlotte's attention that another interpretation could be put on her feelings.

It is of course impossible to pin down Charlotte Brontë's feelings for M. Heger precisely, but the attacks on the basely sensual nature of Belgian women in *The Professor* may reflect her indignation at her noble and pure ideal of friendship being interpreted so crudely. After all, at the beginning of M. Paul's relationship with Lucy Snowe he asks her to be his sister in all but blood, to have 'true friendship' with him, and for Lucy that is indeed enough:

> While he spoke, the tone of his voice, the light of his now affectionate eye, gave me such pleasure as, certainly I had never felt. I envied no girl her lover, no bride her bridegroom, no wife her husband; I was content with this my voluntary, self-offering friend.

And though friendship turns to passion the passion is of a notably cerebral, almost religious nature. The intensely feeling, despairing letters Charlotte wrote to M. Heger from Haworth two years later can only be described as love letters, to the modern eye demanding a response well beyond the bounds of friendship, but they are entirely couched in platonic terms. However full of sublimated sexuality they may be, their demand is actually for friendship.

On the other hand M. Paul Emanuel, Robert Moore and Mr Rochester are powerfully erotic figures, and at least two poems exist, 'Gilbert' and 'At First I did Attention Give', in which the relationship between the two chief protagonists is unlawful in some way, suggesting the recognition of adulterous impulse on Charlotte's part. Nevertheless these characters, whatever has been read into them, were fictional, and the most convincing explanation of them, particularly given Charlotte's maxim that reality must only suggest, never dictate, is that in her writing she was able to project her wish-fulfilment in a way that could never be expressed in life.

Determined clinging to her ideal of friendship can be the only explanation for Charlotte's continued puzzlement at Madame's coolness for the rest of the year, while dimly guessing that this friendship was taking on the nature of emotional obsession. As the warm summer months drew on, and Monsieur remained a remote figure, the Pensionnat garden now truly seemed Edenlike. She could no longer wander happily about it, seeking out his company, following the trail of his cigar. Now, like Lucy Snowe, Charlotte became the haunter of the *allée défendue*, that dark secluded alley at the bottom of the garden, lined by ancient pear trees, which at the Pensionnat Heger, as at the Pensionnat in *Villette*, was forbidden to the younger girls.

By August, as the girls prepared to leave for the summer holidays, Charlotte was in very low spirits. She told Ellen that for the first time she was dreading the vacation. She would be alone for most of the five weeks, and thought she would inevitably 'get downcast, and find both days and nights of a weary length'. For the first time she mentioned her intention to return home, though not for some months. The Hegers were off to the seaside resort of Blankenberg. The warm invitations to consider herself part of the family were now a thing of the past; there had been no question of Charlotte being invited to join them, although the Hegers must have realised how lonely she would be, with no other pupils in the school.

On 15 August, an annual holiday on the Feast of the Assumption of the Virgin Mary, all the Catholic schools broke up for the summer vacation. Perhaps a little remorseful for his having seen so little of her and conscious that a hot August in dusty Brussels would not be agreeable, M. Heger presented Charlotte with the works of the romantic writer Bernardin de St Pierre in a two-volume edition. Later that day he made the Speech Day address at the Athénée Royale; a copy of the speech would become one of Charlotte's most treasured possessions. In the evening a Serenade Concert was given at 10.00 p.m. in the 'Vauxhall' enclosure of the park. The main item was a German mixed choir whose programme included a 'Jagd Chor'[23] or Choeur de Chasseurs, which features in *Villette* on the night of the fête when the drugged Lucy wanders through the park. Charlotte probably attended the concert with the other teachers, and wandering along the broad sandy walks, with their tall thin trees and neo-classical statuary, the whole scene may have taken on a surreal air for her. So great was her feeling of unhappiness that her perceptions were heightened to that painful degree of awareness which is such a feature of *Villette*.

In the next few days the school dispersed, and Charlotte was left alone, with only Mademoiselle Blanche for company. She wrote to Emily two weeks later to say that the holidays which had passed so far had gone rather better than she expected: the weather had not been so 'Asiatically hot' as last year, so she had been able to go for long walks about Brussels. She was probably bravely drawing a veil over her actual experience during those weeks, the real indication of which lay in her telling Emily, while apparently casually dismissing it as 'an odd whim', that she had slipped through the great baroque gates of the vast medieval Cathedral of St Michel and St Gudule and made a confession. It was her habit to wander, as she described it to Emily, aimlessly about the boulevards of Brussels, 'sometimes for hours altogether'. On 1 September she went on a pilgrimage out of town to the cemetery, and

far beyond it on to a hill where there was nothing but fields as far as the horizon. When I came back it was evening; but I had such a repugnance to return to the house, which contained nothing that I cared for, I still kept threading the streets in the neighbourhood of the Rue d'Isabelle and avoiding it. I found myself opposite to Ste Gudule, and the bell whose voice you know, began to toll for evening *salut*. I went in, quite alone (which procedure you will say is not much like me), wandered about the aisles where a few old women were saying their prayers, till vespers began. I stayed till they were over. Still I could not leave the church or force myself to go home – to school I mean. An odd whim came into my head. In a solitary part of the Cathedral six or seven people still remained kneeling by the confessionals. In two confessionals I saw a priest. I felt as if I did not care what I did, provided it was not absolutely wrong, and that it served to vary my life and yield a moment's interest. I took a fancy to change myself into a Catholic and go and make a real confession to see what it was like. Knowing me as you do, you will think this odd, but when people are by themselves they have singular fancies.

Was she overpowered by the splendour of the great cathedral; forced to sudden intimacy with her own thoughts and an equally sudden longing for comfort or at least impersonal human contact?

She could make out a penitent who was confessing through a grating, whispering so low to the priest that she could hardly hear their voices. She stood and watched two or three penitents go and return, as she told Emily, and then in the immense semi-darkness glimmering with yellow candles, 'I approached at last and knelt down in a niche which was just vacated'. She had to kneel there for ten minutes, waiting because there was another penitent on the other side whose presence she had not been aware of.

At last that went away and a little wooden door inside the grating opened, and I saw the priest leaning his ear towards me. I was obliged to begin, and yet I did not know a word of the formula with which they always commence their confessions. It was a funny position. I felt precisely as I did when alone on the Thames at midnight. I commenced with saying I was a foreigner and had been brought up a Protestant. The priest asked if I was a Protestant then.

197

I somehow could not tell a lie, and said 'Yes'. He replied that in that case I could not *jouir du bonheur de la confesse*'; but I was determined to confess, and at last he said he would allow me because it might be the first step towards returning to the true church. I actually did confess – a real confession. When I had done he told me his address, and said that every morning I was to go to the Rue du Parc – to his house – and he would reason with me and try to convince me of the error and enormity of being a Protestant!!! I promised faithfully to go. Of course, however, the adventure stays here, and I hope I shall never see the priest again. I think you had better not tell papa of this. He will not understand that it was only a freak, and will perhaps think I am going to turn Catholic.

The experience would be described almost identically in *Villette*, except that the church in the book is situated down in the medieval part of Brussels, and the priest turns out to be in league with Mme Beck. Lucy would faint on the steps of the great church with the giant spire designed by Rubens. For someone as staunchly Protestant as Charlotte to perform a Roman Catholic act of confession, her mood must have been desperate. Years later she would admit that 'grief' drove her into a depression that made her ill, and was exactly as she described Lucy Snowe's depression in the long vacation. She too had lain in that 'strange fever of the nerves and blood', which almost amounts to madness amidst the white beds in the long dormitory which seemed to turn into death's heads, huge and sun-bleached. Like Charlotte, Lucy Snowe in the end resorts to the confessional.

What was this grief? Was it simply the intolerable pressure of feeling she had no friend to talk to, or was it that she had finally understood what she felt for M. Heger, impossible, unattainable love, and that she was consumed by appalling guilt? Given her own statement that it was 'grief', it is difficult to agree with Miss Fannie Ratchford's assessment that it 'was an effort to ease her mind of a conflict far older than her acquaintance with M. Heger, and rid her conscience of the sin confessed in her Roe Head diary – idolatry, the worship of the creatures of her own imagination. Her statement to Emily that she had made 'a real confession' is hard to interpret as anything but a confession of sin of some kind, yet unless Charlotte's puzzled letters to Ellen later that winter about Mme Heger are taken to be disingenuous, it is almost impossible to credit that her confession was of feelings of adulterous love for M. Heger.

Villette provides a possible clue: when Lucy talks to the priest, it is because she is unhappy; she has no one to love her, she is lonely and distraught:

I said, I was perishing for a word of advice or an accent of comfort. I had been living for some weeks quite alone; I had been ill; I had a pressure of affliction on my mind of which it would hardly any longer endure the weight.

'Was it a sin, a crime?' he inquired, somewhat startled.

I reassured him on this point, and, as well as I could, I showed him the mere outline of my experience.[24]

Furthermore, if it was a confession of adulterous love, it is difficult to see how she could write her later letters to M. Heger, which despite the eroticism with which they are suffused are strikingly innocent of such a connotation. Nor can the concept of Charlotte Brontë as a conscious adulteress be squared with the Charlotte whose female characters in her latest novels were so strictly ruled by duty and conscience, like herself. But perhaps she made her confession of love for M. Heger, and then rigidly decided that hereafter she must think of him only as a friend – but one whom she could not bear to give up.

Her last few months in Brussels appear to have been almost total misery, and yet she was incapable of leaving. A sort of paralysis had overcome her. She wrote to Emily from the school dining room on Sunday morning, 1 October, that she longed now to be back in the dining room at home or in the kitchens. The Charlotte who disliked cooking wouldn't even have minded cutting up the hash 'with the clerk and some register people at the other table, and you standing by, watching that I put enough flour, and not too much pepper, and above all, that I save the best pieces of the leg of mutton for Tiger and Kepper.' And she fell to remembering how Tiger leapt around at the dish, getting in the way of the carving knife, while Kepper would be 'like a devouring flame on the kitchen floor. To complete the picture, Tabby blowing the fire, in order to boil the potatoes to a sort of vegetable glue.' And these homely images, which had once bored and maddened her, in her present mood seemed 'divine'. She was still able to respond with interest to the visit of Queen Victoria to Brussels later in September. She had walked up to the Rue Royale to see her go by in her carriage. Emily, who generally took little note of the greater world, content to dream of Gondal, had expressed curiosity about this visit of the Queen, who at twenty-four was her exact contemporary, and Charlotte wrote approvingly: 'I saw her for an instant flashing through the Rue Royale in a carriage and six, surrounded by soldiers. She looked a little stout, vivacious lady, very plainly dressed, not much dignity or pretension about her. The Belgians liked her very well on the whole. They said she enlivened the sombre court of King Leopold, which is usually as gloomy as a conventicle.'

But at the same time Charlotte told Emily that, although she would like to be at home, 'this place is dismal to me', she had no real pretext for returning; she needed a fixed prospect but it could not be a governess position; she had 'an idea I should be of no use there – a sort of aged person upon the parish'. Emily was sufficiently worried about Charlotte never mentioning her return home to take the unusual step of writing to Ellen suggesting that if she went over for half a year, perhaps she might be able to bring Charlotte back.

Now that the school had reassembled for the autumn, Charlotte's position was more tenable, although she continued to blind herself to its hopelessness. She no longer had any friends in Brussels – Mary Dixon was gone and so were the Wheelwrights. Her feeling for Mme Heger had turned to active dislike. She told Ellen that she was 'a polite, plausible and interested person. I no longer trust her.' In retrospect that feeling would grow into hatred, and the figure of Mme Beck. 'The solitude [which] oppresses me to excess' was the reason she gave to Ellen for going one day, when she could bear it no longer, to Mme Heger and giving in her notice. 'If it had depended on her, I should certainly have soon been at liberty but Monsieur Heger – having heard of what was in agitation – sent for me the day after – and pronounced with vehemence his decision that I should not leave. I could not at that time have persevered in my intention without exciting him to passion – so I promised to stay a while longer.' But she did not know how long that would be. She did not like the idea of returning to England to do nothing; she was obsessed with her age – she said she was 'too old for that now'. If she could hear of a favourable occasion for starting a school she thought she would take it up.

The day after, she scrawled pathetically on the front of her Atlas:

Brussels, Saturday morning, Oct. 14th 1843. First Class. I am very cold – there is no fire – I wish I were at home with Papa – Branwell – Emily – Anne and Tabby – I am tired of being among foreigners – it is a dreary life – especially as there is only one person in this house worthy of being liked – also another, who seems a rosy plum but I know her to be coloured chalk.

November came. She still had not made up her mind to leave. She put off her departure with the thought that it would be as soon as she had acquired as much German as she thought fit. It could be an indefinite period. She had recovered a little of her self-possession. She had worked herself up to be almost affronted by Mme Heger's behaviour to her. On half-holidays, when Charlotte had nowhere to go in Brussels, she thought that Madame could have made an effort to talk to her when she sat by herself in the deserted classrooms, but she never came near her. The first time it happened she was astonished,

200

she told Ellen; Mme Heger was a reasonable and calm woman, but utterly without warm-heartedness. And yet she understood from other people that Madame constantly praised her excellence as a teacher. But now, seven months after the first incomprehensible estrangement, Charlotte said that she finally began 'to perceive the reason of this mighty distance and reserve; it sometimes makes me laugh, and at other times nearly cry. When I am sure of it I will tell you.' Did Charlotte now think that Madame suspected her of being in love with her husband? Presumably.

Charlotte sank into lethargy. Mary Taylor once again came to her rescue, writing from Germany in the rousing language that was what Charlotte needed to rally her. Now Charlotte had got what she wanted, she must leave before she was incapable of doing so. It may be that to Mary Charlotte confided what she could only hint at to Ellen.[25] On 19 December she wrote to tell Emily that she hoped to be home the day after New Year's Day. 'Low spirits have afflicted me much lately, but I hope all will be well when I get home.'

M. Heger in these last days was kind and constructive. He gave her a diploma certifying her abilities as a teacher, with the seal of the Athénée Royale, and to encourage her in her plans for the school for which she had trained so diligently, he suggested that she take one of his little girls with her as a pupil. This, however, Charlotte refused.

As usual, despite her opinion of herself as ill-humoured and misanthropic, she had inspired affection amidst her companions; she was typically surprised at the degree of regret expressed by her pupils when they parted – she had not thought they had it in their phlegmatic natures. The Hegers themselve bade her farewell with the greatest warmth; there were promises to write on both sides, and they generously presented her with another book, an anthology of post-sixteenth-century French poetry. Mme Heger accompanied her, a little grimly, perhaps, all the way in the diligence to the boat at Ostend.

Charlotte's description to Ellen of leaving M. Heger shows that she still could not admit or recognise what she felt for him: 'I suffered much before I left Brussels. I think, however long I live, I shall not forget what the parting with M. Heger cost me; it grieved me so much to grieve him, who has been so true, kind, and disinterested a friend'. For her actual feelings at this terrible parting, which could only gradually be faced once she had returned to Haworth, one must turn to her heartbreaking account in *Villette* of Lucy Snowe's parting with M. Paul; made more heartbreaking by one's consciousness of her recognition that only in her writing could she give a happy ending to her love:

If this were my last moment with him, I would not waste it in

201

forced, unnatural distance. I loved him well – too well not to smite out of my path even Jealousy herself, when she would have obstructed a kind farewell. A cordial word from his lips, or a gentle look from his eyes, would do me good, for all the span of life that remained to me; it would be comfort in the last strait of loneliness; I would take it – I would taste the elixir, and pride should not spill the cup.

The interview would be short, of course: he would say to me just what he had said to each of the assembled pupils; he would take and hold my hand two minutes; he would touch my cheek with his lips for the first, last, only time – and then – no more. Then, indeed, the final parting, then the wide separation, the great gulf I could not pass to go to him – across which, haply, he would not glance, to remember me.

He took my hand in one of his, with the other he put back my bonnet; he looked into my face, his luminous smile went out, his lips expressed something almost like the wordless language of a mother who finds a child greatly and unexpectedly changed, broken with illness, or worn-out by want. A check supervened. . . .

Madame Beck, brought to the spot by vigilance or an inscrutable instinct, pressed so near, she almost thrust herself between me and M. Emanuel. 'Come, Paul!' she reiterated, her eye grazing me with its hard ray like a steel stylet. . . . Pierced deeper than I could endure, made now to feel what defied suppression, I cried –

'My heart will break!'

And in Charlotte's imagination, Mme Heger, dismissed from being M. Heger's wife, could also be dismissed when she, it seemed to Charlotte, made every attempt to prevent a proper leave-taking between what had once been two such close friends. M. Paul turns on Mme Beck: 'Laissez-moi', he orders, and he takes Lucy Snowe in his arms.

CHAPTER XI

A Too Still Existence

Nothing in Charlotte Brontë's life at the beginning of 1844 suggested that she would be the most celebrated author in England three years later. She returned to Haworth convinced by M. Heger that she should be determined to follow the path suitable to her years and sex, and devote herself to teaching, the career for which she had been trained so assiduously by M. Heger and so dear to his own heart. She had suppressed her dream of writing for a living; instead, she day-dreamed obsessively about Brussels and dwelt on the day when she would see her beloved Monsieur again.

But plans for schools which had appeared so workable at parting in the Hegers' drawing room were less practicable in the cold northern light of Haworth. Charlotte arrived back to find that her father's health was increasingly poor and that he was semi-blind from cataracts. He was almost completely dependent on Emily, who had to read all his papers to him, and he could not go out when there was snow on the ground, for the glare hurt his eyes. There were also uncharitable rumours in the village about his drinking habits. John Greenwood, the Haworth stationer, and his wife had told Mr Brontë about these and in a note a few days later he came up with the explanation that he had lately been using a lotion for his eyes, the smell of which had been ascribed to a smell of a more exceptionable character. He intended, he said fiercely, 'to single out one or two of these slanders, and to prosecute them, as the Law directs'. But despite his poor sight he did not neglect his pastoral duties. There is a letter extant of 29 February in which, having tried to console one of his church wardens who had been very recently bereaved, he compassion-ately instructed one of his parishioners to invite him to tea, in order to comfort him. The man was in a state of considerable agitation, in need of some practical help, and was a 'good, well-meaning, and honest man, and in many respects unfit for his present arduous situation.'

It is not clear whether Mr Brontë did drink too much. It might account for his fierceness of temper. Both Ellen Nussey and Mr Nicholls would confirm that Mr Brontë had a tendency to over-conviviality and it may be that this is part of the explanation for Charlotte's unceasing worry about her father's health.

One bright spot amidst the gloom was that Branwell, home with Anne for the Christmas holiday, was, so Charlotte told Ellen, 'wondrously valued' in his situation. Charlotte's frustration, the chafing that the path of duty entailed, was vividly conveyed to Ellen:

Everyone asks me what I am going to do, now that I am returned home; and everyone seems to expect that I should immediately commence a school. In truth it is what I should wish to do. I desire it above all things. I have sufficient money for the undertaking, and I hope now sufficient qualifications to give me a fair chance of success; yet I cannot yet permit myself to enter upon life – to touch the object which seems now within my reach, and which I have been so long straining to obtain. You will ask me why. It is on Papa's account; he is now, as you know, getting old, and it grieves me to tell you that he is losing his sight. I have felt for some months that I ought not to be away from him; and I feel now that it would be too selfish to leave him (at least as long as Branwell and Anne are absent) in order to pursue selfish interests of my own. With the help of God I will try to deny myself in this matter and to wait.

She ended the letter with a second reference to her pathetic desire 'to enter upon life', to gain the object she had been 'so long striving to attain'. She did not know whether Ellen felt as she did, but there were times when it appeared to her as if all her ideas and feelings, except a few friendships and affections, were changed from what they used to be. All her enthusiasm seemed lost – 'tamed down and broken'. Now she was older – she no longer regarded herself as young at twenty-eight – she had fewer illusions: 'What I wish for now is active exertion – a stake in life. Haworth seems such a lonely spot, buried away from the world.' She felt she ought to be working and braving what she called 'the rough realities of the world, as other people did'. But, once again she repeated, as much for herself as for Ellen, it was her duty to restrain this feeling at present, and she would endeavour to do so.

The strain of attending to her duty when every atom of her being was calling out to exercise its faculties, when she was no longer able to find release for her frustration in writing, told severely on her. Brussels took up much of her thoughts. She carried on a correspondence with at least two of her pupils, and was quite overwhelmed by the arrival of a packet of letters from her former pupils in the first class.

She was also exchanging letters with M. Heger. How many letters he wrote in these first months is not clear as none have survived, but there were obviously several, probably written in his usual whimsical, affectionate, intimate style. When Mrs Gaskell went to Brussels to interview M. Heger for her book, he told her about the letters, which he was sure Charlotte would have kept 'as they contained advice about her character, studies, mode of life'.[1]

Charlotte's own letters from this early period are also lost but it is clear from the first surviving letter, of 24 July, that in her mind she was living daily in memory of M. Heger. She told him:

> I greatly fear that I shall forget French, for I am firmly convinced that I shall see you again some day – I know not how or when – but it must be, for I wish it so much, and then I should not wish to remain dumb before you – it would be too sad to see you and not be able to speak to you. To avoid such a misfortune I learn every day by heart half a page of French from a book written in a familiar style: and I take pleasure in learning this lesson, Monsieur; as I pronounce the French words it seems to me as if I were chatting with you.

A visit to Ellen in mid-March helped her a little. To Ellen she could reveal something of her feelings for M. Heger, share an interest in the world and its ways that was lost on Emily, and she returned from Brookroyd in better health and rather more cheerful, laden as usual with Ellen's presents for the household. They included flower seeds for Emily, who was delighted and wanted to know if the Sicilian pea and crimson cornflower were hardy flowers, or if they were delicate and should be sown in warm and sheltered situations. On 25 March, writing back to Ellen, Charlotte gives a vignette of Emily, for whom animals would always be of nearly equal importance to human beings: 'Monday morning. Our poor little cat has been ill two days, and is just dead. It is piteous to see even an animal laying lifeless. Emily *is* sorry.' The weather had cleared up and Charlotte suddenly felt better; Emily and she spent a lot of time walking on the moors, 'to the great damage of our shoes, but I hope to the benefit of our health'.

In April Mary Taylor returned unexpectedly to England, staying at her brother Joe's home at Hunsworth Mills, Cleckheaton, where red army cloth was manufactured. Hunsworth Mill, with Rawfolds Mill at Liversedge, would be the origins of the Hollows Mill in *Shirley*. Although motorways – the M 62 and the M 606 – run past it nowadays, then it was a charming hamlet in this more sheltered, low-lying country – near to the Spen Beck and surrounded by woodland. The house stood above the mill, and a lane led from it to the village green. Mary

205

had made her home there after her father's death, due to her mother's difficult personality; Mrs Taylor continued to live two miles away at the Red House, Gomersal. Charlotte, Emily and Mary soon met up at Hunsworth, but despite Mary's bracing company and her own resolution, Charlotte could not wrest herself out of her debilitating state of mind. As she would express it to M. Heger in a chaotic frenzy of devotion:

> I should not know this lethargy if I could write. Formerly I passed whole days and weeks and months in writing, not wholly without result, for Southey and Coleridge – two of our best authors, to whom I sent certain manuscripts – were good enough to express their approval; but now my sight is too weak to write. Were I to write much I should become blind. This weakness of sight is a terrible hindrance to me. Otherwise do you know what I should do, Monsieur? I should write a book, and I should dedicate it to my literature master – to the only master I ever had – to you, Monsieur. I have often told you in French how much I respect you – how much I am indebted to your goodness, to your advice; I should like to say it once in English. But that cannot be – it is not to be thought of. The career of letters is closed to me – only that of teaching is open. It does not offer the same attractions; never mind, I shall enter it, and if I do not go far it will not be from want of industry. You too, Monsieur – you wished to be a barrister – destiny or Providence made you a professor; you are happy in spite of it.

What appears to have been a hysterical form of near-blindness had her in its grip. Denied her usual release from care, that she had had for more than ten years, 'the strange necromantic joys of fancy', that 'tale my imagination created and narrated continuously', as she would write in *Jane Eyre*, 'quickened with all of the incident, life, fire, feeling, that I desired', she was suffering a paralysis of her normally strong willpower.

The return of Anne and Branwell for a short holiday in June, before they joined their employers at the smart watering place of Scarborough, helped divert Charlotte. Ellen was summoned to Haworth to see them and soon was receiving the attention of Mr Brontë's curate Mr Smith, possibly to make up for the contempt with which Charlotte treated him. She would eventually portray him in *Shirley* as Peter Augustus Malone, one of the three appalling curates. Charlotte disapproved of his worldliness; he made the mistake of saying of Ellen in Charlotte's hearing, 'I suppose she has money', which enraged Charlotte and was immediately reported back to Ellen, who had left for Brookroyd with the present of a puppy born to Anne's dog Flossy.

206

Mr Brontë had his own low opinion of Mr Smith, expressing himself unusually strongly on the subject: he was a very fickle man who if he married would soon get tired of his wife. To Charlotte's great surprise, at breakfast one day he even said he was fearful that Mr Smith's attention to Ellen would perhaps have made an impression on her mind which would interfere with her comfort. Charlotte told him she thought not, believing Ellen to be the mistress of herself in those matters, but he was insistent that Charlotte write to Ellen and dissuade her from thinking of Smith. 'I never saw Papa make himself so uneasy about a thing of that kind before; he is usually very sarcastic on such subjects.' Mr Brontë had perhaps guessed something of his daughter's state of mind, and, noting her depression and altered behaviour since her return from Brussels, was obliquely hinting to her about her own situation.

By July, after much shirt-making by her and Emily, Charlotte had rallied sufficiently to revive the plan of setting up a school. It would be at Haworth, which would thus combine her interests with attending to her father, although she had misgivings that Haworth's retired situation would make the scheme difficult. She began to search her acquaintance for pupils, writing to her old employer Mrs White to ask if she knew of anyone whose children needed a school. She was rather encouraged by Mr White's friendly reply, regretting that she had not informed them a month earlier, otherwise he would have sent his own daughter and that of another local, Colonel Stott, to her, but unfortunately they were now promised to Miss Cockhill's. She also wrote off to a lady in nearby Keighley, Mrs Busfeild, enclosing the precious certificate M. Heger had given her before she left Brussels and asking whether, if she could not consider sending any of her own children, she might recommend other pupils. The Brontës' habit of keeping themselves to themselves was proving a disadvantage, but as soon as Charlotte could get the assurance of just one pupil, she intended to have a card of terms printed and make the necessary changes to the house. She communicated all this to Ellen and asked her to find out the sort of price at which the local schoolmistress Miss Cockhill had fixed board.

Conscious that she was now acting in a way that should bring M. Heger's approval, she wrote describing the scheme to him on 24 July:

I have just been offered a situation as first governess in a large school in Manchester, with a salary of £100 (i.e. 2,500 francs) per annum. I cannot accept it, for in accepting it I should have to leave my father, and that I cannot do. Nevertheless I have a plan (when one lives retired the brain goes on working; there is the desire of occupation, the wish to embark on an active career). Our parsonage is rather a large house – with a few alterations there will be room for five or six boarders. If I could find this number of children of good family, I should devote myself to their education. Emily does not care much for teaching, but she would look after the housekeeping, and, although something of a recluse, she is too good-hearted not to do all she could for the well-being of the children. Moreover, she is very generous, and as for order, economy, strictness – and diligent work – all of them things very essential in a school – I willingly take that upon myself.

That, Monsieur, is my plan, which I have already explained to my father and which he approves. It only remains to find the pupils – rather a difficult thing – for we live rather far from towns, and people do not greatly care about crossing the hills which form as it were a barrier around us. But the task that is without difficulty is almost without merit; there is great interest in triumphing over obstacles. I do not say I shall succeed, but I shall *try* to succeed – the effort alone will do me good. There is nothing I fear so much as idleness, the want of occupation, inactivity, the lethargy of the faculties: when the body is idle, the spirit suffers painfully.

From this first surviving letter of Charlotte's to M. Heger, which she could not resist the opportunity of sending via Mrs Wheelwright – who was on her way back to the continent – even though it was not her turn to write, it is apparent that Charlotte had already stepped beyond the bounds of convention in her previous correspondence. She had earlier sent him, she admits, 'a letter that was less than reasonable, because sorrow was at my heart', and M. Heger, alarmed at the turn this once agreeable relationship was taking and perhaps at last realising what had been plainly manifest for the past year to his wife, seems to have sent her a letter of rebuke. But try though she did to restrain herself, Charlotte could not conceal the obsessional nature of her feelings:

I am very pleased that the school-year is nearly over and that the holidays are approaching. I am pleased on your account, Monsieur – for I am told that you are working too hard and that your health has suffered somewhat in consequence. For that reason I refrain from uttering a single complaint for your long silence – I would rather remain six months without receiving news from you than add one grain to the weight, already too heavy, which overwhelms you. I know well that it is now the period of compositions, that it will soon be that of examinations, and later on of prizes – and during all that time you are condemned to breathe the stifling atmosphere of the class-rooms – to wear yourself out – to explain, to question, to talk all day, and then in the evening you have all those wretched compositions to read, to correct, almost to re-write – Ah, Monsieur! I once wrote you a letter that was less than reasonable, because sorrow was at my heart; but I shall do so no more. – I shall try to be selfish no longer; and even while I look upon your letters as one of the greatest felicities known to me, I shall await the receipt of them in patience until it pleases you and suits you to send me any. Meanwhile, I may well send you a little letter from time to time: – you have authorised me to do so.

By the end of her letter, which included the proper acknowledgement to Mme Heger, Charlotte had virtually abandoned any self-possession in her pitiful pleading for a response:

Please convey to Madame the assurance of my esteem. I fear that Maria, Louise, Claire have already forgotten me. Prospère and Victorine never knew me well; I remember well all five of them, especially Louise. She had so much character – so much naïveté in her little face. – Good-bye, Monsieur,
– Your grateful pupil,

C. Brontë.

I have not begged you to write to me soon as I fear to importune you – but you are too kind to forget that I wish it all the same – yes, I wish it greatly. Enough; after all, do as you wish, Monsieur. If, then, I received a letter, and if I thought that you have written it *out of pity* – I should feel deeply wounded.

It seems that Mrs Wheelwright is going to Paris before going to Brussels – but she will post my letter at Boulogne. Once more good-bye, Monsieur; it hurts to say good-bye even in a letter. Oh, it is certain that I shall see you again one day – it must be so – for as soon as I shall have earned enough money to go to Brussels I shall go there – and I shall see you again if only for a moment.

Meanwhile, she tried to escape her unhappiness by persevering with her plans for the school. Mrs Busfeild replied politely, regretting that her children were already at school in Liverpool while she thought the proposed fee of £35 per annum was very moderate. Like everybody else whom Charlotte had consulted, Mrs Busfeild thought there would be some problems on account of Haworth's retired situation. With spirit Charlotte responded that it was in some ways an advantage: if the school were in the middle of a large town she could not pretend to take pupils on such moderate terms. In a letter to Ellen, she pointed out: 'As it is, not having house-rent to pay, we can offer the same privileges of education that are to be had in expensive seminaries, at little more than half their price; and, as our numbers must be limited, we can devote a large share of time and pains to each pupil.' Ellen had previously sent her a pretty little purse and in return Charlotte now enclosed half a dozen of the cards that she had had printed to show the proposed school's terms and which were modelled on the prospectus for the Pensionnat Heger.

THE MISSES BRONTE'S ESTABLISHMENT
FOR
THE BOARD AND EDUCATION
OF A LIMITED NUMBER OF
YOUNG LADIES,
THE PARSONAGE, HAWORTH,
NEAR BRADFORD.

TERMS.	£ s. d.
Board and Education, including Writing, Arithmetic, History, Grammar, Geography, and Needle Work, per Annum · ·	35 0 0
French ⎫ German ⎬ each per quarter · · Latin ⎭	1 1 0
Music ⎫ Drawing ⎭ each per quarter · ·	1 1 0
Use of Piano Forte, per Quarter ·	0 5 0
Washing, per Quarter · · ·	0 15 0

Each Young Lady to be provided with One Pair of Sheets, Pillow Cases, Four Towels, a Dessert and Tea-Spoon.

A Quarter's Notice, or a Quarter's Board, is required previous to the Removal of a Pupil.

Ellen did her utmost to help, but no pupils materialised. Life for Charlotte went on much as usual. She watched Mr Smith get increasingly on her father's nerves. She read to her father, she taught at the Sunday School, went on walks, and became more and more unhappy. She had now written two letters to M. Heger that had gone unanswered. She began to be convinced that Mme Heger was intercepting them; the other alternative, that M. Heger was no longer interested in her welfare, was inconceivable. Branwell, back for the summer holiday, was irritable and drinking quite heavily. Mary Taylor had returned to Brussels for another half-year, to teach and study music until something better turned up. She was worried about Charlotte's general state of health and wrote to Ellen that she could 'easily imagine that she [Charlotte] is grown low spirited with solitude and want of interesting occupation'.

In September came the doleful news from Brussels that Mary had finally determined to put into action the plan that she had been mulling over for the past three years, and emigrate to the freer climate of New Zealand. Charlotte, trying to express all she felt, wrote that it was 'as if a great planet fell out of the sky'. Mary would be joining her brother Waring in Wellington, where he had set himself up in business, running a general store. It was a far cry from the life she had been brought up to, but Mary had determined to reject such values. She would write after ten years of life as a businesswoman in New Zealand, investing in land and running a store:

I am in better health than at any time since I left school. This difference won't seem much to other people, since I never was *ill* since then; but it is very great to me, for it is just the difference between everything being a burden and everything being more or less a pleasure. Half from physical weakness and half from depression of spirits my judgement in former days was always at war with my will. There was always plenty to do, but never anything that I really felt was worth the labour of doing.

It was just such a life that Charlotte was condemned to. By October she had had to face the fact that although everyone in the vicinity wished the Brontë ladies well, there were no pupils to be had. Resolute as ever, she wrote to Ellen: 'We have no present intention, however, of breaking our hearts on the subject, still less of feeling mortified at defeat. The effort must be beneficial whatever the result may be, because it teaches us experience and an additional knowledge of the world.' Unlike Emily, who continued to be contented, absently performing her household tasks while continuing to enlarge the Gondal writings, never tiring of the bloody activities of its passionate and ferocious denizens, Charlotte seems scarcely to have written anything, except possibly a few melancholy fragments, two or three verses of poetry brooding on M. Heger.

On 24 October she heard that Joseph Taylor was going to Brussels to visit Mary, and Charlotte seized the opportunity to write once again to M. Heger, sure this time that he would personally receive the letter:

211

Monsieur, – I am in high glee this morning – and that has rarely happened to me these last two years. It is because a gentleman of my acquaintance is going to Brussels, and has offered to take charge of a letter for you – which letter he will deliver to you himself, or else his sister, so that I shall be certain that you have received it.

I am not going to write a long letter; in the first place, I have not the time – it must leave at once; and then, I am afraid of worrying you. I would only ask of you if you heard from me at the beginning of May and again in the month of August? For six months I have been awaiting a letter from Monsieur – six months' waiting is very long, you know. However, I do not complain, and I shall be richly rewarded for a little sorrow if you will now write a letter and give it to this gentleman – or to his sister – who will hand it to me without fail.

I shall be satisfied with the letter however brief it be – only do not forget to tell me of your health, Monsieur, and how Madame and the children are, and the governesses and pupils.

My father and my sister send you their respects. My father's infirmity increases little by little. Nevertheless he is not yet entirely blind. My sisters are well, but my poor brother is always ill.

Farewell, Monsieur; I am depending on soon having your news. The idea delights me, for the remembrance of your kindness will never fade from my memory, and as long as that remembrance endures the respect with which it has inspired me will endure likewise. –
Your very devoted pupil,

C. Brontë.

I have just had bound all the books you gave me when I was at Brussels. I take delight in contemplating them; they make quite a little library. To begin with, there are the complete works of Bernardin de St Pierre – the Pensées de Pascal – a book of poetry, two German books – and (worth all the rest) two discourses of Monsieur le Professeur Heger, delivered at the distribution of prizes of the Athénée Royal.

She had evidently heeded well his former rebuke to confine the subject of her letters, chastened by his lack of response. It is a pathetically polite, almost fomulaic, letter. Evidently Branwell was drinking quite heavily judging by her euphemistic 'my poor brother is always ill'.

It now seemed altogether unlikely that the school scheme would ever take place, and the days passed drearily in what Charlotte herself described as hungry anticipation of the postman's knock. Would he bring a letter from Brussels? Charlotte was now the recipient of French newspapers passed on by the Taylors. In a postscript to a letter to Ellen that winter she wrote, 'I have received two French newspapers this week which I shall return to Hunsworth. I am very glad of them.'

When Mary Taylor returned to Hunsworth Mill for her farewell visit at the beginning of January 1845, bearing no letter from M. Heger, something in Charlotte snapped. On 8 January she wrote to him, in her sorrow and anger not even bothering with the convention of a salutation. It is a graphic, almost literary account of the agony she was enduring; quite heartrending in its abandon:

Mr Taylor has returned. I asked him if he had a letter for me. 'No; nothing.' 'Patience,' said I – 'his sister will be here soon.' Miss Taylor has returned. 'I have nothing for you from Monsieur Heger,' says she; 'neither letter nor message.'

Having realised the meaning of these words, I said to myself what I should say to another similarly placed: 'You must be resigned, and above all do not grieve at a misfortune which you have not deserved.' I strove to restrain my tears, to utter no complaint.

But when one does not complain, when one seeks to dominate oneself with a tyrant's grip, the faculties start into rebellion and one pays for external calm with an internal struggle that is almost unbearable. Day and night I find neither rest nor peace. If I sleep I am disturbed by tormenting dreams in which I see you, always severe, always grave, always incensed against me.

Forgive me then, Monsieur, if I adopt the course of writing to you again. How can I endure life if I make no effort to ease its sufferings?

I know you will be irritated when you read this letter. You will say once more that I am hysterical – that I have black thoughts, etc. So be it, Monsieur, I do not seek to justify myself; I submit to every sort of reproach. All I know is, that I cannot, that I will not, resign myself to lose wholly the friendship of my master. I would rather suffer the greatest physical pain than always have my heart lacerated by smarting regrets. If my master withdraws his friendship from me entirely I shall be altogether without hope; if he gives me a little – just a little – I shall be satisfied – happy; I shall have a reason for living on, for working.

Monsieur, the poor have not need of much to sustain them – they ask only for the crumbs that fall from the rich man's table. But if they are refused the crumbs they die of the hunger. Nor do I, either, need much affection from those I love. I should not know what to do with a friendship entire and complete – I am not used to it. But you showed me of yore a *little* interest, when I was your pupil in Brussels, and I hold on to the maintenance of that *little*

213

interest – I hold on to it as I would hold on to life.

You will tell me perhaps – 'I take not the slightest interest in you, Mademoiselle Charlotte. You are no longer an inmate of my house; I have forgotten you.' Well, Monsieur, tell me so frankly. It will be a shock to me. It matters not. It would be less dreadful than uncertainty.

I shall not re-read this letter. I send it as I have written it. Nevertheless, I have a hidden consciousness that some people, cold and sensible, in reading it would say – 'She is talking nonsense.' I would avenge myself on such persons in no other way than by wishing them one single day of the torments which I have suffered for eight months. We should then see if they would not talk nonsense too.

One suffers in silence so long as one has the strength so to do, and when that strength gives out one speaks without too carefully measuring one's words.

I wish Monsieur happiness and prosperity.

C.B.

And Monsieur Heger, either in anger or alarm at the passion he had unleashed, tore up the letter and threw it away, as he did with the other letters. He would later write to Ellen Nussey of Charlotte Brontë's 'pauvre coeur malade', which he then crossed out and more tactfully described as her 'pauvre coeur blessé'.[2] However, his shrewd and practical wife, who had experience of girls conceiving passions for their schoolmaster and perhaps thinking it was more sensible to keep the pitiful letters as a safeguard for the future, picked them out of the wastepaper basket and sewed them back together.

Perhaps writing the letter, itself close to a work of art in its dramatic quality, with its use of inversion and poetic repetition, reminded Charlotte of the solace she derived from writing. Certainly that year of 1845 saw a flood of poetry from Charlotte's pen, examining the themes of love and betrayal. In her poetry she faced what she could not face in real life, that when she spoke of friendship she thought of love. Her first poem written in January 1845 – one of the many versions of the poem in *The Professor* – concerns the relationship between a master and his pupil, and mirrors very poignantly Charlotte's feelings during her time at the Pensionnat: 'His coming was my hope each day / His parting was my pain / The chance that did his steps delay / Was ice in every vein.' The narrator realises that the love she bears for the male figure is morally wrong, though quite why this is so is never explained, but the female narrator nonetheless dares dangers for it – 'Whatever menaced, harassed, warned / I passed impetuous by.'[3] But hate strikes her down; her lover turns cold, and the male figure gives his love to her rival.

It has been argued that this recently discovered poem is evidence of adulterous intentions on Charlotte's part towards M. Heger.[4] It is certainly true that in the poetry written from 1845 onwards, Charlotte concerned herself with illicit love. In 'Frances', a young woman suffering terribly from love longs for death and heaven, where she might 'find love without lust's leaven', an unusually frank and down-to-earth attitude for a Victorian young lady. And the ballad-like 'Gilbert' relates the story of a man who appears to have seduced a young woman, Elinor, before his marriage:

> What he love would name
> Though haply Gilbert's secret deeds
> Might other title claim.

The poem opens quite clearly in the garden of the Pensionnat Heger, soon to be described in *The Professor* and later *Villette*:

> Above the city hung the moon,
>   Right o'er a plot of ground
> Where flowers and orchard-trees were fenced
>   With lofty walls around:
>
> This garden, in a city heart,
>   Lay still as houseless wild,
> Though many-windowed mansion fronts
>   Were round it closely piled;
>
> The city's many-mingled sounds
>   Rose like the hum of ocean;
> They rather lulled the heart than roused
>   Its pulse to faster motion.

Gilbert, now a married man, is pacing up and down; his thoughts turn to love, and then he remembers Elinor. She worshipped him, he had complete power over her life, and he welcomed her worship and revelled in it:

> "'Twas sweet to see her strive to hide
>   What every glance revealed;
> Endowed, the while, with despot-might
>   Her destiny to wield.
> I knew myself no perfect man,
>   Her, as she deemed, divine;

215

I knew that I was glorious – but
   By her reflected shine;

'Her youth, her native energy,
   Her powers new-born and fresh –
'Twas these with Godhead sanctified
   My sensual frame of flesh.
Yet, like a god, did I descend
   At last to meet her love;
And, like a god, I then withdrew
   To my own heaven above.

He leaves her, secure in the knowledge that 'her blinded constancy /
would ne'er my deeds betray', although he sometimes feels the desire
to recreate 'the fond and flattering pain of passion's anguish in her
young breast again' despite now being happily married, with small
children. But he sometimes wonders what has happened to her. He
then receives a chilling vision of her drowned corpse – she has committed suicide. The wicked Gilbert is relieved by this, as he was
relieved that she had vanished, because he feared that his broken vow
might sully his spotless name. But he does not escape justice. By the
end of the poem he has been forced to commit suicide by Elinor's
angry wraith.

Whether this poetry accurately depicts Charlotte Brontë's true feelings and attitude to M. Heger, whether she really contemplated
adultery with him, is debatable. After all, poetry is a fiction; a poem
like 'Gilbert' was a way of escaping from misery, placing it at one
remove by dramatising it. Her poem 'Reason' has been thought to
show that Charlotte left Brussels to flee temptation; but however apt it
might seem, this poem was actually written in 1836, seven years
before she left:

Have I not fled that I may conquer?
Crost the dark sea in firmest faith
That I at last might plant my anchor
Where love cannot prevail to death?

Charlotte did not leave Brussels to flee temptation but on account of
her despair, although how much she wished to refuse temptation back
at Haworth is again debatable.

However, the doubts have centred on where in Brussels Charlotte
sent her letters, whether there was something deliberately underhand
about it. In 1894, a former pupil at the Pensionnat Heger, Frederika
Macdonald, who remained friendly with one of the Heger daughters,

published an article in *The Woman at Home* which scandalised Brontë admirers. In it she claimed that Charlotte had written 'frequent letters' to M. Heger in which her 'strong and enthusiastic attachment to her master in literature' – though she hastened to add that it 'was certainly not tainted nor disfigured by the shadow of any attempt, or desire, to draw to herself affections that were pledged elsewhere' – nevertheless was expressed

> . . . in a tone that her Brussels friends considered it not only prudent but kind to check. She was warned by them that the exaltation these letters betrayed needed to be toned down and replaced by what was reasonable. She was further advised to write only once in six months, and then to limit the subject of her letters to her own health and that of her family and to a plain account of her circumstances and occupations.

This claim sullied the golden, martyr-like image of Charlotte Brontë that Mrs Gaskell had so effectively stamped on the public mind, and it was greeted with outraged disbelief. It would be another twenty-one years before the Heger family finally released those letters which Frederika Macdonald had written about.

In 1895/early 1896, a Brontë scholar, Mr Clement Shorter, interviewed Laetitia Wheelwright about Charlotte's time in Brussels. She immediately came to the rescue of her friend's reputation thus:

> Some time after Charlotte had returned to England, and when at the height of her fame, she met her Brussels schoolfellow in London. Miss Wheelwright asked her whether she still corresponded with M. Heger. Charlotte replied that she had discontinued to do so. M. Heger had mentioned in one letter that his wife did not like the correspondence, and he asked her therefore to address her letters to the Royal Athénée, where . . . he gave lessons to the boys. 'I stopped writing at once,' Charlotte told her friend. 'I would not have dreamt of writing to him when I found it was disagreeable to his wife; certainly I would not write unknown to her.' She added this with the sincerity of manner which characterised her every utterance, and I would sooner have doubted myself than her.

Shorter added sternly, 'Let, then, this silly and offensive imputation be now and for ever dismissed from the minds of Charlotte Brontë's admirers, if indeed it had ever lodged there.'

But in 1914 and 1919 the Heger children, now in their turn eminent members of Belgian society, revived the idea of the Athénée Royale being a poste restante for Charlotte Brontë, but they insisted that it was Charlotte's idea, not M. Heger's. They told Mrs Chadwick, an early Brontë biographer, that the last letter, written in November 1845, was addressed by Charlotte Brontë to the Athénée Royale, 'but it was not at the request of M. Heger, but because Charlotte herself was eager to obtain an answer from him, and she evidently was suspecting Mme Heger as the cause of the delay in getting answers, for it it noticeable that in this last letter Mme Heger is not mentioned at all, although the governess and children are referred to by name.'

In his book, *The Inner History of the Brontë–Heger Letters*, published in 1919, Mr Spielmann, an acquaintance of the Heger family and a scholar of some reputation – who organised the handing over of the Brontë–Heger letters to the British Museum – said that Mlle Louise Heger had told him in an interview in 1913 during arrangements about the letters that one or more of them had been addressed to M. Heger at the boys' grammar school. She was a small child at the time and had been told this by her mother.

The envelopes of the letters themselves yield no clue to this conundrum. Two letters have the Hegers' address, 32 Rue d'Isabelle, on them, and two do not. The last letter, the one which does not mention Mme Heger, does not bear an address. How to weigh up the evidence? On the one hand Laetitia Wheelwright, completely unprompted, volunteered the information that M. Heger had suggested Charlotte write to him in effect secretly at the boys' school. That some kind of suggestion was made to use the boys' school as a poste restante is supported by the fact that both parties agree on it, even if the question of who actually made the suggestion is in dispute. The idea that Miss Wheelwright may have been inventing the story to rescue her friend's reputation from what she felt was Frederika Macdonald's slur seems unlikely in view of this common agreement, although of course it is possible. The Hegers' evidence is tainted by the fact that they may have felt it necessary to spring to their father's defence after Miss Wheelwright had in effect slandered him.

It is also possible that Charlotte was not telling Miss Wheelwright the truth. However, given the one-sided nature of the correspondence, M. Heger was hardly likely to have asked Charlotte to write to him care of the Athénée Royale for an illicit reason; if he did, it probably would have been, as Miss Wheelwright suggested, because the by then hysterical tone of the letters might have suggested to Mme Heger that rather more had been going on between the Professor and his pupil than she had suspected. It may be that this request called Charlotte to her senses, and made her realise how her behaviour could be construed as adulterous overtures to a married man.

Mme Heger's kinder explanation for Charlotte's writing to M.

Heger at the boys' school was, according to her daughter, in order to get him to write to her in his own handwriting; M. Heger usually dictated his correspondence to his wife, who was his amanuensis (in later years Mlle Louise succeeded to the secretarial post). Spielmann's account goes on: 'That is why in one of her letters Charlotte Brontë pleads for the *sight of his own handwriting*, and also why she addressed him at the Athénée Royale: for no other reason.' Yet M. Heger appears to have written Charlotte at least one letter in his own hand, judging from Charlotte's mention of his handwriting in her last surviving letter to him, the context of which suggests that it was not a rare event: '. . . when day by day I await a letter and when day by day disappointment comes to fling me back into overwhelming sorrow, and the sweet delight of seeing your handwriting and reading your counsel escapes me as a vision that is vain. . . .'

Another possibility is that because she feared Mme Heger was interfering with her letters, Charlotte did indeed write to M. Heger at the Athénée Royale. It is conceivable that Mme Heger did intercept Charlotte's letters; that might be the explanation for her not receiving a reply to the letters that arrived in May and August 1844, although another, more plausible explanation is that M. Heger chose not to reply. Since she openly sent her letters with respectable Mrs Wheelwright and Joe Taylor, Charlotte obviously initially felt no guilt about them. Her last letter to survive does, however, pose more of a problem. Written in the desolate winter of 1845, when Branwell had been thrown out of his job and was making life in the small parsonage a misery, it is the most fervent, straightforwardly lover-like of all the letters (though she still attempts to couch her relationship with him in terms of that of a child to its father) and, as Mrs Chadwick says, does not mention Mme Heger. Mrs Chadwick, whose standards of etiquette were far closer to the 1840s than our own, thought this an 'inexcusable' breach of conduct. Perhaps, then, Charlotte was willing M. Heger to reply with something of her passion; perhaps she really did think that she might get to see him.

That summer of 1845 Anne noted in her diary that Charlotte constantly talked of leaving Haworth and obtaining another situation in Paris. In her dreamlike life at Haworth perhaps right and wrong came to have little meaning compared to her love for M. Heger, and Mme Heger almost faded from her memory as the person to whom he was married – M. Paul Emanuel would be unmarried in *Villette* – to re-emerge simply as a woman who was interfering with the course of true love; as Mlle Reuter in *The Professor*, who tries to separate Crimsworth and Frances Henri, and as Madame Beck in *Villette* who behaves similarly to Paul Emanuel and Lucy Snowe. Mr Rochester's wife would be shut away, mad, a hideous encumbrance. At twenty-

one Charlotte had stated her religion of love in a somewhat comic
ballad, 'Apostasy', which she felt was sufficiently important to include
in the selection of her poetry that she would publish in 1846:

> Speak not one word of Heaven above
>> Rave not of Hell's alarms;
> Give me but back my Walter's love,
>> Restore me to his arms!
>
> Then will the bliss of Heaven be won;
>> Then will Hell shrink away . . .
> 'Tis my religion thus to love
>> My creed thus fixed to be;
> Not death shall shake, nor Priestcraft break
>> My rock-like constancy!

Yet it is equally arguable that Charlotte was able to be so passionate,
so fervent and lover-like to M. Heger in the letters because she was in
a sense innocent of what she was actually saying; she repressed the
necessary consequence of such feeling for a married man. She constantly reiterates that their relationship is that of true friendship.
Perhaps she felt something above sexual love, a sort of courtly love of
the purest, most platonic kind. In *Villette* Lucy's relationship with M.
Paul is remarkably cerebral, almost asexual in its exalted passion. He
twice calls her 'petite soeur' and she says she can think of him as a
brother. Perhaps this was Charlotte's highest accolade, given that her
closest emotional relationship with the opposite sex had been with her
brother.

The anguish that Charlotte was suffering throughout this period
was made acute by her isolation and lack of employment. In her
poetry she revealed the desperation:

> For me the universe is dumb,
> Stone-deaf, and blank, and wholly blind;
> Life I must bound, existence sum
> In the strait limits of one mind;
>
> That mind my own. Oh! narrow cell;
> Dark – imageless – a living tomb!
> There must I sleep, there wake and dwell
> Content, with palsy, pain, and gloom.

Time and again she speaks of her need for 'action'. She tormented
herself devouring French newspapers, living in dreams, imagining

A stalwart form, a massive head,
A firm determined face,
Black Spanish locks, a sunburnt cheek,
A brow high, broad, and white

whose furrows alternated between speaking of 'mind and moral might' and cold-hearted libertinage.

Despite her own great personal unhappiness, she gave what advice and comfort she could to Ellen over her youngest brother George, who had become mentally ill and by early 1845 was in an asylum where his condition appeared to be deteriorating. She also reported to Ellen after the New Year of 1845 that 'Branwell has been quieter and less irritable on the whole this time than he was in the summer – Anne is as usual always good, mild and patient'.

In February she went to stay with Mary Taylor at Hunsworth Mill where Mary's many vociferous siblings and cousins were assembled from round about to bid her farewell before she departed for New Zealand. It was the last time, as Charlotte put it picturesquely, that she and Mary Taylor ever met 'under the canopy of heaven'. But even there with the pleasure of seeing her friend, Charlotte could not shake off her depression. She told Ellen: 'I spent a week at Hunsworth not very pleasantly; headache, sickliness, and flatness of spirits made me a poor companion, a sad drag on the vivacious and loquacious gaiety of all the other inmates of the house. I never was fortunate enough to be able to rally, for so much as a single hour, while I was there.' Her usual shyness was exacerbated by her mood – she was sure that everyone with the exception of Mary was very glad when she took her departure – and 'I began to perceive that I have too little life in me, nowadays, to be fit company for any except very quiet people. Is it age, or what else, that changes one so?'

Mary's account of her last meeting with the friend who had often been such sparkling, entrancing company makes bleak reading:

When I last saw Charlotte she told me she had quite decided to stay at home. She owned she did not like it. Her health was weak. She said she would like any change at first, as she had liked Brussels at first, and she thought that there must be some possibility for some people of having a life of more variety and more communion with human kind, but she saw none for her. I told her very warmly that she ought not to stay at home; that to spend the next five years at home, in solitude and weak health, would ruin her; that she would never recover it. Such a dark shadow came over her face when I said, 'Think of what you'll be five years hence!' that I stopped, and said, 'Don't cry, Charlotte!' She did not cry, but went on walking

221

up and down the room and said in a little while, 'But I intend to stay, Polly.'

As the days passed the truth of Mary's attitude to life in England became increasingly self-evident to Charlotte. Yet her desire for action had to be weighed against, and defeated by, what Charlotte would eventually oppose to the enfranchisement of women – self-sacrificing love and disinterested devotion. Her deeply ingrained duty was to stay at home with her father. After Charlotte's death, Mary Taylor wrote to Ellen that she could never 'think without gloomy anger of Charlotte's sacrifices to the selfish old man'. It would do the world good, she went on,

> to know her and be forced to revere her in spite of their contempt for poverty and helplessness. No one ever gave up more than she did and with full consciousness of what she sacrificed. I don't think myself that women are justified in sacrificing themselves for others but since the world generally expects it of them, they should at least acknowledge it. But where much is given, we are all wonderfully given to grasp at more.

In Mary's opinion, if Charlotte had left home 'and made a favour of returning, she would have got thanks instead of tyranny'. And she would write angrily after reading reviews of Mrs Gaskell's *Life of Charlotte Brontë*: 'Neither of them seems to think it a strange or wrong state of things that a woman of first-rate talents, industry, and integrity should live all her life in a walking nightmare of "poverty and self-suppression".' It was the classic nineteenth-century view that the female existence should be subordinate to the male's, and it was encouraged for Charlotte by Mr Brontë's exaggerated fears about his health, which would not prevent him living to eighty.

The strong sense of self and fierce, unfeminine individuality that would so amaze Charlotte Brontë's contemporaries when it surfaced in the character of Jane Eyre was regularly suppressed in real life. Jane Eyre was allowed to reject self-denying Christianity with St John Rivers in favour of her natural self and Mr Rochester; not so Charlotte Brontë. Guilt about M. Heger, social mores, the revelation of vice indulged seen in the ruin of Branwell, perhaps a failure of nerve after great unhappiness, had all come together to teach her never to put her wishes first. Over and over again, between Brussels and the publication of *Jane Eyre* Charlotte reiterated in her letters the paramount importance of self-sacrifice. She speaks of her struggle with 'Conscience' and the happiness she feels when she succeeds in doing what she considers to be right, which in her view must be 'the greatest sacrifice of self-interest – which implies the greatest good to others'. As she wrote to Ellen, in the middle of writing *Jane Eyre*, 'this path, steadily followed, will lead, I believe, in time, to prosperity and to happiness; though it may seem, at the outset, to tend in quite a contrary direction'. Nevertheless she found it a difficult course to follow as the following letter to Ellen recommending that she stay at home and look after her mother, just as Charlotte remained at Haworth, shows:

> Your mother is both old and infirm; old and infirm people have few sources of happiness, fewer almost than the comparatively young and healthy can conceive; to deprive them of one of these is cruel.
>
> If your mother is more composed when you are with her, stay with her. If she would be unhappy in case you left her, stay with her. It will not apparently, as far as short-sighted humanity can see, be for *your* advantage to remain at Brookroyd, nor will you be praised and admired for remaining at home to comfort your mother; yet, probably, your own conscience will approve, and if it does, stay with her. I recommend you to do what I am trying to do myself.

Nowhere could one find the standard Victorian belief that 'the one quality on which woman's value and influence depends is the renunciation of self' more wholly followed, and nowhere to reviewers would it be more denied than in the assertive figure of Jane Eyre whose demands for her claims to happiness was so unusual as to seem to threaten the *status quo*.

The month after Mary left, Charlotte tersely signified to Ellen her approval of the extraordinary step Mary had taken: 'Mary is in her element now. She has done right to go out to New Zealand.' Despite the fact that 'Sickness – Hardship – Danger are her fellow companions', Mary was free. The comparison with her own life of duty and restriction could only be painful. To Ellen she could give some indication of what she felt; Emily would not understand, and she could not tell her father, yet she felt ashamed to admit it:

> I can hardly tell you how time gets on here at Haworth – There is no event whatever to mark its progress – one day resembles another – and all have heavy, lifeless physiognomies – Sunday – baking-day and Saturday are the only ones that bear the slightest distinctive mark – meantime life wears away – I shall soon be thirty – and I have done nothing yet – Sometimes I get melancholy – at the prospect before and behind me – yet it is wrong and foolish to repine – and undoubtedly my duty directs me to stay at home for

the present – There was a time when Haworth was a very pleasant place to me, it is not so now – I feel as if we were all buried here – I long to travel – to work, to live a life of action – Excuse me dear Ellen for troubling you with my fruitless wishes – I will put by the rest and not bother you with them.

Ellen *must* write – if she only knew how welcome her letters were she would write very often, she wrote desperately. 'Your letters and the French newspapers are the only messengers that come to me from the outer world – beyond our Moors, and very welcome messengers they are.'

Charlotte continued to brood on Mary's and her own life, telling Ellen in April that at least real physical danger left a feeling of satisfaction in the mind, of having struggled with a difficulty and overcome it. Strength, courage and experience were positive results which ensued, whereas she doubted whether 'suffering purely mental [h]as any good result unless it be to make us by comparison less sensitive to physical suffering.' At the end of May she was relieved to receive her first letter from Mary, three and a half months after her friend had left England. Mary complained of the oppressive heat and had lived chiefly on oranges on the ship, but she was in excellent spirits and, typically, boasted exuberantly that she was in better health than anyone else on board.

It would be unfair to judge Charlotte's life entirely by her complaints. Undoubtedly this was a particularly difficult period for her but she certainly would have spent some time teaching at the Sunday School and ministering to the poor and sick in the village as she did all her life.

As Mary had predicted, the sole excitements in Charlotte's circle were those concerning marriage, and on this point Charlotte had grown still more worldly wise. The world, she now realised, was run by Mammon and Interest; marriage was decided by money. Her two first novels would rebel against the materialistic world, its hardness and selfishness, which she felt petrified everyone's feelings. Everywhere she turned she was frustrated; it was impossible to behave in a natural fashion, she told Ellen. Ten years ago she would have laughed heartily at Ellen's account of the blunder she made in mistaking the bachelor doctor of Burlington for a married man. She would certainly have thought her over-scrupulous,

and wondered how you could possibly regret being civil to a decent individual merely because he happened to be single instead of double. Now however I can perceive that your scruples are founded on common-sense. I know that if women wish to escape the stigma of husband-seeking they must act and look like marble or clay – cold, expressionless, bloodless – for every appearance of feeling or joy, sorrow, friendliness, antipathy, admiration, disgust, are alike construed by the world into an attempt to hook in a husband. Never mind Nell, well-meaning women have their own consciences to comfort them after all; do not therefore be too much afraid of shewing yourself as you are – affectionate and good hearted – do not too harshly repress sentiments and feelings excellent in themselves because you fear that some puppy may fancy that you are letting them come out to fascinate him; do not condemn yourself to live only by halves because if you shewed too much animation some pragmatical thing in breeches (excuse the expression) might take it into its pate to imagine that you designed to dedicate your precious life to its inanity . . .

More and more she brooded on the lot of women – their lives determined by marriage, and the sort of women who got married, of whom she was becoming convinced that she was not one. Amelia Ringrose, George Nussey's former fiancée, struck her as being the right type for marriage: she was 'an excellent and affectionate girl', notwithstanding her tranquillity, which was so alien to Charlotte as to be incomprehensible. 'If she be lady-like, affectionate and sensible, her decorum and touch of phlegm would have been in decided recommendation not only to George but to most men – as a wife.' Those were the women that were made for marriage – creatures as unlike her own impulsive emotional artistic nature as people on the moon.

She would shortly afterwards make this point in *The Professor*, when Frances interprets Hunsden Yorke's declining to marry Lucia, the actress with whom he was in love, as due to Lucia's gifts not being suited in some way to marriage:

'I am sure Lucia once wore chains and broke them . . . I do not mean matrimonial chains . . . but social chains of some sort. The face is that of one who had made an effort, and a successful and triumphant effort, to wrest some vigorous and valued faculty from insupportable constraint; and when Lucia's faculty got free, I am certain it spread wide pinions and carried her higher than –' She hesitated.

'Than what?' demanded Hunsden.

'Than "les convenances" permitted you to follow.'

'I think you grow spiteful – impertinent.'

'Lucia has trodden the stage,' continued Frances. 'You never seriously thought of marrying her; you admitted her originality, her fearlessness, her energy of body and mind: you delighted in her

225

talent, whatever that was, whether song, dance, or dramatic representation; you worshipped her beauty, which was of the sort after your own heart: but I am sure she filled a sphere from whence you would never have thought of taking a wife.'

The arrival in May 1845 from Ireland of Mr Brontë's new curate, Arthur Bell Nicholls, certainly had no overtones of marriage for Charlotte. Her first description on the 26th of her husband-to-be reads dismissively: 'He appears a respectable young man, reads well and I hope will give satisfaction.' Mr Nicholls, then twenty-seven – two years younger than Charlotte – was in fact a man with admirable qualities – kind, dutiful, hard-working, loyal – an intensely private man of strong beliefs and strong emotions. But his worth was not obvious. It was hidden by his stiff, rather morose manner; nor did his big, heavy-featured, long face hold any romance for Charlotte. In June she wrote to Ellen, who was trying to interest her in the prospect of the Nusseys' new curate: 'I have no desire at all to see your medical–clerical curate – I think he must be like all the other curates I have seen – and they seem to me a self-seeking vain empty race. At this blessed moment we have no less than three of them in Haworth Parish – and God knows there is not one to mend another.' All three had dropped in unexpectedly to tea in what Charlotte clearly felt was a bumptious and presumptuous way.

> The other day they – all three – accompanied by Mr Smidt (of whom by the way I have grievous things to tell you) dropped or rather rushed in unexpectedly to tea. It was Monday and I was hot and tired; still if they had behaved quietly and decently, I would have served them their tea in peace – but they began glorifying themselves and abusing dissenters in such a manner that my temper lost its balance and I pronounced a few sentences sharply and rapidly which struck them all dumb – Papa was greatly horrified also – I don't regret it.

The incident would form the basis for the hilarious opening scene of *Shirley* – the three curates at dinner, which would so horrify Victorian society because of its coarseness. To contemptuous Charlotte there was nothing to admire in these men. As she described them in *Shirley*, instead of expending their energy in performing their pastoral duties, they appeared to do nothing other than be

> rushing backwards and forwards, amongst themselves, to and from their respective lodgings: not a round – but a triangle of visits, which they keep up all the year through, in winter, spring, summer

226

and autumn. Season and weather make no difference; with unintelligible zeal they dare snow and hail, wind and rain, mire and dust, to go and dine, or drink tea, or sup with each other. What attracts them, it would be difficult to say. It is not friendship; for whenever they meet they quarrel. It is not religion; the thing is never named amongst them: theology they may discuss occasionally, but piety – never. It is not the love of eating and drinking; each might have as good a joint and pudding, tea as potent, and toast as succulent, at his own lodgings, as is served to him at this brother's. Mrs Gale, Mrs Hogg and Mrs Whipp – their respective landladies – affirm that 'it is just for nought else but to give folk trouble'. By 'folk' the good ladies of course mean themselves; for indeed they are kept in a continual 'fry' by this system of mutual invasion.

Mr Nicholls, who was the inspiration for Mr Macarthy, who succeeds Mr Malone as curate of Briarfield, would be heard chortling with laughter when the book came out. Meanwhile, however, Charlotte considered him arrogant, stern, narrow-minded and overbearing, with signs of a violent temper. For the first year of their acquaintance relations were very distant: in July 1846 she told Ellen, who saw marriage everywhere, that 'a cold far-away sort of civility are the only terms on which I have ever been with Mr Nicholls'. Her imagination remained in thrall to M. Heger; Mr Nicholls was merely a figure in the unstimulating, unchanging squally landscape of Haworth.

In early June Ellen tried to persuade Charlotte to come and stay with her in the village of Hathersage in Derbyshire. Henry Nussey, Charlotte's old suitor, had at last found himself a bride, Miss Emily Buckhurst, a rich young woman from Sussex, and Ellen had been despatched by her mother to Hathersage, where Henry had recently taken up his post as vicar, to prepare the house for the new bride – to choose the servants and order the furniture. Charlotte was very tempted by the idea – she told Ellen 'I would have given my ears to be able to say yes' – but it was a long journey and not worthwhile because she would have to come back almost immediately on account of her father. Her father's sight was diminishing very rapidly, and she felt reluctant to leave him for a single day.

Charlotte, incapable of criticising him for any selfishness in the way he bore his afflictions, could only feel for him:

. . . can it be wondered at – that as he sees the most precious of his faculties leaving him his spirits sometimes sink? It is hard to feel that his few and scanty pleasures must all soon go – he now has the greatest difficulty in either reading or writing – and then he dreads the state of dependence to which blindness will inevitably reduce

227

him – He fears he will be nothing in his parish – I try to cheer him, sometimes I succeed temporarily – but no consolation can restore his sight or atone for the want of it. Still he is never peevish – never impatient, only anxious and dejected.

Relief came unexpectedly in mid-June when Branwell and Anne came home for a brief holiday with the welcome news that Anne had decided to leave her position as governess to the Robinsons. The presence of calm, capable Anne at home meant that Charlotte felt at liberty to go to Hathersage; she would join Ellen later in the month, after Anne and Emily had made a short expedition together to Ilkley.

Anne never gave much away except to Emily, who was as reserved as herself, and her desire to leave Thorp Green would not have seemed at all strange to Charlotte. She had been there four years, a long time for a Brontë governess, and had wished to leave since she first arrived, even though she had rapidly earned the affection of her two female pupils. From the absence of any references in Charlotte's letters to Ellen, it appears that Anne did not express any strong feelings about leaving, although a month later in her secret diary she would write mysteriously: 'I was then at Thorp Green, and now I am only just escaped from it. I was wishing to leave it then, and if I had known that I had four years longer to stay how wretched I should have been. . . . During my stay I have had some very unpleasant and undreamt-of experience of human nature. . . .'

Charlotte set off south for the beautiful countryside of Derbyshire in high good humour, anticipating an enjoyable holiday with Ellen. The village of Hathersage lies at the edge of the Hallam moors, near the Derbyshire border, about ten miles from the town of Sheffield. Although the rolling moorland, soft green with young heather in summer, gives a bleak tone to the landscape, Hathersage itself is set in a sheltered valley, then enclosed by pasture-land, cornfields and woods. As keenly interested as ever in pictorial effect in landscape, Charlotte was very struck by the romantic hills through which the omnibus bore her, noting with delight the variety and the changes in light – observations which she would eventually put to good use in *Jane Eyre*. Her devoted Ellen was there to meet her, and ahead lay two weeks of agreeable fussing about the number of servants dear Henry should have and the new furnishings appropriate for a bride; there were jellies to be made in the storeroom, beds to be made up, furnishings to be hung.

One can picture Ellen in her snowy white caps and muslin apron, keys jangling at her waist, as she busied herself in preparation for the happy pair's arrival, opening windows to air the rooms and complaining like Mrs Fairfax in *Jane Eyre* that everything gets so damp in apartments that are seldom inhabited. Did part of the plot of *Jane Eyre*, the 'placid-tempered, kind-natured' Mrs Fairfax waiting at Thornfield for the arrival of Mr Rochester, keeping everything fresh in case he should arrive unexpectedly, arise from Ellen waiting for her brother? Was not Charlotte fretting like Jane, as she followed Ellen upstairs and downstairs from room to room, for 'other and more vivid kinds of goodness', for 'the busy world, towns, regions full of life', she scrawled about in her poetry, and meanwhile automatically slipping over her faculties 'the viewless fetters of a uniform and too still existence'.

The chief interest was afforded by going to church, where Charlotte's eyes rested on the many memorials to the Eyre family – on the ancient Charity boards in the tower, the fine fifteenth-century Eyre brasses depicting four couples, four generations of the family with attendant children, while outside in the shady churchyard lay more Eyres beneath their ornate tombs. The name Eyre must have come to have a magical ring when Charlotte heard the legends about the family – the story of the Coat of Arms, the Seven Halls for Seven Sons, the Padley Martyrs.[5] She and Ellen certainly visited members of this ancient squirearchical family still living near Hathersage.

May Eyre, a widow with four unmarried children, inhabited the family seat, North Lees, to which, like Rydings, the description of Thornfield might easily apply: 'It was three stories high, of proportions not vast, though considerable; a gentlemen's manor-house, not a nobleman's seat: battlements round the top gave it a picturesque look.' North Lees was, however, on a grander scale and unlike Rydings, surrounded by quiet and lonely hills as Thornfield is in *Jane Eyre*. It may have been here, although it was a year before she began to write it, that the idea of Bertha Mason began to take shadowy shape in Charlotte's mind, for the first mistress of North Lees was reputed to have become demented and been confined to a room on the second floor where the walls were padded for her comfort; like the mad Mrs Rochester she met her death in a fire. Perhaps it combined with the idea of the obstacles in the way of Henry Nussey's marriage: it had been postponed until 24 May 'in consequence of a death in the lady's family. Those sort of things,' Charlotte had mused at the time, 'never seem to me secure till the knot is actually tied.' Madeira too featured that year. In April Mary Taylor had sailed beyond it. Charlotte was certainly struck by a curious cupboard that the family possessed, which had twelve panels, each depicting one of the twelve apostles. She would reproduce it vividly in the upstairs room at Thornfield where Jane waits with the wounded Mason; 'A great cabinet opposite – whose front, divided into twelve panels, bore, in grim design, the heads of the twelve apostles, each enclosed in its separate panel as in a frame.'

She and Ellen spent some of their time rambling high up on the Hallam moors, probably near the stone pillar known as the Moscar Cross, which marked the crossroads where the old east–west road from Sheffield to Manchester crossed the north–south road from Yorkshire into Derbyshire and which was whitewashed to make it visible in the darkness. Charlotte would later transform this into the place where Jane Eyre wanders for two days and nights before descending into Morton, which bore a distinct resemblance to Hathersage.

After two weeks of pleasurable activity, conscience reasserted itself and on 19 July Charlotte returned home. The journey was enlivened by the presence of a foreigner in the carriage; Charlotte, obsessed by Belgium and thoughts of M. Heger, was delighted to have recognised from this man's features that he was of French origin. She told Ellen with pride that when she had addressed him – 'Monsieur est français, n'est-ce pas?' – he was very surprised and answered in his native tongue, whereupon with an even greater flourish that Sherlock Holmes might have admired, she asked him whether he had not spent the greater part of his life in Germany. He had, and she had guessed it from his speaking French with a German accent.

She got back home at 10 o'clock that night to find Branwell 'ill' (her euphemism for drunk). As he so often was, she was not particularly shocked, but when Anne told her the reason for his illness she was deeply alarmed. Once again, Branwell had been thrown out of his job. Last Thursday, while still at Thorp Green, about to join Mr Robinson and the rest of the family on their summer holiday at Scarborough, he had received a note from Mr Robinson, 'sternly dismissing him, intimating that he had discovered his proceedings, which he characterised as bad beyond expression and charging him on pain of exposure to break off instantly and for ever all communication with every member of his family.'[6] There was now a new burden to add to Charlotte's suffering.

CHAPTER 12

Literary Exertion

Like everything about Branwell, the truth of what happened with the Robinsons is hard to distinguish from his own wild imaginings. It is evident from Charlotte's letters, and Mrs Gaskell, with whom Charlotte had discussed the matter, that she believed the gist of Branwell's own version of events, as related in his letters to his various male friends and drinking companions, which was that he and Mrs Robinson, his employer's wife, had had an affair for the past three years while he was her son's tutor. But even she, once her brother's greatest admirer, admitted as the year went on that she could not distinguish truth from fantasy.

Ever since, moreover, opinion has generally tended to disbelieve Branwell's version of events as the ravings of a consummate fantasist and liar; the combination of the dearth of independent evidence, the unlikely nature of the liaison and all the bizarre subsequent episodes have tended to convince that the greater part of the 'affair' took place only in his imagination. Nevertheless, puzzling facts and details remain which are hard to account for except for the explanation that there were elements of truth, at the very least, in Branwell's story. They will be discussed later in this chapter as they occur chronologically: large, mysterious sums of money sent to Branwell, some definitely from Mrs Robinson's doctor, which Branwell implies came from Mrs Robinson and which no other person of Branwell's acquaintance could have afforded to lend him; and the visit of Mrs Robinson's coachman are the most striking.

The first account of an affair taking place was that of Mrs Gaskell in *The Life of Charlotte Brontë*; some of her information came from Charlotte, some from Mr Brontë. The latter, who shared a room with Branwell for the last year and a half of his son's life and listened to his nightly moanings, approved of the portrait of what he called his son's 'diabolical seductress'. Nevertheless Mrs Gaskell's account had many

231

inaccuracies in it: amongst them she said that Mrs Robinson's daughters threatened to tell their father about 'how she went on with Mr Brontë' – yet it does not square with Charlotte's description in 1847 (two years after Branwell left Thorp Green) of their letters to Anne – they spoke affectionately of their mother and 'never make any allusions intimating acquaintance with her errors. It is to be hoped that they are and always will remain in ignorance of this point.' As Mrs Gaskell does not mention her source, we have no way of knowing whence the information came. Her description of Branwell dying with Mrs Robinson's letters in his pocket is invention; likewise the clandestine meeting at Harrogate between Mrs Robinson and Branwell at which he refused to elope with her is asserted, not proved. Francis Leyland, Branwell's friend and biographer, believed that Mrs Gaskell had simply been picking up Haworth gossip about Mrs Robinson: 'While the lady's reputation was unblemished in the wide circle of her friends or the neighbourhood of her residence, she was being traduced, misrepresented and belied at Haworth and its vicinity alone'.[1] His view was that Branwell made 'statements of circumstances regarding her which had no foundation but in his own heated imagination. The lady, he said, loved him to distraction. She was in a state of inconceivable agony at his loss. Her husband, cruel, brutal and unfeeling, threatened her with his dire indignation, and deprivation of every comfort. Branwell, indeed, told his friend W— by letter that, in consequence of this persecution, the suffering lady "had placed herself under his protection" and many other stories, equally unfounded, extravagant and impossible, were circulated. . . .'[2]

The idea of Branwell being involved in a full-blown affair was evidently difficult for Leyland to envisage. He seems to hint that there was something virginal about him. Thus he wrote, when refuting suggestions that Branwell was Anne's model for Arthur Huntingdon in *Agnes Grey*: 'Even those who have recounted the story of his passion for the wife of his employer, are compelled to say that he remained pure and shrank in horror from the advances which they suppose she made.'[3] It has been supposed that the white-hot heat of indignation in which Mrs Gaskell wrote her description of Mrs Robinson's getting Branwell in her coils must have been occasioned by information given privately to her by Charlotte. Charlotte's letters show that she saw Mrs Robinson as a wicked adulteress; in 1848, writing to Ellen of the Misses Robinson, she stated: 'Of their mother I have not patience to speak; a worse woman, I believe, hardly exists; the more I hear of her the more deeply she revolts me.' Anne was back at the parsonage then, and presumably must have supported some aspects of Branwell's story, otherwise surely Charlotte would not have continued to believe him. But even allowing for Charlotte's anger,

Mrs Gaskell's description of 'the misery she [Mrs Robinson] caused to innocent victims, whose premature deaths may, in part, be laid at her door'[4] seems a trifle strong, particularly if it was based mainly on Haworth gossip.

The truth, however, judging by the following letter, was that Mrs Gaskell had very good reason to believe in Mrs Robinson's guilt, as the quote shows:

> About Lady – (did I tell you the name) [ie. Lady Scott, Mrs Robinson's new name] I see you think me merciless, – but details of her life (past and present) which I heard from her own cousin when I was staying at Sir C. Trevelyans [sic] and which were confirmed by Lady Trevelyan (also a connection) showed her to have been a bad heartless woman for long and long, and to think of her going about calling, and dining out &c. &c. (her own relations have been obliged to drop her acquaintance), while those poor Brontës suffered so – for bad as Branwell was, he was not absolutely ruined for ever, till she got hold of him, and he was not the first, nor the last. However it is a horrid story, and I should not have told it but to show the life of prolonged suffering those Brontë girls had to endure. . . . [Lady Trevelyan's (née Hannah Macauley, sister of Lord Macauley) aunt was married to Lydia Robinson's uncle Thomas Babington.][5]

If then Mrs Robinson did seduce Branwell, and his wild delusions about marriage later were based on promises of hers, she must bear no little responsibility for his decline after the affair. The subsequent messages from Thorp Green about her circumstances may well have been sent by her, worried lest Branwell believe all the vows she could happily make when there was no chance of their being fulfilled, although one continues to wonder why she was so ready to confide in her doctor, and possibly, her coachman.

Lydia Robinson, ironically enough, was the daughter of a great Evangelical, the Reverend Thomas Gisborne, who had been Wilberforce's right-hand man. She had been brought up in wealthy and influential circles, and was rich in her own right. Her sister was married to William Evans, the Member of Parliament for North Derbyshire. On her marriage, her father had fixed £6,000 on her husband for life, and in Edmund Robinson, a landowner of considerable fortune, who had taken holy orders and was of an Evangelical persuasion himself, she had a husband who could certainly provide the same life-style in which she had been brought up.[6]

The Thorp Green estate, in a fertile and well-wooded district twelve miles from York, which included various manors and farms,

233

shooting rights over 2,000 acres and adjoined the estate of Lord Stourton, was sold in 1865 for £116,750, the equivalent of some three million pounds today. From an inventory of contents made in 1846, it was a very large and luxuriously appointed house. The Robinsons were obviously a couple of sophistication who had travelled abroad. The dressing-room off the master bedroom contained a bidet, and there was also a bedstead imported from France. The very large drawing room, laid with a Brussels carpet, contained fine furniture, as did the impressive dining room, which had a more intimate breakfast room opening off it that also housed the piano. On the walls hung expensive oil paintings, beside the bell-pulls used to summon the four or five servants, whose quarters were at the top of the house.

The many guests who came to Thorp Green, often staying for weeks at a time, enjoyed the fine cream and butter from the dairy and Thorp Green's own beer made in the brew house. There were several dogs, and stabling for fourteen horses. Judging by the library's high proportion of sermons, of strong Calvinist bias, including some by Charlotte's old enemy Carus Wilson, a fierce uncompromising religion was much in evidence amidst these pleasant surroundings, which included eleven acres of grounds and lawns. Mr Robinson, like all good Evangelicals, sent monies to convert the poor and unChristian living in misguided darkness both abroad and at home.

Mrs Robinson, who presided over this prosperous, comfortable ménage that was a visible sign of God's grace, was described as a handsome woman by all those who knew her; Mrs Gaskell, informed by her relations, described her as 'a showy woman for her age'. There is a faint overtone of masculinity in her businesslike, pragmatic correspondence. They are hardly the letters of a woman who thought the world well lost for love – romantic poetry is noticeably lacking from the inventory of the Thorp Green bookshelves – and yet it was in such a role that Branwell chose to cast her. But perhaps some romantic impulse, some excitable sexual quality existed in the family beneath the surface calm: both the Robinson daughters were to have a whiff of scandal attached to their names, suggesting a certain flightiness. In 1848, a Mr Milner, a former suitor of Miss Elizabeth Robinson, inserted a notice in the *York Herald* of his intention to publish Miss Robinson's letters, at which Mrs Robinson got an injuction granted against him;[7] he then threatened to bring an action against Miss Robinson for breach of promise of marriage. Even more scandalously, the elder daughter, Lydia, eloped in October 1845, only four months after Branwell's dismissal, with one of a family of travelling actors, Henry Roxby, of Scarborough's Theatre Royal.[8]

Mrs Robinson herself may have possessed considerable attraction, for her second husband, Sir Edward Scott, would marry her very shortly after his wife's death. This second husband was much older than she – she was in her forties – but, like Edmund Robinson, he was a wealthy, well-connected man; he owned a large yacht and they would spend the first winter of their marriage in the Mediterranean. Such marital choices, her background and life, suggest an essentially shrewd, worldly woman, unlikely to have embarked on a serious affair with her son's impoverished young tutor, or to have contemplated marrying him for passionate love when it became clear after Branwell's dismissal that Mr Robinson was dying. That she was also a gracious personality, following at least the outward conventions of the religion in which she was raised, there would seem little doubt.

Branwell's account was as follows:

This lady (though her husband detested me) showed me a degree of kindness which, when I was deeply grieved one day at her husband's conduct, ripened into declarations of more than ordinary feeling. My admiration of her mental and personal attractions, my knowledge of her unselfish sincerity, her sweet temper, and unwearied care for others, with but unrequited return where most should have been given ... although she is seventeen years my senior, all combined to an attachment on my part, and led to reciprocations which I had little looked for. During nearly three years I had daily 'troubled pleasure soon chastised by fear'. Three months since I received a furious letter from my employer, threatening to shoot me if I returned from my vacation, which I was passing at home; and letters from her lady's-maid and physician informed me of the outbreak only checked by her firm courage and resolution that whatever harm came to her, none should come to me. . . . I have lain during nine long weeks utterly shattered in body and broken down in mind. The probability of her becoming free to give me herself and estate never rose to drive away the prospect of her decline under her present grief. I dreaded, too, the wreck of my mind and body, which God knows during a short life have been severely tried. Eleven continuous nights of sleepless horror reduced me almost to blindness, and being taken into Wales to recover, the sweet scenery, the sea, the sound of music caused me fits of unspeakable distress.

Charlotte conveyed some sense of the impact of Branwell's dismissal on the household in her letter to Ellen at the end of July 1845, telling her that they had had 'sad work with Branwell since. He thought of nothing but stunning or drowning his distress of mind. No one in the house could have rest. At last we have been obliged to send him from home for a week, with someone to look after him.' It was Charlotte,

235

always the closest to him and the practical organiser of the home, who took the brunt of his behaviour, and who would be the most critical of it. From Liverpool he wrote to her, expressing 'some sense of contrition for his frantic folly', and though he promised her he would behave better on his return, Charlotte scarcely dared hope for peace in the house while he was there; she was prepared resignedly 'for a season of distress and disquietude'.

Anne's secret diary entry of 31 July, with its mention that at Thorp Green she had had 'some very unpleasant and undreamt of experience of human nature', suggests that she realised that Branwell was having an affair. Or she might possibly have been referring to the beginnings of the romance that led to Miss Robinson's elopement in October, although it seems more likely that this began after Anne had left, when the Robinsons went to stay in Scarborough. In *Agnes Grey*, part of which was written during her time at Thorp Green, Anne gives a fairly frank portrayal of the Misses Robinson and Mrs Robinson in the shape of the frivolous Miss Rosalie Murray and her worldly, attractive mother, Mrs Murray, but the latter's only crime is shallowness, not adultery. However, a poem that Anne wrote on 20 May, called 'If This Be All' shows her at a very low ebb and gives rise to the suspicion that she resigned shortly afterwards because she could not stomach what was going on before her eyes.

> . . . If friendship's solace must decay,
>   When other joys are gone
> And love must keep so far away,
>   While I go wandering on,
>
> Wandering and toiling without gain,
>   The slave of others' will,
> With constant care and frequent pain,
>   Despised, forgotten still;
>
> Grieving to look on vice and sin,
>   Yet powerless to quell,
> The silent current from within,
>   The outward torrent's swell.[9]

Winifred Gerin interviewed the grand-daughter of a Dr William Hall Ryott, who was called in as a consultant for Mr Robinson a number of times. The latter remembered him saying, after Mrs Gaskell's book came out, that Mrs Robinson was wholly to blame for what happened, which seems somewhat thin evidence.[10] The only other material which seemed to show that something had gone on at Thorp Green, a letter from Mrs Robinson to an executor asking that their questioning of her son should be 'less unguarded' than before 'for I am well aware of things he has said to me concerning Thorp Green and *all* which had better not have been said', has been revealed to be a misreading of Mrs Robinson's handwriting: the letter actually concerns the administration of the Thorp Green estate and how much of the cellars Mrs Robinson is entitled to.[11]

At the least, it would appear that there was some flirtation between Branwell and Mrs Robinson. With his ready wit, his charmingly ardent and poetic nature, Branwell would have been quite unlike anyone she had met before, and a welcome contrast to her conventional and dyspeptic husband. Branwell wrote of Mr Robinson's jealousy of him – 'My late employer shrank from the bare idea of my being able to write anything, and had a day's sickness after hearing that Macaulay had sent me a complimentary letter' – yet Charlotte had written in the summer of 1844 how he was 'wondrously valued' in his situation, and if Mr Robinson had such feelings towards the tutor, he could very easily have dismissed him. It did not occur to the vainglorious Branwell, that his employer's sickness and bad-tempered expressions were not due to him but to chronic indigestion, a sign of the illness from which he would die two years later.

Perhaps Branwell and Mrs Robinson shared some furtive embraces; perhaps she allowed more.[12] She may have enjoyed the pleasurable tension of stolen glances; the attentions of the talented and literary tutor may have been particularly flattering to a woman no longer in her prime, particularly when her daughters were just reaching theirs. And perhaps by July 1845 she was tiring of the liaison. It was then that Branwell was left behind at Thorp Green with the Robinsons' son, Edmund, whom he was tutoring for a couple of days before Edmund joined his family at Scarborough. The day after his arrival, on 17 July, Mr Robinson sent the letter to Branwell dismissing him.

Given the timing, it seems plausible that Edmund, having just been alone with Branwell who was very likely drunk and boastfully talkative, reported to his father something of the tutor's ramblings about his mother. Mrs Robinson may then, or possibly before, have told her husband that Branwell had made advances to her, whereupon Mr Robinson acted. Daphne du Maurier's explanation, that Branwell made a pass at the boy and then invented the story of his love for Mrs Robinson because he could not face himself or Charlotte, seems unlikely given the lack of any evidence of Branwell's homosexuality.[13] Charlotte's description of the dismissal to Ellen sounds very much as if she was quoting from what Mr Robinson said: '[Branwell] had last Thursday received a note from Mr Robinson sternly dismissing him, intimating that he had discovered his proceedings, which he characterised as bad beyond expression, and charging him on pain of exposure to break off instantly and for ever all communication with every member of his family.' The words 'on pain of exposure' must suggest that Mr Robinson considered only Branwell to be at fault, since he presumably would not want to expose his own wife.

That the incident did not sour what appear to have been good relations between husband and wife is suggested by the Robinsons' account books. The presents that Mr Robinson gave his wife continued with his customary generosity in July, and 'Darling's bill' appears written by him beside several sums in his cash-book towards the end of 1845.[14] More conclusive is that on 2 January 1846 he changed his will to cut out his daughter who had recently eloped, but showed his continued confidence in his wife in specifying that 'during [his wife's] widowhood every other trustee should attend to [her] wishes in the management of the estate and the execution of the trusts thereby reposed in them'.[15] If she were to remarry, she would lose her income from the estate, ceasing to be a trustee, executor or guardian – a stipulation that was then not uncommon and would not be considered unnatural of him.

Branwell's thoughts, night and day, revolved round Mrs Robinson, her 'inextinguishable love for me', and the terribleness of his loss. He took refuge in drink, indulging in wild drinking bouts followed by maudlin rantings, and he became increasingly dependent on opium, which would leave him semi-comatose. His behaviour made life in the small parsonage almost intolerable. In August 1845 Charlotte wrote to Ellen:

> My hopes ebb low indeed about Branwell – I sometimes fear he will never be fit for much – his bad habits seem more deeply rooted than I thought – The late blow to his prospects and feelings has made him quite reckless.
>
> It is only absolute want of means that acts as any check to him – One ought indeed to hope to the very last and I try to do so – but occasionally hope, in his case, seems a fallacy.

To Branwell it appeared that his formerly understanding family were too insensitive to appreciate the grandeur of the passion that he was at last experiencing. He wrote to his sculptor friend Joseph Leyland of 'the quietude of home, and the inability to make my family aware of the nature of most of my sufferings', and consoled himself with the thought that this suffering would, by some alchemy, be transmuted into great art. He was living out his fantasy, he was the hero of his own romantic odyssey, though the happiness that his nobility of soul deserved was slow in coming. Since his teens, reality and fantasy had been interchangeable, and now at last Angria had come to Yorkshire. He had Joseph Leyland insert a poem that he had written in Wales in the *Halifax Guardian*, and sign it Northangerland. 'I have no other way, not pregnant with danger', he wrote to Leyland in tones reminiscent of Scott, 'of communicating with one whom I cannot help loving.' Had he really told Mrs Robinson of his *alter ego*, the buccaneering Northangerland?

His drunkenness he entitled 'downright illness', brought on by grief and legitimately cushioned by alcohol. He devoted those hours he could snatch from illness, he told his friends, to the composition of a three-volume novel: 'I felt that I must rouse myself to attempt something while roasting daily and nightly over a slow fire – to while away my torment.' By 10 September one volume had been completed of this novel which, he told Leyland, was the result of years of thought and with which he only half-jokingly expected to leap 'from the present bathos of fictitious literature on to the firmly fixed rock honoured by Smollett or Fielding'.

His sisters, meanwhile, were embarked on writing the work which would indeed revivify the present bathos of fictitious literature. Branwell's presence in the parsonage, stretched out half-asleep all day on the sofa and rising only to indulge in his nightly rages, was effectively quelling any last hopes of their starting a school. Ellen, deeply concerned for her friend, suggested a school in Leeds, to which Charlotte told her that their school schemes were 'at rest' for the present. Nor would Charlotte, in her increasing frustration and disgust with Branwell as the year wore on, consider Ellen visiting her: 'While *he* is here – *you* shall not come. I am more confirmed in that resolution the more I see of him. I wish I could say one word to you in his favour but I cannot, therefore I will hold my tongue.' It was equally impossible for her to go to Brookroyd. It was up to her to maintain order in the house, to support her increasingly blind father who was now witnessing with remarkably patient forbearance the disintegration of his once brilliant son.

Branwell's disastrous self-indulgence in his hopeless adulterous love can only have made Charlotte's own sufferings over M. Heger more acute. She began at this time to write the history of her experiences in Brussels, faithfully depicting its scenes but giving herself a happy ending. The curious structure of *The Professor* – it opens with William Crimsworth's letter to a Charles who never appears in the book at all – is explained by the fact that the novel is an amalgam of her Belgian experiences and the world of Angria, the world whose instigating co-creator she now saw with such bitterly disillusioned eyes. Charles is Charlotte's old *alter ego*, the naughty little Lord Charles Wellesley, the narrator of the major proportion of her Angrian tales, just as the brothers Edward and William Crimsworth (the Professor himself) originate in the Percy brothers, the sons of Branwell's own *alter ego*, Alexander Percy, Northangerland. Like the Percy brothers, Edward and William detest one another, and William on the advice of Hunsden Yorke – whose bluff manners were closely modelled on Mary Taylor's father – sets off to seek his fortune in Brussels as a teacher.

Charlotte had certain principles in mind in the construction of her novel: she was making her stand against all the foolish writing she had once devoured, even her hero Scott's romances, which gave no real sense of how life was lived, influenced by her own disillusioning experience, and perhaps the new realism of Dickens and Disraeli. As she later wrote to G.H. Lewes:

> You warn me to beware of melodrama, and you exhort me to adhere to the real. When I first began to write, so impressed was I with the truth of the principles you advocate, that I determined to take Nature and Truth as my sole guides, and to follow their very footprints; I restrained imagination, eschewed romance, repressed excitement; over-bright colouring, too, I avoided, and sought to produce something which should be soft, grave and true.[16]

She would write in a preface to *The Professor*: 'I said to myself that my hero should work his way through life as I had seen real living men work theirs – that he should never get a shilling he had not earned – that no sudden turns should lift him in a moment to wealth and high station.' Art must be true to life and demonstrate experience, unlike the so-called 'Silver Fork' novels which detailed the life supposedly lived in 'high society'. Although it is extremely difficult to ascertain just what Charlotte Brontë did read, it seems likely that her artistic convictions were partly decided in response to a gradual shift in critical opinion towards greater realism. This was as a result of the work of Carlyle and Dickens, whose observation of low life in *Oliver Twist* and *Nicholas Nickleby* broke new ground, which would have been manifest in the various periodicals such as *Blackwood's* and *Fraser's* which she read. And in Frances Henri herself Charlotte created an unusually realistic heroine, just as the girls at the Pensionnat were far from idealised.

The Professor is nevertheless a dream of what might have been for her in Brussels. Frances Henri, the orphan who triumphs over her circumstances and Mlle Reuter's enmity, winning the love of William Crimsworth during class, is Charlotte: Crimsworth himself is an odd mixture of Charlotte and M. Heger. She recreated classroom scenes at the Pensionnat, describing the school exactly and making no attempt, as she would later in *Villette*, to disguise Brussels.

At night as she wrote, sometimes reading out loud to her sisters, sometimes perhaps keeping more private moments to herself, she addressed her imaginary audience, able to pour out her feelings in a way she never could otherwise: 'Reader,' she apostrophised, 'perhaps you were never in Belgium? Happily you don't know the physiognomy of the country? You have not its lineaments defined upon your memory, as I have them on mine?' And she went on: 'Belgium! Name unromantic and unpoetic, yet name that whenever uttered has in my ear a sound, in my heart an echo, such as no other assemblage of syllables, however sweet or classic, can produce. Belgium! I repeat the word, now as I sit alone near midnight.'

She goes on, in the language of death:

It stirs my world of the past like a summons to resurrection: the graves unclose, the dead are raised; thoughts, feelings, memories that slept, are seen by me ascending from the clouds – haloed most of them – but while I gaze on their vapoury forms, and strive to ascertain definitely their outline, the sound which wakened them dies, and they sink, each and all, like a light wreath of mist, absorbed in the mould, recalled to urns, resealed in monuments. Farewell, luminous phantoms.

And in November of 1845 she wrote the last of her surviving letters to M. Heger. It is a moving document, a desperate plea for love in her bleak life of self-sacrifice, but for all its ardour a plea that is couched in terms of his child; perhaps she was consciously avoiding any possible connotation of illicit love, painfully brought home to her by Branwell. In her reference to 'my master', one already hears Jane Eyre using the same address to Mr Rochester:

Monsieur,
The six months of silence have run their course. It is now the 18th of Novr.; my last letter was dated (I think) the 18th of May. I may therefore write to you without failing in my promise.
The summer and autumn seemed very long to me; truth to tell, it has needed painful efforts on my part to bear hitherto the self-denial which I have imposed on myself. You, Monsieur, you cannot conceive what it means; but suppose for a moment that one of your children was separated from you, 160 leagues away, and that you had to remain six months without writing to him, without receiving news of him, without hearing him spoken of, without knowing aught of his health, then you would understand easily all the harshness of such an obligation. I tell you frankly that I have tried

241

meanwhile to forget you, for the remembrance of a person whom one thinks never to see again, and whom nevertheless, one greatly esteems, frets too much the mind; and when one has suffered that kind of anxiety for a year or two, one is ready to do anything to find peace once more. I have done everything; I have sought occupations; I have denied myself absolutely the pleasure of speaking about you – even to Emily; but I have been able to conquer neither my regrets nor my impatience. That, indeed, is humiliating – to be unable to control one's own thoughts, to be the slave of a regret, of a memory, the slave of a fixed and dominant idea which lords it over the mind. Why cannot I have just as much friendship for you, as you for me – neither more nor less? Then should I be so tranquil, so free – I could keep silence then for ten years without an effort.

My father is well but his sight is almost gone. He can neither read nor write. Yet the doctors advise waiting a few months more before attempting an operation. The winter will be a long night for him. He rarely complains; I admire his patience. If Providence wills the same calamity for me, may He at least vouchsafe me as much patience with which to bear it! It seems to me, Monsieur, that there is nothing more galling in great physical misfortunes than to be compelled to make all those about us share in our sufferings. The ills of the soul one can hide, but those which attack the body and destroy the faculties cannot be concealed. My father allows me now to read to him and write for him; he shows me, too, more confidence than he has ever shown before, and that is a great consolation.

Monsieur, I have a favour to ask of you; when you reply to this letter, speak to me a little of yourself, not of me; for I know that if you speak of me it will be to scold me, and this time I would see your kindly side. Speak to me therefore of your children. Never was your brow severe when Louise and Claire and Prosper were by your side. Tell me also something of the School, of the pupils, of the Governesses. Are Mesdemoiselles Blanche, Sophie, and Justine still at Brussels? Tell me where you travelled during the holidays – did you go to the Rhine? Did you not visit Cologne or Coblentz? Tell me, in short, my master, what you will, but tell me something. To write to an ex-assistant-governess (No! I refuse to remember my employment as assistant-governess – I repudiate it) – anyhow, to write to an old pupil cannot be a very interesting occupation for you I know; but for me it is life. Your last letter was stay and prop to me – nourishment to me for half a year. Now I need another and you will give it me; not because you bear me friendship – you cannot have much – but because you are compassionate of soul and you would condemn no one to prolonged suffering to save yourself a few

242

moments' trouble. To forbid me to write to you, to refuse to answer would be to tear from me my only joy on earth, to deprive me of my last privilege – a privilege I never shall consent willingly to surrender. Believe me, my master, in writing to me it is a good deed that you will do. So long as I believe you are pleased with me, so long as I have hope of receiving news from you, I can be at rest and not too sad. But when a prolonged and gloomy silence seems to threaten me with the estrangement of my master – when day by day I await a letter, and when day by day disappointment comes to fling me back into overwhelming sorrow, and the sweet delight of seeing your handwriting and reading your counsel escapes me as a vision that is vain, then fever claims me – I lose appetite and sleep – I pine away.

May I write to you again next May? I would rather wait a year, but it is impossible – it is too long.

C. Brontë.[17]

Then she added the following postscript:

I must say one word to you in English – I wish I could write to you more cheerful letters, for when I read this over, I find it to be somewhat gloomy – but forgive me my dear master – do not be irritated at my sadness – according to the words of the Bible: 'Out of the fulness of the heart, the mouth speaketh' and truly I find it difficult to be cheerful so long as I think I shall never see you more. You will perceive by the defects in this letter that I am forgetting the French language – yet I read all the French books I can get, and learn daily a portion by heart – but I have never heard French spoken but once since I left Brussels – and then it sounded like music in my ears – every word was most precious to me because it reminded me of you – I love French for your sake with all my heart and soul.

Farewell my dear Master – may God protect you with special care and crown you with peculiar blessings.

C.B.

(Professor Heger jotted a couple of notes to himself on the side of the letter, including the name and address of a shoemaker.)

And when no letter came she still wrote to him perhaps once a year. Now in her poetry she expressed her pain, recognising some kind of shame at her actions:

He saw my heart's woe, discerned my soul's anguish,
How in fever, in thirst, in atrophy it pined;

243

Knew he could heal, yet looked and let it languish,
To its moans spirit-deaf, to its pangs spirit-blind.

But once a year he heard a whisper low and dreary,
Appealing for aid, entreating some reply;
Only when sick, soul-worn and torture-weary,
Breathed I that prayer – heaved I that sigh.

He was mute as is the grave, he stood stirless as a tower;
At last I looked up, and saw I prayed to stone;
I asked help of that which to help had no power,
I sought love where love was utterly unknown.

Idolator I kneeled to an idol cut in rock,
I might have slashed my flesh and drawn my heart's best blood,
The Granite God had felt no tenderness, no shock;
My Baal had not seen nor heard nor understood.

In dark remorse I rose – I rose in darker shame,
Self-condemned I withdrew to an exile from my kind;
A solitude I sought where mortal never came,
Hoping in its wilds forgetfulness to find . . .

While Charlotte wrote on, feeling under constant stress from Branwell's behaviour, Emily and Anne had re-established their closeness. Living in their own private worlds, not having Charlotte's jarringly intense reaction to Branwell, they took pleasure in the most ordinary domestic tasks and in their constant writing – Anne was already immersed in *Agnes Grey*, Emily beginning *Wuthering Heights*, and of course there was their poetry. Emily's calm account of her life in her birthday paper of the summer of 1845 makes a strong contrast to Charlotte's feverish agitation:

I am quite contented for myself: not as idle as formerly, altogether as hearty, and having learnt to make the most of the present and long for the future with the fidgetiness that I cannot do all I wish; seldom or never troubled with nothing to do, and merely desiring that everybody could be as comfortable as myself and as undesponding, and then we should have a very tolerable world of it. . . . Tabby has just been teasing me as formerly to 'Pilloputate'. Anne and I should have picked the black-currants if it had been fine and sunshiny. I must hurry off now to my turning and ironing. I have plenty of work on hands, and writing, and am altogether full of business.

Some of the results of that writing Charlotte happened to come across shortly afterwards; she picked up one of Emily's small notebooks containing poetry, which her sister had probably left in the dining room, and began to read. The extraordinary excitement that overcame her at this moment she related in her *Biographical Notice of Ellis and Acton Bell*, written in 1850:

One day, in the autumn of 1845, I accidentally lighted on a MS volume of verse in my sister Emily's handwriting. Of course, I was not surprised, knowing that she could and did write verse: I looked it over, and something more than surprise seized me — a deep conviction that these were not common effusions nor at all like the poetry women generally write. . . . To my ear, they had also a peculiar music — wild, melancholy and elevating.

In a later private letter she would be even more frank:

. . . they stirred my heart like the sound of a trumpet when I read them alone and in secret. The deep excitement I felt forced from me the confession of the discovery I had made. I was sternly rated at first for having taken an unwarrantable liberty. This I expected, for Ellis Bell [Emily] is of no flexible or ordinary materials. By dint of entreaty and reason I at last wrung out a reluctant consent to have the 'rhymes' as they were contemptuously termed, published. The author never alludes to them; or, when she does, it is with scorn. But I know no woman that ever lived ever wrote such poetry before. Condensed energy, clearness, finish — strange strong pathos are their characteristics; utterly different from the weak diffusiveness, the laboured yet most feeble wordiness, which dilute the writing of even very popular poetesses.[18]

Inspired by Emily's work, the genius of which she was the first to recognise, Charlotte went about the difficult task of finding a publisher. She had first to overcome Emily's reluctance, for as she related,

My sister Emily was not a person of demonstrative character, nor one, on the recesses of whose mind and feelings, even those nearest and dearest to her could, with impunity, intrude unlicensed; it took hours to reconcile her to the discovery I had made, and days to persuade her that such poems merited publication. I knew, however, that a mind like hers could not be without some latent spark of honourable ambition, and refused to be discouraged in my attempts to fan that spark to flame.

The plan was to publish a collection of poems by all three sisters, and they set about making their selections and copying them in a fair hand. According to Charlotte, they were aware of the problems ahead: 'Though inexperienced ourselves, we had read of the experience of others.' One difficulty was that the 1840s were a poor time for the publication of poetry; after the extraordinary popularity of Scott and Byron earlier in the century, the demand for poetry had declined. Edward Moxon, the great Victorian publisher of poetry, whose editions the Brontës owned, was unwilling to publish Elizabeth Barrett Browning's poems in 1844, although she was then one of the most famous poets of her era, and he even apparently showed some reluctance to publish Wordsworth.[19] Branwell was aware of this state of affairs, probably on account of his friendship with the Leyland family, who were book publishers as well as booksellers. He wrote in his usual parody of a man of the world to Leyland when talking about his own novel: '. . . in the present state of the publishing and reading world a Novel is the most saleable article, so that where ten pounds would be offered for a work the production of which would require the utmost stretch of a man's intellect – two hundred pounds would be a refused offer for three volumes whose composition would require the smoking of a cigar and the humming of a tune.' By 1848 Charlotte herself would be sufficiently knowledgeable to say that ' "The Trade" are not very fond of hearing about poetry, and that it is but too often a profitless encumbrance on the shelves of the booksellers' shop.'

The first difficulty Charlotte encountered was to get any answers at all from publishers. To her polite enquiries, publishers, like publishers nowadays faced with a mountain of unsolicited correspondence from a public unaware of the huge volume of letters delivered daily to their offices, returned no answer. But Charlotte was made of sterner stuff; she *would* be responded to. 'Greatly harassed by this obstacle, I ventured to apply to Messrs Chambers of Edinburgh for a word of advice [this was the firm who published the encyclopaedia, and Charlotte may have felt that they were in the business of imparting knowledge]; *they* may have forgotten the circumstance, but *I* have not, for from them I received a brief and business-like, but civil and sensible reply, on which we acted, and at last made way.'

Chambers recommended Charlotte to a firm called Aylott and Jones, of 8 Paternoster Row, London, who were stationers and booksellers as well as publishers of classical and theological books, and also did what would nowadays be termed vanity publishing, i.e. the author bears the costs. This was a fairly common practice in the nineteenth century – *Wuthering Heights* and *Agnes Grey* were both published with the authors' bearing some of the expense. Chambers may have suggested this method of publishing to Charlotte, who wrote in businesslike manner to Aylott and Jones on 28 January 1846:

> Gentlemen – May I request to be informed whether you would undertake the publication of a Collection of short poems in I vol. oct.
>
> If you object to publishing the work at your own risk, would you undertake it on the Author's account – I am gentlemen,
> Your obdt. hmble. Servt.
>
> C. Brontë

The publishers replied with alacrity, agreeing that the authors should bear the cost, in effect publishing themselves. By 31 January Charlotte was writing back saying: 'I should wish now to know as soon as possible the cost of paper and printing. I will then send the necessary remittance together with the manuscript.' Long years of fascination with Byron and Wordsworth meant that she knew exactly what sort of production she wanted: 'I should like it to be printed in 1 octavo volume of the same quality of paper and size of type as Moxon's last edition of Wordsworth. The poems will occupy – I should think from 200 to 250 pages.'

In case any problems should arise, she thought she ought to be frank from the outset about the nature of the poetry: 'They are not the production of a Clergyman nor are they exclusively of a religious character – but I presume these circumstances will be immaterial.' She now suggested that she should send them the manuscript in order for them to calculate the expense of publication, but before she did this she said that she would like to have 'some idea of the probable cost' first.

The sisters had to be sure that the cost would not exceed their small means, for all they had was their aunt's legacy. This they had not left idle. Women might not be able to go into business in the 1840s, as Mary Taylor complained, but if they had access to their own money they could not be prevented from attempting to increase it. On the advice of the redoubtable Miss Wooler, they had chosen to speculate in railway shares; as in so many of their affairs, their father was not consulted, perhaps because he still treated them like children, keeping firm hold of the housekeeping purse. Surprisingly, unworldly Emily was the business manager. As usual, she was not put off by her lack of access to information about the great world outside the moors; answers could always be found through the written word. She had gleaned information through the rash of advertisements to be found in every newspaper, tempting optimistic fellow-countrymen to invest in the mighty railways now roaring in every direction across the English landscape. Charlotte told Miss Wooler: 'Emily has made herself mistress of the necessary degree of knowledge for conducting the matter, by dint of carefully reading every paragraph and every advertisement in the newspapers that related to railroads and as we have abstained from all gambling, all mere speculative buying-in and selling-out – we have got on very decently.'[20]

The different characters of Emily and Charlotte showed in their reaction to the Railway Panic of early 1846. Charlotte wrote to Miss Wooler: 'We have never hitherto consulted any one but you on our affairs – nor have we told anyone else of the degree of success our small capital has met with, because, after all, there is nothing so uncertain as railroads; the price of shares varies continually – and any day a small shareholder may find his funds shrunk to their original dimensions.' She wished to sell their shares and invest in a safer investment before it was too late, as her pessimistic and practical nature could not believe 'that even the very best lines will continue for many years at their present premiums'. However, she could not persuade Emily and Anne to see the matter from her point of view, and felt that she would rather run the risk of loss than 'hurt Emily's feelings by acting in direct opposition to her opinion', particularly as Emily had managed Charlotte's affairs 'in a most handsome and able manner for me when I was at Brussels'. Nevertheless, she was nettled enough by what had evidently been quite an argument to make what is tantamount to a rather strong if veiled complaint about her sister's nature:

> Disinterested and energetic she certainly is and if she be not quite so tractable or open to conviction as I could wish I must remember perfection is not the lot of humanity and as long as we can regard those we love, and to whom we are closely allied with profound and never-shaken esteem, it is a small thing that they should vex us occasionally by, what appear to us, unreasonable and headstrong notions.[21]

With advice from Miss Wooler, Charlotte and Emily had also investigated the possibilities of buying a life insurance annuity, apparently as an alternative to railway shares. The 'terms for female lives are very low'. The insurance agent whom they had consulted, Mr Bignold, could only offer $4\frac{1}{2}$ per cent for annuities purchased at twenty-five years of age, and 5 per cent for those at thirty, but as none of the sisters had yet reached the age of thirty they had thought it best to take a year to consider the matter. The insurance agent had also produced an apparently more remunerative plan: 'Mr Bignold also says that an annuity purchased at thirty – and deferred twelve years – would produce 10 per cent.' But Charlotte felt disinclined to run so great a risk: 'It appears to me that, under favourable circumstances and with moderate economy one might in that space of time save the difference out of the interest.' Ironic words. Not even ten more years of life remained to these busy young women making their careful, modest plans for the future.

Money considerations were particularly pressing as Branwell continued to decay, creating a financial as well as emotional burden on the household. At the end of December 1845, Charlotte wrote to Ellen with sympathetic understanding of the problems posed to the family by the mentally ill George Nussey: 'You say well in speaking of Branwell that no sufferings are so awful as those brought on by dissipation – alas! I see the truth of this observation daily proved. Ann and Mercy [Nussey] must have a weary and burdensome life of it in waiting upon their unhappy brother. It seems grievous indeed that those who have not sinned should suffer so largely.' She went on pathetically: 'Write to me a little oftener Ellen. I am very glad to get your notes. Remember me kindly to your Mother and Sisters.'

Branwell had failed to get the secretaryship of a railway committee to which he had applied, and his behaviour was becoming worse. In January Charlotte told Miss Wooler that she feared he 'has rendered himself incapable of filling any respectable station in life . . . if money were at his disposal he would use it only to his own injury. The faculty of self-government is, I fear, almost destroyed in him.' She regretted it, but 'the house must now be barred to visitors'.

Miss Wooler's example was particularly important to her:

I always feel a peculiar satisfaction when I hear of your enjoying yourself, because it proves to me that there is really such a thing as retributive justice even in this world; you worked hard, you denied yourself all pleasure, almost all relaxation in your youth and the prime of your life – now you are free – and that while you have still, I hope, many years of vigour and health, in which you can enjoy freedom – Besides I have another and very egotistical motive for being pleased – it seems that even 'a lone woman' can be happy, as well as cherished wives and proud mothers.

What a terrifying indictment of an age, and how admirable is Charlotte's refusal to give in to custom. She went on bravely:

I speculate much on the existence of unmarried and never-to-be-married women nowadays, and I have already got to the point of considering that there is no more respectable character on this earth

249

than an unmarried woman who makes her own way through life quietly persevering – without support of husband or brother, and who, having attained the age of 45 or upwards – retains in her possession a well-regulated mind, a disposition to enjoy simple pleasures, fortitude to support inevitable pains, sympathy with the sufferings of others, and willingness to relieve want as far as her means extend.

There was diversion from these thoughts, however, in the Brontës' publishing venture. On 6 February, Charlotte sent off the manuscript to Aylott and Jones; it was in two parcels on account of the weight, and accompanied by the following note: 'You will perceive that the Poems are the work of three persons – relatives – their separate pieces are distinguished by their respective signatures.' Those signatures were Currer, Ellis and Acton Bell, being of course Charlotte, Emily and Anne Brontë, and the first name of the author was to appear at the foot of each poem. It has been hazarded that the Brontës chose the name Bell as a joke about the lugubrious Mr Arthur Bell Nicholls, who was particularly proud of his Bell blood (the family had a considerable pedigree) and was wont to emphasise his middle name; certainly it would turn out to have been an ironically appropriate choice for Charlotte. More interesting was the reason for their assumption of *noms-de-plume*, which Charlotte would four years later explain in her *Biographical Notice of 1850*:

> Averse to personal publicity, we veiled our own names under those of Currer, Ellis, and Acton Bell; the ambiguous choice being dictated by a sort of conscientious scruple at assuming Christian names positively masculine, while we did not like to declare ourselves women, because – without at that time suspecting that our mode of writing and thinking was not what is called 'feminine' – we had a vague impression that authoresses are liable to be looked on with prejudice; we had noticed how critics sometimes use for their chastisement the weapon of personality, and for their reward, a flattery, which is not true praise.

Like any anxious new author, Charlotte wrote off asking if the manuscript had arrived safely. On 16 February she received a letter informing her that the manuscript would be a slimmer volume than she had anticipated and suggested that she advise on a more suitable model. Charlotte was rather thrown by this: 'I cannot name another model which I should like it precisely to resemble, yet I think a duodecimo form and a somewhat reduced – though still *clear* type would be preferable.' She thought the publisher's judgement and experience would be better able to tell her what was suitable. She stipulated only '*clear* type – not too small – and good paper'.

On 21 February she finally decided on a 'long primer type' for the poems, and stated that she would send off the cost of the production, £31 10s, which was what the firm's estimate had been. On 3 March, she accompanied the money draft with a note to say that she supposed 'there is nothing now to prevent your immediately commencing the printing of the work'. Once they got the draft, she added with barely concealed impatience, would they please inform her how soon it would take to get the poems printed.

Not a word of this activity was breathed to Ellen, close as their relationship was, but Charlotte had finally acceded to Ellen's pleas to visit her, spending a week at Brookroyd at the end of February. While away she had taken it upon herself to seek the professional opinion of a surgeon named Mr Carr in Leeds about her father's eyesight. Mr Carr, a connection of the Nusseys, had quite sanguine hopes of success for an operation, though he recommended deferring it until later in the year. Surgery in the nineteenth century, particularly eye surgery, was in its puny infancy; such anaesthetics that existed were taken on a voluntary basis and were of an alcoholic nature, although there was ether. It is no wonder that Charlotte reported to Ellen on 3 March, on her return, that her poor father, though cheered by reports of successful operations, could not quite conceal his relief at the idea of putting it off.

The fear that the Brontës might soon be without a roof over their heads if the incumbent failed to minister to his flock hung constantly in the background, to add to the daily problem of Branwell. Charlotte wrote in the same letter to Ellen of 3 March that she had gone into his room 'about an hour after I got home – it was very forced work to address him. I might have spared myself the trouble as he took no notice and made no reply – he was stupified. My fears were not in vain. Emily tells me that he got a sovereign from Papa while I have been away under the pretence of paying a pressing debt – he went immediately and changed it at a public house – and has employed it as was to be expected. Emily concluded her account by saying he was a hopeless being.' From Emily, who never said more than was absolutely necessary, who had such a strong sense of a moral universe, it was a total condemnation. Charlotte wrote on: 'It is too true. In his present state it is scarcely possible to stay in the room where he is. What the future has in store I do not know.'

But by 11 March, some distraction from their immediate circumstances was provided by the arrival of the first proofs of the poetry. Charlotte, still maintaining her front as the Bells' agent, told Aylott and Jones that if there was any doubt at all about the printer's competency to correct errors, 'I would prefer submitting each sheet to the inspection of the Authors – because such a mistake for instance as *tumbling* stars instead of *trembling* would suffice to throw an air of absurdity over a whole poem – but if you know from experience that he is to be relied on, I would trust to your assurance on the subject and leave the task of correction to him.' She said that the printing and the paper appeared satisfactory to her, and though she was anxious to have the work out as soon as possible, the priority was 'that it should be got up in a manner creditable to the Publishers and agreeable to the Authors'. Her next letter informs Aylott and Jones that the authors had finally decided that they would prefer to have all the proofs sent to them in turn, but they need not enclose the manuscript 'as they can correct the errors from memory'.

The bulky packets from London addressed to C. Brontë Esq had clearly caused some confusion among the inquisitive Post Office operatives of Haworth and Keighley, and on 28 March Charlotte decided to disabuse the publishers of their assumption that C. Brontë was a man:

> Gentlemen – As proofs have hitherto always come safe to hand under the direction of C. Brontë *Esq.*, I have not thought it necessary to request you to change it, but a little mistake having occurred yesterday, I think it will be better to send them to me in future under my *real* address which is
> Miss Brontë
Revd. P. Brontë's &c.
> I am Gentlemen Yrs. trly.
> C. Brontë

The proofs of the poetry had evidently set off thoughts of further publication; perhaps, after all, a career in letters was possible. Just over a week later, Charlotte wrote to Aylott and Jones:

> Gentlemen,
> C., E. and A. Bell are now preparing for the Press a work of fiction, consisting of three distinct and unconnected tales which may be published either together as a work of 3 vols. of the ordinary size, or separately as single vols. as shall be deemed most advisable.

The authors, Charlotte told them, were not willing to publish the novels – *Wuthering Heights*, *Agnes Grey* and *The Professor* – 'on their own account', and wished to know if Aylott and Jones would be prepared to publish the tales themselves. With an urgency that denoted the return of her old ambition and a practical determination to earn money, Charlotte said that 'an early answer will oblige as in case of your negativing the proposal, inquiry must be made of other Publishers'.

Aylott and Jones wrote back refusing the novels, for they did not publish work of this type. Years later Mrs Martyn, one of the partners in the firm, told a Brontë scholar that her father had refused to publish novels 'as he was rather old-fashioned and had very narrow views regarding light literature'. However, the publishers offered to give advice, to which Charlotte wrote back eagerly on 11 April:

> It is evident that unknown authors have great difficulties to contend with before they can succeed in bringing their works before the public; can you give me any hint as to the way in which these difficulties are best met? For instance, in the present case, where a work of fiction is in question, in what form would a publisher be likely to accept the MS? Whether offered as a work of three vols. or as tales which might be published in numbers or as contributions to a periodical?
>
> What publishers would be most likely to receive favourably a proposal of this nature?
>
> Would it suffice to *write* to a publisher on the subject or would it be necessary to have recourse to a personal interview?
>
> Your opinion and advice on these three points or on any other which your experience may suggest as important, would be esteemed by us a favour.

Meanwhile, Charlotte's health was far from good. The sharp, cruel winds from the north and east, the prevailing ones at Haworth, had made her ill and nervous, and she longed for mild south and west breezes. She told Ellen in April that she was thankful that her father continued pretty well, although he was often made 'very miserable in mind by Branwell's wretched conduct. There, there is no change but for the worse.'

As his sisters were doggedly beginning to scale the publishing barricades, Branwell, when not ragingly drunk, was passing the hours writing mournful poetry and drawing morbid sketches of funerary sculptures of himself consumed by the flames of hell. Occasionally he could be prevailed upon to write letters on behalf of the sexton. He was being encouraged by Joseph Leyland to write a long epic poem about a Leyland family legend at Morley Hall in Lancashire, and his discussion of the difficulties of getting published makes ironic reading beside his sisters' achievements, of which he would remain totally ignorant:

253

Literary exertion would seem a resource – to while away the unhappy hours – but the depression attendant on it, and the almost hopelessness of bursting through the barriers of literary circles, and getting a hearing among publishers, make me disheartened and indifferent; for I cannot write what would be thrown, unread, into a library fire. Otherwise I have the materials for a respectably sized volume, and if I were in London personally I might perhaps try Henry Moxon – a patroniser of the sons of rhyme; though I dare say the poor man often smarts for his liberality in publishing hideous trash.[22]

By the end of May 1846, *Poems by Currer, Ellis and Acton Bell* had been published. The ever-practical Charlotte, her mood altered by enjoyable occupation, had decided that the price 'may be fixed at 5s or if you think that too much for the size of the volume – say 4s', and directed which periodicals should receive copies and advertisements. Unlike today's newspapers, in order to get editorial attention there was a straightforward *quid pro quo*. Copies were sent to Colburn's *New Monthly*, Bentley's *Miscellany*, *Hood's Magazine*, *Jerrold's Shilling Magazine*, Charlotte's beloved *Blackwood's*, the *Edinburgh Review*, Tait's *Edinburgh Magazine*, the *Dublin University Magazine*, the *Daily News* and the *Britannia Newspaper*. At her request the publishers also added periodicals to which they were in the habit of sending their publications: the *Athenaeum*, the *Literary Gazette*, the *Critic*, *The Times*.

Charlotte wished them to spend only £2 upon advertisements, as she thought that 'the success of a work depends more on the notice it receives from periodicals than on the quantity of advertisements'. She wanted to know as soon as possible when the copies would be sent to the magazines and newspapers; and said she would be grateful if they would send on to her any review that appeared in one of the periodicals, otherwise she might miss it. It was her intention, if the poems were remarked on favourably, to spend some more money on advertising. And she went on, little guessing that a year and a half later England would resound with the Brontës' fame: 'If, on the other hand, they should pass unnoticed or be condemned, I consider it would be quite useless to advertise as there is nothing either in the title of the work or the names of the authors to attract attention from a single individual.'[23]

There is no record of what the Brontë sisters felt on receipt of the copies of their first published work, a slim green volume. Whatever their excitement at this shared secret, it was overshadowed by the news at the same time of Mr Robinson's death. Branwell, Charlotte reported caustically to Ellen on 17 June, had used the death 'for a pretext to throw all about him into hubbub and confusion with his emotions, etc., etc.' Branwell had been told, perhaps by Mrs Robinson's coachman, perhaps by the Robinson doctor, that Mr Robinson had altered his will before he died in order to prevent any chance of a marriage between Branwell and his wife. As Branwell reported to Charlotte, Mr Robinson had stipulated that his wife 'should not have a shilling if she ever ventured to reopen any communication with him'. And to Ellen she went on:

Of course, he then became intolerable. To Papa he allows rest neither day nor night, and he is continually screwing money out of him, sometimes threatening that he will kill himself if it is withheld from him. He says Mrs Robinson is now insane; that her mind is a complete wreck owing to remorse for her conduct to Mr Robinson (whose end it appears was hastened by distress of mind) and grief for having lost him. I do not know how much to believe of what he says, but I fear she is very ill. Branwell declares that he neither can nor will do anything for himself; good situations have been offered him more than once, for which, by a fortnight's work, he might have qualified himself, but he will do nothing, except drink and make us all wretched.

Exactly where the information came from about Mr Robinson's will is unclear. Branwell told his friend Francis Grundy that Mrs Robinson's coachman had come to see him at Haworth and given him 'the statement of her case', but whether this was on Mrs Robinson's order is not certain. It would seem strange in such a formal household for her to entrust the coachman with her intimate affairs. But the coachman certainly seems to have come to Haworth. The owner of the Black Bull, and various others in the village, told Mrs Gaskell in 1856 that a groom arrived from the Robinsons, and sent a messenger up to the parsonage for Branwell. Branwell came down to the inn and was closeted with the man for some time. Then the groom came out, paid his bill, mounted his horse and set off down the steep narrow street. Branwell stayed in the room alone. For about an hour the people outside the room heard no sound; then they heard a noise 'like the bleating of a calf' and, on opening the door, Branwell was found in a kind of fit. The people at the Black Bull informed Mrs Gaskell that it was on account of being forbidden by Mrs Robinson from ever seeing her again.

This visit was not the only communication from Thorp Green. According to Branwell there was a letter from Mrs Robinson's maid describing vows Mrs Robinson had been forced to make at her husband's deathbed never to see Branwell again. There was also a

255

letter from Dr Crosby, the Robinsons' doctor who had attended Mr Robinson in his last illness. According to Branwell this was a 'long, kind and faithful' letter, and he represented Crosby as knowing about the love affair and having been told by Mrs Robinson of her great unhappiness, of her 'inextinguishable love' for him, 'her horror at having been the first to delude me into wretchedness, and her agony at having been the cause of the death of her husband, who, in his last hours, bitterly repented of his treatment of her. . . . Her sensitive mind was totally wrecked. She wandered into talking of entering a nunnery; and the Doctor fairly debars one from hope in the future.'

From this time Branwell gave himself up totally to his obsession with Mrs Robinson; it was the final stage in his deterioration, which would result in his death two years later. He had 'fully expected a change of Will, and difficulties placed in my way by powerful and wealthy men', he ranted with a little of his father's paranoia, 'but I *hardly* expected the hopeless ruin of the mind that I loved even more than its body,' he told Leyland, and anyone else to whom he wrote. In Branwell's eyes: 'For two years (including one year of absence) a lady intensely loved me as I did her, and each sacrificed to that love all we had to sacrifice, and held out to each other HOPE for our guide to the future. She was all I could wish for in a woman, and vastly above me in rank, and she loved me even better than I did her. . . .'

Mrs Robinson showed, however, sufficient possession of her 'totally wrecked' mind to be able to write of her dead husband in her cash books such affectionate jottings as '£18 paid to the Old Servants (for my Angel)', 19 May; 'Edmund's sad funeral', 5 June; 'My Angel Edmund' on 17 June on the blotting paper opposite the accounts; and on 23 August, she spent £2 5s on 'My locket for *My* Edmund's Hair.'

Whatever Branwell's depiction of the affair and his wallowing in the miseries of unrequited love, right up till his death two years later he was the recipient of large sums of money of mysterious provenance, some of which he implied came from Mrs Robinson.[24] According to Mrs Gaskell, who may have been so informed by Charlotte, Branwell was being sent £20 at a time by Mrs Robinson. He himself referred to Dr Crosby as someone from whom he could be absolutely certain of obtaining money; he speaks of 'an advance through his hands which I am sure to obtain'.[25] Branwell would refer to writing to him at least once to ask for money to settle his bills; since he had no reason to lie about getting money from him – the letters in which he talks about this are frantic letters about debt – it seems quite probable that Dr Crosby, a fellow Freemason, did kindheartedly send him money. The only other source of income, who had sometimes helped him out before, was his friend Joseph Leyland, who was himself rapidly sinking into debt in this period and in no position to lend him what

Charlotte described as 'a considerable sum of money'. It has been suggested that Leyland might have drawn on his family, who owned several businesses, but as they did not alleviate his own hard-up state, it seems most unlikely that they would help out his friend. In any case it is in letters to Leyland that Branwell talks of being certain to get money from Crosby and of a settlement which he has reason to hope will be shortly, although this settlement can't do much to 'make a fellow's soul like a calm bowl of creamed milk'.[26]

The Robinson Papers are not particularly helpful on this matter. The only payments to the Brontës are those of Anne and Branwell's wages. Although some biographers have pointed to sums for Dr Crosby for unnamed services in this period, the amounts involved are very small – approximately £3 or £4 – and do not correlate to the dates when Branwell received money. Since Branwell refers to Dr Crosby as a source of funds it seems that one can probably dismiss the fairly unlikely idea of wealthy manufacturers in the Luddenden Bridge area clubbing together to assist the popular Branwell.[27]

Charlotte's increasing disgust with Branwell over the next two years may be partially accounted for by the suspicion that to his now legion faults he had added the crime of blackmail. She, her sisters and father tried vainly to get Branwell to pull himself together. He was asked to do small tasks, such as continuing to do the paperwork for the sexton. In an effort to show affection and interest in him they asked him to get Joseph Leyland to send them the *bas relief* of his head which the latter had sculpted.[28] This life-size relief was, according to Francis Leyland, a perfect likeness, and there is something unusually expressive about what was intended to be a fairly formal portrait medallion. It shows the high forehead, clustered round with red curls *en brosse*, the style favoured by Lord Byron a generation earlier but in this instance cut not by a smart London barber but by Branwell himself; the high-bridged, rather fine Roman nose, a long upper lip, well-moulded mouth and neat though receding chin, surrounded by a bush of red whiskers. He had always been the best-looking of Mr Brontë's children, as would later impress itself so forcefully on Charlotte when she looked on Branwell's corpse and was suddenly overwhelmed at the utter waste of her brother's life and all his gifts. But by 1846, the drink and drugs and irregular hours were taking their toll, and Branwell was appearing increasingly drawn and haggard.

In the face of Branwell's continued wild behaviour, Charlotte's outward adherence to the code of self-sacrifice that she had already articulated grew more and more severe. She noticeably began to make a point of welcoming difficulty, of submitting stoically to fate. To Ellen, who was now wondering whether she should go out into the world as a governess or stay at home and look after her mother,

Charlotte wrote in subdued contrast to her twenty-five-year-old impatient desire to get on in the world:

> . . . It will not, apparently, as far as short-sighted humanity can see, be for *your* advantage to remain at Brookroyd, nor will you be praiscd and admircd for rcmaining at home to comfort your mother; yet, probably, your own conscience will approve, and if it does, stay with her. I recommend you to do what I am trying to do myself.

But on 4 July 1846, it was her refusal to submit to fate which paid off. The sisters received the first two reviews of the Bells' work. The unnamed reviewer of the *Critic* wrote: 'It is long since we have enjoyed a volume of such genuine poetry as this. Amid the heaps of trash and trumpery in the shape of verses, which lumber the table of the literary journalist, this small book of some 170 pages only has come like a ray of sunshine, gladdening the eye with present glory, and the heart with promise of bright hours in store.' The reviewer was pleased to find 'no sickly affectations, no namby-pamby, no tedious imitations of familiar strains, but original thoughts, expressed in the true language of poetry'. Though he/she noted some imitation of great masters, a trace of Tennyson here, Wordsworth there, 'they are *in the manner* only, and not servile copies'.[29] For the most part the Bells were praised for their originality – as their novels would be: 'They have chosen subjects that have freshness in them, and their handling is after a fashion of their own. To those whose love of poetry is more a matter of education than of heart, it is probable that these poems may not prove attractive; they too much violate the conventionalities of poetry for such as look only to form and not to substance.'[30]

The final paragraph of the notice so pleased the Brontës that Charlotte outlaid another £10 on advertisements of the poems with this part of the review appended to it: 'They in whose hearts are chords strung by nature to sympathize with the beautiful and true in the world without, and their embodiments by the gifted among their fellow men, will recognize in the composition of Currer, Ellis and Acton Bell, the present of more genius than it was supposed this utilitarian age had devoted to the loftier exercises of the intellect.' Prefiguring the wild rumours that would run about London a year and a half later on the publication of *Jane Eyre*, the reviewer was most curious about the identity of these mysterious Bells; whether 'the triumvirate' had published in concert, or if their association was the work of an editor, judging them kindred spirits, was not known.

In its review, the *Athenaeum* noted that here was 'a family in whom appears to run the instinct of song'.[31] Ellis was singled out for special praise, a verdict which has stood the test of time. While Acton requires the 'indulgences of affection', and Currer was 'halfway betwixt the level of Acton's and the elevation of Ellis', in Ellis it rose 'into an inspiration, which may yet find an audience in the outer world. A fine quaint spirit has the latter, which may have things to speak that men will be glad to hear, and an evident power of wing that may reach heights not here attempted.'

Charlotte would later tell Mrs Gaskell, with an honest recognition of the weakness beside Emily's of her own poems (which in any case did not show her at her best), that she did not like her share of the book, nor particularly want it read. She thought Ellis Bell's poetry 'good and vigorous', and that Acton's had 'the merit of truth and simplicity'. But as far as her own were concerned, she dismissed them 'as juvenile productions, the restless effervescence of a mind that would not be still. In those days the sea too often "wrought and was tempestuous", and wind, sand, shingle – all turned up in the tumult'.

The two reviews had given them heart. The battlements of the literary world were not down, but the ladders had held. The boiling oil had not appeared. They had been deemed to have talent; the long, long literary apprenticeship seemed at last to be paying off. On 4 July 'Mr Currer Bell' sent, on Aylott and Jones' advice, the now completed manuscripts of *Wuthering Heights*, *Agnes Grey* and *The Professor* to Henry Colburn, beginning what would be a long journey around publishers.

By 18 July, the sisters learned that a princely total of two copies had been sold, out of a total printing of what G.D. Hargreaves, author of the pioneering essay on the Bell poems, has calculated to be probably 1,000 copies;[32] there were 961 copies of the work still left unsold in 1848. Since Matthew Arnold's early poetry was restricted to 500 copies, Hargreaves suggests that the number printed was 'characteristically bold' of Charlotte; however, since Charlotte was dependent for information about appropriate print runs on her publishers, whose judgement she followed on all other matters, it seems probable that she had simply taken Aylott and Jones' advice on this also. However, there was some encouragement to be gleaned from the fact that one of the two purchasers was so impressed by the Bells' work that he requested they send him their autographs.

In October, a third review appeared in the *Dublin University Magazine*, which was pleasing enough. The reviewer, apparently not appreciating the power of some of Emily's inclusions, found the poems to be full of a sort of 'Cowperian amiability and sweetness'; 'their tone of thought seems unaffected and sincere'. After this, there

259

was no more heard, but as Charlotte would later write: 'The mere effort to succeed had given a wonderful zest to existence, it must be pursued.'

CHAPTER XIII

Writing Jane Eyre

As the hot summer of 1846 wore on and initial hopes for publishing success faded – the publishers, it seemed, wanted something a little more exciting, more like Mrs Gore – there were added problems of poor health in the parsonage. Charlotte was suffering from the severe toothache that would plague her for years. It was some kind of gum disease: five years later, when Mrs Gaskell met her, she noticed that she had very few teeth in her head. Charlotte herself found what she described as her irregularly shaped teeth a trial, and used to console herself with the idea that due to the discovery of the property of ether, she might one day have them altered. Meanwhile, she suffered the pain without seeking remedy, more concerned about her father's blindness. She and Emily consulted an eye surgeon, William James Wilson, in Manchester in early August and an appointment was made for Mr Brontë to see him later in the month. Despite her determination not to complain about their circumstances, Charlotte could not forbear from wistfully imagining Ellen and Anne, Emily and she, going to some seaside town, 'without our absence being detrimental to anybody', staying there some weeks, 'taking in a stock of health and strength'.

Leaving with some trepidation Emily and Anne to cope with Branwell, she set off on 19 August with her sixty-nine-year-old father for the hot, dusty metropolis of Manchester. They saw Mr Wilson on the day of their arrival and he pronounced that the cataract was quite ripe enough to be operated on; the operation would take place the next week, on 25 August. He recommended them accommodation in a small lodging house kept by an old servant of his on the comparatively quiet outskirts of the town, 83 Mount Pleasant in Boundary Street. The rooms were very good, as Charlotte told Ellen, but she fretted about her inadequacy in domestic management:

261

I can't tell what the deuce to order in the way of meat etc. I wish you or your sister Anne could give some hints about how to manage. For ourselves I could contrive – Papa's diet is so very simple but there will be a nurse coming in a day or two, and I am afraid of not having things good enough for her – Papa requires nothing you know but plain beef and mutton, tea and bread and butter but a nurse will probably expect to live much better – give me some hints if you can. Mr Wilson says we will have to live here for a month at least – . . .

Feeling ill at east surrounded by the noise and dry, pavemented streets of dark red-brick houses with their tall shadeless trees, and worried about the impending operation, she turned to Ellen for comfort, requesting some lines from her that 'would relieve me from the feelings of strangeness I have in this town'. The only cheer was that Mr Wilson was very hopeful that her father's sight would be restored to him.

The day after the operation, she wrote to Ellen describing it. Mr Wilson had performed it with the assistance of two other surgeons, and it had lasted exactly a quarter of an hour. It was not the more simple operation that the Nusseys' doctor Mr Carr had described 'but the more complicated one of extracting the cataract'. Her father had wanted Charlotte there throughout, an understandable wish from his point of view but a grim ordeal for his daughter, who told Ellen with quiet understatement: 'Of course I neither spoke nor moved till the thing was done – and then I felt that the less I said either to Papa or the surgeons, the better – Papa is now confined to his bed in a dark room and is not to be stirred for four days – He is to speak and to be spoken to as little as possible –'

That morning she had learnt that *The Professor* had been rejected, along with her sisters' novels. If her father did not regain his sight – and there was no certainty that the operation would be successful – the future looked bleak indeed. The other man in the family, who would usually be looked to for some sort of material support in such circumstances, she could only worry about Emily and Anne's ability to control in her absence. Still troubled by toothache, news of her novel's rejection fresh in her mind, her father lying in bed, requiring absolute quiet and, inevitably, as she said, 'depressed and weary' – against this background Charlotte began to write her magical masterpiece *Jane Eyre*.

There are several manuscript fragments at the parsonage dating from around 1844–6 that are about a large house called Gateshead, suggesting that *Jane Eyre* had had a long gestation period, but it was only in the small shabby house in Manchester, so physically similar to

262

her birthplace in Thornton, that she wrote those famous opening lines:

> There was no possibility of taking a walk that day. We had been wandering, indeed, in the leafless shrubbery an hour in the morning; but since dinner (Mrs Reed, when there was no company, dined early) the cold winter wind had brought with it clouds so sombre, and a rain so penetrating, that further outdoor exercise was now out of the question.

And it would of course end with the great eagle Mr Rochester blinded and maimed, just as her father, generally so powerful and alarming a personality, had been rendered helpless by the operation.

The book was the product of two main ingredients, wrought in the crucible of Charlotte Brontë's mind: her overwhelming feeling for M. Heger, which she now was prepared to recognize for what it was, an adulterous love, and the coincidence of Branwell's own guilty passion whose terrible results, like a moral fable, were there for her to witness daily. Her imagination, always with a will and power of its own, began to work on the material, transforming Branwell and perhaps a darker side to Charlotte herself into Bertha Mason, as the following letter indicates:

> I agree [with them] that the character [Mrs Rochester] is shocking but I know that it is but too natural. There is a phase of insanity which may be called moral madness, in which all that is good or even human seems to disappear from the mind and a fiend-nature replaces it. The sole aim and desire of the being thus possessed is to exasperate, to molest, to destroy, and preternatural ingenuity and energy are often exercised to that dreadful end. . . . It is true that profound pity ought to be the only sentiment elicited by the view of such degradation, and equally true is it that I have not sufficiently dwelt on that feeling; I have erred in making *horror* too predominant. Mrs Rochester indeed lived a sinful life before she was insane, but sin is itself a species of insanity: the truly good behold and compassionate it as such.

She could not find it in her to pity Branwell, seeing only a dreadful mirror image of her own incoherent pleas to M. Heger. Nevertheless, on the other hand Charlotte, unlike Branwell, had not sinned herself, but had fled temptation, just as Jane Eyre would do, and at great personal cost.

Evidence of Charlotte Brontë's artistic intentions in *Jane Eyre* is mainly limited to letters written after the publication of the book.

263

Above all things her writing was dedicated almost religiously to the Truth, unpalatable though it might be. In countless letters she reveals how she has been influenced and perhaps emboldened by Dickens' and Thackeray's unvarnished portrayal of society's hypocrisy to champion realism which so appealed to her temperament and parsonage upbringing:

> Yet though I must limit my sympathies, though my observation cannot penetrate where the very deepest political and social truths are to be learnt . . . yet with every disadvantage, I mean still, in my own contracted way, to do my best. Imperfect . . . and poor, and compared with the works of the true masters – of that greatest modern master Thackeray in especial (for it is him I at heart reverence with all my strength) – it will be trifling, but I trust not affected or counterfeit.[1]

Her 'contracted' version of truth would be an astonishingly frank and honest revelation of female character as it was, as opposed to what it was supposed to be, and an equally frank critique of the Evangelical clergy. Deliberately contradicting the usual angelic stereotypes used to portray children – even Dickens, one of Truth's high priests, was guilty of this – she created her unorthodox heroine, the unangelic Jane Eyre, whose courage and honesty she boldly and admiringly contrasted with the unholy behaviour of the Evangelical Calvinistic clergy in an extremely daring fashion. In a puritanical, pious society which tried to suppress it she insisted upon passion, passion which whatever anyone preached could become the strongest thing on earth, stronger even than religion, as she herself knew to her own cost. The Church of England came in for particular criticism through its Evangelical section, whose behaviour was shown to be cruelly unnatural both in the figure of Mr Brocklehurst, and, though rather more sympathetically, in St John Rivers who may have been partly inspired by Ellen's brother Henry. The author's sympathy was with the not particularly reformed reprobate Mr Rochester who, unlike St John Rivers, loves Jane for what she is, and does not try to mould her into what she can never be. The claims of love and proper sexual love are strongly put forward, contrasted favourably with St John Rivers's inability to experience or understand human love.

Although the publishing world was looking for something more exciting than the realism of *The Professor*, *Jane Eyre* was also Charlotte's protest against the stifling convention society imposed, which never allowed true feeling to be voiced. The novelist Geraldine Jewsbury, the best friend of Jane Carlyle, also made a case for strong emotion: 'a real feeling of any kind, is a truth; no matter whether it be

264

compatible or not with received notions of right and wrong,';[2] both Ellen and Charlotte admired her work and it seems probable that Charlotte had perhaps been influenced by her.

Into *Jane Eyre* Charlotte poured much of her own life story: her marvellous sister Maria, reproduced as Helen Burns, the agonies of Cowan Bridge school, the hypocrisy of the people who ran it, the cruel savagery of Mr Carus Wilson. The character of Jane Eyre, as many who knew her would remark after reading the book, was Charlotte herself, struggling for independence, for recognition and for love. Though deeply rooted in Angria, and the ultimate romantic hero fantasy, the erring, harsh Mr Rochester was a supremely potent combination of the more overpoweringly masculine elements of Zamorna and Monsieur Heger placed in the halls and country houses of Charlotte's friends, the Nusseys and their relations. Jane, the unloved orphan, makes all the running. It is she who declares her love for Rochester; she listens unamazed, as reviewers would say in outrage, as Mr Rochester tells her of his affair with a dancer. She claims equality with him, claims equality for all women whatever their social rank:

Do you think, because I am poor, obscure, plain and little, I am heartless and soulless? You think wrong! I have as much soul as you – and full as much heart! And if God had gifted me with some beauty and much wealth, I should have made it as hard for you to leave me, as it is now for me to leave you. I am not talking to you through the medium of custom, conventionalities, nor even of mortal flesh: it is my spirit that addresses your spirit; just as if both had passed through the grave, and we stood at God's feet, equal – as we are!

The book was laced with further protests about women's lot. Charlotte Brontë demanded equal treatment for women, action in their lives, and she articulated her rebellion against the subjugation of women to men, however much she obeyed it in real life:

Nobody knows how many rebellions besides political rebellions ferment in the masses of life which people earth. Women are supposed to be very calm generally: but women feel just as men feel; they need exercise for their faculties, and a field for their efforts as much as their brothers do; they suffer from too rigid a restraint, too absolute a stagnation, precisely as men would suffer; and it is narrow-minded in their more privileged fellow-creatures to say that they ought to confine themselves to making puddings and knitting stockings, to playing on the piano and embroidering bags. It is thoughtless to condemn them, or laugh at them, if they seek to do

265

more or learn more than custom has pronounced necessary for their sex.

In the enforced stillness of the rooms in Manchester, rarely going outside the house, Charlotte wrote incessantly for three weeks, haunted, she said, by 'Sin and Suffering'. Being excessively short-sighted, she wrote in little square paper books, held close to her eyes, and (the first copy) in pencil. She later told Harriet Martineau that when she came to Thornfield and Mr Rochester, she could not stop. And indeed the Thornfield section does give the impression of being written in white heat. Monsieur Heger was transformed, transmogrified, made broader, squarer:

> I knew my traveller, with his broad and jetty eyebrows, his square forehead, made squarer by the horizontal sweep of his black hair. I recognized his decisive nose, more remarkable for character than beauty; his full nostrils, denoting, I thought, choler; his grim mouth, chin and jaw – yes all three were very grim, and no mistake. His shape, now divested of cloak, I perceived harmonized in squareness with his physiognomy. I suppose it was a good figure in the athletic sense of the term – broad-chested and thin-flanked, though neither tall nor graceful.

The famous erotic scene in the garden – no English garden this – was the Pensionnat's garden transplanted, recreated by her lyrical writing into a sort of paradise:

> While such honeydew fell, such silence reigned, such gloaming gathered, I felt as if I could haunt such shade for ever; but in treading the flower and fruit parterres at the upper end of the enclosure, enticed there by the light the now rising moon cast on this more open quarter, my step is stayed – not by sound, not by sight, but once more by a warning fragrance.
>
> Sweet-brier and southernwood, jasmine, pink, and rose have long been yielding their evening sacrifice of incense: this new scent is neither of shrub nor flower; it is – I know it well – it is Mr Rochester's cigar.

And it was the smell of cigar smoke that always heralded M. Heger's presence, just as it would herald M. Paul Emanuel's.

Charlotte wrote on feverishly, until she had carried her heroine away from Thornfield, and was herself in a fever which compelled her to pause. To Ellen she revealed nothing but her constant unhappiness about Branwell. By the end of September she and her father were able

266

to return home. Mr Wilson had pronounced himself well satisfied with the operation, and said that her father would soon be able to read and write. Mr Brontë could shortly resume that endless reading, what Mrs Gaskell called 'his eager appetite for knowledge and information of all kinds'. By November the stout old man was able to take all three church services; the crisis was over, at least for the present, and there was no longer the unwelcome necessity of being reliant on Mr Nicholls to carry on the pastoral duties.

The usual daily round was resumed at the parsonage. Branwell continued to wallow in his self-appointed role as one of The Fallen, to write his mournful poetry and indulge in drink or opium whenever the opportunity arose. Charlotte's contempt and disgust, lashed by guilt, only increased. Anne, more conventionally devout, more detached, more innocent, saw his behaviour in the religious terms of the consequences for his immortal soul, as would be seen in *The Tenant of Wildfell Hall* which she was now embarking on. Neither she nor Emily experienced the extreme reaction of Charlotte, her bitterness and a sort of horror of recognition.

Emily must to some extent have modelled the character of Heathcliff on Branwell in her tale of obsessive love set amidst the wild Yorkshire moors. Charlotte, later describing *Wuthering Heights*, referred to Heathcliff as 'the ever-suffering soul of a magnate of the infernal world',[3] a reference that would have been understood only by her family, including Branwell himself, who with Charlotte had nicknamed their secret world of fantasy 'the infernal world'.

Her very different temperament made it difficult for Charlotte to appreciate the greatness of Emily's novel. In the preface she wrote to the 1850 edition of *Wuthering Heights*, Charlotte vividly recalled how the sisters would read one another the latest chapters of their novels at night in the glow of the firelight and how, listening to Emily, she 'shuddered under the grinding influence of natures so relentless and implacable, of spirits so lost and fallen; if it was complained that the mere hearing of certain vivid and fearful scenes banished sleep by night, and disturbed mental peace by day, Ellis Bell would wonder what was meant, and suspect the complainant of affectation.'[4]

At thirty, Charlotte was as out of sympathy with the strange, wild, heroic world of Gondal transmuted into *Wuthering Heights* as she had been at thirteen when she and Branwell had mocked Emily and Anne's rustic and homely taste. In Charlotte's view, Emily's mind was original but 'unripe . . . inefficiently cultured and partially expanded'. She would write in the *Biographical Notice* of her sisters: 'Neither Emily nor Anne was learned; they had no thought of filling their pitchers at the well-spring of other minds; they always wrote from the impulse of nature, the dictates of intuition, and from such stores of observation as their limited experience had enabled them to amass.'[5]

And Anne's sweet tale of *Agnes Grey* could not be less like the tale of her sister's governess *Jane Eyre*, to which Charlotte was now adding. In *Agnes Grey*, one feels all Anne's touching desire to exercise her faculties, to be taken as a grown-up, as Agnes, like Anne, goes out and triumphs over her shyness to become a much-put-upon governess; like Anne, she was determined to persevere however much she disliked it. Agnes has Anne's religiousity – she determined to teach her charges how to live proper Christian lives, the underlying theme of the novel, whereas it has to be observed of Jane Eyre – everyone's favourite heroine – that she is scarcely interested in her pupil's moral welfare: her aim was to make Adèle obedient and teachable, but the role of governess in the plot distinctly loses out as soon as Mr Rochester arrives on the scene. However, like Charlotte, Anne allowed herself to have a happy ending in fiction, if we may believe that the curate Mr Weston, with whom Agnes falls in love, was based on Willie Weightman.

The reservations that Charlotte later expressed – in veiled terms – of *Wuthering Heights* seemed to be more than shared by publishers: curt rejection letters arrived at intervals over the year from the summer of 1846, but neither were the milder *Professor* or *Agnes Grey* accepted. In October 1846 a not uncritical review of their poetry in the *Dublin University Magazine* gave them some encouragement, even if sales of the poems remained steady at two copies. Charlotte wrote a letter of thanks to the paper's editor: 'After such criticism an author may indeed be smitten at first by a sense of his own insignificance', but then she found that without 'absolutely crushing – it corrects and rouses'.

The three sisters went on writing, holding their nightly confabulations. Yet there were long stretches when Charlotte could not write at all, and she had to wait for inspiration to strike. Those were low periods. As she later told Mrs Gaskell, it was not every day that she could write. Sometimes weeks or even months elapsed before she felt that she had anything to add to that portion of her story which was already written. Then, some morning, she would wake up, and 'the progress of her tale lay clear and bright before her, in distinct vision. When this was the case, all her care was to discharge her household and filial duties, so as to obtain leisure to sit down and write out the incidents and consequent thoughts, which were in fact more present to her mind at such times than her actual life itself'.[6] Mrs Gaskell, anxious to show that this unwomanly writer (according to the standards of the age) never neglected those paramount female domestic obligations, tells us: 'Notwithstanding this "possession" (as it were), those who survive of her daily and household companions, are clear in their testimony, that never was the claim of any duty, never was the call of another for help, neglected for an instant.'

She goes on to give the story of Charlotte picking out the black potato specks which old Tabby would leave in because of her poor sight: '. . . accordingly she would steal into the kitchen and quietly carry off the bowl of vegetables, without Tabby being aware, and breaking off in the full flow of interest and inspiration in her writing, carefully cut out the specks in the potatoes, and noiselessly carry them back to their place.' Given that Charlotte spent little of her time in the kitchen and rather disliked it, this story is perhaps apocryphal. But it belied the image of her as the creator of 'impersonations . . . without the feminine element',[7] which could have no sympathy or true insight into the 'really feminine nature' or 'appreciate the hold which a daily round of simple duties and pure pleasures has on those who are content to practise and enjoy them'.[8]

Unfortunately not everyone was temperamentally suited to these simple duties and pure pleasures. Even Ellen was now considering the idea of setting up a school, for which her brother Richard thought he might be able to procure pupils, and she wrote to ask Charlotte if she was interested in joining her in the scheme. In her reply of 14 October 1846, Charlotte, as usual making no mention of her writing, said that she would have liked to join Ellen but her obligations made it impossible. This was the letter in which she referred to her feelings on her return to Brussels in early 1844, the memory of which she was now seeing in a Calvinistic way as a punishment for pursuing her own interests above other people's: 'I could hardly expect success if I were to err again in the same way.'

There continued to be other worries to occupy her. Mr Brontë's vision was still affected by spots before the eye; though Mr Wilson dismissed it as something of no importance, he did not offer any explanation. The winter of 1846 was particularly severe, and Charlotte wrote poetically to Ellen of a series of North Pole days they had had at Haworth: 'England might really have taken a slide up into the Arctic zone – The sky looks like ice, the earth is frozen, the wind is keen as a two-edged blade – I cannot keep myself warm.' The household all suffered bad colds and coughs, and Anne was badly affected by asthma. She had two nights when her cough and difficulty in breathing were painful to hear for Charlotte in the bed across the narrow hallway. As Charlotte noticed with admiration, she bore it as usual without one complaint, only sighing now and then when she was nearly worn out. Her stoic endurance greatly impressed Charlotte, who thought she could not imitate it.

Charlotte's mood during the writing of *Jane Eyre* had something not a little hysterical in it. Her letters at this time give the impression

269

of vitality rushing off the page, of an almost pathological desire for action, of a vehemence made worse by being confined to the small lonely house. On 28 December she writes quite frenziedly to Ellen in tones very reminiscent of her adolescent religious crisis of her 'haunting terror' lest Ellen imagine Charlotte has forgotten her. She confesses in the rest of the revealing passage how difficult she finds it to govern her temper when fixed in one place and constantly subjected to 'one monotonous species of annoyance' – Branwell. Recognising that her humour snaps a little too easily, it was 'too sore – too demonstrative and vehement', she thinks that perhaps she might be better off if she had some of that serenity of Mrs Joshua Taylor. But then she remembers all she despises about her conventionality and dashes off that 'I would not take her artificial habits and ideas along with her composure – after all I would prefer being as I am' she ends defiantly. She expresses her view that in society 'Nature is turned upside down', that 'well-bred people' seem to walk on their heads, and see everything the wrong way up.

December brought more trouble deriving from Branwell. A sheriff's officer arrived from York, in Charlotte's words to Ellen, 'on a visit to Branwell inviting him to pay his debts, or take a trip to York' – i.e. York prison. It was almost the ultimate disgrace for the parson's family, who were supposed to set a good example to the rest of the community. His family were of course too proud to let him go to prison, and paid up. The terrible wreck of her brother was increasingly awful for Charlotte to witness; as she told Ellen, 'It is not agreeable to lose money time after time in this way but it is ten times worse to witness the shabbiness of his behaviour on such occasions – But where is the use of dwelling on this subject? It will make him no better.'

The debts were mainly of the petty sort, drink bills of a few pounds. Branwell was by now incapable of doing much other than sketches of himself lying on his deathbed or of his cronies debauching themselves at table. He passed much of his time in writing letters. They were confined to three subjects: his depression, his yearning love for Mrs Robinson, and loans. The spring of 1847 was spent weaving unsteadily between the bar of the Black Bull at the bottom of the lane and the druggist, buying the cheaper tonic of opium with the mysterious sum of money he had recently received. His physical condition was appalling. Notes of his survive asking the sexton, his old companion in arms, to get him twists of the opium that he had taken up in slavish imitation of those men of letters amongst whom he had so fondly imagined he would take his place. He was too ill to buy it himself.

One of his last extant letters, written in January 1847, reveals

Branwell to be inhabiting a world which bore no relation to that dwelt in by other human beings. He had once had reason, he told Leyland for the fortieth time, when he had imagined that he would shortly become the husband of Mrs Robinson and (due to her wealth) might live at leisure, 'to try to make a name in the world of posterity, without being pestered by the small but countless botherments, which like mosquitoes sting us in the world of work day toil'. But that hope was gone now. The doctor had told him, as had her brother-in-law, the MP for North Derbyshire, that she was now withering into 'patiently pining decline the hope had to make room for drudgery falling on one now ill-fitted to bear it'.

In fact all the botherments, and they were not small, devolved on his family. In his drunken stupor he set his bed on fire, and was only rescued from incineration by Emily's prompt action. The story of Emily coming down to the Black Bull to escort him home on most nights because he was too drunk to walk may well be apocryphal, but with her dislike of the world and distrust of humanity, she was probably more sympathetic to him in the last years of his life than either Anne or Charlotte could now be.

There were moments when the dream receded and a portion of his native common sense reasserted itself. 'I have been in truth too much petted through life', he wrote regretfully to Joseph Leyland, but then his analysis of his position drifts into hyperbolic, though articulate fantasy:

... in my last situation I was so much master, and gave myself so much up to the enjoyment that now when the cloud of ill-health and adversity has come upon me it will be a disheartening job to work myself up again through a new life's battle, from the position of five years ago to which I have been compelled to retreat with heavy loss and no gain. My army stands now where it did then, but mourning the slaughter of Youth, Health, Hope and both mental and physical elasticity.

The last two losses are indeed important to one who once built his hopes of rising in the world on the possession of them. Noble writings, works of art, music or poetry now instead of rousing my imagination, cause a whirlwind of blighting sorrow that sweeps over my mind with unspeakable dreariness, and if I sit down and try to write, all ideas that used to come clothed in sunlight now press round me in funeral black; for nearly every pleasurable excitement that I used to know has changed to insipidity or pain.

Nevertheless, it was his dreams of glory and his arrogance that origin-ally inspired Charlotte to venture into the great world and try to win

271

a reputation. Without her determination, it seems unlikely that Emily and Anne, with their less ambitious, retiring natures, would ever have got published, just as, without Branwell's sophisticated obsession, his burning desire to be on intimate terms with great men of literature, Charlotte herself would probably not have had the drive to keep pushing for recognition.

It was ironic that knowledge of the manuscripts now passing wearily from publisher back to Haworth, and then sent on again, was kept from Branwell, as was the fact that in March the Misses Robinson had started up again their correspondence with Anne, which had ceased for half a year after their father's death. Despite her fairly low estimation of their abilities and qualities, her disapproval of their worldliness, Anne had won their affection and even in their more glamorous life they had missed the quiet good nature and sincere Christian goodness of their high-minded governess. For a fortnight they sent her a letter almost every day, crammed with warmth and protestations of esteem. They spoke of their mother with affection and never once mentioned their mother's alleged behaviour. Charlotte hoped dourly that they would always remain in ignorance on this point.

As usual kind-hearted Ellen wanted to take Charlotte away, out from the lonely fastness of Haworth and the hills which Charlotte increasingly found to be 'barriers of separation from the living world', into the pleasant social whirl of her home and the neighbourhood of Birstall Smithies. Charlotte, always rather conscious of Ellen's greater social standing, was too proud to accept more invitations from Ellen than Ellen accepted from her, and that spring it was Ellen's turn to come to her. But she wished Ellen to wait until the finer weather came: 'We could go out more, be more independent of the house and of one room' – the one room containing petulant, half-conscious Branwell. Branwell's tendency to speak in an archaic, high-falutin way nowadays was more than ordinarily irritating to her; what once to Charlotte had been a sign of genius and promise was just one more indication of his complete inability to live in the real world. She told Ellen that she expected from the extravagance of his behaviour and from the mysterious hints he dropped – 'he never will speak out plainly' – that they would soon be hearing of fresh debts contracted by him. And she meanwhile continued to castigate herself for her lack of achievement. 'I shall be thirty-one next birthday. My youth is gone like a dream, and very little use have I ever made of it. What have I done these last thirty years? Precious little.'

An incident on 4 April broke up the monotony of life a little. That evening the servant girl Martha came upstairs to Charlotte to tell her that a 'rather ladylike' woman wanted to speak to her in the kitchen. Charlotte went down, to find Mrs Collins, the wife of a former curate of Mr Brontë's, who had abandoned his wife and two children without a farthing in a strange lodging house. Though pale and worn, she was still in Charlotte's eyes interesting looking, as was her little girl. Charlotte was moved by the whole experience: 'I kissed her heartily. I could almost have cried to see her, for I had pitied her with my whole soul when I had heard of her undeserved sufferings, agonies and physical degradation.' It was an age when the victim was likely to be treated as if as besmirched as her unscrupulous husband, 'the wretched and most criminal' Mr Collins, with his 'infamous career of vice, both in England and France'. Charlotte insisted on Mrs Collins taking tea with the family; she stayed for about two hours, and Charlotte was greatly impressed by her. 'Her constitution has triumphed over her illness [which sounds as if it were probably syphilis]; and her excellent sense, her activity and perseverence, have enabled her to regain a decent position in society, and to procure a respectable maintenance for herself and her children.' She was keeping a lodging house in the suburbs of some large town.

Outside such rare incidents, Charlotte relied on Ellen for a vicarious social life of sorts. She demanded that Ellen keep her up-to-date on the Taylors' affairs, particularly enjoying hearing of the shockingly rake-like behaviour of Joe Taylor. Mary Taylor's letters came occasionally, and Charlotte was amused to hear, in view of the Taylors' grandeur and love of good furniture, that Mary was by 1846 living in a log house without a carpet, furnished, it seemed, mainly with wooden stools 'and neither is degraded nor thinks herself degraded by such poor accommodation'. A letter in May, however, worried her. She told Ellen she guessed that Mary was no longer quite as content with her existence in New Zealand as she had been. She seemed to find it too barren and Charlotte detected more homesickness than she would confess. 'Her gloomy ideas respecting you and me prove a state of mind far from gay.'

Ellen at this time had been parading her new friendship with Miss Amelia Ringrose to Charlotte, whose rather distant attitude had evidently upset her. She finally ventured to say that she worried that Charlotte might be jealous. Charlotte was amused by her dear old friend's transparency. 'She and I could not be rivals in your affections. You allot, I know, a different set of feelings to what you allot me. She is peculiarly amiable and estimable. I am not amiable, but still we shall stick to the last, I don't doubt. In short, I should as soon think of being jealous of Emily and Anne in these days as of you.' Meanwhile, she hoped that Ellen would come and visit them at Whitsuntide, for it was the season of fine weather.

Eventually Ellen agreed for the sake of peace. She was warned by Charlotte about Branwell: she must expect to find him considerably weaker in mind, and 'the complete rake in appearance'. Charlotte had no worries that he would be uncivil to her: 'on the contrary, he will be as smooth as oil'. He was somewhat quieter though, as he had run through his money. However, in the event the much looked forward to visit was cancelled because of the call on Ellen from her sister Ann. Charlotte wrote bitterly to Ellen that she did not altogether exempt Ann from reproach. 'I do not think she considers it of the least consequence whether little people like us of Haworth are disappointed or not, provided great nobs like the Briar Hall gentry are accommodated.'

In June, Charlotte and her sisters, aware that their poems had been in print for a year without success, and perhaps also because of having no luck in finding a publisher for their novels, decided to try to revive some interest in their work. In the Brontës' usual grand manner, Charlotte sent the little bottle-green volume of poetry to several of the leading authors of the day – Wordsworth, Tennyson, Hartley Coleridge, De Quincey and John Gibson Lockhart, editor of the *Quarterly Review* – with the following accompanying letter:

Sir,
My relatives, Ellis and Acton Bell, and myself, heedless of the repeated warnings of various respectable publishers, have committed the rash act of printing a volume of poems.

The consequences predicted have, of course, overtaken us; our book is found to be a drug; no man needs or heeds it. In the space of a year our publisher has disposed but of two copies, and by what painful efforts he succeeded in getting rid of these two, himself only knows.

Before transferring the edition to the trunk-makers, we have decided on distributing as presents a few copies of what we cannot sell – We beg to offer you one in acknowledgement of the pleasure and profit we have often and long derived from your works.

I am, sir, yours very respectfully,
Currer Bell.

The next month brought, at last, a publishing offer from a small company named Newby in Cavendish Square, London, but although Mr Newby was willing to accept *Wuthering Heights* and *Agnes Grey*, he did not want *The Professor*. Nor were the terms he offered good: Emily and Anne would have to bear £50 of the production costs. Nevertheless, they felt they could not refuse, even though it lessened the chances for Charlotte's novel, now looking too thin a package for publication on its own. On 15 July Charlotte sent it to the fairly obscure Smith, Elder and Co, in Cornhill, London, very much as a last-ditch hope. It was the sixth publisher to receive it, and the young director George Smith remembered later the extreme naivety of the Bell brothers in not using fresh paper to wrap the manuscripts in, so that the work's previous passage and rejection were to be clearly read in the many crossings out.

Inauspicious as these circumstances looked, this was Charlotte's lucky break, for the manuscript came to the discerning eye of the company's reader, William Smith Williams. To this unassuming, self-educated man, who had clerked to Taylor and Hussey, Keats' publishers, and who had a genuine passion and flair for literature, belongs the credit of discovering Charlotte Brontë. She received his letter at the beginning of August. Although he declined to publish *The Professor* for commercial reasons, he was so encouraging about its merits and demerits that, as Charlotte later put it: 'This very refusal cheered the author better than a vulgarly expressed acceptance would have done. It was added that a work in three volumes would meet with careful attention.'

Charlotte promptly responded on 6 August as follows, describing the novel that would be entitled *Jane Eyre*:

Your objection to the want of varied interest in the tale is, I am aware, not without grounds – yet it seems to me that it might be published without serious risk, if its appearance were speedily followed up by another work from the same pen, of a more striking and exciting character. The first work might serve as an introduction, and accustom the public to the author's name; the success of the second might thereby be rendered more probable. I have a second narrative in three volumes now in progress, and nearly completed, to which I have endeavoured to impart a more vivid interest than belongs to *The Professor*. In about a month I hope to finish it, so that if a publisher were found for *The Professor*, the second narrative might follow as soon as was deemed advisable; and thus the interest of the public (if any interest was aroused) might not be suffered to cool. Will you be kind enough to favour me with your judgement on this plan.[9]

That August Ellen went to stay with the Brontës and, full of suspicions about the sisters' writing activities, she recalled how all four women were out on the moor when a sudden light came into the sky. 'Look,' said Charlotte, and they looked up and saw three suns shining overhead. They all stood still and gazed silently at the parhelion, a phenomenon that has appeared at Haworth intermittently for the past five centuries. Ellen then said boldly: 'That is you! You are the three suns.' 'Hush,' said Charlotte, but as Ellen looked away she noticed that there was a very happy smile on Emily's face.[10]

On 23 August, after the visit from Ellen, who had been bidden to come to celebrate the fine weather – so fine that according to Ellen, Charlotte, in an excess of enthusiasm, suddenly suggested to her father that thanksgiving services should be said throughout the valley – Charlotte finally sent off the manuscript with her usual polite accompanying letter:

Gentlemen,
I now send you per rail a MS entitled *Jane Eyre*, a novel in three volumes, by Currer Bell. I find I cannot prepay the carriage of the parcel, as money for that purpose is not received at the small station-house where it is left. If, when you acknowledge the receipt of the MS, you would have the goodness to mention the amount charged on delivery, I will immediately transmit it in postage stamps. It is better in future to address Mr Currer Bell, under cover to Miss Brontë, Haworth, Bradford, Yorkshire, as there is a risk of letters otherwise directed not reaching me at present. To save trouble, I enclose an envelope.

Did she guess that she was about to have the sort of success that writers dream of, that she, like her idol Byron, would wake up one morning to find herself famous? Surely some strange precognition must have kept up her spirits, beating on doors, without a single contact to help her – unlike the majority of nineteenth-century women novelists, who were in some way connected to publishers. As children she and Branwell had dreamed of belonging to Olympus. There was a kind of genius in Branwell's effrontery, his refusal to be insignificant and obscure as his birth in a wild little village on the edge of the moors had suggested he must be. Now, partly due to his dreams, on that day in late August, Charlotte Brontë began her ascent to her place among the immortals.

CHAPTER XIV

'Conventionality is not Morality'

It could never be said of *Jane Eyre* that it was deficient in 'startling incident' or 'thrilling excitement', the criticisms levelled at *The Professor* by the publishing houses to which it was submitted. Charlotte herself would later ruefully ask Smith, Elder 'if the analyses of other fictions read as absurdly as that of *Jane Eyre* always does'. Its extraordinary qualities were immediately recognised by Mr Williams, who passed the manuscript to Mr Smith to read. He found it equally compelling and once having begun it one Sunday, sat up until he had finished it late in the evening – as many other readers would. Its acceptance was speedily followed by proofs, and the book was published on 16 October 1847 – while Anne's and Emily's novels were still unpublished by Mr Newby, whose behaviour, it was becoming clear, fell far short of the exemplary Smith, Elder company.

Charlotte was delighted with the production standard of the book, writing to her publishers on 19 October, 'if it fails the fault will lie with the author; you are exempt. I now await the judgement of the press and the public.' Smith, Elder had sent out the book to the usual literary editors, adding to their list, at Charlotte's suggestion, the *Dublin University Magazine*, the *Critic* and the *Athenaeum*, which had all reviewed the Bells' poetry. The response was in total contrast to the poems. *Jane Eyre* almost immediately had a success that few novels have enjoyed. The reviews were widespread and the usually caustic literary press high in their praises; sales of the book soared. Ellen Nussey, on a visit to the capital, gave an indication of the waves *Jane Eyre* made at every level of society where books were read, recalling later: 'When I reached London I found there was quite a *fureur* about the authorship of the new novel. The work was quickly obtained, and as soon as it arrived it was seized upon and the first half page read aloud. It was as though Charlotte Brontë herself was present in every word, her voice and spirit thrilling through and through.'

The early, enthusiastic response from Thackeray, who had been sent a review copy, gave Charlotte particular delight when passed on to her by her publishers. He wrote on 23 October to William Smith Williams:

I wish you had not sent me *Jane Eyre*. It interested me so much that I have lost (or won if you like) a whole day in reading it at the busiest period with the printers I know wailing for copy. Who the author can be I can't guess, if a woman she knows her language better than most ladies do, or has had a 'classical' education. It is a fine book though, the man and the woman capital, the style very generous and upright so to speak. I thought it was Kinglake for some time. The plot of the story is one with wh. I am familiar. Some of the love passages made me cry, to the astonishment of John, who came in with the coals. St John the Missionary is a failure I think but a good failure, there are parts excellent. I don't know why I tell you this but that I have been exceedingly moved and pleased by *Jane Eyre*. It is a woman's writing, but whose? Give my respects and thanks to the author, whose novel is the first English one (and the French are only romances now) that I've been able to read for many a day.[1]

Thackeray here pointed to one of the reasons for the outstanding reception that *Jane Eyre* received. It had the good luck – perhaps not entirely luck since again and again Charlotte Brontë had made her contempt for contemporary writing clear – to come out during a dull period in the novel, the desert between Austen and Scott, and just before what has been called its golden age – that of Mrs Gaskell, George Eliot, Dickens, Thackeray (though of course Dickens had published *Nicholas Nickleby* and *Oliver Twist*). Thus the novelists whom Charlotte was competing against were Bulwer (Lytton), G.P.R. James (a Smith, Elder author) and Disraeli, and such now forgotten names as Mrs Marsh, Lady Georgina Fullerton, Marmion Savage and Harriet Smythies.

A young critic sent the book by Mr Williams was so enthusiastic about it that he went down to the editor of *Fraser's* magazine to say that they must review the book, and likewise so must the august *Westminster Review*. This critic was G.H. Lewes, soon to become notorious as the lover of George Eliot, who wrote off to Currer Bell to tell him of the delight with which the book filled him. Charlotte, nervous and strained, took what was intended to be a letter of congratulation as a lecture. It was her first brush with the literary world as a professional author, and she wrote back fervently in answer to his criticisms of her tendency to melodrama, defending the claims of imagination in eloquent and rhetorical fashion: it was, she said, 'a strong, restless faculty, which claims to be heard and exercised: are we to be quite deaf to her cry and insensate to her struggles? When she shows us bright pictures' – pictures the Brontë children had seen so vividly all their lives – 'are we never to look at them, and try to reproduce them? And when she is eloquent, and speaks rapidly and urgently in one ear, are we not to write to her dictation?'[2] Then she wrote off to her publishers with a few enquiries about her critic.

On being told of G.H. Lewes's high standing in the literary world, she wrote to him with endearing candour on 22 November, before he reviewed *Jane Eyre* for *Fraser's*:

> . . . I knew little of your right to condemn or approve. *Now* I am informed on these points.
>
> You will be severe. . . . Well! I shall try to extract good out of your severity; and besides, though I am now sure you are a just, discriminating man, yet being mortal, you must be fallible; and if any part of your censure galls me too keenly to the quick . . . I shall for the present disbelieve it, and put it quite aside, till such time as I feel able to receive it without torture.[3]

To one always pessimistically awaiting the 'mixed cup', one of her father's favourite gloomy sayings which Charlotte had taken for her own, the early reviews of *Jane Eyre* must have exceeded all her hopes. It had an almost extravagantly laudatory reception – 'powerful', 'new', 'original', 'fresh', were the adjectives most frequently used. The first review came from the *Atlas* and was what in modern-day parlance would be called a rave:

> This is not merely a work of great promise, it is one of absolute performance. It is one of the most powerful domestic romances which has been published for many years. It has little or nothing of the old conventional stamp upon it; none of the jaded, exhausted attributes of a worn-out vein of imagination . . . but it is full of youthful vigour, of freshness and originality, of nervous diction and concentrated interest. . . . It is a book to make the pulses gallop and the heart beat, and to fill the eyes with tears.[4]

The *Examiner* and the *Era* were equally pleasing to Charlotte. In the view of the former, *Jane Eyre* was 'a book of decided power', such power that although it was a woman's story, the reviewer could not believe that it had been written by a woman. The moral of the book was found excellent, to Charlotte's particular pleasure:[5] 'Without being professedly didactic, the writer's intention (among other things) seems to be, to show how intellect and unswerving integrity may win their way, although oppressed by that predominating influence in society which is a mere consequence of the accidents of birth or fortune . . . but in the end the honesty, kindness of heart, and perseverance of the heroine are seen triumphant over every obstacle.'[6]

The *Era* was even more enthusiastic. It called *Jane Eyre* 'an extraordinary book. Although a work of fiction, it is no mere novel, for there is nothing but nature and truth about it.' It was a unique story, for 'We have no high life glorified, caricatured or libelled; nor low life elevated to an enviable state of bliss. . . . The tale is one of the heart, and the working out of a moral through the natural affections.' In the *Era*'s opinion, there was an obvious moral lesson to be drawn from the book (which indeed echoed Jane's own reaction to the discovery of a first Mrs Rochester), 'that laws, both human and divine, approved in our calmer moments, are not to be disobeyed when our time of trial comes, however singular the circumstances under which we are tempted to disregard them'.[7]

Charlotte expressed her great pleasure on reading of this kind of approbation, writing to Mr Williams on 17 November: 'An author feels peculiarly gratified by the recognition of a right tendency in his works; for if what he writes does no good to the reader, he feels he has missed his chief aim, wasted in a great measure, his time and his labour.' The fact was, however, that Currer Bell and Victorian society differed on just what was good for the reader. Charlotte Brontë had no intention of upsetting the moral code,[8] yet as other reviewers began to note, *Jane Eyre* is not a book about exercising Christian virtues; the heroine displays not meekness, not the feminine ideal of self-abnegation, but pride and anger. It is a singularly honest book about human love and passion, which is ultimately held up as preferable to a religious life without love. And in an age dominated by the Evangelicals, their supporters were quick to see a threat and to sense an unwelcome change of emphasis.

The *Spectator* was the first of the dissenting voices. The reviewer wrote, somewhat obscurely, that *Jane Eyre* had 'some resemblance to those sculptures of the middle ages in which considerable ability both mechanical and mental was often displayed upon subjects that had no existence in nature, and as far as delicacy was concerned were not pleasing in themselves'. The passages between Mr Rochester and Jane were described as 'a course of hardly "proper" conduct between a single man and a maiden in her teens. . . . There is a low tone of behaviour (rather than of morality) in the book.'[9] Charlotte was not unduly perturbed by this, though she admitted 'it distressed me a little' and wrote resignedly to Mr Williams on 13 November: 'The critique in the *Spectator* gives that view of the book which will naturally be taken by a certain class of minds; I shall expect it to be followed by other notices of a similar nature. The way to detraction has been pointed out, and will probably be pursued. Most future notices will in all likelihood,' she scribbled on pessimistically, 'have a reflection of the *Spectator* in them', but she hoped that if *Jane Eyre* had any solid worth in it, it ought to weather a gust of unfavourable wind.[10]

Future notices had more than a reflection of the *Spectator* in them and although the book's sales flourished, Charlotte was stung by the criticisms. Both the *Sunday Times* and the *Mirror* launched scathing attacks. There was particular objection to the passage between Jane and St John Rivers when Jane tells him that he loves the poor Rosamund Oliver who is unsuited for the life of a missionary's wife: Jane says, 'I could never rest in communication with strong, discreet and refined minds, whether male or female, till I had passed the outworks of conventional reserve, and crossed the threshold of confidence, and won a place by the heart's very firestone.' Unobjectionable enough one would think. But it was seized on by both the *Sunday Times* and the *Mirror* as epitomising the revolutionary and dangerous disregard of custom which was the hallmark of Currer Bell.

The *Sunday Times* quoted in disgust that Currer Bell 'is never content until she "has passed the outworks of conventional reserve" '[11] and that the passages between Mr Rochester and his wife were too disgusting to quote. The *Mirror* said that it would be 'no credit to anyone to be the author of *Jane Eyre*. It is the boast of its writer that she knows how to overstep conventional usages – how in fact to trample upon customs established by our forefathers, and long destined to shed glory upon our domestic circles.' *Jane Eyre* was one of 'the many blows . . . aimed at our institutions, political and social'. In the critic's view – which thirty years ago had been Mr Brontë's own – the purpose of all literature must be didactic, and to further the progress of the state, 'to improve the human race – to elevate its notions, purify its passions, and inculcate the necessity of strong virtue. . . . The question to be decided,' trumpeted the *Mirror*, 'is, whether we shall continue to cherish respect for the faith, the customs, and religion of our ancestors, or go on a steady course of improvement until we reach the perfection of human civilization, or shall we pause in our career, and instead of the dictates of virtue, follow those which a debased nature awakens within us?' The novel was only just escaping from having a bad name. Now it was plunged back into its unsavoury past.

It was the same point on which an increasing number of reviewers would attack Currer Bell. Nature was bad; natural feelings were to be repressed, not acknowledged in what Q.D. Leavis has described as a proto-Lawrencian fashion. Charlotte was too frank for the age, too honest. She was making claims for love, as Leavis points out, in a way which was very new in the Victorian novel. Charlotte could admit that women felt: woman was not idealised by her but 'recognized as an active contributor – fearless, unashamed of passionate feeling, and, while needing to serve, still determined to have her rights acknowledged'. At the end of the novel, when partially blind Rochester realises the force of his feeling that 'I must be aided and by that hand', Jane loves him better than when he 'disdained every part but that of the giver and protector'. Thus Jane says, 'My help had been needed and claimed: I had given it: I was pleased to have done something; trivial, transitory though the deed was, it was yet an active thing, and I was weary of an existence all passive.'

Leavis goes on:

> The general assent to the convention of a sexless ideal produced one of the more unpleasant aspects of the Victorian novel – the idealization of the innocent brother–sister relation, under cover of which only was the married relation tolerable to the imagination . . . the most instructive examples of this perversion are to be found in the very popular novels of the innocent devout Charlotte M. Yonge, with her morbid preference for a relation between brother and sister that precludes marriage for either, with the implication that the kind of love that results in marriage is somehow inferior. To this unwholesome aspect of the Victorian conventions Charlotte Brontë is absolutely hostile, not only free from such a taint herself but also setting out to combat it . . .[12]

The *Mirror* saw Currer Bell as an unwelcome aspect of the modern world. The reviewer, assuming Currer Bell to be a woman, found women to be chief among the new villains of discord: 'The desire of the present generation is to be bold and fearless. Their boast is, that they dare to overstep "conventional rules", and by conventional rules they mean all moral, religious and social laws.' *Jane Eyre* did not encourage vice, but 'the writer evidently seeks throughout to show how impossible it is to reconcile religion with love of mankind. . . .' Currer Bell could not understand 'the pure ennobling influences of true Christianity; she cannot comprehend how his followers can love the Almighty with truth'. The author of *Jane Eyre* was seeking to strike a blow at religion. Instead of showing how religion challenges love and respect, how it purifies and changes the heart, what noble virtues it teaches, the reader was taught to feel 'that it hardens the heart of man, deadens its sympathies and renders him incapable of feeling'. Charlotte's striking a blow for honesty, realism and truth had been misconstrued. In short, the *Mirror* wound up,

Religion is stabbed in the dark – our social distinctions attempted to be levelled, and all absurdly moral notions done away with. The authoress is unacquainted with the commonest rules of society, and affects to present us with specimens of fashionable life, within whose circles she has never entered. The language she puts into the mouth of Blanche Ingram would disgrace a kitchen maid.[13]

This finally was too much for Charlotte. She wrote to Mr Williams that 'the reviewer is mistaken, as he is perverting my meaning, in attributing to me designs I know not, principles I disown'. She was hurt by the bad reviews, and particularly by the accusation that she was the enemy of religion. As she told Mr Williams, 'Whatever such critics as he of the *Mirror* may say, I love the Church of England. Her ministers, indeed, I do not regard as infallible personages. I have seen too much of them for that, but to the Establishment, with all her faults – the profane Athanasian creed *ex*cluded – I am sincerely attached.'[14] A week later on New Year's Eve she was writing rather restrainedly to Mr Williams that she felt a sort of heart-ache when she heard the book called "godless" and "pernicious" by good and earnest-minded men; however, she said firmly, 'I know that heart-ache will be salutary – at least I trust so.'[15]

Concerned that his author's feelings and confidence were being crushed by the reviews, Mr Williams produced a soothing reply. Charlotte quickly wrote back:

It would take a great deal to crush me, because I know, in the first place, that my own intuition was correct; that I feel in my heart a deep reverence for religion, that impiety is very abhorrent to me, and in the second, I place firm ordinance on the judgement of some who have encouraged me. You and Mr Lewes are quite as good authorities in my estimation as Mr Pilke or the editor of the *Spectator*, and I would not under any circumstances, or for any opprobrium, regard with shame what my friends had approved: none but a coward would let the detraction of an enemy outweigh the encouragement of a friend. You must not therefore fulfil your threat of being less communicative in future; you must kindly tell me all.

This was the position she would stick to courageously through thick and thin, despite the considerable opprobrium she would incur in the coming months. Her new relationship with her publishers, in particular William Smith Williams, was something of a hedge against hostility. The correspondence that began with him over the manuscript of *The Professor* developed into a life-long literary exchange which was of great importance to Charlotte, and it was Mr Williams who was responsible for much of her reading matter for the rest of her life. Her trust in him was well-founded and his response in turn was clearly based on affection and respect. She frequently referred to his letters, saying that she could give him 'but a faint idea of the pleasure they afford me; they seem to introduce such light and life to the torpid retirement where we live like dormice'. But, she added with her customary modesty, he must never write to her except when he had both leisure and inclination.

On 10 December she received a payment from Smith, Elder, which was probably part of the advance or perhaps money from royalties, and replied immediately with a dignified statement of gratitude: 'Having already expressed my sense of your kind and upright conduct, I can now only say that I trust you will always have reason to be as well content with me as I am with you. If the result of any future exertions I may be able to make should prove agreeable and advantageous to you, I shall be well satisfied; and it would be a serious source of regret to me if I thought you ever had reason to repent being my publishers.' She was meanwhile writing a short preface, in the event of a second edition.

Further literary excitement came with a note from Thackeray. She told Mr Williams that she had scarcely ever felt delight equal to that when she received his letter; she had never perused his writings 'but with blended feelings of admiration and indignation'. Inspired by *Vanity Fair*, which was appearing in serial form in early 1848, Charlotte in great excitement wrote the following homage to her master: 'The more I read Thackeray's works the more certain I am that he stands alone – alone in his sagacity, alone in his truth, alone in his feeling (his feeling though he makes no noise about it, is about the most genuine that ever lived on a printed page), alone in his power, alone in his simplicity, alone in his self-control. Thackeray is a Titan, so strong that he can afford to perform with calm the most Herculean feats; there is the charm and majesty of repose in his greatest efforts.' Wistfully she wrote that *he* borrowed nothing from fever, unlike herself: 'His is never the energy of delirium – his energy is sane energy, deliberate energy, thoughtful energy ... Thackeray is never borne away by his own ardour – he has it under control. His genius obeys him – it is his servant, it works no fantastic changes at its own wild will, it must achieve the task which reason and sense assign it, and none other. Thackeray is unique. I *can* say no more, I *will* say no less.'

Full of elation, she decided to dedicate the second edition of *Jane Eyre*, in preparation by December 1847, with a wildly enthusiastic paean of praise, to Thackeray. The rest of the preface contained a mighty blast at her critics. She was not the daughter of the volcanic Patrick Brontë for nothing. Having acknowledged those who had helped her, she turned to what she called 'the timorous or carping few' who doubted the tendency of *Jane Eyre*, 'in whose eyes whatever is unusual is wrong, whose ears detect in each protest against bigotry – that parent of crime –' she went on fiercely, 'an insult to piety', which was 'that regent of God on earth'.

With a fearlessness inspired – rather too inspired, she would say later – by the call for liberty across the Channel that triumphed in the 1848 French Revolution, she reminded her critics of 'certain simple truths', every word betraying her parsonage upbringing and profound religious beliefs, had her critics looked a little harder. It was a statement of the religious belief which had been hammered out at the parsonage in the face of the Calvinist creed the inhabitants had found too daunting:

> Conventionality is not morality. Self-righteousness is not religion. To attack the first is not to assail the last. To pluck the mask from the face of the Pharisee, is not to lift an impious hand to the Crown of Thorns. These things and deeds are diametrically opposed: they are as distinct as is vice from virtue. Men too often confound them: they should not be confounded; appearance should not be mistaken for truth; narrow human doctrines, that only tend to elate and magnify a few, should not be substituted for the world-redeeming creed of Christ. There is – I repeat it – a difference; and it is good, and not a bad action to mark broadly and clearly the line of separation between them.

Little notice, however, was taken of the first part of the preface on account of the excitement caused in certain circles by the dedication to Thackeray. Isolated from London, Charlotte Brontë could have no idea that Thackeray's personal life bore an unhappily close resemblance to that of Mr Rochester. He too had a mad wife to whom he was shackled for life – and malicious London gossips whispered that *Jane Eyre* must be written by his mistress. An embarrassed Thackeray finally wrote to Currer Bell via Mr Williams, gently outlining his family circumstances. Charlotte was quite mortified by the consequences of her innocent blunder, telling Mr Williams in a letter of 28 January 1848, 'Well may it be said that fact is often stranger than fiction! . . . The very fact of his not complaining at all and addressing me with such kindness . . . increases my chagrin.' She could not express her real regret properly, constrained by 'the consciousness that that regret was just worth nothing at all – quite valueless for healing the mischief I had done.'

But for someone with such deeply held convictions as Charlotte, the carpings of the critics caused more annoyance than anguish at this early stage a few months after the publication of *Jane Eyre*. The praise outweighed the blame, and she had the mental tranquillity afforded by her anonymity as the country became awake to the name of Currer Bell. The reaction of John Gibson Lockhart, editor of the *Quarterly Review*, was very typical: 'I have finished the adventures of Miss Jane Eyre, and think [the author] far the cleverest that has written since Austen and Edgeworth were in their prime. Worth fifty Trollopes and Martineaus rolled into one counterpane, with fifty Dickenses and Bulwers to keep them company, but rather a brazen Miss.' Nevertheless, despite all the admiration, as Andrew Lang wrote, 'We can only say that in 1848 no critic could have guessed that Currer Bell was neither a man, nor a coarse woman, but the blameless daughter of a rural divine.'

At the end of the *annus mirabilis* of 1847, Charlotte was fairly contented. Complaints about the slow pace of life at Haworth still issued from her sharp tongue, but her boredom was alleviated by the great success. At Christmas there was the unexpected treat of a present from her publishers – Leigh Hunt's *A Jar of Honey from Mount Hylde*. Mr Williams was encouraging her to consider a new novel but, daunted by following up the triumph of *Jane Eyre*, Charlotte was undecided on what form it should take.

By this time, too, her sisters' novels had finally been published. After Emily and Anne had received their first proofs in October, there had been long delays and prevarications by Mr Newby and on 10 November an angry Charlotte had written to Smith, Elder of the way her sisters were being treated. Mr Williams had kindly offered his company's help but by 17 November Mr Newby – spurred on by seeing the success of the novel by the Bells' relative – had at last sent Ellis and Acton Bell the final proofs. Charlotte wrote to Mr Williams to thank him for his offer but saying that there seemed no point taking it up now that the work was finally about to come out. *Wuthering Heights* and *Agnes Grey* were duly published in December. All three sisters were angry about the way the books had been got up. The spelling and punctuation were felt to be embarrassing and almost all the errors that were corrected in the proof sheets appeared intact in what should have been fair copies.

Nevertheless, there was the satisfaction that all three novels were published. According to Mrs Gaskell's account of what Charlotte related to her, Emily and Anne persuaded Charlotte that it was time she told their father about *Jane Eyre*:

Three months after its publication she promised her sisters one day at dinner she would tell him before tea. So she marched into his study with a copy wrapped up and the reviews. She said (I think I can remember the exact words) – 'Papa I've been writing a book.' 'Have you my dear?' and he went on reading. 'But Papa I want you to look at it.' 'I can't be troubled to read manuscripts.' 'But it is printed.' 'I hope you have not been involving yourself in any silly expense.' 'I think I shall gain some money by it. May I read you some reviews.' So she read them; and then she asked him if he would read the book. He said she might leave it and he would see.[16]

It hardly sounded an encouraging reaction, although, Mrs Gaskell's account from Charlotte continues, he was sufficiently impressed to summon them all to tea later that day in the dark little room across from the dining room where they sat – all except Branwell, who was perhaps upstairs lying on a bed or off roistering in Halifax. In his usual teasing way, Mr Brontë delayed his pronouncement till the end of tea. Then he said: 'Children, Charlotte has been writing a book – and I think it is a better one than I expected.'[17] That was all he had to say on the subject, which he didn't mention again until two years afterwards, and according to Mrs Gaskell they never dared to tell him about the other, more scandalous books.[18]

According to Mrs Gaskell, the sisters had kept their venture from their father because of the close interest he took in their welfare and because of his natural pessimism. He might have cast a dampener over the proceedings. Mr Brontë would later tell Mrs Gaskell that he had suspected it all along, for his children were always writing in that small house, and he was convinced that it could not always be letters.

The only other person with whom Charlotte was willing to entrust her publishing secret was Mary Taylor. To Ellen she would confide family problems but she held back from telling her about her writing, feeling that Ellen would not understand and also out of loyalty to Emily's ardent wish for secrecy. Charlotte evidently sent off to New Zealand copies of all the Bells' novels. Back came a pleasingly enthusiastic response from Mary. However, since she was ever a polemicist, she was annoyed at *Jane Eyre* being such a perfect work of art. It was 'impossible to squeeze a moral out of your production', she wrote angrily. 'How have you written through three volumes without declaring war to the knife against a few dozen absurd doctrines each of which is supported by "a large and respectable class of readers"?' There were, she said firmly, 'no good men of the Brocklehurst species' – and she did not believe in Mr Rivers.

She went on jauntily to discuss the mannerless girl she had known who would soon become called the Sphinx of Literature: 'Emily seems to have had such a class in her eye when she wrote that strange thing

Wuthering Heights'. And she continued dismissively: 'Anne too stops repeatedly to preach commonplace truths. She has had a still lower class in her mind's eye. Emily seems to have followed the bookseller's advice.'

Nevertheless, she reported that out in New Zealand *Jane Eyre* had made them cry. With the new-found business acumen that she was enjoying flexing, she pronounced that the price Smith, Elder paid for the book was 'certainly pretty Jewish'. Moreover, she told Charlotte breezily, 'If I were in your place the idea of being bound in the sale of two more would prevent me from ever writing again.'

Charlotte's correspondence with Ellen continued to detail her real life amidst the household cares at Haworth. That winter she expressed her usual nagging concern over her youngest sister's health, hoping that Anne was now a little better in body and spirits but – not mentioning the fact that Anne was immersed in writing *The Tenant of Wildfell Hall* – that she led too sedentary a life, constantly stooped over a book or her desk. 'It is with difficulty one can prevail on her to take a walk or induce her to converse. I shall look forward to next summer with the confident intuition that we shall – if possible – make at least a brief sojourn at the seaside.'

Over Christmas all in the parsonage came down with flu or severe colds and Charlotte again was concerned because of Anne's weak chest; Emily's health did not seem to be such cause for anxiety. Branwell remained in his deplorable state and on 7 January Charlotte wrote to Ellen that he led the household 'a sad life with his absurd and often intolerable conduct. Papa is harassed day and night; we have little peace; he is always sick, has two or three times fallen down in fits. What will be the ultimate end God knows. It remains only to do one's best and endure with patience.'

One difference was that there was an empty place in the curate's pew. The large figure of Mr Nicholls was no longer to be seen there, nor bustling about the village's steep narrow streets in his officious fashion. He had gone home to Banagher in southern Ireland to visit his relations, to the general relief of the parish. His unfortunate ability to put people's backs up by his interfering, high-handed manner had created bad feeling between him and Haworth. Charlotte said tartly to Ellen that he should not trouble himself to recross the Channel but should remain quietly where he was. She was alarmed by relations between him and the village. However much she was traduced for being the enemy of religion, she was the parson's daughter, and she deplored the present situation. It was 'not the feeling that ought to exist between shepherd and flock . . . it is not such as poor Mr Weightman excited.'

Ellen, who strongly suspected the Brontë sisters' writing activities, continued to drop hints to Charlotte about the authorship of *Jane Eyre*. She would later relate that Charlotte had corrected the proofs of the novel in front of her while staying in September 1847 at Brookroyd, the small white suburban villa that Ellen Nussey's mother and family had retired to after the sale of the majestic Rydings. Before the laurels and rhododendrons of its eminently respectable façade, the short-sighted Charlotte had pored over the long galleys, making corrections in her neat careful handwriting to the book which would shake Victorian England. Nearby sat Ellen, her plump, pretty face trained in the art of concealing emotions, but this time trying to conceal her curiosity about her friend's employment. She continued to bend over what was known as women's 'work' – the endless sewing of little cuffs, handkerchiefs, beaded watch-guards. Elizabeth Barrett Browning would sum up this production of thousands of useless gewgaws created by women like her and Ellen in her lifetime:

> We sew, sew, prick our fingers, dull our sight,
> Producing what? A pair of slippers, sir,
> To put on when you're weary – or a stool
> To stumble over and vex you . . . 'curse that stool!'
> Or else at best, a cushion, where you lean
> And sleep, and dream of something we are not
> But would be for your sake. Alas, alas!
> This hurts most, this – that, after all, we are paid
> The worth of our work, perhaps.[19]

Charlotte, conscious of the burden of custom and respectability bearing her friend down, did her best to encourage Ellen in a self-respecting defiance where she thought it merited it. She forthrightly criticised Ellen's brother's fussy, selfish wife, Mrs Henry Nussey, whose house they had prepared two summers ago. Immediately after *Jane Eyre* started to sell she sent off a little money to Ellen, who, like many women of her class, had no income of her own, nor was expected to need any. As Charlotte put it sympathetically: 'An expression in your letter made me conclude that you could probably yourself put a few shillings to a more convenient use than I could do for you, for which reason I send the cash instead of buying what in all likelihood would be useless to you. I know myself how trying it is to be without a shilling of pocket-money'.[20] What vistas such remarks open up into Victorian female life, and at the back of it one hears an echo of Charlotte's father, who, according to Charlotte's reminiscences to Mrs Gaskell, replied when asked by his nineteen-year-old daughter if she could have a penny a week as pocket money, 'What did women want with money?'.[21]

289

Yet, however much Charlotte loved Ellen, she continued to deny hotly that she had done such 'an unkind and ill-bred thing' as publishing.

> The most profound obscurity is infinitely preferable to vulgar notoriety and that notoriety I neither seek nor will have. If then any Birstallian or Gomersalian should presume to bore you on the subject, – to ask you what 'novel' Miss Brontë has been 'publishing' – you can just say, with the distinct firmness of which you are perfect mistress, when you choose, that you are authorized by Miss Brontë to say, that she repels and disowns every accusation of the kind.

Whoever said she was an author wished her ill, Charlotte declared. When Ellen – in London during the spring and early summer of 1848 where *Jane Eyre* was the talk of the town – ventured to ask if Charlotte had read the 'last new novel', she received a sharp reply that Ellen must know that the Brontës did not subscribe to the fashionable diversion of a circulating library at Haworth, and therefore such matters were beyond her ken.

Anonymity gave Charlotte additional confidence to breathe defiance at the world over *Jane Eyre* when, as Mrs Gaskell – who was there to witness it – said, 'the whole reading-world of England was in a ferment to discover the unknown author'. As she told Mr Williams on 20 April, who was kindly telling all and sundry that the only author of *Jane Eyre* was Currer Bell, it was the only name she wished to have mentioned in connection with her writings:

> 'Currer Bell' only I am and will be to the Public; if accident or design should deprive me of that name, I should deem it a misfortune – a very great one. Mental tranquillity would then be gone; it would be a task to write, a task which I doubt whether I could continue. If it were known, I should ever be conscious in writing that my book must be read by ordinary acquaintances, and that idea would fetter me intolerably.[22]

Writing was a way of getting round the social attitudes that made female writers 'notorious', and saying the unsayable. Even Ellen could not be confided in.

Yet the hidden identity created its own problems. What had begun as amusing confusion over the identities of the brothers Bell, by the end of December 1847 had become rather unpleasant: Emily's unscrupulous publisher Newby was putting it about that Ellis Bell was the author of *Jane Eyre*, and allegations began to appear in the press that 'trickery' and 'artifice' were used by the brothers. Charlotte initially took this robustly and found it amusing that the press were confused. They smiled at the confusion at the parsonage, but it had more of an effect than she had anticipated, she would later consider. She wrote in her *Biographical Notice*:

> We laughed at it at first, but I deeply lament it now. Hence, arose a prejudice against the book [*Wuthering Heights*]. That writer who could attempt to palm off an inferior and immature production under cover of one successful effort, must indeed be unduly eager after the secondary and sordid result of authorship, and pitiably indifferent to its true and honourable meed. If reviewers and public truly believed this, no wonder that they looked darkly on the cheat.[23]

Honour had been affronted. But Emily herself refused to show much emotion about the affair; she was too proud to make her feelings known. Charlotte goes on: 'Yet I must not be understood to make these things subject for reproach and complaint; I dare not do so; respect for my sister's memory forbids me. By her, querulous manifestation would have been regarded as an unworthy, and offensive weakness.'

Wuthering Heights had indeed provoked a very strong and condemnatory reaction. Whereas *Agnes Grey* attracted little attention, there had been startling reviews of Ellis Bell's novel, which to Emily, so shy that she would run out of the kitchen if a tradesman came to call and who hated the ridicule of an incomprehending outside world, may well have been lacerating. She had been encouraged by being chosen from her fellow poets for her 'power of wing', but now her very careful work was singled out for its 'want of art', although recognised as having something great, if strange, in it. The *Britannia* said that the characters 'have all the angularity of misshapen growth, and form in this respect a striking contrast to those regular forms we are accustomed to meet within English fiction ... they are so new, so grotesque, so entirely without art, that they strike us as proceeding from a mind of limited experience.' The characters were drawn from the very lowest of life; they were the inhabitants of an isolated and uncivilized district, or were of some demoniac influence. *Douglas Jerrold's Weekly* said that *Wuthering Heights* was a book 'baffling all regular criticism'. Although he admitted its power, which he desired to see put to better use, it was a 'purposeless power'. Readers would be 'disgusted, almost sickened by details of cruelty, inhumanity and the most diabolical hate and vengeance'. Those who loved novelty would enjoy it 'for we can promise them that they have never read anything like it before'. The *Atlas* was of the opinion that

291

the 'general effect is inexpressibly painful', though it had to admit that there were 'evidences in every chapter of a sort of rugged power. . . . We know nothing in the whole range of our fictitious literature which represents such shocking pictures of the worst forms of humanity.'[24]

Emily, it seemed, had been right to distrust the world. It could not understand her; her creation was derided as 'sprawling', it was held together only by the 'singleness of malignity' of the presiding evil genius. 'There is not in the entire *dramatis personae* a single character which is not utterly hateful or thoroughly contemptible. If you do not detest the person you despise him; and if you do not despise him you detest him with your whole heart.'[25]

When they met years later, Charlotte told Mrs Gaskell that her pleasure in the reaction to *Jane Eyre* was quite adulterated by Emily's unhappiness at the reviews of *Wuthering Heights*. 'But Emily – poor Emily – the pangs of disappointment as review after review came out about *Wuthering Heights* were terrible. Miss B. said she had no recollection of pleasure or gladness about *Jane Eyre*; every such feeling was lost in seeing Emily's resolute endurance, yet knowing what she felt.' When Emily's desk was opened after her death, it was found to contain five reviews comparing her book unfavourably to Charlotte's.

Furthermore, Charlotte may well have indicated to Emily that she held a similar opinion of the value of *Wuthering Heights*. On 21 December 1847 she wrote to Mr Williams, approving his judgement of her sister's work:

Ellis has a strong, original mind, full of strange though sombre power. When he writes poetry that power speaks in language at once condensed, elaborated, and refined, but in prose it breaks forth in scenes which shock more than they attract. Ellis will improve, however, because he knows his defects.

In her 1850 preface to *Wuthering Heights*, Charlotte felt the need to explain

to strangers who knew nothing of the author; who are unacquainted with the locality where the scenes of the story are laid; to whom the inhabitants, the customs, the natural characteristics of the outlying hills and hamlets in the West Riding of Yorkshire are things alien and unfamiliar; to all such, *Wuthering Heights* must appear a rude and a strange production. The wild moors of the north of England can for them have no interest; the language, the manners, the very dwellings and household customs of the scattered inhabitants of those districts, must be to such readers in a great measure unintelligible, and – where intelligible – repulsive. Men and women who, perhaps, naturally very calm, and with feelings moderate in degree, and little marked in kind, have been trained from their cradle to observe the utmost evenness of manner and guardedness of language, will hardly know what to make of the rough strong utterance, the harshly manifested passions, the unbridled aversions, and headlong partialities of unlettered moorland hinds and rugged moorland squires, who have grown up untaught and unchecked, except by mentors as harsh as themselves.[26]

To Charlotte, Emily – 'a spirit more sombre than sunny, more powerful than sportive' – was overly influenced by what she absorbed from the people living at Haworth, and in forming the extraordinary beings of *Wuthering Heights*, 'she did not know what she had done'. Anne, to judge from her poetry, was more openly critical towards Emily.[27] She felt that Emily *did* know what she had done in creating her characters and, being closer to Emily than Charlotte, she was probably more aware of her sister's increasing tendency to be possessed by her God of Vision, her 'darling pain'. In her poem 'The Three Guides', Anne seems to be criticising Emily's arrogance, her arrogation of supernatural powers:

> Spirit of Pride! thy wings are strong;
>   Thine eyes like lightning shine
> Ecstatic joys to thee belong
>   And powers almost divine.
> But 'tis a false destructive blaze,
>   Within those eyes I see,
> Turn hence their fascinating gaze–
>   I will not follow thee!

There is a considerable sense of Emily's almost magnetic power, when she chose to assert it:

> 'Cling to the earth, poor grovelling worm
>   'Tis not for thee to soar
> Against the fury of the storm,
>   Amid the thunder's roar,
> There's glory in that daring strife
>   Unknown, undreamt by thee;
> There's speechless rapture in the life
>   Of those who follow me.
>   . . .
> Oh! I have felt what glory then –
>   What transport must be theirs;

293

So far above their fellow men,
   Above their toils and cares,
Inhaling nature's purest breath,
   Her riches round them spread,
The wide expanse of earth beneath,
   Heaven's glories overhead![28]

This closely resembles some of Emily's ecstatic mystic experiences on the moors, which are the subject of her finest poetry. But Anne would not finally follow her sister's path; she distrusted Emily's wild, wilful pantheism, the 'magic power' of the earth to make her happy, summed up by the paradoxical lines written by Emily that epitomised her increasing dilemma:

Few hearts to mortal given
On earth so wildly pine
Yet few would ask a Heaven
More like the Earth than thine.

Then let my winds caress thee;
Thy comrade let me be –
Since nought beside can bless thee
Return and dwell with me.[29]

Is there not something a little sinister about those lines? Anne seems to have thought so. They left a Christian God out of the equation and Anne, with her deep, quietly held religious faith, rejected Emily's vision in the final lines of 'The Three Guides', for the Spirit of Faith:

Spirit of Pride! it needs not this
   To make me shun thy wiles,
Renounce thy triumph and thy bliss,
   Thy honours and thy smiles.
Bright as thou art, and bold, and strong,
   That fierce glance wins not me,
And I abhor thy scoffing tongue –
   I will not walk with thee!

By the end of 1847 Anne was writing her major autobiographical poem, 'Self-Communion', in which she comments on the deepening estrangement between her and Emily, which was mainly due to religious reasons.[30] Anne evidently thought that her sister's worship of imagination and her mysticism had become quite dangerous in its lack of control. What can only be described as visions were increasingly taking over her being.

By 1848 she seems to have been increasingly what Muriel Spark and Derek Stanford have described as 'death-enamoured'. *Wuthering Heights* elaborated many of the themes of the poetry, but they were now more strongly enunciated: the longing to be part of the earth, the longing to escape 'this shattered prison'. It was to this newly emergent Emily that Charlotte referred when she wrote to Mr Williams in early 1848: 'In some points I consider Ellis somewhat of a theorist: now and then he broaches ideas which strike my sense as much more daring and original than practical'. And she went on to say what she would reiterate, that she and Emily were very different writers: 'his reason may be in advance of mine, but certainly it often travels a different road. . . . I should say Ellis will not be seen in his full strength till he is seen as an essayist.'

Charlotte clearly saw many more books coming from Ellis Bell, and the reviews, or in Anne's case paucity of them, did not stop the work of writing continuing. Moreover, both *Wuthering Heights* and *Agnes Grey* were selling well enough to go into second impressions. Anne had begun *The Tenant of Wildfell Hall*, her didactic tale of debauchery intended to warn the young, and inspired by the wreck of her brother, in the summer of 1847; it would be published by Newby in July 1848. It is probable that Emily too had another novel in hand, judging by Newby's letter, which refers to making arrangements for her next novel.

In her *Biographical Notice* Charlotte would write: 'Neither Ellis nor Acton allowed herself for one moment to sink under want of encouragement; energy nerved the one, and endurance upheld the other. They were both prepared to try again. . . .' She herself, though not for want of encouragement, found difficulty in writing again and it was only after several false starts, then the disruptions of family tragedies, that her next book *Shirley* was completed. On 15 February 1848, in response to Smith, Elder's eager enquiries, she told them that she was writing a new novel, and that she supposed it would grow to maturity in time, but that she could not force it. It was not 'every day, nor even every week that I can write what is worth reading'.

Shirley was inspired by Emily, whom Charlotte was now observing with increasing awe, troubled by the darker side of her sister's character that seems to have become apparent from the end of 1847. Perhaps the revulsion expressed in the reviews of *Wuthering Heights*, made all the more painful beside the glowing success of *Jane Eyre*, was the turning point for Emily, who now appeared more outwardly powerful, less amenable and still more withdrawn.

Charlotte's perception of Emily had seemed to change quite radically on reading the poetry that she chanced upon in the autumn of

295

1845. The terse, visionary, musical writing, the wild pantheism, the desire for oblivion, all hinted at another being hidden beneath the childlike, ignorant exterior. Charlotte had always noted what she and Ellen described as Emily's 'peculiarities', and had been quite protective, if patronising, towards them. The opposing strains in her sister's character, of which she was forced into greater and greater awareness, were difficult for Charlotte to reconcile and produced a new, heroic image of Emily. As she wrote in her 1850 preface to *Wuthering Heights*: 'In Emily's nature the extremes of vigour and simplicity seemed to meet. Under an unsophisticated culture, inartificial tastes, and an unpretending outside, lay a secret power and fire that might have informed the brain and kindled the veins of a hero.'

In her portrait of Shirley, the rich heiress who befriends poor Caroline Helstone, niece of the mysogynistic vicar the Reverend Helstone, Charlotte imagined Emily as she might have been if less secluded and better off. The stranger side of her sister's nature was excluded from this portrait, as Charlotte later confided to Mrs Gaskell, but the ignorance that Charlotte stressed in descriptions of both her sisters was a major part of Shirley's character:

> If Shirley were not an indolent, a reckless, and ignorant being, she would take a pen at such moments; or at least while the recollection of such moments was yet fresh on her spirit; she would seize, she would fix the apparition, tell the vision revealed. . . . But indolent she is, reckless she is, and most ignorant, for she does not know her dreams are rare – her feelings peculiar – she does not know, has never known, and will die without knowing, the full value of the spring whose bright fresh bubbling in her heart keeps it green.[31]

But Emily of course did know. And it was her indefinable inner power that remained so fascinating. Ellen Nussey would later give to Mrs Gaskell a description of Emily that reveals her extraordinary and perplexingly contradictory qualities:

> Her extreme reserve seemed impenetrable, yet she was intensely lovable. She invited confidence in her moral power. Few people have the gift of looking and smiling, as she could look and smile – one of her rare expressive looks was something to remember through life, there was such a *depth* of soul and feeling, and yet shyness of revealing herself, a strength of self-containment seen in no other. She was in the strictest sense a law unto herself, and a heroine in keeping to her law. . . .
> If Emily wanted a book she might have left in the sitting room she would dart in without looking at anyone, especially if any guest

were present. Among the curates Mr Weightman was her only exception for any conventional courtesy. The ability with which she took up music was amazing, the style, the touch and the expression was that of a Professor involved heart and soul in his theme.

The two dogs Keeper and Flossy were always in quiet waiting by the side of Emily and Anne during their Scotch breakfast of oatmeal and milk and always had a share handed down to them at the close of the meal. Poor old Keeper! Emily's faithful friend and worshipper – he seemed to understand her like a human being. One evening when the four friends were sitting closely round the fire in C's sitting room, Keeper forced himself in between Charlotte and Emily and mounted himself on Emily's lap. Finding the space too limited for his comfort he pressed himself forward onto the guest's knee making himself quite comfortable. Emily's heart was won by the unresisting endurance of the visitor, little guessing that she herself being in close contact was the inspiring cause of submission to Keeper's preference. Sometimes Emily would delight in showing off Keeper, making him frantic in action and roaring with the voice of a lion – it was a terrifying exhibition within the walls of an ordinary sitting room.

Charlotte's own descriptions of Emily from 1847 onwards have a notably mysterious quality about them, as if she were trying to capture her sister's essence: 'Emily is just now sitting on the floor of the bedroom where I am writing, looking at her apples,' she told Ellen. 'She smiled when I gave them and the collar to her as your presents, with an expression at once well-pleased and slightly surprised.' Was it perhaps the fever of the beginnings of consumption starting to race through Emily's veins which was increasing her tendency to live in a rarefied atmosphere, to live in strange ecstasy, only her mysterious smile sometimes disturbing her pale countenance? An old man who lived in the village remembered seeing her come back along the little green lane that led out from the graveyard, up past the two or three cottages out on to the great moor, with what he described as a look of almost holy rapture on her face.

As the weather grew better that spring of 1848, and the days lengthened into almost painfully fresh, exquisite summer, Emily would have sought the sweeping moors more eagerly than ever. Whether lit up in bright sunlight or washed with the pale-blue aerial tints that swathe the landscape after storms, the moors behind Haworth are a discrete world, completely removed, as Anne had pointed out rather caustically, from worldly cares – the cares that Emily and Branwell so disdained. In summer the landscape has a luminescence – a combination of the clear air and the pale-green

297

shoots and leaves – made more enchanting at evening by the sharp, wavering, violet shadows thrown by each tiny piece of grass, while above and beyond are seemingly endless skies and moorland. To Emily's 'space-sweeping soul', they must indeed have suggested eternity.

More and more perhaps she longed, like Catherine Earnshaw, 'to escape into that glorious world, and to be always there; not seeing it dimly through tears, and yearning for it through the walls of an aching heart; but really with it, and in it'. To be part of the rustling foliage, the mild thaw winds, to fly with the curlew. Emily had rejected the world outside, she had been true to her own nature, above learning, above convention; and when she had tried to give the world her vision, it had been rejected.

From that same mountain eyrie, Charlotte continued to observe her sister and to make hesitant progress with *Shirley*. She decided to set the novel in the Luddite riots of 1811 and 1812, in which her father had played some part, and sent off for old copies of the *Leeds Mercury* in order to research the period. The novel would incorporate many of the places that she had seen when she had lived at Roe Head. Meanwhile, *Jane Eyre*'s popularity was unabated; the second edition had sold well since its publication in December and Charlotte received another £100 from George Smith. There was even a play being made from the novel. Charlotte told Mr Williams that she feared that all her characters would be woefully exaggerated and painfully vulgarised by the players. She could not help thinking that they would make something very pert of Jane Eyre, and as for Mr Rochester – 'the picture my fancy conjures up by way of reply is a somewhat humiliating one'. Nevertheless, she wanted to see it.

By March 1848 her publishers had plans for an unusual third edition – Currer Bell should illustrate it, but this Charlotte refused. She no longer had any illusions about her artistic skills. She was even now rather regretting the strident tone of her preface to the second edition, written in a flush of enthusiasm about the 1848 French Revolution, and encouraged by William Smith Williams. Whatever the high Toryism Charlotte Brontë espoused, a side of her fierce excitable nature could not but respond to revolution, and be exultant: 'Every struggle any nation makes in the cause of Freedom and Truth has something noble in it – something that makes me wish it success', she wrote to Williams.

Reviews of *Jane Eyre* continued to appear through 1848. At the end of March, the review in the Church of England's *Quarterly Review* was, Charlotte decided, 'not on the whole a bad one', at least it was conscientious: 'Some of the ethical and theological notions are not according to his system, and he disapproves of them.' But in April came a renewed attack on the book in the High Church Party's organ, the *Christian Remembrancer*. While recognising the gifts of the author, the reviewer thought he or she had not faced up to the novelists' 'responsibilities as potentially influential directors of moral behaviour', which was particularly important in an age threatened by revolution. In its opinion every page 'burns with moral Jacobinism'. Because *Jane Eyre* had created such a sensation and its remarkable power been so much appreciated by the public, it was obvious that the author could be a powerful influence. She or he ought to be a little more trustful of the reality of human goodness and a little less anxious to detect evil. To Currer Bell all virtue was but masked vice, 'all religious profession and conduct is but the whitening of the sepulchre, all self-denial is but deeper selfishness'. Christianity was seldom evoked except to show that 'all Christian profession is bigotry and all Christian practice is hypocrisy'. Although to say that *Jane Eyre* was positively immoral or anti-Christian would be to do the writer an injustice, 'still it wears a questionable aspect'.

As to the sex of the writer, though the reviewer thought that the book must be written by a woman, and a woman from the north of England, it could not wonder that ladies upheld the notion that it was by a male author –

for a book more unfeminine, both in its excellences and defects, it would be hard to find in the annals of female authorship. Throughout there is masculine power, breadth and shrewdness, combined with masculine hardness, coarseness, and freedom of expression. Slang is not rare. The humour is frequently produced by a use of Scripture at which one is rather sorry to have smiled. The love scenes glow with a fire as fierce as that of Sappho, and somewhat more fulginous. There is an intimate acquaintance with the worst parts of human nature, a practised sagacity in discovering the latent ulcer, and a ruthless rigour in exposing it, which much command our admiration, but are almost startling in one of the softer sex.

This opinion of the powers that be in her father's profession was rather alarming, but Charlotte, as she told Mr Williams, was 'on the whole rather encouraged than dispirited by the review: the hard-wrung praise extorted reluctantly from a foe is the most precious praise of all; you are sure that this, at least, has no admixture of flattery.' She hoped that such reviews would make little difference to her writing, and that if the spirit moved her in the future to say anything about priests, etc., she would say it with the same freedom as before. She went on more threateningly:

299

I hope also that their anger will not make *me* angry; as a body, I had no ill-will against them to begin with, and I feel it would be an error to let opposition engender such ill-will. A few individuals may possibly be called upon to sit for their portraits some time – if their brethren, in general, dislike the resemblance and abuse the artist – '*tant pis!*'.

The opening scene of *Shirley*, with its satirical portrait of the three curates, showed just how little difference such reviews would make to her writing. It may indeed have been written in a spirit of defiance. When Charlotte wrote *Jane Eyre* she cannot have thought that her views would be welcomed, but she had never anticipated this amount of blame. The fact was that the combination of Jane's independent, apparently unfeminine spirit, the attack on the Church of England, the description of passion and tolerance of past vice in Mr Rochester, and the lack of respect for position and rank meant that by mid-1848 an increasing body of opinion had it that *Jane Eyre* was a 'dangerous book', whose author must be 'an alien . . . from society, and amenable to none of its laws.'[32]

All the same, in the late spring of 1848, with the novel in its third edition, Charlotte must have comforted herself that it appealed to some section of the public taste. The future for once seemed to hold some promise. She had no premonition of the personal tragedies that lay so few months ahead.

CHAPTER XV

Dark Shadows

June 1848 opened with the gratifying news from Smith, Elder that *Jane Eyre* had had 'a great run' in America, and that the New York publisher, Harpers, had bid high for the next work from Currer Bell. It was followed by a second, less amiable message. Smith, Elder had received an angry letter from their American friends telling them that the first sheets of a new work by Currer Bell had been received from a rival publisher. The execrable Newby had already been advertising *The Tenant of Wildfell Hall*, just successfully published in England, as if Acton Bell's authorship were interchangeable with that of Currer or Ellis Bell. Now, to Harpers, he had sent Anne's new novel, claiming that to the best of his belief *Jane Eyre*, *Wuthering Heights*, *Agnes Grey* and *The Tenant of Wildfell Hall* were all by one writer. This time Newby had gone too far. There was no author copyright agreement over publication in the States and Charlotte was appalled that Smith, Elder should have been subjected to the implication of double-dealing by the Bell brothers. She received the letter from George Smith on 7 July and on that same day she and Anne set out for London, determined that their business relationships should not be disrupted by that 'shuffling scamp', as Charlotte quaintly called Mr Newby. Emily could not be persuaded to come, but at least Charlotte and Anne could appear in person to prove that they were not one and the same person.

How they disguised what they were doing from Branwell is not clear, but presumably he was either absent or too delirious to notice. He was now well and truly out of control. Mr Brontë had vainly moved his beloved son into his room a year before in an attempt to keep an eye on him after the fire incident, and possibly as a precaution against the threats of suicide. According to one of the servants, this move was only additional aggravation because of the weaponry bristling on the wall of the otherwise unadorned dressing-room. The occupants of the parsonage lived in fear lest one way or another one of the two occupants should not come out next morning. Branwell would tend to stumble downstairs, by now so emaciated that he looked as if he was wearing someone else's clothes, carelessly throwing some word over his shoulder to the household – 'he does his best, the poor old man' being one of his utterances.

From time to time he would sally forth to Halifax and by 17 June he had run up such a bill with Mr Nicholson, the landlord of the Old Cock in Halifax, that the latter sent his father a demand for settlement of the bill or he would initiate court proceedings. The character of Cain-like Northangerland had infected Branwell so deeply as to be part of his constitution, much like the germs of consumption that were slowly invading his lungs. Any pain he might have felt was disguised by the drink running through his veins, which with his opium habit was fatally weakening his resistance. A note written that June to the sculptor Leyland from the Old Cock suggests someone who was nearly a madman:

> For mercie's sake come and see me, for I have sought for you till I dare not risk my knee and my eyesight any more this evening. I shall have a bad evening and night if I do not see you, but I hardly know where to send the bearer of this note so as to enable him to catch you.
>
> Northangerland

No problems at home could, however, deflect Charlotte from her purpose. Packing up a small box with a change of clothes, which they sent on ahead to Keighley, she and Anne set out from Haworth after tea. They walked, almost ran, the four miles to Keighley over the steep hills in their home-made, printed cotton dresses and long narrow shoes. A thunderstorm came on, soaking both delicate women to the skin. They may have had little physical strength and birdlike physiognomies but they had the hearts of lions. When Charlotte burned with moral indignation nothing could stand in her way, as Thackeray would remember. They got to Leeds just in time for the train and, as Charlotte later recounted the whole incident to Mary Taylor, 'whirled up by the night train to London – with the view of proving our separate identity to Smith, Elder and confronting Newby with his lie'.

They arrived in London the next morning at about eight. As usual, impeded by their lack of practical information about London – they knew about art galleries and museums but no comfortable or suitable place to sleep – they made for the Chapter Coffee House in Paternoster Row. There they washed, broke their fast, and then set off, as Charlotte told Mary, 'in queer inward excitement to 65 Cornhill.

Neither Mr Smith nor Mr Williams knew we were coming – they had never seen us, they did not know whether we were men or women – but had always written to us as men.'

They found number 65 to be a large bookseller's shop in a street which was almost as bustling as the Strand. They went in and walked up to the counter past the many young men and boys milling around. Charlotte said to the first one whose eye she could catch:

'May I see Mr Smith.' He hesitated, looked a little surprised – but went to fetch him. We sat down and waited a while – looking a [sic] some books on the counter publications of theirs well known to us, of many of which they had sent us copies as presents. At last somebody came up and said dubiously, 'Did you wish to see me, Madam?' 'Is it Mr Smith?' I said, looking up through my spectacles at a young, tall, gentlemanly man.[1]

By the end of the nineteenth century, the firm of Smith, Elder would become one of the most influential in London, publishing Thackeray, Mrs Gaskell, Matthew Arnold, Ruskin and Browning. George Smith himself would be pre-eminent among publishers, the founder of that typically Victorian monument to the great and the good, the *Dictionary of National Biography* and a convivial figure on the literary scene. But this was chiefly the effect of publishing Currer Bell. In 1848 the firm was in severe financial trouble, the result of inadequate management and actual embezzlement over the years of around £30,000. The publishing arm of Smith, Elder was not nearly so important financially as its role as one of the most important Indian agencies, combining banking with a multifarious export business, the result of the Calcutta connections of the partner in charge of it, Patrick Stewart. When it emerged that Patrick Stewart was the embezzler, from an investigation ordered by George Smith after his father's death in 1846 had left him, aged twenty-two, in charge of the publishing business, it fell to him to run both sides of the operation. Spurred on by the necessity of providing for his mother and four siblings all of whose monies were invested in the firm, under his businesslike approach the company would begin to thrive, but it was at some cost to his health. He frequently worked twenty-two hours a day for around seven or eight years to turn the firm round, and in these circumstances was heavily reliant on the support of his devoted mother.[2]

At the time of his meeting with Charlotte Brontë, George Smith was twenty-four, as genial, kind, handsome, brisk and unimaginative as Dr John Bretton in *Villette*, for whom he would be the inspiration. Nevertheless he had had the foresight to pluck the timorous, melancholy but gifted William Smith Williams out of his job at a lithographers which Smith, Elder used for the many art books that were their speciality, and to give him his head as literary adviser. That Saturday morning in July he was as usual working flat out in his determined way, administering the agency side of the business. He was in the middle of dictating to his clerk, while two others were making fair copies of other letters at their high desks, when a clerk came in and said that two ladies wished to see him. Smith said testily he was very busy, and told the clerk to go and ask them their names. The clerk returned to say the ladies declined to give their names, but wished to see him on a private matter. With a sign of impatience at the irritating ways of the female sex he went into the vestibule. There he saw 'two rather quaintly dressed little ladies, pale-faced and anxious-looking'.

> One of them came forward and presented me with a letter – addressed in my own handwriting to 'Currer Bell, Esq'. I noticed that the letter had been opened, and said with some sharpness: 'Where did you get this from?' 'From the post office,' was the reply. 'It was addressed to me. We have both come that you might have ocular proof that there are at least two of us.'[3]

George Smith looked at the letter, at her, and again at the letter, and Charlotte could not restrain a tiny crow of laughter. For his part, he was simply amazed that this little creature could be the author of that passionate masterpiece *Jane Eyre*. For a moment there was silence. Then he pulled himself together. He now had before him the author for whom all London had been searching. He told Charlotte in a great gabble of excitement, 'If Mr Lewes knew "Currer Bell" was in town he would have to be shut up', likewise Thackeray. He began to make plans: both lions must be invited to dinner forthwith, he must introduce them to his mother and sisters, take them to the Italian opera, the Exhibition. Meanwhile they must come through and meet Mr Williams.

Mr Williams entered, 'a pale, mild, stooping man of fifty', who, as Charlotte told Mary Taylor, strongly reminded her of Tom Dixon, her friend from Brussels. There was a long, heartfelt but nervous shaking of hands. In a sense Charlotte owed this man all. In the small, dusty back room beneath the great skylight, Charlotte saw all her dreams flare up at the thought of a meeting with literary men, with Thackeray her god, with the world of 'literature and critics and fame . . . prominent in my thoughts at the first publication of *Jane Eyre*'. But no, she must deny herself it. She would have to forsake her anonymity in order for Thackeray to come to dinner at such short notice: 'I felt it would have ended in our being made a show of – a thing I have ever resolved to avoid.' The customs of the West Riding of Yorkshire, of womanly behaviour, of publishing not being respectable, were too deeply ingrained to be abandoned in a day. So, even though 'the desire to see some of the names he mentioned kindled in me very strongly',[4] the offer was declined. Mr Williams, with his greater knowledge of his author, immediately understood that 'we are as resolved as ever to preserve our incognito . . . to the rest of the world we must be "gentlemen" as before'.

Now explanations were gone into, the wicked Newby 'being unduly anathematized'. Mr Smith was anxious for them to come and stay at his large and comfortable house in prosperous Bayswater, but Charlotte and Anne were not prepared for a long visit and declined this also. However, Mr Smith would not be put off from getting to know the Bells – those wild brothers who, among other hypotheses, it had been suggested were Lancashire weavers, and insisted on bringing the two elder of his sisters, Eliza and Sarah, to call on them that evening.

The Brontës returned to their inn, purchasing parasols and new gloves on the way. Charlotte's emotions had taken their customary toll on her frail constitution: 'I paid for the excitement of the interview by a thundering headache and harrassing [sic] sickness – towards evening as I got no better and expected the Smiths to call, I took a strong dose of sal volatile – it roused me a little – still I was in grievous bodily case when they were announced.'[5] The two Miss Smiths entered, visions in full evening dress, the low-cut silk in pastel shades popular at that period – bestrewn with ribands and nosegays, ready for that most showy of London occasions, the opera. They were followed by Mr Smith, also in evening costume with white gloves, looking handsome and distinguished, and expecting the Miss Brontës to come too and join them in their box. Here was Angria and Cinderella rolled into one. Charlotte was well aware of the great discrepancy between what she described as she and Anne's 'plain, high-made, country garments' and the glittering dress of the creatures now pressing them to get into the carriage. There was no fairy godmother to come to their rescue and 'we had no fine, elegant dresses either with us or in the world'. But for once she thought it wise to make no objections – 'I put my headache in my pocket' – and off they went.

Despite, as Charlotte related to Mary, feeling that 'they must have thought us queer, quizzical-looking beings' – not helped in Charlotte's case by the wire spectacles defiantly veiling the glowing brown eyes that were her best feature – she could not help but be 'pleasantly excited'. She smiled inwardly at the contrast that must have been apparent between her and Mr Smith as she walked up the crimson carpeted staircase of the Opera House 'and stood amongst a brilliant

305

throng at the box-door which was not yet open. Fine ladies and gentlemen glanced at us with a slight, graceful superciliousness quite warranted by the circumstances.' It was like some delightful dream. Looking round, she saw that Anne 'was calm and gentle, which she always is'.

The opera was Rossini's *Barber of Seville*, which Charlotte thought 'very brilliant', though she guessed that there were performances she would like better. In the darkness of the box she whispered to Mr Smith that he must excuse their reactions, for they really were not used to such things. They got home after one o'clock in the morning, exhausted after being in constant excitement for twenty-four hours and not having slept.

The next two days passed in a whirl of activity, with both Charlotte and Anne now rather strained after the initial excitement. In his impetuously hospitable way George Smith whisked them off in his smart carriage to dine with his mother and sisters, without explaining to his family who the old-fashioned looking spinsters were. They could not even risk being called by their real name for fear of some link being made between Brontë and the Bell brothers by the avid rumour-spreaders, particularly as Ellen Nussey was in London at this time. As Charlotte wrote to Mary, their unexplained presence in the Smith family made for an awkward visit:

> their strange perplexity would have been ludicrous if one had dared to laugh – To be brought down to a part of the city into whose obscure narrow streets they said they had never penetrated before, to an old, dark strange-looking Inn, to take up in their fine carriage a couple of odd-looking countrywomen, to see their elegant, handsome son and brother treating with scrupulous politeness these insignificant spinsters must have puzzled them thoroughly Mr Smith's residence is at Bayswater, six miles from Cornhill – a very fine place – the rooms, the drawing room especially, looked splendid to us.

There were no other guests to dine in the large house at 4 Westbourne Place, just the family – Mrs Smith, Eliza and Sarah, George's brother Alick – 'a lad of twelve or thirteen' – and little sister Isabella, whom Charlotte thought very like her publisher, though they all bore a strong family resemblance: dark-eyed, dark-haired, with clear, pale faces. Mrs Smith, Charlotte found 'a portly handsome woman of her age'; she had handed on her disposition to *embonpoint* to her son, whose convivial life and gregarious disposition meant that he was continually battling against his weight. Charlotte and Anne were scarcely able to eat the fine dinner due to lack of appetite brought on by nerves. Charlotte told Mary: 'I always feel under awkward constraint at table. Dining out would be a hideous bore to me.' She could not, however, altogether conceal the note of triumph which hailed this new possibility.

As Charlotte appraised Mr Smith from behind the array of elaborate silver ornaments weighing down the mahogany table, he in turn had been observing his new charges. 'I must confess,' he wrote somewhat clinically many years later, 'my first impression of Charlotte Brontë's appearance was that it was interesting rather than attractive. She was very small and had a quaint old-fashioned look.' He went on, pointing to the way her missing teeth had spoilt her mouth and to the red complexion noted by Mrs Gaskell:

> Her head seemed too large for her body. She had fine eyes, but her face was marred by the shape of the mouth and by the complexion. There was but little feminine charm about her; and of this fact she was herself uneasily and perpetually conscious. . . . I believe she would have given all her genius and her fame to have been beautiful. Perhaps few women ever existed more anxious to be pretty than she, or more angrily conscious of the circumstance that she was not pretty.[6]

Anne he also found not pretty but of 'a pleasing appearance', with something in her face expressive of an appeal for protection.

Such appraisals reflected George Smith's own system of values and, though acute, did not do full justice to the Brontë sisters' natures. Charlotte may once have been tortured by her consciousness of her poor looks in the world's eyes, feelings that she had struggled not without success to master, but to say that she put such an absolute value on physical beauty was surely to overstate the case. Nor did his notice of Anne's appealing vulnerability allow for her remarkable inner strength. Perhaps, however, Charlotte's sharp appraisal in turn of George Smith's character suppressed an attraction for him that she did not have the confidence to admit to. She thought him 'a firm, intelligent man of business though so young [he was eight years her junior] – bent on getting on – and I think desirous to make his way by fair, honourable means. He is enterprising – but likewise cool and cautious. Mr Smith is a *practical* man.' She wished that Mr Williams, for his own sake, could be more so, 'but he is altogether of the contemplative, theorizing order'. She thought sadly that he 'lives too much in abstractions'.[7]

Nevertheless, Mr Williams was less alarming than his employer. He took them to church on Sunday to hear the famous preacher Dr Croly, Rector of St Stephen's Walbrook,[8] which might have surprised

307

Charlotte's critics. Charlotte found him 'so quiet but so sincere in his attentions, one could not but have a most friendly leaning towards him'. Although he had a nervous hesitation when he spoke, and a difficulty in finding appropriate language in which to express himself – which threw him into the background in conversation – Charlotte knew his worth from his letters and was in no danger of underrating him. She felt that he sympathetically guessed that her life 'is, and always has been, one of few pleasures'.

On the Monday, after visiting the Exhibition of the Royal Academy, and the National Gallery, and dining with the Smiths, Charlotte and Anne went to take tea with the Williamses in their neat, comparatively humble residence. Mrs Williams was ill but they met the eight children of Mr Williams's engaging family, confidences about whom Charlotte had so often received in correspondence. Also there was a daughter of Leigh Hunt, who sang some Italian airs that she had picked up when staying amongst the peasantry in Tuscany. Charlotte was rather charmed by the performance, though not especially by her personality, writing cuttingly that she supposed her 'a rattling good-natured personage enough'.

The next morning they left London, laden with books that the kind-hearted George Smith loaded on to them. Having met with Newby and attempted to dissuade him from further villainy, Charlotte returned home in a state of excitement which she found difficult to quieten. She thought she looked utterly jaded: 'My face looked grey and very old – with strange, deep lines plough [sic] in it – my eyes stared unnaturally – I was weak and yet restless. In a while, however, these bad effects of excitement went off and I regained my normal condition.'[9]

She wrote on the following day, 13 July, to express her thanks to Mr Williams. It had been a somewhat hasty step, she said, to hurry up to town as they had done, but she did not regret having taken it. The candid Charlotte found mystery 'irksome, and I was glad to shake it off with you and Mr Smith, and to show myself to you for what I am, neither more nor less – thus removing any false expectations that may have arisen under the idea that Currer Bell had a just claim to the masculine cognomen he, perhaps somewhat presumptuously, adopted – that he was, in short, of the nobler sex'. She signed the letter in her own name.

The only unpleasant aspect of the affair was Emily's reaction to it. She seems to have been extremely angry that Charlotte had told her publishers that they were three sisters, to judge from Charlotte's plea to Mr Williams on 31 July:

Permit me to caution you not to speak of my sisters when you write

308

to me. I mean, do not use the word in the plural. Ellis Bell will not endure to be alluded to under any other appellation than the *nom de plume*. I committed a grand error in betraying his identity to you and Mr Smith. It was inadvertent – the words 'we are three sisters' escaped me before I was aware. I regretted the avowal the moment I had made it; I regret it bitterly now, for I find it is against every feeling and intention of Ellis Bell.

More and more was Charlotte wondering about Emily. She brought her into her letters far more than she had done as a younger woman. At Mr Williams's urging that all the Brontës should go into society, she admitted there would be an advantage in it, even a great advantage, 'yet it is one that no power on earth could induce Ellis Bell, for instance, to avail himself of'. Meanwhile, she continued to add to *Shirley* and was helped in whiling away the long summer by the books that George Smith repeatedly sent to her. Whatever the impression left by his later published memoir of Charlotte Brontë, he was evidently rather fascinated by her.

She herself was in ebullient mood, rather relishing her new position with her publishers and taking the opportunity to express herself at length on literature to the earnest ear of Mr Williams. A new barrage against the Bell brothers had followed the publication of *The Tenant of Wildfell Hall*, when many critics had interpreted Anne's warning of the perils of dissipation as delight in debauchery. Anne had felt some of the unfavourable notices keenly and Charlotte, who would consistently underrate the novel's worth, told Mr Williams: 'The fact is, neither she nor any of us expected that view to be taken of the book. That it had faults of execution, faults of art, was obvious, but fault of intention or feeling could be suspected by none who knew the writer.'

Though it was becoming obvious to Charlotte that life might be easier if the Bells followed Thackeray's lead, as the 'legitimate high priest of Truth' and only hint at the world's realities, she continued to tell Mr Williams of the Bells' unbowed determination to write as they saw fit:

The first duty of an author is, I conceive, a faithful allegiance to Truth and Nature; his second, such a conscientious study of Art as shall enable him to interpret eloquently and effectively the oracles delivered by those two great deities. The Bells are very sincere in their worship of Truth, and they hope to apply themselves to the consideration of Art, so as to attain one day the power of speaking the language of conviction in the accents of persuasion; though they rather apprehend that whatever pains they take to modify and soften, an abrupt word or vehement tone will now and then occur to

309

startle ears polite, whenever the subject shall chance to be such as moves their spirits within them.

She continued to defend with spirit the character of Mr Rochester against suggestions of any similarities with Mr Huntingdon, telling Mr Williams that there could be no comparison. While Huntingdon was a specimen of the naturally selfish, sensual man, who was sure to grow worse the older he grew, Mr Rochester had 'a thoughtful nature and a very feeling heart. . . . His nature is like wine of a good vintage, time cannot sour, but only mellows him.' Anne, however, was not utterly downcast. *Wildfell Hall* was not only selling well but it had also received some praise: the *Athenaeum* called it 'the most interesting novel which we have read for a month past'. When the *Spectator* and others misunderstood the book's intentions – 'a morbid love for the coarse, not to say the brutal' – she wrote a preface to the second edition in which she demonstrated that her motives for writing the book were as public-spirited and didactic as any critic could wish (though it seems not to have weighed a jot with them). Her object, she pointed out, was not just to amuse the reader or gratify her own taste, or even to produce a perfect work of art; rather it was with God's help to warn against vice. It was better to present a situation offensively than run the risk of a young person falling into such a trap.

She had a robust word or two for those who interested themselves in the sex of the author of *Wildfell Hall*. She was bound to impute much of the severity of her censors to the suspicion that she was a woman, but she intended making no effort to refute this, because 'in my own mind, I am satisfied that if a book is a good one, it is so whatever the sex of the author may be'. All novels are or should be written for both men and women to read, and she was at a loss to conceive 'how a man should permit himself to write anything that would be really disgraceful to a woman, or why a woman should be censured for writing anything that would be proper and becoming for a man'.[10]

Just as Anne spoke out in her own way that summer, there seemed little to shake Charlotte's new-found equilibrium. She was delighted to see Newby's reprehensible publishing manners attacked in the periodicals. There were plans for Smith, Elder to buy up and re-publish the Bells' volume of poetry, which were in fact carried out in October – by which time the lack of critical appreciation of Ellis Bell in the new reviews had taken on bitter overtones for Charlotte. But for now, even the showery weather, which was causing the neighbour-hood to worry about the crops, could not lower her spirits. Concern for her family's health seemed to have faded into the background and her brother's behaviour was almost an accepted pattern. As she wrote to Ellen on 28 July: 'Branwell is the same in conduct as ever. His constitution seems much shattered. Papa and sometimes all of us have sad nights with him.' Mr Brontë, however, was in good form, stimulated by reading a new life of his former mentor, the Evangelical Simeon, which Ellen had lent him. There was considerable agitation in the village because Mr James Greenwood, who owned Woodlands, one of the big houses and estates near Haworth, and who employed a large number of its inhabitants, had gone bankrupt and had to sell up.

Only in September, when the *Rambler* magazine published a review of outright hostility, did it become hard to put a brave face on it. Opining that Acton and Currer Bell were probably one and the same person, probably a woman and a Yorkshire woman at that, and while admitting that the author was a clever and vigorous writer, the review execrated the 'truly offensive and sensual spirit' which was 'painfully prominent' in *Jane Eyre* and *The Tenant of Wildfell Hall*. *Jane Eyre* was, in its opinion, one of the coarsest books the reviewer had ever read, and though the critic could find nothing to pin down in the *professed* religious notions of the writer, there was 'a certain perpetual *tendency* to relapse into that class of ideas, expressions, and circumstances, which is most connected with the grosser and more animal portion of our nature'.[11] *The Tenant of Wildfell Hall* also suffered from this spirit, as well as containing 'disgusting scenes of debauchery' detailed with offending minuteness, and a deathbed scene that was 'neither edifying, nor true to life, nor full of warning to the careless and profligate'. At least, however, it was not so '*bad*' a book as *Jane Eyre*. There was not 'such a palpable blinking of the abominable nature of the morality of its most prominent characters'. The reviewer concluded that he hoped no more novels would issue from the same pen.

Almost simultaneously, *Sharpe's Magazine* declared that *The Tenant of Wildfell Hall* was of such a revolting nature that they had decided to mention it only to warn lady-readers against reading it. The reviewer felt that each brutal or profane expression was chronicled with such hateful accuracy that it could not be 'fit subject matter for the pages of a work of fiction, a popular novel to be obtruded by every circulating library-keeper upon the notice of our sisters, wives, and daughters'. Having been unable to decide on the sex of the writer, the reviewer plumped for a man because 'none but a man could have known so intimately each vile, dark fold of the civilized brute's corrupted nature'; no woman could have displayed such bold coarseness.[12]

Mr Williams sent on the *Rambler* notice, with his own opinion attached. Charlotte replied with dignity:

It is indeed acting the part of a true friend to apprise an author faithfully of what opponents say, and profess to think of his works.

311

Your own comments also demand our best thanks; I have read them with attention and feel their justice.

Defects there are both in 'Jane Eyre' and 'Wildfell Hall' which it will be the authors' wisdom and duty to endeavour to avoid in the future. Other points there are to which they deem it incumbent on them firmly to adhere, whether such adherence bring popularity or unpopularity, praise or blame. The standard heroes and heroines of novels are personages in whom I could never from childhood upwards take an interest, believe to be natural, or wish to imitate. Were I obliged to copy these characters I would simply not write at all. Were I obliged to copy any former novelist, even the greatest, even Scott, in anything, I would not write. Unless I have something of my own to say, and a way of my own to say it in, I have no business to publish. Unless I can look beyond the greatest Masters, and study Nature herself, I have no right to paint. Unless I can have the courage to use the language of Truth in preference to the jargon of Conventionality, I ought to be silent.[13]

There was a sort of rebellious buoyancy to Charlotte's pronouncements of her deepest convictions of artistic truth and integrity – or Truth as she wrote it. She was not to be shaken. And then suddenly the season made the rapid transition from high summer to that melancholy time when the crisp chill is felt beneath each breeze, reminder that autumn and then winter and the close of the year are at hand. With the same remorselessness, on the morning of Sunday, 24 September, Branwell died.

His death was completely unexpected. Although Charlotte had noted that summer that he had less appetite than before and that he was weaker, neither she nor his doctors had realised how far the disease of consumption had eaten into his system. The family had no warning that he was about to die. He was in the village two days before his death, and only confined to his bed for a single day. It took just twenty minutes' struggle, and then his tormented spirit was gone. He had been perfectly conscious till the final agony.

His friend Francis Grundy left the only account of Branwell prior to his death, and though unreliable and highly coloured with hindsight, it is telling of the hopelessly demented state to which Branwell had been reduced:

Very soon I went to Haworth again to see him for the last time. From the little inn I sent for him to the great square cold-looking Rectory. I had ordered a dinner for two, and the room looked cosy and warm, the bright glass and silver pleasantly reflecting the sparkling firelight, deeply toned by the red curtains. Whilst I waited for his appearance, his father was shown in. Much of the Rector's old stiffness of manner was gone. He spoke of Branwell with more affection than I had ever heretofore heard him express, but he also spoke almost hopelessly. He said that when my message came, Branwell was in bed, and had been almost too weak for the last few days to leave it; nevertheless, he had insisted upon coming, and would be there immediately. We parted and I never saw him again.

Presently the door opened cautiously and a head appeared. It was a mass of red unkempt uncut hair, wildly floating round a great gaunt forehead; the cheeks yellow and hollow, the mouth fallen, the thin lips not trembling but shaking, the sunken eyes, once small now glaring with the light of madness – . . . I hastened to my friend, greeted him with my gayest manner, as I knew he liked best, drew him quickly into the room and forced upon him a stiff glass of hot brandy. Under its influence, and that of the bright cheerful surroundings, he looked frightened – frightened of himself. He glanced at me for a moment, and muttered something of leaving a warm bed to come out into the cold night. Another glass of brandy and returning warmth gradually brought him back to something like the Brontë of old. He even ate some dinner, a thing which he said he had not done for long; so our last interview was pleasant though grave. I never knew his intellect clearer. He described himself as waiting anxiously for death – indeed, longing for it, and happy, in these his sane moments, to think that it was so near. He once again declared that that death would be due to the story I knew, and to nothing else. When at last I was compelled to leave, he quietly drew from his sleeve a carving-knife, placed it on the table and holding me by both hands, said that having given up all thoughts of ever seeing me again, he imagined when my message came that it was a call from Satan. Dressing himself, he took the knife, which he had long secreted, and came to the inn, with a full determination to rush into the room and stab the occupant. In the excited state of his mind he did not recognise me when he opened the door, but my voice and manner conquered him and 'brought him home to himself'. . . . I left him standing bareheaded in the road, with bowed form and dropping tears. A few days afterwards he was dead. . . .[14]

Of all Branwell's mourners, Charlotte was the one who collapsed, her illness hastened by 'the awe and trouble of the death-scene – the first I had ever witnessed'. She was quite incapacitated for a week and Anne had to answer all her letters. 'Headache and sickness came on first, on Sunday,' she wrote to Ellen. 'I could not regain my appetite. Then internal pain attacked me. I became at once reduced – it was impossible to eat a morsel – at last, bilious fever declared itself.' She was

313

suffering from jaundice, perhaps expressing unacknowledged guilt for her coldness towards her brother over the past few years. Could she have done more for him? It was her sisters who gathered round to sustain her, who dealt with the dreary practicalities of death. The funeral service was taken once again by their old family friend, the Reverend William Morgan, after which they took Branwell down to lie with his mother and aunt, and with Maria who had haunted him for so long.

Mr Brontë, utterly distraught by the death of his only son who, during his last day, had suddenly consented to pray with him again, cried in agony to Charlotte, 'If *you* fail me Charlotte I know I am done for.' She told Mr Williams a little resentfully: 'My poor father naturally thought more of his *only* son Branwell than of his daughters; much and long as he had suffered on his account, he cried out for his loss like David for that of Absalom – my son! my son! and refused at first to be comforted.' But, she continued, he had been comforted by the change that had come over his son at the very end: 'I myself with painful, mournful joy, heard him praying softly in his dying moments, and to the last prayer which my father offered up at his bedside, he added "amen". How unusual that word appeared from his lips – of course you who did not know him, cannot conceive.'

Charlotte would not allow herself to grieve for Branwell in the normal manner. She told Mr Williams that the removal of their only brother must be regarded as a mercy. Her obituary was frank and short:

> Branwell was his father's and his sisters' pride and hope in boyhood, but since manhood the case has been otherwise. It has been our lot to see him take a wrong bent; to hope, expect, wait his return to the right path; to know the sickness of hope deferred, the dismay of prayer baffled; to experience despair at last – and now to behold the sudden early obscure close of what might have been a noble career.

On his last day, when his mind 'had undergone the peculiar change which precedes death', as Charlotte wrote to Ellen, he had returned to something like his old affectionate self, the terrible bitterness to his family gone. She could not but remember her boon companion, once dearer to her than her own soul, her aider and abetter, her most intimate friend, co-visionary of the literary citadel that they would some day breach. She told Mr Williams that she did not weep from a sense of bereavement, but for what might have been: 'for the wreck of talent, the ruin of promise, the untimely dreary extinction of what might have been a burning and a shining light. My brother was a year my junior. I had aspirations and ambitions for him once, long ago –

314

they have perished mournfully. Nothing remains of him', nothing of that Branwell who had used to enliven them so with his wit and his poetry, 'but a memory of errors and sufferings. There is such a bitterness of pity for his life and death, such a yearning for the emptiness of his whole existence as I cannot describe.'

She went on to Mr Williams: 'My unhappy brother never knew what his sisters had done in literature – he was not aware that they had ever published a line. We could not tell him of our efforts for fear of causing him too deep a pang of remorse for his own time misspent, and talents misapplied. Now he will *never* know. I cannot dwell longer on the subject at present – it is too painful.'

As she had looked on her brother's corpse, his beauty restored in death, she reported to Williams that she had not been able to help asking herself what was the cause of his moral decline 'when he had so many gifts to induce to, and aid in an upward course'. She said that she seemed to receive an oppressive revelation 'of the inadequacy of even genius to lead to true greatness if unaided by religion and principle'. For almost to the very last, Branwell had kept up that swaggering opposition to religious cant 'till within a few days of his end, and then all at once he seemed to open his heart to a conviction of their existence and worth'.

After he had died she suddenly felt, as she had never felt before, that there was peace and forgiveness for him in Heaven. 'A deep conviction that he rests at last – rests well after his brief, erring, suffering, feverish life – fills and quiets my mind now,' she wrote piteously to Ellen.

But it was not the end. Death had not quitted the house. It lingered in the damp stone floors, hung in the humid air. It was encouraged by the stone privy, by the water drawn from a contaminated well whose source came through a channel in the too closely packed graveyard. Branwell had died of tuberculosis, a notoriously contagious disease. He may have contracted it from the village, where it was endemic, which would explain the speed with which it killed Emily and Anne. The other conceivable sources were either Emily or Charlotte herself, who was carrying a form of chronic fibrotic tuberculosis which periodically flared up, or Mr Brontë, who is now believed to have suffered from chronic tubercular bronchitis.[15] Whoever the carrier, the bacteria literally hangs in the air in a miasma for hours after a consumptive breathes his deadly germs into it. People are most at risk from tuberculosis in damp crowded conditions, and the cosy little parsonage became a death trap.

Within weeks of her brother's death, still stunned by grief, Charlotte was expressing deep unease to Mr Williams about her sisters' health. Emily had caught a cold at Branwell's funeral; at first dismissed, above all by Emily herself, as nothing serious, it was in fact the first stage of her rapid decline. She became extraordinarily thin and pale, obviously desperately ill, but refused, with a power that seemed almost a will to die, to try any of Charlotte's proffered remedies or even to reply to questions about her health. On the evening of 2 November, Charlotte wrote to Mr Williams that she thought she might see a little improvement in her sister's haggard face. Finding a cure was made more difficult by Emily's ruthless stoicism, which refused to accept or ask for sympathy. As she gazed at her, she told him that she thought 'a certain harshness in her powerful and peculiar character only makes me cling to her more. But this is all family egotism (so to speak) – excuse it, and, above all, never allude to it, or to the name Emily, when you write to me. I do not always show your letters, but I never withhold them when they are inquired after.'

Charlotte, her work abandoned, looked on in agony, her active executive nature frustrated by her sister's mystery, her anxiety made greater by Anne's great delicacy of constitution. Emily would not abandon any of her household tasks – the cleaning, the baking, feeding the animals – even though by the end of November she could scarcely perform them. She never left the house after Branwell's death, gradually becoming too weak even to read, but not for one day would she take to her bed. Charlotte was more and more impressed by the terrible majesty of her sister, now so gaunt and silent, but wished, as she wrote to Mr Williams, that Emily added 'to her many great qualities the humble one of tractability'. Emily said she would have no 'poisoning doctor' near her. Homeopathic remedies, suggested by Mr Williams, were also rejected, labelled 'another form of quackery'.

Meanwhile notices continued to arrive berating the Bells. On 22 November, after the receipt of one such, and reading its description of the general 'fever of moral and religious indignation produced by *Jane Eyre*',[16] Charlotte ironically described the scene at the parsonage to Mr Williams:

The North American Review is worth reading; there is no mincing the matter there. What a bad set the Bells must be! What appalling books they write! Today as Emily appeared a little easier, I thought the *Review* would amuse her, so I read it aloud to her and Anne. As I sat between them at our quiet but now somewhat melancholy fireside, I studied the two ferocious authors. Ellis, the 'man of uncommon talents but dogged, brutal, and morose', sat leaning back in his easy-chair drawing his impeded breath as best he could and looking alas! piteously pale and wasted; it is not his wont to laugh but he smiled half-amused and half in scorn as he listened.

316

Acton was sewing, no emotion ever stirs him to loquacity, so he only smiled too, dropping at the same time a single word of calm amazement to hear his character so darkly portrayed. I wonder what the reviewer would have thought of his own sagacity could he have beheld the pair as I did.

To Ellen five days later, she was writing: 'Emily continues much the same . . . I hope still – for I *must* hope – she is dear to me as life.' By now the thought that Charlotte could not allow herself was physically undeniable. The slightest exertion meant that Emily's breath became a rapid pant; her pulse was 115 a minute. By 10 December diarrhoea had set in, weakening her still further; in addition to tuberculosis of the lungs (pulmonary tuberculosis), Emily had contracted generalised miliary tuberculosis in the bowel, either by contagion through the bloodstream or possibly by swallowing her own sputum. Even if Emily had co-operated by eating, and lying up, thus giving the fibres in her lungs a remote chance to knit themselves together, there was no escape from this secondary infection.

Charlotte would later write in her obituary notice of her sisters of the ordeal of witnessing Emily's illness and her refusal to allow her to speak of it:

The details of her illness are deep-branded in my memory, but to dwell on them either in thought or narrative, is not in my power. Never in her life had she lingered over any task that lay before her, and she did not linger now. She sank rapidly. She made haste to leave us. Yet while physically she perished, mentally she grew stronger than we had yet known her. Day by day, when I saw with what a front she met suffering, I looked on her with an anguish of wonder and love. I have seen nothing like it; but, indeed, I have never seen her parallel in anything. Stronger than a man, simpler than a child, her nature stood alone. The awful point was, that, while full of ruth for others, on herself she had no pity; the spirit was inexorable to the flesh; from the trembling hand, the unnerved limbs, the faded eyes, the same service was exacted as they had rendered in health. To stand by and witness this, and not dare to remonstrate was a pain no words can render.[17]

Eventually Charlotte could bear the situation no longer and, unknown to Emily, wrote to an eminent physician in London giving as minute a statement of Emily's case and symptoms as she could draw up. At this point, to compound her anxiety, Anne began to have frequent pains in the side. Ellen anxiously sent presents of crabcheese, messages of comfort. The Misses Robinson came to see Anne. 'They are attractive

317

and stylish looking girls,' Charlotte noted. 'They seemed overjoyed to see Anne; when I went into the room, they were clinging round her like two children – she, meantime, looking perfectly quiet and passive.' The father fretted; Charlotte continued to manage to control her health by a supreme effort of will; Anne shivered in the December winds attacking the house with repeated vehemence. The physician sent his opinion, 'which was expressed too obscurely to be of use'. He sent some medicine which Emily would not take.

When Charlotte came back from a long search on the moors with a tiny sprig of heather, to find that Emily did not recognise the once beloved flower, she realised that there was to be no averting death. Emily could scarcely move without coughing but on Monday 18 December she was still about the house, going through the habitual motions of her day's duties. In the evening she got up to feed the dogs, walking slowly, with her usual apronful of bits of meat and bread held out in her now skeletal hands. But when she got outside into the stone passage she staggered against the wall, thrown by the extreme cold and the unevenness of the floor. Charlotte and Anne tried to get her to go back to the sofa in the dining room, but she refused; she *would* give Flossy and Keeper their supper. Then, that last night, Charlotte read one of Emerson's soothing and inspiring essays to her. She read on till she noticed that the figure on the sofa was not listening, and she shut the book and put it away, thinking that she would start it again the next day.

But it was not to be. On Tuesday morning, the 19th, Emily insisted on dressing herself without help, as usual. Each movement occasioned a pause, a gasp for breath, but nevertheless she came down the stairs unaided to the drawing room. There, although her breath was rattling in her throat, she took up her sewing, even though her eyes were too glazed to see, and Charlotte's first glance at her told her 'what would happen before nightfall'. Her sisters dared not say a word. Charlotte scribbled agonisedly to Ellen: 'I should have written to you before, if I had but one word of hope to say; but I had not. She grows daily weaker. The physician . . . sent some medicine which she would not take – Moments so dark as these I have never known. I pray for God's support to us all. Hitherto he has granted it.' The dark December morning grew lighter. When it was almost noon Emily at last said faintly to Charlotte 'If you will send for a doctor, I will see him now.' About two o'clock she died, on the sofa in the dining room.[18]

She was buried three days later, in a service conducted by Mr Nicholls. So wasted was Emily's body by the time of her death that her coffin measured only sixteen inches wide. Her devoted Keeper, whom she had treated with the sort of feeling usually reserved for

318

human beings, walked in the short cortège of Charlotte, Anne, the servants and Mr Brontë, behind the wooden coffin through the graveyard in the biting wind. He was taken into the church and the Brontës' own pew, where he sat quietly while the burial service was read. And for the next week he lay outside Emily's bedroom and howled.

For Charlotte her grief for Emily was compounded by anxiety about Anne's health and the necessity to appear well herself for her father's sake. He implored her 'almost hourly' to 'bear up', saying 'I shall sink if you fail me.' On Christmas Day from the house now missing two of its inhabitants Charlotte wrote passionately to Mr Williams:

Emily is nowhere here now – her wasted mortal remains are taken out of the house; we have laid her cherished head under the church-aisle beside my mother's, my two sisters', dead long ago, and my poor, hapless brother's. But a small remnant of the race is left – so my poor father thinks.

Well, the loss is ours, not hers, and some sad comfort I take, as I hear the wind blow and feel the cutting keenness of the frost, in knowing that the elements bring her no more suffering – their severity cannot reach her grave – her fever is quieted, her restless-ness soothed, her deep hollow cough is hushed for ever; we do not hear it in the night nor listen for it in the morning; we have not the conflict of the strangely strong spirit and the fragile frame before us – relentless conflict – once seen, never to be forgotten. A dreary calm reigns round us, in the midst of which we seek resignation. . . .

So I will not ask why Emily was torn from us in the fullness of our attachment, rooted up in the prime of her own days, in the promise of her powers – why her existence now lies like a field of green corn trodden down – like a tree in full bearing – struck at the root; I will only say, sweet is rest after labour and calm after tempest, and repeat again and again that Emily knows that now.

In her desolate state, she asked Ellen to come to stay, a plea that her loyal friend immediately complied with. The consolation she was able to give was all the more needed, for on 5 January 1849, just over two weeks after Emily's death, a doctor whom Mr Brontë had sent for from Leeds examined Anne and confirmed that she too had been infected by tuberculosis. On hearing the news, Mr Brontë simply drew his youngest child to him with the words 'my *dear* little Anne'. Dr Teale of Leeds suggested some sea air when the weather grew milder in the spring; there seemed hope that the disease might not be so far advanced as to rule out the possibility of a cure.

319

There began a regime of trying all the unpleasant remedies that nineteenth-century medicine had contrived for consumption: castor oil, blisters applied to the side, carbonate of iron. Ironically, the first hospital for consumption, the Brompton Hospital in London, had just been founded, although most of the remedies in use still dated from the seventeenth and eighteenth centuries. The great break-through in discoveries of the nature and transmission of consumption were not made till sixteen years after Emily's death, and even then very little could be done to treat it, notwithstanding sanatoria and theories of rest and dry fresh air. Only a hundred years later, with the revolution brought about by chemotherapy, did any real cure come about.

Anne, unlike Emily, willingly and uncomplainingly submitted to all the medical treatments advised. It made the situation less terrible for Charlotte, who never relaxed her vigilance. She wrote to Mr Williams, with the sad hindsight: 'unused any of us to the possession of robust health, we have not noticed the gradual approaches of decay; we did not know its symptoms; the little cough, the small appetite, the tendency to take cold at every variation of atmosphere have been regarded as things of course – I see them in another light now.'

She dared not let herself think about the future. In a memorable phrase to Mr Williams, she wrote on 18 January: 'I must not look forwards, nor must I look backwards. Too often I feel like one cross-ing an abyss on a narrow plank – a glance round might quite unnerve.' Her 'literary character was effaced for a time,' she told him; 'care of Papa and Anne is necessarily my chief present object in life to the exclusion of all that could give me interest in my Publishers or their connexions – Should Anne get better, I think I could rally and become Currer Bell once more – but if otherwise – I look no farther – suf-ficient for the day is the evil thereof.'

A swingeing attack on Currer Bell and the Bells' novels had mean-while appeared in the *Quarterly Review* of December 1848, the initial impact of which had been blunted by grief for Emily's death. Because of the high social standing of the magazine and the reviewer, Elizabeth Rigby, Charlotte's publishers were particularly agitated by the article. Miss Rigby, while admiring the power of the writing and conceding that *Jane Eyre* was a remarkable book, like other reviewers, criticised its moral and religious deficiencies. It was the work, she said, of a person who 'with great mental powers combines a total ignorance of the habits of society, a great coarseness of taste', which characterised all the Bell brothers, and a 'heathenish doctrine of religion'. *Jane Eyre* was a dangerous picture of 'a natural heart', i.e. one where religion failed to reign over the passions; Jane was a 'mere heathen mind' dangerously masquerading as a woman of self-control and principle.

Wuthering Heights was even worse, and should be only singled out if it were for more reprobation; Catherine and Heathfield [sic] were 'the Jane and Rochester animals in their native state . . . too odiously and abominably pagan to be palatable even to the most vitiated class of English readers.'[19]

Jane's independent spirit and proud equality appalled her: 'The doctrine of humility is not more foreign to her mind than it is repudiated by her heart. It is by her own talents, virtues, and courage that she is made to attain the summit of human happiness, and, as far as Jane Eyre's own statement is concerned, no one would think that she owed anything either to God above or to man below.' Miss Rigby came to the conclusion that altogether the autobiography of Jane Eyre was 'pre-eminently an anti-Christian composition'. Throughout it she found a murmuring against the rich and of the deprivation of the poor which went against the God-given order, what she called 'a proud and perpetual assertion of the rights of man . . . that pervading tone of ungodly discontent which is at once the most prominent and the most subtle evil . . . civilised society . . . has at the present day to contend with.' She did not hesitate to say that 'the tone of the mind and thought which has overthrown authority and violated every code human and divine abroad, and fostered Chartism and rebellion at home, is the same which has also written *Jane Eyre*'.[20]

Although, she wound up ferociously, it was possible that all the mistakes of etiquette – no woman trusses game and garnishes dessert dishes with the same unwashed hands, or when roused in the night hurries on a 'frock' – were deliberately assumed to disguise the female, if it were written by a woman she had no alternative 'but to ascribe it to one who has, for some sufficient reason, long forfeited the society of her own sex'.[21]

This attack hit Charlotte very hard indeed. She hid the review from her father, anxious not to upset him. The old chestnut that she was Thackeray's governess had also been thrown into the article and although she dismissed it to Smith, Elder – 'slander without a germ of truth is seldom injurious; it resembles a rootless plant and must soon wither away' – the reference had stung. She was dissuaded by her publishers from writing a reply to the *Quarterly Review* but she found an outlet for her anger by incorporating in *Shirley* many of Elizabeth Rigby's words into Mrs Prior's description of the contempt in which she was held by a family to whom she had been governess. Caroline Helstone, who goes into a near fatal decline on account of being repressed and having so little to do, has a long monologue in which Charlotte challenges the status quo; single women should have more to do – better chances of interesting and profitable occupation than they possess now.

As her beloved, virtuous little sister slowly faded before her eyes, Charlotte became increasingly bellicose in defence of her standards and attitudes. Her work on *Shirley* continued intermittently through the spring, often laid aside before her far more pressing concern for Anne. Correspondence with her publishers was all the more important in the absence of Emily's critical judgement and she now had a new receptive ear in James Taylor, Smith, Elder's manager, whom she had met on the visit to London. In February she sent the first part of *Shirley* to her publishers, asking for their honest opinion. All concerned at Smith, Elder disliked the opening scene of three very unholy curates at tea, and they asked her to remove it.

Charlotte appreciated their candour but, as she explained to Mr Williams, the curates and their ongoings were merely photographed from life, just as Lowood had been; curates *were* just as badly behaved as she showed them to be, and it was her duty to the Truth to tell it. Was his reservation, she asked, because he thought that this chapter would render the work liable to severe handling by the press, or because 'knowing as you now do the identity of "Currer Bell", this scene strikes you as unfeminine? . . . I am afraid the two first reasons would not weigh with me.' She had clung to her allegiance to the Truth in the face of the hostility in 1848; the article of faith she had begun articulating then was now a battle cry which would echo through *Shirley* and *Villette*.

To Mr Williams's protestations about artistry she produced her credo: 'Say what you will, gentlemen, say it as ably as you will – Truth is better than Art; Burns's songs are better than Bulwer's Epics. Thackeray's rude, careless sketches are preferable to thousands of carefully finished paintings. Ignorant as I am, I dare to hold and maintain that doctrine.' When she read Carlyle that spring, she found that she liked him a little more than she had, admiring him for his 'manly love of the truth', his 'honest recognition and fearless vindication of intrinsic greatness, of intellectual and moral worth'.

To her new correspondent James Taylor, she stated of *Shirley* that she anticipated 'general blame and no praise'. Were her principal motives in writing 'a thirst for popularity', or were the chief check on her pen a dread of being censured, she would never have written what she had. Though she could not say 'whether the considerations that really govern me are sound, or whether my convictions are just; but such as they are, to their influence I must yield submission. They forbid me to sacrifice truth to the fear of blame. I accept their prohibition.'

No doubt, she said, her handling of the surplice would stir up such publications as the *Christian Remembrancer* and the *Quarterly*

Review – 'those heavy Goliaths of the periodical press', she wrote sarcastically. If she alone were concerned, this would not trouble her 'for a second'. Recoursing to the language of the Bible, which might have surprised her critics, the tiny Charlotte declared that she would welcome 'the Giants to stand in their greaves of brass, poising their ponderous spears, cursing their prey by the gods, and thundering invitations to the intended victim to "come forth" and have his flesh given to the fowls of the air and the beasts of the field; Currer Bell, without pretending to be a David, feels no awe of the unwieldy Anakim'. She finished a little lamely that, as others than herself were involved, her publishers could be certain that she would not act rashly. She found it much harder to write nowadays in any case, she told Williams in May. 'That absorption in my employment to which I gave myself up without fear of doing wrong when I wrote *Jane Eyre*, would now be alike impossible and blamable.' If the Bells possessed real merit, she didn't worry about impartial justice being rendered them one day. She was far less uneasy at the idea of 'public impatience, misconstruction, censure etc.' than disappointing her kind supporters in Cornhill. But the brave words were at a cost to her nerves. The woman who could hardly bear to go into a room if it was full of strangers had the full glare of publicity on her: 'What the sensations of the nervous are under the gaze of publicity none but the nervous know; and how powerless reason and resolution are to control them would sound incredible except to the actual sufferers.'

Such literary preoccupations did not, however, begin to compare with those over Anne, who continued to get paler and thinner, although it sometimes seemed as if she were getting better. Ellen, ever solicitous, had been commissioned to buy a respiratory contraption. Gobbold's vegetable balsam, cod liver oil, were assiduously poured down poor Anne's throat. Sometimes they seemed to alleviate the pain and fever, stop the terrible cough. But it was all an illusion. Night after night the same deep cough rang out between the quiet bedrooms, heard by the sleepless Charlotte.

Charlotte clung to the hope of the benefits of sea air, when the milder weather came in the late spring, a trip to be financed by the legacy of £200 left by Anne's godmother Miss Outhwaite. Meanwhile she forced Anne to go out every day: 'we creep rather than walk', she told Ellen. The warmer weather of May, however, to Charlotte's alarm, made Anne worse. Her symptoms were beginning to be all too like Emily's shortly before she died: lethargy in the mornings, fever in the evenings, and sleepless nights. But Anne seemed to rally again; she was set on seeing the sea, and Charlotte, with a heavy heart, made plans for the expedition to Scarborough. Ellen was to go with them, and Charlotte warned her that she would 'be shocked when she saw Anne – but be on your guard dear Ellen not to express your feelings – indeed I can trust both your self-possession and your kindness'.

They left home on 24 May. Anne was so weak that she had to be carried downstairs by her seventy-two-year-old father. They travelled to York, relying on the good will of kindly passers-by to lift her in and out of trains and carriages, since Charlotte herself could not manage it. But Anne was able to see the great York Minster, a happy reminder to her of the power of God, which brought her tranquillity. The next day they arrived at Scarborough, the scene of Anne's pathetically happy imagining of Mr Weston's proposal to Agnes Grey, and now to be the scene of her own death. They had booked lodgings at No. 2 Cliff – with a pleasant, airy double-bedded room (if Charlotte was ever to have avoided consumption there was no hope for her now) and a view over the bay. Anne's difficulties with breathing became steadily worse, but she would sit quietly at the window looking down at the sea, which at the end of May was clear as glass, and on the day after her arrival she drove on the sands in a donkey cart.

Ellen later narrated the heart-breaking scene as Anne, realising her death was imminent, returned to her seat by the fire and calmly discussed with Charlotte the propriety of going home. She said that she did not wish it for her own sake, but she feared that others might suffer more if her death occurred where they were. To Charlotte, still unable to believe the end was so near, this was nearly intolerable. Ellen's narrative, related by Mrs Gaskell, continues:

The night was passed without any apparent occasion of illness. She rose at seven o'clock, and performed most of her toilet herself, by her expressed wish. Her sister always yielded such points, believing it was truest kindness not to press inability when it was not acknowledged. Nothing occurred to excite alarm till about 11 a.m. She then spoke of feeling a change. 'She believed she had not long to live. Could she reach home alive, if we prepared immediately for departure?' A physician was sent for. Her address to him was made with perfect composure. She begged him to say 'how long he thought she might live – not to fear speaking the truth, for she was not afraid to die'. The doctor reluctantly admitted that the angel of death was already arrived and that life was ebbing fast. She thanked him for his truthfulness, and he departed to come again very soon. She still occupied her easy chair, looking so serene, so reliant: there was no opening for grief as yet, though all knew the separation was at hand. She clasped her hands, and reverently invoked a blessing from on high; first upon her sister, then upon her friend, to whom she said, 'Be a sister, in my stead. Give Charlotte as much of your company as you can.' She then thanked each for her kindness and attention.

Ere long the restlessness of approaching death appeared, and she was borne to the sofa. On being asked if she were easier she looked gratefully at her questioner, and said, 'It is not *you* who can give me ease, but soon all will be well through the merits of our Redeemer'. Shortly after this, seeing that her sister could hardly restrain her grief, she said, 'Take courage, Charlotte; take courage.' Her faith never failed, and her eye never dimmed till about two o'clock, when she calmly, and without a sigh, passed from the temporal to the eternal. So still and so hallowed were her last hours and moments. There was no thought of assistance or of dread. The doctor came and went two or three times. The hostess knew that death was near, yet so little was the house disturbed by the presence of the dying, and the sorrow of those so nearly bereaved, that dinner was announced as ready through the half-opened door as the living sister was closing the eyes of the dead one. She could no more stay the welled-up grief of her sister with her emphatic and dying 'Take Courage', and it burst forth in brief but agonising strength.

Anne died on Monday 28 May, and on the following day Charlotte wrote to her father, telling him that she had decided to bury Anne at Scarborough. As the internment would take place almost immediately, and he would scarcely arrive in time and also had an annual church solemnity to take, she suggested that he did not come. She wanted to spare him the ordeal of seeing his third child buried, his 'dear little Anne', within six months of Emily's death. The funeral was finally attended only by Charlotte, Ellen and a kind friend of Ellen's from Birstall who was staying in the area and came to stand at the back of the church to lend sympathy.

Mr Brontë, responding to Charlotte's own ordeal, wrote ordering her to stay on at the seaside a while to recover her health. And there she stayed, very shaken, accompanied by Ellen, dreading what she knew must be the life to come: 'It will be solitary – I cannot help dreading the first experience of it – the first aspect of the empty rooms which once were tenanted by those dearest to my heart – and where the shadow of their last days must now, I think, linger for ever.'

She took some consolation in thinking of the religious nature of Anne's death. She thought that from childhood Anne had been preparing for an early death, and she seemed to have died without severe struggle, that she was resigned, trusting in God – thankful for release from a suffering life – deeply assured that a better existence lay before her. Her quiet, Christian death 'did not rend my heart as Emily's stern, simple, undemonstrative end did,' she told Williams. 'I let Anne go to God, and felt He had a right to her. I could hardly let Emily go. I wanted to hold her back then, and I want her back now.'

Charlotte was so numb as to be almost incapable of revolt. Just a whisper of it escaped her: 'Why life is so blank, brief and bitter I do not know', but increasingly she allowed herself to relax into a doctrine of impotence in the face of God. At least such belief meant that some life continued afterwards. She had battled against a hostile fate, hostile circumstances, but fate had beaten her. The idea that she had pushed past the remote moorland hills, the obscurity, the poverty, to the fame and happiness her talent deserved was all an illusion. Still, she could never have foreseen just how cruelly the deity looking down over the hills would take his revenge for her attempt to escape, to throw a challenge to him.

She meditated:

A year ago – had a prophet warned me how I should stand in June 1849 – how stripped and bereaved – had he foretold the autumn, the winter, the spring of sickness and suffering to be gone through – I should have thought – this can never be endured. It is over. Branwell – Emily – Anne are gone like dreams – gone as Maria and Elizabeth went twenty years ago. One by one I have watched them fall asleep on my arm – and closed their glazed eyes – I have seen them buried one by one and – thus far – God has upheld me. From my heart I thank Him.

CHAPTER XVI

Shirley

Charlotte remained on the Yorkshire coast with Ellen until the third week of June 1849. They went to stay at Filey, where the days were passed in long walks on the solitary beach of the wild, rocky coast. The quietness suited Charlotte's mood better than Scarborough, which she found too gay. After two weeks they went on to Burlington, the seaside resort which Charlotte had found so pleasing ten years before when she and Ellen had stayed there. As in the past, they stayed with the kindly Hudsons at nearby Easton, but this time Charlotte went reluctantly, on Ellen's insistence. The bleakness of her spirits was made worse by catching a cold, but she was determined that after a week at Easton she would return home, to where her duty lay. Refusing Ellen's offer to accompany her, she left for Haworth on 21 June, in dread of the solitary future. Two days later, she wrote to Ellen:

I got home a little before eight o'clock. All was clean and bright waiting for me – Papa and the servants were well – and all received me with an affection which should have consoled. The dogs seemed in strange ecstasy. I am certain they regarded me as the harbinger of others, the dumb creatures thought that as I was returned, those who had been so long absent were not far behind.

I left Papa soon and went into the dining room – I shut the door – I tried to be glad that I was come home. I have always been glad before – except once; even then I was cheered, but this time joy was not to be the sensation. I felt the house was silent – all the rooms were all empty. I remembered where the three were laid – in what narrow dark dwellings – never were they to reappear on earth. So the sense of desolation and bitterness took possession of me – the agony that *was to be undergone*, and *was not* to be avoided, came on. I underwent it and passed a dreary evening and night and a

327

mournful morrow; today I am better.

Her father thought that she looked a little stronger; her eyes were not quite so sunken. She managed to get through the day. It was the time when darkness fell that was almost unmanageable. That had been the hour when all the family used to assemble together in the dining room, and used to talk. 'Now I sit by myself; necessarily I am silent,' she told Ellen.

All around her were mementoes of those who were no longer there. Keeper made daily visits to Emily's little bedroom, and Flossy looked wistfully around for Anne, expressing Charlotte's own feelings. 'They will never see them again – nor shall I – at least the human part of me,' Charlotte wrote to Mr Williams on 25 June. She said that she wished she did not write to him so sadly, but how could she help thinking and feeling so? In the daytime her occupation, what she called the great boon of writing, took her out of herself. But at evening, she told Mr Williams, 'something within my heart revolts against the burden of solitude – The sense of loss and want grows almost too much for me. I am not good or amiable in such moments – I am rebellious – and it is only the thought of my dear father in the next room, or of the kind servants in the kitchen – or some caress of the poor dogs, which restores me to softer sentiments and more rational views.'

The conflict between her rage against fate and the necessity of subduing that rage had been a skein in her life since Brussels, and her philosophy came to contain more and more pride in endurance. She would increasingly seek consolation in religion; although she found it far from an easy comfort. She had confessed to Mr Williams in July 1848: 'I perceive myself that some light falls on earth from Heaven – that some rays from the shrine of truth pierce the darkness of this life and world; but they are few, faint, and scattered.' Now, almost a year later, religious solace for her grief could only be more difficult to find. As she went on in her letter to Mr Williams:

As to the night – could I do without bed, I would never seek it – waking I think, sleeping I dream of them – and I cannot recall them as they were in health – still they appear to me in sickness and suffering – Still, my nights were worse after the first shock of Branwell's death. They were terrible then, and the impressions experienced on waking were at that time such as we do not put into language.

Under these conditions, so different from *Jane Eyre*, was the last third of *Shirley* written. Artistically, the novel is quite a failure, lacking the unity of *Jane Eyre*; its disjointed nature partly reflects the disjointed manner of its creation. It never quite makes up its mind whether it is primarily a novel of social protest or a straightforward love story, and uneasily combines the two. In its emphasis on feeling and truth it continues many of the themes of *Jane Eyre*, only this time they are developed into a portrait and analysis of a wretched society, where two classes, women and workers, are trapped and miserable. The mood is generally defiant and Charlotte Brontë's views are scarcely disguised in the speech of characters; there is much protest and much philosophising.

It is perhaps less than surprising that Charlotte Brontë undertook to write a 'condition-of-England' novel in 1848, even if she was not particularly suited to do so. Her personal circumstances, the impression made upon her by Thackeray's masterly *Vanity Fair* and the plight of the Chartists after the failure of their petition seem to have given her a more burning sense of the 'warped system of things'. Although she rarely discussed contemporary British politics in her letters (and was quick to say politics were not her study), on 20 April 1848 after the failure of the Chartists' petition she told Williams that she saw 'this fact plainly' that the government must make concessions 'as justice and humanity dictate' and 'mutual kindliness' be substituted for ill feeling. It would be one of the themes of the novel.

Although Charlotte considered herself anticipated in subject matter by Mrs Gaskell's *Mary Barton* her approach is in fact far more carefully balanced. She displays nothing like the sympathy for the workers of the former. Although she shows that conditions in the mills could be brutal, which she, as a daughter of the centre of the manufacturing industry could not but be aware of, as the friend of many mill-owning families such as the Taylors and Nusseys she refused to present the situation in exaggerated terms and condemn all. Although Robert Moore is shown to be ruthlessly selfish in his introduction of new machinery into the mill at such a date, she nevertheless defends the fact of progress. As a Tory she could not see the Luddites as a spontaneous working-class movement, only as the result of work by sinister agitators.

Perhaps inspired in her historical themes by Scott, the novel was set round the Spen Valley, focused on the Taylors's mill at Hunsworth, transformed into Rawfold's, and celebrated the Yorkshire character – which was seen at its finest in the Yorkes, the 'racy, vigorous' Taylors themselves.

The snobbery of the London critics and the accusations of crudeness in the Bells' work accounts for the promotion of plain Yorkshire virtues, for all their 'wanting polish'. The action of the novel was set quite straightforwardly in Oakwell Hall the Jacobean home of relations of the Nusseys, which became Shirley Keeldar's Fieldhead,

329

and The Red House, Gomersal, which was Briarmains. Mary Taylor would amusedly complain that Charlotte had got the disposition of the bedrooms wrong and put Robert Moore in the servant's bedroom, but said that Charlotte had made them all talk as they would have done, and that she had not seen their 'matted hall and painted parlour windows so plain these five years'.[1]

But one of the most striking and personally inspired themes of the book is the use Charlotte makes of the two chief female characters Caroline Helstone and Shirley Keeldar to attack the treatment of women by society.

The savage attacks on the Bell brothers, coinciding with the deaths of Emily and Anne, and the doubts expressed as to the propriety of the presumed woman author of *Jane Eyre* helped to radicalise Charlotte's attitude to the 'Woman Question'. Her naturally rebellious, Romantic, passionate nature, her dislike of cant, her unconventional upbringing, all made her a natural candidate to dislike middle-class female life in the mid-nineteenth century. By the time she wrote *Shirley*, the tentacles of its absurd conventions seemed to be threatening every aspect of her life that was important to her – her writing, her reputation and that of her sisters, her daily life – and in *Shirley* she launched a blistering denunciation of the evils of the age.

After the death of Anne, Charlotte wrote to Mr Williams of the 'noble legacies' she felt her two sisters had left in their memories. Were she all alone in the world even without her father, there was something 'in the past I can love intensely and honour deeply – and it is something which cannot change – which cannot decay – which immortality guarantees from corruption'. Whatever the critics might have said, their 'short lives were spotless – their brief career was honourable – their untimely death befell amidst all associations that can hallow, and not one that can desecrate'.[2]

The sorrow and the anger showed in the book. The chapter, 'The Valley of the Shadow of Death' was written after Anne died, and Chapter 18 was headed by the warning: 'Which the Genteel Reader is Recommended to Skip, Low Persons being Here Introduced'. Charlotte used the character of Caroline Helstone to remonstrate about the condition of women and stereotyped ideas of them, a subject which she had told Mr Williams last summer was currently occupying her. The only problem, she felt, was that there had been so much cant talked about the subject. Charlotte did not produce cant, though some might call it so; instead streams of protest about what was and what was not allowed to women came out in undigested chunks, heavily influenced by Harriet Martineau's proto-feminist *Deerbrook*, by Mary Taylor's views, perhaps George Sand, and by her own experience of precisely what was expected from that curious new phenomenon, the woman author.

The 'Woman Question' was one currently agitating Victorian society, and with *Shirley* Charlotte added her own views to it. How far women were capable of being educated, and what sort of education they should receive, was fermenting as an issue in the 1840s, with figures such as Harriet Martineau and Tennyson, in his poem 'The Princess', contributing to the vigorous debate, a debate that would end in establishing the first institute for the higher education of women, the Governesses Institution, which would eventually become Bedford College, London. Meanwhile, alongside female radicals demanding a position in the workplace, there was a far more flourishing phenomenon, the Women's Mission school of thought, part of what has been identified by historians as the 'cult of domesticity', which reached its apogee in the 1860s. It was promoter of the angelic nature attributed to women and concomitant housebound idleness.

During the eighteenth and early nineteenth century, views about female nature underwent a substantial change from that of the seventeenth century. The standard seventeenth-century view of women – their weaker moral natures, due to Eve's legacy (being the first to transgress) – was replaced by an emphasis on other women in the Bible, whose noble lives were an example of how women were suited to the religious impulse. And with the increasing importance since the middle of the eighteenth century of the doctrine of separate spheres into public and private, and with the tendency to categorise the sexes in a far more polarised fashion, by the end of the eighteenth century the idea of woman's sphere had been completely established by a flood of didactic pamphlets and books of etiquette addressed to the female sex. Books such as Dr John Gregory's *A Father's Legacy to his Daughters* (1774), and the Reverend James Fordyce's *Sermons to Young Women* (1765) had firmly delineated the division (challenged only by a few brave hearts like Mary Wollstonecraft) between the 'hard and masculine spirit' and feminine 'softness and sensibility of heart', and said that woman's true 'empire' had 'the heart for its object', which was 'secured by meekness and modesty by soft attraction and virtuous love', and that this should be the object of their attention, 'not politics, commerce, abstract intellectual pursuits or exercises of strength'.

The cult of sensibility gave unprecedented attention to the heart and raised esteem of women; with the perils of the French Revolution apparently threatening Britain, women were eagerly roped in to help battle for the nation's soul. Rousseau had drawn attention to the important influence the mother had on the child. Each child was a potential citizen and, to the pessimist, conceivably a voter.

'"Female influence" had been a popular feature of bourgeois prescriptive writing well before revivalist didacts developed it into the campaigning gospel of "Woman's Mission" which shored up Britain against revolution,' to quote the historian Barbara Taylor.

As Nancy Cott has pointed out, the Evangelicals 'transformed the truism of etiquette books, that individual women influenced individual men's manners, into the proposition that the collective influence of women was an agency of moral reform'. More specifically, they developed a concept of femininity based on the identification of womanliness with godliness, and both with the private virtues of domestic life.[3]

The 'moral power' of women, Sarah Stickney Ellis argued in her enormously influential popularisations of this thesis, derived first from God (who had endowed women with all the basic Christian attributes of love, compassion and self-abnegation and almost none of the more suspect masculine virtues such as intelligence, humour and resourcefulness) and secondly from the sexual division of labour, which provided women with the duties appropriate to a loving, self-denying nature and insulated them from the harsh realities (and unsavoury 'pecuniary objects') of male existence. 'What then, is the true object of female education?' Sarah Lewis demanded rhetorically, '. . . conscience, the heart and the affections. . . . Leave to men the grimy life of intellect and action, 'the moral world is ours'. In the performance of home duties women were not merely fulfilling their natural function but realising a divine purpose: as chaste wives and mothers they became (in the words of William Wilberforce) 'the medium of our intercourse with the heavenly world, the faithful repositories of the religious principle, both for the benefit of the present and the rising generation'.[4]

Women were praised for their Christ-like qualities, for their 'compassion and self-abnegation'; according to Sarah Lewis's enormously popular book *Woman's Mission* 'the one quality on which women's value and influence depends is the renunciation of self'.[5]

That this notion of women had reached absurd and unhealthy proportions is shown by John Stuart Mills' trenchant comment on it in 1861 in *On The Subjection of Women*: the 'exaggerated self-abnegation which is the present artificial ideal of feminine character'.

Brave Mary Taylor had found England intolerable under this regime, and had emigrated; Charlotte now took up the standard. She had already foreshadowed her ideas in *Shirley* in that famous passage in *Jane Eyre* where she defended the right of women to 'feel just as men feel', to exercise their faculties.

In *Shirley* Charlotte took up this theme to show us a typical woman, Caroline Helstone, who is perfectly intelligent but is treated like a doll

332

by her uncle, Reverend Helstone. Through her she satirised many of the ideas holding Britain's women in a grip of iron. She showed the asinine nature of attributing high moral purpose to sewing: Hortense Moore, like Aurora Leigh's aunt, wishes Caroline to use 'her angelic reach of virtue ... to sit and darn'; she worries about Caroline because 'There is about her an occasional something – a reserve, I think – which I do not quite like, because it is not sufficiently girlish and submissive.' Hortense Moore's ideas about life and education are shown by Charlotte Brontë to be almost a travesty of the words. In a passage of great sarcasm, the preoccupations of the Woman's Mission school of writers are held up to scorn:

> She by no means thought it waste of time to devote unnumbered hours to fine embroidery, sight-destroying lace-work, marvellous netting and knitting, and, above all to most elaborate stocking-mending. She would give a day to the mending of two holes in a stocking at any time, and think her 'mission' nobly fulfilled when she had accomplished it. It was another of Caroline's troubles to be condemned to learn this foreign style of darning ... to imitate the fabric of the stocking itself ... wearifu' process, but considered by Hortense Gerard and by her ancestresses before her for long generations back, as one of the first 'duties of woman' ... when she first discovered that Caroline was profoundly ignorant of this most essential of attainments, she could have wept with pity over her miserably neglected youth.

Such an outlook does not accord well with Caroline's natural instinct for expanding her mind and horizons. As she confesses in an interesting passage to the heiress Shirley Keeldar, she is sure that if she had more to do she would not be so dependent on obsessional romance for stimulation. Although her uncle tells her to 'stick to the needle – learn shirt-making and gown-making and pie-crust making and you'll be a clever woman one day', Caroline cannot see this as a purpose in life: 'I often wonder what I came into the world for. I long to have something absorbing and compulsory to fill my head and hands and to occupy my thoughts.' She wishes that she had a trade; not that she thinks that labour alone can make woman happy, but it can give 'varieties of pain' and 'prevent us from breaking our hearts with a single master torture'. At least successful labour had its recompense: 'a weary lonely hopeless life has none'. When Shirley Keeldar says that hard labour and learned professions make women masculine, coarse and unwomanly, Caroline replies that it doesn't matter what unmarried women look like, as long as they don't offend men in the street (Mary Taylor would take Charlotte to task for this!).

Caroline Helstone's views are echoed, though in more positive form, in the figure of Rose Yorke, who was based on Mary Taylor, as was well-nigh universally recognised shortly after publication. In this character Charlotte seems to hint that she foresees a future when women will revolt against their biological destiny, when there will be a new kind of woman – a woman similar to that foreseen by Princess Ida in "The Princess' when looking at the bones of a prehistoric monster. Rose Yorke's mother 'wants to make of her such a woman as she is herself – a woman of dark and dreary duties, and Rose has a mind full-set, thick-sown with the germs of ideas her mother never knew. It is agony to her often to have these ideas trampled on and repressed. She has never rebelled yet; but if hard driven, she will rebel one day and then it will be once for all.' It is Rose Yorke who, like Mary Taylor, calls a spade a spade and tells Caroline that her life is a long slow trance, a long slow death in Briarfield Rectory, like a toad's buried in marble – the same metaphor Charlotte would use about her own life in the terrible summer of 1849 to Mr Williams. The description of Caroline's life as a long slow death would be echoed by Elizabeth Barrett Browning, who wrote that, 'Certain of your feebler souls/Go out in such a process.'[6]

Rose Yorke says to Caroline that it is a sin to 'leave your life blank' and not to use her God-given talents, and she reminds her of the Lord who will one day demand an account from all of the use to which their talents have been put. In a striking passage she says that the place for women's talents is not in household chores:

> . . . if my Master has given me ten talents, my duty is to trade with them, and make them ten talents more. Not in the dust of household drawers shall the coin be interred. I will *not* deposit it in a broken-spouted tea-pot, and shut it up in a china closet among tea-things. I will *not* commit it to your work-table to be smothered in piles of woollen hose. I will *not* prison it in the linen press to find shrouds among the sheets: and least of all . . . will I hide it in a tureen of cold potatoes, to be ranged with bread, butter, pastry, and ham on the shelves of the larder.

Mrs Yorke then asks: 'Do you think yourself oppressed now? A victim? . . . as far as I understood your tirade, it was a protest against all womanly and domestic employment.'

Although Caroline is able to falter towards these ideas, she is not strong enough or rich enough to resist her destiny; when her only salvation from her life of nothingness, her relationship with Robert Moore, seems to be lost, she goes into a terrifying and morbid decline because she has nothing else to live for. Realising that her life must now be that of the spinster, she examines the position of the spinster in society, and finds much to criticise. She is at least able to see through the Victorian doctrine that the beauty of women's existence consists of self-abnegation. 'Is this enough?' she says, and we hear Charlotte's challenge to the critics of *Jane Eyre*:

> Is it to live? Is there not a terrible hollowness, mockery, want, craving, in that existence which is given away to others, for want of something of your own to bestow it on? I suspect there is. Does virtue lie in abnegation of self? I do not believe it! Undue humility makes tyranny, weak concession creates selfishness . . . each human being has his share of rights. I suspect it would conduce to the happiness and welfare of all, if each knew his allotment, and held to it as tenaciously as the martyr to his creed.[7]

Radical thoughts indeed.

As the days go by Caroline realises that old maids remain happy by keeping their thoughts on Heaven. But she herself refuses to believe that 'God creates us, and cause[s] us to live, with the sole end of wishing always to die.' Finally, she exhorts the men of England to

> look at your poor girls, many of them fading around you, dropping off in consumption or decline; or what is worse, degenerating to sour old maids. . . . Fathers! Cannot you alter these things? Perhaps not all at once, but consider the matter well when it is brought before you. . . . You would wish to be proud of your daughters and not blush for them . . . cultivate them, give them scope and work – they will be your gayest companions in health; your tenderest nurses in sickness; your most faithful prop in age.[8]

As usual with Charlotte, she expressed in her novels a more radical view than in her letters and her day-to-day existence. After all Mary Taylor had condemned Charlotte's tendency to self-sacrifice – and Charlotte would constantly promote its virtues. She would later say on reading John Stuart Mill's/Harriet Taylor Mill's article, 'The Enfranchisement of Women', that though it was clearly argued, 'vast is the hiatus of omission; harsh the consequent jar on every finer chord of the soul'. What was this hiatus? 'I think I know and will venture to say. I think the writer forgets there is such a thing as self-sacrificing love and disinterested devotion.'[9] She could not wholly avoid the trap.

But she was in a more extreme, angry mood by 1849, with the deaths of Emily and Anne. The spectacle of Ellen was constantly before her, now piteously very nearly accepting that the husband she had waited for in her white frocks, priding herself that she still had a youthful enough look to wear them, might never come. What had it all been for, her preservation in a state of perpetual ready maidenhood, filling the day with all the domestic little tasks, waiting for a husband, unable to work? Youth, Charlotte said in 1848, for her and Ellen was 'gone – gone!' She told Ellen she found it painful at first to hear of her wanting to obtain a little pocket money,

> but on second thoughts I discover this to be a foolish feeling. You are doing right – even though you should not gain much, the effort is in the right direction; it will do you good, you will never regret it – no one ever does regret a step towards self-help; it is so much gained in independence. I do not wonder at your saying you are happier – the feeling is an honourable one.

Her rather cautious and pessimistic attitude towards female employment, which she had discussed in various letters with Mr Williams in 1848, was now less moderate. She had earlier agreed with Mr Williams that the present female labour market was overstocked, but she had no idea where or how another could be opened: although many said that 'the professions now filled only by men should be open to women also', she felt that there were more than enough male occupants and candidates to answer every demand. She wondered whether there was any room for more female lawyers, female engravers, for more female artists, more authoresses. It was an evil, but she had no idea who could point out the remedy. Marriage and a family were still her *beau idéal*, the sum of female happiness. 'When a woman has a little family to rear and educate and a household to conduct, her hands are full, her vocation is evident' – though Frances Henri in *The Professor*, written two years earlier, had insisted on working after marriage: she was not one who could live 'quiescent and inactive. . . . Duties she must have to fulfil, and important duties . . . exciting, absorbing, profitable work'.

The other possibility for women was presented as very bleak: 'When her destiny isolates her, I suppose she must do what she can, live as she can, complain as little, bear as much, work as well as possible.' That life seemed as miserable to her as that of the factory operative. As she wrote later to Ellen, she did not mind being single, it was the loneliness of the life she found depressing. In a period in which life was organised around the family group, the single woman had very little to look forward to.

On 15 June 1848 Charlotte had once more addressed the question of women and employment (still in the character of Currer Bell) in a letter to Mr Williams. She felt it was most desirable that women should not simply add to the weight of male responsibilities, particularly if it was too great a strain on the husband. Although Mr Williams feared that his daughters would suffer if they were sent out to be governesses, she who had suffered now strongly recommended that she should go: though a governess's experience was frequently bitter, in retrospect she felt that it was a precious discipline. She wholeheartedly agreed with Mr Williams that girls without fortune should be brought up to support themselves, and that if they marry poor men, it should be with a prospect of being able to help their partners. If all parents thought so, girls would not be reared on speculation with a view to making mercenary marriages, and consequently 'women would not be piteously degraded as they now too often are'.

Caroline Helstone, perhaps rather like Charlotte, perhaps rather like Ellen – on whom the character of Caroline was first modelled – has no real ideas of how the situation should be changed, but thinks that changed it must be. 'Nobody in particular,' Caroline says, 'is to blame, that I can see, for the state in which things are; and I cannot tell, however much I puzzle over it, how they are to be altered for the better; but I feel there is something wrong somewhere. I believe single women should have more to do – better chances of interesting and profitable occupation than they possess now.' And, Charlotte wrote on, boldly challenging the serried ranks of the *Spectator*, *The Times* and the *Mirror*, mindful of being denounced as irreligious: 'When I speak thus, I have no impression that I displease God by my words; that I am either impious or impatient, irreligious or sacrilegious. My consolation is, indeed,' – Charlotte's, Ellen's, the Ringrose girls, all her many single acquaintances who were now the old maids who 'should not ask for a place and an occupation in the world' – 'that God hears many a groan, and compassionates much grief which man stops his ears against'.

Charlotte always maintained that she could not write novels with messages, but nevertheless the message of *Shirley* seems to be loud and clear enough. In some ways, Shirley is a fantasy figure who represents the impossible, the future, the new. She mocks male stereotypes: she was not tied to one sex at birth, she points out, she was given a boy's name; she does business, with Mr Moore her tenant (whom she will save from financial disaster).

Business! Really the word makes me conscious I am indeed no longer a girl, but quite a woman and something more. I am an Esquire; Shirley Keeldar Esquire ought to be my style and title. . . . I hold a man's position: it is enough to inspire me with a touch of manhood; and when I see such people . . . gravely talking to me of business, really I feel quite gentleman-like.

She demands that she be chosen as a magistrate: 'Tony Lumpkin's

337

mother was a Colonel, and his aunt a Justice of the Peace – why shouldn't I be?'

Charlotte Brontë made several historical comparisons between past and present attitudes to women, as further indication of the unnaturally passive nature of Victorian life. Caroline Helstone looks for precedents in the Bible for this life of unmitigated weariness and finds that Solomon's 'virtuous woman' is a worthy model: 'but she had something more to do than spin and give out portions: she was a manufacturer – she made fine linen and sold it: she was an agriculturist – she bought estates and planted vineyards. That woman was a manager. . . . But are we, in these days, brought up to be like her?'

Shirley sees that all the enjoyment of life is to be got by men. She rebels against marriage because she could not be her own mistress any more; she could no longer have her independence. She sees woman as majestic, and criticises Milton's version of the first woman as being far too domestic. He must have based her on his cook, she says. Her first woman is a 'woman-Titan', a giantess: 'vast was the heart whence gushed the well-spring of the blood of nations', a woman who had 'the strength that would bear a thousand years of bondage'.

All the same, Shirley, like Charlotte – perhaps the assonance of the name is no coincidence – would surrender mastery to the man she loves: 'I tell you when they are good, they are lords of creation – indisputably a great good handsome man is the first of created things.' 'Above us?' asks Caroline. Shirley replies that she would scorn to contend with him for empire. 'Shall my left hand dispute for precedence with my right? Shall my heart quarrel with my pulse – shall my veins be jealous of the blood that fills them?'

But Caroline, or perhaps Charlotte's own conscience, will not be put off: 'But are we man's equals, or are we not?' Laughing, Shirley tries to avoid the issue. Her notions of equality are undermined by her need to worship. Although she has not yet met the man she can call her superior, she wants to. And to some extent her problems are resolved by the figure of Louis Moore, her former tutor, and intellectual superior, whom she, like Jane Eyre and Lucy Snowe, can call 'Master'.

Despite all the opprobrium arising from *Jane Eyre*, Charlotte clung in *Shirley* to her stated resolution to write honestly about human nature. As she would repeat to G.H. Lewes, it was not with the idea of being elegant and charming that she ever took pen in hand – nor, she might have added, didactic; if those were the only terms on which her writing would be tolerated, she would 'pass away from the public and trouble it no more'. From obscurity she had come and, she threatened her publishers, to obscurity she could return.

In *Shirley* she specifically challenged the notion that her detractors

338

had been so keen to emphasise: that novels must have a moral. Her book did have a moral, but it was not the kind they wanted. Thus Caroline Helstone wants to read Shakespeare with Robert Moore. He asks if it is to make him better, 'to operate like a sermon', and Caroline replies that on the contrary, 'It is to stir you; to give you new sensations. It is to make you feel your life strongly, not only your virtues, but your vicious perverse points.'

Unintimidated by reviewers, Charlotte still further challenged the feminine image in literature, hinting that sensuality, passion, were simply part of human nature. Jane Eyre's passion, any woman's passion, was something which was not meant to exist, which was not countenanced by polite society, but in *Shirley* she once again, but at greater length, reiterated that women were misrepresented:

> ... if men could see us as we really are they would be amazed; ... the cleverest and acutest men are often under an illusion about women; they do not read them in a true light; they misapprehend them, both for good and evil; their good woman is a queer thing, half doll, half angel, their bad woman almost always a fiend. . . . If I spoke all I think on this point, if I gave my real opinion of some first rate female characters in first-rate works, where should I be? Dead under some cairn of avenging stones in half an hour.[10]

Or a cairn of angry newspaper reviews at least.

In Shirley's version of the mermaid, the 'Temptress-terror! monstrous likeness of our selves!', Charlotte Brontë seems to be moving towards an emancipated, new kind of heroine who hints at embarking on an examination of the taboo subject of sexuality. Shirley asks half-teasingly, 'Are you not glad, Caroline, when at last, and with a wild shriek she dives?' Caroline's conventional mind is sure of its ground: 'but Shirley, she is not like us: we are neither temptresses, nor terrors, nor monsters'. 'Some of our kind, it is said, are all three,' says Shirley.

Nevertheless, Charlotte did make a few revisions to the manuscript after the harshest of the reviews of the Bells' works had appeared, so that the book could not be accused of being coarse. As Margaret Smith has revealed, although Shirley still stands on the hearthrug with her hands behind her, Charlotte has deleted 'very much in the gentleman's fashion'; the breast of the woman Titan 'no longer yields daring "with her milk" '.[11]

It was only her work, her writing, that sustained Charlotte in the dreadful, silent house after her sisters' deaths. Where would she have been if she had listened to the advice urged upon women? As she wrote to Mr Williams on 3 July:

Lonely as I am – how should I be if Providence had never given me courage to adopt a career, perseverance to plead through two long, weary years with publishers till they admitted me? How should I be with youth past – sisters lost – a resident in a moorland parish where there is not a single educated family? In that case I should have no world at all: the raven, weary of surveying the deluge and without an ark to return to, would be my type. As it is, something like a hope and motive sustains me still. I wish all your daughters – I wish every woman in England, had also a hope and motive: alas there are many old maids who have neither.

Charlotte's lonely defiance was not continued without personal cost. Despite her brave words about critical reviews, she found it a different matter when her acquaintance used hard language about *Jane Eyre*. She heard from Ellen that the daughter of another local clergyman, Margaret Hall, had called *Jane Eyre* a 'wicked book' on the authority of the article in the *Quarterly Review*. Charlotte confessed to Mr Williams that, coming from someone she knew, the condemnation struck deep; it opened her eyes to the harm that the *Quarterly* had done, for she did not think Margaret would have called the book wicked if she had not been told to do so. 'No matter,' she told Mr Williams resolutely, 'whether known or unknown – misjudged or the contrary – I am resolved not to write otherwise. I shall bend as my powers tend. The two human beings who understood me, and whom I understood, are gone.' She still had some who loved her yet, whom she loved, without expecting them to perfectly understand her. She would accept that, but she would *not* sacrifice what was now her only form of expressing her true self. She went on grimly:

I am satisfied, but I must have my own way in the matter of writing. The loss of what we possess nearest and dearest to us in this world produces an effect on the character: we search out what we have yet left that can support, and, when found, we cling to it with a hold of new-strung tenacity. The faculty of imagination lifted me when I was sinking, three months ago; its active exercise has kept my head above water since; its results cheer me now, for I feel they have enabled me to give pleasure to others. I am thankful to God, who gave me the faculty; and it is for me a part of my religion to defend this gift and to profit by its possession.[12]

Five days later she wrote even more fiercely: 'Meantime, though I earnestly wish to preserve my incognito, I live under no slavish fear of discovery. I am ashamed of nothing I have written – not a line.'

Then a day later, when Martha went down with a serious inflamma-

340

9a 'Le grand berceau' in the Pensionnat garden, where lessons were held.

9b Pupils in the Pensionnat garden at the end of the nineteenth century.

10a The gates of the Parc and the statue of General Belliard marking the steps down to the Rue d'Isabelle, up and down which Charlotte Brontë, William Crimsworth and Lucy Snowe travelled.

10b Charlotte Brontë painted by one of Branwell's friends, the Bradford artist J. H. Thompson, between 1840 and 1855.

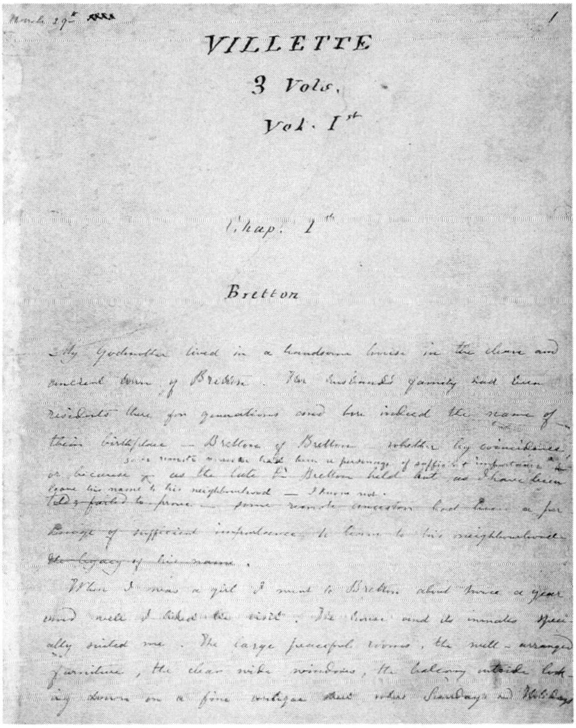
March 29th

VILLETTE

3 Vols.

Vol. 1st

Chap. 1st

Bretton

My Godmother lived in a handsome house in the clean and ancient town of Bretton. Her husband's family had been residents there for generations and bore indeed the name of their birthplace — Bretton of Bretton — whether by coincidence or because some remote ancestor had been a personage of sufficient importance to leave his name to his neighbourhood — I know not.

When I was a girl I went to Bretton about twice a year and well I liked the visit. The house and its inmates specially suited me. The large peaceful rooms, the well-arranged furniture, the clear wide windows, the balcony outside looking down on a fine antique street where Sundays and holidays

11a The first page of the autograph fair copy of *Villette*.

11b *left* William Smith Williams.

11c *right* George Smith as a young man, at about the time when he first met Charlotte Brontë. Artist unknown.

12a Rydings, Ellen Nussey's home, which provided some of the inspiration for Mr Rochester's house, Thornfield Hall, in appropriately romantic weather.

12b A selection of Charlotte's jewellery: a brooch of polished stone, possibly quartz; a small plaited gold ring; a mourning brooch which probably originally contained Anne Brontë's hair, and now contains Charlotte's; a necklace of cornelian beads.

13a Mrs Gaskell in 1851, about the time when she became friends with Charlotte Brontë, by George Richmond.

13b Harriet Martineau in 1849, the year she met Charlotte, by George Richmond.

13c William Makepeace Thackeray by Samuel Laurence, date unknown.

13d 112 Gloucester Terrace, Hyde Park, the former home of George Smith, the worse for wear after an air raid during the Second World War.

14a *left* A photograph of Mary Taylor in late middle age, the only known likeness of her.

14b *right* A recently discovered photograph of Ellen Nussey, probably in her late forties.

14c *left* The Rev. Patrick Brontë, c. 1860, in his eighties.

14d The dining-room where Charlotte did much of her writing. The photograph shows her writing desk on the table, and J. B. Leyland's relief of Branwell on the wall.

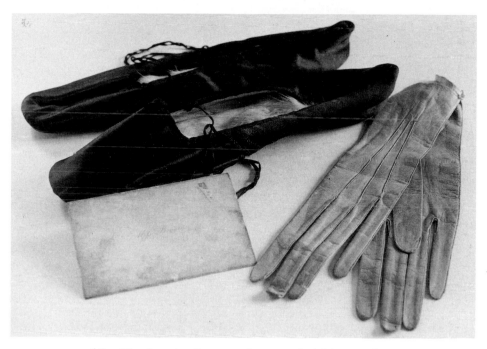

15a Charlotte's slippers, gloves and visiting card.

15b Charlotte's wedding bonnet, trimmed with white lace, white flowers and green leaves.

15c A dress of sober mauve and brown silk, made for Charlotte's honeymoon.

16a Arthur Bell Nicholls in 1854. This portrait was taken on his honeymoon in Ireland.

16b This photograph is almost certainly of Charlotte Brontë, and is likely to be the companion piece to the one next to it and to have been taken at the same time. Photograph by Emery Walker after an unknown photographer.

16c Cuba House, Banagher, County Offaly, Eire, home of the Royal School. Arthur Nicholls was brought up here by his uncle the headmaster. Charlotte Brontë visited it on her honeymoon, and was agreeably surprised by its splendour.

tion and Tabby's lame leg became so bad that the old lady could neither stand nor walk, Charlotte suddenly collapsed under the strain. She had a headache and felt sick; Martha's illness was at its height, and a cry from Tabby had called her into the kitchen where she found her lying on the floor, her head under the kitchen grate, having fallen from a chair when she was trying to get up. Her father had just declared Martha in imminent danger of death; and it was suddenly all too much. She broke down for ten minutes and cried, she told Ellen, like a fool. 'That day I hardly knew what to do, or where to turn,' she confessed.

Her father, frantic at the possibility of losing this last, most beloved and theoretically weakest child, never stopped asking about her health, which alarmed and irritated her. The cold she had caught at Easton had lingered on, with concomitant cough and sore chest and pains between her shoulders, but her own nervousness was made worse by not being able to talk about it to her constantly worried father. Likewise her pain over the ongoing attacks on the Bells' works was suffered alone. She told Mr Williams that she would grieve to see her father's peace of mind perturbed on her account, so she kept her existence as an author very much out of his way. She had always given him what she described as a 'carefully diluted and modified account of the success of *Jane Eyre* – just what would please without startling him'. The book was not mentioned between them once a month.

Yet something in Charlotte's nature thrived on challenge. Although the attitude of the world to her books caused her anguish, there was never any real question of capitulation to opinion. Her father's training had resulted in a toughness of mind: as long as conscience approved, then the world's opinion could go hang, and she continued to write what she wanted and to wage war for a sexless standard for authorship. By 29 August she was able to report to Mr Williams that *Shirley* was finished – 'thank God'. She told him that 'Whatever now becomes of the work, the occupation of writing it has been a boon to me. It took me out of dark and desolate reality into an unreal but happier region' – although it had left her with rather weak eyes and a tendency to headache because of such close work. The trouble was that she could write nothing of value unless she gave herself 'wholly to the theme' – and in her case this resulted in loss of appetite and sleep.

It had been arranged that James Taylor, one of the office managers of Smith, Elder should collect the manuscript in person on his way back to London from a holiday in Scotland. Charlotte was perfectly prepared to put him up for a few days, as she told Mr Williams, who was arranging the plan, but she was worried that he would not be sufficiently entertained. There would be no one to accompany him on walks on the moors – Charlotte was mistress enough of the proprieties to know that any walking out by herself and Mr Taylor alone would be unbecoming – and although, she said, Mr Brontë was not in the least misanthropical, the fact was that her father's peculiarly retiring habits – sitting alone in the study all day – could not be disturbed. He would find it irksome to have to entertain anyone.

In the event Mr Taylor came for the day, on 8 September. Small, red-headed and sharp-witted – rather too like Branwell for Charlotte not to feel a *frisson* – he duly departed with the manuscript, and Charlotte waited with some trepidation for the response from Smith, Elder. She had already corresponded with Mr Williams about her intended preface to the book, 'A Word to the *Quarterly*'. Her publishers had been rather alarmed by its flippant tone – the *Quarterly* was a very influential Establishment paper – and they desired her to reveal in the preface a little more of her own tragic situation to counteract the Bells' bad reputation. Charlotte replied indignantly to Mr Williams on 31 August. She would, she said, shed no tears before the public gaze: ' "C. Brontë" must not here appear; what she feels or has felt is not the question – it is "Currer Bell" who was insulted – he must reply.' She continued: 'Ellis and Acton Bell were, for me, Emily and Anne; my sisters – to me intimately near, tenderly dear – to the public they were nothing – worse than nothing – beings speculated upon, misunderstood, misrepresented. If I live, the hour may come when the spirit will move me to speak of them, but it is not come yet.'

She was curious to know whether Smith, Elder thought *Shirley* an improvement on *Jane Eyre*, and whether the book would tend to strengthen the idea that Currer Bell was a woman or have the opposite effect. Smith, Elder were kind enough to express satisfaction, and hope of sales, though they wanted her to remove the incident where Shirley cauterises her arm with a red-hot poker after she has been bitten by a dog; they thought it untrue. Charlotte was furious. It was true. She had seen Emily do so.

Her mood and expectations for the book were very low, her antici-pations of what the critics would say 'somewhat sad and bitter'. Her publishers were suggesting that she came to London but nowadays, she told Mr Williams, she recoiled from the literary coteries, though she admitted she longed to see 'some of the truly great literary charac-ters', but it was not to be yet, because she could not sacrifice her incognito. In any case she felt that she was unfit for anything other than her retired life at Haworth, where she had at last achieved a little mental tranquillity after the terrible turbulence of the last months.

In this time of trouble Charlotte's practical side had not deserted her. On receipt of £500 for the English copyright of *Shirley*, she asked Mr Smith for some advice on how to invest it; she had lost faith in the railways, as her shares in the York and North Midland Railway had had an erratic history and sunk to less than 50 per cent of their original value after an apparently impressive high. After a letter in which Smith outlined the possibilities open to her, Charlotte decided to settle for $3\frac{1}{4}$ per cent reduced bank annuities – because she wanted a 'safe permanent investment' as a foundation for a future small independency, rather than large interest. Although George Smith was still not quite sure of Currer Bell's real name, he still kindheartedly undertook to handle all the business pertaining to the funds on her behalf, and also offered to seek a professional opinion for her as to how she should proceed with the railway shares.[13]

Ellen had been pressing her for weeks to come for a visit and Charlotte finally decided to make the twenty-mile journey to Gomersal and the bustle of society around Brookroyd. Her father's poor health that September prevented her leaving home and it was not until late October that she was able to leave Haworth, first going to Leeds to have the lamentable state of her teeth attended to. Ellen met her there and bore her back to Brookroyd to stay for a week – during which, on 26 October, *Shirley* was published.

The visit was not unmixed pleasure. It appeared that Ellen's ready tongue had not been able to keep the secret of her friend's occupation, and Charlotte found to her amazement that *Jane Eyre* had been read all over the district, 'a fact of which I never dreamt', she told Mr Williams on 1 November. Though it was sometimes enjoyable to be praised, her anonymity had gone. Opinion among the clerical society in which the Nusseys moved was divided: Charlotte sometimes met with new deference, with greater kindness, and sometimes with angry looks from vicars who, however, would never say what they thought outright. She wished that they would speak out plainly; the Irish in her longed for debate.

She returned home to receive the first review of *Shirley* in the *Daily News*. It sickened her, she told Mr Williams almost hysterically:

Are there no such men as the Helstones and Yorkes?
Yes, there are.
Is the first chapter disgusting or vulgar?
It is not, it is real.

Still weakened by grief, she found it impossible to take adverse criticism calmly. She admitted that she felt defenceless; any shock had the force of a knock-out blow.

In general, however, the reviews – though much less euphoric than for *Jane Eyre* – were also less condemnatory. Various church organs were relieved to report that they could find no pernicious moral tendency in the book; the Church of England *Quarterly Review* kindly notified its readers that *Shirley* enlisted 'the purer sympathies of our nature, instead of appealing to its baser passions', as *Jane Eyre* had, though it could not help noting that it was less exciting than *Jane Eyre* – false excitement of course, it said hurriedly. A contemporary reader, Catherine Winkworth, the translator of many hymns from the German, and friend of Mrs Gaskell, wrote that: 'In power and in descriptions of scenery, there is nothing in "Shirley" which seems to me to come up to some parts of "Jane Eyre", but then there is nothing also in "Shirley" like the disagreeable parts of "Jane Eyre".'

The vulgarity and coarseness of the tea scene with the three curates was remarked on by many, as was the novel's construction, its lack of unity. The 'emancipation' theme was noticed by some not for its radical nature and explanation, but as 'the malady of unrest and dissatisfaction – on the prevalence of which among women of the nineteenth century so many protests have been issued, so many theories of "emancipation" set forth'.[14] The *Athenaeum* suggested languidly that it was a book that women would admire as very passionate, and men might regard as somewhat prosy. Others missed much of the feminist theme. *The Times* was at a loss to see quite what was the matter with Caroline Helstone and thought the entire performance 'a mental exercise that could bring the author no profit'.

Albany Fonblanque's view in the *Examiner* was more pleasurable. He continued to see similarities to William Godwin in the author's interest in psychology, but he saw no signs of a revolutionary attitude towards society. Despite the book's coarseness, and the rather unnatural characters, the reviewer thought that it possessed 'an irresistible grasp of reality', that the writer 'works upon a very limited range of rather homely materials yet inspires them with a power of exciting, elevating, pleasing and instructing, which belongs only to genius of a most unquestionable kind'.[15] Like all the other reviewers, to Charlotte's surprise, he thought that Currer Bell must be a woman.

Charlotte meanwhile tried to follow an alarmed Mr Williams' advice and be less excited by the reviews. She was pleased by a notice from a dissenter who described *Shirley* as being written by a woman 'endowed not only with the finest and, we trust, the most tender sensibilities of her sex, but with the intellectual power of a man', but also one who was a churchwoman, who while 'she does not hesitate, as a faithful delineator of manners, to smile at the foibles of individual clergymen . . . she draws the principal characters of the clerical class in a manner that makes you respect them'.[16]

Charlotte took the greatest pleasure from the notes of appreciation she received from two of the most eminent women writers of the time, Harriet Martineau the great educationist, and Mrs Gaskell, the sympathetic author. She had sent both of them copies of her novel, telling Harriet Martineau in her accompanying note:

Currer Bell offers a copy of *Shirley* to Miss Martineau's acceptance, in acknowledgement of the pleasure and profit he has derived from her works. When C.B. first read *Deerbrook* he tasted a new and keen pleasure, and experienced a genuine benefit. In his mind *Deerbrook* ranks with the writings that have really done him good, added to his stock of ideas and rectified his views of life.

Harriet Martineau would later say that she guessed from the handwriting – and from the passage with Grace Poole sewing on curtain rings – that *Jane Eyre* was written either by a woman or an upholsterer.

After receiving their replies, Charlotte wrote to Mr Williams on 24 November, that when Mrs Gaskell told her that she would keep her works 'as a treasure for her daughters, and when Harriet Martineau testifies affectionate approbation, I feel the sting taken from the strictures of another class of critics'. Her resolution of seclusion prevented her from communicating further with them at present, 'but I now know how they are inclined to me – I know how my writings have affected their wise and pure minds. The knowledge is present support and, perhaps, may be future armour.'[17]

On the whole, however, Charlotte felt that the reviews had been favourable and a little stir of pleasure seems to have come back into her life. Her name in the newspaper acted as an intoxicant; something of her old spirit and gaiety returned, deliberately encouraged by her. She seems to have decided that since she had very little in life she might as well capitalise on what she had. She told G.H. Lewes at the beginning of November that for the past year and a half she had passed 'some black milestones in the journey of life', when there had been 'intervals when I have ceased to care about literature and critics and fame; when I have lost sight of whatever was prominent in my thoughts at the first publication of "Jane Eyre"; but now I want these things to come back vividly'. This explains her sudden boldness in hinting to George Smith in several letters in the middle of November that with a little persuasion she might be lured down to London.

A genial letter from George Smith urged her to come and stay at his home, where his mother and sisters would be delighted to have the honour of her presence under their roof. Charlotte was slightly dubious about accepting, since a few months ago her Brussels friends, the Wheelwrights, had written, inviting her to stay with them in their new home in London, a pleasant house in Kensington. However, she went on, in a tone which might have surprised the kindly

345

Wheelwrights, 'they are of the class, perfectly worthy but in no sort remarkable, to whom I should feel it quite superfluous to introduce Currer Bell; I know they would not understand the author'. Under those circumstances she thought that her movements would have been very much restrained. However, if she were to stay with Mr Smith she would still be able to see them, and they could put down her staying at a publisher's to her literary tastes.

She set about marshalling a small trousseau for the visit. She asked Ellen, who was deeply involved in the ongoing off and on romance between the irresponsibly flirtatious Joe Taylor and Miss Amelia Ringrose, if she would help oversee her wardrobe for the occasion. Ellen, who had supervised Charlotte's first purchase of a fur earlier that year, and was a great believer in the consolatory effect of material possessions, was delighted. For the first time in her life, the abstemious, parsimonious Charlotte was to be seen indulging herself in Ellen-like pursuits – purchases of new materials, card cases, browsing over patterns that Ellen pressed on her. Ellen with her rather girlish taste would doubtless have preferred that the theme of Charlotte's clothing should not have been austere simplicity. 'The dressmaker has done my small matters pretty well,' she told Ellen, 'but I wish you could have looked over them and given a dictum. I insisted on the dresses been [sic] made quite plainly.' She had not liked the dressmaker whom Ellen had sent over to Haworth; her manners were not to her taste.

On Thursday, 29 November she set out for London, armed with her new wardrobe, including the sable boa and cuffs that she had commissioned Ellen to buy for her that summer with money from *Jane Eyre*, along with a squirrel tippet for everyday use. She liked the sables very much and told Ellen that ' "to save them" [I] shall keep the squirrel, as you prudently suggested', though she hoped it was not too much like using the steel poker to save the brass one.

When she arrived in London, she went straight to the Smiths' house in Westbourne Place, which she and Anne had visited in 1848. She told Ellen that Mrs Smith received her as if she had had the strictest orders to be scrupulously attentive, and that she and her two large daughters looked at her, the author of books which called forth the wrath of Victorian England, with a mixture of respect and alarm. She was taken upstairs to see her bedroom, which had the uncommon and delightful luxury for her of fires in it, morning and evening, and two wax candles.

In the midst of this comfort and splendour, she revealed to Mrs Gaskell later, she felt rather worried that her clothes were wrong. Furthermore, it was a large house with many confusing doors, which she remembered studying in tribulation, not knowing which to open.

But after a few days she felt that Mrs Smith's attitude had changed, reporting in her letter to Ellen, 'the attention and politeness continue as great as ever, but the alarm and estrangement are quite gone'. Mrs Smith had seen that, emancipated and free-thinking as their authoress visitor might be in her work, in life or at least in society she was as proper as one could expect any daughter of the clergy to be, whatever her reprehensible remarks in print about the cloth. Charlotte told Ellen that Mrs Smith now treated her as if she liked her, and in turn Charlotte, ever rather poignantly susceptible to being liked, began to like her – 'kindness is a potent heart-winner'.

The special nature of the relationship between Mrs Smith and her son was rapidly made manifest to Charlotte. They had been drawn together during the days of economic struggle after Mrs Smith's husband's illness, when she was as supportive as any wife of her young unmarried son, and there continued to be something rather conjugal about their reliance upon one another. Despite the kindness, Mrs Smith continued to observe closely the notorious authoress's behaviour amidst the guests whom George Smith invited to the house to meet the literary phenomenon – from whom they were clearly expecting the sort of extravagant behaviour and brilliant conversation of a Madame de Staël. In fact Charlotte's tendency to be retiring in company meant that she behaved as timidly and quietly as was appropriate for any lady. Mrs Smith was reassured. At first she was 'rather stern', so Charlotte told Ellen, 'but she has sense and discrimination; she watched me very narrowly when surrounded by gentlemen, she never took her eye from me.' Charlotte liked the 'surveillance for its chaperonage: both when it kept guard over me amongst many, or only with her cherished one. She soon, I am convinced, saw in what light I received all, Thackeray included.'[18]

Mrs Smith's formidableness lent countenance to what could have been an awkward situation – an unattached female staying in a bachelor's home, and the authoress of what was now widely considered a 'naughty' book. In his Memoirs George Smith recalled that when Lady Herschel saw *Jane Eyre* lying about in his mother's drawing room, she said, 'You surely do not leave such a book as *this* about, at the risk of your daughters reading it?'[19] Whatever, too, Mrs Gaskell had told Charlotte about treasuring *Shirley* to give to her daughters, it was only after requesting their mother's permission that they were allowed to read *Jane Eyre*.

Charlotte was still trying to retain her anonymity, even though London was buzzing with rumours about Currer Bell and the literary guests were fully aware of her authorship. When she went to visit the Wheelwrights shortly after her arrival, on 3 December, she discovered that, for all her worries about their being insufficiently sophisticated to understand her life as an author, they had read the *Illustrated London News* that month which had named her as the author of *Jane Eyre* and *Shirley*. But they said that they had realised immediately who Currer Bell must be on reading *Shirley*, as Hortense Moore was quite obviously the odious Mademoiselle Haussée at the Pensionnat.

The Wheelwrights were living not far away from the Smiths in a similar, large stucco villa, 29 Phillimore Gardens, Kensington. It was about two miles away from Bayswater, over the two great rises of Ladbroke Grove, then indeed grove-like and tree-lined, and Campden Hill, near the High Street thoroughfare. The large house was set back off the road, with a handsome linen motif moulding around the top storey, wrought-iron balconies and a creeper.[20] The Wheelwrights – the girls still unmarried and almost all grown up; Laetitia was now twenty-one, Emily twenty, Frances eighteen and Sarah-Anne fifteen – were as welcoming and kind as ever. Despite her previous reservations, Charlotte found that the family were pleasurably impressed by their little friend being the object of so much attention, rather than in any way disapproving. She left, after planning a future visit, in a state of excitement and anxiety, for that night she was to meet that 'Titan of mind', Thackeray.

Nervousness had prevented her eating anything since breakfast and by the evening she was, she confessed to Ellen, 'almost faint with inanition'. She dressed in her candle-lit chamber in elegant Westbourne Place and, wearing one of those costumes that made no concessions to evening dress, her brown hair bandolined smoothly if unbecomingly on either side of her broad pale face, she made her way downstairs to meet her idol for the first time.

George Smith had assembled an illustrious party of guests and at 7 o'clock the arrival of Thackeray was announced. When Charlotte saw him enter, looked up at his tall figure, the chubby, quizzical face, heard his voice, she found that 'the whole incident was truly dream-like', as she later told Mr Williams. She was only certain that it was true because of her usual miserable destitution of self-possession. She felt that if she had not been obliged to make reply to his remarks, generally sallies, she would have been able to answer intelligently, but as it was, overcome by the presence of her hero, she thought she spoke stupidly.

To Ellen, she later wrote: 'I do not see him or know him as a man.' He was pure intellect; 'his presence and powers impress me deeply in an intellectual sense'. Unfortunately this inability of Charlotte's to see him as anything other than the great regenerator of the warped social system, for which she had hailed him so enthusiastically in the preface to *Jane Eyre*, and whose words had spoken to her so deeply alone by the fireside at Haworth, impeded any really intimate relationship being established between them. Charlotte wanted him to be the heroic figure she had estimated him from his novels, and Thackeray was all too human. The side of himself that he chose to present in company was one of genial conviviality, a lover of pretty women, especially pretty young aristocrats. There was no place at the noisy dinner parties Thackeray adored for that rapport which Charlotte had imagined would exist between two such like-minded spirits.

For Thackeray's part, he wrote in his kindly way of their first meeting:

> I saw her at first just as I rose out of an illness from which I had never thought to recover. I remember the trembling little frame, the little hand, the great honest eyes. An impetuous honesty seemed to me to characterize the woman. . . . I fancied an austere little Joan of Arc marching in upon us, and rebuking our easy lives, our easy morals. She gave me the impression of being a very pure, and lofty, and high-minded person.[21]

George Smith had had to impress upon Thackeray that he must avoid all mention of Currer Bell and his works when talking to Miss Brontë. Nevertheless it appears that Thackeray felt that some kind of recognition was in order, for Charlotte, reporting the meeting to her father on 4 December, said that she saw him looking at her through his spectacles, 'and when we all rose to go down to dinner he just stepped quietly up and said, "Shake hands"; so I shook hands.' She told her father that he 'is a very tall man – above six feet high – with a peculiar face – not handsome, very ugly indeed, but capable also of a kind look' – in all very formidable looking.

What she did not tell her father was that although she thought that most people knew who she was, and were 'far too well bred to show that they know me, so that there is none of that bustle or that sense of publicity I dislike', Thackeray's behaviour later that evening had been less than exemplary. George Smith later described the scene:

> When the ladies had left the dining-room I offered Thackeray a cigar. The custom of smoking after dinner was not common then, but I had been told he liked a cigar, and so provided for his tastes. To my dismay, when we rejoined the ladies in the drawing-room he quoted a . . . passage from *Jane Eyre*. It was that in which she describes 'the warning fragrance' which told of the approach of Mr Rochester. . . . The quotation . . . did credit to Thackeray's memory . . . but not to his memory of his agreement with me. Miss Brontë's face showed her discomposure, and in a chilly fashion she turned off the allusion. . . . She cast an accusing look at me.[22]

349

Thackeray was not alone in finding Miss Brontë disconcertingly severe. In his Memoirs George Smith would relate that his mother and sisters had found Miss Brontë rather a difficult guest because of her nervousness. In his opinion she was never perfectly at ease with them – though one of his sisters was sufficiently fond of her to give her a pair of boots to keep her warm on her journey back north. 'Strangers used to say that they were afraid of her,' he went on. 'She was very quiet and self-absorbed, and gave the impression that she was always engaged in observing and analysing the people she met.'[23]

To Ellen, discussing her visit, Charlotte said that Mr Smith was constantly worried that her silence suggested some insensitive or care-less remark had been made about her writing which upset or annoyed her, whereas in fact it was usually exhaustion from so much stimulus after the seclusion she had been used to for so long. In fact, she told Ellen, she had met 'with perfect good breeding even from antagonists, men who had done their best or worst to write me down'.[24] Her manner in general had been to 'have esteem for some, and I trust, courtesy for all'. Though she did not know what they made of her, she believed that 'most of them expected me to come out in a more marked, eccentric, striking light'. She thought they desired 'more to admire and more to blame'.[25]

George Smith and Mr Williams put themselves out to entertain their author; they took her to the theatre, to the new Houses of Parliament, to the National Gallery, where Charlotte particularly enjoyed the exhibition of Turner's paintings. James Taylor fell ill during Charlotte's visit, so she saw little of him, rather to her relief. Ellen's romantic heart had seen potential husband material in both James Taylor and George Smith and doubtless would have in Mr Williams had not the eight children and the wife settled what would otherwise still be food for thought. Charlotte was speedy to disabuse her about Mr Taylor, who appeared to her as one 'of the Helstone order of men – rigid, despotic and self-willed'. He ruled the pub-lishing operation of Smith, Elder and had forty men under him. Though he was obviously interested in Charlotte, there was some-thing about him that made her shrink from him. She told Ellen innocently that he had 'a determined, dreadful nose in the middle of his face which when poked into my countenance cuts into my soul like iron'. He tried to be sympathetic and kind but he could not quite manage it – 'Still, he is horribly intelligent, quick, searching, saga-cious, and with a memory of relentless tenacity. To turn to Williams after him, or to Smith himself, is to turn from granite to easy down or warm fur.' And it was to George Smith that she was increasingly to turn.

Charlotte learned from the Smiths that the other great female

350

phenomenon of the age, Harriet Martineau, was staying with her brother around the corner in Paddington, and on 8 December, with a new boldness, she sent her a note:

My Dear Madam,

I happen to be staying in London for a few days; and having just heard that you are likewise in town, I could not help feeling a very strong wish to see you. If you will permit me to call upon you, have the goodness to tell me when to come. Should you prefer calling on me, my address is. . . . Do not think this request springs from mere curiosity. I hope it has its origin in better feelings. It would grieve me to lose this chance of seeing one whose works have so often made her the subject of my thoughts.

I am, my dear Madam,
  Yours sincerely,
   'CURRER BELL'[26]

Charlotte had perhaps been able to pluck up her courage a little because Harriet Martineau's brother, the Reverend James Martineau, had been a supporter of Branwell's; he had encouraged him to write verse. Round came the servant to the Smiths' the next day, a Sunday, with a note asking Currer Bell to come to an early tea at six, as was the custom amongst dissenters, or to visit on any other day; and back came a breathless note from Currer Bell saying that he would come at six that day, 'and I shall try now to be patient till six o'clock comes'.

Harriet Martineau was at the height of her fame in 1849. Then forty-six, astonishingly ugly, half-deaf and always accompanied by the inconvenient ear-trumpet into which she forced her interlocutors to bellow, she had been a nationally famous figure since the publication of her best-seller, *Illustrations of Political Economy*. This twenty-four-part series comprised the economic theories of Adam Smith in fictionalised form for easy assimilation by lay people. From leading the obscure life of a scribbling daughter of an impoverished Unitarian Norwich manufacturer, she had shot to prominence; she was consulted by Lord Brougham over the 1832 Reform Bill, had moved to London and become part of the circle of London society that included John Stuart Mill, Coleridge and Darwin. She was completely fearless in her writing, and an indefatigable champion of the rights of women, whether in her articles, her books or her speech. She was a heroine of Charlotte's, probably partly because she was one of the lone respectable voices to say that women must be allowed to use the talents they were given for grander objects than housework. Charlotte told Williams that 'For her character, as revealed in her works, I have a lively admiration, a deep esteem'.

351

Harriet Martineau described the scene that December:

'This is a woman's note,' we agreed. We were in a certain state of excitement all day, and especially towards evening. The footman would certainly announce this mysterious personage by his or her right name; and, as I could not hear the announcement, I charged my cousins to take care that I was duly informed of it. A little before six, there was a thundering rap: – the drawing room door was thrown open, and in stalked a gentleman of six feet high. It was not 'Currer', but a philanthropist, who had an errand about a model lodging house. Minute by minute I, for one, wished him away; and he did go before anyone else came. Precisely as the time-piece struck six, a carriage stopped at the door; and after a minute of suspense, the footman announced 'Miss Brogden'; whereupon, my cousin informed me that it was Miss Bronti [sic]; for we had heard the name before, among others, in the way of conjecture. – I thought her the smallest creature I had ever seen (except at a fair) and her eyes blazed, as it seemed to me. She glanced quickly round; and my trumpet pointing me out, she held out her hand frankly and pleasantly. I introduced her, of course, to the family; and then came a moment which I had not anticipated. When she was seated by me on the sofa, she cast up at me such a look, – so loving, so appealing, – that, in connexion with her deep mourning dress, and the knowledge that she was the sole survivor of her family, I could with utmost difficulty return her smile, or keep my composure. I should have been heartily glad to cry. We soon got on very well; and she appeared more at her ease that evening than I ever saw her afterwards, except when we were alone together.[27]

Her cousin's wife was considerate enough to leave them alone together after tea in case Miss Brontë wished to have a private conversation with Miss Martineau. She raised the problem of the reviewers' strictures and 'besought me then, and repeatedly afterwards, to tell her, at whatever cost of pain to herself, if I saw her afford any justification of them'. Harriet wrote afterwards that 'I did not approve the spirit of those strictures; but I thought them not entirely groundless'.

She said that the reviews sometimes puzzled her, and that some imputed to her what made her think she must be very unlike other people, or cause herself to be misunderstood. She could not make it out at all, and wished that I could explain it. I had not seen that sort of criticism then, I think, but I had heard *Jane Eyre* called 'coarse'. I told her that love was treated with unusual breadth, and that the kind of intercourse was uncommon, and uncommonly described, but that I did *not* consider the book a coarse one, though I could not answer for it that there were no traits which, on a second leisurely reading, I might not dislike on that ground. She begged me to give it that second reading, and I did on condition that she would regard my criticisms as made through the eyes of her reviewers.[28]

Harriet later wrote that 'our intercourse then confirmed my deep impression of her integrity, her noble conscientiousness about her vocation, and her consequent self-reliance in the moral conduct of her life.' However, she said that at the same time she also saw tokens of a morbid condition of mind.

How much influence Harriet Martineau had on Charlotte is difficult to estimate. It does seem, however, that after her interview with this admirable and emancipated woman she did pause and begin to be a little more circumspect about what was suitable and what was not suitable for women. A definite friendship was established by the meeting, which for Charlotte was the high spot of her London visit.

By the end of her stay, she was exhausted by the whirl of social life. She saw one or two private collections of Turner's water-colours, as well as his later oil paintings, which she had been anxious to see after reading Ruskin, but thought them 'strange things'. Modern art was not much discussed at the parsonage, despite her enthusiasm for painting. Showing further resistance to the new she loathed Macready's acting in *Macbeth* and *Othello* and astonished a dinner party by saying so. Her unfashionable pronouncement that his acting was false and artificial produced a blank silence. In general, she found her tastes very dissimilar to those of Londoners and 'was obliged to dissent on many occasions', she told Miss Wooler, 'and to offend by dissenting.' It culminated on her last evening in a dinner party to which the Smiths had invited the critics of *The Times*, *Athenaeum*, *Spectator*, *Atlas* and *Examiner* – 'Men more dreaded in the world of letters than you can conceive', as Charlotte proudly told Laetitia Wheelwright. She seems to have been determined to prove the critics wrong in their estimation of the sort of woman who could write *Jane Eyre*: she was not to be worsted by these 'Literary Rhadamanthi', and she clearly held her own during the dinner. In the account written by Mrs Gaskell, ever anxious to dispose of the idea that her friend ever behaved in a reprehensible and unfeminine fashion in company, she stressed the point, on information from Mrs Smith, that Charlotte behaved in a most orthodoxly feminine way: her natural place would have been at the bottom of the table by her host, 'but on entering the dining-room, she quickly passed up so as to sit next to the lady of the house, anxious to shelter herself near someone of her own sex. This slight action arose out of the same womanly seeking after protection on

353

every occasion, when there was no moral duty involved in asserting her independence.'[29]

But however correct Charlotte's behaviour, she was evidently very exhilarated by the conversation. She told Laetitia Wheelwright that the dreaded evening had passed off better than she expected:

> Thanks to my substantial lunch and cheering cup of coffee, I was able to wait the eight o'clock dinner with complete resignation, and to endure its length quite courageously, nor was I too much exhausted to converse; and of this I was glad, for otherwise I know my kind host and hostess would have been much disappointed. There were only seven gentlemen at dinner besides Mr Smith, but of these, five were critics – a formidable band. . . . I did not know how much their presence and conversation had excited me till they were gone, and the reaction commenced. When I retired for the night I wished to sleep; the effort to do so was vain – I could not close my eyes. Night passed, morning came, and I rose without having known a morning's slumber.

In fact she was so utterly worn out that she had to spend the night in Derby on her way home. She reached Haworth on 15 December, to find her father quite well, and she settled back with some initial relief into her lonely life. Meanwhile London was left in a ferment. Harriet Martineau, who shortly after wrote a long, warm letter to Haworth to invite Miss Brontë to her home in the Lake District, told almost everyone she knew about her visit from Currer Bell – and the hints she had had of the strange, solitary life she led. Stories flew about of her shyness and strangeness. None of them was known to the object of their interest, who had returned to her quiet life of daily duties at the parsonage, having disburdened herself of a description of some of the great national armouries to her father, as he had requested. At least at home she did not have to undergo what she described as 'mental pain', for Charlotte an accompaniment to all excitement.

CHAPTER 17

The She-Artist

The secret of the authorship of the notorious *Jane Eyre*, and now *Shirley*, was out; by the time Charlotte had spent her first solitary Christmas at the silent parsonage, the news was spreading to the British reading public, to reach her neighbours and acquaintances from Haworth across to Leeds. Over the New Year of 1850 Ellen came to stay, the one person to have shared something of Charlotte's terrible personal losses. As Charlotte reflected on her memorable visit to London, she thought of the strange plant of friendship. When she had first seen Ellen, she told Mr Williams on 3 January, she did not care for her much, but now she thought 'no new friend, however lofty or profound in intellect – not even Miss Martineau herself could be to me what Ellen is, yet she is no more than a conscientious, observant, calm, well-bred Yorkshire girl'.

During Ellen's stay came the first evidence of intense local curiosity, with a letter to Ellen from Canon Heald of Birstall. Referring to Charlotte Brontë as 'the renowned Currer Bell, the "great unknown" of the present day', he claimed the character of Mr Hall in *Shirley* for either himself or his father: 'Mr Hall is represented as black, bilious, and of dismal aspect, stooping a trifle, and indulging a little now and then in the indigenous dialect. This seems to sit very well on your humble servant – other traits do better for my good father than myself. However, though I had no idea that I should be made a means to amuse the public, Currer Bell is perfectly welcome to what she can make of so unpromising a subject.' However he thought that he was owed the secret of who made up the rest of the persons and localities in *Shirley*, other than the Taylors for the Yorkes, Mr Cartwright for Robert Moore, Canon Roberson for the Reverend Helstone, and Cecilia Crowther and Miss Johnstone for the two old maids.

What Charlotte and Ellen made of this impertinent piece of writing, history does not relate, but when Ellen related to Charlotte on her return to Brookroyd of the 'notoriety' of *Shirley* in Dewsbury, she responded that it was 'almost as good as an emetic to me – I should really "go off at side" if I thought too much about it'. It seemed that Charlotte's commitment to the Real and True had doomed her to endless explanation as the presumed originals of her characters scrutinised her depiction of them. By 22 February she was reporting sardonically to Mr Williams that 'various folks are beginning to come boring to Haworth, on the wise errand of seeing the scenery described in "Jane Eyre" and "Shirley".'

Worse, however, was that Mr Nicholls, having finished *Jane Eyre*, was crying out for her other book. Much good may it do him, Charlotte said crossly to Ellen. To her surprise, though, since he served as the model for an admittedly pleasanter clergyman, Macarthy, Mr Nicholls raced through *Shirley* and was delighted with it. 'John Brown's wife seriously thought he had gone wrong in the head as she heard him giving vent to roars of laughter as he sat alone, clapping his hands and stamping on the floor.' More irritatingly, 'He would read all the scenes about the clergy to Papa; he triumphed in his own character.'

Not one of the curates showed resentment; characteristically, she noted, each found solace for his wounds in crowing over the others. Mr Grant, far from flatteringly represented as Mr Donne, was at first a little disturbed, and sulked for a week or two, but Charlotte reported sarcastically to William Smith Williams that she had recently had the pleasure of making him a comfortable cup of tea, and seeing him sip it 'with renewed complacency'. It was a curious fact that since he had read *Shirley* he had come to the house more often than ever and had been remarkably meek and eager to please: she had expected to have had 'one good scene at least with him', but regretfully this had not yet occurred.

In fact, the clergy of her acquaintance seemed to have few reservations about the book, despite the attacks from their official organs. To her great surprise, that thoroughgoing Evangelical, the rotund, tract-loving Reverend Morgan, had written about *Jane Eyre* 'not in blame, but in the highest strains of eulogy!' she informed Ellen. 'He says it thoroughly fascinated and enchained him.'[1]

In general the pleasure that most of her Yorkshire friends took in the book – *they* approved of the depiction of rough manners which southern critics had once again taken exception to – helped make up for the snipings of the critics. Nevertheless, grief and loneliness continued to weigh her down, causing her to react over-sensitively. Her greatest pain had come with the review of *Shirley* by G.H. Lewes, her correspondent and former champion, in the January edition of the *Edinburgh Review*. She sent him a single line: 'I can be on guard against my enemies, but God deliver me from my friends.' He had prefaced his criticisms by saying that he considered Currer Bell to be 'one of the most remarkable of female writers'. Nevertheless, she had felt 'cold and sick' at his opinion that, as in *Jane Eyre*, the writing was coarse; his criticisms of her artistry, as well as his view of the place of the woman author; and his dismissal of the likelihood of Mrs Pryor disposing of her baby in that way – with its imputation that Charlotte as a spinster could not understand the mysterious maternal instinct. Later, on 19 January, she wrote to him telling him that she was so hurt by the review, not because praise was stinted, but 'because after I had said earnestly' – and had written to him expressly so doing – 'that I wished critics would judge me as an *author*, not as a woman, you so roughly – I even thought so cruelly – handled the question of sex.'

In contrast, she told Mr Williams that more than once she had been touched by 'manifestations of even enthusiastic approbation' from her local circle. Although she thought it 'unwise' to dwell on such things, she said that she must at least permit herself to remark that 'the matter has been such as to awake and claim my gratitude, especially since it has afforded a source of reviving pleasure to my father in his old age'.

It was nevertheless in some horror that her long-cherished privacy as an author was invaded on her own doorstep. She wrote to Ellen on 4 February that Martha had come in to her room yesterday, puffing and blowing, and much excited:

'I've heard sich news,' she began. 'What about?' 'Please ma'am, you've been and written two books, the grandest books that ever was seen. My father has heard it at Halifax, and Mr George Taylor and Mr Greenwood, and Mr Merrall at Bradford; and they are going to have a meeting at the Mechanics' Institute, and to settle about ordering them.' 'Hold your tongue, Martha, and be off.' I fell into a cold sweat. 'Jane Eyre will be read by John Brown, by Mrs Taylor, and Betty. God help, keep, and deliver me!'

The Haworth people seemed to have rushed off in a body to storm the Mechanics Institute at Keighley. Since all the members wanted the books, they cast lots for each of the three volumes making up the whole, and whoever got a volume was allowed to keep it for only two days, being fined a shilling if they kept it longer. Miss Brontë heard all this from excited villagers with a very faint smile on her lips. But she was moved by an opinion of *Jane Eyre* written by a working man in the village. She had spoken to him three times in her life, and knew him to have financial problems; on account of delicate health he was

357

not able to card wool like the rest of his family and so spent a lot of time reading. In a letter to Ellen, in which she enclosed the scrap of paper from this man, Charlotte wrote: 'He feared that if "Miss Brontë saw what he had written she would laugh it to scorn", but Miss Brontë considers it one of the highest, because one of the most truthful and artless tributes her work has yet received.' (Unfortunately, it is lost to posterity.)

In her kind-hearted way, Charlotte had befriended the Haworth stationer Mr Greenwood, who had supplied all the Brontës with reams of paper for as long as both could remember. He had always been curious about the use they put it to. Now he knew, and through Charlotte's help he began to sell Smith, Elder's cheap edition of *Jane Eyre* – though she had to admit she still felt 'twinges' at the idea of 'all the worthy folk of Haworth and Keighley' reading it. Nevertheless she thought that it would benefit this 'good and intelligent though poor man' to use more of his faculties by getting a living through bookselling than the wool-combing by which he presently supplemented his income.

The only friend who acted in an untoward fashion was Miss Wooler. There was a restrained but angry little correspondence between the former headmistress and pupil, which Charlotte had to confess to Ellen 'nettled' her. Miss Wooler had written assuring her in what Charlotte considered an 'unnecessarily earnest' fashion that in spite of all that she had written she still retained Miss Wooler's esteem. Charlotte wrote back that she could never have feared that she would have forfeited it; such a thought would do justice neither to her nor Miss Wooler. And, she pointed out loftily, when she had been in London, 'a woman whose celebrity is not wider than her moral standard is elevated – and in each point she has no living superior [Miss Martineau] – said to me, *I have ever observed that it is to the coarse-minded alone – "Jane Eyre" is coarse.*'

She went on pointedly: 'This remark tallied with what I had myself noticed; I felt its truth; And, feeling it, be assured my dear Miss Wooler – I was at ease on the secret opinion of *your* heart.' Though Miss Wooler might and did object to certain phrases, exclamations, etc., they were phrases and exclamations which 'viewing them from an artistic point of view, my judgement ratifies as consistent and characteristic'. She was not disposed to think well of any who made an exaggerated outcry about *Jane Eyre*. The clergy who did so were evidently men in whom 'the animal obviously predominates over the intellectual'.

She was nevertheless at pains to convince her old teacher that she still understood what was proper and what was not. It certainly was not quite proper to be lionised. Thus she told Miss Wooler that it had been proposed that she should meet Dickens, Lady Morgan, Mesdames Trollope and Gore, and some others, 'but I was aware these introductions would bring a degree of notoriety I was not disposed to encounter; I declined therefore with thanks'.[2] She said she thought that she should scarcely like to live in London, but were she obliged to live there, 'I should certainly go little into company – especially I should eschew the literary coteries'.

It was a somewhat partial picture, rather different from that of the woman who had evoked fame to Mr Williams in terms of 'the solemn blast of her trumpet – sounding long, and slowly waxing louder'; who would tell Ellen Nussey that one of the treats that she was looking forward to on her visit to London in the summer of 1850 was the dinner of the Royal Literary Fund Society: 'I should have seen all the great literati and artists gathered in the hall below, and heard them speak. Thackeray and Dickens are always present among the rest. . . . I don't think all London can afford another sight to me so interesting.'[3]

The fact was that Charlotte, as her later letters reveal, very much adhered in some ways to the age's concept of the feminine. In one letter to Mr Williams, she made claims for a more refined and different feminine sensibility – despite denying to Lewes that women should be judged by separate standards. 'Against the teaching of some (even clever) men, one instinctively revolts. They may possess attainments, they may boast varied knowledge of life and the world; but if of the finer perceptions, of the more delicate phases of feeling, they may be destitute and incapable, of what avail is the rest?'

That spring an incident took place that curiously touched her. Her father had somewhat mysteriously been moved suddenly to produce a little packet of letters and papers saying that they were her mother's, and that she might read them.

> I did read them, in a frame of mind I cannot describe. The letters were yellow with time, all having been written before I was born; it was strange now to peruse, for the first time, the records of a mind whence my own sprang; and most strange, and at once sad and sweet, to find that mind of a truly fine, pure, and elevated order. They were written to Papa before they were married. There is a rectitude, a refinement, a constancy, a modesty, a sense, a gentleness about them indescribable. I wish she had lived; and that I had known her.

The losses that she had suffered, her loneliness, caused her such heaviness of spirit that she was unable to write. As the new year progressed and letters and parcels of reading matter from London became less frequent, she confessed herself ashamed to find how dependent upon their stimulus she had become. She told Ellen wretchedly on 16 February, a month and a half after her London visit, that she could not help feeling excitedly expectant until the post hour arrived, and then 'when day after day, it brings nothing, I get low'. She was enraged by her weakness, lucidly recognising that it was the result of being alone so much, but helpless to change the situation: 'It is so bad for the mind to be quite alone, and to have none with whom to talk over little crosses and disappointments, and laugh them away.' She told Ellen that 'the solitude of the room has pressed on me with a weight I found it difficult to bear'. She spoke of bodily weakness and terrible sadness, intensified by the bad weather. The only occurrence which had broken her anchorite-like seclusion had been a rowdy clergyman who had desired to visit the wild country round Haworth and had urged Mr Brontë and his daughter to visit him at Bradford. Charlotte suspected him darkly of being a curiosity seeker.

Such was her lethargy that even Mr Brontë was sufficiently alarmed to welcome an invitation for his daughter to stay away from home. It came at the beginning of March with the descent upon Haworth of the eminent do-gooder Sir James Kay Shuttleworth. He had already written to her about *Shirley* and his desire to meet the renowned author. Undeterred by Charlotte's rebuffs, which seem to have been for no particular reason other than a desire to guard her privacy, he arrived with his wife at the parsonage. They lived only ten miles away, at Gawthorpe Hall, near Burnley, across the moors leading into east Lancashire. Sir James was at this time forty-four, although Charlotte thought he looked as hale and hearty as if he were ten years younger; he had been made a baronet in 1849 on resigning the secretaryship of the Committee of the Council on Education. As a young doctor he had won honours for his unflagging work among the poor in Manchester, where he had become especially aware of problems of hygiene, and as one of the first Poor Law Commissioners he had seen the need for opening schools in workhouses. It was perhaps typical of the man's drive, and his slightly inhuman quality, that he had formulated a scheme to separate pauper children from their parents on the grounds that the latter must be a bad example to them. A great social reformer, founder of the Manchester Provident Society, he was a tireless lobbyist for free libraries and free education and in fact probably the man more than any other to whom credit for the Education Bill of 1870 is due. It was in the same indefatigable spirit that he now insisted that Miss Currer Bell should come to stay at Gawthorpe, though Charlotte scarcely bothered to conceal that it was against her will.

Mixed in with Sir James' extraordinary drive and slightly mechanical efficiency there was a strange quirk in his nature which made him want to write fiction and to actively hunt out the company of writers such as Mrs Gaskell and Currer Bell. Charlotte would later say that she thought one-tenth of his nature was artistic and constantly warring with the rest of it – she could never feel any real sympathy with him. But on this first sight in March 1850 she was chiefly struck by his white teeth, which she thought he showed in too frequent a smile – the 'snapping teeth' much remarked on by his contemporaries. The conflict with his artistic, imaginative side may have been partly responsible for the successive nervous breakdowns that he suffered throughout his life, brought on largely as a result of the superhuman amount of work he carried out. When he met Charlotte Brontë he was recuperating from his most recent breakdown and by the end of the visit, knowledge of it disposed her to be a little more sympathetic to him than she otherwise would have been.

On 6 March she went to stay with the Kay Shuttleworths for a few days, her nervousness increased by a disagreeable consciousness of being patronised. Sir James met her from the train to Burnley and a drive of about three miles brought them to the gates of Gawthorpe, through which they passed along what appeared to Charlotte as rather a desolate avenue up to the great Hall. The devourer of Scott's historical romances could not help being captured by this magnificent monument to the Jacobean age, which towered 'grey, antique, castellated and stately' before her. Inside, the arms and strange crest of the Shuttleworths were carved on the oak panelling of each room. Rather against her will, the novelist in her began to be fascinated by the ménage she found there, even though the entire expedition was such a strain on her nerves.

Sir James improved upon closer acquaintance, though not so much for Charlotte to see any of his schemes for her to visit them in London during the season as other than a 'perfect terror'. She found it very hard to relax in his presence. Though she admired his high mental cultivation, and his grace and dignity, she found his taste capable of elevation. Her own painful self-consciousness was not helped by his irritability, the result of the illness which had weakened already very sensitive nerves. She was less pleased by his wife, a little woman, thirty-two years old, with a pretty, smooth, lively face. Though she was frank and good-humoured and not full of aristocratic pretension, which she might well have been – Gawthorpe Hall had belonged to her family for over two centuries and Sir James had taken her name, Shuttleworth, in order to inherit the place – Charlotte did not find her congenial. She lacked grace, dignity and fine feeling, she told Ellen. Her real sympathy went out to the German governess looking after the four children; she had, Charlotte told Ellen, 'the usual pale, despondent look of her class'; her charges, she said, were all fine children in their way. The governess, who would later acquire a rather sinister influence over Lady Shuttleworth, told Charlotte that she was homesick, a plight she could empathise with, although the latter had to admit that she was very well treated.

Although what had been intended out of the most kindly of motives was often 'painful and trying', Charlotte considered that the visit had bettered her spirits. On the whole she had got on well with her host. On account of his poor health all the expeditions they made were by carriage, which Charlotte rather disliked, but it had been pleasant to visit old ruins and old halls set amongst woods, and she had admired her host's clear intellect. 'The dialogues (perhaps I should say monologues for I listened far more than I talked) by the fireside in his antique oak-panelled drawing room, while they suited him, did not too much oppress and exhaust me,' she reported to a curious Mr Williams on 16 March, though she does not seem to have found his schemes for factory children or education in general sufficiently interesting to discuss. Her only worry was what she described as the 'menace hanging over my head of an invitation to go to them in London during the season' – an invitation that Sir James continued to press over the next two months.

As March and April drew on, the chill east winds showed little signs of abating; Charlotte was almost constantly feverish and suffering from minor colds. A letter from that free spirit, Mary Taylor, who had only just received the news of Anne's death, helped rally Charlotte. Robustly rejecting the idea of her friend resting her thoughts on Heaven, in favour of the here and now, she told Charlotte that she simply must not be as indifferent to everything, even the success of her last book, as she said she was. Mary was convinced that money would bring happiness, give her 'great and noble pleasures':

> Look out then for success in writing. You ought to care as much for that as you do for going to Heaven. Though the advantages of being employed appear to you now the best part of the business you will soon please God have other enjoyments from your success. Railway shares will rise, your book will sell and you will acquire influence and power – and then most certainly you will find something to use it in, which will interest you and make you exert yourself.

Mary's own concerns were thriving. Her cousin Ellen had just arrived; like Mary, she had bravely decided to emigrate to earn her own living. Mary reported that Ellen had secretly thought herself coming woefully down in the world when she came out to New Zealand, but now she found herself better received than she ever was in her life before. The two women had rented some land and built a house in the heart of the 'town', which, despite the grand nomenclature, had the usual cart road going through the middle of it. Mary enclosed a diagram of her clapboard house, describing the groceries in the back room downstairs and the ideas for the rest of the dwelling. Since the Mechanics' Institute was 'the only place of (respectable) amusement in the town we encourage it with all our hearts – we encourage everything about it but the objects it was instituted for,' she said naughtily. One of these 'not-objects' was dancing. They were going to open the new hall with a dance, and Mary was to find young ladies for young gentlemen. 'I cannot tell you with what zeal I labour to spite the "uneasy virtues" that are always saying something against "promiscuous dancing" – what a phrase,' she wrote with her usual iconoclastic gaiety. She had, she said, got into all this social trickery since Ellen arrived, never having troubled her head before about the comparative numbers of young ladies and young gentlemen. Their acquaintances were decent well-to-do people – one grocer, one draper, two parsons, two clerks, two lawyers and so on: 'All these but one have families to "take tea with" and there are a lot more single men to flirt with,'[4] she added frankly to her intimate friend, as modern as if she were alive today. When she had time on her hands, she said that she continued to think of her novel, which she intended should 'revolutionise society'.[5]

The contrast was painfully vivid with Charlotte's own life, where the arrival of a parcel of books from Smith, Elder often formed the only break in the monotony. Delight in their arrival was mixed with pain, for she would often be reminded of those familiar voices who had once commented 'mirthfully and pleasantly; the room seems very still, very empty'. On 12 April she wrote to Mr Williams after reading the copy he had sent her of Jane Austen's *Emma*. Her reaction against it was quite violent. It was an impassioned defence of her own romantic art, ladylike or not.

I have . . . read it with interest and with just the degree of admiration which Miss Austen herself would have thought sensible and suitable – anything like warmth or enthusiasm; anything energetic, poignant, heartfelt, is utterly out of place in commending these works: all such demonstration the authoress would have met with a well-bred sneer, would have calmly scorned as *outré* and extravagant. She does her business of delineating the surface of the lives of genteel English people curiously well; there is a Chinese fidelity, a miniature delicacy in the painting: she ruffles her reader by nothing vehement, disturbs him by nothing profound: the Passions are perfectly unknown to her; she rejects even a speaking acquaintance with that stormy Sisterhood; even to the Feelings she vouchsafes no more than an occasional graceful but distant recognition; too frequent converse with them would ruffle the smooth elegance of her progress. Her business is not half so much with the human heart as with the human eyes, mouth, hands and feet; what sees keenly, speaks aptly, moves flexibly, it suits her to study, but what throbs fast and fully, though hidden, what the blood rushes through, what is the unseen seat of Life and the sentient target of death – *this* Miss Austen ignores, she no more, with her mind's eye, beholds the heart of her race than each man, with bodily vision, sees the heart in his heaving breast. Jane Austen was a complete and most sensible lady, but a very incomplete, and rather insensible (*not senseless*) woman; if this is heresy – I cannot help it. If I said it to some people (Lewes for instance), they would directly accuse me of advocating exaggerated heroics, but I am not afraid of your falling into any such vulgar error.

Lewes had earlier sent her *Pride and Prejudice*; he had a strong didactic streak, and thought that Charlotte needed guidance in reading matter to prevent her style becoming too overblown. A dose of Jane Austen he thought might redress the balance. It was a clash between two opposites: the arch-romantic and the arch-classicist. Jane Austen was only 'shrewd and observant', and she was contrasted unfavourably with George Sand, whom Charlotte could 'very deeply respect: she is sagacious and profound'. To Charlotte all great artists had to have what she termed poetry and for her Georges Sand had some kind of truth, some kind of poetry, whereas Jane Austen was 'without "sentiment"', 'without *poetry* . . . sensible, real (more *real* than *true*), but she cannot be great'.

Towards the end of April the keen frosts and cold east winds about Haworth began to die down. The slight colds she had had all spring continued, but her headaches became less frequent. Her father's health continued to worry her, and her mood was anxious and far from calm. A frenzied religious feeling continued to be a predominant theme in her letters – such phrases as 'the hope of re-union in eternal life', 'the Great Hope', echo through them, as does a heightened unnatural anxiety about her friends' health and a pessimistic submission to all-powerful death, which lurked so near, it seemed. Even a tooth operation that Ellen was to have made her fear for her friend's life.

She realised, perhaps roused by Mary Taylor's letter, that though she dreaded the idea of revisiting London, she ought to take up Sir James' invitation, a visit that was being encouraged by her publishers. She told Mr Williams on 12 April that 'my conscience tells me it would be the act of a moral poltroon to let the fear of suffering stand in the way of improvement'. She knew she would suffer, but suffer she must. Her father too was eager and restless for her to go, and to take her place in the world: 'The idea of a refusal quite hurt him.'

While Sir James continued to press her, Charlotte paid a visit to Ellen for a week. The talk before a cosy fire was mainly limited to the Lothario, Joe Taylor, whose extremely slow-moving romance with Miss Ringrose seemed at last to be nearing a declaration. He seemed to be trying to talk himself into being in love with her, Charlotte thought. On her return, Joe Taylor himself called and while Charlotte sewed and said very little, he repeated over and over again that Amelia Ringrose had looked 'very nice' last time he saw her, and he commended her conduct to the servants and to all round her. Charlotte found it all rather unconvincing, telling Ellen that he said, in short what was true and right, but he said it so often that she was sometimes at a loss for responses.

At the end of April Mr Brontë went down with chronic bronchitis and Charlotte could not countenance leaving him to stay with the Shuttleworths while he was ill. The plan was for a slow progress to London from Gawthorpe, staying at the houses of friends and relatives en route – 'I would as lief have walked among red-hot ploughshares,' Charlotte told Ellen on 11 May. But she submitted to the idea of joining Sir James and his wife in London later, after her father's recovery.

George Smith had meanwhile written to her from Cornhill saying that he had dreamt that she was coming to town, and she wrote back alarmedly that she had to confess that she had so much superstition in her nature as to make her reluctant to hear of the fulfilment of a dream, however pleasant. It was partly because if the good dreams came true, so might the bad ones, and she had many more of the bad than the good. But she was very well disposed to Cornhill, perhaps even a little more than that to its proprietor. He continued to give her advice on railway shares and investments, in which she still interested herself.

The London visit was again postponed when Sir James himself became ill, although he pleaded with Charlotte that once he was better he alone should be allowed to introduce his pet celebrity into the 'Oceanic life of London' – a phrase that she could not help smiling at, she told Ellen. But whatever Charlotte's reluctance to join him, without any imminent prospect of going away she was reduced to severe depression. On 22 May she told James Taylor, who had made bold once more to strike up a correspondence with her by sending her literary newspapers, that she often wished she could taste 'one draught of oblivion, and forget much that, while mind remains, I shall never forget'. Even going out on the moors in the now beautiful weather was a sort of torture to her; there was not a knoll of heather, or a branch of fern, which did not remind her of Emily. The distant views had been Anne's particular delight, and when she looked round she felt her presence 'in the blue tints, the pale mists, the waves and shadows of the horizon'. Up on the moors, amidst the silence, their poetry came line by line into her mind: once she loved it, she said, but now she dared not read it. It was a long and perhaps intentionally prolonged mourning, preventing her having to think of the future.

Her plight seems to have been recognised by her publishers, for warm invitations were now repeated by Mrs Smith to come to stay in their new house in elegantly porticoed Gloucester Terrace, off Hyde Park Square. Despite almost daily bulletins from Sir James, still postponing the visit, his nervous illness was such, Charlotte explained to Mrs Smith, that she felt that she must stay with him and allow him to make the introductions into fashionable life that he was so looking forward to. However, in the event Sir James finally became completely prostrated, and it seemed simpler to avail herself of the Smiths' invitation, now that her father was so much better and able to preach twice on Sunday. He was extremely anxious that she should get the visit over as soon as possible, and on Thursday, 30 May Charlotte left to stay with the Smiths on what was intended to be a very brief visit. In fact, in turned out to be for the best part of a month.

Of all Charlotte Brontë's visits to London, this was the one that she enjoyed the most. Although she said that feverishness and exhaustion beset her somewhat, she was more relaxed than before, and the tone of the letters that she sent speeding north relaying her adventures became increasingly euphoric. Despite her request for quiet, the days passed in a whirl of engagements, many of them the result of her celebrity. George Smith abandoned the office in Cornhill where he would sometimes work for thirty-six hours at a stretch, sustained only by green tea and mutton chops, to escort her about town. Although his mother and sisters would always find Currer Bell difficult, and though he himself would report that she could seem rather offputting, he would write that her personality 'as well as, or even more than, her literary gifts, was always peculiarly interesting to me'. In his company, Charlotte found herself at her most vivacious, as her letters show.

Knowing of her passionate admiration for the Duke of Wellington, he took her to the Chapel Royal St James, which the hero of Waterloo generally attended on Sundays, and indulged Charlotte by arranging their walk so that she met the great Iron Duke twice on his way back to Apsley House. The idol of her youth lived up to all her expectations: 'he is a real grand old man,' she told Ellen. They went to the Exhibition of the Royal Academy, to the opera, to the Zoological Gardens. The weather, Charlotte wrote delightedly, 'is splendid'. She had not lost her childhood enthusiasm for John Martin and she described a new picture of his in the Academy, an illustration to Campbell's poem the 'Last Man', to her fellow-enthusiast father as 'a grand wonderful picture'. The Secretary of the Zoological Society had sent her an honorary ticket of admission to the gardens (naughty or not, *Jane Eyre* had somehow contrived to get beneath every waistcoat and stiff shirt) and for her father's benefit Charlotte described the collection at length, knowing his love of the macabre – the camelopard, with an Egyptian for its keeper, the laughing hyena, which every now and then uttered a 'hideous peal of laughter such as a score of maniacs might produce'; a snake that darted its tongue in and out 'incessantly, like a fiend'.

Charlotte arranged to see the Wheelwrights, and she met Mr Williams again at a ball given by Mrs Smith shortly after her arrival. His family had been present but, apart from his daughter Fanny, Charlotte could not quite take to them; she sensed an unspecified lack of refinement about them. Mr Williams himself she excepted but socially she found him quite trying in anything but small doses. The little red-headed James Taylor she felt rather guilty about almost completely ignoring during her visit, but she was being more than well looked after by Mr Smith. By 21 June he had become George, whose boundless enthusiasm, 'buoyant animal spirits and youthful vigour' Charlotte looked on with delight, whose good temper she found pleasure in humouring. With such an ally critics could be dismissed: she had written to her father on 4 June that she hoped 'you don't care for the notice in "Sharpe's Magazine"; it does not disturb me in the least. Mr Smith says it is of no consequence whatever in a literary sense. Sharpe, the proprietor, was an apprentice of Mr Smith's father.'

Even the meeting with G.H. Lewes had not been as terrible as she had imagined. As befitted an early admirer and promoter of Currer Bell's genius, he had been asked to lunch at the Smiths. It had proceeded well until G.H. Lewes had 'the indiscretion to say across the table, "There ought to be a bond of sympathy between us, Miss Brontë; for we have both written naughty books!" ' George Smith had noticed that Miss Brontë generally shrank from being drawn out, and seemed to place herself under his mother's care for her protection. 'My mother accepted the position, and was generally equal to it, but sometimes, when accident left Charlotte Brontë exposed to a direct attack, the fire concealed beneath her mildness broke out.' This occasion was the first time it happened and he was not a little surprised by it. Lewes had said the unthinkable to her face. George Smith remembered well the tremendous explosion that followed: 'I listened with mingled admiration and alarm to the indignant eloquence with which that impertinent remark was answered.'[6]

Charlotte however forgave Lewes because, astonishingly enough, his face was 'so wonderfully like Emily – her eyes, her features, the very nose, the somewhat prominent mouth, the forehead – even at moments the expression'. She had been moved almost to tears, she told Ellen: 'whatever Lewes does or says I believe I cannot hate him', although she did not mention to her friend what he had said, on paper at least; perhaps she may have told her later when they met in person.

Perhaps because of her extreme short sight, perhaps because the painful past was always fresh in her mind, Charlotte had a tendency to fancy resemblances everywhere. George Smith related that she had wept on seeing the portrait of her that had been drawn by George Richmond, for it was so like her sister Anne. When, at Mr Williams' suggestion, she had called on a poor authoress, Miss Julia Kavanagh, she had found a little dwarfish figure who met her half frankly, half trembling, and within five minutes of talking to her, 'that face was no longer strange but mournfully familiar – it was Martha Taylor in every lineament'. She lived in a poor but clean and neat lodging with her old mother, and feeling sorry for her Charlotte determined to call again.

One of the first callers Charlotte herself received that June was Thackeray, who made a morning visit to the Smiths' house and bravely stayed for over two hours. Charlotte was still bent on improving him, on making the 'good angel' in his nature predominate over the bad. She told Ellen that Mr Smith had been in the room the whole time, and had told her afterwards that it was 'a queer scene'. On reflection, she supposed it was, for she had been 'moved to speak to him [Thackeray] of some of his shortcomings (literary of course); one by one the faults came into my mind and one by one I brought them out and sought some explanation or defence. He did defend himself like a great Turk and heathen – that is to say, the excuses were often worse than the crime itself.'[7]

George Smith remembered entering the room to find the tiny figure of Currer Bell furiously scolding a chastened Thackeray, who towered over her. Continuing to be intrigued by the woman whose work was considered to be so savage and free thinking and yet who had so many of the predominant traits of the most schoolmarmish of church-going country spinsters, Thackeray was nevertheless touched by her sincerity and the interview ended amicably enough with an invitation for her to dine with him on the night of 12 June.

Both Thackeray and George Smith were evidently rather amazed by the high principles animating every attitude of their new acquaintance, so unlike their usual careless sophisticated circle. Both men noted that she expected a great deal of her literary idols. Thackeray would write of her later with some admiration: 'New to the London world she entered it with an independent, indomitable spirit of her own . . . she was angry with her favourites if their conduct or conversation fell below her ideal.' He would admit to having been quite frightened of her after the lecture. In George Smith's view:

Thackeray shocked Charlotte Brontë sadly by the fashion of his talk on literary subjects. The truth is, Charlotte Brontë's heroics roused Thackeray's antagonism. He declined to pose on a pedestal for her admiration, and with characteristic contrariety of nature he seemed to be tempted to say the very things that set Charlotte Brontë's teeth, so to speak, on edge, and affronted all her ideals. He insisted on discussing his books very much as a clerk in a bank would discuss the ledgers he had to keep for a salary. But all this was, on Thackeray's part, an affectation; an affectation into which he was provoked by what he considered Charlotte Brontë's high-falutin. Miss Brontë wanted to persuade him that he was a great man with a 'mission'; and Thackeray, with a great many wicked jests, declined to recognize the mission.[8]

Thackeray could not be expected to know that without that sense of mission, the responsibility for her Gift, which both Mrs Gaskell and Harriet Martineau observed, it was unlikely that Charlotte Brontë would have continued to write all alone in the small bare dining room of the windswept parsonage. Yet something about Charlotte Brontë did appeal to Thackeray's better nature. He would publish the fragment 'Emma', Charlotte Brontë's last piece of writing, in the *Cornhill Magazine* with a tribute to her 'burning love of the truth, the bravery, the simplicity, the indignation at wrong, the eager sympathy, the pious love and reverence, the passionate honour so to speak, of the woman'. At the same time he said that he thought that she was often mistaken in her opinions, and judged too quickly and too harshly: 'She spoke her mind out. . . . Often she seemed to me to be judging the London folk prematurely. . . . A great and holy reverence of right and truth seemed to be with her always.'

It was perhaps inevitable that the grand dinner given in Charlotte's honour was not a great success. It was held at Thackeray's home at 13 Young Street, off Kensington Square, a fine mellow redbrick eighteenth-century building, within which convened the lions of the day, literary ladies and society favourites. George Smith in his memoirs would say that Charlotte Brontë was quite capable of 'chilling' a dinner party if she was in the mood to so do, and she was at this one. The quietness and self-absorption, the impression that she was always engaged in observing and analysing the people she met, made conversation, not surprisingly, difficult, particularly as Charlotte

Brontë was 'sometimes tempted to confide her analysis to the victims'. At this dinner her new tendency to talk in company failed her. Millais the painter, one of the illustrious guests, described her, a little glibly, as looking 'tired with her own brains', though he thought that he would like to paint her.

Another guest, the sophisticated Mrs Brookfield with whom Thackeray had just fallen madly in love, remembered her odd appearance: 'There was just then a fashion for wearing a plait of hair across the head, and Miss Brontë, a timid little woman with a firm mouth, did not possess a large enough quantity of hair to enable her to form a plait, so therefore wore a very obvious crown of brown silk.' If Mrs Brookfield's memory is to be trusted, Thackeray addressed Charlotte on their way to dinner as Currer Bell: 'She tossed her head and said she believed there were books being published by a person named Currer Bell . . . but the person he was talking to was Miss Brontë – and she saw no connection between the two.' The demure little personage, in modest, high-necked, sober print dresses adorned only with a small mourning brooch, who said very little, was scarcely to be credited with creating the wondrous whirl of passion of *Jane Eyre*, as Thackeray's daughter Anne, later Lady Ritchie, makes plain from her childhood recollection of the evening:

I can still see the scene quite plainly – the hot summer evening, the open windows, the carriage driving to the door as we all sat silent and expectant; my father, who rarely waited, waiting with us; our governess and my sisters and I all in a row, and prepared for the great event. We saw the carriage stop, and out of it sprang the active well-knit figure of Mr George Smith, who was bringing Miss Brontë to see our father.

My father, who had been walking up and down the room, goes out into the hall to meet his guests, and then, after a moment's delay, the door opens wide, and the two gentlemen come in, leading a tiny, delicate, serious little lady, pale, with fair straight hair, and steady eyes. She may be a little over thirty; she is dressed in a little *barège* dress, with a pattern of faint green moss. She enters in mittens, in silence, in seriousness; our hearts are beating with wild excitement. This, then, is the authoress, the unknown power whose books have set all London talking, reading, speculating; some people even say our father wrote the books – the wonderful books. To say that we little girls had been given *Jane Eyre* to read scarcely represents the fact of the case; to say that we had taken it without leave, read bits here and read bits there, been carried away by an undreamed-of and hitherto unimagined whirlwind into things, times, places, all utterly absorbing, and at the same time absolutely unintelligible to us, would more accurately describe our state of mind on that summer's evening as we look at Jane Eyre – the great Jane Eyre – the tiny little lady. The moment is so breathless that dinner comes as a relief to the solemnity of the occasion, and we all smile as my father stoops to offer his arm, for though genius she may be, Miss Brontë can barely reach his elbow. My own personal impressions are that she is somewhat grave and stern, especially to forward little girls who wish to chatter. Mr George Smith has since told me how she afterwards remarked upon my father's wonderful forbearance and gentleness with our uncalled-for incursions into the conversation. She sat gazing at him with kindling eyes of interest, lighting up with a sort of illumination every now and then as she answered him. I can see her bending forward over the table, not eating, but listening to what he said as he carved the dish before him.

I think it must have been on this very occasion that my father invited some of his friends in the evening to meet Miss Brontë – for everybody was interested and anxious to see her. Mrs Crowe, the reciter of ghost stories, was there. Mrs Brookfield, Mrs Carlyle, Mr Carlyle himself was present, so I am told, railing at the appearance of cockneys upon Scotch mountain sides; there were also too many Americans for his taste, 'but the Americans were as Gods compared to the cockneys', says the philosopher. Besides the Carlyles, there were Mrs Elliott and Miss Perry, Mrs Procter and her daughter, most of my father's habitual friends and companions. In the recent life of Lord Houghton I was amused to see a note quoted in which Lord Houghton also was convened. Would that he had been present – perhaps the party would have gone off better. It was a gloomy and a silent evening. Every one waited for the brilliant conversation which never began at all. Miss Brontë retired to the sofa in the study and murmured a low word now and then to our kind governess, Miss Trulock. The room looked very dark, the lamp began to smoke a little, the conversation grew dimmer and more dim, the ladies sat round still expectant, my father was too much perturbed by the gloom and the silence to be able to cope with it at all. Mrs Brookfield, who was in the doorway by the study, near the corner in which Miss Brontë was sitting, leant forward with a little common-place, since brilliance was not to be the order of the evening. 'Do you like London, Miss Brontë?' she said; another silence, a pause, then Miss Brontë answers, 'Yes and No', very gravely. Mrs Brook-field has herself reported the conversation. My sister and I were much too young to be bored in those days; alarmed, impressed we might be, but not yet bored. A party was a party, a lioness was a lioness; and – shall I confess it? – at that time an extra dish of

371

biscuits was enough to mark the evening. We felt all the importance of the occasion: tea spread in the dining room, ladies in the drawing room. We roamed about inconveniently, no doubt, and excitedly, and in one of my incursions crossing the hall, after Miss Brontë had left, I was surprised to see my father opening the front door with his hat on. He put his fingers to his lips, walked out into the darkness, and shut the door quietly behind him. When I went back to the drawing room again, the ladies asked me where he was. I vaguely answered that I thought he was coming back. I was puzzled at the time, nor was it all made clear to me till long years afterwards, when one day Mrs Procter asked me if I knew what had happened once my father had invited a party to meet Jane Eyre at his house. It was one of the dullest evenings she had ever spent in her life, she said. And then with a good deal of humour she described the situation – the ladies who had all come expecting so much delightful conversation, and the gloom and the constraint, and how, finally, overwhelmed by the situation, my father had quietly left the room, left the house, and gone off to his club. The ladies waited, wondered, and finally departed also; and as we were going up to bed with our candles after everybody was gone, I remember two pretty Miss L—s, in shiny silk dresses, arriving, full of expectation. . . . We still said we thought our father would soon be back, but the Miss L—s declined to wait upon the chance, laughed, and drove away again almost immediately.

Mrs Brookfield somewhat condescendingly opined that the failure of the party was probably due to Charlotte's inability 'to fall in with the easy *badinage* of the people with whom she found herself surrounded.' She thought that, accustomed to the narrow literalness of her own circle, she must have found it hard to keep up with 'the rapid give and take, the easy conversational grace, of these new friends'. And it may be that Charlotte found the informality of their manners difficult to respond to, since she knew them so little.

Part of the chill of the evening may have also been caused by George Smith's attentions to Miss Procter. As George Smith related the incident:

If Miss Brontë did not talk much, as was usual with her, she kept her eyes open. One of Mr Thackeray's guests was Miss Adelaide Procter, and those who remember the lady's charming personality will not be surprised to learn that I was greatly attracted to her. During our drive home I was seated opposite Miss Brontë, and I was startled by her leaning forward, putting her hands on my knees, and saying, 'she would make you a very nice wife'. 'Whom do you mean?' I replied. 'Oh! you know whom I mean,' she said; and we relapsed into silence. Though I admired Miss Procter very much, it was not a case of love at first sight, as Miss Brontë supposed.[9]

The fact was that Charlotte was becoming increasingly drawn to George Smith. Mrs Gaskell heard gossip about it – two months later she would quiz Charlotte about 'the Editorial party' – which George Smith with his attentions to his house guest was doing little to dispel. He had commissioned George Richmond the portrait painter to draw her likeness; he paid for visiting cards for her. They went everywhere together, and sufficient intimacy had arisen, no doubt aided by Charlotte's sparkling frankness, for him to invite her on a trip to Edinburgh – chaperoned by his sister Eliza – to fetch his young brother home from school for the vacation.

George Smith had proposed the scheme quite suddenly one evening. Charlotte, thinking at first that he was joking, laughed and refused. Mrs Smith, who was sitting in the drawing room and who Charlotte sensed was not in favour of great intimacy between her son and the forthright, strange Miss Brontë, also did not favour it, and united with Charlotte against her son's wild schemes. 'You may easily fancy how she helped me to sustain my opposition,' Charlotte wrote privately to Ellen on 21 June. But George Smith only became more determined. The next morning Mrs Smith came into her bedroom and entreated Miss Brontë to go: 'George wishes it so much'. Her son, 'master of his mother', said Charlotte, had begged her to use her influence. With his sister Eliza in attendance the trip would be perfectly proper.

Charlotte protested a little too much to Ellen for conviction, telling her: 'George and I understand each other very well, and respect each other very sincerely. We both know the wide breach time has made between us; we do not embarrass each other, or very rarely'. Her 'six or eight years of seniority', her 'lack of all pretension to beauty' were a 'perfect safeguard'.[10] She would not in the least fear to go with him to China. He would have his way – 'I dare say I shall get through somehow' – and trial though it was, she would join him at Edinburgh after spending a few days at Brookroyd with Ellen.

In later years George Smith would tell Mrs Humphrey Ward that he was never in love with his authoress.

. . . . the truth is, I never could have loved any woman who had not some charm of grace or person, and Charlotte Brontë had none – I liked her and was interested in her, and I admired her – especially when she was in Yorkshire and I was in London. I was never coxcomb enough to suppose that she was in love with me. But I

373

believe my mother was at one time rather alarmed.[11]

Nevertheless, he admitted that her personality 'as well as, or even more than, her literary gifts, was always peculiarly interesting to me'. To anyone, particularly one as lonely, susceptible and mentally fragile as Charlotte Brontë, the wish to prolong an acquaintance naturally yielded favourable expectations.

She made her cheerful farewells to Mrs Smith, and early in the morning of Tuesday, 17 June, she left for Leeds by the express train which arrived there at thirty-five minutes past two. The next day she wrote buoyantly to Mrs Smith that she had performed the journey with less inconvenience from headache and stress than she could ever remember. Mrs Smith cannot have liked any further indications of the happiness her son was creating by his attentions to Miss Brontë. She was very unsuited for the role of a wife for her beloved son. Indeed it was difficult to think of anyone who could really suit his every need – except perhaps herself! Certainly, what Lewes had described as 'a little, plain, provincial, sickly-looking old maid' without any fortune to aid the house of Smith, Elder was not desirable. It was perhaps partly to appease Mrs Smith that Charlotte informed her that she was modifying George Smith's original plan, of meeting him at Tarbert in Argyllshire and then going up the west coast to Oban with him. Instead, she met him in Edinburgh, and spent only a couple of days sightseeing, on 4 and 5 July.

They had, for Charlotte's part, one of the most enjoyable times she could remember. She wrote to Mr Williams on 20 July that she had always liked Scotland as an idea 'but now, as a reality, I like it far better; it furnished me with some hours as happy almost as any I ever spent'. It was an extraordinary and rare thing for Charlotte to say. She must indeed have been very happy in George Smith's company for all the pain she had undergone so recently to be so effectively cancelled.

Edinburgh sent her into raptures: with its marvellously dramatic and romantic vistas, opening everywhere the thirsty eye turns, it was poetry compared to the prose of London, she thought. It was glorious Dun Edin, 'mine own romantic town'. London was 'a great rumbling, rambling, heavy Epic – compared to a lyric, brief, bright, clear and vital as a flash of lightning'. London had nothing like Scott's monument, or if it had that and 'all the glories of architecture assembled together, you have nothing like Arthur's Seat', she told Mr Williams. The party had ventured up the volcanic outcrop that looks over the city in a carriage driven by a Scot with a dry sense of humour whom Mr Smith remembered Charlotte finding very amusing. She thought Queen Victoria had been quite right to climb it with her husband and children, which she had done quite recently. Writing to James Taylor in September, she said: 'I shall not soon forget how I felt, when, having reached its summit, we all sat down and looked over the city, towards the sea and Leith.'

In a sense the experience symbolised a magical and rather illusory apogee to her life. It was a romantic climax, in a city imbued with the magic of Scott, with a man whom she found attractive. A more sensitive, more imaginative, less businesslike man might have seen that he was giving rise to some sort of expectation. Not George Smith. They journeyed on, to Abbotsford and Melrose. With her love of Scott, Charlotte found such charm of 'situation, association, and circumstances that I think the enjoyment experienced in that little space equalled in degree and excelled in kind all which London yielded in a month's sojourn'; and still Mr Smith said nothing.

They parted – Charlotte to go back to her life at Haworth, stopping off at Brookroyd, and George Smith to London. She stayed at Brookroyd for a couple of days, to find that Mr Brontë had replied in high anxiety to Ellen's report of Charlotte not being well, though it was not entirely clear which was the greater worry pressing on his mind – that Charlotte was being courted, or that she was ill. To her scarcely concealed irritation, by the time Charlotte got to Haworth her father's panic had wrought on the stationer Mr Greenwood so that as the cab was coming up Bridgehouse Lane she met him, staff in hand, walking to Brookroyd to check on the parson's daughter. 'I found on my arrival that Papa had worked himself up into a sad pitch of nervous excitement and alarm – in which Martha and Tabby were but too obviously joining him – I can't deny but I was annoyed; there really being small cause for it.'

After such activity it was an effort to adjust again to the terrible solitude. The post hour once again became the most meaningful moment of the day, but as she told Ellen, it was so painful to be dependent on the small stimulus of letters that at first she put off writing to London to tell them she was returned. She sometimes thought she ought to 'close all the correspondence on some quiet pretext'.

At the end of July George Smith sent her a framed engraving of the Duke of Wellington as well as the portrait that he had commissioned of her by Richmond, which was a present for Mr Brontë. Who would not construe such an act as out of the ordinary personal interest and kindness, and continue to hope? Mr Brontë was very pleased. Both heads, he assured Mr Smith in a stately and laborious letter of thanks, had been safely hung up in the best light and most favourable position. His daughter's portrait was not only a 'correct likeness' but had 'succeeded in a graphic representation of mind as well as matter, and with only black and white has given prominence and seeming life, and

375

speech, and motion'. He might be partial but he fancied on looking on the picture, which he thought improved upon acquaintance, 'as all real works of art do', that he saw strong indications of the genius of the author of *Shirley* and *Jane Eyre*.

Privately, to Charlotte, he said that he considered that it made her look much older. Tabby too thought the drawing aged her, but, as a grateful Charlotte told George Smith, since Tabby thought the engraving of the Duke of Wellington was of 'the Master', not much weight was to be ascribed to her opinion. Mr Brontë also commented that the features were far from flattered, although he did think the expression 'wonderfully good and lifelike'. If so, even this period of happiness could not erase the sadness and anxiety that haunts the face, recalling the constant references to pain, both physical and mental – the sick headaches, the tortured nerves, the mental anguish. The mouth is controlled, steeled; the soft reddish hair is worn uncompromisingly, unbecomingly swept down in bandeaux on either side of the calm pale face. Only the eyes, those large compelling eyes, have been drawn with a rather unearthly gleam, suggesting what Mrs Gaskell would call the 'piercing observation', that 'vehemence and power'. In combination with the brows ruched in concentration, they give a sharp, almost fiery, character to the face, which one might otherwise pass by in the general air of soft sadness.[13]

The days continued to be passed in a dull sort of unhappiness. Time hung heavy on her now that she was again faced by the loneliness of home, the interminable ticking of the clock out in the hall. From a letter to Ellen written on 7 August it appears that Charlotte had let slip that she did not count on a long life. She immediately regretted it, for Ellen, with a flurry of letters from Brookroyd, then nagged her more about her health than her father did. Charlotte told her that she must dismiss it from her mind, and unless it was *very* disagreeable to her, not mention it to her any more. Her father's, Tabby's and Martha's anxiety about her made her still more anxious; it was like living under a sword suspended by a horsehair, she said. She had had to beg her father to consider her own feelings, and then finally command it, that he should not talk about his fears for her, for when he did she found it difficult to suppress terrifying thoughts, against which 'every effort either of religion or philosophy must at times totally fail'. As she said, it was a situation over which she could have no control.

She struggled to settle into the parsonage routine but as she told Ellen, 'the solitude seems heavy as yet – it is a great change, but in looking forward I try to hope for the best'. George Smith inevitably remained in her thoughts. He had evidently forbade her expressing any more thanks to him, but on finding that he had sent her the original Richmond drawing and not the copy, she wrote: 'You thought inaccurately about the copy of the picture as far as my feelings are concerned, and yet you judged rightly on the whole; for it is my intention that the original drawing shall one day return to your hands.' She said modestly, 'As the production of a true artist it will always have a certain worth, independently of subject.' And a cheery letter came back from him, wishing they could have seen Glencoe and Loch Katrine together.

She would later base the character of Dr John Bretton in *Villette* on George Smith. Let the passage describing the effect of Dr Bretton on Lucy Snowe as they begin to know one another sum up Charlotte's state of mind that summer:

> . . . a new influence began to act upon my life, and sadness, for a certain space, was held at bay. Conceive a dell, deep-hollowed in forest secrecy; it lies in dimness, and mist: its turf is dank, its herbage pale and humid. A storm or an axe makes a wide gap amongst the oak trees; the breeze sweeps in, the sun looks down; the sad, cold dell becomes a deep cup of lustre; high summer pours her blue glory and her golden light out of that beauteous sky, which till now the starved hollow never saw.

By the middle of August, unable to control a strange restlessness, Charlotte had reluctantly acquiesced to Sir James Kay Shuttleworth's invitation to stay in the house he had rented at Windermere in the Lake District. She told Ellen that she was going only in order to please her father, and was not at all cheered by the prospect. But it was there that she would meet her great and sympathetic biographer, the novelist Mrs Gaskell, for whom she had already conceived a fervent admiration.

CHAPTER XVIII

New Friendships

Charlotte arrived at Windermere on 18 August after a long and tedious journey during which she had had to change carriages three times and to wait an hour and a half at Lancaster. Sir James met her at the station and bore her off to Briery Close, where she was received by Lady Shuttleworth with a warmth equal to her husband's. The house, made out of the local Westmoreland stone, with gables and windows surmounted by fretted wood giving it a chalet-like air, was superbly situated high above Low Wood, with panoramic views over Windermere Lake, Coniston Fell, the Langdale Pikes and the hills above Ullswater. It had been built only a few years before, one of the new holiday homes in the area, which had been made fashionable by the extraordinary popularity of the Lake Poets and had been recently opened up by property developers. Scattered nearby were the houses of the famous, including those of Harriet Martineau and the Arnolds at Ambleside; countless humbler buildings were host to those who sought to emulate the simple life of the Wordsworths at Dove Cottage some forty years before.

Although it was August, the views of water and fell for which the area is justly celebrated were shrouded in cloud and mist on Charlotte's arrival; stormy weather sent jets of rain lashing across the land, but she found it exquisitely beautiful when the sun occasionally broke through to show the hills and lake. Sir James, whose only aim was to please his often difficult, celebrated guest, decided that it was more sensible to show her the countryside by carriage. Charlotte, used to roaming the moors at Haworth and never at ease with Sir James, was frustrated at not being able to walk about this 'glorious region – of which I had only seen the similitude in dreams', as she later told Miss Wooler:

I find it does not agree with me to prosecute the search of the picturesque in a carriage. A waggon, a spring-cart, even a post-chaise might do – but the carriage upsets everything. I longed to slip out unseen, and to run away by myself in amongst the hills and dales. Erratic and vagrant instincts tormented me, and these I was obliged to control, or rather, suppress – for fear of growing in any degree enthusiastic, and thus drawing attention to the 'lioness', the authoress – the she-artist. Sir J.K. Shuttleworth is a man of ability and intellect, but not a man in whose presence one willingly unbends.[1]

It was perhaps lucky for the atmosphere of the party that the gay and soothing presence of Elizabeth Gaskell joined it the evening after Charlotte arrived. Elizabeth Cleghorn Gaskell was at the height of her beauty, though not her fame, in 1850. Then a woman of forty, she was married to the brilliant Unitarian minister William Gaskell and had begun to achieve literary eminence only quite recently with some short stories in Dickens' magazine *Household Words*, in which her delicacy and lyric gift allied to her large-hearted comprehension of human nature had rapidly won her many admirers. It had been followed by her first novel, *Mary Barton*, published two years previously in 1848. A portrait of the miseries of life in what would be termed the industrial revolution, based on her observations as a minister's wife in Manchester, it was remarkable for its compassionate depiction of the bewildered factory workers and the poor. It would have been in liberal intellectual circles that she became friendly with Sir James.

The following description by her intimate friend Susanna Winkworth conveys something of the charm and wisdom of the future author of *Wives and Daughters*:

She was a noble-looking woman with a queenly presence, and her high, broad, serene brow, and finely cut mobile features, were lighted up by a constantly varying play of expression as she poured forth her wonderful talk. It was like the gleaming ripple and rush of a clear deep stream in sunshine. Though one of the most brilliant persons I ever saw, she had none of the restlessness and eagerness that spoil so much of our conversations nowadays. There was no hurry or high-pressure about her, but she seemed always surrounded by an atmosphere of ease, leisure, and playful geniality, that drew out the best side of everyone who was in her company. When you were with her, you felt as if you had twice the life in you that you had at ordinary times.[2]

It was almost dark when Mrs Gaskell arrived at Windermere station, full of anticipation at the thought of meeting the greatly daring writer

379

for whom she already felt so much sympathy; ever since the publication of *Jane Eyre* her letters had been sprinkled with references to Currer Bell. Her husband had been preaching in Birmingham on Sunday, and as he did not like them both to be absent from their five children, he had returned to their large comfortable villa, leaving his impulsive, unconventional wife to make the trip to the Lakes alone. It was at the suggestion of Lady Shuttleworth that she had been invited to meet Currer Bell, who would perhaps have been surprised to realise that her hostess had thought Mrs Gaskell could do their strained guest some 'good', and perhaps strengthen her in some way. Mrs Gaskell had written: 'I should like to hear a great deal more about her, as I have been so much interested in what she has written. I don't mean merely in the story and mode of narration, wonderful as that is, but in the glimpses one gets of *her*, and her modes of thought, and, all unconsciously to herself, of the way in which she has suffered. I wonder if she suffers now.'[3]

Mrs Gaskell's concern over some tendencies in *Jane Eyre* had made her at first unable to decide whether she too had liked or disliked it;[4] she had disliked a good deal in the plot of *Shirley* but she found 'the expression of her own thoughts in it is so true and brave, that I greatly admire her'. She had been further reassured about Miss Brontë by hearing 'such a nice account' of her soon after she had seen Lady Kay Shuttleworth, from a gentleman who had gone over to see her father and who had stayed in the village for a night.[5] She now very much wanted to know her, and arrived almost pen in hand to take down her own impressions of the phenomenon and transmit them to friends eagerly awaiting a description of the woman who had said the unsayable about feeling and passion.

As the cab clambered up the steep wooded lane to Briery Close, she must have reviewed the rumours she had heard from London: Miss Brontë was 'frightfully shy, and almost cries at the thought of going among strangers';[6] she and Harriet Martineau had sworn vows of eternal friendship – this suggested a more boisterous nature, and indeed Harriet Martineau had relayed that she was 'full of life and power'; she was supposed to be a 'little, very little, bright-haired sprite, not looking above fifteen, very unsophisticated, neat and tidy'; her father was a Yorkshire clergyman who apparently had never slept out of his house for twenty-six years; she kept her name 'a profound secret; but Thackeray does *not*'.[7] Mrs Gaskell had no idea what to expect, but she was already predisposed to see Charlotte Brontë in a protective, romantic light.

On her arrival, she was shown into the pretty drawing-room where were Sir James and Lady Kay Shuttleworth, and 'a little wee dark person' in a black silk gown sitting behind the tea things, whom she could not see at first for the dazzle in the room. Charlotte immediately came up and shook hands with Mrs Gaskell, who then went upstairs to take off her bonnet. When she returned, Charlotte was busy at her sewing and scarcely spoke, so Mrs Gaskell had time to observe her closely.[8] She noted the touchingly small, childlike chest which could not fill an adult chemise, the hands so thin and delicate that she described them as bird's claws, and the myopia 'she cannot see your face unless you are close to her'.

Mrs Gaskell's fullest description of Miss Brontë was in a long, excited letter she wrote to Catherine Winkworth on 25 August after she had returned home to Plymouth Grove:

> She is (as she calls herself) *undeveloped*; thin and more than half a head shorter than I, soft brown hair not so dark as mine; eyes (very good and expressive looking straight and open at you) of the same colour, a reddish face; large mouth, and many teeth gone; altogether *plain*; the forehead square, broad, and *rather* overhanging. She has a very sweet voice, rather hesitates in choosing her expressions, but when chosen they seem without an effort, *admirable* and *just* befitting the occasion. There is nothing overstrained but perfectly simple.

For her part, Charlotte, never particularly given to favourable first impressions – if anything the reverse, was quite captivated by this warm, impulsive and determined woman, who had all the confidence of great physical beauty, during their three-day acquaintance. She told Ellen that she had been 'truly glad of her companionship. She is a woman of the most genuine talent, of cheerful, pleasing and cordial manners and – I believe – of a kind and good heart.'

Because Lady Shuttleworth was ill with a cold, on top of having a difficult time with pregnancy, she was confined to her room during Charlotte's stay and as a result the two women guests had much of the day to themselves, except when Sir James took it upon himself to lecture the two artistic ladies. The ebullient Mrs Gaskell was only amused by this 'eminently practical man' talking earnestly to them of 'bringing ourselves down to a lower level' and of 'the beauty of expediency', but Charlotte was irritated. To nerves strained to the limits by the events of the last year and a half, Sir James' hard-headed, kindly meant advice was wearying and insensitive. She had to admit to Mrs Gaskell's point that he had a 'strong and sincere friendship' for her, but she felt, as she told Ellen, that 'to authors as a class (the imaginative portion of them) he has a natural antipathy'. She thought the substratum of his character was hard as flint, and that she would not be sad if this man for whom she felt no sympathy, though she admired his intellect, were never to invite her to stay again. She found it difficult to understand his thirst for her company, which would continue until the end of her life. His artistic ambitions seemed so at odds with the rest of his distinctly utilitarian nature; in her view the artistic part of his nature was just enough to make him want to seek out the artist class, but it was too little to make him one of them. His inability to do what he admired, to paint, to write, had embittered him, she thought.

But the friendship between Charlotte and Mrs Gaskell flourished in the informal atmosphere of the Lakes. It was Mrs Gaskell who made breakfast in the morning, and on the first day they were joined by one of Sir James' former colleagues, Mr Moseley, an Inspector of Schools. He lectured the company on the evils of Mr Newman, brother of Cardinal Newman, for trying to acquire various branches of knowledge, which 'savoured of vanity and was a temptation of the D'. Mrs Gaskell described this thunderer with her usual brio as 'an old jolly'. After breakfast, all four of them went out boating on Lake Windermere – the house had its own landing stage – and, doubtless encouraged by a conspiratorial twinkle in Mrs Gaskell's eye, the two ladies found themselves in frank agreement that Mr Moseley was 'a good goose', that they both liked Newman's *Soul*, Ruskin's *Modern Painters* and the idea of the Seven Lamps. Charlotte then told Mrs Gaskell about Father Newman's lectures in a quiet, succinct fashion.

Mrs Gaskell found herself increasingly impressed, and intrigued. Here was the woman who had been denounced as an enemy of religion, as a moral Jacobin, showing herself to be as serious minded and moral as any of her acquaintance. She was sure that Miss Brontë 'works off a great deal that is morbid *into* her writing, and *out* of her life; and my books are so far better than I am that I often feel ashamed of having written them and as if I were a hypocrite'.[9] The more she found out about Charlotte on the visit, the more she felt admiration and pity for this 'very little and very plain' creature who had been so maligned and who had such nobility of character despite the wretchedness of her life. Her life was the self-denying fulfilment of filial duties towards her father, the poor and the old servants.

After lunch on the first day there was great excitement on Mrs Gaskell's part at the idea of going to see Tennyson and his wife, who, it had just been learnt, were staying nearby at Coniston. As Sir James knew the Poet Laureate, he thought that they might pay a call, and off they set in the carriage, Sir James sitting on the box, and Mrs Gaskell and Miss Brontë inside 'very cosy', as Mrs Gaskell said. However, much to Mrs Gaskell's annoyance, halfway there it started to rain and Sir James, ever mindful of his health, decided to turn back. Mrs Gaskell bit her lip to check her very considerable irritation, but

Charlotte herself was rather less interested by the idea. She did not share Mrs Gaskell's enthusiasm for Tennyson, thinking him far too measured. She preferred the exuberance and feeling of Wordsworth – who had died only a few months previously at neighbouring Rydal Mount. In Mrs Gaskell's words, 'She and I quarrelled and differed about almost everything – she calls me a democrat, and cannot bear Tennyson – but we like each other heartily, I think, and I hope we shall ripen into friends.'

An intimate friendship born of a sort of natural affinity was indeed established during their three days together. Between carriage rides and chats in the drawing room, supplemented by whispered consultations with Lady Kay Shuttleworth upstairs, a picture of Charlotte's life was revealed to Mrs Gaskell that quite overcame her with pity. She had never heard of so hard and dreary a life; she thought she was very like a friend of hers, Miss Tottie Fox, the daughter of a Unitarian divine, if one could imagine her to have gone through enough suffering to have taken out every spark of merriment, and become shy and silent from the habit of extreme solitude. Miss Brontë had, she said, a calm resigned air, especially when being given advice by Sir James; she thought her 'noble' and 'sterling' and 'true', 'and if she is a little bitter she checks herself, and speaks kindly and hopefully of things and people directly'. The wonder to Mrs Gaskell was how she could have kept heart and power alive in her life of desolation. The impression she received of Mr Brontë was particularly unfavourable, but whether Charlotte herself realised what a poor idea she was giving of her father is impossible to know. She told Mrs Gaskell that she and her father both dined and sat alone. The idea of an early death was still, in her future biographer's words, preying on Charlotte's mind. Mrs Gaskell said Charlotte was resigned to the idea that 'her death [would] be quite lonely; having no friend or relation in the world to nurse her, and her father dreading a sick room above all places'.

After observing her small, pale companion for some time, Mrs Gaskell also had little doubt that Miss Brontë was already tainted by consumption. She was greatly struck by the idea of the loneliness of the life in the cold grey parsonage stuck up on the bleak moor, and the tragedy of the Brontës' brief lives which Charlotte related to her. She noticed Miss Brontë's careful examination of the shape of the clouds and the signs of the heavens 'in which she read, as from a book, what the coming weather would be'. Charlotte told Mrs Gaskell that she could have 'no idea what a companion the sky became to anyone living in solitude – more than any inanimate object on earth – more than the moors themselves'.

When they were invited to tea with Mrs Arnold, widow of the great headmaster of Rugby, Dr Thomas Arnold, Mrs Gaskell witnessed how severely Miss Brontë's nerves were taxed by the effort of going among strangers. They knew beforehand that the number of the party going to the Arnolds' house, Fox How, would not exceed twelve – but Charlotte suffered the whole day from an acute headache brought on by apprehension of the evening. Charlotte herself would remember the situation of Fox How very well on account of its exquisite loveliness. She would write on 6 November to James Taylor, after he had just sent her Dean Stanley's *Life* of Dr Arnold: 'It was twilight as I drove to the place, and almost dark ere I reached it. . . . The house looked like a nest half-buried in flowers and creepers, and, dusk as it was, I could feel that the valley and the hills round were beautiful as imagination could dream. Mrs Arnold seemed an amiable, and must once have been a very pretty, woman.' Despite her nervousness she had liked the Arnold daughters very much. She thought that the whole visit would have interested her more if she had read Dr Arnold's *Life* beforehand, but it was nevertheless stimulating. A son of Chevalier Bunsen, the Prussian ambassador, had been there with his wife; his father had lately been in the news after Lord Brougham had behaved with outrageous impertinence to him in the House of Lords.

On the last day a large party came over to see Charlotte, consisting of Mrs Ferrand and some of her guests. Mrs Ferrand was the wife of a considerable landowner who owned a large country place four miles away from Haworth. With the party was Lord John Manners, who had brought two brace of grouse for Charlotte to present to Mr Brontë, a welcome gift, for her father had just mentioned wanting some. Charlotte duly left on 25 August after her week's visit, reporting to Ellen that it had 'passed off very well'; and for once she was 'very glad I went'.

She had found a new friend, and the future champion of Currer Bell. Mrs Gaskell would shortly be writing to her extremely curious friends defending the author of the scandalous *Jane Eyre*, anxious to convince them that Miss Brontë '*is* a nice person', who had 'high, noble aims'; who was 'truth itself' and of a 'sterling nature', which had never been called out 'by anything kind or genial'. Charlotte Froude was told firmly, 'Miss Brontë I like. Her faults are the faults of the very peculiar circumstances in which she has been placed; she possesses a charming union of simplicity and power; and a strong feeling of responsibility for the Gift, which she has given her.'[10] The woman who would go on to dare to tackle the taboo subject of the fallen woman in *Ruth* found her sympathy aroused by Charlotte Brontë's 'strong feeling of the duty of representing life as it really is, not as it ought to be'.[11]

Her championship would amount to a plea for understanding for her friend, an *apologia* on her behalf to her contemporaries. In her posthumous biography of Charlotte, her professed aim was 'to show her as a very noble, true Christian woman firstly, and as an author secondly': 'If the "Public" only will see Charlotte as she really was and as I meant to show that she was I shall feel my work has succeeded and I shall be happy. A noble Christian woman was what she was even more than a gifted author and it is in the first character I wish her to be thought of . . .'[12] Thus she would say that it was hardly surprising, given the father, the debauched brother, the wild villagers and the strange life so removed from any kind of normal or decent society, that Miss Brontë should write as she did. People should try to imagine her as she would have been had God spared her, 'rather than censure her because circumstances had forced her to touch pitch, as it were, and by it her hand was for a moment defiled', because it was but skin-deep. And she continued, questionably to a modern view, 'Every change in her life was purifying her', although Mrs Gaskell admitted that it could 'hardly raise her'.[13]

Mrs Gaskell achieved her object. After reading her biography of Charlotte Brontë, a typical commentator, Charles Kingsley, who had refused to continue reading *Shirley* after the 'coarseness' of the first scene, would write that here was a portrait of a woman made 'perfect by sufferings'. Emily Winkworth's reaction to Mrs Gaskell's first enthusiastic description of Charlotte gives an insight into the average middle-class woman's reaction to Charlotte Brontë: 'Poor Miss Brontë. . . . One feels as if one ought to go to her at once, and do something for her. . . . One feels that her life at least *almost* makes one like her books, though one does not want there to be any more Miss Brontës.'[14]

On her return to Haworth, Charlotte wrote off immediately in reply to Mrs Gaskell's first letter, clearly delighted with her new friendship and wishing to cement the bonds:

> . . . Papa and I have just had tea; he is sitting quietly in his room, and I in mine; 'storms of rain' are sweeping over the garden and churchyard: as to the moors, they are hidden in thick fog. Though alone, I am not unhappy; I have a thousand things to be grateful for, and, amongst the rest, that this morning I received a letter from you, and that this evening I have the privilege of answering it.

And Mrs Gaskell, surrounded by her pretty possessions and her noisy cheerful children in her large comfortable house filled with the many brilliant people who were part of her Manchester salon, felt the sort of tug at her heart strings that would never be disentangled. 'Poor, poor creature,' she would exclaim, while devising plans for quiet visits for her new friend.

Charlotte now took up with her in writing many of the things that they had discussed while in the Lake District, among them, not surprisingly, the problems facing women writers. She told Mrs Gaskell that there was an article entitled 'Woman's Mission' in the *Westminster Review* containing a great deal that seemed just and sensible to her. She thought that men were beginning to regard the position of women 'in another light than they used to; and a few men, whose sympathies are fine and whose sense of justice is strong, think and speak of it with a candour that commands my admiration. They say, however – and to an extent truly – that the amelioration of our condition depends on ourselves.' She agreed that 'Certainly there are evils which our own efforts will best reach; but as certainly there are other evils – deep-rooted in the foundations of the social system – which no efforts of ours can touch; of which we cannot complain; of which it is advisable not too often to think.'

It seems very likely that Charlotte was here thinking of the passiveness required of the female sex, the conventions which hedged women around, which prevented them from ever publicly discussing their intimate feelings, without deserving to 'forfeit the company of their own sex'. After all, her writings had shown that that was what happened. The article on 'Woman's Mission'[15] in fact in many ways proceeded from all the conventions that Charlotte had offended against and criticised in *Shirley*. It depicted women's real 'genius' as 'influence' of a quasi-heavenly kind: 'Many mistakes will be made, many kinds of work attempted unsuited to her woman's nature', warbled John Parker, 'as the years pass by, but always with nearer and nearer approaches to the true. Writing, speaking, governing, the warehouse and the mart, with art and science, may each be taken up and laid down again, and a life of *Being* be found the finest result of her nature, for her own and the world's joy, an atmosphere of light and love, from which her sons shall go forth into the world to act, as from the temple of the living God.'

Charlotte's response to an article in the *Westminster Review* a year later on the Emancipation of Women, which she believed to be by John Stuart Mill (it was in fact by his wife to be, Harriet Taylor) shows similar contradictions, and fears of losing aspects of her feminine role which were more important to her than emancipation: the article was well argued, the greater part of it spoke 'admirable sense', that careers should be open to all regardless of sex; nevertheless she complained of a great lacuna in the piece which grated on her and indicated Mill's deficiencies; the writer forgot the existence of 'self-sacrificing love and disinterested devotion'. When she had first read the paper she thought it must be written by a woman with 'nerves of bent leather . . . who longed for power, and had never

386

felt affection. To many women,' she continued, 'affection is sweet, and power conquered indifferent – though we all like influence won.'

Mrs Gaskell was much of her persuasion. Although she was willing to sign petitions to improve the legal position of women, particularly wives, she is on record as saying that they 'have no judgement'. They had tact, 'and sensitiveness and genius, and hundreds of fine and lovely qualities' but were 'angelic geese as to matter requiring serious and long scientific consideration'. Consequently she was not in favour of 'Female Medical Education'.

During their conversations, Mrs Gaskell had been greatly struck by the difference in their experience of publishers and Charlotte now evidently rather hoped that Mrs Gaskell would offer her next work to Smith, Elder – both out of affection for Mrs Gaskell and from a strong desire to be useful to the firm that had done so much for her. (Mrs Gaskell's biography of Charlotte would be published by Smith, Elder but not her novels.) Meanwhile, Charlotte sent her a copy of the Bells' poetry, whose co-authors she had told Mrs Gaskell so much about.

Her thoughts were focused even more closely on her sisters when, within a few days, Mr Williams wrote suggesting that she edit a new edition of Ellis and Acton Bell's works, with a 'Biographical Notice' written by Charlotte to set at rest all erroneous conjectures about the Bells' identity and character. In a burst of sudden enthusiasm, Charlotte accepted the idea. She did not, however, wish *Wildfell Hall* to be included; she hardly thought it worth preserving. The choice of subject had been a mistake; Anne had written it 'under a strange conscientious half-ascetic notion of accomplishing a painful penance and severe duty'. Going through Anne's papers after her death had confirmed her own suspicions that this delicate, blameless creature's nature had contained a degree of severe religious melancholy, owing much to Calvinism.

Charlotte's enthusiasm for the new project was given an unexpected boost by a eulogy of *Wuthering Heights* in a review of the work of Currer Bell by Sydney Dobell in the September edition of the *Palladium*. It was, Charlotte said, 'of such warm sympathy, high appreciation as I had ever expected to see'. Though he refused to accept the disclaimer Charlotte had published in the third edition of *Jane Eyre* that it was that book alone of which she was the author and none of the other Bells' books, it was a wonderful review for Charlotte, and to Emily's memory. She told Mr Taylor on 5 September that it was

. . . one of those notices over which an author rejoices with trembling. He rejoices to find his work finely, fully, fervently appreciated, and trembles under the responsibility such appreciation seems to devolve upon him. I am counselled to wait and watch. D.V., I

387

will do so. Yet it is harder work to wait with the hands bound and observant and reflective faculties at their silent unseen work, than to labour mechanically.

The critic's words on *Wuthering Heights* 'woke the saddest yet most grateful feelings; they are true, they are discriminating; they are full of late justice – but it is very late – alas! in one sense too late.' Quivering with emotion, she wrote a long letter of gratitude to him.

Dobell was a most sensitive critic, anticipating much of the later praise of *Wuthering Heights*: he admired the 'admirable combination of extreme likelihood with the rarest originality'; the brilliant handling of a double narrative from the opening of Chapter Two to Lockwood's settling for the night in the kitchen; he was at a loss to find anywhere in modern prose in the same space such wealth and such economy, such apparent ease, such instinctive art. He told Currer Bell to prize the young intuition of character he perceived in the character of Cathy, finding 'a deep unconscious philosophy' in some of her speeches.

Wuthering Heights he thought was 'the flight of an impatient fancy fluttering in the very exultation of young wings; sometimes beating against its solitary bars, but turning, rather to exhaust in a circumscribed space, the energy and agility which it may not yet spend in the heavens – a youthful story written for oneself in solitude'. Catherine Earnshaw was praised as wonderfully fresh, so new, 'as if brought from other spheres'; 'the involuntary art with which her two natures are so made to coexist, that in the very arms of her lover we dare not doubt her purity . . .'

It was nectar to Charlotte's ears – at last Emily was understood. He went on, 'Not a subordinate place or person in this novel, but bears more or less the stamp of high genius.' Like Charlotte, he thought that the author needed more time to develop: 'It is the unformed writing of a giant's hand; the "large utterance" of a baby God.'[16]

Meanwhile a letter arrived from Mrs Gaskell thanking Charlotte for the book of the Bells' poetry, and sending her some flowers. When put in water they revived, Charlotte told her, and looked quite fresh and beautiful. She especially prized the bit of heliotrope for its incomparable perfume. But such kindnesses from the outside world could not compensate for the lonely reality of her existence. She admitted to Mr Williams on 2 October that she found to her humiliation that 'it is not in my power to bear the canker of constant solitude'. She had calculated that when shut out from every enjoyment, every stimulus other than that from intellectual exercise, her mind would rouse itself and she would be able to write. But it was not so: 'even intellect, even imagination, will not dispense with the ray of domestic cheerfulness –

with the gentle spur of family discussion.'

Unable to continue with her own writing, she immersed herself in the 'sacred task' of re-publishing her sisters' work. Re-reading their writings brought back the worst pangs of bereavement. She told Ellen on 25 October that there were some nights when she scarcely knew how to get through to morning: 'the deadly silence, solitude, desolation were awful – the craving for companionship – the hopelessness of relief – were what I should dread to feel again.' But to the alarmed Ellen, who scribbled back frantically in her near-illegible handwriting, Charlotte wrote that she was *not* to worry about her. Her health was actually quite good; it simply was necessary for her sometimes to find relief by telling Ellen about such things. And she went on, 'Dear Nell, when I think of you, it is with a compassion and tenderness that scarcely cheer me – mentally, I feel you also are too lonely and too little occupied. It seems our doom for the present at least. May God in his mercy help us to bear it!'

Miss Wooler wrote asking her to come for a holiday – also at the Lakes – but Charlotte felt that she must press on with her task; nor was she willing to leave her father. Both Harriet Martineau and Mrs Gaskell also asked her to come to stay that winter but Charlotte was equally reluctant to accept an invitation from them. She fell into a condition of mind that turned entirely to the past. Re-reading *Wuthering Heights* she found that its power filled her with renewed admiration, she told Williams, 'but yet I am oppressed: the reader is scarcely ever permitted a taste of unalloyed pleasure; every beam of sunshine is poured down through black bars of threatening cloud; every page is charged with a sort of moral electricity; and the writer was unconscious of this – nothing could make her conscious of it'.[17] She would stand by her view that Emily had no real sense of the amorality of her characters.

In the preface that she wrote to the new edition of the novel, she defended it as a product of its environment, the result of time spent among rude moorland squires, incomprehensible perhaps to those whose feelings were calm and orderly; it was as knotty as a piece of moorish heath; her sister had rarely gone out; all she knew of was the tragic and strange annals of village life. Furthermore, she said, the book contained delightful domestic passages of tranquillity, contrasting with the atmosphere of great horror brooding over the whole. The sister she proudly defended to the unkind world perhaps would have written differently placed in different circumstances; all she could say was that she was genuinely good and great.

In her desire to present her sister in what she felt was the best possible light, she modified much of the original punctuation and spelling, and the dialect of *Wuthering Heights*, so that, she argued, the character of Joseph would not be lost on southern readers. She excised all mentions of Gondal in the poems, of which she included only a small selection of the whole and avoiding the most personal of Anne's. *Wuthering Heights, Agnes Grey, together with a selection of Poems by Ellis and Acton Bell*, 'Prefixed with a Biographical Memoir of the authors by Currer Bell', was published in early December 1850; and although Charlotte's editing may have done no literary service to her sisters, the book left no doubt as to the individual identities of the Bells.

By December Charlotte recognised that she should go away to try to counteract the illness and depression into which she had fallen, broken only by the diversion of correspondence and the books that continued to arrive from Cornhill. She wrote intermittently, fancifully and amusingly to George Smith, reserving her literary letters for Mr Williams and for Mr Taylor, whose interest in her clearly remained strong. On reading the *Life* of Dr Arnold that he had sent her in November, she had been very struck by the uneventful happiness of Arnold's life, containing none of 'those deep and bitter griefs which most human beings are called upon to endure'. There were no lack of invitations – from Ellen, Mrs Gaskell, Harriet Martineau and, inevitably, Sir James Kay Shuttleworth. She accepted the long-standing one from Miss Martineau to visit her at her house, The Knoll, at Ambleside, which prevented her from taking up that from Mrs Gaskell for a quiet stay with friends in Essex. Mrs Gaskell immediately wrote off a long warm letter of advice which touched Charlotte very much. Mrs Gaskell intended to have her to stay as soon as possible, with the family, and without all the bother of curiosity.

Charlotte left for Ambleside on 16 December and shortly after she arrived she was writing to Ellen that her depression of that autumn had entirely lifted. She stayed for a week. To her, Miss Martineau appeared quite 'exhaustless in strength and spirit, and indefatigable in the faculty of labour. She is a great and good woman; of course not without peculiarities, but I have seen none as yet that annoy me.' She was 'both hard and warm-hearted, abrupt and affectionate – liberal and despotic'. Altogether it was a far more cheerful Charlotte who informed Ellen that when she told Miss Martineau of her absolutism she denied it warmly and then laughed at her. Miss Martineau almost ruled Ambleside.

The Knoll itself was a pleasant, comfortably appointed house, which Harriet Martineau had had built for herself. Visitors to it were allowed to behave exactly as they pleased, like their eccentric hostess. Miss Martineau was up at five, took a cold bath, 'a walk by starlight', and had finished breakfast and was at her desk by 7.00. Charlotte rose whenever she pleased, breakfasted alone, and then spent the morning in the drawing-room while Harriet Martineau was in her study. At 2.00 in the afternoon, they met, worked, talked and walked together till five, which was her hostess's dinner hour. They spent the evening together, 'when she converses fluently, abundantly and with the most complete frankness', Charlotte wrote with pleasure and slight amazement. Charlotte went to her room about 10.00 while Miss Martineau stayed up writing her voluminous correspondence till midnight. In awe she wrote that in spite of 'the unceasing activity of her colossal intellect she enjoys robust health'.

In this unconventional household Charlotte for once was completely at her ease. The only cloud on the horizon was Sir James Kay Shuttleworth, who was planning to carry her off to his house, which his quarry was equally determined to prevent happening. She succeeded by accepting instead to go out for a drive in his carriage almost every morning, and by the end of her stay she began to have a more kindly feeling towards this strange man, whose nervous illness meant that he seemed to be wasting away before her eyes. She had now to admit that she thought he was 'sincerely benignant' to her and wanted to be her friend. Lady Shuttleworth she did not see at all, for she was now close to the end of her pregnancy and unable to leave the house.

Otherwise, Charlotte had the bracing company of Harriet Martineau whom, she told Ellen, 'I relish inexpressibly'.[18] With her brusque contempt for convention, she was like 'some sovereign medicine – harsh, perhaps, to the taste, but potent to invigorate'. It was delightful, Charlotte told Mr Williams, to sit near her in the evenings 'and hear her converse, myself mute'. This was perhaps just as well given that interlocutors were obliged to shout down Miss Martineau's large ear-trumpet. The two women together must have been a faintly comic sight – the one so large, the other so small. Miss Martineau was taller and more strongly made than Charlotte had imagined from the first interview that they had had. She told her father that 'she is very kind to me, though she must think I am a very insignificant person compared to herself' – which was in fact far from the truth. She related to her father that Harriet Martineau had just been into the room to show her a chapter of her *History of England during the Thirty Years of Peace*, relating to the Duke of Wellington and the Peninsula War. She wanted Miss Brontë's opinion of the work. According to Harriet Martineau's later account of the incident to Mrs Gaskell, she read a page or two to Charlotte as they stood before the fire and to her amazement when she looked up she saw tears running down Charlotte's cheeks. 'She said, "Oh! I do thank you! Oh! we are of one mind! Oh! I thank you for justice to this man." I saw at once there was a touch of idolatry in the case, but it was a charming enthusiasm.'

391

For whatever reasons, nerves, ill health, her depression that autumn, her intensely emotional nature, Charlotte had a tendency to burst into tears at moments of excitement. It was on account of her excessive sensibility and receptiveness that Miss Martineau was particularly reluctant to experiment with her in mesmerism, the practice of which was one of Harriet Martineau's many interests, although she did tell Charlotte that she thought she would be an excellent subject. According to Miss Martineau,

> she was strangely pertinacious about that, and I *most* reluctant to bring it before her at all, we being alone, and I having no confidence in her nerves. Day after day she urged me to mesmerize her. I always, and quite truly, pleaded that I was too tired for success, for we had no opportunity till the end of the day. At last, on Sunday evening, we returned from early tea somewhere; I could not say I was tired, and she insisted. I stopped the moment she called out that she was under the influence, and I would not resume it.[19]

Perhaps her guest was so anxious to undergo it because it must have reminded her of the trance-like state she went into when she wrote.

The topic that Charlotte could not share her hostess's enthusiasm for was that of atheism. Harriet Martineau's large and energetic mind had wrestled boldly with the subject and her thoughts emerged in her controversial book *Letters on the Laws of Man's Social Nature and Development*, the proofs of which were arriving during Charlotte's stay. Charlotte said valiantly that in judging her lengthy exposition on 'disbelief in the existence of a God or a Future Life', 'one would wish entirely to put aside the sort of instinctive horror they awaken, and to consider them in an impartial spirit and collected mood'. But this she found difficult to do. Her view was inevitably coloured by her bereaved state. Her only crutch nowadays was the surety that she would meet her loved ones in heaven. She said wonderingly that the strangest thing to her was that 'we are called on to rejoice over this hopeless blank, to receive this bitter bereavement as great gain, to welcome this unutterable desolation as a state of pleasant freedom. Who could do this if he would? Who would do it if he could?'

She rather trembled for Miss Martineau's reputation. Though she admired that indomitable courage that made Miss Martineau ready to meet the shock of opposition for the sake of her 'Truth', in the end she thought that she would regret the book's publication for 'it gives a death-blow to her future usefulness. Who can trust the word, or rely on the judgement, of an avowed atheist?'[20] She herself wished to know the Truth, but if this was the Truth, anyone who believed it must rue the day they were born.

Miss Martineau's contempt for organised religion could take a less attractive form, as Matthew Arnold found when the two literary ladies were invited to tea at Fox How on 21 December. The Doctor's son wrote:

At seven came Miss Martineau and Miss Brontë (*Jane Eyre*); talked to Miss Martineau (who blasphemes frightfully) about the prospects of the Church of England, and, wretched man that I am, promised to go and see her cow-keeping miracles tomorrow – I who hardly know a cow from a sheep. I talked to Miss Brontë (past thirty and plain, with expressive grey eyes, though) of her curates, of French novels, and her education in a school in Brussels, and sent the lions roaring to their dens at half past nine.[21]

This rather cheeky comment would perhaps not have surprised the object of his cynosure – Matthew Arnold's manner had at first displeased her 'from its seeming foppery', as she told James Taylor. She thought that 'the shade of Dr Arnold seemed to me to frown on his young representative'. Nevertheless after a while she thought 'a real modesty appeared under his assumed conceit and some genuine intellectual aspirations, as well as high educational attainments, displaced superficial affectations'.

On 23 December Charlotte left Ambleside for a Christmas visit to Ellen at Brookroyd before returning home. Her spirits were buoyed up by her stay, which she told her father that she had enjoyed exceedingly. She admired Harriet Martineau's sincerity, her 'fine mind and noble powers', and considered her to be a better writer than Mrs Gaskell. Harriet Martineau had probably given her courage in her new role as a literary woman, as a 'she-artist', but she could not help reflecting that 'neither solitude nor loss of friends would break her down'; the physically fragile and emotionally sensitive Charlotte could not hope to match Miss Martineau's strength, and she would constantly chastise herself for her inability to cope with solitude.

Back at Haworth for the New Year of 1851, she continued to be unable to work on a new novel. However, the first months of the year took a different turn: they were occupied almost exclusively with matters of the heart, albeit the principals involved were three hundred miles from Haworth. Mr Taylor continued to press his suit through the medium of literary newspapers that he sent to the parsonage. Now that Charlotte's coldness had made his manner more respectful and less familiar, his constancy, she told Ellen jokily, added a foot to his height and turned his red hair dark. It was, however, to her handsome young publisher that she had to confess she was increasingly drawn. Charlotte passed on most of her letters to Ellen for entertainment, and the latter was pleased to detect 'undercurrents' in George Smith's letters, 'fixed intentions'. In January he suggested that they voyage down the Rhine together in the summer. Ellen was immediately bubbling with excitement. Charlotte wrote back to her on 20 January:

Dear Nell, Your last letter but one made me smile. I think you draw great conclusions from small inferences. . . . I think those 'fixed intentions' you fancy – are imaginary – I think the 'undercurrent' amounts simply to this – a kind of natural liking and a sense of something congenial. Were there no vast barrier of age, fortune, etc. there is perhaps enough personal regard to make things possible which are now impossible. If men and women married because they liked each other's temper, look, conversation, nature and so on – and if besides, years were more nearly equal – the chance you allude to might be admitted as a chance but other reasons regulate matrimony – reasons of convenience, of connection, of money. Meantime I am content to have him as a friend – and pray God to continue to me the common sense to look on one so young, so rising, and so hopeful in no other light.

But she had to admit to Ellen that his hint about the Rhine disturbed her. As in all her relationships, she recognised that 'what is mere excitement to him is fever to me'. Although the matter was out of the question for many reasons, she did wonder at his proposing it – his mother and sister would not like it, 'and all London would gabble like a countless host of geese'. Meanwhile she counselled herself to resist the lure of pleasure when it came in the shape of which judgement would disapprove. Nevertheless she was more amenable to his ensuing invitations to come to London in June, although she would not commit herself.

If George Smith had been wondering about the progress of the next novel from Currer Bell, he might after a little thought have concluded that some of his author's imaginative energy was going into the writing of enchanting, whimsical, flirtatious letters to him, which impelled him to respond. She had fascinated the world with her pen, and she was now using it to mesmerise a more intimate audience. When he suggested that he publish *The Professor*, to which Charlotte had told him that she felt like a doting parent towards an idiot child, whose merits would never be owned by anyone but Mr Williams and herself, she replied on 5 February:

You kindly propose to take *The Professor* into custody. Ah no! His modest merit shrinks at the thought of going alone and unbe-

394

friended to a spirited Publisher. Perhaps with slips of him you might light an occasional cigar, or might remember to lose him someday, and a Cornhill functionary would gather him up and consign him to repositories of waste paper, and thus he would prematurely find his way to the 'butter man' and trunk-makers. No, I have put him by and locked him up, not indeed in my desk, where I could not tolerate the monotony of his demure Quaker countenance, but in a cupboard by himself.

Something you say about going to London; but the words are dreamy and fortunately I am not obliged to hear or answer them. London and summer are many months away: our moors are all white with snow just now, and little red-breasts come every morning to the window for crumbs. One can lay no plans three or four months beforehand. Besides, I don't deserve to go to London: nobody merits a change or treat less. I secretly think, on the contrary, I ought to be put in prison, and kept on bread and water in solitary confinement – without even a letter from Cornhill – till I have written a book. One of the two things would certainly result from such a mode of treatment pursued for twelve months; either I should come out at the end of that time with a 3 vol. MS in my hand, or else with a condition of intellect that would exempt me ever after from literary efforts and expectations.

Cornhill must not worry, she continued light-heartedly, that Currer Bell might think its proceedings a rich field for satire; although he had been tempted by its possibilities, he had decided against it.

In her enthusiasm for her correspondence with Mr Smith, however, Charlotte failed to calculate what effect it might have upon Mr Smith's employee. There was silence from Mr Taylor for several weeks, and then in March she learned from Mr Smith that Mr Taylor would shortly be going to India to man the Smith, Elder office out there. This was rather unexpected, if not a little hurtful. A letter of farewell was despatched by Charlotte. The ever-hopeful heart of the pugnacious Mr Taylor leapt up. Detecting something more beneath the polite formal phrases, he announced that he must be in Scotland next week. Might he call on his way back south?

Perhaps wanting to talk it over with Ellen, Charlotte invited her to stay, receiving at the same time another affectionate invitation from Mrs Gaskell to come to Manchester for a visit, which she was obliged to refuse. Comforted by the effects of Ellen's visit, she received James Taylor at the parsonage on Friday morning, 4 April. He looked much thinner and older to her. She saw him very near and once through her glasses, and the marked resemblance he bore to Branwell struck her very forcibly, too forcibly. He was not ugly, she thought, but very peculiar, and once again she noticed his inflexibility and hardness of character, this time in the lines on his face. He had come to propose, and propose he did.

But as he stood near her, and he looked at her in his keen way, it was, she told Ellen, 'all I could do to stand my ground tranquilly and steadily, and not to recoil as before'. Although she had vaguely entertained the idea of embarking on a courtship, when it came to the moment she found that his personal presence and manners scarcely pleased her more than at the first interview. There was something not gentlemanly, something second-rate about him, something jarring; 'stern and abrupt little man as he is'. Perhaps he made his desire, his passion, too obvious, even though he might be forgiven for thinking that the creator of Mr Rochester would prefer a rough wooing. In her letter to Ellen of 9 April, she agonised:

> Would Mr T— and I ever suit? Could I ever feel for him enough love to accept of him as a husband? Friendship – gratitude – esteem, I have – but each moment he comes near me, and that I could see his eyes fastened on me, my veins ran ice. Now that he is away I feel far more gently towards him – it is only close by that I grow rigid – stiffening with a strange mixture of apprehension and anger – which nothing softens but his retreat and a perfect subduing of his manner. I did not want to be proud nor intend to be proud – but I was forced to be so.

He gave her a book when he left, asking her in his brief way that she would keep it for his sake and adding hastily, 'I shall hope to hear from you in India – your letters *have* been, and *will* be, a greater refreshment than you can think or I can tell.'

She had gathered from hints that he had dropped that there had been some kind of fracas between him and Mr Smith. She noticed that he studiously avoided all mention of Mr Smith personally, and there seemed little doubt that he was going abroad unwillingly. Although she could not reciprocate his regard, Charlotte confessed to Ellen that 'his withdrawal leaves a painful blank'; the idea of him at the back of her mind had been some support to her and she was now left 'in deeper solitude than before'. Her father, on hearing that Mr Taylor was sailing out of his daughter's life forever, had grown very warm towards him, throwing his usual catechism of questions at him. But curiously, very soon after Mr Taylor had left the house that evening Mr Brontë, although apparently in rather better health, suddenly took ill and retired to bed. It was a graphic warning of what might happen if Charlotte ever were to leave him. Never able to articulate her feelings about his behaviour, his daughter followed his tall black figure up the stairs and sat by him until the sickness passed, and he began to doze. Then she came down through the dark hall, into the dining room, where she sat churning with what she could only call 'a sense of weight, fear and desolation hard to express and harder to endure'.

Over the next few weeks, to Charlotte's surprise, Mr Brontë raised the subject of Mr Taylor on most days, speaking enthusiastically of him and even hinting that perhaps when he came back, something might come of it. The 'marked kindness of his manner to the little man when he bid him goodbye – exhorting him to be "true to himself, his Country, and his God" and wishing him all good wishes, struck me with some astonishment at the time,' she told Ellen on 5 May:

> When I alleged that he was 'no gentleman' he seemed out of patience with me for the objection. You say Papa has penetration – on this subject I believe he has indeed. I have told him nothing, yet he seems to be *au fait* to the whole business – I would think at some moments his guesses go farther than mine. I believe he thinks a prospective union, deferred for five years, with such a decorous reliable personage would be a very proper and advisable affair. However I ask no questions and he asks me none, and if he did, I should have nothing to tell him.

It has been suggested that Mr Brontë's curious behaviour over his daughter's suitors was motivated by fear that his daughter would not survive childbirth – a fear wisely founded as it proved. From this point of view, he would naturally welcome Mr Taylor in the role of lover if he were not to assume it till five years later, since Charlotte would then probably be past childbearing age. However, given the alarm that he displayed at any idea of Charlotte's suitors, it seems that at the age of seventy-three he was determined – consciously or unconsciously – that nothing was going to come between him and his settled life with the last of his surviving flesh and blood. The old man who had been through so much upheaval and tragedy may have thought no further than that, although he may well have calculated that five years would see him out and he could have the comfort of knowing Charlotte would then be taken care of.

Charlotte herself, once the reality of Mr Taylor began to retreat, once more pondered on the possibility of a liaison. She found that she could not get him out of her thoughts. The optimistic Ellen reminded her that perhaps in five years' time. . . . No, Charlotte wrote sternly to herself as much as to Ellen. Common sense told her that 'an absence of five years – a dividing expanse of three oceans – the wide difference between a man's active career and a woman's passive existence – these

397

things are almost equivalent to an eternal separation'. For his part Mr Taylor had not quite lost hope; on his arrival back in London he had immediately dispatched his usual token of love to Miss Brontë – a parcel of books. He was due to leave England on 20 May and he asked whether there was any chance of seeing her in London before that time.

But there was no possibility of that. Charlotte had other plans about when she would come to London. Once again, despite all her caveats, her thoughts had been whirled away by the dashing Mr Smith, though the wherefores of a high forehead, large heavy-lidded but unremarkable eyes, neat features and reported charm against Mr Taylor's vigour must remain to us mysterious. On 17 April she was writing to his mother accepting her kind invitation to stay with them. Although she had been determined to resist, and could not come in the spring when her father's health was so uncertain – until the warm weather set in she would hardly think it right or feel happy to leave him – she had decided that she could come in June.

Haworth immediately took on a more carefree atmosphere, as Charlotte prepared for her visit with the ritual sewing that preceded her every outing to London. Indeed such was her optimism that she ventured into Leeds alone on a shopping expedition to the emporium of Hunt & Hall to purchase a bonnet for the many outings which she would undoubtedly be taken on by George Smith. She bought one with a pink lining. It had seemed 'grave and quiet there amongst all the splendours', she told Ellen, but now she got home to the parsonage it suddenly seemed infinitely too gay. Like Lucy Snowe Charlotte wanted nothing to draw attention to herself, to show she expected anything. A dress of shadow was more suitable. In the shop she had also seen 'some beautiful silks of pale sweet colours but had not the spirit or the means to launch out at the rate of 5s. per yd. and went and bought a black silk at 3s. after all'. Nevertheless, back home she now rather regretted that she had not indulged that rare impulse to prettify herself. Her father, for once not thinking of himself, moved by his tiny anxious daughter, said that he would have lent her a sovereign if he had known. But she would not expose herself to ridicule. She was like an elder sister to George Smith. That was it.

Ellen was commanded to buy one of the new lace cloaks, either black or white, which had rather taken Charlotte's fancy in Leeds. She supposed timidly that the shop in Leeds which stocked them would hardly like to send a selection to Haworth to try, and indeed if they cost very much it would be useless, but if it were possible she would like to see them. She would also like 'some chemisettes of small size (the full woman's size don't fit me) both of simple style for everyday and good quality for best'. But Mr Stocks of Leeds was quite happy to accede to the ladylike Miss Nussey's request and the mantles found their way to Haworth, where Charlotte decided on one of the black lace ones. However, when she came to try it with the black satin dress with which she chiefly intended to wear it, the effect to her dismay was not pleasing. The beauty of the lace was lost. It looked brown and rusty against the black satin. She wrote to Mr Stocks asking him to change it for a white mantle of the same price. 'He was extremely courteous, and sent to London for one, which I have got this morning,' she told Ellen happily. 'The price is less, being but £1.14s.; it is pretty, neat and light, looks well on black; and upon reasoning the matter over, I came to the conclusion, that it would be no shame for a person of my means to wear a cheaper thing; so I think I shall take it, and if you ever see it and call it "trumpery",' she said to the sartorially exacting Ellen, 'so much the worse.'

She was, however, looking strained – grey and washed out; it was 'her London look', she told Ellen with heavy irony. Headaches and occasional sickness continued to oppress her and however careful she was with her diet, her stomach would not 'keep right', as she described it. But at least her father's health was better. The wily old man sent her off with the cheerful words that if she got married, he would go into lodgings. Charlotte bid farewell to Ellen by letter, smiling at old Mrs Nussey's mysterious hints which echoed the knowing looks in the parsonage. All fancied that 'I am somehow, by some mysterious process, to be married in London – or to engage myself to matrimony. How I smile internally! How groundless and impossible is the idea!' Strong words. But perhaps a little of the internal smile was because it was not quite impossible, was it?

CHAPTER XIX

Villette

The weather at least made the visit seem to promise fair. Charlotte left Yorkshire for the long journey from Leeds to London on Wednesday, 28 May, and the day stayed beautiful and warm the whole way. She was met at Euston by a cordial Mrs Smith chaperoning her handsome son, who was full of plans to entertain her. The next afternoon, Thursday, she was to see one of the sights of London – Thackeray lecturing – she had been summoned a day sooner so as not to miss him. Of course one of the first items on her agenda must be the eighth wonder of the world, the Great Exhibition, Prince Albert's brainchild intended to celebrate peace and the spiritual and material progress of mankind. Full of anticipation that even her disciplined nature could not quite subdue, Charlotte exuberantly wrote a cursory note from Gloucester Terrace to her father to let him know that she had arrived safely.

To Ellen she confided a few days later that 'Mr S' was 'rather changed in appearance'. He seemed to her to look 'a little older, darker and more careworn'. His manner was graver, though in the evening the high spirits bubbled back a bit, which with his energetic, extrovert manner made him so attractive. All seemed much as usual in the comfortable house but she fancied that there had been some kind of crisis through which he had sustained them, for his doting mother and sisters were even more bound to him than before and his slightest wish was an unquestioned law.

The next day it was Mrs Smith who escorted her to Thackeray's lecture on Congreve and Addison, the second in his series of lectures on English humorists of the eighteenth century, held at Almack's Assembly Rooms, St James. The audience, to her secret delight, was composed of the cream of London society: 'Duchesses were there by the score, and amongst them the great and beautiful Duchess of Sutherland, the Queen's Mistress of the Robes,' ran her excited description to her father; the lecture took place in 'a large and splendid kind of saloon', where the walls were all painted and gilded, and the benches and sofas stuffed and cushioned and covered with blue damask.

Under such circumstances she had not expected Thackeray to notice her, but on the contrary he met her as she came in, shook hands and brought her to meet his mother. Charlotte thought her a 'fine, handsome, young-looking old lady' who was very gracious; the next day she would favour Miss Brontë with a call in the company of one of her granddaughters. There was a little ripple of notice about her presence – glasses were put up to look at her – and it seemed that Thackeray had been putting it about that 'Jane Eyre', as he referred to Charlotte, was in the audience. She turned to Mrs Smith resignedly to say, 'I am afraid Mr Thackeray has been playing me a trick'. They settled themselves on one of the sofas dotted about the room, now buzzing with the low hum preceding a hush of the many spectators, but there was further recognition in store for Charlotte. She told Ellen: 'Just before the lecture began, somebody came up behind me, leaned over and said, "Permit me, as a Yorkshireman, to introduce myself." I turned round, saw a strange, not handsome face which puzzled me for a half a minute, and then I said, "You are Lord Carlisle".'[1] He smiled and said he was in what his critical interlocutor considered a 'courteous, kind fashion'. He went on to ask after Mr Brontë, whom he recalled from 1835 when they had been on the same platform during the election campaign at Haworth. He was followed by two other admirers, who also claimed the privilege of being fellow countrymen: Richard Monckton Milnes, later Lord Houghton, one of the MPs for Yorkshire and a poet and friend of many writers; and Dr Forbes, whose advice she had sought during Emily's final illness.

Such attentions were forgotten once the lecture began. She thought it 'truly good' and that Thackeray spoke 'with as much simplicity and ease as if he had been speaking to a few friends by his own fireside'; it was a sort of essay characterised by his own peculiar originality and power, and delivered with admirably finished taste. But as soon as it was over, Thackeray bounded down to where she was sitting to ask her what she thought of the lecture, thus causing all heads to turn in the way she most disliked. She described the experience a couple of days later to Mrs Gaskell, who would be fascinated to see the entire experience incorporated into *Villette*, when a near-identical action and words were performed by M. Paul Emanuel.

As they were beginning to leave the room, Mrs Smith noticed with dismay that many of the audience were forming themselves into two lines on each side of the aisle down which the two ladies would have to pass to reach the door. Aware that if she hesitated, the now trembling

Miss Brontë might not reach the exit, Mrs Smith took her firmly by the arm, and they went through 'the avenue of eager and admiring faces'. During their passage through this unique guard of honour of the highest of the land, Mrs Smith remembered that Miss Brontë's hand had trembled to such a degree that she was worried that she might turn faint and be unable to proceed. She dared not say a word of sympathy in case it should bring on the crisis of nerves she feared.

Of this latter event, Charlotte, with her dread of notoriety and in the habit of concealing so much from her father about her life as an author, she said nothing to him, or to Ellen. He probably would have been delighted at his daughter being honoured in such a way. It was a different matter with Thackeray. He called the next afternoon, to find a very angry Miss Brontë awaiting him. George Smith, who arrived back from the office shortly afterwards, entered the drawing-room to find Thackeray standing on the hearth-rug, 'looking anything but happy'. Charlotte Brontë was standing close to him, her head thrown back, her face white with anger. The first words he heard from the furious little authoress were:

'No, Sir! If *you* had come to our part of the country in Yorkshire, what would you have thought of me if I had introduced you to my father, before a mixed company of strangers, as "Mr Warrington"?' Thackeray replied, 'No, you mean Arthur Pendennis.' 'No, I don't mean Arthur Pendennis!' retorted Miss Brontë. 'I mean Mr Warrington, and Mr Warrington would not have behaved as you behaved to me yesterday.' The spectacle of this little woman, hardly reaching to Thackeray's elbow, but somehow looking stronger and fiercer than himself, and casting her incisive words at his head, resembled the dropping of shells into a fortress.

By this time I had recovered my presence of mind, and hastened to interpose. Thackeray made the necessary and half-humorous apologies and the parting was a friendly one.[2]

Despite the great Turk's lamentable behaviour, Charlotte was spell-bound by his lectures, and attended all of them that she was able to while in London. He came to Gloucester Terrace again the following week for dinner, full of the triumphant success of the lectures, which he estimated would earn him enough to enable him to give his daughters a dowry. He was planning to postpone the next lecture for the sake of the duchesses, who would not be able to attend because they had to accompany the Queen to Ascot. Charlotte thought he was wrong to put it off on their account, and told him so severely: he was far too much enslaved by them. Her castigation was perhaps partly out of pique, for his fascination with the *beau monde* meant that he left the Smiths' dinner party very early to see some of his grand friends before they left for a fancy-dress ball at Buckingham Palace. Where now was the great reformer of the social system? Surely he was joining in with it much too much for his own good. Charlotte was quite dismayed to find her idol to have such feet of clay, and so susceptible to dancing slippers. She wrote to Mrs Gaskell and her father complaining of his behaviour. She thought Thackeray had become spoiled by the 'furor' his lectures had created. In his convivial way he had offered two or three times to introduce the 'little woman of genius', as he called her affectionately, if somewhat carelessly, to some of his great friends, and said he knew many great ladies who would receive Charlotte with open arms if she would go to their houses. Charlotte responded austerely; she told her father on 14 June, 'seriously, I cannot see that this sort of society produces so good an effect on him as to tempt me in the least to try the same experiment, so I remain obscure'. She at least would adhere to seeing society as it was, and rather critically. Thackeray was off to America shortly to give some talks and scandalising Charlotte's notions of the fitness of things by talking of appearing with Barnum's Circus.

It was evident to Thackeray at least that whatever the fascination for each other, they could never be close. Some months later he would forward one of Charlotte's enthusiastic letters to a friend, Mary Holmes, with the following note:

You see by Jane Eyre's letter don't you why we can't be very great friends? We had a correspondence – a little one; and met, very eagerly on her part. But there's a fire raging in that little woman, a rage scorching her heart wh[ich] doesn't suit me. She has had a story and a great grief that has gone badly with her.[3]

It was a perceptive remark, particularly as it was made long before the publication of *Villette*. Nevertheless, her opinion remained very important to him, and his letters are full of scattered references to her ideas.

On Charlotte's second day in London, she was taken to the Great Exhibition at Crystal Palace. News had reached the north of the great palace of glass which Prince Albert had had the architect of the Duke of Devonshire's conservatory, Joseph Paxton, build in the middle of Hyde Park, and Charlotte must have read Thackeray's 'May Day Ode' greeting to 'the blazing arch of lucid glass' leaping like a fountain from the grass. Besides Thackeray's lectures, it was the Exhibition, its ton-lump of coal at the entrance standing alongside a statue of Richard the Lionheart, which was the talk of the London season. Never very interested in factories or manufactures, Charlotte's first reaction to the 'outstanding sign of the mind of the age' was that 'it is not much in my way', marvellous though it was.

She was, however, far more interested on her second visit – altogether she would be taken to the Exhibition five times during her London stay – and although by the time she emerged her only desire was, she said, to fall on to a chair, or better still get into bed, she now found it 'a famous and wonderful sight'. It was almost impossible to describe – its grandeur did not consist in one thing,

> but in the unique assemblage of *all* things. Whatever human industry has created, you find there, from the great compartments filled with railway engines and boilers, with mill-machinery in full work, with splendid carriages of all kinds, with harness of every description – to the glass-covered and velvet-spread stands loaded with the most gorgeous work of the goldsmith and silversmith, and the carefully guarded caskets full of real diamonds and pearls worth hundreds of thousands of pounds.

Charlotte went on to report to her father, gloomily living in her sitting room while his parlour was being repainted, that all other sights seemed to give way to it. To her romantic eye, the multitude filling the great aisles seemed ruled and subdued by some invisible influence: 'Amongst the thirty thousand souls that peopled it the day I was there, not one loud noise was to be heard, not one irregular movement seen – the living tide rolls on quietly, with a deep hum like the sea heard from a distance.' Altogether the Exhibition would attract six million visitors; to her it seemed like a living version of Thackeray's fairground image of the world in *Vanity Fair*. On 13 June she herself saw members of the ex-French royal family there, when the wife of King Louis-Philippe, with her daughter-in-law the Duchess d'Orléans and her two sons, passed down the transept.

Although she scarcely saw George Smith, who was sometimes in his office until three in the morning because of the absence of Mr Taylor and the new company in East India, the visit at first was a success. On Saturday 31 May she saw the exhibition at Somerset House in the Strand. Sunday, she wrote to Ellen, 'was a day to be marked with a white stone – through most of the day I was very happy without being tired or over-excited'. George Smith was plainly at home and being agreeable. In the afternoon she went to hear D'Aubigny, the famous French Protestant preacher, telling Ellen that it was 'half sweet, half sad, and strangely suggestive to hear the French language once more'. Her health was really not too bad, in her opinion. There was an enjoyable visit to Mr Williams in the evening, when a little shop was talked: Mr Taylor, it seemed, had rather a short temper. The brief visit suited Charlotte, for fond and grateful towards Mr Williams as she was, she still found too much of his company and his little foibles a tiny bit irritating.

By 7 June, however, the plans for Miss Brontë tailed off. The visit which had begun so auspiciously had become very quiet, almost as quiet as Haworth. That evening, though, George Smith was to take her to see Rachel, the most famous French actress of her epoch, an expedition to which Charlotte was keenly looking forward. The impression Rachel made upon her was very great; she would see her twice during her visit and far from being shocked by this sinuous, devilish creature, Charlotte was attracted to the point of almost feeling a strange affinity with her: 'The strong magnetism of genius drew my heart out of its wonted orbit; the sunflower turned from the south to a fierce light.'[4] In various descriptions she told friends how much the performance had stirred her, even though she felt it was evil, because it was so genuine. Almost exactly the same words she burst out with to Ellen about her reaction to Rachel would be used in *Villette* in her description of Vashti. To Ellen she wrote on 24 June:

On Saturday I went to hear and see Rachel – a wonderful sight, 'terrible as if the earth had cracked deep at your feet and revealed a glimpse of hell'. I shall never forget it. She made me shudder to the marrow of my bones: in her some fiend has certainly taken up an incarnate home. She is not a woman – she is a snake – she is the —.

In *Villette* Lucy is both horrified and admires the power and passion of Vashti: 'It was a marvellous sight: a mighty revelation. It was a spectacle low, horrible, immoral.' Here was a woman unafraid of convention, powerful, altogether unVictorian, and one who most emphatically did not believe in the philosophy of suffering which Charlotte felt impelled to adhere to:

I have said that she does not *resent* her grief. No; the weakness of that word would make it a lie. To her, what hurts becomes immediately embodied: she looks on it as a thing that can be attacked, worried down, torn in shreds. Scarcely a substance herself, she grapples to conflict with abstractions. Before calamity she is a tigress; she rends her woes, shivers them in convulsed abhorrence. Pain, for her, has no result in good; tears water no harvest of wisdom; on sickness, on death itself, she looks with the eye of a rebel.

Beneath the surface of the neat, mittened spinster, so Quaker-like in appearance, there was concealed a good deal of Vashti.

405

But while Charlotte looked on quite transfixed, George Smith, if her description of Dr John's reaction is based on his, seems to have been quite unmoved by the greatness of the artist they saw that evening. Charlotte would write in *Villette* that Dr John was not 'a serious, impassioned man . . . for what belonged to storm, what was wild and intense, dangerous, sudden and flaming, he had no sympathy, and held with it no communion'. Had she reassessed George Smith's character after that night? Did she, like Lucy Snowe, her pale face and large brown eyes lit up by the excitement of her response, ask what Mr Smith felt, and he 'in a few terse phrases . . . told me his opinion of, and feeling towards, the actress: he judged her as a woman, not an artist: it was a branding judgement'.

Probably Charlotte, herself branded for her artistry, saw which way the land lay. Certainly, judging by indirect indications, 7 June was the fatal night when it was confirmed to her that she could never be more to George Smith than friend and author. From the 9th onwards she began to complain of terrible nervous headaches, migraines that were 'rampant and violent', ending with 'excessive sickness'; to Ellen she wrote on 11 June that she intended to end her visit that weekend. The weather, mimicking her mood, was wet and dark, the air oppressive and close. She told Ellen to disabuse herself of ideas that she was in an enviable position: 'pleasant moments I have, but it is usually a pleasure I am obliged to repel and check, which cannot benefit the future, but only add to its solitude, which is no more to be relied on than the sunshine of one summer's day. I pass many portions of the night in extreme sadness.' She even had so little 'pith' in her as to be incapable of summoning up the energy to describe Rachel.

A depression settled on her spirits. By the 14th she was again making plans to return to Haworth, plans which were not eventually carried out until 27 June, when she was to go to Manchester to stay for a few days with Mrs Gaskell. Although she knew that the Kay Shuttleworths were in London, she had not called on them, writing angrily and irrationally to Mrs Gaskell that 'calling on people who can't possibly want you seems to me a grievous waste of exertion'. Instead she went to hear more preachers: Henry Melvill and Cardinal Wiseman. Charlotte had lost none of her loathing for Rome in the seven years since she had left Brussels. She told her father that Cardinal Wiseman was a big portly man rather like Mr Morgan: 'he has a very large mouth with oily lips, and looks as if he would relish a good dinner with a bottle of wine after it. He came swimming into the room smiling, simpering, and bowing like a fat old lady, and sat down very demure in his chair, and looked the picture of a sleek hypocrite.' Surrounded by a bevy of 'very dark-looking and sinister men', the Cardinal spoke 'in a smooth whining manner, just like a canting Methodist preacher'. She was amazed to find that 'a spirit of the hottest zeal pervaded the whole meeting'. The Protestants better look to their laurels, she told her father, if this was the spirit of the new army.

By 19 June Sir James Kay Shuttleworth had found out his authoress. Not unnaturally he was a little hurt at her curious behaviour, but as usual it was swallowed in his passion for Currer Bell. He could only be stopped with difficulty from carrying her off to his own house by Mrs Smith pleading extra engagements for Miss Brontë; in return, however, for the next week he seized his chance to lionise Charlotte, who scarcely had a minute to herself. Somewhat against her inclinations she had to confess some pleasure in having some of the great and the good lay their tribute at her feet. Her mood lifted, the headache was no longer heard of.

The Marquis of Westminster asked her to a party, and though she resolutely declined it, she thought she could not be criticised for having breakfast with Samuel Rogers, the 87-year-old patriarch poet, and the beautiful Mrs Davenport and Lord Glenelg – 'a most calm, refined and intellectual treat'. The breakfasts, she told her father, were famed throughout Europe for their 'peculiar refinement and taste': there were never more than four people at them – Mr Rogers himself and three other guests. After breakfast Sir David Brewster came to show her round the Great Exhibition; she rather dreaded that being a man 'of the profoundest science' it would be almost impossible to understand his explanations. She found instead that he gave information 'in the kindest and simplest manner'; as she admitted to her father:

An attention that pleased and surprised me more I think than any other was the circumstance of Sir David Brewster, who is one of the first scientific men of his day, coming to take me over the Crystal Palace, and pointing out and explaining the most remarkable curiosities. You will know, dear Papa, that I do not mention those things to boast of them, but merely because I think they will give you pleasure.

Nobody, I find, thinks the worse of me for avoiding publicity and declining to go to large parties.

After Crystal Palace, it was on to Lord Westminster's to look at pictures in his 'splendid gallery'. 'Everybody seems truly courteous and respectful, a mode of behaviour which makes me grateful, as it ought to do,' she told her father. She did not tell him that she had also been to Richmond for the day with the Smiths. George Smith, she told Ellen, had persuaded her to stay on because Wednesday, 25 June,

407

was his only holiday and he wanted to take the whole party from Gloucester Terrace out on an excursion. He and Charlotte, adopting the names of Mr and Miss Fraser, then went to see a phrenologist, Dr Browne at 367 The Strand, who was much in vogue. A strong believer in bumps being revelatory of personality, Charlotte was much excited with the treat. A little of the old happy intimacy between her and Mr Smith seemed to return before she left two days later for her brief visit to Mrs Gaskell.

A letter from George Smith pursued her to Manchester. Much to Charlotte's surprise she found it waiting for her on her return from church, shortly before the Unitarian Gaskells returned from chapel. Perhaps he felt guilty at not seeing so much of her and had observed her quietness, for it was plain that she had not enjoyed the visit as she did the last; perhaps it was mixed with worry that he might lose such a lucrative author. He enquired about her plans for her next book, to which Charlotte responded with a gush of fantasy. She told him that she secretly wished that a sort of 'Chamber in the Wall' might be prepared at Cornhill, fitted up with all suitable appurtenances for when 'the spirit' seized her:

> There the prophet might be received and lodged, subject to a system kind (perhaps) yet firm; roused each morning at six punctually, by contrivance of that virtuous self-acting couch which casts from it its too fondly clinging inmate . . . served with a slight breakfast then with the exception of a crust at one, no further gastronomic interruption till 7 p.m., at which time the greatest and most industrious of modern authors should be summoned by the most spirited and vigilant of modern publishers to a meal, comfortable and comforting – in short, a good dinner . . . of which they should partake together in the finest spirit of geniality and fraternity – part at half-past nine and at that salutary hour withdraw to recreating repose. Grand would be the result of such a system pursued for six months.

The truth was that she was finding it extremely difficult to write her next book.

The short visit to Mrs Gaskell provided a cheering break in the journey home, and was greatly enjoyed by Charlotte. The Gaskells had moved to their lovely and spacious home at 42 Plymouth Grove, on the outskirts of Manchester, a year before. The eighteenth-century house, its front door with Adam moulding surmounted by a portico, stood in its own grounds and was surrounded by open fields. Charlotte described it to George Smith as large, airy and cheerful, 'quite out of the Manchester smoke; a garden surrounds it, and, as in this hot weather the windows were kept open, a whispering of leaves and perfume of flowers always pervaded the rooms'. To the right of the square hall was Mr Gaskell's study and library, and to the left Mrs Gaskell's morning room. Further on was the large drawing room with adjoining conservatory, furnished in elaborate Victorian style and containing a grand piano and elegant furniture by Chippendale and Sheraton; on the walls were drawings by Ruskin. In the middle was the famous dining room with four doors always open so that Mrs Gaskell never felt she was neglecting her household. Upstairs lay seven bedrooms, and attics for the servants.

Charlotte's hostess was as charming as her home; Charlotte's opinion of her became still higher: she was 'kind, clever, animated and unaffected', and William Gaskell was 'a good and kind man too'. Mrs Gaskell not only turned out her novels and organised the busy household, anxious to ensure that she was always accessible to her four daughters, but she was also Manchester's most eminent hostess. Plymouth Grove normally throbbed with the vitality of the city's famous intellectual life, which partly owed its existence to Manchester's small German colony, many of whose members had adopted the Unitarian faith practised by the Gaskells as being nearest to their own ardent Protestantism and tradition of intellectual biblical criticism. The lions of Victorian society came to stay at Plymouth Grove: the Brownings, Matthew Arnold, the Carlyles, Dickens and many others. Furthermore, once a week she gave classes to girls from the worst areas of Manchester, as well as doing social work which involved the Winkworths, Dickens and Angela Burdett Coutts.[5]

For Charlotte's visit, however, the house was deliberately kept quiet, so that Miss Brontë should be relaxed and not bothered by curiosity. Consequently she saw a great deal of her hostess and her family, and she became quite unashamedly infatuated with the children, particularly Julia, the youngest, then aged seven. She described to Mrs Smith Mrs Gaskell's four little girls: 'all more or less pretty and intelligent – these scattered through the rooms of a somewhat spacious house seem to fill it with liveliness and gaiety'. Charlotte would later tell Mrs Gaskell that Julia 'surreptitiously possessed herself of a minute fraction of my heart which has been missing ever since I saw her'; she reminded Charlotte very much of Mrs Gaskell. Mrs Gaskell herself would report the strong and mutual attraction which existed between Miss Brontë and her youngest daughter:

The child would steal her little hand into Miss Brontë's scarcely larger one, and each took pleasure in this apparently unobserved caress. Yet once when I told Julia to take and show her the way to some room in the house, Miss Brontë shrunk back: 'Do not *bid* her

409

do anything for me,' she said; 'it has been so sweet hitherto to have her rendering her little kindnesses spontaneously.'[6]

Several of Charlotte's letters would enquire after 'the small sprite Julia', whose antics Mrs Gaskell took as much delight in relating as her correspondent took in hearing. This 'dear but dangerous little person' was almost certainly the inspiration for the character of Paulina Home in *Villette*, the germ for which was slowly building in Charlotte Brontë's mind.

Mrs Gaskell's daughters almost matched their mother for quality. Her affection for them is obvious from her letters. Her second daughter, the fourteen-year-old Meta was very musical[7] and also gifted with her pencil, both in drawing, and in writing. Mrs Gaskell sent Charlotte some of her letters home from school the next year and Charlotte responded delightedly:

> . . . that little maiden – Meta – has inherited Mamma's gift. What is her age? It cannot be more than fourteen, and with a few strokes she can put on paper a lively little sketch of character. I read her letters with pleasure – they seem to me remarkable: I might well use the word 'companion' in speaking of her; there is something specially conversible, *companionable*, interesting in these letters.[8]

Rather fittingly it would be the same Meta who would be so helpful to her mother in preparing *The Life of Charlotte Brontë*, copying out many of the letters that would be lent to Mrs Gaskell by Ellen Nussey.

Florence, the third daughter, Mrs Gaskell said frankly, 'has no talents under the sun; and is very nervous and anxious; she will require so much strength to hold her up through life; everything is a terror to her. . . . Julia is witty, and wild and clever and droll, the pet of the house; and I often admire Florence's utter absence of jealousy, and pride in Julia's doings and sayings.' Charlotte, unused to children and always made nervous by them, found herself unexpectedly enchanted. A year later she would write to Mrs Gaskell that whenever she saw Florence and Julia again she would feel like

> a fond but bashful suitor, who views at a distance the fair personage to whom, in his clownish awe, he dare not risk a near approach. Such is the clearest idea of my feelings towards children I like, but to whom I am a stranger. And to what children am I not a stranger? They seem to me little wonders; their talk, their ways are all matter of half-admiring, half-puzzled, speculation.

This was very evident in her enchanting and delicate portrait of the

410

astonishing miniature grown-up Paulina, who is so self-possessed, yet suffers acute grief in her tiny but marvellously dignified person.

Mrs Gaskell, with her usual sensitivity, had seen how lonely Miss Brontë was, how much she missed the gentle pleasures of family life, and she endeavoured during her guest's visit to replace a little of that loss with her own sunny domesticity. In her company, Charlotte was able to be almost as relaxed as she was with Ellen. It seems highly likely that one of the subjects they would have discussed was the conflict for women between home duties and the individual life, something which concerned both of them so nearly. In many letters to her friends Mrs Gaskell stresses her gratitude that she became a wife and mother: 'I am so happy in the performance of those clear and defined duties', for she saw life without those things as difficult. Yet how were these duties to be reconciled with an independent life of work? It was her belief that women must give up living an artist's life, if home duties are to be paramount, which to some extent she felt that they should be, judging by the following passage on the subject from *The Life of Charlotte Brontë*: 'no other can take up the quiet regular duties of the daughter, the wife or the mother, as well as she whom God has appointed to fill that particular place: a woman's principal work in life is hardly left to her own choice; nor can she drop the domestic charges devolving on her as an individual, for the exercise of the most splendid talents that were ever bestowed.' It was different with men, whose homes were so small a part of their lives. On the other hand, she was sure that it was healthy for women to have

... the refuge of the hidden world of Art to shelter themselves in when too much pressed upon by daily small Lilliputian arrows of peddling cares; it keeps them from being morbid as you say ... and soothes them with its peace. I have felt this in writing, I see others feel it in music, you in painting, so assuredly a blending of the two is desirable (Home duties and the development of the Individual I mean), which you will say it takes no Solomon to tell you. The difficulty is where and when to make one set of duties subserve and give place to the other.

And the peculiar difficulty in Victorian England was to convince the masculine world that it was possible to combine the two.

Mrs Gaskell's own strong religious beliefs made her naturally sympathetic to Miss Brontë's strongly Evangelical character, and now that she was convinced that her new friend was truly religious, Charlotte Brontë's desire to write what she considered to be 'the truth' was admirable. It was part of the dilemma of whether women should fulfil themselves: although part of the danger of cultivating the

411

individual life was thinking of the self only, and exertions on behalf of the self only were unholy, she nevertheless believed that:

> we all have some appointed work to do, whh [sic] no one else can do so well; wh. is *our* work, what *we* have to do in advancing the Kingdom of God; and that first we must find out what we are sent into the world to do, and define it and make it clear to ourselves, (*that's* the hard part) and then forget ourselves in our work, and our work in the End we ought to strive to bring about.[9]

Her own work alternated between writing and teaching children from the slums of Manchester, but she admitted rather sweetly that discovery of one's exact work in the world is the puzzle. 'I long (weakly) for the old times where right and wrong did not seem such complicated matters; and I am sometimes coward enough to wish that we were back in the darkness where obedience was the only seen duty of women. Only even then I don't believe William would ever have *commanded me*.'[10]

Mrs Gaskell's remarkable personal gifts enabled her to combine a happy marriage and home life with a kind of career. So relaxing was the atmosphere she created at Plymouth Grove that after her visit there, even Haworth did not seem so depressing to Charlotte. Writing her thank-you letter to Mrs Smith, Charlotte said that although it was still a little gloomy, the weather was bright and sunny, and with the window open she could hear birds singing on the thorn trees in the garden. Her father and Martha and Tabby all thought that her looks were much improved.

A second letter rapidly followed to George Smith, who, hot on the heels of his writing to Charlotte in Manchester, had sent her the phrenologist Dr Browne's estimation of the character of 'Mr Fraser'. She returned it to him but told him with her sincerity that usually forgot decorum that she had taken a copy of it, 'which (DV) I mean to keep always. I wanted a portrait and have now got me one very much to my mind.' It was a sort of 'miracle', she wrote ecstatically: 'Like – LIKE – LIKE as the very life itself. . . . I am glad I have got it. I wanted it.' In return, she sent him Dr Browne's estimation of 'the Lady's' character. She was said to be endowed with an exalted sense of the beautiful and ideal, to have a nervous temperament, and excellent understanding. Her attachments were 'strong and enduring' – indeed, this was 'a leading element of her character'.

That summer and autumn Charlotte continued her correspondence with George Smith. To him her letters were always sprightly, allowing little or no trace of the great depression of spirits that she had felt during the past year, and still continued to suffer from, to surface. She kept to her appointed elder sister role with him, though much of the history of her feeling for him can be read in the pages of *Villette*, which she was now very slowly beginning to write. Having been expelled from school at the age of fourteen,[11] he had doubts about his intellect and education, however much he dined with Thackeray, which she was swift to comfort him about: if other people over-whelmed him with acquired knowledge such as he had not had the opportunity, perhaps not the application, to gain, he should derive support from the thought that if books had never been written some of these minds would themselves have remained blank pages.

He should not, she told him, over-task himself with reading dry heavy books, or deny himself holidays. She herself found that setting herself to study a book for only an hour a day – in his case she kindly suggested half an hour – would make it finish sooner than one thought.

She acted as an intermediary between Harriet Martineau and Smith, Elder, luring the great woman away from her usual publishers, and acted as a literary adviser on the novel (*Oliver Weld*) when it came in, though it was in fact never published. Safe in such a role, as elder sister/confidante and author, she was able to be quite frank about his importance to her: in July she told him that before she received his last letter she had made up her mind to tell him that she would expect no letter for three months to come, 'intending afterwards to extend this abstinence to six months, for I am jealous of becoming dependent on this indulgence: you doubtless cannot see why because you do not live my life'. There was a slightly lecturing side to her relations with him, which she herself noticed on occasion and slightly regretted: 'I may venture to confess that after I had written that PS and sent the letter off, some severe qualms came over me as to whether I had not taken a small liberty.'[12]

Nevertheless the correspondence did not flag. To her delight, he wrote back quite lengthy letters, in one detailing a fire that had broken out at the Guildhall. She wrote to him on 9 August, using their 'brother and sister' names assumed for the phrenologist: 'The incident at the Guild Performance amused me; it was one of those occasions which, while startling people out of their customary smooth bearing, elicit genuine touches of character. Mr Fraser and the panic-struck young lady both revealed themselves according to their different natures. It is easy to realize the scene.' So easy that it was incorporated into the incident when Lucy Snowe and Graham Bretton go to see Vashti, just as Charlotte and George Smith had indeed gone to see Rachel, but without the fire breaking out.

In September, in response to his suggestion that she should write her book for publication in serial form, she told him:

Can I help wishing you well when I owe you directly or indirectly most of the good moments I now enjoy? Or can I avoid feeling grieved – mortified – when the chance of aiding to give effect to my own wishes offers itself and, for want of strength, vitality, animal spirits, I know not what in me, passes by unimproved.

But the very idea of writing in serial form! It alarmed her terribly. She had neither the requisite experience of Thackeray nor the animal spirits of Dickens, she said, to do so. But, she went on,

. . . . though Currer Bell cannot do this you are still to think him your friend, and you are still to be *his* friend. You are to keep a fraction of yourself – if it be only the end of your little finger – for *him*, and that fraction he will neither let gentleman or lady, author or artist . . . take possession of, or so much as meddle with. He reduces his claim to a minute point, and that point he monopolizes.

Invitations to London continued to flow from the gallant George Smith, but she refused them all. Finally, she replied in a way which could not have made her feelings clearer: 'There is the pain of that last bidding good-bye, that hopeless shaking hands, yet undulled and unforgotten. I don't like it. I could not bear its frequent repetition.' And elder sister or no, she gave him to understand that during her last time in London she had been harassed by frequent headaches.

To the rest of her correspondents, Mrs Gaskell, Ellen Nussey and Mr Williams – though the latter had been mainly superseded by George Smith as her chief Smith, Elder correspondent – she gave a fuller picture of herself. Much of the terrible painful pessimism that so permeates the pages of *Villette* hung over her letters that autumn. To Mrs Gaskell she said simply on 20 September, repeating what she said to Ellen: 'You charge me to write about myself. What can I say on that precious topic? My health is pretty good. My spirits are not always alike. Nothing happens to me. I hope and expect little in this world, and am thankful that I do not despond and suffer more.' To Ellen's account of the now married Amelia Taylor's happy life at Hunsworth, she wrote, 'It somewhat cheers me to know that such happiness does exist on earth.' It was her constant refrain.

She indicated what she had been going through in a letter to Mrs Gaskell of 6 November:

I feel greatly better at present than I did three weeks ago. For a month or six weeks about the equinox (autumnal or vernal) is a period of the year which, I have noticed, strangely tries me. Sometimes the strain falls on the mental, sometimes on the physical

414

part of me; I am ill with neuralgic headache, or I am ground to the dust with deep dejection of spirits (not, however, such dejection but I can keep to myself). That weary time has, I think and trust, got over for this year. It was the anniversary of my poor brother's death, and of my sister's failing health: I need say no more.

Mrs Gaskell had invited her to stay, to which Charlotte wrote that if anyone could tempt her away from home, her friend would, but at the moment she could not leave. Mrs Gaskell's kind letters, she said, had had a truly healing effect, but as to running away from home every time she had a battle of this sort to fight, it would not do. Besides, the 'weird' would follow; she could not shake it off. And, true daughter of her father, she rallied her martial spirit, that spirit which would emerge against the fatalism battling for possession of Lucy Snowe: life was a war, and though it was 'a war, it seemed my destiny to conduct it single-handed'. She had declined other invitations that autumn, and she must decline to go to Mrs Gaskell.

She had, however, been visited by Miss Wooler at the beginning of October. After advising her former pupil to end her friendship with that avowed atheist Miss Martineau, and receiving another sharp letter from Miss Brontë, Miss Wooler appears to have decided to put away her advice. There was a reconciliation, and after her stay at the parsonage Charlotte thought that she really was like good wine: she got better with age. Surprisingly something about her took Mr Brontë's fancy and he most unexpectedly asked her to stay again. Another visitor to the parsonage that month was one of the Branwells from Cornwall; meanwhile, the health of the servants as well as of her father gave her cause for anxiety. She worried about giving Martha too much to do, and about Tabby's feeble constitution; on the other hand, she could not do much herself.

But amidst an autumn during which she frankly admitted to Mrs Gaskell that she sometimes wished she might die came a tiny sliver of hope, for from India came two letters from Mr Taylor. She was extremely surprised by this and could not decide what to do about the matter; prudence, her own low opinion of her marital prospects, suggested that despite her earlier reservations further investigation of his character might perhaps be sensible, though the errors of taste in the letters continued to make her shudder. She got up her courage, she told Ellen on 19 November, to write to Mr Williams for his frank and impartial judgement of Mr Taylor's character and disposition, 'owning that I was very much in the dark on these points and did not like to continue correspondence without further information'. His complimentary answer, together with Mr Taylor's letter, she enclosed for Ellen's perusal and interest, and told her that she had replied to Mr

Taylor 'in a calm civil manner'.

Calm and civil it certainly was, far too calm and civil to encourage any suitor, particularly one who had been refused so unquestionably a few months before; in fact it verged on coldness. She expressed herself sorry that the society in Bombay should be so deficient in intellectual interest; no doubt there would be moments when he would look back 'to London and Scotland and the friends you have left there', she wrote, carefully avoiding Yorkshire, but business must have its interest, as must the new country and new scenes, she said impersonally. 'You will not expect me to write a letter that shall form a parallel with your own either in quantity or quality; what I write must be brief, and what I communicate must be commonplace and of trivial interest.' She briskly gave him a short account of her time in London. Although she said her father sent his very kind remembrances, and had been interested in hearing portions of the letter that she had read out to him, only a clairvoyant would have seen that as encouragement, for the letter ended in the most non-committal fashion, though perhaps reading between the lines there was a little hurt:

> I had myself ceased to expect a letter from you. On taking leave at Haworth you said something about writing from India, but I doubted at the time whether it was not one of those forms of speech which politeness dictates; and as time passed, and I did not hear from you, I became confirmed in this view of the subject. With every good wish for your welfare.
> I am, yours sincerely, C. Brontë.

There was nothing in this to make the most imaginative person's heart beat a little faster. And yet, Charlotte told Ellen that she expected to hear from Mr Taylor some time in March, and looked forward to doing so – not a little, it would transpire.

In contrast, to George Smith – now to her alarm proposing to advertise her new novel – she continued in the brilliant, intimate, analytical vein that was the hallmark of her letters to him. Whether she was ill or well, and she was mostly ill, she wrote regularly, sometimes once a week, to him. There was in his nature, she told him on 7 November, 'an undercurrent of quiet raillery, an inaudible laugh to yourself, a not unkindly but somewhat subtle playing on your correspondent or companion for the time being – in short, a sly touch of a Mephistopheles with the fiend extracted.' Poor Charlotte. Nothing seems less like Mephistopheles than the bonhomous George Smith. In the intoxicated eyes of a provincial Miss though, he was suave and debonair and full of dazzling metropolitan dash.

Meanwhile, she told him, she wrote her novel when she could, waiting Quaker-like for the spirit to come to her. The spirit had so far taken her back to Brussels, now viewed in a tender, affectionate light as the little town – Villette. M. Heger was now seen amusedly, glimpsed at the beginning of the book as M. Paul Emanuel – just as George Smith himself was glimpsed – in the Park Royal, leading her heroine to the Pensionnat. The heroine who despite the mysterious fate that has left her without any friends or relations, entirely alone, and who is as unobtrusive as a shadow, 'still felt life at life's sources', just as her creator did. She still had hopes for happiness, just as her creator had. Hope in the shape of George Smith, of Dr John.

But, she told George Smith at the end of November, she was not very pleased by the novel's progress. There were 'blank intervals' when she could not write. Although he had again asked her to come to stay in London before Christmas, she felt she must stay at home to finish the book. Like Lucy Snowe, in catalepsy and a dead trance, Charlotte studiously held the quick of her nature. As she wrote in *Villette*:

> Even to look forward was not to hope. The dumb figure spoke no comfort, offered no promise, gave no inducement to bear present evil in reliance on future good. A sorrowful indifference to existence often pressed on me – a despairing resignation to reach betimes the end of all things earthly. Alas! When I had a full leisure to look on life as life must be looked on by such as me, I found it but a hopeless desert.

The religious reader, she wrote, would preach a long sermon about her attitude. To that, this woman who had so bravely tried the panacea of religion in the face of unimaginable disaster wrote defiantly: 'I accept the sermon, frown, sneer and laugh; perhaps you are all right: and perhaps, circumstanced like me, you would have been, like me, wrong.' And, as she would later tell Mrs Gaskell, she stoically tried to welcome her cruel fate, and made Lucy embrace hers: fate was her 'permanent foe, never to be conciliated': 'I concluded it to be a part of this great plan that some must deeply suffer while they live, and I thrilled in the certainty that of this number I was one.'

In the small parsonage so far from London she meditated on the difference between her life and that of George Smith's mother, transforming her into Lucy Snowe's godmother Louisa Bretton. She felt that the difference between her and Mrs Smith might be figured

> ... by that between the stately ship cruising safe on smooth seas, with its full complement of crew, a captain gay and brave, and venturous and provident; and the life boat, which most days of the

year lies dry and solitary in an old, dark boathouse, only putting to sea when the billows run high in rough weather, when cloud encounters water, when danger and death divide between them the rule of the great deep.

It was indeed the Slough of Despond she was going through.

All through the severe winter, into the New Year of 1852, Charlotte in her deliberately self-imposed isolation was acutely depressed and ill. At the beginning of December Emily's dog Keeper died; after being ill all night, he went gently to sleep in the morning, and they buried the faithful old animal in the garden. She was glad that he had met a natural fate – others had hinted that he ought to be put down but neither her father nor she had liked to think of doing so – but she found that there was something very sad in losing the old dog, last living memento of his mistress, and Anne's dog Flossy, missing her lifelong companion, was dull and listless too.

As December advanced, the illness that Charlotte had felt slowly creeping up on her began to affect her severely. As she told Mr Williams on 1 January, she was never able all winter 'to stoop over a desk without bringing on pain and oppression in the chest'; she was finding it hard to sleep at nights. Her deepest fear was that she was suffering from the consumption that killed her sisters, but her doctor, Mr Ruddock, repeatedly stressed that there was no organic disease, only a highly sensitive and irritable condition of the liver, and recommended her to take more of the prescribed medicine. Despite her illness, she continued to correspond with George Smith over his publication of Harriet Martineau's novel.

She recognised how much she longed for company but had not allowed herself to send for Ellen, feeling it was selfish. By 17 December, however, convinced that a little cheerful society would do more good than gallons of medicine, she wrote asking Ellen to stay. And with Ellen in the house, she would later tell Mrs Gaskell, she could at last sleep calmly and deeply. In an attempt to cheer up the parsonage in these dreary winter months, she had ordered some crimson curtains to be made for the dining-room-cum-sitting-room where she sat all day, paid for out of her earnings. But like everything else that winter they did not please her: the colour was wrong, they had been poorly dyed at the local factory in Keighley and looked shoddy. It was the first time in her life that there had been curtains at the window.

Her illness seems to have been largely psychosomatic. While Ellen was there in late December, Charlotte recovered remarkably, but she grew worse again immediately on her departure. Her headache returned, which the doctor said was due to inertness in the liver, and he gave her some pills containing mercury. She took them every day, hoping to benefit, but instead rapidly grew worse. Before the week was over she was unable to swallow any nourishment except a few teaspoonfuls of liquid. Her mouth became sore, her teeth loose, her tongue swelled, raw and ulcerated, while water welled continually into her mouth. When Dr Ruddock found her in this state he was absolutely amazed and perhaps disbelieving of the sensitivity of her constitution, since the amount of mercury in the dose was not enough to salivate a child. But with her usual refusal to be a burden to Martha or her father, Charlotte insisted on staying out of bed: 'It was enough to burden myself – it would have been misery to me to have annoyed another.'

Finally, near the end of January, Ellen persuaded her to come to Brookroyd for a change and a rest. To Charlotte's chagrin, while she was absent from home, George Smith, grown restive about the manuscript, made the long journey over to Haworth to see his authoress. She invited him to call in at Brookroyd, but he declined. To Mrs Smith, who had again invited her to London, she wrote poignantly on 29 January: 'The solitude of my life I had certainly felt very keenly this winter – but every one has his own burden to bear – and where there is no available remedy, it is right to be patient and trust that Providence will in His own time lighten the load.' It was the same message as in *Villette*. In recompense for the utter lack of activity, in memory Charlotte saw action. She returned to the bustle of the school in Brussels and recreated it in minutest detail, but overlaid by the heightened atmosphere of her pain. It is seen through the eyes of the fated Lucy Snowe. She still has some fire buried in her, remnants of Jane Eyre's rebelliousness, but it is now banked down beneath misery and hopelessness and an ominously grim religion. As an astute reviewer would write, 'Her talk is of duty – her predilections lie with passion.'

To Mrs Gaskell Charlotte wrote that if she had the prospect of living this time over again, 'My prayer must necessarily be "Let this cup pass from me".' She felt that if good weather were restored, she would be better, but the long storms of February and the 'incessantly howling winds depress the nervous system much'. She was unable to write. March brought the upsetting news from New Zealand that Mary Taylor's cousin and companion Ellen had died out there of consumption. Mary wrote to Charlotte that she feared now in her dreary solitude she would become 'a stern, harsh, selfish woman'. Charlotte told Ellen how her fear struck home – 'again and again I have felt it for myself – and what is *my* position to Mary's?' She would, she continued to Ellen, have sent energetic wishes that Mary should return to England, 'if reason would permit me to believe that prosperity and happiness would there await her – but I see no such

419

prospect. . . . May God help her as God only can help!' It was a recourse she now made frequently.

March also brought no letters from India. She confessed to Ellen that any uneasiness she felt was 'not that of confirmed and fixed regard, but that anxiety which is inseparable from a state of absolute uncertainty about a somewhat momentous matter'. The lack of response from Mr Taylor bred a new interest in him. She now became painfully interested in what appeared to be her last hope of marriage; although she was still not sure that 'any other termination would be better than lasting estrangement and unbroken silence – yet a good deal of pain has been and must be gone through in that case.' The month wore on and no news came; she could not think of making enquiries at Cornhill. India remained in the back of her mind to resurface in M. Paul Emanuel's destination, the 'Indian isle'. Meanwhile her physical health reflected her mental life. She drank hop tea for her liver, but headaches still afflicted her; she had a swollen face and a tick in the cheekbone. Her doctor decided to experiment with the benefits of quinine on her constitution and then, just as suddenly, took her off it, perhaps seeing that it was an illness as much of the mind as of the body.

She would not be lured to Sussex by Ellen; Dr Ruddock had told her that southern warmth would not do her constitution any good, the bracing north would be better, and she must follow his instructions to the letter. But in any case she must try to write. Her publishers were now besieging her with enquiries as to when the book would be finished, and yet it was still impossible for her to make progress. Ellen tried to rouse her from the lethargy which possessed her: she suggested that she 'chat' on paper. Charlotte wearily replied, 'How can I? – Where are my materials – Where is my life fertile in subjects of chat? What callers do I see, what visits do I pay?' From the depths of her depression she was amused by Ellen's interest in politics – 'Don't expect to rouse me – to me all ministries and all oppositions seem to be pretty much alike,' wrote the former little girl who had been such an ardent politician. She continued to follow the government ministries, but now with the cynicism born of experience and depression: 'Disraeli was factious as Leader of the Opposition; Lord J. Russell is going to be factious now that he has stepped into DI's shoes. Confound them all. Lord Derby's "christian tone and spirit" is worth 3 halfpence.' The strain of disciplining herself shows in the writing of *Villette*, as Lucy Snowe herself struggles with personified abstractions and fears in a heightened, often surreal atmosphere, and in her letters correspondingly Charlotte would write of 'Disappointment' as if she were a real being.

Meanwhile Mary Taylor wrote to Charlotte, bringing her news of

420

life in New Zealand. She was forcing herself to rally under her own affliction and, reading in the newspaper Charlotte's name amongst the 'notables' who attended Thackeray's lecture and hearing of her new life, which seemed like a 'new country' to her, one which she could not even picture, she could not understand why her friend was so full of gloom: 'It is really melancholy,' she wrote briskly, 'that now in the prime of life, in the flush of your hard-earned prosperity, you can't be well! Did not Miss Martineau improve you? If she did, why not try her and her plan again? But I suppose if you had hope and energy to try,' she said, remembering her friend's lack of them, 'you would be well.'

For herself she began to wonder if Charlotte still looked as she used to; she and Ellen were beginning to seem very far off, 'O for one hour's talk,' she exclaimed. In the meantime, when not working in her shop, and now that she no longer had Ellen to nurse, she had written about a volume and a half of her novel. It was full of 'music, poverty, disputing, politics, and original views of life', she said. The trouble was that she could not bring 'the lover' into it, nor tell what he would do when he came. Indeed, she said airily, 'of the men generally, I can never tell what they do next'; she knew about women, certainly, and their lives. New Zealand had not turned out to be quite the land of milk and honey she had hoped for, but at least with her occupations, she was not melancholy.

At last, at the end of May, in order to get the bracing change of scene that her doctor thought she required, Charlotte decided to go north-east to Filey, staying in the same lodgings, although not in the same rooms, where she and Ellen had stayed after Anne's death. Ellen would certainly have disapproved of the almost masochistic revisiting of the scene of Anne's death, which certainly was not guaranteed to make her health better. It was a somewhat melancholy pilgrimage with a partly practical purpose: Charlotte had been worried for some time about the letters on the headstone of Anne's grave being properly cut and when she went to Scarborough to visit the grave, she found that it had been incorrectly lettered, and needed to be redone.

At first she felt tremendously desolate and melancholy, almost prostrate. She was troubled with the same pain in the side that had made its appearance last winter, and the same headaches – also probably of psychosomatic origin. But gradually, under the influence of the sun and the sea and long long walks, her spirits and physique began to improve. To Ellen she said she believed that she could stay there two months and get something like her 'social cheerfulness' back, though of course this could not be. She swam once from 'a peculiar bathing contraption', and felt that it had done her good, although she had been told that it was much too early in the season. She had walked for hours by the sea, writing to her father that it was 'very grand'. She watched an unusually high tide, and stood for about an hour on the cliffs lost in the rushing on of 'great tawny turbid waves, that made the whole shore white with foam and filled the air with a sound hollower and deeper than thunder'. There were so few visitors at Filey that she and a few fishing boats often had the whole expanse of seashore and cliff to themselves. When the tide was out the sands were wide, long and smooth, and very pleasant to walk on. She had seen a great dog rush into the sea 'and swim and bear up against the waves like a seal. I wonder what Flossy would say to that.'

It was in her letter to her father that June that there first appears a sign of interest in her father's curate. She usually confined herself to sending Mr Nicholls her good wishes, but now she wrote that she had been to a church on Sunday that she would like Mr Nicholls to see. It was a tiny church, not more than three times the length and breadth of their passage at home – the walls green with mould, and at one end there was a little gallery for the singers; when the singers stood up to perform, they all turned *their* backs on the congregation, and the congregation turned *their* backs on the pulpit and parson. 'The effect of this manoeuvre was so ludicrous, I could hardly help laughing; had Mr Nicholls been there he certainly would have laughed out loud.' And the letter closes with a request for her father to give 'my kind regards, dear Papa, to Mr Nicholls, Tabby and Martha'.

She returned home at the end of June, looking, she thought, as sunburnt and weather-beaten as a fisherman or bathing woman from being out in the open air. She had obeyed the anxious Ellen's instructions to walk three or four hours a day to lift that congestion of the liver, even though one result had been being frightened by two cows on the way to Filey Bridge, and she felt considerably better physically, even if not with renewed spirits to write.

Some time during the first six months of 1852 Charlotte evidently finally came to the conclusion that George Smith was beyond her reach. By July the correspondence, which on his part seems to have been partly actuated by desire to get the manuscript from his best-selling author as soon as possible, had largely lapsed. Nothing came from India, and nothing came from Cornhill. Charlotte told Ellen bitterly, 'We must not rely upon our fellow-creatures, only on ourselves, and on Him who is above both us and them', and she waited with increasing desperation for the spirit to come to help her write. To Laetitia Wheelwright she said that there were 'some long stormy days and nights when I felt such a craving for support and companionship as I cannot express'. She lay awake sleepless, night after night; 'weak and unable to occupy myself, I sat in my chair day after day, the saddest memories my only company'. Again and again she said she trusted in God – that had there been no world beyond this one, she would despair. Somehow, suddenly the creative urge reappeared and she turned herself to work. The main part of *Villette* was written between August and October. Her mood was very low: 'submission, courage, exertion when practicable, these seem to be the weapons with which we must fight life's long battle'. It summed up Lucy Snowe's philosophy, and Charlotte's own.

In mid-August to her great alarm her father suddenly had an apoplectic fit. It began with acute inflammation of the eye, but when Dr Ruddock was sent for, he said that Mr Brontë's pulse was up to 150 a minute and that there was strong pressure of blood on the brain. In short, he was having a stroke. Mr Brontë did not know his condition, as Charlotte thought that the shock of knowing he had been in danger of apoplexy might kill him. He was kept very quiet, and there was partial paralysis for a couple of days. Then to everybody's relief, his sight returned. It was the threat of losing this which had chiefly alarmed him.

Charlotte continued to write on, utterly exhausted though she was. The future was sometimes appalling to her, a 'pale blank', 'a very weary burden', was how she described it to Ellen on 25 August. It was not that she was a *single* woman and likely to remain a single woman, but because she was a *lonely* woman and likely to remain *lonely*. She remembered the pleasure that the Smiths' friendship had brought to her. Lucy Snowe was made to relive the agony when she realised that George Smith's letters, his friendship, would lead no further than that. In her imagination M. Heger, M. Paul was there, watching her efforts. He saw what George Smith, John Bretton could never see – the passion and feeling that lurked beneath the grey being whom Graham Bretton sees only as 'inoffensive as a shadow'; stepping up to Lucy, to Charlotte, as she basks in the friendship of the Brettons, he whispers that he 'had his eye on me: *he* at least would discharge the duty of a friend. . . . My proceedings seemed at present very unsettled.' All this life with Counts and Countesses.[13]

Eventually, out of weariness and solitude, Charlotte yielded to the temptation of seeing Ellen, of enjoying the calm sleep she brought, just for a week, and then 'disgusted with myself and my delays' she despatched her and ploughed on with the task. On 30 October she finally sent George Smith the first two volumes of *Villette*; she told him that he must notify her honestly what he thought of the book. She had set him an impossible task. He was not so insensitive as to miss the resemblance between his mother and himself. As he would later say – and it was all he said – many of his mother's and his expressions were used *verbatim*. Charlotte told him how she longed to hear some opinion of the novel beside her own, and how she had sometimes despaired because there was no one to read a line to, or ask counsel of: '*Jane Eyre* was not written under such circumstances, nor were two-thirds of *Shirley*.' She had become so miserable about *Villette* that she could scarcely bear any allusion to it and she now proposed it should be published anonymously, if it would not harm its chances of material success, interfere with booksellers' orders, etc. She did not want to press the point, but 'if no such detriment is contingent I should be much thankful for the sheltering shadow of an incognito. I seem to dread the advertisements – the large-lettered "Currer Bell's New Novel" or "New Work by the author of *Jane Eyre*".'

He would see, she said a little enigmatically, that *Villette* touched on no matter of public interest – 'I cannot write books handling the topics of the day; it is of no use trying. Nor can I write a book for its moral. Nor can I take up a philanthropic scheme, though I honour philanthropy; and voluntarily and sincerely veil my face before such a mighty subject as that handled in Mrs Beecher Stowe's work, *Uncle Tom's Cabin*.' To write that sort of book, the subject it addressed would not only have to be studied very carefully, but its evils would have to be genuinely felt.

She had paused at a crucial moment in the novel. George Smith wrote back with a flicker of that Mephistophelean aspect of his nature, enquiring as to why Lucy Snowe should not marry Dr John; what did she intend to happen in the third volume? Rather provocatively she wrote back:

> Most of the third volume is given to the development of the 'crabbed Professor's' character. Lucy must not marry Dr John; he is far too youthful, handsome, bright-spirited, and sweet-tempered; he is a 'curled darling' of Nature and of Fortune, and must draw a prize in life's lottery. His wife must be young, rich, pretty; he must be made very happy indeed. If Lucy marries anybody it must be the Professor, a man in whom there is much to forgive, much to 'put up with'.

But, she told him, 'I am not leniently disposed towards Miss *Frost*; from the beginning I never meant to appoint her lines in pleasant places.'

George Smith had a couple of criticisms of the internal logic of the book, which coincided with Charlotte's own worries about it – the discrepancy between Graham's boyhood and manhood – and his very sudden change of heart towards Miss Fanshawe. 'You must remember, though,' Charlotte told him, 'that in secret he had for some time appreciated that young lady at a somewhat depressed standard – held her a *little* lower than the angels.' Still she admitted that the reader ought to have been made to feel better prepared for this change of mood. But she submitted to her name appearing on the jacket, and the advertisements in large letters, although, she had to confess, with an ostrich-like longing for concealment.

To Mr Williams three days later she gave a little more idea of her views of *Villette*. Wearily when he told her that he would have preferred more of a climax, which he hoped might appear in the third volume, she agreed that she doubted whether the regular novel-reader would consider 'the "agony piled sufficiently high" (as the Americans say) or the colours dashed on to the canvas with the proper amount of daring.' Somewhat ironically she went on that unless she was mistaken, the emotion in the novel

> . . . will be found to be kept throughout in tolerable subjection. As to the name of the heroine, I can hardly express what subtlety of thought made me decide upon giving her a cold name; but at first I called her 'Lucy Snowe' (spelt with an 'e'), which Snowe I afterwards changed to 'Frost'. Subsequently I rather regretted the change, and wished it 'Snowe' again. A *cold* name she must have; partly, perhaps, on the '*lucus a non lucendo*' principle – partly on that of the 'fitness of things', for she has about her an external coldness.

If it was not too late she would like the name altered back to Snowe, as it now appears.

Mr Williams objected that Miss Snowe would be thought morbid and weak, unless the history of her life be given more fully. Charlotte replied that she thought that she *was* both morbid and weak at times; 'her character sets up no pretensions to unmixed strength, and anybody living her life would necessarily become morbid'. In a sense Lucy Snowe was a paradigm for all those single women who lived alone like her, like Ellen, like Mary, like Miss Wooler.

As she wrote to Mr Williams: 'It was no impetus of healthy feeling which urged her [Lucy Snowe] to the confessional, for instance; it was the semi-delirium of solitary grief and sickness.' If, however, the book did not explain all this, she added, there must be a great fault somewhere. She might explain a few other points, but it would be rather like drawing a picture and then writing underneath the name of the object intended to be represented.

One of her most virulent critics, Anne Mozley, would write angrily in a review, that the moral purpose of the book seemed to be to demand for a certain class of minds a degree of sympathy not hitherto accorded to them. Charlotte Brontë would not stop herself reacting against the Victorian ideal of women now articulated everywhere around her. She was not to be restrained by the straitjacket of sex roles being put round women. Her extraordinary, too-feeling nature could not but express the passion that she felt, passion made more intense by its restriction, by her practical historical circumstances, by her lonely life.

By 20 November she had finished *Villette* and sent it off to George Smith. She did not know whether it was good or bad, she told Ellen; her verdict was that it would not be considered pretentious, nor was it of a character to excite hostility. Her father, to whom she had read some passages, was partly responsible for its enigmatic finale. He could not bear a sad ending, and in the first version M. Paul had died in the shipwreck. Charlotte faithfully made the conclusion apparently ambivalent, although it must be obvious to most readers that M. Paul dies in the Indian Ocean, the way Mr Taylor was now dead to her.

But no answer came from London, only a receipt without a line of acknowledgement. Charlotte nervously anticipated the worst, and had made up her mind to take the train to London to see what was the matter, when the desired letter suddenly arrived on Sunday. In his scarcely legible handwriting Mr Smith complained about the transfer of interest in the third volume from one set of characters to a new, i.e. from Graham Bretton to M. Paul Emanuel. She had asked him teasingly what he thought about the female character, to which he replied that 'she is an odd, fascinating little puss', but said that he was 'not in love with her': a curiously flirtatious discussion about a novelist's work. He also said, Charlotte told Ellen, that he would answer no more questions about *Villette*, almost as if *Villette* had become a means of her communicating with him. He was apparently not at all offended by the suggestion that he, Dr John, did not have enough depth for Lucy Snowe.

Meanwhile, to his letter complaining about the transfer of interest, Charlotte responded rather pointedly: 'It is not pleasant, and will probably be found as unwelcome to the reader as it was, in a sense, compulsory upon the writer.' She went on, 'The spirit of romance would have indicated another course, far more flowery and inviting; it would have fashioned a paramount hero, kept faithfully with him, and made him supremely worshipful; he should have an idol, and not a mute, unresponding idol either, but this would have been unlike real life – inconsistent with truth – at variance with probability.'

She did, though, consent to go and stay with the Smiths shortly after Christmas. Mr Smith had been urging her to come and she now received a 'very kind' note from Mrs Smith. As she told Ellen, she almost wished that she could still look on that kindness as she used to – 'it was very pleasant to me once'. Her letter to Mrs Smith accepting the invitation has something a little grim about it: 'It will be about eighteen months since I bid you good-bye in Euston Square: the interim has not always been one of good health to me, and I must expect that friends who have not seen me for a year and a half, will find some change.' Still she had to admit that her health was better – that brief stay at Brookroyd in early December had improved it. The sight of her old friends, Ellen – now growing a little stout – and kindly Miss Wooler, and their cheerful gossip of the doings of their relatives, the same gossip that had provided a lifetime's interest to Ellen, ebbed and flowed like a calming stream around her.

But the year which in a sense had been a long, slow exploration of the single female life did not end on a celibate note. Or at least it ended with a vigorous attempt to break rough masculine life through the priestess-like concentration on sorrow, a clash of cymbals amidst the dithyrambs. Admittedly the man who dared to trespass in the groves of Diana was not the sort to rouse many to Dionysian frenzy – least of all the goddess herself, who was more disposed to be amused than angry. Not so her guardians though.

Although in her loneliness Charlotte had paid a little more attention to this man, the curate Mr Nicholls, who had been present through so many of her family's tragedies, it was not until the latter half of 1852 that he penetrated her consciousness. But recently she had begun to observe, and thought her father had too, that there was something in the way this great ox-like man looked at her that contained more meaning than the usual small-talk that tea with the curates demanded. As usual scenting danger where his way of life was concerned, Mr Brontë had recently expressed himself with a good deal of sarcasm on the subject of Mr Nicholls. The latter was continuously in mysteriously low spirits and threatening most inconveniently to return to Ireland.

On Monday evening, 13 December, Mr Nicholls came to tea. Charlotte, reporting to Ellen two days later, said that she vaguely felt, without clearly seeing, the meaning of his constant looks and 'strange feverish restraint'. After tea she withdrew to the dining room as usual, and as usual Mr Nicholls sat with her father between eight and nine o'clock.

I then heard him open the parlour door as if going. I expected the clash of the front door. He stopped in the passage: he tapped: like lightning it flashed on me what was coming. He entered – he stood before me. What his words were you can guess; his manner – you can hardly realize – never can I forget it. Shaking from head to foot, looking deadly pale, speaking low, vehemently yet with difficulty – he made me for the first time feel what it costs a man to declare his affection where he doubts response.

427

The spectacle of this supremely immovable man, whom she thought of as statue-like in his mien, trembling before her, so racked by feeling, gave her a strange kind of shock, she told Ellen. The great heavy features, the ponderous bulk before her encased in thick tweed clothes, shook as he spoke of sufferings he had borne for months, of 'sufferings he could endure no longer, and craved leave for some hope'. Here was someone who could match her in feeling at least.

But Charlotte was too amazed and alarmed by him to do anything other than beg him to leave and hastily to promise him a reply the next day. She asked him if he had spoken to her father. He said he dared not. She half led, half put him out of the little room. When he had stumbled out, she immediately went to her father and told him what had happened. As she told Ellen graphically:

> Agitation and anger disproportionate to the occasion ensued; if I had *loved* Mr Nicholls and had heard such epithets applied to him as were used, it would have transported me past my patience; as it was, my blood boiled with a sense of injustice, but Papa worked himself into a state not to be trifled with, the veins on his temples started up like whipcord, and his eyes became suddenly bloodshot.

Naturally his daughter quickly promised that Mr Nicholls would have a distinct refusal the next day. But though she did her father's will, the vehemence of his antipathy to the idea of anyone considering Charlotte for a wife distressed her, as did the idea of Mr Nicholls suffering, and suffering for so long. It made her quite uncomfortable.

But the matter was not over. Lumbering though Mr Nicholls was, he was also a man of iron will, who refused in effect to take no for an answer. Instead of behaving gracefully, he gave vent to his unhappiness with the whole of Haworth for an audience. He was horrifying his landlady, Charlotte learned via the furious Tabby and Martha, by 'entirely rejecting his meals'. Mr Brontë, anxious to despatch his foe with a knock-out blow, followed Charlotte's note with a cruel note of his own. Charlotte was quite astonished by his hardness and contempt for the unfortunate man. However, she was not quite so much at her father's bidding that she did not decide to do something, and the note from her father was accompanied by a line from her: while Mr Nicholls must never expect her to reciprocate the feeling he had expressed, at the same time she wished to disclaim participation in sentiments calculated to give him pain. In her kind-hearted way she had to exhort him to maintain his courage and spirits. Mr Nicholls handed in his resignation in a gesture worthy, and most surprisingly so, of any romantic hero. To Charlotte, had she not been aware of this brewing in the back of her mind, it would have all seemed quite dreamlike. Mr Nicholls, the impassive, solitary, massive curate, hid a heart as passionate seemingly as her own beneath the solid flesh. It quite puzzled her to comprehend 'how and whence comes this turbulence of feelings'.

Unlike the rest of Haworth, who were filled with possessive rage at the man's presumption – Martha was bitter against him, John Brown the sexton had actually said he would like to shoot him, her father was disgusted that an Irish curate with no prospects and no money had dared to raise his eyes to his daughter! – Charlotte continued to feel sorry for him. The analyst of emotion suddenly became more interested by him. The others did not understand his feelings, she told Ellen, but she saw now what they were: 'Mr N.- is one of those who attach themselves to very few, whose sensations are close and deep – like an underground stream, running strong but in a narrow channel.' Mr Nicholls continued to be restless and ill. He could scarcely perform his duties, only managing to carry on through immense concentration and care. He did not come near the old black church; a substitute performed his duties every Sunday.

Mr Brontë meanwhile ranted and raved, and as a result secured even more sympathy from his daughter for the unlucky curate than before. Charlotte could not go along with her father's views on her marriage: to wit, if she married at all it must be very differently – as indeed would befit a daughter of Patrick Brontë and authoress who had the greatest in the land lining up to watch her go by. She herself had only a little patience with this. Her own objections arose from a 'sense of incongruity and uncongeniality in feelings, tastes, principles'.

Mr Nicholls, however, was not to give up hope so easily. He had loved Miss Brontë for too long, waited for too long, to abandon it all in a day. He cunningly wrote to Mr Brontë, whom he had still not seen, asking permission to withdraw his resignation. The proud old man said he would agree only on condition of Mr Nicholls giving his written promise never again to broach the subject of marriage either to him or his daughter. This the rash Mr Nicholls equally firmly refused to do. And thus the matter rested.

By good luck Charlotte's presence was now demanded in London, for there were alterations Mr Smith wished her to make to her novel at proof stage. It was with a sense of relief that she quitted the suddenly tense atmosphere of the usually quiet little village and set out for Leeds on 5 January 1853.

CHAPTER XX

The Eye of a Rebel

Charlotte stayed in London until early February, on what was to prove her last visit. Though something of the old raillery persisted between her and George Smith, the convivial intimacy of the past was at an end. Given Charlotte's not totally flattering portrayal of him and his mother, it probably could not be otherwise. She scarcely saw him except when going over the proof sheets of her book. He was frequently working till all hours in the office, his physical appearance quite altered by the strain. Mrs Smith's accounts to Charlotte of the work weighing on him had been quite alarming, and bore out the reports in his own letters, but Charlotte had thought they might be an exaggeration. They were not.

None of the entertainments that George Smith had laid on for her benefit on previous visits were repeated this time. Charlotte would sum up her stay to Ellen as having passed pleasantly enough but it had left 'some sorrowful impressions'; by the end of 1853 their correspondence would become pretty desultory.

Correcting the proofs of *Villette* kept Charlotte busy for much of her time in London. Publication had been delayed until 28 January to avoid coinciding with the publication of Mrs Gaskell's *Ruth*. Charlotte wrote grandly to Mrs Gaskell: 'We shall not be able wholly to prevent comparisons; it is the nature of some critics to be invidious; but we need not care: we can set them at defiance; they *shall* not make us foes, they *shall* not mingle with our mutual feelings one taint of jealousy: there is my hand on that: I know you will give clasp for clasp.' And to Ellen she said, taking some pleasure from being in the position of benefactress to her gracious literary friend: 'Mrs Gaskell wrote so pitifully to beg that it should not clash with her "Ruth" that it was impossible to refuse to defer the publication a week or two.'

Although her visit was quiet, it was not without diversions. Sir James Kay Shuttleworth as usual insisted on entertaining her, as did

Dr Forbes; but despite Sir James's benevolence nothing could prevent her dreading what she called 'the excited fuss' he would put himself into for her. Charlotte herself determined on visiting sights of her own choice, announcing perhaps a little aggressively to Mrs Smith that this time she wished to see the *real* rather than the decorative side of life. Accordingly, she went to see two prisons, 'ancient and modern' – Newgate and Pentonville – the Bank, the Exchange, the Foundling Hospital and Bethlehem Hospital. She wrote to Ellen: 'Mrs S. and her daughter are – I believe – a little amazed at my gloomy taste, but I take no notice.'

This defiance was symptomatic of a change in Charlotte, a new toughness. *Villette* was not only a book about destroying illusion, in a sense it also destroyed any illusions about her personal life. It was the frankest book, in an autobiographical sense, that she had written. Thackeray said he thought he could read her life's history there, and indeed he could. She had concealed nothing in *Villette*; it was the history of a woman who had suffered so deeply that she had become almost deranged, and this was revealed in raw, painful detail to the public. But she no longer cared. The toughness permeated her attitude to her friends. She had been assaulted beyond caring by critics and by life, and this time, with the publication of *Villette*, she refused to lie down before her friends' references to sniping reviews and indeed before the reviewers themselves.

Her disillusion with life and with the literary world whose luminaries had dazzled her so long ago was made acute when her idol and friend Harriet Martineau betrayed her. Although in the course of their correspondence Charlotte's views on her friend had undergone some modification – she thought there was a certain tendency to monomania in Miss Martineau so that she only really cared for people to agree with her – she continued to admire her writing above that of any female contemporary; as she said on a number of occasions, she thought her 'truly great'.

On 21 January from Gloucester Terrace Charlotte wrote excitedly to her heroine:

I know that you will give me your thoughts upon my book, as frankly as if you spoke to some near relative whose good you preferred to her gratification. I wince under the pain of condemnation, like any other weak structure of flesh and blood; but I love, I honour, I kneel to truth. Let her smite me on the one cheek – good! the tears may spring to the eyes; but courage! there is the other side; hit again, right sharply.

Ironically, a few days later on 27 January she wrote to Miss Wooler

431

defending her friendship with Miss Martineau; her former teacher was still worried about Charlotte's relationship with this avowed atheist. Charlotte did not feel that it would be right to give Miss Martineau up entirely; there was much that was noble in her nature. Hundreds had forsaken her, more out of fear of their names suffering from connection with her, rather than from horror at her sin; with these fair-weather friends, Charlotte told Miss Wooler, she could not bear to rank, and as for her sin, it was for God to judge that. She went on, more confidentially, that if Miss Wooler knew Miss Martineau as she did, and had proofs of her rough but genuine kindliness, she would be the last to give her up. In any case Charlotte thought Miss Martineau one of those people whom 'opposition and desertion make obstinate in error'.

In a couple of days she was repaid for her kindness and understanding. Harriet Martineau replied to her enquiry about 'womanly delicacy or propriety' in connection with *Villette* without mincing her words. In her impulsive, clumsy, high-minded way, she stated the truth as she saw it, without thought for Charlotte's feelings:

> As for the other side of the question, which you so desire to know, I have but one thing to say; but it is not a small one. I do not like the love, either the kind or the degree of it; and the prevalence in the book, and the effect on the action of it, help to explain the passages in the reviews which you consulted me about, and seem to afford *some* foundation for the criticisms they offered.

This was wounding in the extreme. Charlotte wrote back immediately, enclosing Miss Martineau's letter:

> I . . . have marked with red ink the passage which struck me dumb. All the rest is fair, right, worthy of you, but I protest against this passage; and were I brought before the bar of critics in England to such a charge I should respond, 'not guilty'.
>
> I know what *love* is as I understand it; and if man or woman should be ashamed of feeling such love, then is there nothing right, noble, faithful, truthful, unselfish in this earth, as I comprehend rectitude, nobleness, fidelity, truth, and disinterestedness.
>
> Yours sincerely,
> C. Brontë.
> To differ from you gives me keen pain.

Harriet Martineau had shown herself to be monstrous. Charlotte knew what passion was; she had written about it, she thought it necessary to write about it, but in her view *Villette* was not the same sort of book as

Jane Eyre. Perhaps her anger was given added edge by the way she had transformed her feeling for M. Heger into a holier, more cerebral love – which had now been reduced to low, base passion. The friend who had said that she saw nothing coarse – i.e. improper – in *Jane Eyre* had joined the most poisonous of critics who maintained that *Jane Eyre* was improper. The theoretically free-thinking Miss Martineau was far less so than her reputation suggested.

The trouble was that Charlotte had come up against Miss Martineau's deepest feminist convictions, as the latter revealed in her anonymous review of *Villette* in the *Daily News*. In fact, she misrepresented her criticism of the book to Charlotte in her letter. Her chief criticism was not its coarseness – its sensuality – but that it was degrading to women to be represented as seeing life in terms of one thing only, i.e. love. She wrote indignantly: 'There are substantial, heartfelt interests for women of all ages, and under ordinary circumstances, quite apart from love: there is an absence of introspection, an unconsciousness, a repose in women's lives – unless under peculiarly unfortunate circumstances – of which we find no admission in this book.' To the absence of this, the great campaigner scribbled on, 'may be attributed some of the criticism which the book will meet from readers who are not prudes, but whose reason and taste will reject the assumption that events and characters are to be regarded through the medium of one passion only'.

She proceeded in fact to praise the book highly, despite the atmosphere of pain that hung about it, which reminded her of Balzac. All else was 'power, skill and interest', which only needed 'the cheerfulness of health' to return the author to her best performance. But for her this emphasis on love pointed to nothing but a willing return to the domestic bondage that so many women were trying to escape. The same point was made by the *Athenaeum* reviewer, who lauded the book, as did the majority of the critics:

> Currer Bell will be surprised to be told that the burden of her Pindaric concerning 'Woman's mission' is virtually identical with that sarcastic and depreciating proverb (born among bachelor monks) which ranged Man's help-mate with the ass and the walnut-tree, as 'three things that do nothing rightly if not beaten'. But such is the case. From the moment when M. Paul Emanuel begins to insult Miss Lucy Snowe, we give up her heart as gone.

The indignation that Charlotte felt at the betrayal by her friend – she swiftly found out that Miss Martineau was the reviewer – was not to be gainsaid. Despite Harriet Martineau's subsequent attempts at reconciliation, she never would see her again. The respect for truth

433

which had brought the two apostles together had broken them asunder; and on this occasion Charlotte's reverence of the truth deserted her. In her rage she repudiated every point Miss Martineau had made, and wrote angrily to George Smith about Miss Martineau's suggestion that *Villette* showed the influence of Balzac, 'whose works I have not read' – although in a letter of 1852 she had discussed two of his novels which G.H. Lewes had lent her.

In general, however, the first notices of *Villette* were all that Charlotte could hope for, and to Ellen she wrote on 15 February that 'the import of the notices is such as to make my heart swell with thankfulness to Him who takes note both of suffering and work and motives'. Most of the reviews agreed on the book's remarkable power, freshness and skill in creating such 'living' characters – which are indeed drawn with even greater subtlety. It was confirmation of the genius which had written *Jane Eyre*, even if many also deplored the female characters' obsession with love. Most agreed that the coarseness which had 'disfigured' *Jane Eyre* had largely vanished. George Eliot wrote on 15 February: 'I am only just returned to a sense of the real world about me, for I have been reading *Villette*, a still more wonderful book than *Jane Eyre*. There is something almost preternatural in its power . . . '; and then on 12 March, '*Villette* – *Villette* – have you read it?' A few reviewers quarrelled with Miss Snowe's belief that happiness was not something to be cultivated, but 'manna' shining from Heaven. Indeed, one said earnestly, 'Exertion is the indispensable condition of all healthy life, mental or bodily.' Mary Taylor would have agreed with them. Nevertheless *Villette* partly owes its great and extraordinary power to the fatalism and unhappiness which broods over it.

To Matthew Arnold, however, *Villette* was a 'hideous, undelightful convulsed constricted novel', which reminded him of repulsive aspects of American feminism: 'It is one of the most utterly disagreeable books I ever read – and having seen her makes it more so. She is so entirely – what Margaret Fuller was partially – a fire without aliment – one of the most distressing barren sights one can witness.' The book seemed to him an unpleasant instance of female frustration in a time of change and unrest: 'Religion or devotion or whatever it is to be called may be impossible for such women now: but they have at any rate not found a substitute for it and it was better for the world when they comforted themselves with it.'

Much of Charlotte's misery which had been so evident in 1851 and 1852 seems to have been exorcised by the book, helped now by its favourable reception. She was able to tell Mrs Gaskell on 24 February that whereas the winter of 1851 had passed like a painful dream, 'the corresponding months in '52–53 have gone over my head quietly and not uncheerfully'. Although Lucy Snowe undoubtedly reflected a side of Charlotte's personality – as Lewes said, 'Every page, every paragraph, is sharp with *individuality*. It is Currer Bell speaking to you' – the fact is that the other, gregarious side of Charlotte continued to exist. She was now sufficiently distanced from her creation Lucy Snowe to be amused by her – her coldness, her unhappiness, her pain, her prickliness. Thus, discussing the question of whether Lucy does or does not marry M. Paul, which was now obsessing fashionable London society, she wrote to George Smith light-heartedly: 'The merciful . . . will of course choose the former and milder doom – drown him to put him out of pain. The cruel-hearted will, on the contrary, pitilessly impale him on the second horn of the dilemma, marrying him without ruth or compunction to that – person – that – that – individual – "Lucy Snowe".'

The new pragmatism and new calm enabled Charlotte to meet the criticisms that did arise more equably, and at the same time more formidably. Accusations of being unladylike were now sneered at, where six years ago they had caused acute misery and unhappiness. She was what she was. She had, perhaps, been given courage by the acclaim for her genius. Once again, though, in March she had to ask the tactful Mr Williams not to withhold bad reviews, such as that in the *Guardian* which accused her of moral faults – even her best characters, it said, adopted practices no 'really high-minded and virtuous person would consent to'; 'differences in religion were treated as immaterial'. Surely few authors, she said, would be so weak as to be shaken by reviews such as these. She told Mr Williams, perhaps a little morbidly, that she *must* also see the reviews which were unsatisfactory and hostile: 'these are for my own especial edification – it is in these I best read public feeling and opinion. To shun examination into the dangerous and disagreeable seems to me cowardly – I long always to know what really *is*, and am only unnerved when kept in the dark.' She went on that she now smiled at her 'friends',

with their little notes of condolence, with their hints about 'unmanly insult.' Surely the poor *Guardian* critic has a right to lisp his opinion that Currer Bell's female characters do not realize his notion of ladyhood – and even 'respectfully to decline' the honour of an acquaintance with 'Jane Eyre and Lucy Snowe' without meriting on that account to be charged with having offered an 'unmanly insult'.

Ah, I forgive the worthy critic very freely – his acquaintance and his standard of refinement are two points that will not trouble me much; perhaps ere tomorrow I shall even have forgiven my 'Kind friends' their false alarm.

Even Ellen indulged in *schadenfreude*, pointing out the bad reviews. Was *Sharpe's* small article like a bit of sugar-candy too, or did it have 'the proper wholesome wormwood taste'? Charlotte wrote sarcastically to her, adding that she could not wait for *The Times* to castigate her. To her annoyance, too, the odious curate Mr Grant had already been into her father's study and read the *Guardian*'s criticisms out to her father, when she had intended, as was her custom, to keep it from him.

Taking a fairly resigned view of the ire her work aroused in organs of the Church, Charlotte wrote to Miss Wooler of the reception of *Villette*: 'There is a minority – small in number but influential in character – which views the work with no favourable eye. Currer Bell's remarks on Romanism have drawn down on him the condign displeasure of the High Church Party – which displeasure had been unequivocally expressed through their principal organs the "Guardian", the "English Churchman" and the "Christian Remembrancer".' She said she could well understand 'that some the charges launched against me by these publications will tell heavily to my prejudice in the minds of most readers', but she courageously decided 'that this must be borne, and for my part – I can suffer no accusation to oppress me much which is not supported by the inward evidence of Conscience and Reason.'

The *Christian Remembrancer*'s review was a particularly swingeing attack. Like the attacks on *Jane Eyre*, it may partly be accounted for by the continued political unrest in Britain during the 'hungry forties' and early fifties; after the revolutions of 1848, anything which appeared to echo the romantic rhetoric of the Chartists seemed dangerous. Anne Mozley, author of the review of *Villette* in the *Christian Remembrancer*, described *Jane Eyre* as 'a dangerous book', for its 'outrages on decorum, the moral perversity, the toleration of, nay indifference to, vices which deform her first powerful picture of a desolate woman's trials and sufferings . . . and which must leave a permanent mistrust of the author on all thoughtful and scrupulous minds'. She thought, however, that 'in many important moral points' *Villette* was an improvement on its predecessors: 'The author has gained both in amiability and propriety since she first presented herself to the world – soured, coarse, and grumbling; and alien, it might seem, from society, and amenable to none of its laws.'

Miss Mozley went on to say that she would be sorry to subject any child of hers to the teaching of Lucy Snowe, 'whose religion is without awe, who despises and sets down every form and distinction she cannot understand, who rejects all guides but her Bible, and at the same time . . . plays with its sacred pages, as though they had been given to the world for no better purpose than to point a witticism or furnish ingenious illustration'. Lastly, she criticised Lucy's lack of femininity:

> We want a woman at our hearth; and her impersonations are without the feminine element, infringers of modest restraints, despisers of bashful fears, self-reliant, contemptuous of prescriptive decorum; their own unaided reason, their individual opinion of right and wrong, discreet or imprudent, sole guides of conduct and rules of manners, – the whole hedge of immemorial scruple and habit broken down and trampled upon.

She could sympathise with Lucy Snowe being fatherless and penniless, but she could not offer 'the affections of our fancy . . . to her unscrupulous, and self-dependent intellect'.

By July, however, as the following letter shows, there had been enough reviewers who followed the *Christian Remembrancer*'s lead for Charlotte to feel that a letter defending her morals and putting speculation at rest was necessary. Now that she was no longer anonymous it was beholden upon her to clear her name; as it was, the buzz of rumour between Leeds and Haworth was something she would no longer tolerate:

> . . . When first I read that article I thought only of its ability, which seemed to me considerable, of its acumen, which I felt to be penetrating; an occasional misconception passed scarce noticed, and I smiled at certain passages from which evils have since risen so heavy as to oblige me to revert seriously to their origin. Conscious myself that the import of these insinuations was far indeed from the truth, I forgot to calculate how they might appear to that great Public which personally did not know me.
>
> The passage to which I particularly allude characterizes me by a strong expression. I am spoken of as 'an alien – it might seem from society, and amenable to none of its laws'.
>
> The 'G—' newspaper gave a notice in the same spirit. The 'E—' culled isolated extracts from your review, and presented them in a concentrated form as one paragraph of unqualified condemnation.
>
> The result of these combined attacks, all to one effect – all insinuating some disadvantageous occult motive for a retired life – has been such, that I at length find it advisable to speak a few words of temperate explanation in the quarter that seems to me most worthy to be thus addressed, and the most likely to understand rightly my intention. Who my reviewer may be I know not, but I am convinced he is no narrow-minded or naturally unjust thinker.
>
> To him I would say no cause of seclusion such as he would imply

437

has ever come near my thoughts, deed, or life. It has not entered my experience. It has not crossed my observation.

Providence so regulated my destiny that I was born and have been reared in the seclusion of a country parsonage. I have never been rich enough to go out into the world as a participator in its gaieties, though it early became my duty to leave home in order partly to diminish the calls on a limited income. That income is lightened of claims in another sense now, for of a family of six I am the only survivor.

My father is now in his seventy-seventh year; his mind is clear as it ever was, and he is not infirm; but he suffers from partial privation and threatened loss of sight; and his general health is also delicate, he cannot be left often or long; my place consequently is at home. These are reasons which made retirement a plain duty; but were there no such reasons in existence, were I bound by no such ties, it is very possible that seclusion might still appear to me, on the whole, more congenial than publicity; the brief and rare glimpses I have had of the world do not incline me to think I should seek its circles with very keen zest – nor can I consider such disinclination a just subject for reproach.

This is the truth. The careless, rather than malevolent insinuations of reviewers have, it seems, widely spread another impression. It would be weak to complain, but I feel that it is only right to place the real in opposition to the unreal.

Will you kindly show this note to my reviewer? Perhaps he can now find an antidote for the poison into which he dipped that shaft he shot at 'Currer Bell', but when again tempted to take aim at other prey – let him refrain his hand a moment till he has considered consequences to the wounded and recalled the 'golden rule'.[1]

Nine days earlier Charlotte had written meditatively to Mrs Gaskell, whose own *Ruth* had outraged decorum, about the difficulties of relations with her milieu. Although she did not say precisely what was on her mind she hoped for some sympathy in her predicament:

Do you, who have so many friends – so large a circle of acquaintances – find it easy, when you sit down to write, to isolate yourself from all those ties, and their sweet associations, so as to be quite *your own woman*, uninfluenced, unswayed by the consciousness of how your own work may affect other minds; what blame, what sympathy it may call forth? Does no luminous cloud ever come between you and the severe Truth as you know it in your own secret and clear-seeing soul? In a word, are you never tempted to make your own characters more amiable than the Life, by the inclination

438

to assimilate your thoughts to the thoughts of those who always *feel* kindly, but sometimes fail to *see* justly? Don't answer the question; it is not intended to be answered.

There is, unfortunately, no record of Mrs Gaskell's reply.

Nowadays Charlotte was constantly being taken for something far more radical than she was. One of Miss Wooler's many clergyman brothers had written to her, trying to adjust to the new view of little Miss Brontë as an authoress. Charlotte responded swiftly to his sister: 'Mr Wooler thinks me a much hotter advocate for *change* and what is called "political progress" than I am. However, in my reply I did not touch on these subjects.'

In fact the literary side of her life was fast retreating to its periphery. On her return from London in February 1853, the focus of her attention had shifted to events in Haworth, where both Mr Nicholls and her father were behaving in an increasingly bizarre fashion. They were like two offended potentates who had the misfortune to share the same kingdom. Mr Nicholls refused to moderate his feeling in any wise, or to conceal it.

The Bishop of Ripon, the Reverend Dr Charles Longley had paid a visit to the parish, and Mr Nicholls had not let up his brooding air of injury for a minute, inappropriate though it was for such an occasion. He seems to have seized the chance of the episcopal visit to carry his warfare into the enemy's camp, staying at the parsonage for supper as well as tea. He sat in the little dining room with his long face in lines of such dejection as to draw notice from the Bishop, whom Charlotte noticed was most puzzled by the usually sensible curate's behaviour. He also 'showed temper once or twice in speaking to Papa', Charlotte wrote to Ellen. Outside the dining room, garrulous Martha excitedly started to tell her of certain 'flaysome' looks she had observed Mr Nicholls giving her until her mistress quickly hushed her up.

Charlotte told Ellen that she would be most thankful when he had departed. She pitied him but she didn't like 'that dark gloom of his'. She had been quite alarmed by the way he had dogged her up the lane after the evening service 'in no pleasant manner' so she almost felt his hot breath on the back of her neck. He had also stopped in the little passage after the Bishop and the other clergy had gone into the dining room, 'and it was because I drew away and went upstairs that he gave that look which filled Martha's soul with horror'. As he stared greedily after her little mistress Martha made it 'her business to watch him from the kitchen door', Charlotte told Ellen with the tremor of a laugh. It was a pity, she thought, that if Mr Nicholls was a good man at bottom, nature had not given him the faculty to put goodness into a more attractive form. He had managed into the bargain to get up a 'most pertinacious and needless dispute with the Inspector, in listening to which all my old unfavourable impressions revived so strongly, I fear my countenance could not but show them'.

By April the pugnacity had subsided somewhat. He had got himself another curacy, but Charlotte did not know where. Meanwhile, he had to await the appointment of his replacement, and he sat drearily in his rooms, from time to time still allowing Flossy to go there to be taken for a walk out on the moors, and occasionally going over to visit his friend Mr Sowden, the clergyman at Oxenhope. But that was all. He had allowed 'late circumstances so to act on him as to freeze up his manner and overcast his countenance not only to those immediately concerned but to everyone,' Charlotte reported to a curious Ellen on 6 April. 'If Mr Croxton or Mr Grant or any other clergyman calls to see, and as they think, to cheer him, he scarcely speaks. I find he tells them nothing, seeks no confidant, rebuffs all attempts to penetrate his mind.' She had to admit that she respected him for this. She thought he looked ill and miserable, and pitied him inexpressibly. They never met nor spoke, nor dared she look at him when she saw him at church or in the village. She could not make up her mind whether the gloom was due to true affection 'or only rancour and corroding disappointment at the bottom of his chagrin'. Because of this doubt, she reasoned, conscience would not allow her to take one step in opposition to her father, to whose happiness inevitably she was bound to cater. She might be losing 'the purest gem, and to me far the most precious life can give – genuine attachment – or I may be escaping the yoke of a morose temper.' Nevertheless in letters to Ellen she came very near expressing deep disapprobation of her father's behaviour – the 'bitter and unreasonable prejudices' did not put her father in a very good light. Mr Brontë considered the affair so degrading that he would not have it hinted at or known to his old friend Mr Morgan. 'This circumstance serves as a tolerably pointed illustration of his painful way of viewing the matter,' she wrote wearily.

The unreasonable behaviour of the household to Mr Nicholls – her father's 'perfect antipathy', Martha's hatred: 'I think he might almost be *dying* and they would not speak a friendly word to or of him' – made the atmosphere very uncomfortable. Mr Nicholls had never been 'agreeable or amiable', she thought, but now he had grown so gloomy and reserved that absolutely nobody seemed to like him; his fellow curates shunned him, and the lower orders loathed him. And he and her father were like a pair of angry cats together. Towards the end of April Charlotte decided to flee this unhappy situation by going to visit Mrs Gaskell at Plymouth Grove in Manchester.

Charlotte had expected to find the Gaskells alone and was, according to Mrs Gaskell, made nervous and shy by another woman guest, even though this friend was 'gentle and sensible after Miss Brontë's own heart'. Mrs Gaskell described how both her guests were unusually silent; a little shiver ran from time to time over Miss Brontë's frame 'and the next day Miss Brontë told me how the unexpected sight of a strange face had affected her'.

Mrs Gaskell wrote of Charlotte's meeting with Catherine and Susanna Winkworth, Mrs Gaskell's friends, who were great performers of Scottish ballads:

Miss Brontë had been sitting quiet and constrained till they began 'The Bonnie House of Airlie', but the effect of that and 'Carlisle Yetts' which followed, was as irresistible as the playing of the Piper of Hamelin. The beautiful clear light came into her eyes; her lips quivered with emotion; she forgot herself, rose, and crossed the room to the piano where she asked eagerly for song after song. The sisters begged her to come and see them the next morning, when they would sing as long as ever she liked; and she promised gladly and thankfully. But on reaching the house her courage failed. We walked some time up and down the street; she upbraiding herself all the while for her folly, and trying to dwell on the sweet echoes in her memory rather than on the thought of a third sister who would have to be faced if we went in. But it was of no use; and dreading lest this struggle with herself might bring on one of her trying headaches, I entered at last and made the best apology I could for her non-appearance.[2]

Mrs Gaskell ascribed much of this nervous dread of encountering strangers to Charlotte's conviction of her own personal ugliness, which, according to Mrs Gaskell, had been strongly impressed upon her imagination early in life, and which she exaggerated to herself in a 'remarkable manner'. Mrs Gaskell remembered her saying: 'I notice that after a stranger has once looked at my face he is careful not to let his eyes wander to that part of the room again.' And Mrs Gaskell added that nothing could be more untrue – 'Two gentlemen who saw her during this visit, without knowing at the time who she was, were singularly attracted by her appearance; and this feeling of attraction towards a pleasant countenance, sweet voice, and gentle timid manners was so strong in one as to conquer a dislike he had previously entertained to her works.'

Mrs Gaskell also related another incident about her guest, 'which told secrets about the finely strung frame'. One night she was about to tell a ghost story just before they went to bed, but her guest shrank from hearing it. She confessed that she was superstitious, and had a tendency for gloomy thoughts and ideas to recur constantly and involuntarily when they had been suggested to her. 'She said that on first coming to us she had found a letter on her dressing table from a friend in Yorkshire containing a story which had impressed her vividly ever since – that it mingled with her dreams at night and made her sleep restless and unrefreshing.'

Charlotte's alarm in the company of strangers also showed itself at a dinner to which the Gaskells had asked two gentlemen with whom they thought Miss Brontë would have much in common. Mrs Gaskell reported that their guest was able to reply to their questions and remarks only 'in the briefest possible manner till at last they gave up their efforts to draw her into conversation in despair', and talked to each other and Mr Gaskell on subjects of recent local interest. It was the old problem of Charlotte being unable to come to terms with her celebrity. However, when the company began to discuss some of Thackeray's lectures which had recently been given in Manchester, and in particular the one on Fielding, which had greatly obsessed Charlotte in letters, she threw herself warmly into the discussion. The question of morality in art was one about which she felt increasingly strongly as the years went by; by the end of her life she was quite convinced that it was his reading matter which had sent Branwell to the bad. 'The ice of her reserve was broken, and from that time she showed her interest in all that was said, and contributed her share to any conversation that was going on in the course of the evening.'

Although Charlotte still found it difficult to relax in the company of strangers, her friendship with Mrs Gaskell waxed warmer than ever on her visit. She wrote to her hostess that the week she 'spent in Manchester has impressed me as the very brightest and healthiest I have known for these five years past' – that is, since her sisters died. On her way back home, she stopped to visit a low-spirited Ellen, having just like Charlotte turned thirty-seven. Then she returned to the strained atmosphere of Haworth – 'to barbarism, loneliness and liberty', as she described it to Mrs Gaskell, urging her friend to 'take leave of the domestic circle and turn your back on Plymouth Grove' for a return visit. Charlotte longed to see her.

Mrs Gaskell in turn expressed her feelings for Miss Brontë in a letter to her friend John Forster:

. . . she is so true, she wins respect, deep respect, from the very first – and then comes hearty liking – and last of all comes love. I thoroughly loved her before she left, and I was so sorry for her! She has had so little kindness and affection shown to her; she said that she was afraid of loving me as much as she could, because she had never been able to inspire the kind of love she felt. She has had an uncomfortable kind of coolness with Miss Martineau, on account of some *very* disagreeable remarks Miss M. made on *Villette*, and this has been preying on Miss Brontë's mind as she says everything does prey on it, in the solitude in which she lives. She gave Mr Thackeray the benefit of some of her piercingly keen observation. My word! he had reason when he said he was afraid of her. But she was very angry indeed with that part of the *Examiner* review of Esmond (I had forgotten it) which said his works would not live; She is not going to write again for some time. She is thoroughly good; only made bitter by some deep mortifications, and feeling her plainness as 'something almost repulsive'. I am going to see her at Haworth, at her father's particular desire. Mr Smith has got her £100 for a (French) translation of *Villette* . . .[3]

Back at Haworth, Mr Nicholls was seeing out his last weeks of duty, and on Sunday 15 May he was still taking the communion service. His behaviour gave Charlotte some concrete evidence of his great feeling for her, and as she wrote to Ellen the following day, she felt 'as if I were to be punished for my doubts about the nature and truth of poor Mr Nicholls' regard'. When she went up to the communion rail to receive the sacrament, he 'struggled, faltered, then lost command over himself, stood before my eyes and in the sight of all the communicants, white, shaking, voiceless. Papa was not there, thank God! Joseph Redman spoke some words to him. He made a great effort, but could only with difficulty whisper and falter through the service.' Round about her Charlotte could hear the women sobbing, and she could not quite check her own tears. But she could not prevent the incident reaching her father, who flew into a rage, calling the unfortunate man, among other choice epithets, 'unmanly driveller'. Charlotte wrote restrainedly that 'Compassion or relenting is no more to be looked for from Papa than sap from firewood'.

She felt a certain satisfaction when she found out that the people of Haworth were getting up a subscription to offer a testimonial of respect to Mr Nicholls on his leaving. She had heard that the church wardens had asked him about the affair and had admired the straight way in which he said that it was not Mr Brontë's fault, but that the whole matter continued to give him great pain. Nevertheless, when Charlotte argued herself round to Mr Nicholls' side out of the pity she felt for the underdog, she speedily had to remind herself that Mr Nicholls was not always right. She could not help being irritated by the curious mixture of honour and obstinacy in his character, of 'feeling and sullenness'. When her father had made a point of addressing him at the Sunday School tea, with constrained civility, but still civility, Mr Nicholls had cut him short. This was a mistake, Charlotte thought; her father's pride simply would not forget or forgive such

443

treatment in public. It had the effect of inspiring him with a silent bitterness not to be expressed. She told Ellen she was afraid that both solemn Anglican clergymen were now actually quite unchristian in their feelings; 'Nor do I know which of them is least accessible to reason or least likely to forgive.'

Eight days later, on 27 May, Mr Nicholls left Haworth. Charlotte found the whole episode extremely painful. There was a public meeting to present the testimonial – a gold watch – which Mr Brontë did not attend; he was not very well and Charlotte had advised him to stay away. On the last Sunday before he left, Mr Nicholls had taken the service, and once again it was a cruel struggle for him to keep his composure. Charlotte, watching helplessly, thought he ought not to have had to take any duty. The evening before his departure, he called at the parsonage to deliver the deeds of the National School to Mr Brontë, and to say goodbye. Just so much would he do. The servants were busy cleaning and washing the paintwork in the dining room so he did not find Charlotte there; she was upstairs, not wanting to say goodbye to him in her father's presence and thinking that it was better not to see him at all. Then, at the last moment, seeing that he was lingering outside the house before going out at the gate, and 'remembering his long grief, I took courage and went out trembling and miserable'.

She continued her account to Ellen: 'I found him leaning against the garden door in a paroxysm of anguish, sobbing as women never sob. Of course I went straight to him. Very few words were interchanged, those few barely articulate. Several things I should have liked to ask him were swept entirely from my memory.' He wanted hope and encouragement that she could not give him, but she trusted that he now knew that she was not 'cruelly blind and indifferent to his constancy and grief'. And indeed she was not. Although she told Ellen that that was an end of it – he was going south, and then taking a curacy somewhere in Yorkshire, and she saw no chance of hearing a word about him in the future – he had evidently left some impression not wholly unfavourable on her. By the time Mrs Gaskell arrived in September, Charlotte was in a state of some perturbation about him.

Mr Nicholls, undaunted, and with surprising cunning, had written to Charlotte informing her that in August he was to become the curate to the Reverend T. Cator, vicar of Kirk Smeaton near Pontefract. She did not reply. Nor to the next letter, nor the next, but on the sixth letter, perhaps impressed by his persistence, she wrote to him, counselling 'heroic submission to his lot'. Mr Nicholls immediately wrote back, saying that her letter had so comforted him in his affliction that she must write to him some more; his wily appeal paid off. By the autumn they were in regular correspondence, and Charlotte's feelings were evidently not wholly neutral.

But the rule Mr Brontë had had over his daughter for so long was not to be gainsaid. She told Ellen that she became so 'miserable' at deceiving her father by carrying on a clandestine correspondence and it had weighed so greatly on her mind that in the end she had to tell him that she was writing to Mr Nicholls. It had been 'sheer pain' which made her gather courage to break the news. 'I told all. It was very hard and rough work at the time, but the issue after a few days was that I obtained leave to continue the communication.' Here was a thirty-seven-year-old woman – the Currer Bell whose passion had so shocked Victorian England – obtaining leave from her seventy-six-year-old father to continue to write to her would-be curate lover. Mrs Gaskell, arriving in the middle of the conflict over Mr Nicholls, would be amazed by the way Mr Brontë continued to treat Charlotte as a child, which was made more curious on account of his proprietorial pride in her success.

Charlotte had written to Mrs Gaskell that she had waited for 'the purple signal' of the heath in bloom before asking her friend to come to stay. Her father, she said, although sickly all summer, was much looking forward to her visit and she herself would be particularly glad of her friend's company, since her recent proposed trip to Scotland with Joe Taylor and his wife and baby had had to be cut short when the baby became ill in Carlisle and they had had to turn back. Mrs Gaskell arrived on 19 September, on what she described as a 'dull, drizzly, Indian-inky day all the way on the railroad to Keighley', the sky was lead-coloured, and everything looked particularly grey and dull and hungry looking 'with stone fences everywhere, and trees nowhere'. A thunderstorm had blighted the purple heather bloom two days before and the moors were a livid brown colour instead of the burnished purple glory they should have been.

Charlotte had warned her humorously that she must come to Haworth 'in the spirit which might sustain you in case you were setting out on a brief visit to the backwoods of America', and that the change would do her good 'if not too prolonged'. The warning was perhaps needed. Mrs Gaskell found the country cold and bleak-looking, and very isolated. There was the 'pestiferous' graveyard, surrounding the house, the moors sweeping away everywhere – moors everywhere beyond and above the house: 'Oh! those high, wild, desolate moors, up above the whole world, and the very realms of silence', she exclaimed in the *Life*. She recalled being half blown back by the vehemence of the wind which howled round the house and along the narrow gravel walk. She noted the garden of a small plot of grass enclosed within a low stone wall, gravestones towering over it and all around, and then she went up the steps, through the door into the

445

'exquisitely clean passage' and into the square parlour, where Miss Brontë rose to greet her. She thought that the room looked the perfection of warmth and snugness, crimson predominating in the furniture. Charlotte informed her that everything was new within the last few years, paid for by the £1,500 she had earned as an authoress. It was about the equivalent amount per annum as Mr Brontë's own income, although she was never allowed to do the household accounts, which were always entered in the shabby little notebook by Mr Brontë.

Mrs Gaskell noticed the same air of 'the most delicate and scrupulous cleanliness' throughout the house. Miss Brontë was so neat herself that Mrs Gaskell became quite ashamed of any touches of her own exuberant untidiness. She could see that a chair out of place, work left on the table, were annoyances to her hostess's sense of order. She observed the three drawings in her room – Miss Brontë's likeness by Richmond, the print of Thackeray and the engraving of the Duke of Wellington – all presents from Mr Smith at the height of his enthusiasm.

Mrs Gaskell's room was above the parlour, and thus looked out on the same view, i.e. the graveyard, which she said valiantly was really beautiful in certain lights, moonlight especially. She asked Martha to take her into the church to look at the graves of the Brontës, though all she could see was the tablet put up at the communion rails, since they were buried beneath the aisle. Tabby, whom Mrs Gaskell thought was ninety – she was in fact eighty-two – described how, since 'they were little bairns, Miss Brontë and Miss Emily and Miss Anne used to put away their sewing after prayers and walk all three one after the other round the table in the parlour till near eleven o'clock'. With a poetic flourish, she concluded – 'and now my heart aches to hear Miss Brontë walking, walking, on alone'. On enquiring, Mrs Gaskell found out that after the rest of the household had gone to bed, Miss Brontë *did* come downstairs and begin the slow, monotonous, incessant walk, in which Mrs Gaskell felt sure she would fancy hearing the footsteps of the dead following her.

Mr Brontë's custom of having his dinner sent to him in his sitting room, when there were only two of the family left, rather scandalised Mrs Gaskell, though during her visit he came into tea as an honour to her and they all three breakfasted together at 9 am. She could not imagine what he did with himself all day – brooded perhaps; his room contained very little – there was no sign of engraving, map, writing materials, beyond a desk, and no books except for those contained on two hanging shelves between the windows, along with his two pipes and a spittoon. She found him 'a tall fine looking old man, with silver bristles all over his head; nearly blind; speaking with a strong Scotch accent'. He told her that he had been rather intimate with Lord

Palmerston at Cambridge, which she thought was 'a pleasant soothing reflection now, in his shut out life'. Her description in a letter to a friend, which was much toned down for her biography of Miss Brontë, goes on:

He was very polite and agreeable to me; paying rather elaborate old-fashioned compliments, but I was sadly afraid of him in my inmost soul; for I caught a glare of his stern eyes over his spectacles at Miss Brontë once or twice which made me know my man; and he talked at her some times. . . . He won't let Miss Brontë accompany him in his walks, although he is so nearly blind; goes out in defiance of her gentle attempts to restrain him, speaking as if she thought him in his second childhood; and comes home moaning and tired: having lost his way; 'Where is my strength gone?' is his cry then. 'I used to walk 40 miles a day' &c. There are little bits of picturesque affection about him — for his old dogs for instance. . . .

Though she was rather alarmed by this being whom she brushed against in the passages or saw for tea, she had to admit that it was 'rather an admiring fear after all'.

Mrs Gaskell could also see the rough, rather crude side of Mr Brontë. He was not all stately compliments. In her letter, she wrote that when Charlotte had refused to see a pushy young author who intended to call on her on his way back from Hull, Mr Brontë had 'abused us both for "a couple of proud minxes" when we said we would rather be without individual patronage if it was to subject us to individual impertinence'. And then, dismayed at her indiscretion, she wrote, 'Oh, please burn this letter as soon as you have read it!'[4]

In the day they went up on the moors for long walks and Mrs Gaskell got to know more — and feel even more pity — for Charlotte as she heard more of the 'wild, strange facts' about the family's lives. She thought that Miss Brontë had 'the most original and suggestive thoughts of her own; so that, like the moors, I felt on the last day as if our talk might be extended in any direction without getting to the end of any subject'. Before tea one day they had a wonderful talk

. . . right against the wind on Penistone Moor which stretches directly behind the Parsonage going over the hill in brown and purple sweeps and falling softly down into a little upland valley through which a 'beck' ran, and beyond again was another great waving hill — and in the dip of that might be seen another yet more distant, and beyond that the said Lancashire came; but the sinuous hills seemed to girdle the world like the great Norse serpent, and for my part I don't know if they don't stretch up to the North Pole.

447

They met no one up on the moors. Here and there from the high moorland summit Mrs Gaskell noticed newly built churches tended to by the curates described in *Shirley*. Miss Brontë pointed out faraway hollows where grey houses were to be glimpsed, often with a few Scotch firs growing near them, and told her guest such tales of the wild ungovernable families living there 'that *Wuthering Heights* even seemed tame comparatively'. It emerged that Miss Brontë spent some time visiting the poor, and taught at the schools during the day.

In the evening Mr Brontë retreated, as was his custom, to his sitting room to smoke a pipe and the two women sat by the fire and talked of how the room had once been full of children. At half past eight they went into his study for prayers, and soon after nine everyone was in bed but them. Charlotte told Mrs Gaskell that in general she sat there quite alone thinking over the past, because her eyesight was now so bad as to prevent her reading or writing by candlelight; the knitting she did for occupation was very mechanical and did not keep the thoughts from wandering. At one point Mrs Gaskell asked her if she had ever taken opium, as the description of its effects in *Villette* was so exactly like what she herself had experienced on once taking opium – 'vivid and exaggerated presence of objects, of which the outlines were indistinct or lost in golden mist etc'. Charlotte replied no, but that she had followed the process she always adopted when she had to describe anything not within her own experience: she thought intently about it for many a night before falling asleep, 'till at length, sometimes after the progress of her story had been arrested at this one point for weeks, she wakened up in the morning with all clear before her, as if she had in reality gone through the experience, and then could describe it, word for word, as it had happened'.

Other literary subjects preoccupied Charlotte that September. She was very curious about Harriet Beecher Stowe's personal appearance; it evidently harmonised with some theory of hers when she heard that the author of *Uncle Tom's Cabin* was small and slight. Perhaps she considered that there was an inverse proportion between literary power and size. Charlotte also told Mrs Gaskell that she had dreaded the charge of plagiarism after she had written *Jane Eyre*, when she read the thrilling effect of the mysterious scream at midnight in Mrs Marsh's story *The Deformed*. Likewise when she read *The Neighbours* by Miss Bremer she thought everyone must imagine that she had taken her conception of Jane Eyre's character from that of Francesca.

On their walks they sometimes met the poor people of the hills, and Mrs Gaskell noted how well known Charlotte was, and how kindly and warmly greeted. Charlotte for her part knew which members of the family to enquire after. 'Her quiet gentle words, few though they might be, were evidently grateful to those Yorkshire ears. Their welcome to her, though rough and curt, was sincere and hearty.'

In the course of the four-day visit Miss Brontë revealed her new theory of disappointment. They talked about the different courses through which life ran:

> She said in her own composed manner, as if she had accepted the theory as a fact, that she believed some were appointed beforehand to sorrow and much disappointment; that it did not fall to the lot of all – as Scripture told us – to have their lines fall in pleasant places; that it was well for those who had rougher paths to perceive that such was God's will concerning them, and try to moderate their expectations, leaving hope to those of a different doom, and seeking patience and resignations as the virtues they were to cultivate.

But as various reviewers noticed, in *Villette* its author showed how difficult it was to be subdued when her natural bent was to be ambitious, to desire, to expect much, as was obvious from the way she had forged out her own life. Nothing could be more alien to the fiery personality who had expressed herself in *Jane Eyre*, *Shirley* and *Villette* than to cultivate patience and resignation. *Villette* revealed the extent of it; as Matthew Arnold wrote, the book is full 'of hunger, rebellion and rage'. Nevertheless, this was what she must do.

Beautiful, benevolent Mrs Gaskell, with her busy happy life, could not allow this. Although she would admit the great discrepancy between their lives and would say privately that she was sure that, 'even with my inferior vehemence of power and nature', she could not have borne Miss Brontë's life of monotony and privation of anyone to love, she had worried about Miss Brontë's lack of repose after reading *Villette*. 'Her craving for keen enjoyment of life – which after all comes only in *drams* to anyone' would inevitably leave 'the spaces between most dreary and depressing'. Probably for this reason Mrs Gaskell insisted on differing with her friend's pessimism, and furious, almost aggressive stoicism:

> I took a different view: I thought that human lots were more equal than she imagined; that to some happiness and sorrow came in strong patches of light and shadow (so to speak), while in the lives of others they were pretty equally blended throughout. She smiled, and shook her head, and said she was trying to school herself against ever anticipating any pleasure; that it was better to be brave and submit faithfully; there was some good reason which we should know in time, why sorrow and disappointment were to be the lot of some on earth. It was better to acknowledge this, and face out the truth in a religious faith.

The visit gave Charlotte temporary cheer and encouragement. Mrs Gaskell departed with a present for Charlotte's favourite little Julia, and with many intentions, in Mrs Gaskell's words, of 'renewing very frequently the pleasure we had in being together. We agreed that when she wanted bustle, or when I wanted quiet, we were to let each other know, and exchange visits as occasion required.' Charlotte was again left alone to wrestle with her doubts about her feelings for Mr Nicholls. In her restlessness she went to stay that autumn with Ellen and with Miss Wooler; and on Mrs Gaskell's advice she had notified a Mrs Dove at 36 Bloomsbury Square, London, who kept lodgings, to ask for rooms some time in November. Apparently she wished to visit London independent of George Smith.

Meanwhile she pondered on the many differences between Charlotte Brontë and the man who proposed to be her husband – his narrow religious views, his lack of intellectual pursuits. Nevertheless, over the next few months she began to form a better notion from his letters of the kind of man Mr Nicholls was. She might not find his tastes or thoughts 'congenial', but at least she could be sure of his 'tender love for me'. There was genuine affection there. He was an affectionate conscientious, high-principled man' beneath the moroseness. As she wrote to Ellen, all she learnt of him 'inclined me to esteem and if not love – at least affection'.

Mrs Gaskell had returned home full of even greater pity for her friend and with a picture of Mr Nicholls from what Charlotte had told her as 'very good, but *very* stern and bigoted'. 'He sounds vehemently in love with her . . . Mr N never knew, till long after *Shirley* was published, that she wrote books; and came in, cold and disapproving one day, to ask her if the report he had heard at Keighley was true etc. Fancy him, an Irish curate, loving her even then, reading the beginning of *Shirley*!'[5] Mr Brontë's particular insistence on Mr Nicholls' lack of money set Mrs Gaskell thinking and by the end of October she had contacted Richard Monckton Milnes, since he was a patron of writers and as fascinated by the lonely bold genius of little Currer Bell as she was, about giving Mr Nicholls a pension, in order to make him a little more of a proposition as a husband. Sending Monckton Milnes Mr Nicholls' address so that he could be summoned for an interview, she wrote:

I am quite sure that *one* hundred a year given as acknowledgement of his merits, as a good faithful clergyman, would give her ten times the pleasure that *two* hundred a year would do, if bestowed upon her in her capacity as a writer. I am sure he is a thoroughly good hard-working, self-denying curate. . . . Her father's only reason for his violent and virulent opposition is Mr Nicholls' utter want of money, or friends to help him to any professional advancement.[6]

The entire project was to be a complete secret: 'If my well-meant treachery becomes known to her I shall lose her friendship, which I prize most highly.' And in Mrs Gaskell's view Mr Monckton Milnes's kind words must have made Mr Nicholls feel that he was not entirely friendless, and made him rouse himself to fresh effort. Charlotte Brontë would later tell Mrs Gaskell of the interview and of his puzzle to account for the interest in him.

The correspondence with Mr Nicholls continued and towards the end of the autumn Charlotte told Mrs Gaskell that 'the matter was again brought prominently forward'. It appears from this that Mr Nicholls had decided to make a bold foray after his long slow war of attrition. He wanted a meeting, and it seems likely from Charlotte's cryptic reference, the only one to the affair, that she at last dared suggest such a thing to her father. This turn of events may account for her sudden changes of plans over her trip to London, although equally another explanation may be called for. On 21 November Charlotte wrote two letters. One was to Mrs Emily Shaen (née Winkworth), a friend of Mrs Gaskell's, who had offered her assistance in obtaining rooms in London for her. Charlotte apologised for not writing back by return – she had still been awaiting a reply from Mrs Dove – but 'as I have little time to lose, I think it better at once to avail myself of the information you have so kindly collected for me. I am quite sure I can trust your opinion better than my own, and shall therefore be truly obliged if you will engage for me the front sitting room and bedroom at 30s. a week at Mrs Joyce's, 37 Bedford Place, for next Thursday.' If she had nothing available, could she make alternative arrangements.

And she refers to 'my business in town', though what the business was is not specified. There is no surviving letter from Smith, Elder suggesting that her presence was necessary in London for business reasons; there was no work going through the press. Charlotte had, however, evidently received a letter from George Smith that same day, 21 November, as appears from her concerned reply not to him, but to his mother:

Haworth Nov 21st 1853.

My dear Mrs Smith,
    I had not heard from your son for a long time – and this morning I had a note from him which though brief and not explicit was indication of a good deal of uneasiness and disturbance of mind. The cover was edged and sealed with black but he does not say what relative he has lost. As it is not deep mourning I trust no harm has

451

befallen any one very dear to him, but I cannot resist writing to you for a word of explanation. What ails him? Do you feel uneasy about him, or do you think he will soon be better? If he is going to take any important step in life – as some of his expressions would seem to imply – is it one likely to conduce to his happiness and welfare?

I hope your daughters and yourself are well. My Father's health was very infirm throughout the summer, but I am thankful to say he is better now. Remember me kindly to your circle, and believe me,
    Sincerely yours,
C. Brontë[7]

Charlotte might have received George Smith's letter by a second post after she had written off to Mrs Shaen, but it seems more likely that she wrote to Mrs Shaen after, and as a result of, the post arriving bearing George Smith's letter. Alarm for his welfare could explain the sudden urgency of her desire to go to London, the next week. However, on 24 November, only three days later, she wrote to Mrs Shaen saying, 'At the last moment when my portmanteau was packed and all ready – circumstances have taken a turn which will prevent my intended journey to London.' Possibly at this moment a tremendous row broke out between Charlotte and her father about Mr Nicholls; but another reason for the sudden change of plan may well be found in the draft of a letter from Mrs Smith to Miss Brontë, which although undated, seems to be her drafted reply to Charlotte's letter of 21 November. In it Mrs Smith struggles to convey, without actually stating the news, that George Smith is about to announce his engagement. (According to his memoirs George Smith proposed to the Paulina-like Elizabeth Blakeway, the daughter of a wine merchant, in November and they were married in February.)

. . . . I shall answer your kind enquiries about my son with a great deal of pleasure – he is quite well and very happy – *there is every prospect* [crossed out] he is thinking of *his* [crossed out] taking a very important step in life. The most important and *I think* [crossed out] with every prospect of happiness. I am very thankful and pleased about it – I am sure he will as soon as it is quite settled enter *fully* [crossed out] into all the particulars with you – it is not *fully* [crossed out] yet tho' I have no doubt in my own mind all be as his best friends could wish and you will soon hear *soon* [crossed out] from him again . . .[8]

Mrs Smith went on to give details of how they closed earlier at Cornhill than they used to. The family were in mourning for her mother-in-law who had died last September, hence the black-edged paper. They had been to the Isle of Wight for a holiday and enjoyed themselves very much, and had managed to entice George down for a holiday; they sent him back all the better for the change. They were all well and her daughters wrote with her in kind love and respects.

If Charlotte had still nursed some hopes about Mr Smith, receipt of this letter would effectively have put an end to them. She had perhaps intended something when she went to London, perhaps hoping that if Mr Smith was 'uneasy', as he appeared to be, all was not totally lost. Perhaps this speculation is unjust to Charlotte, but a couple of weeks later, on 6 December, she suddenly sent a note to Mr Williams, telling him: 'Do not trouble yourself to select or send any more books. These courtesies must cease some day, and I would rather give them up than wear them out.' Evidently she felt that the connection with Cornhill must now be severed, but the brusqueness with which she did this suggests emotional hurt. It may simply be that she realised that the intimate, personal relationship which once existed between her and Mr Smith must of necessity end with his marriage. Certainly, by 10 December she had been told of his engagement. Her note of congratulation was perfunctory to the point of hostility:

10 December 1853

My dear Sir,
    In great happiness, as in great grief, – words of sympathy should be few. Accept my meed of congratulation – and believe me,
    Sincerely yours,
                        C. Brontë[9]

Her mood, as revealed in a letter to Miss Wooler two days later, was rather savage, and more akin to the desperate letters of late 1851 and 1852 than her more cheerful frame of mind in 1853:

I wonder how you are spending these long winter evenings. Alone – probably – like me. The thought often crosses me, as I sit by myself, how pleasant it would be if you lived within walking distance, and I could go to you sometimes, or have you to come and spend a day and night with me. . . . I fear you must be very solitary at Hornsea. How hard to some people of the world it would seem to live your life – how utterly impossible to live it with a serene spirit and an unsoured disposition! It seems wonderful to me – because you are not like Mrs Ruff – phlegmatic and impenetrable – but received from nature feelings of the very finest edge. Such feelings when they are locked up – sometimes damage the mind and temper. They don't with you. It must be partly principle, partly self-

453

discipline, which keeps you as you are.

George Smith's marriage announcement may have helped finally to pave the way for Mr Nicholls; from now on Charlotte decided to concentrate on matters closer to home, to shelve her other life as an author to meet the emotional demands on her at Haworth. For whatever reasons, she braved her father's wrath and demanded to be allowed the meeting for which Mr Nicholls had been relentlessly pushing. Just as she had argued for several days about being allowed to continue to write to him, it took several days before her father finally gave his acceptance to a meeting. This time she was less worried about the effect upon his health, as he had passed the winter without particular illness, and she, rather to her surprise, had only suffered from headache and a little dyspepsia, but not a single cold, so she may have felt stronger to do battle with the pugnacious old man. There was also another factor that disposed Mr Brontë to think of his former curate with a little more favour: he found Mr Nicholls' replacement, Mr De Renzy, even more intolerable. So, with her father's reluctant compliance, Charlotte arranged to see Mr Nicholls in early January.

CHAPTER XXI

Marriage

In January Mr Nicholls came to stay for ten days with his friend Mr Sowden at Oxenhope, the hamlet which is part of the Haworth parish on the other side of the valley, about a mile beyond the parsonage going towards Lancashire. Here in the bitterly cold weather, surrounded by the bleak moors, the ardent Mr Nicholls and his reluctant inamorata met and walked, far from the suspicious glare of the old parson hunched up in his study. Charlotte had the opportunity she had demanded from her father to become better acquainted, although Mr Brontë remained 'very, very hostile – bitterly unjust'. She told Mr Nicholls during their meetings of the great obstacles which stood in his way, but he persevered, in the process winning her admiration because he proved himself to be disinterested and forbearing, and 'that while his feelings are exquisitely keen, he can freely forgive'.

Mrs Gaskell, whom Charlotte visited four months later, recounted how Miss Brontë revealed something of the way she had finally made her father relax his upsettingly 'vehement antipathy to the bare thought of anyone thinking of me as a wife':

> To hear her description of the conversation with her father when she insisted on her right to see something more of Mr Nicholls was really fine. Her father thought that she had a chance of somebody higher or at least farther removed from poverty. She said 'Father I am not a young girl, nor a young woman even – I never was pretty. I now am ugly. At your death I will have £300 besides the little I have earned myself – do you think there are many men who would serve seven years for me?' And again when he renewed the conversation and asked her if she would marry a curate? – 'Yes I must marry a curate if I marry at all; not merely a curate but *your* curate: not merely *your* curate but he must live in the house with you, for I cannot leave you.' The sightless old man stood up and said solemnly

'Never. I will never have another man in this house,' and stalked out of the room. For a week he never spoke to her. She had not made up her mind to accept Mr Nicholls and the worry on both sides made her ill – then the old servant interfered, and asked him, sitting blind and alone, 'if he wished to kill his daughter?' and went up to her and abused Mr Nicholls for not having 'more brass'.[1]

By 18 April Charlotte wrote stiffly to Mrs Gaskell: 'Things have progressed I don't know how. It is of no use going into detail. After various visits and as the result of perseverance in one quarter and a gradual change of feeling in others, I find myself what people call "engaged".' Nevertheless it was not absolutely what she wanted. She confessed to Mrs Gaskell that 'there was much reluctance, and many difficulties to be overcome. I cannot deny that I have had a battle to fight with myself; I am not sure that I have not even yet conquered certain inward combatants.' And she went on to say:

I could almost cry sometimes that in this important action in my life I cannot better satisfy papa's perhaps natural pride. My destiny will not be brilliant, certainly, but Mr Nicholls is conscientious, affectionate, pure in heart and life. He offers a most constant and tried attachment – I am very grateful to him. I mean to try and make him happy, and papa too. . . .

The fact was that she herself, like her father, still had a remembrance of grand dreams which showed in all the letters she wrote announcing her engagement. To Miss Wooler she wrote almost apologetically that 'The destiny which Providence in His goodness and wisdom seems to offer me will not – I am aware – be generally regarded as brilliant – but I trust I see in it some germs of real happiness', and to Ellen she explained that 'The feeling which had been disappointed in Papa was *ambition*, paternal pride – ever a restless feeling, as we all know.' As one who had once so much of it, it was perhaps unsurprising that she should have desired more for herself. However, she had at least found a solution to her worry about her father, for Mr Nicholls was to return to Haworth as curate and would live at the parsonage. To her great relief, now that the matter was settled Mr Brontë appeared to have begun to respect Mr Nicholls.

Charlotte had as usual been confiding her anxieties to Ellen, who was proving a rather unhelpful counsellor. Later letters reveal Ellen's jealousy of Mr Nicholls; she and Charlotte had had after all the sort of relationship which in some ways was close to a marriage – it had been full of intimacy and emotion which both parties had not been able to find elsewhere. To Mary Taylor, Ellen clothed her sense of betrayal in high-flown Victorian maidenly talk, wallowing in the cult of self-sacrifice, to the former's unconcealed and healthy rage. 'You talk wonderful nonsense about Charlotte Brontë in your letter,' Mary blasted superbly from New Zealand on 24 February:

> What do you mean about 'bearing her position so long, and enduring to the end?' and still better – 'bearing our lot, whatever it is.' If it's C's lot to be married, shd n't she bear that too? or does your strange morality mean that she should refuse to ameliorate her lot when it lies in her power. How would she be inconsistent with herself in marrying? Because she considers her own pleasure? If this is new for her to do, it is high time she began to make it more common. It is an outrageous exaction to expect her to give up her choice in a matter so important, and I think her to blame in having been hitherto so yielding that her friends can think of making such an impudent demand.[2]

And with that Mary went back to ticketing and arranging the new silk mantles for the ladies of Wellington in her store, to which she had lately built a magnificent twenty-foot extension.

Charlotte announced her engagement in a letter to Ellen of 11 April. The creator of Rochester said that 'what I taste of happiness is of the soberest order'. Nevertheless she had made up her mind, marry him she would. Mr Nicholls, now that he had finally won his cause, wanted the wedding to be as soon as possible, and although Charlotte shrank from the imminence of July, she had yielded to his wish. She told Ellen that during the week when she had taken her decision, she had longed for her friend's presence but Mr Nicholls – 'Arthur as I now call him' – had put his foot down. He said 'it was the only time and place when he could not have wished to see you'. With marriage as unknown territory rearing suddenly before her, Charlotte felt both apprehensive and oddly melancholy. She asked Ellen to be her bridesmaid, and told her that she intended the wedding to be 'literally *as quiet as possible*'. Almost thirty-eight, she was about to share her life, her bed, her person, with a man for the first time. There was a strange half-sad feeling in making the engagement announcements. 'The whole thing is something other than imagination paints it beforehand; cares, fears, come mixed inextricably with hopes', particularly when her own rich imagination was at work. She longed to talk it over with her dear Nell. But the fact that Ellen was prevented from seeing her friend because of Mr Nicholls' attentions to his fiancée cannot have eased her jealousy.

The only person who appears to have taken a sanguine view of the whole affair was Mrs Gaskell. Despite Charlotte's worries about congenial thoughts and taste and lack of talent, in conjunction with the threat of concealed marital mysteries, Mrs Gaskell was sure that 'Miss Brontë could never have borne not to be well ruled and ordered . . . she would never have been happy but with an exacting, rigid, law-giving, passionate man'. The only fly in the ointment were Mr Nicholls' narrow religious views, which she thought meant Mr Nicholls would not allow her to remain friends with 'us heretics'.[3]

On the same day, 18 April, that Charlotte wrote her rather anguished letter to Mrs Gaskell announcing her engagement, she also wrote to George Smith. Her method of conveying the news to him was strange and constricted, asking for all monies due to her to be trans-ferred to another name (a requirement upon marriage under British law, until the Married Woman's Property Act of 1872):

It having become necessary that my Stock in the Funds should be transferred to another name, I have empowered Mr Metcalfe – my Solicitor – the Bearer of this note – to ask such particulars as are required to fill up the Power of Attorney for a transfer, a Statement of the exact amount standing in my name in the Government Books is also required: I have Bank-Receipts for the following sums in my possession, viz.

£500 The price of the copyright of 'Shirley' invested in the Funds Octbr 1849.

£480 Recd for the copyright of 'Villette' invested Decr 1852.

£521.17s. 6d The proceeds of the sale of Railway Shares – invested Jany 1853.

£82.10s Recd for Foreign Copyright of 'Villette'; invested April 1853.

Besides these there is a further Sum of £100 which became due to me in July 1851 – and which I find by reference to a letter of yours dated Novr 15th 1851 – was for the small edition of 'Jane Eyre'. You asked me – I remember – what should be done with this sum – and I said it might be put in the Bank with the rest – but for it I have never had a receipt, and should feel obliged if you will now ascertain whether such a document is in your possession.

Apologising for the unavoidable trouble this gives

I am, my dear Sir

Yours sincerely

C. Brontë[4]

Rather surprised at this brusque way of announcing an engagement, George Smith must have written a warm letter back, for on 25 April Charlotte wrote a long, quite intimate letter to him, more pessimistic in tone than letters to her other correspondents:

. . . There has been heavy anxiety – but I begin to hope all will end for the best. My expectations however are very subdued – very different, I dare say, to what *yours* were before you were married. Care and Fear stand so close to Hope, I sometimes scarcely can see her for the shadows they cast. And yet I am thankful too, and the doubtful future must be left with Providence.

On one feature in the marriage I can dwell with unmingled satisfaction, with a *certainty* of being right. It takes nothing from the attention I owe to my Father. I am not to leave him – my future husband consents to come here – thus Papa secures by the step a devoted and reliable assistant in his old age.

She ended the letter very much with a farewell, as if she never intended to see her publishers again, as if with marriage her writing career had come to an end:

I hardly know in what form of greeting to include your wife's name, as I have never seen her. Say to her whatever may seem to you most appropriate and expressive of goodwill. I sometimes wonder how Mr Williams is, and hope he is well. In the course of the year that is gone, Cornhill and London have receded a long way from me; the lines of communication have waxed very frail and few. It must be so in this world. All things considered, I don't wish it otherwise.

    – Yours sincerely,

C. Brontë.

So, as an escape from loneliness, to relieve a suffering and faithful heart, to secure in its fidelity a solid good, rather than pursuing the vain, empty shadow of ambition – as she told her father, Charlotte Brontë began to prepare for her wedding. Mr Brontë continued cheerful and quiet; apparently he had come to terms with his daughter's marriage. She was impressed by Mr Nicholls' dutifulness. He *would* look after her father, and had been a most assiduous curate. She found it touching that he wanted to prove his gratitude to her father by offering support and consolation in his declining age. She felt that it really would not be 'mere talk with him; he is no talker, no dealer in professions'.

At the beginning of May she went to pay a last visit to the Gaskells, perhaps to hear a few comforting words about the strange estate she was about to enter into. Catherine Winkworth, Mrs Gaskell's friend and the authoress of many hymns, gave the following account of Miss Brontë a month and a half before her wedding; it suggests that Miss Brontë still half longed for that hint of Mephistopheles. Catherine Winkworth was taken up to Miss Brontë's bedroom by Mrs Gaskell, who whispered, 'Say something about her marriage':

. . . I began: 'I was very glad to hear something Mrs Gaskell told me about you.' 'What was it?' 'That you are not going to be alone any more.' She leant her head on her hand and said very quickly: 'Yes, I am going to be married in June.' 'It will be a great happiness for you to have someone to care for, and make happy.' 'Yes; and it is a great thing to be the first object with any one.' 'And you must be very sure of that with Mr Nicholls; he has known you and wished for this so long, I hear.' 'Yes, he has more than once refused preferment since he left my father, because he knew he never could marry me unless he could return to Haworth; he knew I could not leave my father.'

She stopped, and then went on: 'But Katie, it has cost me a good deal to come to this.' 'You will have to care for his things, instead of caring for yours, is that it?' 'Yes, I can see that beforehand.' 'But you have been together so long already that you know what his things are, very well. He is very devoted to his duties, is he not? – and you can and would like to help him in those?' 'I have always been used to those, and it is one great pleasure to me that he is so much beloved by all the people in the parish; there is quite a rejoicing over his return. But those are not everything, and I cannot conceal from myself that he is *not* intellectual; there are many places into which he could not follow me intellectually.' 'Well; of course everyone has their own tastes. For myself, if a man had a firm, constant, affectionate reliable nature, with tolerable practical sense, I should be much better satisfied with him than if he had an intellect far beyond mine, and brilliant gifts without that trustworthiness. I care most for a calm, equable atmosphere at home.' 'I do believe Mr Nicholls is as reliable as you say, or I wouldn't marry him.' 'And you have had time to prove it; you are both not acting in a hurry.' 'That is true; and indeed, I am quite satisfied with my decisions; still' – here Lily [Mrs Gaskell] came in, and Miss Brontë repeated what I had been saying, ending with – 'still such a character would be far less amusing and interesting than a more impulsive and fickle one; it might be dull!' 'Yes, indeed,' said Lily. 'For a day's companion, yes,' I said, 'But not for a life's: one's home ought to be the one fixed point, the one untroubled region in one's lot; at home one wants peace and settled love and trust, not storm and change and excitement; besides such a character would have the advantage that one might do the fickleness required one's self, which would be a relief sometimes.' 'Oh, Katie, if *I* had ever said such a wicked thing,' cried Lily; and then Miss Brontë: 'Oh, Katie, I never thought to hear such a speech from *you*!' 'You don't agree with it?'

'Oh, there is truth in it; so much that I don't think *I* could ever have been so candid,' Miss Brontë said; 'And there is danger, too, one might be led on to go too far.' 'I think not,' I said; 'the steadiness and generosity on the other side would always keep one in check.'

But they made a great deal of fun and laughing about this, and then Lily was called away again, and Miss Brontë went on: 'he is a Puseyite and very stiff; I fear it will stand in the way of intercourse with some of my friends. But I shall always be the same in heart towards them. I shall never let him make me a bigot. I don't think differences of opinion ought to interfere with friendship, do you?' 'No.' And we talked about this a little, and then I said: 'Perhaps, too, you may do something to introduce him to goodness in sects where he has thought it could not be.' 'That is what I hope; he has a most sincere love of goodness wherever he sees it. I think if he could come to know Mr Gaskell it would change his feeling.' Then, quite suddenly, she said: 'Tell me about your sister [Emily Shaen]. Is she happy in her married life?' 'Yes, very happy indeed.' 'Sincerely?' 'Yes, she not only says so, but it shines out in everything that she is happier than ever before in her life.' 'And what is your brother-in-law like?' So I had to describe Will, thinking privately that it did not sound as though Mr Nicholls would make half such a good husband, but did not say so, and to tell her a good deal about their engagement. What she cared most about hearing about Will was, whether he was selfish about small things, whether he took his share of small economies, or whether he appreciated Emily's endeavours and small denials, &c. Concerning which he had been praising Emily to me the last time he was here, so I edified her with reporting that, and gave him generally 'an excellent character', as people say of servants.

About Emily she wanted to know what variations of mood, what doubts and fears, she had felt about her marriage beforehand. Had she felt any, or was she always light-hearted during the time? So I said that no one could be exactly always light-hearted, I thought, who was not very young and thoughtless, whereat it came out that she thought Emily not twenty-five now. And then we talked over all the natural doubts that any thoughtful woman would feel at such a time, and my own mother's early married life, and when Lily returned she said she felt greatly comforted; and whereupon Lily set off praising *her* husband for being a good sick nurse and so good to the children, and how very winning that was to the mother. . . .

Catherine Winkworth went on to relate what she had gleaned from Mrs Gaskell about the affair: when Miss Brontë saw Mr Nicholls again in January she decided that she could make him happy, and that his love was too good to be thrown away by one so lonely as she is. He thinks her intellectually superior to himself, and admires her gifts, and likes her the better, which sounds as though he were generous. And he has very good family connections, but they will be very poor, for the living is only £250 a year. If only he is not altogether too narrow for her, one can fancy her much more really happy with such a man than with one who might have made her more in love, and I am sure she will be really good to him. But I *guess* the true love was Paul Emanuel after all, and is dead; but I don't know, and don't think that Lily knows. . . .[5]

If Catherine Winkworth was describing the entire substance of the conversation between her and Charlotte, it was not perhaps very satisfactory or informative for an anxious Charlotte suffering from pre-wedding nerves. From Mrs Gaskell's house she went on to visit Joe Taylor and his wife, then Ellen, before returning to Haworth and all the hustle and bustle of preparations. The little room under the stairs, formerly used to store peat, had been transformed into a study for Mr Nicholls, with green and white curtains and matching paper. Charlotte thought they looked 'clean and neat enough'. Joseph Taylor had been consulted about her financial position on marriage; she and perhaps more so Mr Brontë evidently felt quite strongly that her marriage should not prevent her controlling the not inconsiderable money she had made as an author, all in all £1,684 7s 6d. A document was drawn up on 24 May 1854 in which the conflicts of her position are revealed. It was signed by Charlotte Brontë, Arthur Nicholls and Joseph Taylor, and basically prevented Mr Nicholls touching a penny of her money, whether she was alive or dead.

All the money which Charlotte possessed in her own right was to be paid into a trust for herself and any children she might have. The money, which had been invested for her by George Smith in $3\frac{1}{4}$ per cent reduced bank annuities, was transferred into Joseph Taylor's name, who was to act as trustee. The interest and dividends arising from the capital sum were to be paid to whomsoever Charlotte directed in writing, regardless of her marriage. In default of such action, the money was to be paid to Charlotte personally 'for her sole and separate use independent of the said Arthur Bell Nicholls, her intended husband, who is not to intermeddle therewith'; the money was not to be 'subject or liable to his debts, Control Contracts or Engagements', so that Charlotte alone controlled its expenditure. If she were to become a widow and had no living children, then the capital sum with any interest arising was to be transferred to her 'absolute and proper use and benefit', free of all trusts. If she died in her husband's lifetime leaving living children and no written direction to the trustee, the capital was to remain in trust for the children. Shares of children dying before becoming entitled to receive them were to be divided between remaining children. If the share had already vested, it was to be kept in trust for Charlotte's grandchild until it came of age. If there were no living children of the marriage on Charlotte's death, then the entire trust funds were to be paid out according to the Intestacy Statutes as if Charlotte had died unmarried and intestate. If Joseph Taylor died or otherwise relinquished his position as trustee, then Charlotte could appoint another in his stead, regardless of her marriage.

The terms of the trust to benefit Charlotte's children were in fact quite normal;[6] fathers giving daughters a dowry on marriage usually specified that the children should be the beneficiaries in the event of the daughter's death. However, the clause that prevented Mr Nicholls from receiving any money in the event of Charlotte Brontë's death was very unusual, and it has been suggested by Dr Juliet Barker, the Curator of the Brontë Parsonage Museum, who discovered and published the document, that 'this clause, more than any other, indicates the depth of doubt Charlotte felt about Nicholls' motives in marrying her, as this [i.e that Charlotte would die childless in her husband's lifetime], given their respective ages, states of health and risks of childbirth, was the likeliest outcome'. This seems a rather harsh judgement on Mr Nicholls for Charlotte to make; in her letters she made a point of stressing his high-mindedness. Another explanation is that she was appeasing the tyrannical Mr Brontë, who could not view with equanimity the idea of Mr Nicholls controlling money which had hitherto been as good as his.

Charlotte continued to have pre-wedding nerves about Mr Nicholls, which manifested themselves in curious ways. She suddenly thought that he probably had the sort of rheumatoid arthritis which might prove fatal. She wrote melodramatically to Ellen that 'if he is doomed to suffer, it seems so much the more will he need care and help. And yet the ultimate possibilities of such a case are appalling. You remember your aunt,' she said darkly, 'well, come what may, God help and strengthen both him and me.'

But she had met her match for nervous excitability. Mr Nicholls was as agitated as she, which rather dissipated her own anxieties. A month before the wedding he arrived looking so strange – nervous and wasted – that she told Ellen she was 'thoroughly frightened' by his look. But inquiry relieved her: although he could not give his ailment a name, he had not one touch of rheumatism; that fear was quite groundless. He said, though, that he was going to die, 'or something like it', Charlotte wrote dismissively to Ellen; 'I took heart on hearing this – which may seem paradoxical – but you know, dear Nell – when people are really going to die they don't come a distance of some fifty miles to tell you so.' And as the conversation progressed, she elicited the information from her enormous fiancé that he had been to his doctor, who told him (confirming her own suspicions) 'that he had no manner of complaint whatever except an over-excited mind. In short I soon discovered that my business was – instead of sympathizing – to rate him soundly. He had wholesome treatment while he was at Haworth – and went away singularly better.'

Depite his calling, Mr Nicholls was no less human than other men impatient to be married, as might have been guessed from his passionate temperament. Miss Brontë appears to have had some difficulty restraining him, to judge from the following passage in her letter to Ellen of 27 May:

> Perfectly unreasonable however on some points – as his fallible sex are not ashamed to be – groaning over the prospect of a few more weeks of bachelorhood, as much as if it were an age of banishment or prison. It is probable he will fret himself thin again in the time – but I certainly shall not pity him if he does; there is not a woman in England but would have more sense, more courage, more sustaining hope than to behave so.
>
> Man is indeed an amazing piece of mechanism when you see – so to speak – the full weakness – of what he calls – his strength. There is not a female child above the age of eight but might rebuke him for the spoilt petulance of his wilful nonsense.

Her irritability and anxiety about the proceedings seem to have increased as the day drew nearer. Her wedding clothes were to come from Leeds but she deputed Ellen to choose the bonnet and dress she would wear – 'something that can be turned to decent use and worn after the wedding will be best, I think.' Although she could have afforded something quite costly, she stipulated firmly that the purchases should be neither 'expensive nor extensive'. Ellen, typically, chose wedding clothes that were both pretty and traditional. The bonnet was covered in white flowers, trimmed with greenery, and over it would go a white lace veil, with a motif of ivy leaves, which matched the border of the white muslin dress. Charlotte's own choice of clothing for the honeymoon, a heavy silk dress of the soberest brown and mauve, had nothing bridal about it. It was the result of an expedition to Halifax, where rather grudgingly she had some more dresses made up.

Then there were all the other details: she ordered fifty wedding cards from Ellen, which displeased her on account of the gaudy

464

amount of silver on them. She would have preferred the envelope to be perfectly plain with a silver initial. And then she found she should have ordered twice the number because of Mr Nicholls' string of clerical friends. Moreover, there was the white sealing wax to buy, which she thought would be appropriate, but since Haworth didn't stock it, once again Ellen had to be commissioned to obtain it.

The date of the wedding was finally determined for 29 June, to fit in not with the bride but with curacy arrangements. Mr De Renzy, who was expected to remain in his post until Mr Nicholls and his bride returned from their month-long honeymoon, had proved himself even more self-centred than had first been suspected. Although his quarter would not be up until 20 August, he had decided to take a holiday and would be leaving on 25 June, which threw all arrangements for services and parish duties into confusion. Mr Brontë fretted, and to the dismay of Charlotte, who wished to delay the ceremony until the second week of July, he was now exceedingly anxious to get the whole business over. But to her warm approval, Mr Nicholls 'with his usual trustworthiness' took all the trouble of providing curate substitutes on his own shoulders.

Every day she found new good points about him. To Miss Wooler she wrote on 16 June:

I hope Mr Carter and Mr Nicholls may meet some day – I believe mutual acquaintance would, in time, bring mutual respect – but one of them at least requires *knowing* to be *appreciated* – and I must say that I have not yet found him to lose with close knowledge – I make no grand discoveries – but I occasionally come on a quiet little nook of character which excites esteem. He is always reliable, truthful, suadable – and open to kind influence. A man never indeed to be driven – but who may be led.

On that date Charlotte had still not decided upon whom she should invite.[7] There were eighteen recipients of invitations, among them the Reverend William Morgan, her father's old friend now living at Aylesbury, Buckinghamshire, and her cousin Joseph Branwell, living at Launceston in Cornwall. The Wheelwright family were invited, as was George Smith, and, by separate invitation, Mrs Smith and her children and Mr Williams. Naturally she asked Mrs Gaskell, but not the James Kay Shuttleworths. Richard Monckton Milnes, however, was invited, as was, rather oddly, Francis Bennoch. This was the man whom Mrs Gaskell had reported that Miss Brontë had tried not to see when he said that he would call at the parsonage on his way back from Hull; Mr Brontë however had liked him and probably he was the latter's choice. Six invitations went to local Haworth residents, and of course one went to the Wooler family and one to the Nussey family at Brookroyd. The Taylors, and other relations of the Nusseys, were not invited. It was a very small list, only partially reflecting Charlotte's circle of acquaintance, and perhaps by sending out the invitations so late, Charlotte made sure that few of the invitees would be able to attend, and she would thus ensure the quiet she desired. In contrast, good Mr Nicholls seemed to have no end to his parson friends. Strangely, Mrs Gaskell, who usually immediately scribbled down anything about Miss Brontë, makes no mention of her marriage until 21 July. Did she really receive an invitation?

Charlotte's half reluctant attitude to the proceedings as well as a sense of decorum made her very anxious for the entire affair to take place as quietly as possible; short though her list of invitations was, she wished only her closest friends actually to attend. She told Miss Wooler that 'Mr Nicholls enters with true kindness into my wish to have all done quietly and he has made such arrangements as – I trust – will secure literal privacy'. The only persons to be present at the ceremony were to be Miss Wooler, whose presence Mr Brontë particularly wished for, Ellen Nussey, Mr Sowden who would marry them, and Mr Brontë. The ceremony would take place at eight in the morning, after which the tiny party were to adjourn to the small grey parsonage.

Ellen and Miss Wooler were brought over on the afternoon of 28 June, in order to be present for the wedding early the next day, and the long, hot summer afternoon and evening were spent with these two ladies who had known the bride since she was fifteen. Physically she had changed very little, looking still very like the diminutive schoolgirl of 1831. Mr Nicholls and Mr Sowden were installed at Oxenhope with the curate Mr Grant and his wife, and as had been arranged, the eager bridegroom had sent a note up to Miss Brontë telling her that they had arrived. Mr Nicholls, Charlotte had noted with approval, had been very kind and considerate about her wishes on every point; he had anticipated her desire to make arrangements for Ellen and Miss Wooler's departure, and in deference to his fiancée's evident nervousness about the whole affair, he had kept the day of the wedding secret from the villagers.

Finally, at the end of the evening, when all had been finished – the arrangements made conscientiously for Mr Brontë's routine during Charlotte's honeymoon, her trunk with the new dresses from Halifax packed, the white wedding dress laid out, with the lace veil and bonnet, and the wedding breakfast prepared, Mr Brontë suddenly announced that he could not give away the bride. He claimed to be unwell. What was to be done? He would not be persuaded, and there was no obvious substitute. At least in this ultimate crisis Charlotte had the kind and commonsensical Miss Wooler and an indignant Ellen to support her. The *Prayer Book* was rapidly consulted, which revealed that all that was required was for the minister to receive 'the woman from her father's or *friend's* hand,'; nothing was specified about the sex of the friend. Miss Wooler, with all the despatch that had made her such an admired headmistress, promptly volunteered to give away her pupil.

On 'that dim June morning' of the 29th, as Charlotte remembered it, she, Ellen and Miss Wooler stepped quietly down the path, beneath the shady green trees to the church, where awaited Mr Nicholls. It was perhaps pleasing for Charlotte that she was attended by these two sister substitutes. There, at eight o'clock in the morning, Charlotte Brontë became Mrs Arthur Nicholls, or Charlotte Brontë Nicholls as she signed herself thereafter.

For all her and Mr Nicholls' care, news of the wedding had leaked out into the small village, and its inhabitants stood below the church in the cobbled street waiting for her to come out. It was said that she looked like a snowdrop, and perhaps the diminutiveness of her appearance, clothed in white embroidered muslin, with the lace veil and the pretty white bonnet ornamented with green leaves, suggested something of that brave little winter flower; at least Mrs Gaskell, imagining the scene later, thought so.

The only other memento of that day, apart from Charlotte's veil and bonnet which linger at Haworth behind a glass case, is the note which Charlotte wrote that evening to Ellen when she and her husband had arrived at Conway in Wales, en route to Ireland. It cannot have made a particularly auspicious start to the honeymoon that the bride asked her close female friend, who was always threatening her fiancé's intimacy, to write by return of post:

I scribble one hasty line just to say that after a pleasant enough journey we have got safely to Conway – the evening is wet and wild, though the day was fair chiefly with some gleams of sunshine. However, we are sheltered in a comfortable inn. My cold is not worse. If you get this scrawl tomorrow and write by return – direct to me at the Post-Office, Bangor, and I may get it on Monday. Say how you and Miss Wooler got home. Give my kindest and most grateful love to Miss Wooler whenever you write. On Monday, I think, we cross the Channel. No more at present.
    – Yours faithfully and lovingly,
                    C.B.N.

It is hardly a letter that conveys the ecstasy of honeymoon. Moreover, the bride's cold cannot have been conducive to intimacy, and perhaps may have been used as a way of deferring sexual intercourse. Indeed, although Charlotte found some pleasure in the Welsh scenery, which she thought surpassed the English Lakes, the first part of the honeymoon was far from smooth. By the time that the Nichollses arrived at Mr Nicholls' uncle's house at Banagher in the south of Ireland, Charlotte was sufficiently ill to require nursing by Mrs Bell, the wife of Mr Nicholls' uncle. She wrote to Miss Wooler on 10 July: 'I was not well when I came here – fatigue and excitement had nearly knocked me up – and my cough was become very bad – but Mrs Bell has nursed me both with kindness and skill, and I am greatly better now.' That cough was so often brought on by stress and unhappiness that it seems more than likely that it was brought on by similar factors on her honeymoon. The letter to Miss Wooler continues rather doubtfully: 'I trust I feel thankful to God for having enabled me to make what seems a right choice'.

After spending the first few days in Wales, they had crossed from Holyhead to Dublin. It was a calm crossing and the weather was good. There they had been met by three of Mr Nicholls' relatives, who took them about the city to see the sights – the College library, the museum, the chapel, and would have seen much more had not Charlotte's cold been such a restriction on them. Mr Nicholls' brother was the manager of the Grand Canal from Dublin to Banagher, 'a sagacious well-informed and courteous man'; the other male cousin was a student of the University. The third member of the party was a female cousin whom Charlotte, anxious to keep her end up before the socially aware Woolers, said was 'a lady-like girl with gentle English manners'. It was perhaps in Dublin that Mr Nicholls posed for two photographic portraits, and it seems likely[8] that the only known photograph of Charlotte was also taken then. Mr Nicholls looks full of triumph; Charlotte, in her quiet outfit with a very small frill at the neck, somewhat subdued.

Mr Nicholls' relatives then accompanied the newly-weds down to Banagher, in County Offaly, where Mr Nicholls had been brought up, and where Charlotte now saw her husband in a new light, as she had to confess. The house was an imposing Stuart mansion, with a mansard roof and exquisite pedimented classical façade; it was as grand as any of the houses that she had ever stayed in. The degradation which her father had talked of, and which she had sensibly and robustly dismissed, had nevertheless worried her a little, perhaps because of Mr Brontë's own treatment as an Irish clergyman, for she wrote frankly to Miss Catherine Wooler: 'I was pretty much pleased with what I saw. I was also greatly surprised to find so much of English order and repose in the family habits and arrangements. I had heard a great deal about Irish negligence &c.' Mrs Bell was also pronounced socially acceptable to Miss Wooler. There was nothing Irish about her, the half-Irish Charlotte observed relievedly: 'Mrs Bell is like an English or Scotch matron, quiet, kind and well-bred – It seems she was brought up in London'; and both her daughters were 'strikingly pretty in appearance' – no wild pipe-smoking Irish hoydens! She found their manners very amiable and pleasing, and thought that the male members of the family, such as she had seen, seemed 'thoroughly educated gentlemen'.

In this pleasant spot, which looked 'externally like a gentleman's country-seat – within most of the rooms are lofty and spacious and some – the drawing-room, dining-room, &c., handsomely and commodiously furnished', she more than once had 'deep pleasure in hearing his [Mr Nicholls'] praises on all sides', while his aunt spoke of him 'with a mixture of affection and respect most gratifying to hear'. Servants and old retainers excitedly told her that she was a most fortunate person 'for that I have got one of the best gentlemen in the country'.

Nevertheless, Charlotte evidently continued to be less than enthusiastic about her partner. To her many correspondents she expressed earnest hopes of being able to continue to be grateful to him for his attentions. She worried that he might not understand her need to be alone at times, particularly in the face of nature. But by the end of the honeymoon both parties were far more at their ease. When they went on to stay at Kilkee, in County Clare on the wild west coast and found that their hotel, splendidly designated 'the West End Hotel', was in fact a shoddy little inn, Charlotte wrote gaily to Miss Catherine Wooler that 'there is a good deal to carp at if one were in a carping humour – but we laugh instead of grumbling – for out of doors there is much indeed to compensate for any indoor shortcomings; so magnificent an ocean – so bold and grand a coast – I never yet saw. My husband calls me. . . .' In that letter is a touch of the charming, impulsive, old Charlotte, instead of the frozen unhappy woman of the past three years. Mr Nicholls and she evidently shared a sense of humour – after all she had thought he would be amused despite his stern Puseyite religion by the strange church on the sea at Filey; and he had roared with laughter at *Shirley* – and as time went on, she would find that they shared a pleasantly similar view of their fellow creatures' foolishness.

Mr Nicholls, treading on eggshells where his sharp, delicate wife was concerned, deserves much credit for their increasing happiness. Nothing was too much for him. His own description of the 'finest shore he ever saw . . . completely girdled with stupendous cliffs – it was most refreshing to sit on a rock and look out on the broad Atlantic boiling and foaming at our feet' shows that the beauties of nature were not utterly lost on him, but Charlotte was not slow to indicate that her very romantic reaction must be allowed to be a solitary communing, uninterrupted by husbands – and Mr Nicholls humbly and readily agreed. Charlotte described the incident rather disloyally to Catherine Winkworth on 27 July, ending by saying she would try 'with God's help to be as indulgent to him whenever indulgence is needed':

> My husband is not a poet or a poetical man and one of my grand doubts before marriage was about 'congenial tastes' and so on. The first morning we went out on to the cliffs and saw the Atlantic coming in all white foam, I did not know whether I should get leave or time to take the matter in my own way. I did not want to talk – but I *did* want to look and be silent. Having hinted a petition, licence was not refused – covered with a rug to keep off the spray I was allowed to sit where I chose – and he only interrupted me when he thought I crept too near the edge of the cliff. So far he is always good in this way – and this protection which does not interfere or pretend is I believe a thousand times better than any half sort of pseudo-sympathy.

From Kilkee, they had continued their tour, and ventured up to the Gap of Dunloe in Killarney. It was there that an alarming incident had occurred. The guide had warned Mrs Nicholls to alight from her horse as they went through the Gap, as the path was very broken and dangerous, but Charlotte did not feel afraid and would not do so. They passed the dangerous part; the horse trembled and slipped once, but did not fall, and though soon afterwards it started and became unruly for a minute, she managed to keep her seat. Mr Nicholls, rather alarmed, went to the mare's head and led her, but suddenly without cause the beast seemed to go mad, rearing and plunging, and Charlotte was thrown on the stones right under her. Mr Nicholls did not see that she had fallen, and still held on to the mare. Charlotte, recounting the incident to Catherine Winkworth, shows a proper sense of priorities.

> I saw and felt her kick, plunge, trample round me. I had my thoughts about the moment – its consequences – my husband – my father. When my plight was seen, the struggling creature was let loose – she sprung over me. I was lifted off the stones neither bruised by the fall nor touched by the mare's hoofs. Of course the only feeling was gratitude for more sakes than my own.

She used curious words to describe the incident. It was a 'sudden glimpse of a very grim phantom'. Alas, it was indeed a warning glimpse.

Writing the next day, 28 July, to Ellen, she said: 'I have been longing, *longing intensely* sometimes, to be at home. Indeed, I could enjoy and rest no more, and so home we are going.' She was worried about her father's health. Nevertheless, when describing the honeymoon to Ellen, she said that more pleasure perhaps even than the splendid scenery had sprung from 'the kind and ceaseless protection which has ever surrounded me, and made travelling a different matter to me from what it has heretofore been.' It boded well.

CHAPTER XXII

The Final Months

Charlotte and her husband reached Haworth on 1 August and eight days later she was giving her first truly positive report of marriage to Ellen:

> Since I came home I have not had an unemployed moment; my life is changed indeed – to be wanted continually – to be constantly called for and occupied seems so strange: yet it is a marvellously good thing. As yet I don't understand how some wives grow so selfish. As far as my experience of matrimony goes, I think it tends to draw you out, and away from yourself. . . .
>
> Dear Nell – during the last 6 weeks – the colour of my thoughts is a good deal changed: I know more of the realities of life than I once did. I think many false ideas are propagated perhaps unintention- ally. I think those married women who indiscriminately urge their acquaintance to marry much to blame. For my part I can only say with deeper sincerity and fuller significance – what I always said in theory – Wait God's will. Indeed – indeed Nell – it is a solemn and strange and perilous thing for a woman to become a wife. Man's lot is far, far different.

The postscript to the letter runs:

> Have I told you how much better Mr Nicholls is? He looks quite strong and hale – he gained 12 lbs during the 4 weeks we were in Ireland. To see this improvement in him has been a main source of happiness to me, and to speak truth a subject of wonder too.

Although this letter has been interpreted, using unrepresentative extracts, to show that Charlotte was unhappy in her marriage, its overall tone is one of considerable contentment. She had indeed waited God's will, and He had brought her Arthur. The delighted exclamations over the rest of this year at her remarkable good health and the affectionate references to the man who was becoming 'my dear Arthur' all point to her happiness. In November she told Miss Wooler amazedly that 'it is long since I have known such comparative immunity from headache, sickness and indigestion, as during the last three months'.

With marriage the whole tone of her letters changed, as did her existence. By September so thoroughly had the practical Mr Nicholls taken over his wife's life that anything not to do with his needs had gone by the board. Those French newspapers, once a key to another world, to the 'necromantic joys of fancy', were now just a heap of yellowing old newspapers. On 7 September Charlotte wrote cheerfully to Ellen that her friend might have thought that she had given them up, it was so long since one was sent to Brookroyd, but the truth was 'they had accumulated to quite a pile during my absence. I wished to look them over before sending them off, and as yet I have scarcely found time.' That side of her life had quite vanished. As she told Miss Wooler, 'the fact is my time is not my own now; somebody else wants a good portion of it – and says we must do so and so. We *do* "so and so" accordingly, and it generally seems the right thing – only I sometimes wish that I could have written the letter as well as taken the walk.' And over the next five months she does indeed scarcely seem to have had a moment to herself to write a letter, let alone any new book.

Nevertheless a new, contented Charlotte was emerging, amused now even by the village social round. After a tea that Mr and Mrs Nicholls gave to the village to thank them for the goodwill shown to Mr Nicholls on his return, one of the villagers had proposed Mr Nicholls' health, describing him as 'a consistent Christian and a kind gentleman'. His sophisticated, often sarcastic wife listening to this had to own that she was very touched by these words. She told Miss Wooler:

I thought – (as I know *you* would have thought – had you been present) – that to merit and win such a character was better than to earn either Wealth or Fame or Power. I am disposed to echo that high but simple eulogium *now*. If I can do so with sincerity and conviction *seven years* – or *even a year hence* – I shall esteem myself a happy woman. Faultless my husband is not – faultless no human being is; but as you well know – I did not expect perfection.

Even Mr Brontë, who was not well when they had arrived back from Ireland but had soon got better on their return, now had an excellent understanding with Mr Nicholls. Charlotte, ever anxious for her

473

father, told Miss Wooler: 'The wish for his continued life – together with a certain solicitude for his happiness and health seems – I scarcely know why – stronger in me now than before I was married.' Mr Brontë had taken no church duties since Mr Nicholls' return, and Charlotte felt comforted every time she saw her husband put on gown or surplice to think that the marriage had secured her father such good aid in his old age. She told Ellen on 7 September that 'Papa continues greatly better; my husband flourishes, he begins indeed to express some slight alarm at the growing improvement in his condition. I think I am decent, better certainly than I was two months ago; but people don't compliment me as they do Arthur; excuse the name, it has grown natural to use it now.'

Now she wished that Miss Wooler had 'some kind faithful companion' to enliven her solitude at Richmond – 'some friend to whom to communicate your pleasure in the scenery, the fine weather, the pleasant walks. You never complain, never murmur, never seem otherwise than thankful, but I know you must miss a privilege none could more keenly appreciate than yourself.' She had one final thought on Fame, as she called it with a capital F, for Miss Wooler. In retrospect it seemed that it had not been wholly without its pleasures. Responding to Miss Wooler's enquiry about what visitors they had had, she wrote:

> a good many amongst the clergy &c. in the neighbourhood, but none of note from a distance. Haworth is – as you say – a very quiet place; it is also difficult of access and unless under the stimulus of necessity or that of strong curiosity – or finally that of true and tried friendship – few take the courage to penetrate to so remote a nook. Besides, now that I am married I do not expect to be an object of much general interest. Ladies who have won some prominence (call it either *notoriety* or celebrity) in their single life – often fall quite into the background when they change their names; but if true domestic happiness replace Fame – the exchange will indeed be for the better.

In the same letter she added that she now believed that it was not bad for her that Mr Nicholls' bent should be 'so wholly towards matters of real life and active usefulness – so little inclined to the literary and contemplative'. It was tantamount to abdication. She confessed that she had much less time for thinking. She was obliged to be more practical, for 'my dear Arthur is a very practical as well as a very punctual, methodical man'. Every morning he was in the National School by nine o'clock, and gave the children religious instruction till half past ten. Almost every afternoon he paid visits among the poor parishioners, and he often found work for his wife, of which she wrote rather tenderly, 'and I hope she is not sorry to help him'. Indeed, she was very happy. The weather that September was 'glorious'. Charlotte thought she had never seen the moors fuller of purple bloom. The strange low spirits she had undergone each equinox had quite vanished. The parsonage, once so silent, was now full of the noise of the large and busy Mr Nicholls.

Her life now centred on Arthur, and the simple pleasures of domestic life. Amelia Taylor had come to visit, and had spent much of her time singing the praises of a former girlfriend of Joe Taylor's – her fine clothes, open pink muslin gown, worked petticoat, velvet cape, carriage and pairs. Both Arthur and she found the cultivation of the wicked Joe Taylor's former flames odd and unnatural. Arthur was 'very strong upon it'. Their relationship was becoming more and more intimate: By 11 October she told Ellen:

I don't know whether I shall be able to keep him at home now whenever she [Amelia] does come. He threatens to bolt. He flourishes, and desires his kind regards to you. He often says he wishes you were well settled in life. He is just gone out this morning in a rather refractory mood about some Dissenters. On Sunday, we had a pair of very sweet sermons indeed, really good, and touching the better springs of our nature. Just before going to Church he menaced me with something worse than the preceding Sunday. I was agreeably disappointed.

Another visit from Amelia Taylor, this time accompanied by the miscreant Joe and their small daughter, Tim, had Charlotte writing to Ellen:

Tim behaved capitally on the whole. She amused Papa very much – chattering away to him very funnily – his white hair took her fancy. She announced a decided preference for it over Arthur's black hair, and coolly advised the latter to 'go to the barber and get his whiskers cut off'. Papa says she speaks as I did when I was a child – says the same odd unexpected things.

It conjures up a scene of domestic happiness, but the contented married woman, always being interrupted by Arthur, to go for walks, to visit the sick, so that she could call but a very small portion of her time her own, had not quite lost her firecracker quality. She told Ellen that when she paid her intended visit to Brookroyd, 'if I hear Mr Clapham [Ellen's brother-in-law] or anybody else say anything to the disparagement of single women, I shall go off like a bomb shell, and as for *you* –

475

but I won't prophesy.'

It seems that Charlotte and Mr Nicholls may have had schemes to match Ellen with his friend the Reverend Sowden, who was a regular visitor to the parsonage and in early November came with his brother; Charlotte particularly mentions in her letter to Ellen that he had asked after Miss Nussey. Mr Nicholls' brother also came to stay and Charlotte found him too a charming, gentlemanly man. Ellen herself had come for a visit in early October, but the friendship was now under the vigilant eye of Mr Nicholls, who had sufficiently consolidated his position in his wife's affections as to now interfere with Charlotte's correspondence with Ellen. Their married relationship was such that he had begun to read his wife's letters and was duly horrified by the revelations they contained of the feminine tendency to character analysis. He thought that she had written much too freely about Amelia Taylor, and that letters like hers were 'as dangerous as lucifer matches'. He told Charlotte to write to Ellen that if she did not burn them, there would be no more. Rather than reacting angrily to this domineering, Charlotte seems to have rather enjoyed it. As Mrs Gaskell had suspected, Charlotte liked being ruled. 'I can't help laughing,' Charlotte wrote to Ellen on 7 November, 'this seems to me so funny. Arthur, however, says he is quite "serious" and looks it, I assure you; he is bending over the desk with his eyes full of concern. I am now desired "to have done with it", so with his kind regards and mine, goodbye, dear Ellen.'

A furious Ellen's next letter contained no distinct pledge that she would destroy the letters, so Charlotte again wrote to her, asking her to make the promise to Mr Nicholls, otherwise he threatened to elect himself the censor of their correspondence. Charlotte told Ellen that she

> must give the promise . . . or else you will get such notes as he writes to Mr Sowden, plain, brief statements of facts without the adornment of a single flourish, with no comment on the character or peculiarities of any human being, and if a phrase of sensibility or affection steals in, it seems to come on tiptoe, looking ashamed of itself, blushing 'pea-green' as he says, and holding both its shy hands before its face. Write him out his promise on a separate slip of paper, in a legible hand, and send it in your next. Papa, I am glad to say, continues pretty well. I hope your mother prospers, and that Ann is better, with love to all. Mr Clapham included.

Ellen duly wrote her frosty pledge:

My dear Mr Nicholls, – As you seem to hold in great horror the

476

ardentia verba of feminine epistles, I pledge myself to the destruction of Charlotte's epistles, henceforth, if you pledge yourself to *no* authorship in the matter communicated.

– Yours very truly,

E. Nussey

And, fortunately for us, the ever-obedient, dutiful Ellen disobeyed. But the letters were anyway becoming less frequent, as Charlotte devoted herself to her husband. By December she would write: 'It is almost inexplicable to me that I seem so often hurried now, but the fact is, whenever Arthur is in, I must have occupations in which he can share, or which will not at least divert my attention from him; thus a multitude of little matters get put off till he goes out, and then I am quite busy.' And she wrote to Miss Wooler as frankly as ever: 'My life is different to what it used to be. May God make me thankful for it! I have a good, kind attached husband and every day makes my own attachment to him stronger.'

Her identity was becoming quite submerged in her husband's. The driving ambition, the burning desire for fame, seem to have died down; she was mellow and contented, almost proving the truth of that nineteenth-century dictum that women only wrote if they were unhappy, single, or had some hereditary tendency. She seems quite deliberately to have slowly allowed all aspects of the professional and literary side of her life to lapse, perhaps thinking it impossible to combine with being a proper wife to a curate. It was easy enough to happen, for apart from her friendships with Miss Martineau and Mrs Gaskell and her publishers, she had successfully rebuffed overtures which would have brought her into a wider circle, whether through reviewing or social gatherings. In the case of Mrs Gaskell their friendship foundered on the rocks of Mr Nicholls' high Anglicanism. At first after her marriage Charlotte continued to frequently extend invitations to Mrs Gaskell, which the latter did not accept 'partly because it required a little courage to face Mr Nicholls' since Charlotte had told her that he 'did not like her intimacy with us dissenters',[1] though she was sure that he would change his mind upon acquaintance. But with Mrs Gaskell's letter in response to her own praising *North and South*, which in Mrs Gaskell's words 'was a sort of explanation of my way of looking at her Church (the Establishment) and religion; intended for husband's benefit'[2] (appropriately enough, as dissent forms some of the novel's subject matter) she seems to have felt that as Arthur's wife she could not countenance further correspondence along those lines and she did not reply.

Perhaps out of pique Mrs Gaskell would later claim that Mr Nicholls prevented Charlotte from writing further novels, but he denied this.

In 1899 he would write to Mrs Humphrey Ward (Matthew Arnold's niece who was then preparing introductions to a new Haworth edition of the Brontë novels) on similar lines, in response to her queries about Mrs Gaskell's claims:

> Since the receipt of your letter I have re-read my wife's letters written after her marriage & published by Mrs Gaskell.
>
> I must say that I fail to see any confirmation in them of the statement that 'I encouraged her to give up novel writing.'
>
> There was no such understanding between us – of course. We talked of her Literary Work – on one occasion she read for me the MS (afterwards published in 'The Cornhill'); when she concluded I merely said 'I fear the critics will accuse you of repetition' – but not a word of discouragement.
>
> I never interfered in the slightest degree with her liberty of action – I shall feel obliged if you will endeavour to remove the misconception which you say exists in this respect.[3]

Mr Nicholls was right in suggesting that *Emma*, which begins in a girls' school with a pathetic abandoned girl, seemed repetitious. The manuscript (of around 5,000 words) has the curious, rather effeminate figure of Willie Ellin and the realistically drawn figure of Miss Wilcox, the headmistress, who cannot really like the little girl who turns out to be a 'pseudo-heiress', Matilda Fitzgibbon. There are the beginnings of a dramatic plot, when Miss Wilcox writes to Miss Fitzgibbon's father at May Park only to have her letter returned, as no such place exists, which suggest a return to the atmosphere of *Jane Eyre* from the everyday realism of her other books. But it is impossible to say what Charlotte might have done with this work had she lived.

It is hard to believe that she would not have continued to write, even if, according to Ellen Nussey, Mr Nicholls was against it. In an interview Ellen gave to Sir Wemyss Reid fifteen years later, she said that Mr Nicholls had tried to stop Charlotte writing, saying 'I did not marry Currer Bell, the novelist, but Charlotte Brontë, the clergyman's daughter. Currer Bell may fly to heaven tomorrow for all I care.' By that time, however, there was no love lost between Ellen Nussey and Arthur Nicholls, and her statement must be read in that context; furthermore the energetic part Mr Nicholls played in the selection of Charlotte's poetry after her death suggests the pride he took in her fame.

Although she might no longer have felt the need of writing to take herself out of her desperate circumstances, Charlotte would surely have found it difficult to abandon the supreme literary gift that had given her so much pleasure, and she would at some point have taken up her pen again; *Villette* after all shows her at her subtlest in her creation of character. But this must remain supposition; by the end of 1854, her time and her emotional energies were understandably absorbed in the novelty of married life.

As the autumn progressed, rainy, wild weather set in. Mr Brontë was well, now going slightly deaf, but 'settled and content', Charlotte wrote with relief. The marriage *had* been the right step. Only her father's cough persisted, but he had had that for many years. In mid-November Sir James Kay Shuttleworth and a friend came to stay; the former had had a frightful accident and had lost the sight of one eye. His chief errand was to see Currer Bell's husband, and to Charlotte's great pleasure he took a fancy to him, before he left making him a formal offer of the living of Padiham, which was near Sir James' home at Gawthorpe. The living was £200 per annum, twice the amount Mr Nicholls was getting (he was paid £90 per annum out of Mr Brontë's stipend at Haworth). But of course it was not to be thought of while Mr Brontë was alive. Mr Nicholls had, however, suggested Mr Sowden in his place and, as Charlotte had told Ellen, the latter had been summoned to Haworth to talk about it.

Husband and wife were drawing ever closer together. Worship of nature together was now quite permitted; their tastes were more congenial than Charlotte had thought. On 29 November she wrote to Ellen describing their walk to the waterfall out on the moor:

We set off not intending to go far, but though wild and cloudy it was fair in the morning. When we had got about half a mile on the moors, Arthur suggested the idea of the waterfall – after the melted snow he said it would be fine. I had often wanted to see it in its winter power so we walked on. It was fine indeed – a perfect torrent raving over the rocks white and beautiful. It began to rain while we were watching it, and we returned home under a stormy sky. However I enjoyed the walk inexpressibly, and would not have missed the spectacle on any account.

But despite her good health and good spirits Charlotte caught a cold at the waterfall. She felt a chill afterwards, even though she immediately changed her wet things on arriving back, and the same night she had a sore throat and a cold which lingered. Arthur did not want her to accept Ellen's invitation to Brookroyd partly because of it and partly on account of Ellen's sister Mercy having a fever; he insisted that she stay away from Brookroyd for at least a few weeks while all contagion passed. If it just depended on her, she would come, Charlotte told Ellen on 7 December, 'but these matters are not quite in my power

479

now, another must be consulted, and where his wish and judgement have a decided bias to a particular course, I make no stir, but just adopt it.' In the same letter she told Ellen that her father continued pretty well, and proudly that 'my dear boy flourishes; I do not mean that he continues to grow stouter, which one would not desire, but he keeps in excellent condition'. Even Flossy's death could not really disturb her equilibrium: 'He drooped for a single day, and died quietly in the night without pain. The loss even of a dog was very saddening, yet perhaps no dog ever had a happier life or an easier death.'

By Boxing Day Charlotte was quite better; it was a very happy Christmas. She told Ellen that Arthur joined her in sincere good wishes – 'many of them to you and yours. He is well, thank God, and so am I, and he is "my dear boy" certainly, dearer now than he was six months ago. In three days we shall actually have been married that length of time! Good-bye, dear Nell.' The only occurrence marring the end of an eventful year was the appalling weather. For three weeks they had had 'little less than a succession of hurricanes'. But nothing it seemed, not even the weather, could affect the contentment of Mr and Mrs Nicholls.

Early in the New Year the Nicholls were prevailed upon to go and stay for a few days with Sir James Kay Shuttleworth at Gawthorpe. Soon after their return, Charlotte became unwell; on 19 January she wrote to Ellen:

> My health has been really very good ever since my return from Ireland till about ten days ago, when the stomach seemed quite suddenly to lose its tone, indigestion and continual faint sickness have been my portion ever since. Don't conjecture – dear Nell – for it is too soon yet though I certainly never before felt as I have done lately. But keep the matter wholly to yourself – for I can come to no decided opinion at present.

Although the implication is that she was pregnant, Charlotte was still hoping to make her intended visit to Ellen, and then to Amelia Taylor, at the end of the month, and she described the pleasure of having Arthur's clergyman cousin from Banagher, James Adamson Bell, staying at Haworth: 'The visit was a real treat. He is a cultivated, thoroughly educated man with a mind stored with information gathered from books and travel – and what is far rarer – with the art of conversing appropriately and quietly and never pushing his superiority upon you.' It was an hourly happiness, she told Amelia Taylor, to see how well 'Arthur and my Father get on together now – there has never been a misunderstanding or wrong word.'

Despite her expressions of happiness, sickness was once again battering at the house. Shortly after Charlotte began to have sensations of nausea and recurring faintness, indigestion and loss of appetite, Tabby too fell ill and it was clear that the doughty old woman, now eighty-four, was dying. By 23 January Charlotte was so incapacitated by illness that she was confined to bed and Mr Nicholls had to answer her letters. She yielded to her husband's demands that she should see a second doctor and on 29 January he sent to Bradford for Dr Mac-Turk, writing to Ellen that he wished 'to have better advice than Haworth affords'. Dr MacTurk came the next day and according to Mrs Gaskell, 'assigned a natural cause for her miserable disposition – a little patience and all would go right'.[4] MacTurk's opinion, so Mr Nicholls told Ellen Nussey, was that her illness would be 'of some duration, but that there was no immediate danger. I trust therefore that in a few weeks she will be well again.'

But instead of getting better in a few weeks, Charlotte got steadily worse. She became very emaciated, her illness punctuated by continuous vomiting. To Amelia Taylor she managed to write a brief letter, asking for the advice of a married woman with a child: 'Let me speak the plain truth – my sufferings are very great – my nights indescribable – sickness with scarce a reprieve – I strain until what I vomit is mixed with blood. Medicine I have quite discontinued. If you can send me anything that will do good – do.' It was not clear what the complications were, and in the parsonage there was confusion about the causes of Charlotte's condition. To Ellen's anxious enquiries, Mr Nicholls wrote on 14 February: 'It is difficult to write to friends about my wife's illness, as its cause is yet uncertain – at present she is completely prostrated with weakness and sickness and frequent fever – all may turn out well in the end, and I hope it will; if you saw her you would perceive that she can maintain no correspondence at present.'

From the great bed upstairs, her parents' marriage bed for only eight years and hers for such a short while, Charlotte managed to write a few faint pencilled notes, to Laetitia Wheelwright, and to Ellen to comfort her. And there seems no reason to doubt that these few last notes from her hand, in which she speaks in such loving terms of her husband, reflect anything except the brief happiness she had at last found in marriage. On 15 February, she told Laetitia:

A few lines of acknowledgement your letter *shall* have, whether well or ill. At present I am confined to my bed, and have been so for three weeks. Up to this period, since my marriage, I have had excellent health – my husband and I live at home with my Father – of course I could not leave *him*. He is pretty well – better than last summer. No kinder, better husband than mine, it seems to me, can

481

there be in the world. I do not want now for kind companionship in health and the tenderest nursing in sickness.

To Ellen she wrote on 21 February, the penultimate letter of the twenty-four-year-long correspondence which had sustained her through so much:

I must write one line out of my weary bed. The news of Mercy's probable recovery came like a ray of joy to me. I am not going to talk about my sufferings, it would be useless and painful – I want to give you an assurance which I know will comfort you – and that is that I find my husband the tenderest nurse, the kindest support – the best earthly comfort that ever woman had. His patience never fails, and it is tried by sad days and broken nights.

That day, Tabby had been buried, Mr Nicholls taking time away from his dying wife to perform the funeral service. The old servant had died on 17 February, the same day that Charlotte changed her will: if she died without children, all her property would go to her husband; if she died leaving issue, he should have the interest of her property during his lifetime and after his death the principal should go to their surviving child or children. Arthur had won his colours.

Meanwhile Charlotte slowly weakened. She could only say a few words at once 'even to my dear, patient, constant Arthur'. Then, for a very few days, she seemed to rally and would accept a very little to eat – 'Some beef-tea – spoonfuls of wine and water – a mouthful of light pudding at different times.' She was not eating enough to keep a bird alive, and still she vomited. For a little while at the end of February, in milder weather, she seemed to get better, and then, as the equinoctal March winds started to roar in round the house, she began to sink. By the third week in March delirium came on, and she seemed to become hungry, strangely asking now for food constantly, but it was too late. On 30 March, Mr Brontë took over as the transmitter of news to Ellen, as his son-in-law could no longer control his grief:

My dear Madam, – We are all in great trouble, and Mr Nicholls so much so that he is not so sufficiently strong and composed as to be able to write. I therefore devote a few moments to tell you that my dear Daughter is very ill, and apparently on the verge of the grave. If she could speak she would no doubt dictate to us while answering your kind letter, but we are left to ourselves to give what answer we can. The Doctors have no hope of her cause, and fondly as we a long time cherished hope that hope is now gone, and we have only to look forward to the solemn event with prayer to God that He will give us grace and strength sufficient to our day.

Will you be so kind as to write to Miss Wooler, and Mrs Joe Taylor, and inform them that we requested you to do so, telling them of our present condition?

– Ever truly and respectfully yours,

P. Brontë.

In the early hours of Saturday 31 March 1855, the frail little body finally gave up the valiant spirit which had battled with it for so long. She had spoken little during the last few days, but she continued quite conscious.[5] There seems no reason to disbelieve Mr Nicholls' account of her deathbed. As he brokenly asked God to spare her, Charlotte suddenly seemed to rally: 'Oh!' she said, 'I am not going to die, am I? He will not separate us, we have been so happy.' But the fate ever hovering over Charlotte Brontë waiting to play its last and cruellest trick was not to be dissuaded by such a plea. She was not to be allowed to attain her thirty-ninth birthday, nor to produce her and Arthur's child. The epitaph she had written for Lucy Snowe must be hers as well: 'The orb of your life is not to be so rounded; for you the crescent-phase must suffice.'

The official cause of death was pronounced to be pthisis (duration two months), that is, tuberculosis. Nevertheless, there has been furious debate about the real cause of death, with opinions ranging from plain tuberculosis, the tuberculosis she had suffered intermittently from all her life exacerbated by pregnancy, and the pregnancy itself. In recent years Professor Rhodes' view[6] that the severe vomiting in Charlotte's pregnancy (*hyperemesis gravidarum*) was the sole cause of death has achieved great currency, with its corollary that such vomiting is often a sign of subconscious rejection of the foetus. Despite an attempt by John Maynard in his interesting book to prove that Charlotte Brontë was not pregnant and died of a wasting disease,[7] as Mr Gallagher has pointed out he has failed to take into consideration that Mr Nicholls, Mr Brontë and (from them) Mrs Gaskell all believed Charlotte to be pregnant. Furthermore, Gallagher goes on, destroying the case against tuberculosis alone killing Charlotte, there is 'no tuberculosis lesion that causes retching and vomiting of the type and severity described by Charlotte'.[8] It seems most likely then that Charlotte Brontë's actual cause of death was exhaustion and dehydration. Whether, though, it had its origins in rejection of the baby remains a moot point. The latest thinking is that it is only in a second pregnancy that *hyperemesis gravidarum* is a sign of the individual rejecting the child.

Ellen arrived at Haworth in the late morning of the 31st to make her final farewell. She had begged to come before but Mr Brontë and Mr Nicholls had refused, fearing the effect on Charlotte of the excitement. Mr Brontë did not appear at first; after being the one who had taken charge during the terrible hours of his daughter's leaving him, he had then retired. Now he sent Ellen a message from his study asking her to stay in the house until the interment, which was to be on the Wednesday.

Ellen went up to the bedroom where Charlotte's body lay. Martha Brown had been out to get evergreens and whatever flowers were growing at Haworth, and silently brought the tray of them to Ellen for her to strew about Charlotte's lifeless form. At first poor Ellen recoiled, suddenly remembering the flowers Martha had gathered last summer from all the village gardens to decorate the wedding breakfast. Charlotte had been so pleased by the display Ellen had made. And then collecting herself, and mindful that this 'tender office' had been given to her by the devoted Martha before Mr Nicholls, or Mr Brontë,[9] she set about her dreadful task.

Mrs Gaskell records that one member out of most of the families in the far-flung moorland parish was asked to attend the funeral. Those not in the formal train of mourners stood in the churchyard and outside the church to see that short journey out through the little low gate of the dead, connecting the garden of the parsonage to the graveyard. The pathetically small coffin, not much larger than a child's, was born up the aisle which Charlotte had stepped up only nine months before as a bride, and finally was placed in the crypt.

Ellen left an hour later, making her last journey down the steep grey street, past the severe millstone grit houses, to cross the leafy valley bottom and climb away from the wild, rugged place which had so amazed her when she had first come there twenty-two years ago to meet her new friend's curious family. She never saw the two survivors again.

Mr Nicholls and Mr Brontë retired to the parsonage, where they would live together for another six years until Mr Brontë's death. 'For better for worse' had turned out to mean they two, but they had their shared grief if nothing else, and Mr Nicholls had his promise to Charlotte to look after her blind old father. To Mrs Gaskell, who had learned with shocked sadness of Charlotte's death from Mr Greenwood, the Haworth stationer, Mr Brontë wrote: 'My daughter is indeed, dead, and the solemn truth presses upon her worthy and affectionate husband and me, with great, and, it may be unusual weight. . . .' She must, he said, excuse his brief scrawl as he was not fit at present to write much, nor to write satisfactorily. 'The marriage

484

that took place seemed to hold forth long and bright prospects of happiness, but in the inscrutable providence of God, all our hopes have ended in disappointment, and our joy, in mourning.'[11]

CHAPTER XXIII

Epilogue

The months after Charlotte Brontë's death brought a flood of speculative articles about Currer Bell. Harriet Martineau's tribute stood
alone; recognising as a fellow pioneer Charlotte's struggles, she pointed out, for the benefit of the clergy, how misunderstood she had
been. She had been no wanton, but a woman of conscience, who, far
from bringing disgrace to a form which had only just become respectable, had made it glorious:

> Currer Bell is dead! The early death of the large family of whom she
> was the sole survivor prepared all who knew the circumstances to
> expect the loss of this gifted creature at any time: but not the less
> deep will be the grief of society that her genius will yield us nothing
> more. . . . She had every inducement that could have availed with
> one less high-minded to publish two or three novels a year. Fame
> awaited upon all she did; and she might have enriched herself by
> very slight exertion: but her steady conviction was that the publica-
> tion of a book is a solemn act of conscience – in the case of a novel as
> much as any other kind of book. She was not fond of speaking of
> herself and her conscience; but she now and then uttered to her
> very few friends things which may, alas! be told now, without fear
> of hurting her sensitive nature; things which ought to be told in her
> honour. Among these sayings was one which explains the long
> interval between her works. She said that she thought every serious
> delineation of life ought to be the product of personal experience
> and observation of a normal, and not of a forced or special kind. 'I
> have not accumulated, since I published "Shirley",' she said, 'what
> makes it needful for me to speak again, and, till I do, may God give
> me grace to be dumb.' She had a conscientiousness which could not
> be relaxed by praise or even sympathy – dear as sympathy was to
> her sensitive nature. She had no vanity which praise could

486

aggravate or censure mortify. . . . From her feeble constitution of body, her sufferings by the death of her whole family, and the secluded and monotonous life she led, she became morbidly sensitive in some respects; but in her high vocation, she had, in addition to the deep intuitions of a gifted woman, the strength of a man, the patience of a hero, and the conscientiousness of a saint. In the points in which women are usually most weak – in regard to opinion, to appreciation, to applause – her moral strength fell not a whit behind the intellectual force manifested in her works. Though passion occupies too prominent a place in her pictures of life, though women have to complain that she represents love as the whole and sole concern of their lives, and though governesses especially have reason to remonstrate, and do remonstrate, that their share of human conflict is laid open somewhat rudely and inconsiderately and sweepingly to social observation, it is a true social blessing that we have had a female writer who has discountenanced sentimentalism and feeble egotism with such practical force as is apparent in the works of Currer Bell. Her heroines love too readily, too vehemently, and sometimes after a fashion which their female readers may resent; but they do their duty through everything, and are healthy in action, however morbid in passion.

Elsewhere in the press, conjecture about Currer Bell was again the order of the day. After a particularly pejorative article was published in *Sharpe's Magazine* in June, Ellen Nussey – ultra-sensitive where her friend's reputation was concerned – suggested that Mrs Gaskell write a reply. At first Mr Brontë would not hear of it. Mr Nicholls told her: 'The remarks respecting Mr Brontë excited in him only amusement indeed, I have not seen him laugh as much for some months as he did while I was reading the article to him.' But by July there had been so many false articles about Charlotte that Mr Brontë asked Mrs Gaskell to write a life of his daughter to put the record straight; he now thought it necessary. Should she refuse, he said that he intended to write one himself, bad though he thought it would be.

In fact Mr Brontë's request coincided precisely with Mrs Gaskell's own wishes. As the months had passed she had felt increasingly strongly the need to do justice to her friend. In May she had written to George Smith that one day, if she lived long enough and if no one was living whom such a publication would hurt, she would like to publish what she knew of Charlotte Brontë and 'make the world (if I am but strong enough in expression) honour the woman as much as they have admired the writer'.[1] She was haunted by the thought of her, whose 'thanks came more through her eyes and the grasp of her hand than her tongue', by a consciousness of thwarted potential, of the 'transcendent grandeur' that would have been hers, if she had been brought up in a healthy and happy atmosphere. She wished, as she told several correspondents, that she had known about Charlotte's illness sooner: she thought that if she had come, she could have induced Charlotte to terminate the pregnancy.[2]

In early June Mrs Gaskell had again written to George Smith – feeling that he must be suffering from a similar regret, that of not cultivating Charlotte Brontë's intimacy more assiduously. She had determined to 'put down everything I remembered about this dear friend and noble woman, before its vividness had faded from my mind: but I *know* that Mr Brontë, and I *fear* that Mr Nicholls, would not like this made public, even though the more she was known the more people would honour her as a woman, separate from her character of authoress'.[3] Once she had been asked by Mr Brontë to write Charlotte's life, Mrs Gaskell's task was very different from that of writing her own personal recollections with no intention of immediate publication. As she told George Smith: 'I shall have now to omit a good deal of detail as to her home, and the circumstances, which must have had so much to do in forming her character. All these can merely be indicated during the lifetime of her father, and to a certain degree in the lifetime of her husband'.[4]

Mr Nicholls was averse to the idea of publishing a life of Charlotte Brontë – he himself had taken no notice of the accounts of his wife as he was 'well aware of how the subject of them would have acted'[5] – but he finally acquiesced because Mr Brontë desired it. When Mrs Gaskell came to Haworth to discuss the matter, he told her plainly that he did 'not approve of the project, but that out of deference to Mr Brontë's wishes', he should give her every facility in his power.[6]

Mrs Gaskell, as she told Ellen Nussey, saw that Mr Brontë, unlike Mr Nicholls, did not perceive 'the full extent of the great interest in her personal history felt by strangers. . . . Mr Nicholls was far more aware of the kind of particulars which people would look for; and saw how they had snatched at every gossiping account of her, and how desirable it was to have a full and authorised history of her life, if it were done at all.'[7] To Mr Brontë and Mr Nicholls she gave a hint of trouble to come. She had long ago made up her mind that Miss Brontë's faults were those of the strange circumstances she had been brought up in: 'I told Mr Brontë how much of the task I had undertaken, yet how much I wished to do it well, and make his daughter's most unusual character (as taken separately from her genius) known to those who from their deep interest and admiration of her writings would naturally, if her life was to be written, expect to be informed as to the circumstances which made her what she was.' Both men agreed, Mr Brontë saying with his usual vigour, 'No quailing, Mrs Gaskell.

No drawing back.'[8]

And Mrs Gaskell set to, with Ellen Nussey's co-operation. Ellen allowed her to see three hundred of what she said was a total of five hundred letters from Charlotte, and on 6 September 1855 Mrs Gaskell told her, after reading them through: 'They gave me a very beautiful idea of her character. . . . I am sure the more fully she – Charlotte Brontë – the *friend*, the *daughter*, the *sister*, the *wife*, is known, and known where need be in her own words, the more highly she will be appreciated . . . the more her character and talents are known the more thoroughly will both be admired and reverenced.'[9] The letters had only confirmed her own view of Charlotte's highly principled nature. The woman that emerged from the letters was no sensualist but instead a high-minded woman devoted to duty. As she began to write, she hoped that she 'carefully preserved the reader's respect of Mr Brontë, while truth and the desire of doing justice to her, compelled me to state the domestic peculiarities of her childhood, which (as in all cases) contributed so much to make her what she was.'[10]

Ellen Nussey approved the 'righteous work' that Mrs Gaskell had undertaken, and said that she would try to obtain a reproduction of the portrait of Charlotte by Richmond: it would be 'such a satisfaction to people to see something that would settle their ideas of the personal appearance of the dear departed one. It has been a surprise to every stranger, I think, that she was so gentle and lady-like to look upon.'[11]

In the early summer of 1856 Mrs Gaskell's researches took her to Brussels. There she saw the letters which Charlotte had written to M. Heger. These were a side to her subject's character which did not harmonise with the portrait of her friend. She devoutly hoped he would never allow his friends to persuade him to publish, in response to and as a defence against *Villette*. Madame Heger had refused to see her, though M. Heger had been very charming. In her *Life* of Charlotte, Mrs Gaskell would deliberately obscure this part of her subject's life, fearing how it would come across to readers of the time. Meanwhile she was having difficulty getting material out of the 'dogged' Mr Nicholls, whom she found a very 'ticklish' person to deal with despite his warm affections and her liking and respect for him. In the end she enlisted the aid of Sir James Kay Shuttleworth, and when they visited Haworth in the summer of 1856 he successfully carried off for her the manuscript of *The Professor*, the manuscript fragment of fifty pages called *Emma*, and a packet the size of a lady's travelling case full of paper books of all sizes: 'the wildest and most incoherent things, all purporting to be written . . . to some member of the Wellesley family. They give one the idea of creative power carried to the verge of insanity.'[12]

But Mr Nicholls suffered anguish at the thought of the book. On

1 December he wrote to George Smith, after he had been asked to sign copyright documents in connection with it:

> I trust I shall not be required to do anything more in a matter which from beginning to end has been such a source of pain and annoyance to me; as I have been dragged into sanctioning a proceeding utterly repugnant to my feelings – indeed nothing but an unwillingness to thwart Mr Brontë's wishes could have induced me to acquiesce in a project, which in my eyes is little short of desecration.[13]

He would afterwards say that he read the work with 'inexpressible pain'.

After Brussels it had been a particular worry to Mrs Gaskell that *The Professor* would be about M. Heger. She was relieved to find, on reading it, that although set in the school in Brussels, it had no direct relation to him. In her view George Smith should publish it because it was a curious link in Charlotte's literary history, showing the promise that was afterwards realised; another advantage was that it contained what she considered 'the most charming woman she ever drew'. On the other hand, Mrs Gaskell thought it 'disfigured by more coarseness – and profanity in quoting texts of Scripture disagreeably than in any of her other works',[14] and because of her avowed aim to defend Charlotte Brontë from just such accusations in her *Life*, she was particularly concerned at the possible consequences of publishing *The Professor* as it stood.

She intimated something of this to Mr Nicholls, whose consent as the copyright owner would be needed to any extirpations by her and Sir James. Mr Nicholls wrote robustly to her that while he could not consent to any revision of the work, at the same time he did not wish 'to give occasion for malignant criticism – If therefore it should appear to Mr Brontë and myself, that any such result would be likely to accrue, we should hesitate before giving the work to the public.' However, after Mr Nicholls had conscientiously consulted Mr Brontë on the matter and read over the book to him, neither clergyman could find much to object to: their opinion was that with 'the exception of two or three strong expressions which might be open to misinterpretation', no revision of the MS was necessary. If any extensive alteration had been requisite they could not have consented to the publication of the tale.[15]

Mrs Gaskell's original intention was that *The Professor* should be published before the *Life*; then, without appearing to take notice, she could answer any objections and criticisms that might be raised by the novel.[16] However, after Mr Nicholls had altered very little, she thought after all it should not be published, writing to George

Smith, that the book had 'a lovely female character – and glimpses of home and family life in the latter portion of the tale. – But oh! I wish Mr Nicholls wd have altered more! . . . I fear he has left many little things . . . likely to make her misunderstood. For I would not, if I could help it, have another syllable that could be called coarse to be associated with her name. Yet another *woman* of her drawing – still more a *nice* one, still more a *married* one, ought to be widely interesting'.[17] (Mr Nicholls had failed to remove Hunsden Yorke's irreverent quotations from the Bible, and Frances Henri's repetition of the word Hell. *The Professor* was in fact published in June 1857, soon after Mrs Gaskell's *Life*, with a brief preface by Mr Nicholls.)

Mrs Gaskell had anyway gone ahead with her tirade against Lady Eastlake, formerly Miss Rigby, whose swingeing criticisms of Currer Bell had appeared in the *Quarterly Review*, for in Mrs Gaskell's view, 'whatever Miss Brontë wrote, Lady E. had no right to make such offensive conjectures as she did'.[18] She angrily attacked Lady Eastlake's gossiping speculations about who Currer Bell really was, her lack of Christian charity that made her presume herself able to decide what the writer may be away from the book and to make the cruel judgement that the author 'must be one who for some sufficient reason has long forfeited the society of her sex'. And she asked rhetorically, was the reviewer one who had 'led a wild and struggling and isolated life – seeing few but plain and outspoken Northerners, unskilled in the euphuisms which assist the polite world to skim over the mention of vice?' Had she 'striven through long weeping years to find excuses for the lapse of an only brother; and through daily contact with a poor lost profligate, been compelled into a certain familiarity with the vices his soul abhors?' She defended the irreligiousness reviewers had been disgusted by as unsurprising lapses of faith in a life so tragic: 'Has he, through trials, close following in dread march through his household, sweeping the hearthstone bare of life and love, still striven hard for strength to say, "It is the Lord! let Him do what seemeth to Him good" – and sometimes striven in vain, until the kindly Light returned? If through all these dark waters the scornful reviewer has passed clear, refined, free from stain, – with a soul that has never in all its agonies, cried "lama sabachthani", – still, even then let him pray with the Publican rather than judge with the Pharisee.'[19]

Mrs Gaskell went on to present Charlotte Brontë as the picture of purity, using her marriage to a clergyman of Mr Nicholls' character to make her point:

. . . Mr Nicholls was one who had seen her almost daily for years;
. . . as a daughter, a sister, a mistress and a friend. He was not a man to be attracted by any kind of literary fame. I imagine that this,

491

by itself, would rather repel him when he saw it in the possession of a woman. He was a grave reserved, conscientious man, with a deep sense of religion, and of his duties as one of its ministers. . . . The love of such a man – a daily spectator of her life for years – is a great testimony to her character as a woman.[20]

The way that Charlotte accepted the marriage proposal provided yet further testimony: '. . . quietly and modestly did she, on whom such hard judgements had been passed by ignorant reviewers, receive this vehement, passionate declaration of love, – thus thoughtfully for her father, and unselfishly for herself, put aside all consideration of how she should reply, excepting as he wished!'[21]

Miss Brontë, according to Mrs Gaskell, was 'utterly unconscious . . . of what was, by some, esteemed coarse in her writings'.[22] She was 'invariably shocked and distressed' to hear any disapproval of *Jane Eyre* on grounds of propriety. 'The misunderstanding with Miss Martineau on account of *Villette* was the cause of bitter regret to Miss Brontë. Her woman's nature had been touched, as she thought, with insulting misconception; and she had dearly loved the person who had thus unconsciously wounded her.'[23] Mrs Gaskell had told George Smith that she particularly wanted to include the reference in one of Charlotte's letters to how she liked the chaperonage of Mrs Smith when meeting strangers at Westbourne Place – 'which is a piece of womanliness (as opposed to the common ideas of her being a "strong-minded emancipated" woman) which I should like to bring out'.[24] And indeed the 'clever bold girl' who had opinions every bit as strong as her father, who had passions as strong as Branwell, and who found the affections of most people insipid, was most successfully camouflaged.

Mrs Gaskell said that she wished to be out of the country for the reviews of the *Life*, which in this case would have 'a double power to wound, for if they say anything disparaging of *her*, I know I shall not have done her and the circumstances in which she was placed justice; that is to say that in her case more visibly than in most her circumstances made her faults, while her virtues were her own'.[25] On that score she need not have worried. The general reaction to the book was excellent; the public responded with wholehearted sympathy to the image Mrs Gaskell had created of a shrinking domestic woman who had suffered terribly and who could write books such as *Jane Eyre* while her purity remained unimpaired. The attacks came from those who felt themselves injured parties in the story. The portrayal of Cowan Bridge School brought threatened legal action and a battle in the newspaper correspondence columns between the Carus Wilson faction and a majestic and cutting Mr Nicholls, who unhesitatingly defended the descriptions of the school given by Charlotte to Mrs Gaskell. Harriet Martineau wrote sheet after sheet about her quarrel with Charlotte; and Mrs Robinson (now Lady Scott) threatened a suit unless a revised edition of the *Life* was prepared. Mrs Gaskell was very upset, writing to Ellen Nussey: '*I did so try* to *tell the truth*, and I believe *now* I hit as near the truth as any one *could* do. And I weighed every line with all my whole power and heart, so that every line should go to its great purpose of making *her* known and valued, as one who had gone through such a terrible life with a brave and faithful heart.'[26]

Mr Brontë's reaction to the not altogether uncritical account of him was to do nothing, though privately he protested to Mrs Gaskell and to George Smith about his depiction as a man of explosive rages, as did Mr Nicholls. Mr Nicholls also said that Haworth and its environs might be queer places, but they were nowhere near as queer as Mrs Gaskell had made them out to be.[27] But Mr Brontë was determined not to give further ammunition to the Carus Wilson party, and said he would do nothing, although he asked Mrs Gaskell to remove the statement that he had not allowed his children to eat meat, that he had burnt their coloured boots, and that he had burned the hearthrug and sawn off the chairs. Mrs Gaskell, for his forbearance, pronounced him a 'brick'.

To a visiting Methodist minister Patrick Brontë said, 'Mrs Gaskell is a novelist, you know, and we must allow her a *little* romance, eh?' And he wrote to her: 'Why should you disturb yourself concerning what has been, is, and ever will be the lot of eminent writers. . . . Above three thousand years since, Solomon said, "He that increaseth knowledge, increaseth sorrow". . . . So you may find it, and so my Daughter Charlotte found it. . . .'[28]

He was magnanimous about the errors in the book, which he otherwise thought 'full of truth and life'. Before he read the reviews, he had 'formed my own opinion, from which you know I am not easily shaken. And my opinion and the reading World's opinion of the "Memoir", is that it is in every way worthy of what one Great Woman should have written of Another, and that it ought to stand, and will stand, in the first rank of Biographies till the end of time.'[29]

Mr Nicholls, too, said that Mrs Gaskell had done justice to her subject, although she had inserted some things that ought never to have been published. Mary Taylor sent praise from New Zealand, telling Ellen on hearing the news of Mrs Gaskell having to do a new edition: 'Libellous or not, the first edition was all true, and except the declamation all, in my opinion, useful to be published. Of course I don't know how far necessity may make Mrs Gaskell give them up. You know one dare not always say the world moves.'[30] Mary Taylor had written to Mrs Gaskell of Charlotte:

She thought much of her duty, and had loftier and clearer notions of it than most people, and held fast to them with more success. It was done, it seems to me, with much more difficulty than people have of stronger nerves, and better fortunes. All her life was but labour and pain; and she never threw down the burden for the sake of present pleasure. I don't know what use you can make of all I have said. I have written it with the strong desire to obtain appreciation for her. Yet, what does it matter? She herself appealed to the world's judgement for her use of some of the faculties she had, – not the best, – but still the only ones she could turn to strangers' benefit. They heartily, greedily enjoyed the fruits of her labours and then found out she was much to be blamed for possessing such faculties. Why ask a judgement on her from such a world?[31]

Having read the book, she congratulated Mrs Gaskell on giving such a true picture of such a melancholy life, while being in her view forced to skirt round the truth of Mr Brontë's selfishness. She had seen two reviews of the *Life* out in New Zealand: 'neither of them seems to think it a strange or wrong state of things that a woman of first-rate talents, industry and integrity should live her life in a walking nightmare of "poverty and self-suppression". I doubt whether any of them will.'[32]

A couple of years later Mary Taylor gave up life in New Zealand and returned to England, where she lived a quiet existence at Gomersal, close to Ellen Nussey, with whom she soon quarrelled. She remained faithful to her ardent feminist principles and the articles she contributed to the *Victorian Magazine* were collected in 1870 and published under the title *The First Duty of Women*.[33] By then, the main theme of her writing – women's duty to earn money – which had been revolutionary in 1837, was becoming a commonplace. The novel over which she had long brooded and delighted finally came out three years before her death in 1890. By then she had required a reputation for being very eccentric and was said to keep a pistol by her bed. She had steadfastly refused to discuss Charlotte Brontë with newspaper hounds, just as she had deliberately burnt all her friend's letters.

Not so Ellen Nussey. For the rest of her long life – she died aged eighty, in 1897, forty-two years after Charlotte – she would talk of her friend, and it is to her that we owe so much information about the Brontës. Perhaps it was a desire for attention, her later impoverishment and her concern that Mrs Gaskell had not really shown how very religious Charlotte was, but with time her behaviour with regard to Charlotte Brontë became rather unattractive. In particular she became embittered towards Arthur Nicholls and by the end of their lives she seems to have been set on besmirching his memory.

After Charlotte's death Mr Nicholls and Mr Brontë established a *modus vivendi* in the small parsonage which had once echoed to the racket of Branwell's footsteps and the soft rustle of his sisters' skirts as they tripped about the passages neatly performing their daily tasks to keep the house in running order. The faithful Martha Brown continued to serve the two men, and Mr Brontë still preached every Sunday. The fame of Charlotte Brontë continued to bring visitors to the parsonage. The Duke of Devonshire called with a brace of grouse; there were requests from all over the world for samples of Charlotte's handwriting and Mr Brontë spent much time cutting up letters of his daughter in order to send them to well-wishers.

Between them, Mr Nicholls and Mr Brontë took a great deal of trouble to exhume and read over some of Emily's and Charlotte's poems, sending them with the manuscript fragment *Emma* to George Smith for submission to the *Cornhill Magazine*. Whatever Ellen Nussey may have said, Mr Nicholls' pride in his wife and reverence for the fame of the family show in his letters; it particularly pleased him that Thackeray was to write an introduction to the *Emma* fragment, for 'he both can and will do justice to the character and genius of the writer'. He wished to have the fragment returned to him because 'I prize it very much as being the last thing of its kind written by the Author'.[34] He went through Emily's poetry and willingly transcribed it for Mr Smith, in case he might be interested in publishing it in the *Cornhill Magazine*.

On 23 December 1859 Mr Nicholls reported to George Smith that he had been amusing himself with a microscope lately, and that Mr Brontë was still making his weekly sermon. The following month he described Mr Brontë as 'wonderfully well',[35] but owing to the very severe frost he was very much confined to the parsonage and had not been able to preach. Mr Nicholls hoped that with the return of a milder season, the old man would again be able to give his afternoon sermon.

The publication of the *Emma* fragment in the *Cornhill Magazine* that spring gave both men great pleasure. On 26 March 1860 Mr Brontë wrote to thank George Smith:

Though writing is to me now something of a task, I cannot avoid sending you a few lines, to thank you for sending me the magazines, and for your gentlemanly conduct towards my daughter in all your transactions with her, from first to last. . . . The 'Last Sketch' took full possession of my mind. Thackeray, in his remarks in it, has excelled even himself. . . . And what he has written does honour both to his head and heart – thank him kindly both in Mr Nicholls' name and mine.

Touchingly he adds:

> If organless spirits see as we see, and feel as we feel, in this material clogging world, my daughter Charlotte's spirit will receive additional happiness on scanning the remarks of her Ancient Favourite.[36]

The remarkable old man finally took formal leave of his parishioners from the pulpit of St Michael and All Angels in August 1860. For the next eighteen months he was almost continually confined to his bed, but despite illness and his great age his mind was as sharp as ever. We have a last glimpse of him through the eyes of Mrs Gaskell's daughter, Meta. Mrs Gaskell had fancied that he might not wish to meet her when she visited Haworth with Meta, but on 6 November 1860 there came a few tremulous lines saying that he would be glad to see them.

> . . . we were taken into his bedroom; where everything was delicately clean and white, and there he was sitting propped up in bed in a clean nightgown, with a clean towel laid just for his hands to play upon – looking Oh! very different from the stiff scarred face above the white walls of cravat in the photograph – he had a short white growth of beard on his chin; and such a gentle, quiet, sweet, half-pitiful expression on his mouth, a good deal of soft white hair, and spectacles on. He shook hands with us, and we sat down, and then said how glad he was to see Mama – and she said how she had hesitated about coming, – feeling as if he might now have unpleasant associations with her – which never seemed to have entered into his head – then he asked her how, since he last saw her, she had passed through this weary and varied world – in a sort of half grandiloquent style. . . .

Then he talked of Charlotte and the numerous requests he had received for her handwriting; he repeated that Mrs Gaskell's book would hand her name down to posterity. He went on to talk about politics, before expressing his pleasure at Thackeray's notice in the *Cornhill* – he thought it showed 'heart', but that Thackeray was 'an odd man, a very odd man'. He alluded with a certain pride to his own 'eccentricity' and 'independence' of other people's opinion.

> Mama said: 'Yes – I was just telling my daughter as we came up the hill, that I thought you had always done what you thought right.' – 'And so I have,' he said, 'and I appeal to God.' There was something very solemn in the way he said it; and in him altogether – None of the sternness I had fancied – Mama said something about

496

our not staying too long to tire him and that we were going, for me to make a sketch; And he said, 'There are certain circumstances, you see,' looking very knowing, 'which make it desirable that when you leave in 5 minutes or so, we should shake hands – and I give your daughter free leave to make a sketch, or do anything *outside* the house. Do you understand Latin? Mrs Gaskell does at any rate, well *verbum sap.*, a word to the wise,' and then he chuckled very much; the gist of it was, as Mama saw, and I guessed, that he feared Mr Nicholls' return from the school – and we were to be safely out of the house before that. . . .[37]

They saw Mr Greenwood before leaving the village and his wife volunteered that they all disliked Mr Nicholls. The sexton said 'Aye, Mester Brontë and Mr Nicholls live together still *ever near* but *ever separate*'. Mrs Gaskell thought that Mr Nicholls held Mr Brontë rather in terror, as he seemed to hold many in the village by his fiercely uncompromising stance. Nevertheless, the fact remains that the old man left everything in his will to his son-in-law rather than to his next of kin, who were living on both the Branwell and Brontë sides. Ellen Nussey suggested that Mr Brontë's arm had been twisted, but this seems out of character for the tough and wilful Patrick Brontë, who survived through another severe winter in 1860–61, confined to bed but, as Mr Nicholls said on 4 April 1861 with some pride, with 'his mental faculties unimpaired'. Mr Brontë finally died on 7 June, the death certificate giving the cause as 'chronic bronchitis; dyspepsia; convulsions, duration nine hours'.

He was buried five days later, the coffin, like his daughter's six years before, being brought out of the eastern gate of the garden leading into the churchyard. And as for Charlotte's funeral, there were great numbers of people collected in the small churchyard. The Bradford paper reporting the event noted that as a sign of respect all the shops in Haworth were closed, and that the people 'filled every pew, and the aisles in the church, and many shed tears during the impressive reading of the service for the burial of the dead, by the vicar [of Bradford, Dr Burnet]'. Then the body of Mr Brontë was taken down to be laid by the side of his daughter Charlotte, within the altar rails, the last person to be buried there before the crypt and graveyard were sealed up for ever.

Mr Nicholls, the chief mourner, did not however go on to take over the parish. The Church Trustees decided against him, nor did the people of Haworth want him as incumbent after Mr Brontë. By November of that year he was back in Ireland, at his childhood home at Banagher, and had left Holy Orders to be a farmer. He took with him all his wife's effects including her dresses, and Mr Brontë's dog,

Plato, which the old man had bought after Charlotte's death; it was perhaps Mr Nicholls' last playing out of his promise to Charlotte to take care of her father. Nor did he forget Martha Brown, to whom he would write several times a year for the rest of her life and who would come to Ireland to stay with him on several occasions.[38] In August 1862 he revisited Haworth for the last time, staying with Mr Grant, the other curate. And when questions of his wife's fame arose, as they did sporadically over the next forty years, he would write to the newspapers.

Two years later he married his cousin, Mary Bell, and rather curiously he took her on their honeymoon to Upper Bangor in North Wales, the same place where he had taken Charlotte Brontë ten years before. Perhaps he wanted to remember his small, fiery, nervous first wife. Certainly he did not forget her, despite marrying again; he wrote to Mr Greenwood after being asked to send one of the little magazines written by the Brontë children: 'I got one to enclose to you: but when I looked at the handwriting I could not bring myself to part with it.' Mr Nicholls would live to see out the century, dying at the great age of eighty-eight in Banagher on 2 December 1906.

Charlotte Brontë's existence was peculiarly sad, though her name is now touched with peculiar glory. Her childhood was blighted by domestic tragedy, as, with terrible symmetry, was her adulthood some twenty years later. In a sense tragedy was a prerequisite for the flowering of genius from natural talent, for it forced that retreat into imagination in early youth and the long literary apprenticeship in Angria, to which in no small degree is owed her facility and stylistic excellence. To the lack of discipline of her infernal Byronic world too, allied to a naturally ardent temperament, can be attributed unreasonable expectations of life, and a hatred of cant and convention. While it gave great force to the novels, in everyday existence it produced a sense of being thwarted and created much sometimes self-imposed unhappiness – albeit in a life which could offer few pleasures. But it was perhaps Charlotte Brontë's doom to be born with an extraordinary sensibility and an almost unmanageably passionate nature, and to have little or nothing to spend it upon.

She published her views at considerable cost to herself, for though her innovative realism was admired, it was also considered dangerous. Her extraordinary, original writing made her a contemporary phenomenon, and she reached an eminence difficult to imagine today, being one of a handful of women writers who confounded the expectations of their sex's capabilities.

After the adulation of the 1850s and 1860s, however, Charlotte

Brontë's reputation declined in relation to her sister Emily's. It was no longer considered possible to place her in the first rank of writers: her canvas is too narrow, she writes too much in the grip of one emotion; she has no great themes, or ideas, none of the philosophical range of Tolstoy (for example), none of Dickens's prolific invention, none of George Eliot's ability to create character; the great Mr Rochester himself has been unkindly described as speaking like an overwrought governess. Yet, the masterly handling of narrative tempo and prosody, the magnificence and eloquence of her writing, with its great symbolism and potent use of imagery, cannot be denied. Few but the most hardy would dismiss the claims of Jane Eyre and Lucy Snowe to be two of the greatest and most living characters in the pantheon of world literature. Whatever her novels' faults, the incandescent power of her writing gives *Jane Eyre* in particular a uniquely favoured niche in the affections of the reading public. Her vigorous, disadvantaged heroines appeal to a strong, if not always visible, component of the English psyche – what has been called 'a rugged intellectual republicanism'.

Charlotte Brontë herself was well aware of the limitations imposed by her small experience and her poor health. But as her juvenilia, letters and some of *Shirley* and particularly *Villette* demonstrate, she possessed humour, wit, subtlety and an ability to sketch the broadest range of character and subject matter. Much of the 'hunger, rebellion and rage' which Matthew Arnold detected in her writing, and which he prophesied would be fatal to her in the long run, vanished after Charlotte's marriage to Mr Nicholls. That she would have extended her palette had she lived to take up her craft again is hard not to believe, since much of *Villette*, with its well-rounded, independent, brilliantly individualized creations, points to such a development.

Nevertheless, as the body of her work stands, Charlotte Brontë's genius was for expressing a rare intensity of feeling, the result of emotional and spiritual deprivation; she was a powerful poet of suffering, and she was uniquely well placed for that position. Her remote situation added to a tragedy begun by her family's feeble constitutions and exacerbated by a morbidity which was partly physical in origin. Hers was an excitable, vehement nature – too vehement, as Mrs Gaskell observed – full of intellectual interests, which fretted for lack of stimulation in the wild hilltop village where there was not a single educated family; full of artistic, creative urges, but also hysterical fears and dreads. For those urges could also torment her, and weave the chimera which plagued her before she wrote *Villette*; though imagination was her saviour, it was also a savage god.

The little she did see of society was of a kind antipathetic to her restless spirit, for it was composed of petty bourgeois, small manufacturers' daughters and unadventurous curates. Her chief experience

499

outside her narrow circle during her formative years was a girls' school in Brussels – which, while headed by an exceptional schoolmaster, provided company scarcely less provincial than that in the environs of Leeds. She was not fitted for provincial manners any better by her extraordinary literary precocity and obsessions, and she became the foe of convention, which she felt frustrated her at every turn. Her intellectual honesty and sophistication alienated her from many of her circle, particularly in the area of religious belief and behaviour, which conflicted with a strangely modern, hedonistic sensuality that was the legacy of Byron. Her experience at the hands of the Evangelicals as a child, the discrepancy between their caveats and her own needs, bred religious fear and hatred of hypocrisy; in conjunction with an upbringing very much centred on the Bible, her father's missionary commitment to religious truth became an equally religious commitment to the truth of the nature of human beings. Eventually her unending, romantic quest for the real behind the conventional led to the creation of female characters that gave the lie to current anaemic, falsely idealized representations of them. On the other hand, perhaps much of her boldness in championing truth was the effect on her of her Yorkshire surroundings, of bluff north-country attitudes and plain-speaking.

Charlotte Brontë's war with convention was intensified by the excessive restrictions on middle-class women during her lifetime, which had little or no place for an unmarried, undomesticated, intelligent woman. Under these circumstances she produced novels of an autobiographical kind and of rare power and analysis, which astonished her contemporaries, unused to revelation of such feeling from feminine lips. In the hullabaloo that followed, she refused to tone down her unorthodox writing, faithful to truth against accusations of impropriety, though it cost her dearly. She had not become a writer in order to conform to contemporary standards of feminine authorship, standards which she despised. Her novels held up to critical examination two facets of Victorian life considered sacred – women and the clergy, and exposed the realities of the one and the flaws of the other, in a society inimical to them.

For all the recognition of her greatness in her lifetime, Charlotte Brontë's 'unfeminine' heroines, with their 'self-dependent intellects' and their lack of respect for rank, gave her a reputation for being a 'dangerous'[39] writer, the 'treacherous advocate of contempt of established maxims and disregard of the regulations of society' – *Jane Eyre* was an 'immoral production'.[40] Though no political thinker, still less a feminist, she was, as many critics since have noticed, feminist in the deepest psychological sense; although she may have been conventional enough in life, in her books, particularly *Villette*, she strongly challenges male authority. As Tony Tanner has pointed out, though she did not 'finally succeed in redefining the whole social context . . . the challenge and resistance contained in her narrative are sufficiently painful to show up the need for such radical definition and this to some extent makes it possible'.[41]

To the self-denying, sexless, womanly ethos of her day, she opposed what appeared to be an unsettling individualism, revolutionary in its implications. Two months after Charlotte Brontë's death, Mrs Oliphant commented that *Jane Eyre* had 'turned the world of fancy upside down'; she had 'dashed into our well-ordered world, broke its boundaries, and defied its principles . . . the furious love-making was but a wild declaration of the "Rights of Woman" in a new aspect'.[42] For Charlotte's part, she was simply giving expression to a suppressed inner life, revealing the problems posed by Victorian society, of, as another female poet wrote, 'the inner life with all its ample room for heart and lungs, for will and intellect, Inviolable by conventions'.[43] For this contribution, Tanner has seen *Villette* as one of the 'great fictional studies, not of the self and society, but the self without society, in our literature'.[44]

Despite the opprobrium her work drew upon her, Charlotte remained bloody but unbowed by the criticism of her epoch, faithful to what had become a near-religious feeling of responsibility for her gifts of perception and writing. As she wrote in *Villette*, 'Whatever my powers – feminine or the contrary – God had given them, and I felt resolute to be ashamed of no faculty of his disposal.' Mrs Gaskell often wondered what Charlotte Brontë might have been if she had been born into health and happiness, 'what would have been her transcendent grandeur?'. What, indeed?

Notes

For the most part I have used the imperfect text of the Shakespeare Head edition of the Brontë letters. As is well known, it is riddled with inaccuracies but in many cases it is the only text available. Since it would be outside the scope of this book to correct the text, I have only supplemented a more accurate reading occasionally. For reasons of space, unless otherwise indicated the Shakespeare Head should be taken to be the source of information. Manuscript sources are indicated in the notes.

I have relied on the Penguin editions of Charlotte Brontë's novels, excepting *The Professor* (Dent), and quotations are from those texts. Mrs Gaskell's *The Life of Charlotte Brontë* is also the Penguin unexpurgated first edition. Until Christine Alexander finishes preparing the definitive edition of the juvenilia it is necessary to rely on the Shakespeare Head edition, as well as the transcribed versions published in a diversity of forms, for which see the Bibliography. Charlotte Brontë's poetry is published in a scholarly edition by T.J. Winnifrith, *The Poems of Charlotte Brontë* (Blackwell, 1984). Mrs Gaskell's letters are taken from the edition by J.A.V. Chapple and Arthur Pollard, *The Letters of Mrs Gaskell* (Manchester University Press, 1966); Mary Taylor's letters from *Mary Taylor, Friend of Charlotte Brontë*, ed. Joan Stevens (Oxford University Press, 1972).

Abbreviations used in the notes
ABN — Arthur Bell Nicholls
DPM — Brontë Parsonage Museum
BST — Brontë Society Transactions
CB — Charlotte Brontë
ECG — Mrs Gaskell
EN — Ellen Nussey
GS — George Smith
Life — Mrs Gaskell, *The Life of Charlotte Brontë*
MT — Mary Taylor
PB — Patrick Brontë
SHCBM — Shakespeare Head, *The Miscellaneous and Unpublished Writings of Charlotte and Patrick Branwell Brontë*
SHCBP — Shakespeare Head, *The Poems of Charlotte Brontë and Patrick Branwell Brontë*
SHLL — Shakespeare Head, *Lives and Letters*

Chapter One
For Patrick Brontë's life I am indebted to the extensive researches of John Lock and Canon W.T. Dixon in *A Man of Sorrow*. Dr Edward Chitham's *The Brontës' Irish Background* elucidates his early life, and Horsfall Turner's *Brontëana* and Erskine Stuart's essay on the Brontë nomenclature in Brontë Society Transactions (BST) 1:3:13 are also of interest. Patrick Brontë's correspondence with Mrs Gaskell, informing her about his early life and that of his children as well as his reactions to her *Life* of Charlotte, are reprinted in their entirety in BST 8:43:83 and

8:44:125. Information about Mr Brontë at Cambridge and the Evangelical movement derives mainly from Ford K. Brown's magisterial history *Fathers of the Victorians* and Charles Smyth's *Simeon and Church Order*. G. Elsie Harrison's *The Clue to the Brontës* points up Patrick Brontë's Wesleyan connections and further evidence of it is to be found in William Morgan's *Life of John Crosse*.

Patrick Brontë's writings – his sermons, poetry and novelettes, are mainly reprinted in Horsfall Turner's edition of his *Collected Works*; for the rest see the Bibliography. W.W. Scruton is useful on his early ministry. For information on Mr Brontë's attempts to invent a new musket see BST 14:1:13.

The Branwells are very nearly as poorly documented as the Bruntys. Besides Winifred Gerin's biographies of Branwell and Anne Brontë the following BST articles contain information: J. Hambley Rowe's 'The Maternal Relations of the Brontës' (6:33:135); Ivy Holgate's 'The Branwells at Penzance' (BST 13:70:425); a little more light is shed by articles about Charlotte Brontë's first cousin Eliza Jane Kingston in BST Volumes 11, 12 and 13, particularly Fanny Ratchford's (13:67:200). Thomas Branwell's Will is helpful for his financial position. The Cornish historian P.A.S. Pool's article in the BST 18:3:93, 'The Branwell Connection' is particularly important. J.S. Courtney's nineteenth-century *History of Penzance* contains an interesting description of the Branwell shop at the corner of Market Place and Causeway Head.

1. Meta Gaskell to Emily Shaen, 6 Nov. 1860, Shakespeare Head Lives and Letters (SHLL) IV, p. 240
2. Patrick Brontë (PB) to Mrs Gaskell (ECG), 3 Nov. 1856, quoted in Lock, *op. cit.*, p. 503
3. Chitham, *op. cit.*; Horsfall Turner, *Brontëana*; Lock, *op. cit.*
4. John Greenwood's diary, quoted in Lock, *op. cit.*, p. 6
5. Chitham, *op cit.*, p. 90
6. Lock, *op cit.*, p. 11
7. *Ibid.*, p. 18
8. Morgan, *Life of John Crosse*; Harrison, *op. cit.*
9. Henry Venn quoted in Brown, *op. cit.*
10. Sydney Smith quoted in F. W. Smith, *Wilberforce*, p. 41
11. Smyth, *op. cit.*, p. 257
12. The Journals and Letters of Henry Martyn
13. Brown, *op. cit.*, p. 80 and p. 308n.
14. 1844, quoted in Smyth, *op. cit.*, p. 6
15. See Harrison *op. cit.*, p. 20 and Morgan, *op. cit.*
16. Ellen Nussey (EN), 'Recollections of Charlotte Brontë' (CB), SHLL I
17. PB to ECG, 30 July 1857
18. For information on the Branwells see above
19. Although the Branwells are not recorded as so being in the Morrab Library records at Penzance
20. Quoted in Harrison, *op. cit.*, p. 29
21. SHLL I, p. 68; her box was lost at sea during a shipwreck
22. Chitham, *A Life of Emily Brontë*, p. 12

Chapter Two
1. Defoe's *Tour through the Whole Island of Great Britain* (1724–6), quoted in G.G. Cragg's *Grimshaw of Haworth*, p. 27
2. Introduction to her selection of Ellis Bell's 'Literary Remains' in *Wuthering Heights* (1850), p. 471 *et seq.*
3. EN's narrative, SHLL I, p. 110
4. Chitham, *Emily Brontë*, p. 16, from J. Kellett, *Haworth Parsonage*
5. EN narrative, SHLL
6. Eulogy for Willie Weightman, Horsfall Turner, *Collected Works*
7. ECG Sept. 1853, SHLL IV, p. 88
8. 'the cutting up of the silk gown . . . told me by CB herself; and not only to me, but to Miss Nussey and Miss Wooler', ECG to M. Martineau, *Letters*, Pollard, No. 368 (23 August 1857), p. 467. Francis Leyland, Branwell's biographer and contemporary, interviewed Nancy Garrs, the maid who went from Thornton to Haworth, who confirmed the story,

though according to her it was a print dress that was not new, and the episode was intended as a joke. Mr Brontë disliked its enormous sleeves and cut them off. She also said that 'Mr Brontë was a "most affectionate husband; there was never a more affectionate father, never a kinder master" and "he was not of a violent temper at all; quite the reverse". He also immediately bought his wife a new dress.' Leyland, *The Brontë Family*, p. 48

9. Mr Brontë's own reaction to Mrs Gaskell's book was not that of a madman. While he had 'no objection whatever to your representing me as a little eccentric since you and your learned friends will have it so; only don't set me on in my fury to burning hearthrugs, sawing the backs of chairs, and tearing my wife's silk gowns', PB to ECG, 30 July 1857, Lock, *op. cit.*, p. 508. He did not refute Mrs Gaskell publicly as some of his friends would have liked him to do, because it would have given more of a handle to the Carus Wilson camp and Lady Scott. He complained to Mr Smith among others about Mrs Gaskell's insistence on his passionate rages, which he felt made him look ridiculous (John Murray archives)

10. See Lock, *op. cit.*, *passim* for Mr Brontë's record

11. Gaskell, *The Life of Charlotte Brontë*, p. 496

12. John Murray archives, Arthur Nicholls to George Smith, 2 April 1857

13. *Life*, p. 90

14. *Ibid.*, p. 91

15. CB's preface to the 1850 edition of *Wuthering Heights* (Penguin), p. 32

16. SHLL IV, p. 91

17. *Life*, p. 87

18. ECG, Pollard, No. 166, p. 245

19. Chadwick, *In the Footsteps of the Brontës*; Gerin, *C. Brontë*, p. 19

20. EN, narrative, SHLL

21. The portrait of a woman of forty-odd at the parsonage is no longer considered to be that of Miss Branwell

22. Confidential notes to Sir Wemyss Reid from Ellen Nussey, the Berg Foundation, New York Public Library

23. PB to ECG, 20 June 1855

24. PB to ECG, 1855, BST 8:44:127

25. PB to ECG, 24 July 1855

26. Preface to 'The Phenomenon, or An account in verse of the Extraordinary Eruption of a Bog', Horsfall Turner, *Collected Works*

27. SHLL IV to EN, October 1854, p. 155

28. PB to ECG, 24 July 1855

29. *Ibid.*

30. Carus-Wilson Shepheard Walwyn, *Memorials of a Father and Mother*, p. 37

31. Dame Myra Curtis, 'Cowan Bridge School: An Old Prospectus Re-examined', BST 12.63.107

32. SHLL I, p. 69

33. Brown, *op. cit.*, p. 455

34. SHLL IV, Appendix

35. Chitham, *E. Brontë*, p. 46

36. Chadwick, *op. cit.*

37. CB to Miss Wooler, 28 Aug. 1848, SHLL II, p. 248

38. According to Brown the Evangelicals were engrossed with deathbed scenes 'in an inconceivable degree' and the 'youthful deathbed scene was almost a special province of several juvenile publications', *Fathers of the Victorians*, p. 461

39. 'Thoughts Suggested to the Superintendent and Ladies of the Clergy Daughters School' quoted SHLL I, pp. 71 *et seq.*

40. *Life*, p. 98

41. See article by Brett Harrison and note by Dr T. Winnifrith, BST 85 (1975)

42. Harrison, 'The Real Miss Temple', BST 16:85:361

43. Letter to W.S. Williams, 4 Jan. 1848, SHLL II, p. 174

Chapter Three
For the texts of the juvenilia, I have used the Shakespeare Head *Miscellaneous and Unpublished Writings of Charlotte and Branwell* (SHCBM) volumes I and II, various printed transcrip-

tions, and Dr Christine Alexander's *The Early Writings of Charlotte Brontë* as well as various manuscripts in the Brontë Museum. Where the text is particularly well known, such as 'The History of the Year 1829', I have not identified it in the notes.

1. 'Misery' (Part 2) by Branwell Brontë in Winnifrith edition of the *Poems* of Branwell Brontë, 11. 225–8, p. 29
2. 'Caroline' (Calm and clear the Day declining) *ibid.* 11. 239–42, p. 72
3. I. Holgate, 'The Brontës at Thornton', BST 13:69:323
4. EN's narrative, SHLL
5. Information from Patrick Brontë's notebook at Brontë Parsonage Museum (BPM)
6. Letter to Rev. J.C. Franks, 10 Jan. 1839, Lock, *op. cit.*, p. 292
7. Winnifrith, *The Brontës and Their Background*, p. 37
8. P. Brontë, *The Maid of Killarney*
9. Gerin, *Anne Brontë*, p. 37
10. William Scruton, 'Reminiscences of Ellen Nussey', BST 1:8:23 (1898)
11. T. Balston, *John Martin*, p. 63
12. *Life*
13. D. Cecil, *Early Victorian Novelists*, pp. 105–6
14. Quoted in Thomas Bewick's Vignettes – tail pieces engraved principally for his *General History of Quadrupeds and History of British Birds* edited with an Introduction by I. Bain
15. 7 Dec. 1835, SHLL I, p. 133
16. 'History of the Year 1829', quoted in *Life*, p. 117
17. C. Alexander, *Early Writings*
18. 'The Play of the Islanders', quoted in C. Alexander, *ibid.*, pp. 42–3
19. 'History of the Year 1829', quoted in *Life*, pp. 116–17
20. 'Tales of the Islanders', from *Life*, p. 118–19
21. Manuscripts at BPM
22. See SHCBM I; MS at BPM; Ratchford, *The Brontës' Web of Childhood*, and C. Alexander, *op. cit.*
23. SHCBM I, pp. 40–1
24. Leyland, *op. cit.*, p. 88
25. *Life*, p. 111
26. SHLL I, p. 82
27. *Life*, p. 119
28. M. Monahan, ed., *The Poetaster*
29. Lord Charles Wellesley, 'Strange Events', 2nd series of the *Young Men's Magazine*, Dec. 1830; SHCBM I, p. 19

Chapter Four
Mary Taylor's narrative is printed in its entirety in SHLL and Joan Stevens' *Mary Taylor*.

1. SHLL I, EN, pp. 92 *et seq.*
2. Mary Taylor (MT) narrative, SHLL
3. *Ibid.*
4. *Ibid.*
5. PB to ECG, 7 April 1857
6. W.W. Yates, 'Dewsbury and the Brontës', BST 1:3:8
7. SHLL I, p. 87
8. M. Blakeley, 'Memories of Margaret Wooler and her Sisters', BST 12:62:113
9. 17 May 1831 to B. Brontë, SHLL I, p. 87
10. SHCBP, pp. 129–31
11. SHCBP, pp. 132–3

Chapter Five
1. 1 Jan 1833, SHLL I, pp. 108–9
2. Ellen Nussey, 'Reminiscences of Charlotte Brontë', reprinted from *Scribner's Monthly*, May 1871, BST 2:10:58
3. Series of 17 letters from EN to T. Wemyss Reid, 1870, Berg Collection, New York Public Library

4. *Ibid.*
5. See C. Alexander, *op. cit.*, pp. 91 *et seq.*
6. C. Alexander, ed., *Something about Arthur*
7. Berg Collection, EN to T. Wemyss Reid, *op. cit.*
8. *Ibid.*
9. *Ibid.*
10. MS fragment concerning CB [to Meta Gaskell? c. 1855/6], Brotherton Collection
11. Berg Collection *op. cit.*
12. *Ibid.*
13. *Ibid.*
14. *Ibid.*
15. Facsimile in SHCBM Vol. I, p. 331, quoted in C. Alexander, *op. cit.*, p. 115
16. G.E. MacLean, ed., *The Spell*, p. 42
17. The son of Mr Brontë's tailor in interview, *Bradford Observer*, 17 Feb. 1894
18. 'My Angria and the Angrians', SHCBM II, p. 12
19. Leyland, *op. cit.*, p. 119
20. In W. Gerin, *B. Brontë*; facsimile only in SHCBM II, p. 64
21. S. Foister, 'The Brontë Portraits', BST 18:5:95, pp. 339 *et seq.*
22. MT to ECG, Letter 30, 30 July 1857, Stevens, *op. cit.*, p. 133
23. See F. Ratchford, *Gondal's Queen*
24. For greater elucidation see C. Alexander, *op. cit.*, pp. 122–39
25. *Bradford Observer*, 1894, *op. cit.*

Chapter Six
1. The *Roe Head Journal*, BPM
2. SHCBP, pp. 182–3
3. Introduction to 'Selections from the Literary Remains of Ellis . . . Bell', *Wuthering Heights* (1850)
4. *Ibid.*
5. Leyland, *op. cit.*
6. D. du Maurier, *B. Brontë*, p. 50
7. *The Adventures of Charles Wentworth*, May 1836, Gerin, *B. Brontë*, pp. 99–105
8. Chadwick, *op. cit.*
9. Winnifrith ed., B. Brontë poetry, p. 210
10. See C. Alexander, *op. cit.*, p. 141
11. Hitherto unpublished MS at the State University of New York at Buffalo, 19 Jan 1836, Winnifrith, *C. Brontë*
12. From 'My Dreams', SHCBP, p. 201
13. See T.J. Winnifrith Notes and Queries, Jan 1970, p. 17. Winnifrith argues that examination of CB's letter to EN, No. 53 p. 147 in SHLL I, written probably late December 1836, shows that the letter probably says 'your ghastly Calvinistic doctrines are true'. Since Ellen was apparently a 'model of Church of England orthodoxy', he believes she must have been repeating the opinions of her brother Henry, whose diary reveals his Calvinistic tendencies, and who most probably served as a model for the Calvinistic St John Rivers
14. 'Passing Events' in W. Gerin, ed., *Five Novelettes*, p. 46
15. *Roe Head Journal*, BPM
16. *Ibid.*
17. Quoted in H. Björk, *The Language of Truth: Charlotte Brontë, the Woman Question and the Novel*
18. Quoted in Björk, p. 41
19. *Life*, p. 334
20. CB to Robert Southey, 16 March 1837, SHLL I, pp. 157 *et seq.*
21. Southey to Caroline Bowles, SHLL I, pp. 156 *et seq.*
22. *Roe Head Journal*, BPM
23. 4 Jan 1838, SHLL I, p. 163
24. 9 June 1838, SHLL I, p. 166

Chapter Seven
Information derived from Francis A. Leyland, *The Brontë Family with Special Reference to*

Patrick Branwell Brontë; Daphne du Maurier, *The Infernal World of Branwell Brontë*; Winifred Gerin, *Branwell Brontë*; Christine Alexander, *The Early Writings of Charlotte Brontë*.

1. MS known as 'Stanclyffe's Hotel' at BPM, No. B114
2. *Ibid.*
3. *The Duke of Zamorna*, SHCBM, Vol. II, p. 375
4. 'Stanclyffe's Hotel', *op. cit.*
5. *Duke of Zamorna*, *op. cit.*, p. 390
6. Fragment, BPM: No. B113 (7)
7. Quoted in SHLL I, note p. 172
8. SHLL I, p. 173
9. 'Henry Hastings' in *Five Novelettes*, p. 242
10. *The Life of Edward White Benson*, quoted in SHLL I
11. Wroot, *The Persons and Places in the Brontë novels*, p. 19
12. See C. Alexander in *The Early Writings*, *op. cit.*, Chapter 25
13. 'Caroline Vernon' in *Five Novelettes*, p. 268
14. SHCBM II, pp. 403–4

Chapter Eight
For female life in the nineteenth century, its taboos and restrictions, and attitudes towards women and women writers, the following are particularly important: Harriet Martineau's *Autobiography*, Elaine Showalter, *A Literature of their Own: British Women Novelists from Brontë to Lessing*; Ellen Moers, *Literary Women*; Barbara Taylor, *Eve and the New Jerusalem*; Martha Vicinus, ed., *Suffer and Be Still: Women in the Victorian Age*; M. Vicinus, *Independent Women: Work and Community for Single Women 1850–1920*; Harriet Björk, *Charlotte Brontë*.

1. Letter 10 Jan. 1839, quoted in Lock, *Man of Sorrow*, p. 292
2. Aubrey de Vere quoted in W. Gerin, *Branwell Brontë*, p. 173
3. F. Carlock Stephens, 'Hartley Coleridge and the Brontës', *TLS*, 14 May 1970
4. *Ibid.*
5. *Ibid.*
6. C. Alexander, *op. cit.*, Chapter 26; M. Monahan, ed., *Ashworth: An Unfinished Novel by Charlotte Brontë*
7. I. Pinchbeck, *Women Workers and the Industrial Revolution*
8. See also M. Vicinus, *Suffer and Be Still* and *Independent Women*; Nancy F. Cott, *The Bonds of Womanhood*; E. Showalter, *op. cit.*; B. Taylor, *op. cit.*
9. J.S. Mill, *The Subjection of Women* (1869), quoted in Kate Millett, 'The Debate over Women: Ruskin vs. Mill', in M. Vicinus, ed., *Suffer and Be Still*
10. M. Vicinus, *Independent Women*, p. 3
11. Quoted in *ibid.*, p. 2
12. Quoted in *ibid.*, p. 16
13. W.R. Greg, 'Why are Women Redundant?', *National Review* 15 (1862):436; quoted in Vicinus, *op. cit.*, pp. 3–4
14. In H. Björk, *op. cit.*, p. 45; B. Taylor, *op. cit.* p. 321
15. In H. Björk, *op. cit.*
16. Harriet Martineau, *Household Education*, p. 243
17. *Ibid.*
18. H. Martineau, *Deerbrook*
19. Mary Taylor, *Miss Miles*
20. *Ibid.*
21. J.S. Mill, *op. cit.* in Vicinus, *Suffer and Be Still*, p. 137

Chapter Nine
1. Notebook at BPM
2. Stevens, *op. cit.*, p. 172
3. Thackeray, 'Little Travels and Roadside Sketches' in *Punch* magazine, Wroot, p. 152
4. Wroot, *Sources of Charlotte Brontë's novels*, p. 153. He quotes Victor Tahon on the quartier Isabelle thus: 'longuement, nous avons erré par l'ancien et curieux quartier aux rues étroites,

montantes et tortueuses, mal pavée, pauvrement éclairées, aux antiques maisons . . . aux aspects archaïques ou pittoresques . . . Marché-au-Bois, Montagne-des-Aveugles, rue des XII Apôtres, rue de Parchemin, rue des Sols, rue de la Cuillers-à-pot, rue Terarcken, rue Isabelle, rues et ruelles aux vieux noms bruxellois' (*La Rue Isabelle et le Jardin des Arbaletriers*, Brussels, Rossignol et Van den Bril, 1912). Also see M.H. Spielmann, *Charlotte Brontë in Brussels*

5. *Life*, p. 227
6. Chadwick, *op. cit.*, p. 226 and Chapters 15–20
7. M. Heger's obituary in *L'Indépendence Belge*, 9 May 1896
8. *Indépendence Belge*, 4 Sept. 1886
9. Information about M. Heger derived from M. René Pechère, M. Heger's great grand-son personally and from family papers, and from his brother M. Paul Pechère in BST 90:5:17; also E. Duthie, *The Foreign Vision of Charlotte Brontë*; Gerin, *C. Brontë*; F. Macdonald, *The Secret of Charlotte Brontë*; Chadwick, *op. cit.*
10. *Life*, p. 229
11. F. Macdonald, *op. cit.*
12. Duthie, *op. cit.*; M. Albert Colin, editor of *L'Etoile Belge*, reprinted in the *Sketch*, quoted in Wroot, *op. cit.*, p. 172
13. *Life*, p. 230
14. Stevens, *op. cit.*, pp. 172–3; according to her calculations the present Rue Schmitz leading to the Place des Étangs Noirs was the old allée of the Château
15. Mrs Chadwick, information from Mrs Jenkins, *op. cit.*
16. Macdonald, *op. cit.*
17. *Life*, p. 231
18. *Ibid.*, pp. 230–1
19. *Ibid.*
20. BPM
21. Duthie, *op. cit.*, p. 208
22. *Ibid.*, pp. 44–5, 59. CB's *devoirs* are in the British Library and BPM; see also BST Nos 6:34:236, 12:62:88, 12:64:273, 12:65:361
23. Duthie, *op. cit.*, p. 164
24. Macdonald, *op. cit.*, pp. 95 and 133
25. Stevens, *op. cit.*, Mary Taylor to Mrs Gaskell, p. 166
26. Chadwick, *op. cit.*
27. J.J. Green, 'The Brontë/Wheelwright Friendship', *Friends Quarterly*, November 1915
28. BST 5:23:26, Mlle Louise de Bassompierre, letter to W.T. Field
29. *The Professor*, p. 83
30. G. Charlier, 'Brussels life in *Villette*; a Visit to the Salon in 1842', BST 12:65:386
31. Mary Taylor, *Miss Miles*, p. 340
32. Horsfall Turner, ed., *Works*, *op. cit.*, sermon preached at Willie Weightman's funeral

Chapter Ten
1. Gerin, *Branwell Brontë*, p. 203; Leyland, *op. cit.*, p. 292; Grundy, *Pictures of the Past*
2. SHLL I, pp. 278 *et seq.*
3. *Ibid.*
4. 14 October 1846, CB to EN, quoted in SHLL II, pp. 114–15
5. *Ibid.*
6. 10 July 1846 to EN, SHLL II, p. 101
7. Gerin, *C. Brontë*, p. 219
8. Wroot, *op. cit.*, p. 163
9. Green, 'The Brontë/Wheelwright Friendship'
10. 6 March 1843, SHLL I, p. 293
11. Heger family papers owned by M. René Péchère
12. *Devoirs*, *op. cit.*
13. Duthie, *op. cit.*, p. 40
14. BST 6:34:236
15. *Ibid.*, comment written at foot of essay
16. BST 14:73:32 and 11:59:249

17. Macdonald, *op. cit.*
18. Edith M. Weir, 'The Heger Family: New Brontë Material Comes to Light. Letters from Constantin and Zoë Heger to former pupils and from Louise Heger', BST 11:59:249
19. *Ibid.*
20. Janet Harper, 'Charlotte Brontë's Heger family', *Blackwood's Magazine*, April 1912
21. BPM
22. BST 11:59:249
23. W. Gerin, *C. Brontë*, pp. 238–9
24. *Villette*, p. 176
25. If so, this may explain why Mary Taylor felt nervous about possessing the letters, and eventually burnt them

Chapter Eleven
Charlotte Brontë's letters to M. Heger are now in the British Library (MS Add. 38732). Translations of the letters are taken from the Shakespeare Head Volume II, by M.H. Spielmann.

1. ECG to EN, 9 July 1856, SHLL IV, p. 201
2. SHLL IV, p. 248
3. E. Chitham and T.J. Winnifrith, *Brontë Facts and Brontë Problems*, ch. I
4. *Ibid.*
5. M. F. H. Hulbert, *Jane Eyre and Hathersage*
6. SHLL II, p. 43.

Chapter Twelve
1. Leyland, *op. cit.*, p. 144
2. *Ibid.*, p. 56
3. *Ibid.*, p. 218–19
4. *Life*, p. 283
5. 29 Dec 1856, ECG to G. Smith, Pollard, p. 432
6. Robinson Papers at BPM; Gerin, *B. Brontë*, *op. cit.*
7. Robinson Papers
8. Gerin, *B. Brontë*, p. 252
9. 'If this be all', 20 May 1845, Chitham, ed., *The Poems of Anne Brontë*, p. 111
10. Gerin, *B. Brontë*, pp. 241–2
11. *Ibid.*, pp. 235–6; Robinson Papers. For letter see BST Vol. 19, Parts 1 & 2, Rebecca Fraser, 'Mrs Robinson and Branwell Brontë: Some Mistaken Evidence'
12. Dr Mildred Christian has dismissed Winifred Gerin's notion (*B. Brontë*, pp. 236–7) that large payments made to Ann Marshall, Mrs Robinson's maid, by Mr Robinson were her price for spying into his wife's affairs, as having no special significance 'since similar promissory notes to numerous other persons connected with Thorp Green over a long period of time are preserved in the Deed Box and appear to be connected with liabilities on the estate'. BST part 72, No. 2 Vol. 14, p. 16, 'Further thoughts on Branwell Brontë's story'.
13. D. Du Maurier, *The Infernal World of Branwell Brontë*
14. Mr Robinson's cashbook, BPM
15. Robinson Papers
16. Letter G.H. Lewes, 6 Nov. 1847, SHLL II, p. 152
17. SHLL II, p. 69–71
18. To W.S. Williams Sept. 1848, SHLL II, p. 256
19. G. D. Hargreaves, 'The Publishing of Poems, by C., E. and A. Bell, BST, 1969'
20. SHLL II, pp. 31 *et seq.*
21. SHLL II, p. 76
22. 28 April 1846, SHLL II, p. 92
23. 24 May 1846, SHLL II, p. 94
24. SHLL II, p. 121 (circa Jan. 1847): 'I wish Mr Thos Nicholson of the "Old Cock" would send me my bill of what I owe to him, and, the moment that I receive my outlaid cash, or any sum which may fall into my hands through one I may never see again, I shall settle it.'
25. To J.B. Leyland, 17 June 1848, SHLL II, p. 223: 'my receipt of money on asking, through Dr Crosby, is morally certain'

26. SHLL II, p. 121, M. Leyland, Transactions, Halifax Antiquarian Society
27. Du Maurier, *op. cit.*
28. BPM
29. *The Critic*, 4 July 1846 in Miriam Allott, *The Critical Heritage*, p. 59
30. *Ibid.*, p. 60
31. *Athenaeum* 4 July 1846, Allott, *op. cit.* p. 61
32. G.D. Hargreaves, BST, *op. cit.*

Chapter Thirteen
1. 28 Jan. 1848, SHLL II, p. 184
2. Geraldine Jewsbury, *The Half Sisters* (although this was not published until 1848) chap. xii, quoted p. 61, Kathleen Tillotson, *Novels of the 1840s*
3. 1850 preface to *Wuthering Heights* (Penguin, p. 40)
4. *Ibid.*
5. 'Biographical Notice of Ellis and Acton Bell' (*Wuthering Heights*, Penguin, p. 36)
6. *Life*
7. Anne Mozley from an unsigned review of *Villette* in the *Christian Remembrancer*, April 1853, in Allott, *The Critical Heritage*, p. 207
8. *Ibid.*
9. 7 August 1847, BST 18:2 (1982), A. Pollard, 'The Seton–Gordon Brontë Letters'
10. Mary Duclaux, *Emily Brontë, A Memoir*

Chapter Fourteen
1. SHLL II, p. 149
2. 6 Nov. 1847, SHLL II, p. 153
3. SHLL II, p. 156
4. *Atlas*, Allott, *op. cit.*, pp. 67 *et seq.*
5. SHLL II, p. 158 'The notice in the *Examiner* gratified me very much'.
6. *Examiner*, Allott, pp. 76 *et seq.*
7. *Era*, Allott, pp. 78–9
8. One of the reviewers CB felt best understood *Jane Eyre* was Eugene Forcade in the *Revue de deux mondes*; he praised it expressly for its moral qualities, and thought it 'completely English in the moral sense of the word. One feels all through it the spirit of that Anglo-Saxon race, crude if you will . . . but masculine, inured to suffering and hardship. . . . They firmly implant in the hearts of their children the feeling for freedom and responsibility . . . this book proves once more that there are infinite resources for fiction in the depiction of the upright morals and straightforward events of real life and the simple and open development of the passions.'
9. 6 Nov. 1847, Allott, pp. 74–5
10. SHLL II, p. 155
11. *Sunday Times*, 5 December 1847
12. Q.D. Leavis, Introduction to the Penguin edition of *Jane Eyre*
13. The *Mirror*, p. 376 *et seq.*
14. 23 Dec. 1847, SHLL II, p. 166
15. 31 Dec. 1847, SHLL II, p. 170
16. ECG to Catherine Winkworth 25 Aug. 1850, Pollard, *op. cit.*, p. 126
17. *Ibid.*
18. *Ibid.*
19. *Aurora Leigh*, p. 52
20. SHLL II, p. 193
21. Pollard, *op. cit.*, p. 125
22. 20 April 1848, SHLL II, p. 204
23. Penguin edition *Wuthering Heights*, p. 33
24. *Atlas*, 22 Jan. 1848, Allott, pp. 230–1
25. *Ibid.*
26. *Wuthering Heights*, p. 37
27. See E. Chitham, *The Poems of Anne Brontë*, p. 36
28. 'The Three Guides', *ibid.*, pp. 144–5

29. From 'Shall Earth no more inspire thee', in P. Henderson, ed., *The Complete Poems of Emily Brontë*, pp. 152–3
30. See Chitham, *The Poems of Anne Brontë*, introduction pp. 7–8
31. *Shirley*, p. 400
32. *Christian Remembrancer*, April 1853, Allott, pp. 203 *et. seq.*

Chapter Fifteen
1. Quoted from J. Stevens, *op. cit.* Letter CB to MT 4 Sept. 1848, p. 178.
2. New light on the operations of Smith, Elder has been cast by Jenifer Glynn in *Prince of Publishers: A Biography of the Great Victorian Publisher*; see also George Smith's reminiscences in *Cornhill Magazine* Dec. 1900
3. *Cornhill Magazine*, Dec. 1900
4. Letter CB to MT, Stevens, *op. cit.*, p. 179
5. *Ibid.*
6. *Cornhill Magazine*, Dec. 1900
7. Stevens, *op. cit.*
8. W. Gerin, *C. Brontë*, p. 367
9. Stevens, *op. cit.*, p. 181
10. Preface to the second edition, in Penguin pp. 29–31, ed. G.D. Hargreaves
11. *Rambler*, 'Mr Bell's New Novel', Sept. 1848, Allott, *op. cit.*, pp. 266–7
12. Unsigned review, *Sharpe's London Magazine*, July–Oct. 1848 pp. 181–3
13. Letter to WSW Sept. 1848, SHLL II, p. 255
14. F. Grundy, *Pictures of the Past*; Grundy's dates were wrong and Branwell did not die a few days later as he stated
15. See BST part 95:18 (1985); H.W. Gallagher, 'Charlotte Brontë: A Surgeon's Assessment'; A.S. McNalty, 'The Brontës: A Study in the epidemiology of tuberculosis' (1934), *British Journal of Tuberculosis* **28**, pp. 4–7; Sir Ian Fraser (ex-President of Royal College of Surgeons in Ireland), 'Disease is good for you' (1978), *Ulster Medical Journal* **47**, pp. 141–50, who with Dr N. Oswald, Consultant Physician to the Brompton Hospital, in 'Seeker of the Art of Living' (1980), *BMJ* **2**, p. 1080, believe that Patrick Brontë's chronic bronchitis 'was tubercular and that he was the focus of infection for the rest of the family' (Gallagher)
16. 'Novels of the Season', *North American Review*, Allott, p. 97 *et seq.*
17. *Biographical Notice* to 1850 edition of *Wuthering Heights* and *Agnes Grey*, Penguin edition pp. 34–5
18. Information about EB's deathbed from Mrs Gaskell, *Life*, who was presumably informed by CB
19. Elizabeth Rigby, from an unsigned review, *Quarterly Review*, Allott, pp. 106 *et seq.*
20. *Ibid.*
21. *Ibid.*

Chapter Sixteen
1. MT to CB, 13 August 1850, Stevens, *op. cit.*, p. 97
2. 13 June 1849, SHLL II, p. 340
3. B. Taylor, *Eve and the New Jerusalem*, p. 125 from Nancy F. Cott, 'Passionless: an Interpretation of Victorian Sexual Ideology 1790–1850', *Signs*, Vol. 4, no. 2 (Winter 1978); see also Cott's *The Bonds of Womanhood*
4. Taylor, *op. cit.*, p. 126
5. *Ibid.*, p. 124
6. Elizabeth Barrett Browning, *Aurora Leigh* (Women's Press edition), pp. 470–1
7. *Shirley*, p. 190
8. *Ibid.*, pp. 378–9
9. 20 Sept. 1851 to ECG, SHLL III, p. 278
10. *Shirley*, p. 343
11. M. Smith, 'The Manuscripts of Charlotte Brontë's Novels', BST (1983) p. 199 Part 93, No. 3 of Vol. 18
12. 21 Sept. 1849 to WSW, SHLL III, pp. 23–4

13. Letters to George Smith from CB, 14 Sept. – 27 Sept. 1849, published in A. Pollard, 'The Seton–Gordon Brontë letters', BST (1982) Part 92, No. 2 of Vol. 18, pp. 104–106
14. *Athenaeum*, Allott, *op. cit.*, p. 123
15. Albany Fonblanque – *Examiner*, Allott, *op. cit.*, pp. 125 *et seq.*
16. William Howitt in *Standard of Freedom*, Allott, *op. cit.*, p. 133
17. SHLL III, p. 45
18. CB to EN, 18 Dec. 1849, SHLL III, p. 60
19. *Cornhill Magazine* Dec. 1900
20. Gerin, *C. Brontë*, p. 403
21. Thackeray, 'The Last Sketch', *Cornhill Magazine*, published in Everyman edition of *The Professor*
22. George Smith, *Cornhill Magazine*, Dec. 1900
23. *Ibid.*
24. SHLL III, p. 60
25. *Ibid.*
26. Harriet Martineau, *Autobiography*, p. 325
27. *Ibid.*
28. *Life*, p. 618, letter from Miss Martineau to Mrs Gaskell, added as footnote in Third Edition
29. *Ibid.*, p. 393

Chapter Seventeen
1. SHLL III, p. 73. Queen Victoria herself would have nothing but praise for *Jane Eyre*: in her diary in 1858 she said she found it 'melancholy' and 'most interesting', and in 1880, though 'very peculiar in parts', it was 'really a wonderful book . . . such a fine tone in it, such fine religious feeling'. To her, Mr Rochester's character was simply 'a very remarkable one' and Jane's 'a beautiful one'. M. Allott, *op. cit.*, p. 390–1
2. SHLL III, p. 76
3. *Ibid.*, p. 109
4. MT to CB, 5 April 1850, J. Stevens, *Mary Taylor*, p. 90
5. J. Stevens, *op. cit.*, p. 86
6. *Cornhill Magazine*, Dec. 1900
7. SHLL III, p. 118
8. *Cornhill Magazine*, *op. cit.*
9. *Ibid.*
10. SHLL III, p. 121
11. Quoted in W. Gerin, *Charlotte Brontë*, p. 436
12. SHLL III, p. 128
13. In a letter to Clement Shorter in the Brotherton Collection Arthur Nicholls would later call it 'Richmond's admirable likeness . . .' He also describes her forehead as 'exceptionally broad – indeed so much so that she endeavoured to cover it by the arrangement of her hair.'

Chapter Eighteen
1. CB to Margaret Wooler, 27 Sept. 1850, SHLL III, p. 163–4
2. Quoted in A.B. Hopkins, *Elizabeth Gaskell*, p. 312
3. To Lady Kay Shuttleworth, 14 May [1850], Letter 72, Pollard, p. 116
4. No. 25a, *ibid.*, p. 57
5. No. 72, *ibid.*, p. 116
6. No. 77, *ibid.*, p. 127
7. No. 60, *ibid.*, p. 96–7
8. No. 75, *ibid.*, p. 123
9. No. 154, *ibid.*, p. 228
10. See Letters 79 to Eliza Fox, Pollard p. 130, and 78 to Charlotte Froude, Pollard p. 128
11. *Life*, p. 496
12. See Letter 242 to George Smith, Pollard p. 347, and unpublished autograph letter to Mrs Hooper, telling her of Mrs Gaskell's pleasure at the latter's interest in her Memoir of Charlotte Brontë, 24 June [1857]
13. *Life*, p. 496
14. Emily Winkworth to Catherine Winkworth, SHLL III, p. 151

15. J.W. Parker, 'Woman's Mission', *Westminster Review*, Jan. 1850
16. Sydney Dobell on 'Currer Bell' and *Wuthering Heights*, *Palladium*, Sept. 1850, M. Allott, pp. 277 *et seq.*
17. 29 Sept. 1850, SHLL III, p. 165
18. 21 Dec. 1850, SHLL III, p. 190
19. Insertion in third edition of Mrs Gaskell's *Life*, in Penguin edition, p. 610
20. To James Taylor, 24 March 1851, SHLL III, p. 214
21. 21 Dec. 1850, SHLL III, p. 198

Chapter Nineteen
Information about Mrs Gaskell derives mainly from A.B. Hopkins, *Elizabeth Gaskell* and W. Gerin, *Elizabeth Gaskell*, as well as her letters edited by Chapple and Pollard. The Phrenological Estimate of Charlotte Brontë is in the Brontë Parsonage Museum.

1. SHLL III, p. 241
2. *Cornhill Magazine*, Dec. 1900
3. From Letters and Private Papers of W.M. Thackeray, iii 12 quoted W. Gerin, *C. Brontë*, p. 479
4. *Villette*, p. 340
5. Hopkins, *op. cit.*, p. 317
6. *Life*, p. 457
7. *Pollard, op. cit.*, p. 160–1
8. CB to ECG, 22 May 1852, quoted in W. Gerin, *C. Brontë*, p. 491 (in Manchester University Library)
9. No. 68, Pollard, p. 106
10. No. 69
11. Jennifer Glynn, *Prince of Publishers*, p. 17
12. To George Smith, 9 Aug. 1851, SHLL III, p. 270
13. *Villette*, p. 387. Judging by the MS fragment at the BPM, Bonnell Collection 124 (2) [1850], one of the preliminary drafts of *Villette*, the visionary quality which had been so vital a part of her creative processes in adolescence remained important in middle age: 'It was in the cold weather which follows the shortest day that we first came to England. . . . We came from a place where the buildings were numerous and stately – where before white house fronts there rose here and there trees straight as spires, where there was one walk broad and endlessly long – down which on certain days [?] two tides – one of people on foot brightly clad – with shining silks – delicate bonnets with feathers and roses . . . little parasols gay as tulips – and the other of carriages rolling along, refined and quiet – indeed all was quiet in this walk – it was a mysterious place – full of people but without noise.'

Chapter Twenty
1. Letter to the *Christian Remembrancer* of 18 July 1853, quoted in an unsigned review in the *Christian Remembrancer*, July 1857
2. *Life*, p. 507
3. To John Forster, No. 155, [late April 1853?] Pollard, p. 230
4. No. 166, Pollard, pp. 243 *et seq.*
5. No. 191, *ibid.*
6. To Richard Monckton Milnes, 29 Oct. 1853, Pollard, p. 252
7. BST (1982) Part 92 No. 2 of Volume 18 – Arthur Pollard, 'The Seton–Gordon Brontë Letters', p. 113
8. Incomplete draft of letter from Mrs Smith at the Brontë Parsonage Museum, Seton–Gordon Collection No. 87, undated
9. BST (1982), 'The Seton–Gordon Brontë Letters', p. 113

Chapter Twenty-one
1. Quoted in No. 195, to John Forster, Pollard, p. 289
2. No. 26, J. Stevens, 24 February 1854, p. 120
3. No. 191, Pollard, p. 280–1
4. A. Pollard, 'The Seton–Gordon Brontë Letters', BST (1982), p. 113

5. Catherine Winkworth to Emma Shaen, 8 May 1854, SHLL IV, pp. 121 *et seq.*
6. Dr Juliet R.V. Barker, 'Subdued Expectations: Charlotte Brontë's Marriage Settlement', BST (1986)Vol 19 Parts 1 and 2, p. 35
7. SHLL IV, p. 131
8. This is the suggestion of Dr Barker. *See* 'Charlotte Brontë's Photograph', BST (1986) pp. 27–8

Chapter Twenty-two
The Seton–Gordon Collection at John Murray contains letters from Ellen Nussey to George Smith relating her impression of Haworth immediately after Charlotte's death, as well as a series of letters from Mr Nicholls to George Smith showing his pride in his wife's reputation and shedding light on the lives of Mr Brontë and Mr Nicholls together after Charlotte's death.

1. No. 242, Pollard, p. 347
2. Pollard, p. 327
3. Letter to Mrs Humphrey Ward in W. Gerin, *C. Brontë*, p. 554
4. *Life*, p. 523
5. ABN to Mary Hewitt, SHLL IV, p. 178
6. See P. Rhodes, 'A Medical Reappraisal of the Brontës', BST (1972) 16, pp. 101–109; also A.S. McNalty, 'The Brontës: A study in the epidemiology of tuberculosis' (1934), *British Journal of Tuberculosis* **28**, pp. 4–7; I. Fraser, 'Disease is good for you' (1978), *Ulster Medical Journal* **47**, pp. 141–150; N. Oswald, 'Seeker of the art of living' (1980), BMJ **2**, p. 1080.
7. H.W. Gallagher, Honorary Consultant Surgeon, Ards Hospital, Newtonards, Co. Down, Northern Ireland, 'Charlotte Brontë: A Surgeon's Assessment', BST part 95:18 (1985)
8. *Loc. cit.* and see J. Maynard, *Charlotte Brontë and Sexuality*
9. I am indebted for this information to Dr Peter Dally, of the Department of Psychological Medicine at Westminster Hospital
10. Letter from Ellen Nussey to GS in John Murray archives, 28 March 1860
11. J. Lock, *Man of Sorrow*, p. 479

Chapter Twenty-three
1. Mrs Gaskell to GS, No. 241, Pollard, p. 343
2. Mrs Gaskell to John Greenwood, 12 April 1855, No. 223; Pollard, p. 337 'I do fancy . . . I could have induced her, – even though they had all felt angry with me at first, – to do what was so absolutely necessary, for her very life'.
3. No. 242, Pollard, p. 347
4. No. 245, *ibid.*
5. ABN to GS, 28 Nov. 1856, John Murray archives
6. *Ibid.*
7. No. 257 to E.N. Pollard
8. *Ibid.*
9. Nos. 267 and 294, Pollard
10. No. 294, *Ibid.*
11. SHLL IV, p. 203
12. No. 297, Pollard
13. 1 Dec. 1855, to GS, John Murray archives
14. No. 308, Pollard
15. ABN to GS, 21 Aug. and 20 Sept. 1856, John Murray archives
16. No. 309, Pollard
17. No. 314, *Ibid.*
18. No. 303, *Ibid.*
19. *Life*, p. 360
20. *Ibid.*, p. 490
21. *Ibid.*, p. 491
22. *Ibid.*, p. 495
23. *Ibid.*, p. 496
24. No. 326, Pollard

25. No. 313, *Ibid*.
26. No. 352, *Ibid*.
27. John Murray archives
28. Letter 24 Aug. 1852, quoted in Lock, *Man of Sorrow*, p. 511
29. Letter 30 July 1857, quoted in Lock, *op. cit.*, pp. 508–9
30. Letter 31, 28 Jan. 1858, J. Stevens, p. 134
31. J. Stevens, *op. cit.*, Appendix B pp. 161–2
32. Letter 30, 30 July 1857, Stevens, *op. cit.*, p. 132
33. Stevens, p. 141
34. ABN to GS, 11 Nov. 1859, John Murray archives; see particularly Margaret Smith, 'New Light on Mr Nicholls', BST 1987 Vol. 1 part 3, pp. 97 *et seq*. And see Brotherton Collection 11 April 1855, 'Our loss is indeed great – the loss of one as good as she was gifted'. See also ABN to C. K. Shorter, 8 June 1896
35. ABN to GS, 27 Jan. 1860, John Murray archives
36. Lock, pp. 491–2
37. Meta Gaskell's account quoted in Lock, *Man of Sorrow*, pp. 519–20
38. Letters from ABN to Martha Brown at BPM
39. Anne Mozley in the *Christian Remembrancer* April 1853, in M. Allott, *op. cit.*, p. 203
40. The *Oxford and Cambridge Magazine* 1856, in M. Allott, p. 316
41. Introduction to Penguin edition of *Villette*
42. Mrs Oliphant in *Blackwood's Magazine*, May 1855 in M. Allott, pp. 311 *et seq*.
43. Elizabeth Barrett Browning, *Aurora Leigh*, 11. 478–80
44. Tony Tanner, Introduction to Penguin edition of *Villette*

Select Bibliography

Manuscript sources

Unpublished: At the Brontë Parsonage Museum: Charlotte Brontë's juvenilia and fragments of her writing, including most of the *Roe Head Journal*; part of the Seton–Gordon Collection; the Robinson Papers; documents of the Brontë family, including Branwell's notebook and juvenilia; Mr Nicholls' commonplace book and letters to Martha Brown. The Brotherton Collection, Leeds University: letters from Mr Nicholls to C.K. Shorter, additional Ellen Nussey material and Branwell Brontë manuscripts (also in British Museum). The Berg Collection, the New York Public Library: letters from Ellen Nussey to Sir T. Wemyss Reid. John Murray archives (Seton–Gordon Collection): letters from Mr Brontë and Mr Nicholls to George Smith, and from Ellen Nussey to Mrs Gaskell.

Published: Charlotte Brontë's letters to M. Heger, circa 1844–5, British Museum Add. 38732; 'William Wallace and Other Essays in Prose and Verse' (1842) B.M. Ashley 160; 'Portrait. Pierre l'Ermite' (1842) B.M. Ashley 2444.

Newspapers and periodicals

The bulk of the reviews of Charlotte Brontë's novels are cited at length in the endnotes as are particular issues of the Brontë Society Transactions referred to.

Blackwood's Edinburgh Magazine for 1826–31; *The Edinburgh Review*, 1802–31; *The Methodist Magazine*, 1798–1812; *The Pastoral Visitor*, 1815, Bradford, W. Yorks; *Fraser's Magazine for Town and Country*, 1830–3; *The Children's Friend*, 1824–6; Kirkby Lonsdale; *The Leyland Family* 1954; Mary Leyland, Transactions of the Halifax Antiquarian Society; *Scribner's Monthly Magazine*, May 1871; the *Bradford Observer*, 17 Feb. 1894; T.J. Winnifrith, 'Charlotte Brontë and Calvinism', Notes and Queries 1970; Frederika Macdonald, 'The Brontës in Brussels', *Woman at Home*, July 1894; J.J. Green, 'The Brontë/Wheelwright Friendship', *Friends' Quarterly*, Nov. 1915; Janet Harper, 'Charlotte Brontë's Heger family', *Blackwood's* April 1912; *L'Indépendence Belge*, 4 Sept. 1886, 9 May 1896; Benjamin Herschel, Report to the General Board of Health on the sanitary condition of Haworth, 1850; *Cornhill Magazine*, Dec. 1860 and 1900; the *Quarterly Review*, Dec. 1848; the *Sunday Times*, 13 Dec. 1847; George Eliot, 'Silly Novels by Lady Novelists', *Westminster Review*, 1856; G.H. Lewes, 'The Lady Novelists', *Westminster Review*, 1852; John Parker, 'Woman's Mission', *Westminster Review*, 1850; Harriet Taylor Mill, 'Enfranchisement of Women', *Westminster Review*, 1851; the *Christian Remembrancer*, July 1857; *Blackwood's*, 1855; *Sharpe's London Magazine*, 1855; Lucile Dooley, 'Psychoanalysis of Charlotte Brontë as a Type of Woman of Genius', *American Journal of Psychology*, July 1920; *The Times*, 29 July 1913.

Published works

Unless otherwise stated London is the place of publication.

Christine Alexander, *A Bibliography of the Manuscripts of Charlotte Brontë* (the Brontë Society in association with Meckler, 1982)
  The Early Writings of Charlotte Brontë (Basil Blackwell, 1984)
  An Edition of the Early Writings of Charlotte Brontë Vol. 1 (Oxford, Shakespeare Head Press, Basil Blackwell, 1987)

Miriam Allott, *The Brontës: The Critical Heritage* (Routledge and Kegan Paul, 1974)

Matthew Arnold, *The Letters of Matthew Arnold*, ed. G.W.E. Russell (1895)

Thomas Balston, *John Martin His Life and Works* (Duckworth, 1947)

Patricia Beer, *Reader I married him* (Macmillan, 1974)

Ellis and Acton Bell, *Wuthering Heights and Agnes Grey* (Smith, Elder, 1850)

Bessie Rayner Belloc, *Essays on Women's Work* (1865)

E.F. Benson, *Charlotte Brontë* (Longmans Green and Co., 1932)

Phyllis Bentley, *The Brontës* (Home and Van Thal, 1947)
  The Brontë Sisters (Longmans Green, 1950)

Thomas Bewick, *General History of Quadrupeds and History of British Birds*, ed. I. Bain (London, 1969)

L. Elliott-Binns, *Religion in the Victorian Era* (Lutterworth Press, 1936)

Augustine Birrell, *The Life of Charlotte Brontë* (Walter Scott, 1887)

Harriet Björk, *The Language of Truth: Charlotte Brontë, the Woman Question and the Novel* (Lund Studies in English)

Jacques Blondel, *Emily Brontë – Expérience spirituelle et création poétique* (Presses Universitaires de France, 1955)

Asa Briggs, *The Age of Improvement* (Weidenfeld, 1965)
  Victorian People (Weidenfeld, 1974)

Anne Brontë, *The Poems of Anne Brontë*, ed. Edward Chitham (Macmillan, 1979)
  Agnes Grey, with an introduction by Margaret Lane (Dent, 1958)
  The Tenant of Wildfell Hall, ed. G.D. Hargreaves (Penguin, 1979)

519

Emily Brontë, *The Complete Poems of Emily Brontë*, ed. Philip Henderson (Folio Society, 1951)
  Wuthering Heights, ed. David Daiches (Penguin, 1967)
Patrick Branwell Brontë, *Poems – annotated and enlarged edition of the Shakespeare Head Brontë*, ed. T.J. Winnifrith (Basil Blackwell, 1983)
Revd Patrick Brontë, *A Funeral Sermon for the Late Rev. William Weightman, MA* (JU Walker Halifax, 1842)
  The Signs of the Times (Aked Keighley, 1835)
  Collected Works, ed. J. Horsfall Turner (T. Harrison & Sons, Bingley, 1898)
  'On Halley's Comet in 1835', *The Bradfordian*, August 1861
  The Maid of Killarney (Baldwin, Cradock and Joy, 1818)
  'On Conversion' *The Pastoral Visitor, 1815*
  The Brontë Family, A Selection of Poetry, ed. Dr Juliet Barker (Dent, 1985)
Brontë Society Transactions 1895–1987
Ford K. Brown, *The Fathers of the Victorians: The Age of Wilberforce* (Cambridge University Press, 1961)
Elizabeth Barrett Browning, *Aurora Leigh* (Women's Press, 1978)
Charles Burkhart, *Charlotte Brontë: A Psychosexual Study of her Novels* (Gollancz, 1973)
Lord Byron, *Poetical Works*, ed. Frederick Page (Oxford University Press, 1970)
Thomas Carlyle, *Works*, ed. Grant Richards (Oxford University Press, 1902–9)
David Cecil, *Early Victorian Novelists* (Collins, 1964)
Mrs Ellis H. Chadwick, *In the Footsteps of the Brontës* (Sir Isaac Pitman and Son Ltd, 1914)
Mrs Hester Chapone, *Letters on the Improvement of the Mind* (John Anderson, Edinburgh, 1823)
Edward Chitham, *A Life of Emily Brontë* (Basil Blackwell, 1987)
  The Brontes' Irish Background (Macmillan, 1986)
E. Chitham and T.J. Winnifrith, *Brontë Facts and Brontë Problems* (Macmillan, 1986)
Mildred G. Christian, *A Census of Brontë MSS in the United States* (reprinted from *The Trollopian*, Berkeley, California, 1947–8)
Nancy F. Cott, *The Bonds of Womanhood* (Yale University Press, 1977)
R. Coupland, *Wilberforce: A Narrative* (Oxford University Press, 1923)
George G. Cragg, *Grimshaw of Haworth – A Study in Eighteenth-Century Evangelicalism* (Canterbury Press, 1947)
W.A. Craik, *The Brontë Novels* (Methuen, 1968)
Valentine Cunningham, *Everywhere Spoken Against: Dissent in the Victorian Novel* (Clarendon Press, Oxford, 1975)
E.M. Delafield, *The Brontës: Their Lives Recorded by their Contemporaries* (Hogarth Press, 1935)
Benjamin Disraeli, *Coningsby* (Penguin, 1983)
  Sybil (Penguin, 1980)
Enid Duthie, *The Foreign Vision of Charlotte Brontë* (Macmillan, 1975)

George Eliot, *The Letters of George Eliot*, ed. Gordon S. Haight (Oxford University Press, 1954)

Inga-Stina Ewbank, *Their Proper Sphere: A Study of the Brontë Sisters as Early Victorian Female Novelists* (Edward Arnold, 1965)

Antoine Galland, *The Arabian Nights Entertainment* (Nuttall, Fisher and Dixon, Liverpool, 1914)

Mrs Gaskell, *The Letters of Mrs Gaskell*, eds. J.A.V. Chapple and Arthur Pollard (Manchester University Press, 1966)
The Life of Charlotte Brontë (Penguin, 1975)
Mary Barton (Penguin, 1970)
North and South (Penguin, 1970)
Ruth (Oxford University Press, 1985)

William Gaskell, 'Strong Points of Unitarian Christianity' (a lecture, British and Foreign Unitarian Association, 1873)
Protestant Practices Inconsistent with Protestant Principles (Liverpool, 1836)

Winifred Gerin, *Anne Brontë* (Nelson, 1959)
Branwell Brontë (Nelson, 1961)
Charlotte Brontë: The Evolution of Genius (Oxford University Press, 1967)
Emily Brontë (Clarendon Press, Oxford, 1971)
Elizabeth Gaskell (Clarendon Press, Oxford, 1976)

Jenifer Glynn, *Prince of Publishers: A Biography of the Great Victorian Publisher George Smith* (Allison and Busby, 1986)

Dr John Gregory, *A Father's Legacy to his Daughters* (John Anderson, Edinburgh, 1823)

Francis H. Grundy, *Pictures of the Past* (Griffith and Farrar, 1879)

L. and E.M. Hanson, *The Four Brontës* (Oxford University Press, 1949)

G. Elsie Harrison, *The Clue to the Brontës* (Methuen, 1948)
Haworth Parsonage – A Study of Wesley and the Brontës (The Epworth Press, 1937)

Annette B. Hopkins, *Elizabeth Gaskell Her Life and Work* (John Lehmann, 1952)
The Father of the Brontës (Johns Hopkins University Press, Baltimore, 1958)

Laura L. Hinkley, *The Brontës: Charlotte and Emily* (Hammond, 1947)

Walter E. Houghton, *The Victorian Frame of Mind* (Yale University Press, New Haven, 1966)

Martin F.H. Hulbert, *Jane Eyre and Hathersage* (Hathersage Parochial Council, 1983)

Robert Keefe, *Charlotte Brontë's World of Death* (University of Texas Press, Austin, 1979)

Jocelyn Kellett, *Haworth Parsonage* (Haworth, 1977)

Margaret Lane, *The Brontë Story: A Reconsideration of Mrs Gaskell's 'Life of Charlotte Brontë'* (Heinemann, 1953)
The Druglike Brontë Dream (John Murray, 1980)

Francis A. Leyland, *The Brontë Family: With Special Reference to Patrick Branwell Brontë* (Hurst and Blackett, 1886)

John Lock and W.T. Dixon, *A Man of Sorrow: The Life, Letters and Times of the Rev. Patrick Brontë* (Nelson, 1965)

Angus MacKay, *The Brontës: Fact and Fiction* (Service and Paton, 1897)
Frederika Macdonald, *The Secret of Charlotte Brontë* (T.C. and E.C. Jack, 1914)
John Martin, *A Descriptive Catalogue of Pompeii and Herculaneum* (1822)
R. Martin, *The Accents of Persuasion: Charlotte Brontë's Novels* (Faber and Faber, 1966)
Henry Martyn, *Journals and Letters* ed. S. Wilberforce (Thames Ditton, 1837)
Harriet Martineau, *Household Education* (1849)
  Society in America (1837)
  Deerbrook (1839)
  Autobiography (1877; reprinted with an introduction by Gaby Weiner, Virago, 1983)
Daphne du Maurier, *The Infernal World of Branwell Brontë* (Gollancz, 1960)
John Maynard, *Charlotte Brontë and Sexuality* (Cambridge University Press, 1984)
Joseph H. Miller, *The Disappearance of God: Five Victorian Novelists* (Cambridge, Mass., Harvard University Press, 1963)
Kate Millett, *Sexual Politics* (Virago, 1977)
Ellen Moers, *Literary Women* (Women's Press, 1978)
Revd William B.D. Morgan, *Christian Instructions, consisting of sermons, essays, addresses, reflections etc.* (Bradford, 1824)
  The Parish Priest: pourtrayed in the life, character and ministry of the Revd John Crosse, late vicar of Bradford (Bradford, 1841)
Stephen C. Neill, *Anglicanism* (Penguin, 1965)
Mrs Oliphant, *Annals of a Publishing House* (Macmillan, 1897)
Margot Peters, *Style in the Novel* (University of Wisconsin Press, Wisconsin, 1973)
  Unquiet Soul: A Biography of Charlotte Brontë (Hodder and Stoughton, 1975)
Ivy Pinchbeck, *Women Workers and the Industrial Revolution* (1933; reissued by Virago, 1978)
Arthur Pollard, *Charlotte Brontë* (Routledge and Kegan Paul, 1968)
  Mrs Gaskell: Novelist and Biographer (Manchester University Press, 1965)
Thomas De Quincey, *Memorials etc.* ed. Alexander Hay Japp (Heinemann, 1891)
Fannie E. Ratchford, *The Brontës' Web of Childhood* (Columbia University Press, New York, 1941)
  Gondal's Queen (University of Texas Press, Austin, 1955)
Ernest Raymond, *In the Footsteps of the Brontës* (Rich and Cowan, 1948)
A.M.F. Robinson, *Emily Brontë* (W.H. Allen and Co., 1883)
T. Wemyss Reid, *Charlotte Brontë* (Macmillan, 1877)
Aina Rubenius, *The Woman Question in Mrs Gaskell's Life and Work* (Lund Essays and Studies on English Language and Literature Vol. 5, 1950)
William Scruton, *Pen and Pencil Pictures of Old Bradford* (Thos Brear and Co., Bradford, 1889)

Thornton and the Brontës (John Dale and Co., Bradford, 1898)

Margaret J. Shaen, *Memorials of Two Sisters* (1908)

Clement Carus-Wilson, Shepheard Walwyn, *Henry and Margaret Jane Shepheard: Memorials etc.* (Elliot Stock, 1882)

Elaine Showalter, *A Literature of their Own: British Women Novelists from Brontë to Lessing* (Virago, 1982)

Charles Simeon, *Memoirs of the Life of Charles Simeon* ed. Rev. William Carus (Hatchard, 1847)

May Sinclair, *The Three Brontës* (Hutchinson, 1912)

Frank Smith, *The Life and Work of Sir James Kay Shuttleworth* (John Murray, 1923)

F.W. Smith, *Wilberforce the Philanthropist* (Hamish Hamilton, 1974)

Charles Smyth, *Simeon and Church Order: A Study of the Evangelical Revival in Cambridge in the Eighteenth Century* (Cambridge University Press, 1940)

M.H. Spielmann, *The Inner History of the Brontë–Heger Letters* (Chapman and Hall, 1919)

Sir James Stephen, *Essays in Ecclesiastical Biography* (reissue, Longmans, 1949)

Joan Stevens, *Mary Taylor: Letters from New Zealand and Elsewhere* (Oxford University Press, 1972)

J.A. Erskine Stuart, *The Brontë Country: Its Topography, Antiquities and History* (Longmans Green and Co., 1888)

Algernon Swinburne, *A Note on Charlotte Brontë* (1877)

Barbara Taylor, *Eve and the New Jerusalem* (Virago, 1983)

Mary Taylor, *The First Duty of Women* (a series of articles reprinted from the *Victoria Magazine*, 1865–70)
    Miss Miles, or a Tale of Yorkshire Life 60 years ago (C. Remington and Co., 1890)

William Makepeace Thackeray, *The Letters and Private Papers of W.M. Thackeray*, ed. Gordon N. Ray (Oxford University Press, 1945)

Alfred Lord Tennyson, *The Princess* (Moxon, 1848)

Kathleen Tillotson, *Novels of the 1840s* (Oxford University Press, 1954)

J.M.S. Tompkins, *The Popular Novel in England 1770–1800* (Methuen, 1962)
    The Fawcett Lectures 1961–62 on Aurora Leigh 28 Nov., 1961 (1962)

G.M. Trevelyan, *English Social History* (Longmans Green, 1944)

J. Horsfall Turner, *Haworth Past and Present: A History of Haworth, Stanbury and Oxenhope* (Bingley, 1897)

Martha Vicinus (ed.), *Suffer and Be Still: Women in the Victorian Age* (Methuen, 1980)
    Independent Women: Work and Community for Single Women 1850–1920 (Virago, 1985)

Robert K. Webb, *Harriet Martineau, A Radical Victorian* (Heinemann, 1960)

T.J. Winnifrith, *The Brontës and their Background: Romance and Reality* (Macmillan, 1973)

523

D.A. Winstanley, *The University of Cambridge in the Eighteenth Century* (Cambridge University Press, 1922)
Unreformed Cambridge: A Study of Certain Aspects of the University in the Eighteenth Century (Cambridge University Press, 1935)

Butler Wood (ed.), *Charlotte Brontë 1816–1916: A Centenary Memorial* (Fisher Unwin Ltd, 1918)

Revd William Wright, *The Brontës in Ireland* (Hodder and Stoughton, 1893)

Hubert E. Wroot, *Persons and Places: Sources of Charlotte Brontë's Novels* (Shipley, publication of the Brontë Society, 1935)

W.W. Yates, *The Father of the Brontës – His Life and Work at Dewsbury and Hartshead* (Fred R. Spack and Son, Leeds, 1897)

G.M. Young, *Victorian England: Portrait of an Age* (Oxford University Press, 1957)

Editions of Charlotte Brontë's work used in this book

Jane Eyre (with an introduction by Q.D. Leavis, Penguin, 1968)

The Professor and Emma (a fragment with an introduction by Margaret Lane, Dent, 1969)

Christine Alexander (ed.), *Something about Arthur* (University of Texas, Austin, 1981)

T.A.J. Burnett (ed.), *The Search after Happiness: A Tale by Charlotte Brontë* (Harvill Press, 1969)

Winifred Gerin (ed.), *Five Novelettes* (Folio Press, 1971)

William Holtz (ed.), *The Secret and Lily Hart* (University of Missouri Press, 1977)

Andrew and Judith Hook (eds), *Shirley* (Penguin, 1974)

Mark Lilly (ed.), *Villette* (with an introduction by Tony Tanner, Penguin, 1979)

George MacLean (ed.), *The Spell: An Extravaganza* (Oxford University Press, 1931)

Melodie Monahan (ed.), *Ashworth: An Unfinished Novel by Charlotte Brontë* (PhD dissertation for the University of Rochester, 1976)

'Charlotte Brontë's The Poetaster: Text and Notes', *Studies in Romanticism, 20* (Winter, 1981)

Edward A. Newton (ed.), *Derby Day and Other Adventures* (Boston, Little, Brown, 1934)

W. Robertson Nicoll, *'Jane Eyre' to which is added 'The Moores'* (Hodder and Stoughton, 1902)

Fannie E. Ratchford and William C. DeVane (eds), *Legends of Angria: Compiled from the Early Writings of Charlotte Brontë* (Yale University Press, New Haven, 1933)

Clement Shorter (ed.), *The Four Wishes: A Fairy Tale* (privately printed, 1918)

C. Shorter and C.W. Hatfield (eds), *The Twelve Adventurers and Other Stories* (Hodder and Stoughton, 1925)

T.J. Winnifrith (ed.), *The Poems of Charlotte Brontë* (Basil Blackwell, 1984)

Thomas J. Wise (ed.), *The Adventures of Ernest Alembert: A Fairy Tale* (privately printed, 1896)

Thomas J. Wise and J.A. Symington (eds), *The Brontës: Their Lives, Friendships and Correspondence* 4 Vols. (The Shakespeare Head Brontë – Oxford, Basil Blackwell, 1932)

The Poems of Charlotte Brontë and Patrick Branwell Brontë (The Shakespeare Head Brontë – Oxford, Basil Blackwell, 1934)

The Miscellaneous and Unpublished Writings of Charlotte and Patrick Branwell Brontë 2 Vols. (The Shakespeare Head Brontë – Oxford, Basil Blackwell, 1936 and 1938)

Index

Addison, Joseph, 400
Aesop's Fables, 53
Agnes Grey see Brontë, Anne
Albert, Prince Consort, 400, 403
Alexander, Christine, xi, 103
Allerton Hall, 44
Almack's Assembly Rooms, Charlotte attends Thackeray's lecture at, 400–2
Ambleside, Harriet Martineau's home, The Knoll, at, 390–3
Angria, Charlotte's and Branwell's writings about imaginary kingdom of, 88, 95–6, 102–4, 107, 108, 117, 118–19, 127, 163, 182, 188, 192, 239–40, 498; transplanted to Yorkshire, 131–2, 136, 138–9; *see also* Glass Town
Arabian Nights, 49, 50
Arminian theology, 46
Arnold, Matthew, 259, 303, 393, 409, 434, 499
Arnold family of Fox How, Ambleside, 378; Charlotte's visits to, 383–4, 393
Arnold, Dr Thomas, 383, 384, 393
Arnold, Mrs Thomas, 383, 384
Athenaeum, 254, 258–9, 277, 310, 344, 353, 433
Athenée Royale, Brussels, 152, 158, 159, 161, 162, 196, 201, 212, 217; M. Heger's Speech Day Address at, 196; as poste restante for Charlotte's letters, 217–19
Atkinsons (Charlotte's godparents), 62, 68
Atlas, 279, 291–2, 253
Austen, Jane: *Emma*, 363–4; *Pride and Prejudice*, 364

Akroyd, Tabitha *see* Tabby
Aylott & Jones, publication of *Poems by Currer, Ellis and Acton Bell* (1846), 245–7, 250–4, 259

Balzac, Honoré de, 133, 134
Banagher, County Offaly, 480; Charlotte's honeymoon in, 468–9; Arthur Nicholls' return to, 497–8
Barbauld, Mrs, *A Legacy for Young Ladies. . .*, 110
Barrett-Browning, Elizabeth, 126, 246, 289, 334, 409; *Aurora Leigh*, 145–6
Barthélémy, Abbé, 167
Bassompierre, Louise de, 171
Belgian War of Independence (1830), 160–1
Bell, Acton *see* Brontë, Anne
Bell, Currer *see* Brontë, Charlotte
Bell, Ellis *see* Brontë, Emily
Bell, James Adamson, 480
Bell, Mary *see* Nicholls, Mrs
Bell, Mrs, 468–9
Bell Chapel, Thornton, 17
Bennoch, Francis, 465
Benson, A. C., 126
Benson, Archbishop, 126
Bentinck, Lord, 54
Bernardin de St Pierre, 196, 212
Bethlehem Hospital, London, 431
Bewick, Thomas, 51, 89; *History of British Birds*, 51–2; *General History of Quadrupeds*, 51
Bible, 47, 50, 73, 112, 323, 331, 500
Bignold, Mr, insurance agent, 247–8
Black Bull, Haworth, 91, 96, 255, 270–1

527

in political issues, 54–5, 74, 95–6; relations with Branwell see Brontë, Patrick Branwell; short-sightedness of, 58, 63, 65, 266, 368; visit to Cross-Stone, 58–9; attends Roe Head school (1831–2), 61–75, 76; friendships and correspondence with Ellen Nussey and Mary Taylor see Nussey, Ellen, and Taylor, Mary; appearance of, 63, 64, 67, 93, 307, 376, 381; drawing ability, 65, 92; visit to Rydings (1832), 78–80; Ellen's visit to Haworth (1833), 81–7; Branwell's portrait of, 93; as teacher at Roe Head (1835–8), 96–100, 104–9, 111, 112–14; and religious crisis, 103–4, 106–7; sends Glass Town poetry to Southey and his response, 109–12; Mary and Martha Taylor's visit to Haworth (1838), 115; visits Branwell in Bradford, 116; stays with Ellen and visits Lascelles Hall, 118; refuses Henry Nussey's marriage proposal, 19–21; employed as governess by Sidgwick family (1839), 123–7; turns down Bryce's proposal of marriage, 127–8; Burlington holiday with Ellen, 128–30; Henry Nussey's literary correspondence with, 130–1, 139; and William Weightman, 134–6, 139, 140, 142; Ellen's visit to Haworth (1840), 134–5; Hartley Coleridge's comments on Angrian MS, 138–9; Mary Taylor's visit to Haworth, 140; employed as governess by White family (1841), 143–4, 151; plan to open school, 144, 150, 182, 203, 204, 207–8, 209–10, 211, 212, 239; proposes trip to Brussels with Emily, 150–2; and father accompanies them on journey, 152–9; and her first year at Pensionnat Heger (1842), 157–77; visits and excursions in Brussels, 170–1, 184–6, 193; and death of Martha Taylor, 176; Aunt Branwell dies, and returns home, 177–8, 180–1; and her second year at Pensionnat Heger (1843), 184–202; her relations with and feelings for M. Heger, 182–3, 187–91, 195–6, 198–9, 200, 201–2, 208–20; and letters to M. Heger from Haworth, 195, 199, 205, 206, 207–9, 210–14, 217–19, 220, 241–3; returns

to Haworth (1844), 201–4; and worries over father's health and blindness, 203–4, 222, 227–8, 242, 251, 253, 261, 364; visits Mary at Hunsworth Mill, 206, 221–2; her opinion of Arthur Nicholls, 226–7, 288; stays with Ellen at Hathersage, 228–30; and Branwell's dismissal as tutor, and alleged affair with Mrs Robinson, 230, 231, 232, 235–6, 237; investment in railway shares, 247–8, 343, 365; and life insurance, 248–9; stays with Ellen at Brookroyd (1846), 251; toothache suffered by, 261, 262; and father's cataract operation in Manchester, 261–2, 266–7; her reservations about Wuthering Heights, 267–8, 292–3; and concern over Anne's health, 288; and her changing perception of Emily, 295–6, 297, 298, 309, 316; trip to London to meet publishers (1848), 301, 302–8; attends Opera, 305–6; and dinner at Westbourne Place, 306–7; death of Branwell, 312, 313, 314–6; and Emily's illness and death, 315–19; and Anne's illness (TB), 319–20, 322, 323–4; and death of Anne in Scarborough (1849), 323–6; stays at Filey and Easton with Ellen, 327; her loneliness and low spirits at Haworth, 327–8, 359–60, 365–6, 375, 376, 383, 388–9, 390, 414–15, 417–8, 320, 423; and collapses under strain, 341; James Taylor collects MS of Shirley from Haworth, 341–2; invests £500 copyright money, 342–3; stays with Ellen at Brookroyd, 343; and stays with Smith family in London (1849), 345–55; and her new wardrobe, 346, 398–9; visits Wheelwrights in Kensington, 347–8; and meets Thackeray, 348–50; and visits Harriet Martineau, 351–3, 354; and dinner party with critics, 353–4; local reactions to her books, 355–6, 357–8; her reaction to Jane Austen's writing, 363–4; stays with Ellen at Brookroyd, 365, 375, 393; and with Smith family at Gloucester Terrace (1850), 366–74; meeting with G. H. Lewes, 367–8; Richmond's portrait of, 368, 373, 375–6, 489; and Thackeray invites her

Brontë, Charlotte – *cont.*
to dinner, 368–73; George Smith's
relations with, 372–7, 393–5, 398,
400, 406–7, 412–14, 416–17, 418,
422, 430, 451–4; and Edinburgh trip,
373, 374–5; her expectations of an
early death, 376, 383; stays with
Shuttleworths at Windermere, 377–
84; first meeting and friendship with
Mrs Gaskell, 377, 379–85, 387; and
visits Arnolds of Fox How, 383–4,
393; sends Bells' poetry to Mrs
Gaskell, 387, 388; editing and
republication of sisters' work (1850),
387, 389–90; stays with Harriet
Martineau at Ambleside, 390–3; and
Christmas visit to Ellen, 393; James
Taylor's visit to Haworth and his
interest in her, 395–7, 415–16; stays
with Smiths in London (1851), 398–
408; attends Thackeray's lectures,
400–3; and visits Great Exhibition,
403–4, 407; impressed by Rachel,
405–6; visits phrenologist, 408, 412;
stays with Mrs Gaskell at Plymouth
Grove, 406, 408–12; psychosomatic
illness of, 418–19, 420, 421; visits
Ellen at Brookroyd, 419, 427; and
stays at Filey, 421–2; her father has
apoplectic fit, 423; turns down Arthur
Nicholl's proposal of marriage, 427–9;
stays with Smiths in London (1853),
429–30; quarrel with Harriet
Martineau over *Villette,* 431–4, 442–3,
492, 493; her letter to *Christian
Remembrancer* defending her morals,
437–8; stays with Mrs Gaskell at
Plymouth Grove, 440–2; and her
dread of meeting strangers, 440–1,
442; Arthur Nicholls' relations and
correspondence with, 443–5, 450–1,
454–6, 457–8, 459–62, 463–4, 469–70,
472–3, 479; Mrs Gaskell's visit to
Haworth, 445–50; and George
Smith's engagement to Elizabeth
Blakeway, 451–4; her engagement to
Mr Nicholls, 455–6, 457–9; and
financial arrangements, 458, 462–3;
pre-marriage visit to Mrs Gaskell,
459–62; and wedding, 462, 463, 464–
7; and honeymoon in Ireland, 467–
71; and married life, 472–7, 479–80,
481–2; and her writing lapses, 477–9;

stays at Gawthorpe, 480; pregnancy,
illness and death of (1855), 480–5;
Harriet Martineau's tribute to,
486–7; and Mrs Gaskell's *Life* of,
487–94

Brontë, Charlotte: WRITTEN
WORKS (in alphabetical order)
'Albion and Marina', 61
Angria, writings about, 88, 95–6,
102–5, 107, 117, 118–19, 127, 131–
2, 136, 138–9, 182, 188, 192, 239–
40, 498
'Apostasy', 220
'At First I did Attention Give', 195
*Biographical Notice of Ellis and Acton
Bell* (1850), 163, 245, 250, 267–8,
291, 295, 387, 390
'The Bridal', 78
'Caroline Vernon', 127, 131
Emma (fragment pub. in *Cornhill
Magazine*), 369, 478, 489, 495;
Thackeray's introduction to,
495–6
'The Farewell to Angria', 131
'The Foundling', 80–1
'Frances', 215
'Gilbert', 195, 215–16
Glass Town, writings about, 48–50,
55–7, 58, 60, 61, 63, 73, 74, 78,
80–1, 88–9, 95, 109–12, 190
'Henry Hastings', 121–2
'High Life in Verdopolis', 87–8
'History of the Year (1829)', 49, 54
Jane Eyre (1847), x, 24, 29, 42, 48,
50, 51–2, 61, 68, 72, 79, 126–7,
146, 172, 190, 206, 219, 222, 223,
228–30, 241, 258, 275–6, 277–91,
295, 298, 304, 310, 323, 328, 329,
330, 332, 335, 339–49 *passim,* 352–
3, 355, 356, 357–8, 367, 370–1,
376, 380, 384, 424, 433, 434, 436,
448, 449, 458, 478, 492, 499, 500,
502; 'Lowood', 36–42; writing of,
262–6, 270; publication of (1847),
277–84; and reviews, 277–83, 286,
292, 298–300, 311–12, 316, 320–1,
340, 343, 344, 352, 353, 357, 436;
preface to 2nd edition of, 284–5,
298, 348; 3rd edition of, 298, 300;
American publication of, 301;
cheap edition of, 358
'Lines on Bewick', 51
'My Angria and the Angrians', 91–2

530

and letter to Wordsworth, 109, 112; settles in Bradford as portrait painter, 115–16; and takes opium, 116–17, 267, 271, 302; as tutor to Postlethwaite family, 132, 136–7, 138; Horace's *Odes* translated by, 137–8; and dismissed, 138; works as railway booking clerk, 142, 143, 152; and fired from job, 175, 178–9; and death of Weightman, 175, 176, 178; and death of Aunt Branwell, 178, 179–80; 'Afghan War', 179; employed as tutor to Edmund Robinson, 182, 204, 206; Charlotte's letters from Brussels to, 191–2, 193–4; dismissed as tutor by Robinsons, 230, 231; and alleged affair with Mrs Robinson, 231–40; moral and physical decline of, 249, 251, 253, 256, 257, 267, 270–1, 288, 301–2, 310–11, 312–13, 315, 442; and death of Mr Robinson, 253 4; and his obsession with Mrs Robinson, 254–5, 262, 270–1; and mysterious payments of money to, 255–6; Leyland's *bas relief* of head of, 256; family pay his debts, 269–70, 302; death from TB of (1848), 312–15, 316, 326

Brontë Parsonage Museum, 95, 463
Brookfield, Mrs, 370, 371, 372
Brookroyd (Nussey home), 289, 356; Charlotte's visits to, 180 1, 204, 250, 343, 365, 375, 393, 419, 427, 442, 450, 462, 476
Brougham, Lord, 384
Brown, Ford K., 37
Brown, John, sexton, 136, 179, 429
Brown, Martha, servant at Parsonage, 272, 340–1, 357, 376, 412, 415, 419, 428, 429, 439, 446, 484, 495, 498
Browne, Dr, phrenologist, 408, 412
Browning, Robert, 303, 409
Brunty, Alice, 4–5
Brunty, Hugh, 4–5
Brussels, 240–1; Mary's letters from, 144–5, 149, 211; Charlotte and Emily stay at Pensionnat Heger in (1842), 150–77; and Charlotte's second year in (1843), 183–202, 269; Queen Victoria's visit to, 199–200; Mrs Gaskell's visit to (1856), 489
Brussels Triennial Salon (1842), 173–4
Bryce, Mr, curate: Charlotte turns

down his proposal of marriage, 127–8; death of (1840), 133
Buckhurst, Emily *see* Nussey, Mrs Henry
Bunsen, Chevalier, Prussian Ambassador, 384
Burns, Robert, 323
Busfield, Mrs, 207, 209
Butler, Bishop, 7
Butler, Samuel, 10; *The Way of All Flesh*, 7
Byron, George Gordon, Lord, 50, 61, 74, 78, 89, 109, 246, 247, 257, 276

Calvinism, 46, 100, 106, 119, 133–4, 234, 264, 387
Cambridge University, Revd Patrick Bronte's student years at St John's College, 6–7, 8, 9, 10, 150
Carlisle, Lord, 401
Carlyle, Jane, 264, 371
Carlyle, Thomas, 240, 322, 371, 409
Carne, Anne *see* Branwell, Mrs Thomas
Carne family, 12
Carr, Mr, eye specialist, 251, 262
Carter, Anne, death of, 133
Carter, Revd Edward and Mrs, 123–4
Casterton Hall, Cowan Bridge, 34
Catholic Emancipation Bill (1829), 54–5
Cator, Revd T., 444
Chadwick, Mrs, 218, 219
Chambers of Edinburgh, Messrs, 246–7
Chapel Royal, Brussels, 170
Chapone, Mrs, *Letters on the Improvement of the Mind*, 73
Chapter Coffee House, Paternoster Row, 153, 184, 302, 305
Chartists, 329, 436
Chateaubriand, François, Vicomte, 167
The Children's Friend, 34, 38
Christian Remembrancer, 299, 322, 436–7; Charlotte's letter to, 437–8
Church Missionary Society (CMS), 8
Church of England, 264, 283, 300, 393, 436–7; High Church Party, 8, 436; rates fracas (1840), 135–6; *see also* Evangelicals
Cobbe, Frances Power, 146–7
Cockhill, Miss, schoolmistress, 207
Colburn, Henry, 259
Coleridge, Hartley, 137–9, 142, 274
Coleridge, Samuel Taylor, 137
Collins, Mr, curate, 135, 136, 273

533